MASTERING THE INTERNET, XHTML, AND JAVASCRIPT

Second Edition

Ibrahim Zeid
Northeastern University

PEARSON
Prentice
Hall

Upper Saddle River, NJ 07458

Library of Congress Cataloging-in-Publication Data

CIP Data on File

Vice President and Editorial Director, ECS: *Marcia Horton*
Senior Acquisitions Editor: *Kate Hargett*
Assistant Editor: *Sarah E. Parker*
Editorial Assistant: *Michael Giacobbe*
Vice President and Director of Production and Manufacturing, ESM: *David W. Riccardi*
Executive Managing Editor: *Vince O'Brien*
Managing Editor: *Camille Trentacoste*
Production Editor: *Lakshmi Balasubramanian*
Director of Creative Services: *Paul Belfanti*
Creative Director: *Carole Anson*
Art Director and Cover Manager: *Jayne Conte*
Managing Editor, AV Management and Production: *Patricia Burns*
Art Editor: *Gregory Dulles*
Manufacturing Manager: *Trudy Pisciotti*
Manufacturing Buyer: *Lisa McDowell*
Marketing Manager: *Pamela Hersperger*

© 2004 Pearson Education, Inc.
Pearson Prentice Hall
Pearson Education, Inc.
Upper Saddle River, NJ 07458

The author and publisher of this book have used their best efforts in preparing this book. These efforts include the development, research, and testing of the theories and programs to determine their effectiveness. The author and publisher make no warranty of any kind, expressed or implied, with regard to these programs or the documentation contained in this book. The author or publisher shall not be liable in any event for incidental or consequential damage in connection with, or arising out of, the furnishing, performance, or use of these programs.

Product names mentioned herein are the trademarks or registered trademarks of their respective owners.

AceHTML, Acoustica, Active Movie, Adobe Illustrator, Adobe Photoshop, AIM, AOLserver, Apache, CoffeeCup, Commerce-Server, CoolEdit, Crazy Browser, Domino, Enterprise Server, Eudora, FrontPage, GoldWave, HotDog Pro, Hotmail, HotMetal Pro, Indeo video, Internet Information Server, Java Web server, Kamboo! Factory, Lview, Macromedia, Mapedit, Maplay 32, Media Player, MicroServer, Microsoft Access, Microsoft Excel, Microsoft Internet Explorer, Microsoft Outlook Express, mIRC, MSN Messenger, NCSA HTTPD, Netscape Communicator, Netscape Composer, Netscape Enterpirse Server, Netscape Navigator, Opera, Oracle Web Application Server, Page Mill, Paint, Paint Shop Pro, Personal Web Server, SnagIt, Sound catcher, SoundEdit Pro II, Sound Forge, Sound Recorder, Sox, Synchrome's Maestro V, ThumbsPlus, Tomcat, VMPEG, Web-EditPRO, WebImage, Winamp, Windows, wintel32, winzip, WS FTL LE, ws_ftp32, Yahoo! Mail, and Yahoo! Messenger.

Printed in the United States of America
10 9 8 7 6 5 4 3 2 1

ISBN: 0-13-140086-X

Pearson Education Ltd., *London*
Pearson Education Australia Pty. Ltd., *Sydney*
Pearson Education Singapore, Pte. Ltd.
Pearson Education North Asia Ltd., *Hong Kong*
Pearson Education Canada, Inc., *Toronto*
Pearson Educación de Mexico, S.A. de C.V.
Pearson Education—Japan, *Tokyo*
Pearson Education Malaysia, Pte. Ltd.
Pearson Education, Inc., *Upper Saddle River, New Jersey*

To all my students
who taught me
how to teach.

Brief Contents

v

Part III: JavaScript

Contents

Part III: JavaScript

Preface

This second edition has been redesigned from the ground up to reflect and respond to many of the suggestions the author has received since the first edition was written. It has also been rewritten to accommodate the new Internet concepts that have been developed since the first edition was released.

This edition has many new pedagogical and content features:

- The page design and layout are completely new, with many eye-catching graphics features for section and example headings.
- Abundant figures and screen captures have been included to illustrate concepts.
- Each chapter begins with a goal, a set of objectives, and a list of section titles; and ends with tutorials, FAQs, a summary, a progress checklist, and problems.
- Many chapters have a "Quick reference" section at the end that summarizes software use (Part I of the book), syntax of XHTML tags (Part II), and JavaScript syntax (Part III).
- Each section has at least one pedagogical tool, be it an image insert, a figure, a table, an example, a tutorial, an FAQ, or a piece of advice. These tools make it easy to follow and understand the material and minimize the need to thumb through pages in order to find material.
- Each example and tutorial in the book has three pedagogical elements that inspire interactivity and deeper understanding. "Code explained" describes what particular code lines and sections do. "Discussion" provides insight on why certain segments of code are written the way they are. It also provides tips on running the code and cites pitfalls to avoid. "Hands-on" asks the reader to extend the existing code to accomplish a new task. This element is a confidence builder, as it is hard to write completely new code during the learning process.

- Each example focuses on one chapter concept only, while each tutorial combines a few chapter concepts together to provide a more practical application.
- Concepts are explained first and then applied, using many existing software tools in one place, so that the reader can have a conceptual overview and can compare the available tools.
- The "FAQs" are organized by chapter sections and serve as a stimulus for discussion.
- The "Blackbox" (summary) section is tightly integrated with the chapter material. It lists the section and example numbers where the corresponding detailed information can be found.
- The "Check your progress" section is tightly integrated with the chapter sections. It can serve to focus group discussions in class or as a review for exams.
- The text is written in an easy-to-follow writing style.
- All topics are covered with great attention to both depth and breadth.
- The book covers three essential elements of today's Web pages: the Internet, XHTML, and JavaScript.
- The book covers four major leading browsers: IE 6.0, Netscape 4.8 & 7.0, Opera 7, and Crazy Browser 1.05.
- The book covers seven major leading e-mail tools: Eudora, Hotmail, Outlook Express 6.0, Yahoo! Mail, Netscape 4.8 Messenger, Netscape 7.01 mailer, and Opera 7 M2.
- The book covers three major leading HTML editors: FrontPage 2002, Composer 7.01, and AceHTML 5.0.
- The book covers two leading servers: Apache server version 2.0.45 and Tomcat server version 4.1.24, both from the Apache Software Foundation.

The rationale behind this edition is simple, but effective: We need to provide a comprehensive and complete source of Web knowledge for students to be able to learn the basics that allow them to be proficient in client-side technologies. These technologies include Internet literacy, XHTML, and client-side JavaScript—three essential elements that one begins studying in order to understand the Web and Web pages today. As the Web matures and its users become more sophisticated, both students and instructors should continue to find this book useful as a single source for all their learning and teaching needs.

The purpose of this edition is to present the fundamental concepts of the Internet and its scripting tools (XHTML and JavaScript) in a generic framework. These concepts and tools are supplemented with examples, tutorials, and problems to provide readers with hands-on experience so that they can master the concepts. The book strikes a delicate balance between subject depth and breadth, and between generic and practical aspects of the Internet. As an example of the book's coverage of depth and breadth, the text covers the basic topics pertaining to the Internet and its effective use in daily tasks such as e-mail and searching, as well as all aspects of client-side XHTML and JavaScript. As an example of its coverage of generic and practical aspects, the book always relates the generic concepts to their use in technology, software, and practical applications. For instance, the book discusses the generic concepts behind e-mail tools and then covers the details of seven popular tools today, including e-mail clients and Web-based mail. Another example is the use of XHTML editors: After covering the generic aspects of XHTML, the book presents some of the commonly used HTML editors and relates their user interfaces to the raw XHTML.

This book fills an important need in the market. Students need a book that explains the subject matter in a simple, yet comprehensive and coherent, way, with ample examples and hands-on tutorials. As a matter of fact, this book's approach is a response to the nature of surfing the Web: If surfers do not find what they need on a Web page in about 30 seconds, they move on to another one. So, if a Web site does not offer visitors concentrated services and information, it loses them. This book offers concentrated knowledge to its readers so that they can find what they need very quickly. Students can also use the book's companion website, located at `http://www.prenhall.com/zeid`, to download the source code for each chapter and can use the chapter's multiple-choice questions to study and prepare for exams.

Instructors need a book that provides them with ample topics, examples, tutorials, problems, and pedagogy. For example, the instructor may use the examples, tutorials, or exercises in a lab setting. Or the instructor may use the "Blackbox" (summary) section at the end of each chapter as the basis for class discussion and review to prepare students for exams. The instructor can also access the book's companion website to download a complete set of PowerPoint slides and all the book's source code, or to use the online test bank to prepare quizzes and exams. A solutions manual accompanies the book as well. Moreover, instructors who wish to have only portions of the book, such as individual parts or selected chapters, can do so through custom publishing—a request that Prentice Hall handles with ease through its sales representatives.

The book covers three topics: Internet literacy, XHTML, and JavaScript. If you cover the three topics in one course, use the book as is. If you cover each topic in a separate course, order one part per course through Prentice Hall's custom-publishing service. Why should instructors use this three-part volume instead of three separate books? Consistency in style, format, and pedagogy is the reason. This consistency significantly increases the ease of using the book for both instructors, who must prepare the material, and students, who must learn it. Reducing the overhead of preparation and learning allows both instructors and students to devote their scarce time to using and learning the material instead of weaving through page after page trying to follow and understand three styles of three different books and authors. With the three parts of this book, instructors and students know what to expect and where to find it.

Professionals, who are usually pressed for time, need a book that they can use for self-teaching purposes. They also need a book that provides them with answers to specific questions they may have when developing websites and Web pages. With this volume, professionals can tap into the "Blackbox" (summary) and "FAQs" sections for quick consultation. In fact, many of the questions in the "FAQs" sections of this book are questions asked by past students and professionals.

The book is organized into three related parts. Part I covers the effective use of the Internet. This part develops the basic skills required for using the Internet. While many readers have been using the Internet for a long time, Part I formalizes this experience. Part II discusses, in detail, XHTML and Web-page design and development. Part III covers client-side JavaScript. This organization is beneficial in accommodating different course requirements and reader back-grounds. Those who want to focus on XHTML can also use the early chapters of Part III. Those who want to focus on JavaScript can use Part II as a review. As stated previously, if instructors or professionals want only portions of the book, the solution is custom publishing.

As in the first edition, the problems section is divided into two parts: exercises and home-work. The exercises can be used in a lab where class time is limited. The homework problems are designed to be more extensive, and some of them are open ended in nature, as students have more time outside the classroom to do them.

I am indebted to all the people who helped directly and indirectly to improve this book. I would like to thank the following reviewers (of both the first and second editions) for their valu-able comments, suggestions, and advice throughout the project: Floyd LeCureux of California State University at Sacramento, Harold Grossman of Clemson University, Rayford Vaughn of Mississippi State University, Scott Henninger of the University of Nebraska–Lincoln, Michelle Ratliff Lee of Sante Fe Community College, Patricia Gregory of Anne Arundel Community Col-lege, Denny Czejdo of Loyola University, and Hayden Schultz of Northeastern University. There is no doubt that their suggestions have influenced and enhanced this book.

I would also like to thank all my students and colleagues who contributed to both editions of this book in many ways through seminars, discussions, and courses. Special thanks are due to the following former students who gave me their generous permission to use their work in this book: Janet Beaudoin, Debra Buchanan, Ted Catino, John Daley, Cindy Desmond, John Doyle, Roger Eames, Lisa Evans, Walter Frank, Adrian Goneau, Linda Haviland, Anatoli Kurkil, Regina Lagakos, Tim Martel, Rick Mashburn, Tom Medlar, Lissa Pierson, Stephanie Rogers, Margery Rosenblatt, David Shadmon, Suzanne Sigman, John Trainor, Donna Waugh, and Paul Wikstrom. I also would like to acknowledge the following readers of the first edition who informed me of typos and errata: Mohamed Assim, Lass Hellvig, Donna Mistal-Houle, Bob Sherman, and Arnold Worsley.

Thanks are due to the Prentice Hall staff for its patience and professional help. The valu-able experience and vision of Petra Recter permitted the successful completion of the manu-script. Her e-mail messages and phone calls kept the project moving, and her coordination of the review process ensured the reception of valuable feedback in a timely manner. I would also like to thank Marcia Horton for her support of the project. In addition, I greatly appreciate the efforts and support of Kate Hargett in finishing the review process and the project. I would like to thank Camille Trentacoste and Lakshmi Balasubramanian for helping with all production issues as well. Many thanks are also due to Jessica Fitzpatrick for editing the early chapters of the book and providing very valuable feedback and suggestions.

Last, but not least, very special thanks are due to my family and friends, who supported me from start to finish with their love and encouragement, which are greatly appreciated.

IBRAHIM ZEID
Boston

PART I

Internet Literacy

This part covers all the plumbing of the Internet, an important foundation that students must understand. This part helps put Parts II and III in context. The goal of this part is to provide a solid and clear understanding of the basic concepts of the Internet and World Wide Web. To achieve this goal, this part helps readers accomplish the following objectives:

1. Understand and master the client/server model, IP addresses, URLs, e-mail addresses, file protocols and compression, and Internet connections **(Chapter 1)**.
2. Understand and master four Web browsers (Internet Explorer 6.0, Netscape 4.8 and 7.01, Crazy Browser 1.05, and Opera 7) **(Chapter 2)**.
3. Understand and master e-mail concepts, e-mail clients (Eudora 5.2, Outlook Express 6.0, Netscape 4.8 and 7.01, and Opera 7), and Web-based e-mail (Hotmail and Yahoo! Mail) **(Chapter 3)**.
4. Understand and master synchronous Web communication such as instant messaging, Web chat (BBS, chat rooms, and IRC channels), and Webcasting **(Chapter 4)**.
5. Understand and master asynchronous Web communication such as mailing lists, discussion groups, and Usenet newsgroups **(Chapter 5)**.
6. Understand and master the security and privacy issues associated with using the Internet **(Chapter 6)**.
7. Understand and master searching the Internet via a number of techniques **(Chapter 7)**.
8. Understand and master FTP and Telnet concepts **(Chapter 8)**.

Overview of the Internet

Goal

Understand and master some of the basic concepts of the Internet and the World Wide Web in order to be able to use them effectively in ordinary life, as well as in professional activities.

Objectives

- Client/server model
- Data and file transmission across the Internet
- URLs and IP addresses as unique Internet IDs
- The structure of e-mail addresses
- File protocols and compression and decompression of files
- Inranets and extranets
- Requirements and types of Internet connections
- Modem types

Outline

1.1   Introduction

The Internet has been acknowledged as the source of a profound information revolution. It has already changed our lives and the ways in which we communicate and conduct business. For example, many of us send e-mail messages back and forth to friends, colleagues, customers, clients and relatives all over the world. The Internet provides an instant mode of communication in the form of electronic mail—or e-mail for short—and instant messaging. You can even meet people on the Internet. Web pages clutter the Internet. Today, Internet Yellow Pages assist in helping people sift through the clutter. There is no doubt that this medium of communication will dominate and surpass any other medium. The Internet had more users in its first 5 years than the telephone did in its first 30 years, and the volume of e-mail sent everyday already outnumbers that of regular mail.

While hearing and reading about the Internet is exciting, putting all its related pieces together is often confusing. This chapter provides an overview of the structure of the Internet, explains how the Internet works, and discusses the different types of connections to the Internet.

1.2   The Internet and the World Wide Web

The **Internet** encompasses diverse computers and programs working together seamlessly as a network. A **network** is a collection of devices (such as computers and printers) that are connected together by communication paths. These devices are called the nodes of the network, and the communication paths may be wires, fiber-optic cables, or wireless connections. The **Internet** is a network of networks. These networks include various federal networks, a set of regional networks, campus networks, and foreign networks. The Internet connects many geographical regions; sometimes it is known as the "information superhighway." It also enables worldwide international networks to communicate with each other.

This definition of the Internet typically does not mean much to the end user. The user only wants to do something specific, such as run a program, access a website, or download a particular file. As such, an end user does not need to worry about how the Internet is put together. A good analogy is the telephone system; it, too, is a network. Phone companies such as AT&T, MCI, and Sprint are all separate corporations running pieces of the telephone system. They worry about how to make it all work together; all the user has to do is dial the number. The user begins to worry only when a problem occurs, such as when a phone call cannot be completed. In such cases, the company that owns the part of the phone system causing the problem should fix it. The same is true for the Internet: Each network has its own operations center. If something goes wrong with the network, the center that operates it should fix the problem.

The Internet's driving force is the World Wide Web (also known as WWW, W3, or the **Web**), the section of the Internet that features multimedia capabilities (i.e., has video, audio, images, graphics, and text). The Web began to take off after Mosaic, the first graphical Web viewer (browser), came out in 1994 and has quickly become a vast network of data, news, shopping guides, promotional materials, periodicals, and Web pages, displayed in colors, often with audio and video output. As described in detail in Part II of the book, extensible hypertext markup language (XHTML) allows website creators to link their Web pages to other pages, with each page accessed by a simple click of the mouse button.

The Internet links powerful servers in every part of the world. A **server** is a program that resides on a computer and provides services for other computer programs known as **clients** A particular computer may contain both client and server programs. Web users can transfer files to and from other computers (known as uploading and downloading, respectively), send electronic messages to the e-mail addresses of other users, and set up their own Web pages for whatever purpose they desire. Companies, universities, government agencies, and individuals throughout the world now maintain pages on the Web, and the demand for Web access is increasing PC (personal computer) use.

The methods for finding and accessing information on the Internet are very unique. Traditionally, as found in libraries, information is organized in books that are indexed and shelved in order, according to a standard classification system. Unlike information in libraries, however, information on the Internet is not organized at all. Information is contained in Web pages. In order to find a particular piece of information, a Web surfer uses a search engine. A **Web surfer** is a person who uses the Internet to find desired information. A **search engine** is a computer program that helps you find specific information on the Web. The Web surfer types a search string (one or more words that might be found in websites containing the information), and the search engine returns links to the Web pages that contain the string (usually known as hits).

The conclusion drawn from the foregoing analogy is that we need to use a different mental model when dealing with information on the Web. The heart of this model is a dynamic nature and randomness of information. Thus, one should not tend to memorize the addresses and titles of websites, but rather learn how to search for information effectively.

1.3 Internet Jargon

The Internet field is full of acronyms and new words. The chapters of this book introduce definitions as we need them, and these definitions are listed again in the glossary in *Appendix A*. For additional information on Internet jargon, refer to the following websites or use a search engine: `http://www.whatis.com` and `http://www.webopaedia.com`.

1.4 Client/Server Model

The client/server model is central to Internet communication, distributed networked computing, and services. This model uses two computer programs installed on two separate, but networked, computers at different locations. The client program (or client, for short) installed on one computer (known as the client computer) communicates with the server program (or server, for short) installed on the other computer (known as the server computer), as shown in Figure 1.1. The client requests services from the server. While the server is running, it acts as a daemon. A **daemon** is a process that awaits ("listens" to) client requests. When it receives a request from a client, it grants the request and sends a response back to the client. A common example of client/server communication is a Web browser acting as a client when requesting a Web page from a Web server.

Multiple clients can access a server concurrently. This situation increases the demand (known as the server load, traffic, or number of hits) on the server and may slow its response time significantly. In such a case, the server computer (also known as the host computer or host machine, or host for short) must be upgraded or replaced with a faster computer to handle the increased demand. Balancing a server's load to improve its response time is a very interesting and practical problem, but is beyond the scope of this book.

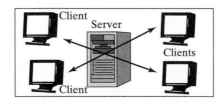

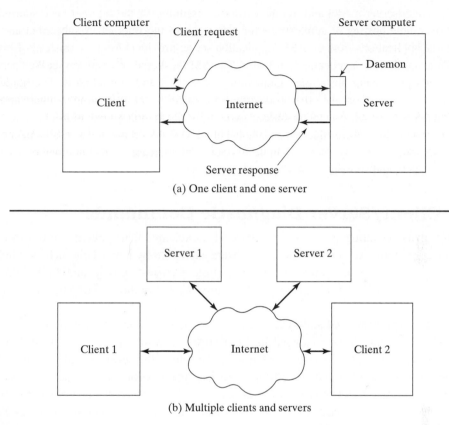

(a) One client and one server

(b) Multiple clients and servers

Figure 1.1   Client/server model.

Client/server databases are used extensively on the Web. A **database** is a set of data that is organized and stored in a file or many files. For example, a bank customer can use a browser to access the bank's database, installed on a server, to check his or her account balance. A common architecture of a client/server database is the **two-tier model**, where two networked computers are used as shown in Figure 1.1(a). The client, running as an application in a browser, sends requests (queries) to the database. The database, accessed through a server, sends the query results back to the client. Another architecture is the **three-tier model**, where a middle server is added between the database and the client for security purposes.

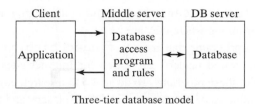

Three-tier database model

The client/server model and the increasing accessibility of the Internet have spurred the concept of remote hosting of applications for delivery over the Internet. A subscriber can rent any of these applications from an **ASP** (application server provider) for a fee, instead of installing and maintaining the applications in-house. The ASP hosts the software on its Web servers, which entails purchasing, installing, maintaining, managing, and upgrading it. The burden of computing then shifts from the client (subscriber) to the ASP server. Renting software applications from ASPs frees subscribers' resources, saves subscribers money, and allows them to focus on their core activities. The evaluation and choice of an ASP should include an assessment of the service, support, scalability (can it handle a significant increase in the number of users or amount of data?), and security the ASP provides.

1.5 Client/Server Diagnostic Commands

There are many operating system–level (OS-level) commands that a client can use to probe communication with a server. These commands are supported by major OSs such as Windows and Unix. We cover three commands in this section: `finger`, `ping`, and `traceroute`. Refer to Tutorial 1.17.1 for an exercise in their use. We cover the `nslookup` command in Section 1.8.

The `finger` command allows you to find out who is currently logged into a given host or whether a particular user is logged in. To `finger` a host, use the command `finger hostname`—for example, `finger neu.edu`, for which the result would be a list of the users currently logged into the `neu.edu` host. To `finger` a particular user, use the command `finger username@hostname`—for example, `finger zeid@coe.neu.edu`. If the user is logged in, you will receive back the login name, the last name, and the logging time of the user. You need to realize that some computers may reject the `finger` command, for security reasons.

The `ping` command allows a client to check whether a server is up and running. The general command syntax is `ping hostname`—for example, `ping neu.edu`. The command returns whether the host is up or down. This command is helpful to use before you connect to a host.

The `traceroute` (Unix) and `tracert` (Windows) commands trace the transmission route that data take from a client to a server. The general command syntax is `traceroute hostname`—for example, `traceroute www.mit.edu`. The route is measured in term of hops. A **hop** is the trip that data take from one router to another. Alternatively, a hop is an intermediate network node that data pass through. The command also calculates and displays the amount of time each hop takes. `traceroute` is useful in debugging network problems, especially with respect to determining where they are.

There are computer programs that include `finger`, `ping`, `traceroute`, and other diagnostic commands. Interested readers can search for Internet sites from which they may download and install one of these programs. To do so, go to a search engine and enter the string "ping and trace tools". Examples of the programs include NetMaps and CyberKit.

Example 1.1 Use client/server diagnostic commands.

Check the status of the following two hosts: `mit.edu` and `neu.edu`. How many hops it takes to connect to each host?

Solution 1.1 Type the following two commands in a DOS window: `ping mit.edu` and `ping neu.edu`. Observe the output. Then enter these two commands: `tracert mit.edu` and `tracert neu.edu`. Count the number of hops for each command. See Tutorial 1.17.1 for more details.

1.6 Evolution of the Internet and the World Wide Web

This section provides a brief history of the Internet and some of its milestone events. For further information, the reader can enter a search string such as "history of the Internet" into a search engine. Early research on the concept of the Internet began in 1962 at the Advanced Research Project Agency (ARPA; then known as DARPA) within the Department of Defense (DoD). Researchers sought to study the feasibility of communication using packets (see page 11 for definitions). This concept is what fueled computer networking. The Internet was born when ARPA established ARPAnet in an effort to connect together the U.S. DoD networks. In 1969, four computers were connected via ARPAnet, and in 1971 this connection was successfully demonstrated to military personnel 1971 also brought the invention of e-mail.

Much of the time during the 1970s was spent on researching the idea of open-architecture networking, as well as on the development of Ethernet (the most widely installed network technology today) by Xerox. With ARPAnet and Ethernet, the United States was able to develop a working network, and academic and research users had access to it. Other networks were soon developed in the late 1970s and early 1980s, including CSNET, USENET, and BITNET. At about the same time, Ethernet local area networks (LANs) were developed to allow computers, printers, and other hardware to communicate. When desktop computers and workstations became available, local networking exploded. Users wanted to connect their LANs to ARPAnet. Many companies and organizations began building private networks.

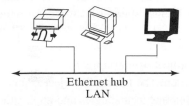

Ethernet hub
LAN

NSFnet, one of the important networks developed in 1980s, was created in 1986 by the National Science Foundation (NSF) to connect five supercomputer centers at major universities. NSFnet was built as a result of collaboration between the NSF and ARPA. NSFnet divided the United States into five regions. Each region had a supercomputer center as a hub or gateway. Universities and organizations belonging to a region could connect to the designated center via a regional network. Because of the overloading of these centers in 1987, NSFnet was upgraded with faster telephone lines and more powerful computers. By 1990, NSFnet replaced ARPAnet, with a well-developed set of regional and metropolitan area networks feeding into the NSF backbone. NSFnet's major objective was to serve educational, research, and government networking needs. In 1991, the CIX (Commercial Internet Exchange) Association was formed by Internet service providers to commercialize the Internet and establish the legitimate uses of the Internet for business and profit purposes.

PCs, which become a major platform in the 1980s, helped promote the widespread use of the Internet. LANs became available from major players in the market such as Novell. These LANs were connected to Ethernet, which allowed PCs to connect to the Internet. PCs at home could access the Internet via modems and telephone lines.

In 1989, the World Wide Web was conceived by Tim Berners-Lee of the European Laboratory for Particle Physics, or CERN (an acronym for the group's original name in French), in Geneva, Switzerland. By the end of 1991, CERN released a line-by-line text browser. The actual explosive growth of the Web started when the first graphically oriented browser, Mosaic, was developed at the National Center for Supercomputing Applications (NCSA) at the University of Illinois at Urbana-Champaign (UIUC) in 1994. The Web has quickly become the predominant part of the Internet, since it supports documents with multimedia elements: text, graphics, colors, images, and sounds. In addition, the tools needed to utilize the Web, such as browsers and search engines, are fairly easy to use. With the wide use of the Web, an organization called the World Wide Web Consortium (W3C) has taken the responsibility for evolving the various protocols and standards related to the Web.

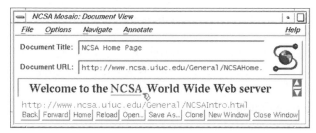

Mosaic Browser window (Courtesy of the National
Center for Supercomputing Applications (NCSA) and
the Board of Trustees of the University of Illinois)

In 1996, the Internet2 project was established. This project developed the NSF High-Performance Connections program. The Internet2 project is a collaborative effort by many universities to develop advanced Internet technologies and applications. The target next-generation applications for Internet2 include health care, national security, distance learning, digital libraries, video teleconferencing, virtual laboratories, and manufacturing. Internet2 is not intended to replace the current Internet. Instead, they are expected to complement each other.

During the 1990s, the wireless World Wide Web (WWWW) began to evolve in response to the need for instant communication anytime and anywhere by many Web users. The concept of the mobile Internet has been possible because of the availability of many wireless gadgets such as PDAs (personal digital assistants), cell phones, and other handheld mobile devices and the accessibility of wireless networks, satellite communications, and GPS (Global Positioning System) technology.

During the late 1990s and early 2000s, the "connected home" concept started to emerge, wherein home devices and appliances can be connected to the Internet by using a home gateway. A home gateway is a black box that connects home devices and appliances to each other and to the Internet. The Internet and smart embedded devices are the key drivers of the connected home. The home gateway enables dynamic delivery of network services on demand, including communication (e.g., phones, e-mail, voice mail, fax, and answering service), entertainment (e.g., video on demand and digital video recorders), home control (e.g., monitoring and integration of home devices, such as the alarm clock telling the coffeemaker to turn on), and information services (e.g., clicking a button on the TV remote control in order to store items like recipes and TV programs).

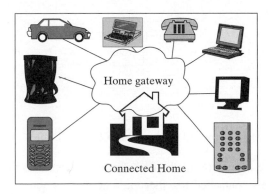

Example 1.2 Become familiar with the World Wide Web Consortium (W3C).

What are W3C technologies, and what are some of the W3C's latest developments?

Solution 1.2 Visit `http://www.w3c.org` to find information on current Web technologies and much more. Familiarize yourself with the W3C website, and visit it frequently to stay current.

1.7 Transmission across the Internet

The best way to understand how the Internet works is to think of mail delivery via a postal service. The postal service has its network of offices, its hardware (mail trucks, cars, sorting machines, etc.), and its distribution system, consisting mainly of letter carriers. Similarly, the Internet has its network of computers, its hardware (computers, routers, telephone lines, etc.), and its software needed to distribute the data (files) from one location to another.

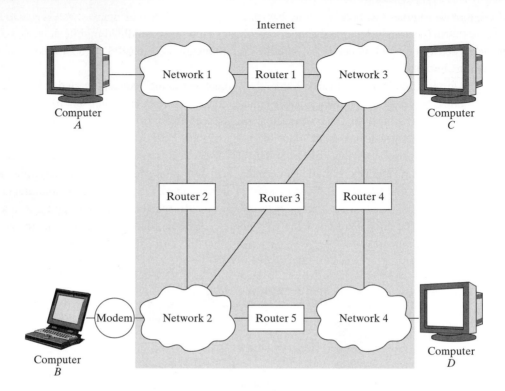

Figure 1.2   A four-network model of the Internet.

As shown in Figure 1.2, the basic idea of communication across the Internet is to have two remote sites or computers connected together via a network. Figure 1.2 shows four networks, five routers (a **router** is a computer that decides how to route data across the Internet), one modem, and four computers. The four networks resemble the Internet. They could be LANs, regional networks, national networks, or international networks. Computers A, C, and D are connected to the Internet via dedicated lines. Laptop computer B is connected to the Internet via a modem and a typical telephone line. The dedicated and telephone lines are equivalent to postal trucks and cars. They move the data from one place to another. The routers are the postal substations. They decide how to route the data transmitted through the network lines, finding the shortest and best way to deliver the data. To do so, the routers use sophisticated routing software and algorithms.

How does the Internet know where data are coming from and going to? It uses a communication protocol (a **protocol** is a set of telecommunication rules that two computers use to communicate) called **TCP/IP** (transmission control protocol/Internet protocol) that allows the inclusion of the IP addresses (see page 12 for definition) of the sending and receiving computers in the transmitted data, be they an e-mail message, a Web page, or any other file. A TCP program residing on the sending computer breaks the data to be transmitted into one or more chunks, called **packets**. It numbers the packets and adds both the sender's and receiver's IP addresses to each packet. It then forwards the packets to an IP program that resides on the same sending computer. The IP program delivers them to the receiving computer, using the IP address that is included in each packet.

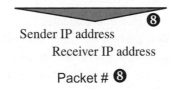

Sender IP address
Receiver IP address

Packet # **8**

TCP/IP handles packets in a similar way to how the traditional postal service handles mail. The postal service receives envelopes, addressed with both sending and receiving addresses, and delivers them to the right destinations. Similarly, TCP/IP is a two-layer protocol. The lower layer, IP, delivers the packets. The higher layer, TCP, breaks the data into packets and manages their transmission for efficient routing through the Internet. Although each packet has the same receiver's IP address, it may get routed differently than the other packets. A TCP program residing on the receiving computer awaits the delivery of the packets and then collects and reassembles them together in the right order, thus generating the original data that were sent and making them available on the receiving computer. A user can utilize an application program to view the data (e.g., an e-mail tool to read an e-mail message, or a Web browser to view a Web page) at a convenient time. Figure 1.3 shows the steps of the transmission process.

Packet transmission across the Internet employs the Internet's heterarchical structure. A **heterarchical network** has its nodes connected randomly, which implies that no one node is more important than another in the network. When a part of the Internet is down, packets are routed to avoid it. Only the users of the down part are affected. Packets are routed dynamically at

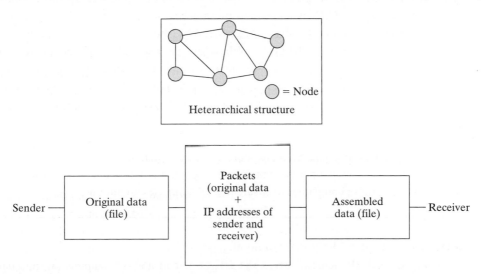

Figure 1.3 Transmission across the Internet.

the time of transmission, based on the conditions of the networks. Dynamic routing is done to ensure robust communication.

1.8 IP Addresses and URLs

The IP protocol uses a logical address scheme to guarantee that a host or a node in any network has a unique address. An **IP address** is a 32-bit integer composed of four 8-bit numbers written in base 10 and separated by periods. A **bit** is a computer storage space that holds a binary value of 0 or 1. A **byte** is an 8-bit storage space. Thus, each of the four numbers of an IP address holds a value between 0 and 255, inclusive (2^8 = 256 values). An example of an IP address is `155.33.227.141`. Like a house address, an IP address is assigned to one and only one host.

While numbers are convenient for machines and computers, they are not for humans. Therefore, we use names to refer to IP addresses. The **DNS** (domain name system) is a software application that converts names to IP addresses, and vice versa, by using a technique called reverse lookup. Both Windows and Unix OSs provide the command `nslookup`, which converts a host name to an IP address. Linux OS uses the `dig` and `host` commands. The `nslookup` command and its equivalents can also do reverse name lookup to find the name for an IP address. Tutorial 1.17.2 provides instruction in use of this command. DNS servers maintain the lookup tables of name and address correspondences. For example, the name `www.neu.edu` corresponds to an IP address of `155.33.227.141`. So if a client requests to be connected to `www.neu.edu`, the DNS server converts this address into an IP address, locates the site, and connects the client to it. This conversion is sometimes known as DNS name resolution. If the site is down or the given address is incorrect, no communication takes place between the client and the site, and a communication error is reported.

The name version of an IP address is a part of what is commonly known as a uniform resource locator, or URL. A **URL** is an address of an accessible file, say a Web page, on the Internet. An example of a valid URL is `http://www.neu.edu`. A URL consists of the protocol name required to access the file (`http` for Web pages), the name of the server computer that hosts the file (`www.neu.edu`), and the file name, including its directory name (none for `www.neu.edu`). When no file is specified in the URL, a default file name in a default directory is used. The webmaster (the administrator in charge of the Web server's operations) sets up the default file name, usually as `index.html` or `index.htm`.

The entire system of assigning and managing IP addresses is managed and controlled by national and international organizations. There are companies that sell IP addresses around the globe. These companies charge a purchase price and an annual fee to maintain an IP address. It is the responsibility of these companies to ensure that IP addresses are unique.

Example 1.3 Use the `nslookup` command.

Find the name of the IP address `66.135.192.83` and the IP address of the name `www.harvard.edu`.

Solution 1.3 Type the following two commands into a DOS window: `nslookup 66.135.192.83` and `nslookup www.harvard.edu`. The name of the IP address is `www.ebay.com`; use `nslookup www.ebay.com` to confirm. The IP address of Harvard is `128.103.60.24`. See Tutorial 1.17.2 for more details.

1.9   Internet Domain Names

The name version of an IP address is also known as the domain name. A **domain name** consists of subdomains (usually fewer than five) separated by periods. The first subdomain (on the far left of the domain name) is the host name, and the last subdomain (on the far right) is the top-level domain (**TLD**). The second-level domain name excludes the host name of the domain name. For example, the domain name of the College of Engineering at Northeastern University is `www.coe.neu.edu`. The host name is `www`, and `edu` is the TLD. The second-level domain name is `coe.neu.edu`.

Anatomy of domain names

As a general rule, the subdomains in a domain name get more general from left to right; for example, the College of Engineering (`coe`) is part of Northeastern University (`neu`), which, in turn, is part of the education sphere (`edu`). Within the college itself, there are many hosts, including `www` (`www.coe.neu.edu`) and `ftp` (`ftp.coe.neu.edu`).

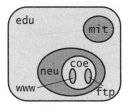

The TLD can be geographic if needed. For international use, the TLD is the country code, e.g., `au` for Australia and `uk` for the United Kingdom. Thus, in general, the format of a domain name looks as follows: `h.p1.p2.....oo.tt.cc`, where each element is defined as follows:

`h` is the host name. The host name is usually `www`.

`p1.p2....` are parts of an organization tree, e.g., `dept1.coe`. That tree organization can be as deep as needed. For example, `dept1` may be broken down into a number of groups, and each group may have subgroups for both faculty and students. In this case, we keep adding different subdomains separated by periods, i.e., p1.p2.p3.p4.....

`oo` is the organization name, e.g., `neu`, `harvard`, `mit`, `sun`, `ibm`, or `dell`.

tt is the TLD (unless we have a cc). It is usually three characters long. The most common top-level domain names used are as follows:

.com: commercial organization;
.edu: educational institution;
.gov: government agency;
.org: nonprofit organization;
.net: network service provider;
.mil: U.S. military.

cc is the country code. This code identifies countries or geographical zones. While the country code us is optional for the United States, it is mandatory for other countries. Here are some sample codes: at (Austria), au (Australia), nz (New Zealand), ca (Canada), ch (Switzerland), dk (Denmark), es (Spain), fr (France), de (Germany), gr (Greece), jp (Japan), uk (United Kingdom), se (Sweden), and ie (Republic of Ireland). Country codes are defined in the ISO-3166-1 standard.

With the explosive growth of the Internet, available domain names using the top-level domains .com, .net, and .org are running out. To address this problem, new top-level domains have been created—for example, .web, .shop, .firm, .rec, .biz, .tv, .inc, and .law.

Example 1.4 **Find the latest TLDs.**

What are some TLDs that exist or have been proposed?

Solution 1.4 Perform a Web search, using a search engine. Use search strings such as "new TLD". Some of the TLDs you may find are as follows:

.pro: accountants, lawyers, and physicians;   .name: individuals;
.museum: museums;   .aero: air-transport industry;
.coop: cooperative businesses;   .info: unrestricted use.

1.10 E-mail Addresses

The aforementioned naming scheme for a domain name is extended by the Internet to assign e-mail addresses to its users. Each node or user on the Internet has a unique e-mail address. Often, e-mail addresses employ the username@second-levelDomainName format. The username could be a combination of the user's first and last names, or any fictitious name. Some usernames employ the first letter of the user's first name followed by a period or an underscore and then the user's last name, e.g., p.smith or p_smith for Paul Smith. Others use the user's last name only. The author's e-mail address is zeid@coe.neu.edu. In general, an e-mail address can be represented in one of the following formats:

username@organization.extension, e.g., smith@company.tt;
username@organization.extension.country-code,
  e.g., smith@company.tt.cc;
username@organizational-unit.organization.extension,
  e.g., smith@sales.company.tt;
username@server.organization.extension.country-code,
  e.g., smith@alpha.company.tt.cc.

1.11 File Protocols on the Internet

While the TCP/IP protocol transmits files between servers and clients, **file protocols** determine the formats and rules of exchanging files between them. For example, exchanging a Web-page file is different from exchanging a plain-text file, although both files are transmitted as packets. The concept of a file protocol is analogous to making a phone call. While the voices of both the caller and the recipient are transmitted as sound waves, both the caller and the recipient must speak the same language in order to exchange the phone call correctly, i.e., understand each other. Relative to TCP/IP, a file protocol is an application protocol. Several types of file protocols are used on the Web, including the following:

1. **HTTP** (hypertext transfer protocol): Allows a client to request a Web page from a server. An example is http://www.neu.edu.
2. **HTTPS** (secure HTTP): Ensures secure communication between a client and a server. An example is https://www.amazon.com.
3. **Mailto**: Sends an e-mail message to a specified address, e.g., mailto:zeid@coe.neu.edu. When this command is typed in a browser, it invokes the client's default e-mail tool.
4. **NNTP** (network news transfer protocol): Allows a client to read (post) messages from (to) newsgroups and bulletin boards. Refer to Chapter 5 for an explanation of how to use this protocol.
5. **FTP** (file transfer protocol): Allows you to receive (download) and send (upload) files from a remote computer. An example is ftp://ftp.coe.neu.edu.
6. **Telnet**: Allows you to access a remote computer. An example is telnet://gate-way.coe.neu.edu.
7. **File**: Displays a file that exists on any of a client's local drives, such as a hard or floppy drive. An example is c:\dir1\dir2\filename.txt.

Tutorial 1.17.3 demonstrates how to use some of these protocols. The default protocol is HTTP. If a user does not specify a protocol, the browser uses HTTP to send and receive information from the Web server. In addition to protocols, URLs may occasionally use port numbers. A port is a logical connection or channel that allows a client to communicate with a server. For example, HTTP communication occurs through port 80. An example is http://www.neu.edu:80.

Port numbers used by the Web are standard and do not have to be specified. They are 80, 25, 110, 119, 21, and 23 for HTTP, SMTP (send mail), POP (retrieve mail), NNTP, FTP, and Telnet, respectively. The TCP/IP protocol hands off packets to a server through the standard port number. This arrangement guarantees that the server is able to handle the packets successfully. Some servers may request that packets of a certain type go to a nonstandard port number. In this case, this number is used as part of the server's URL. A port number may be used in a URL when the website is experimental, in a development stage, or otherwise not ready for public use.

1.12   File Compression and Decompression

Users surfing the Internet often find music and video files to download. Multimedia files can be very large, making them slow to download. File transfer depends on factors such as the speed of the Internet connection transferring the file, the file size, and the server traffic. In particular, the file size affects both the transfer time and the disk space required to store the file on a computer. File compression (encoding) and decompression (decoding) are two techniques that control the size of a file. File compression reduces the file size and therefore its downloading time. Typically, large files available on server computers are stored in compressed mode in order to speed up their transfer. A user decompresses them after downloading in order to use them.

File compression software, such as WinZip, uses complex algorithms to scan a file for repeating patterns and redundancy in the data. An algorithm may replace the repeating patterns with a code storing their content and locations more efficiently. A repeating pattern could be composed of either characters (in text files) or pixels (in image files). For example, consider the following string of characters:

> AAAAAAAAAAGGGGWWZZZZZ

We can compress (encode) this string in a more compact form by writing it as

> 10A4G2W5Z

where 10A means 10 A's, 4G means 4 G's, and so on.

As another example, consider the following single-color bit-mapped image:

> 000000000000000000000000000000
> 000000000011111111110000000000
> 111110000000000000111111111111
> 111111111111111111111111111111

This image file can be compressed to 30 0; 10 0, 10 1, 10 0; 5 1, 13 0, 12 1; 30 1, where rows of data are separated by semicolons. The first row of the image has 30 0's. The second row has 10 0's followed by 10 1's followed by 10 0's, and so on for the other rows.

To view compressed files, a compatible decompression program is required to read the codes stored and restore the file to its orginal state. Typically, the same program can perform both compression and decompression. For example, we can use the WinZip program to decompress (unzip) and compress (zip) files on Windows OS, or we can use a zip command on Unix OS.

Two types of compressed files exist: self-extracting and non-self-extracting. A **self-extracting** zip file has a zip program built into it. It has the .exe file extension. This file unzips and installs itself. Executable files of application programs are zipped in this way. Examples include browser and Java software. A **non-self-extracting** file requires a zip–unzip program to decompress it. Examples include large text and multimedia files. To find out if a zipped file is self-extracting or not, simply double-click on it. If it is self-extracting, then, as stated previously, it will unzip and install itself. If not, a dialog box will appear stating that the file must first be unzipped before it can be open.

The most commonly used extensions for compressed files are `.zip`, `.sit`, and `.gzip` (or `.zip`) for PC, Mac, and Unix, respectively. File extensions used on Linux OS include `.arc`, `.arj`, `.lzh`, `.rar`, `.sit`, `.zip`, and `.zoo`.

When we package multiple files together, we create an archive (one file) that holds them. Archives can maintain a file directory structure. Archive programs provide their users with this option. WinZip, for example, can maintain a file directory structure, or it can flatten it (i.e., put all of the files at one level). WinZip uses the `.zip` file extension for archives. On Unix OS, archives use the `.tar` (tape archive) extension. In the Java community, archives use the `.jar` (Java archive) extension. While compression is not required in order to create archives, it is commonly used. For example, as started previously, WinZip compresses archives and then uses the `.zip` file extension for them; see Tutorial 1.17.4.

Example 1.5 Zip a file.

Choose a file on your computer and zip it. What is the file size before and after zipping?

Solution 1.5 Use WinZip and Windows OS. Follow this sequence to create a zip file with the name `zipFile`: Right-click on the desktop => Select `New` => Select `WinZip File`. The file we will compress is an Excel file and has the name `mim3140new`. Drag and drop it onto the `zipFile` icon. To find the file size, right-click on the file icon => Click `Properties` => Click `OK`. The file sizes before and after zipping are 19.5 KB (1KB = 1024 bytes, and 1 byte = 8 bits) and 3.88 KB, respectively. The compression ratio (19.5/3.88) is not constant and depends on the file type.

1.13 Intranets and Extranets

The underlying concept for the Internet, intranets, and extranets is the same. They are all networks using the same hardware and software. The differences occur with respect to their geographical domains and the level of security they use. Figure 1.4 shows the three types of networks. An **intranet** is a network that is contained within an organization; that is, it is an internal or private network. Organizations use intranets to share information and computing resources among employees in different departments and widespread offices.

Like the Internet, intranets connect heterogeneous computer hardware, including server computers, workstations, and PCs. Because intranets provide companywide (intracompany) access to the internal private information of the entire company, they must be protected from outside intruders. Thus, it is typical for companies to install firewalls around their intranets in order to prevent unauthorized access. A **firewall** is a collection of related computer programs installed on a server computer that acts as a gateway to the intranet. The firewall intercepts each incoming packet and examines the sender's IP address to determine whether to forward it to its destination.

An **extranet** is an organization network that allows access to outside networks such as the Internet. It allows users outside a company to communicate with its employees, and vice versa. The users can access the company's internal information and resources as well. An extranet facilitates intercompany relationships. Extranets typically link companies and businesses with their customers, suppliers, vendors, partners, and other businesses over the Internet. Extranets provide secure and private links via advances in network security and the use of firewalls. An extranet may be viewed as an intermediate network between the Internet and an intranet.

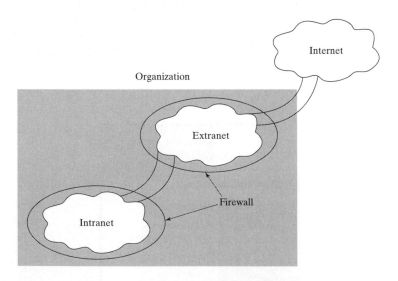

Figure 1.4   The Internet, intranets, and extranets.

1.14 Connecting to the Internet

Organizations, such as companies and universities, and individuals need an Internet service provider (**ISP**) in order to connect to the Internet. Organizations connect their networks to one of the ISP networks. Individuals typically connect their computers at home to an ISP network. Individuals who own more than one computer at home can network them first before connecting them to an ISP network.

ISPs can offer Internet access (connection) only or both access and content. Organizations usually select access only, while individuals may select both access and content. America Online (AOL) and the Microsoft Network (MSN) are examples of ISPs that offer both types of service. These ISPs offer extensive categorized online services, including information, sports, finance, news, and shopping, to end users. Phone and cable companies that act as ISPs provide online access only. End users who have online access through these ISPs surf the Internet on their own to find the content they need. This process can be time consuming for some users. If you think of the Internet as a city, a content-providing ISP would be its directory. Once you remove the directory, you are on your own in finding your way around the city.

The choice of an ISP for individual use depends largely on the individual's particular needs. It is out of the scope of this book to compare commercial ISPs. Interested readers can search the Internet itself for answers. However, some of the general features one should consider when choosing an ISP include the maximum connection speed; the type of connection (dial-up or broadband); whether there is an available 800-number help line; the software provided, if any, for browsing and other online activities; the monthly service charges and hourly rates (both peak and off-peak), the search tools and Web services provided; the extent of technical support provided, whether there are any trial accounts one can use before deciding to purchase the service; the procedure for installation and orientation (e.g., via a CD-ROM); and the supported newsgroups and forums.

After choosing an ISP, organizations connect their employees' PCs and workstations to network (known as Ethernet) ports. These ports provide dedicated broadband (high-speed) connections that are available 24 hours a day. The PCs and workstations have Ethernet cards to allow communication with the network. Organizations also install Web browsers on the PCs and workstations in order to complete the Internet access requirements. They also provide in-house training and support for their employees on using the companywide Web tools such as e-mail tools, online databases, and Web-based software.

Individuals who set up Internet connections at home need a modem and a browser. Refer to the next section for information on modem types and specifications. Three types of home connections exist. A **dial-up connection** requires a telephone line and a modem. The modem speed is usually 56K. (See the next section for more details.) This type of connection is slow, crash prone, and ties up phone lines. The user must dial a phone number provided by the ISP in order to establish a connection. After he or she is done surfing the Web, the user must disconnect the phone line.

The other two types of home connections are cable and DSL. (See the next section for more details.) Both types are dedicated (i.e., available 24 hours a day) and high speed (i.e., broadband). **DSL connections** use existing phone lines; they require DSL modems. **Cable connections** use TV cables and require cable modems. Both connections have comparable speeds. Telephone companies usually offer DSL services, and cable-TV companies offer cable services.

1.14.1   T-Carrier System

ISPs use T lines to provide dedicated high-speed access to the Internet. The T-carrier system is the easiest, fastest, and most convenient way to connect to the Internet. The system was introduced by Bell phone companies in the United States in the 1960s. A **T line** supports digital transmission at high speeds. Large organizations typically lease T lines at a speed of their choice from a commercial provider. The provider places a routing computer (router) at an organization site. This computer takes communications from the site and sends them to their final destinations. All site computers can be connected to the router via the site's LANs. The LANs are the responsibility of the site. Once the site is up and running, the provider is responsible for only the router and the T line.

How fast are T lines? Two of the existing technologies are T1 and T3 lines. A **T1 line** provides a bandwidth of 1.5 million bits per second. A **T3 line** has a bandwidth of 45 Mbps (45 megabits, or 45 million bits, per second).   A bandwidth of 45 Mbps means that a T3 line transmits 45 million bits of data, voice, and video per second. A T1 line uses 24 64-Kbps channels (24×64 Kbps = 1.5 Mbps) to deliver its data throughput. A T3 line uses 672 64-Kbps channels (the equivalent of 28 T1 lines). The channels of a T line can be divided or allocated between data, video, and voice, depending on a company's needs. A T1 line provides enough speed for a small company that has a Web server that gets more than 1500 hits a month. A T3 line is good for a large company with an active website that gets more than 25,000 hits per month. The cost of a T1 line includes installation fees and a monthly fee that depends on the traffic (number of bits) that goes through the line. A T3 line costs more than a T1 line and can handle much more traffic.

1.14.2   Point-to-Point Dial-Up Connection

All Internet dial-up connections via a modem and a telephone line use the PPP (point-to-point) protocol. ISPs issue PPP accounts to their dial-up customers. Whether you configure the PPP connection yourself or through your ISP, it is beneficial that you know the basics of the procedure.

The **PPP protocol** enables the connection of two hosts, say, your PC and a Web server, over a direct link such as a telephone line. Your PC becomes a host on the network. The PPP protocol was introduced in 1992. It allows the user to specify the network protocol—that is, whether it is TCP/IP or something else. It can negotiate connection parameters and compression, and it can protect against transmission errors.

You need a PPP account in order to be able to use a PPP connection. Your ISP provides you with the account and its information. The ISP also gives you a phone number, a username, and a password. With this information, you can log into your service provider's server. The phone call you make to connect to the server may be a local call to you, and, depending on your phone billing plan, the call may not add charge to your phone bill. To minimize or eliminate charges to users for phone calls during connection time, all ISPs have many POP (point of presence) access points in many regions of the country.

It does not take too much effort to make a home PC Internet ready. A computer program that uses the TCP/IP protocol is typically part of the OS (e.g., Windows). Configuring a PPP connection is systematic and simple, as shown in Tutorial 1.17.5. The connection uses sockets to connect two computers. A **socket** is a method of communication between a client and a server. Think of a socket as the end of a virtual wire that goes into a computer. A client/server communication requires two sockets, one on each end. They are known as a client socket and a server socket.

OSs (e.g., Windows and Unix) provide users with built-in computer programs that handle socket communication. Windows uses the Winsock (Windows socket) API (application programming interface). **Winsock** is an adaptation of the Berkeley Unix socket interface. Winsock became available in 1993 and became part of the OS with Windows 95. Stand-alone versions of Winsock, such as Trumpet Winsock, also exist. Unix OS does not require a Winsock equivalent, because TCP/IP and sockets are designed to run directly with Unix application programs.

Winsock runs between a browser and the program that uses the TCP/IP protocol, as shown in Figure 1.5. It runs as a Windows DLL (dynamic link library) file—that is, it is loaded and executed when, say, a TCP/IP program needs it.

The main bottleneck for dial-up users is the access speed. Downloading or uploading Web pages with many graphics, a lot of animation, and high sound content is very slow when using modem speeds. Access speeds are directly dependent on the wires that make up the telephone system. They are typically twisted-pair copper wires. These wires are not the ideal medium for moving data at high speeds. As a result, telecommunication companies such as Cisco, Lucent Technologies, and Northern Telecom as well as telephone and cable-television companies compete to upgrade transmission methods and speeds.

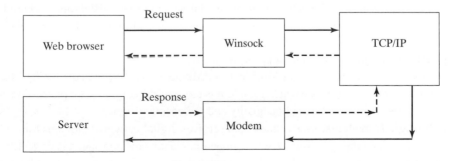

Figure 1.5   Windows Winsock communication.

1.15   Types of Modems

Different types of modems exist. What most people refer to as just "a modem" is and analog modem. In this book, when we say a modem, we mean an analog modem. A **modem** is a device that is used to transfer data from one location to another through phone lines. On the sending end, the modem converts the data into sound (analog) waves that can be transmitted through the phone lines. Thus, the modem acts as a modulator. On the receiving end, the modem performs the opposite operation: It converts the sound waves back to data. Here, the modem acts as a demodulator. The name modem originates from the words "*mo*dulator" and "*dem*odulator."

The battle for faster dial-up connections has resulted in many technologies and ways to access the Internet. Here is a list of the available modem types for dial-up users:

1. **Telephone (analog) modems.** This is the most common and least expensive way to connect to the Internet, but it is also the slowest. The fastest modem speed today is 56K; that is, the modem can transmit 56,000 bits of data per second. Slower modem speeds, such as 28.8K and 14.4K, also exist. The slower the modem speed, the longer it takes to download Web pages. Most home PCs come with a 56K modem. All 56K modems use the ITU V.90 analog modem speed standard.

2. **Cable modems.** Cable-television wires, made of coaxial cables, can be adapted to transfer data at access speeds as high as 10 Mbps. Cable companies charge monthly fees for using cable modems and may charge installation fees as well. With cable modems, the cable company becomes one's ISP. Users who are interested in utilizing cable modems should check with their local cable companies to make sure that the service exists in their area or neighborhood. Cable modems share the bandwidth with many users; thus, ISPs that offer cable connections usually prohibit running a server. DSL providers (see the next item) do not.

3. **DSL and ADSL modems.** Digital subscriber line (DSL) and asynchronous DSL (ADSL) are technologies that allow Internet users to tap into the Internet over an ordinary phone line, at speeds significantly faster than those of the existing V.90 modems. DSL modems use existing phone lines. A DSL modem takes an electronic signal and splits it so that a single phone wire can transmit voice (regular phone calls) and data (Internet content) simultaneously. A DSL modem uses the same speed for both downloading and uploading. An ADSL modem splits the bandwidth so that more of it is dedicated to downloading. Thus, ADSL modems allow faster downloads than uploads. Use of DSL and ADSL modems enables one family member to chat on the phone or fax a document while another member in the same house is surfing the Web, using the same phone line. Speeds of DSL and ADSL modems range from 144K bits to 1.5Mb per second, with plans for 7.1 Mbps in the works. DSL works best when the modem is close to the origin of the phone line and suffers greatly with decreasing line quality and increasing distance.

4. **ISDN (digital) modems.** ISDN (integrated services digital network) modems transmit data, voice, and video over ordinary telephone lines. Transmission speed is up to 128 Kbps. An ISDN line is a digital line. It uses twisted-pair copper wires. The monthly fee for an ISDN line depends on its speed and use.

5. B-ISDN modems. These modems are broadband ISDN modems. (The previously mentioned ISDN modems are narrowband ISDN modems.) B-ISDN lines use fiber optics instead of twisted-pair copper wires. B-ISDN is much faster than ISDN.

6. Satellite modems. Satellite-based Internet access uses a satellite dish to receive data at an average speed of 300 Kbps. A satellite Internet connection requires a special receiver, a PC adapter card, and special software. Each one of these components has a price associated with it, in addition to a monthly fee. The advantage of satellite-based Internet connection is that it allows rural areas and the developing world, where phone lines are rare or nonexistent, to access the Internet.

7. Wireless (cellular) modems. Cellular modems are used to connect a laptop computer or a cellular phone to the Internet. This capability alleviates the need to plug the laptop into a wall socket. Users can check their e-mail while on the road, on a boat, in a plane, etc. Wireless modems are slow. While connected, the modem may transfer data at a rate of 9600 bits per second over a cellular phone line, thus costing you a lot just to check your e-mail, for example. To try to bring the cost down, the cellular phone companies have developed a replacement for the TCP/IP protocol. The new protocol is called CDPD (cellular digital packet data). The CDPD packets are IP packets encrypted for security purposes. This technique allows cellular phone companies to charge customers by packets transferred and not by the number of minutes of connection.

Example 1.6   Understand home broadband networking.

How do you network multiple computers at home to share the same cable or DSL modem?

Solution 1.6   You can buy a home broadband networking kit from an electronics store. The kit typically comes with a router (hub), network cables, and LAN cards. A cable or DSL line connects your ISP to the cable or DSL modem at home. Another cable connects the modem to the router. A LAN card is installed into each computer at home. Each card is connected to the router via a separate cable. In addition, LAN software is installed on each computer. The software must be configured before successful communication through the network can be achieved. It is preferred that the kit provide wireless networking, because a wireless setup is more convenient to use around the house.

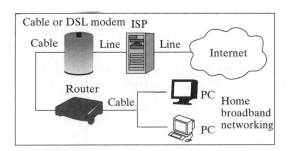

1.16 Internet Tools

The effective daily use of the Internet requires some essential tools. These tools are primarily computer programs. While many readers have already used them extensively, we list them here as a reminder. These tools, and others, are covered in more detail throughout the book. The basic tools are a Web browser, a virus-scan program, a zip–unzip program, a screen-capture program, an FTP program, a Telnet program, and a graphics program. A **screen capture** is an image of the entire computer screen or parts of it.

Some of these programs are shareware, while others are freeware. **Shareware** is software that is distributed for free on trial basis for a period of time, usually 30 days. The user may purchase a copy of the shareware at the end of the trial period. **Freeware**, on the other hand, is software that is offered free, at no cost on a permanent basis. Freeware is copyrighted, and you cannot use it in any of your own software development without permission from its developer.

The easiest way to generate a screen capture in Windows OS is to use the `Print Screen` key on the computer keyboard. Simply hit the key. This places the screen capture (the image in a bit-map format) in the system clipboard. You can then open, for example, a Word document and paste the screen capture into it. (See Tutorial 1.17.6.) Alternatively, you can open a graphics program, such as Paint, and paste in the clipboard content.

1.17 Tutorials

Note that we print command, icon, and button names in roman Courier font and file names in italic Courier font.

1.17.1   Use Client/Server Diagnostic Commands (Study Sections 1.4 and 1.5)

We use three commands in this tutorial: `finger`, `ping`, and `traceroute`. We use Windows OS throughout this book. When we say "click," we mean click the mouse left button of the mouse. "Right-click" means to click the right button of the mouse. When we need you to type an input, we use "type" followed by the input. We separate a sequence of clicks by =>. Follow these steps:

1. **Open a DOS window.** `Start` (Windows `Start` button) => `Run` => Type `cmd` => `OK`.

2. **Use the `finger` command.** Let us check if the user `zeid` is logged into the `coe.neu.edu` host. Type `finger zeid@gateway.coe.neu.edu` at the DOS prompt. Although `zeid` is a current user on `gateway.coe.neu.edu`, Figure 1.6 shows that the command fails, because it is not permitted by the host. The system administrator has disabled it.

Figure 1.6   The finger command.

```
C:\WINDOWS\System32\cmd.exe                              _ □ ×
Microsoft Windows XP [Version 5.1.2600]
(C) Copyright 1985-2001 Microsoft Corp.

C:\Documents and Settings\Z>tracert gateway.coe.neu.edu

Tracing route to Free.coe.neu.edu [129.10.33.202]
over a maximum of 30 hops:

  1     8 ms    12 ms    26 ms   10.221.112.1
  2     8 ms    10 ms     9 ms   24.62.0.1
  3     9 ms    14 ms     9 ms   65.96.1.149
  4    10 ms     9 ms     9 ms   bar02-p7-0.ndhmhe1.ma.attbb.net [24.91.0.46]
  5     8 ms    11 ms    11 ms   bar02-p2-0.cmbrhe1.ma.attbb.net [24.91.0.157]
  6     8 ms    12 ms    14 ms   192.5.89.137
  7    11 ms    10 ms     9 ms   NU-GIGAPOPNE.NOX.ORG [192.5.89.18]
  8    10 ms    20 ms    54 ms   129.10.6.49
  9     9 ms    10 ms     9 ms   129.10.6.11
 10     *         *        *     Request timed out.
 11     *         *        *     Request timed out.
 12     *         *        *     Request timed out.
 13     *         *        *     Request timed out.
 14    21 ms    32 ms    16 ms   13-sn-1.cne.neu.edu [129.10.24.38]
 15    11 ms    11 ms    11 ms   Gamma.coe.neu.edu [129.10.33.202]

Trace complete.
```

Figure 1.7   The tracert command.

3. **Use the tracert command.** Type the command tracert gateway.coe.neu.edu at the DOS prompt in order to examine the route between you (the client) and the gateway server. The route has 15 hops, 4 of which are timed out (Figure 1.7). Some hops have both host names and IP addresses. The last hop is gamma.coe.neu.edu, which is another name (alias) for gateway.coe.neu.edu. The number of hops depends on the route; it changes all the time.

4. **Use the ping command.** Check whether the gateway.coe.neu.edu server is up and running before using it. Type ping gateway.coe.neu.edu at the DOS prompt. The server responds (Figure 1.8), which means that its IP address is valid and that it can accept requests.

Figure 1.8   The `ping` command.

1.17.2   Use DNS Lookup Tables (Study Sections 1.7, 1.8, and 1.9)

In this tutorial, we use the `nslookup` command to convert a host name to an IP address and vice versa. First, find the IP addresses of both `www.mit.edu` and `www.yahoo.com`. Type `nslookup  www.mit.edu` at the DOS prompt. The MIT IP address is `18.181.0.31` (Figure 1.9). Then type `nslookup  www.yahoo.com`. This time, the command returns multiple IP addresses, as also shown in Figure 1.9. Companies that expect heavy Web traffic, such as Yahoo!, map their host name to many servers in order to balance the traffic load on these servers.

We now use the `nslookup` command to find the host name of an IP address. Type `nslookup 205.188.145.215`. Figure 1.9 shows that this is the IP address of `www.aol.com`.

To learn more, type `nslookup` at the DOS prompt and then hit `Enter`. Next type `?` and hit `Enter` again. Windows displays many other useful commands. Try some or all of them. For example, if you type `name` and hit `Enter`, the name and IP address of your current server are displayed. When you are done, type `exit` to get back to the DOS prompt.

1.17.3   Use File Protocols in a Browser (Study Section 1.11)

In this tutorial, we use the File and Mailto protocols. Open a browser window on your computer. Find a text file on your computer's hard drive, and open it in the browser window. Observe the URL that the browser uses for the file. It is presented in the File protocol. You cannot open a file whose format is not supported by the browser.

The Mailto protocol allows you to use a browser to open your e-mail tool. Type `mailto:zeid@coe.neu.edu` in the browser. Type a message after the mail-tool window is open.

Figure 1.9   The nslookup command.

1.17.4   Using WinZip to Zip and Unzip Files (Study Section 1.12)

If you do not have the WinZip program already installed on your computer, download and install a copy. Follow these steps to compress three files into one zip file with the name testZip:

1. **Create testZip as an empty zip file.** Right-click on your computer's Desktop => New => WinZip File. Type the file name testZip and hit Enter. The extension of this file is .zip.
2. **Add the three files to testZip.** Drag and drop each of the three files onto the testZip icon.
3. **Check the content of testZip.** Double-click the testZip file icon. Follow the prompts to open the file in WinZip. You should see the three files if testZip was successfully created.

To unzip the file you just created, double-click it and follow the WinZip prompts.

In some cases, we need to zip entire directories (folders) while maintaining the directory structure in the resulting zip file. We now use WinZip to create the testFolder zip file that contains and maintains all subfolders of the myDir folder. To do so, follow this sequence: Start WinZip => Click New => Type testFolder as the name of the zip file we want to create => Click OK => Select the myDir folder from the combo box (drop-down list) => Check Include subfolders => Click Add with wildcards. Unzip testFolder to verify its correct creation.

1.17.5 Create a PPP Dial-Up Connection in Windows (Study Section 1.14)

Windows makes creating a dial-up connection transparent to the user. But first you need to obtain a PPP account from your service provider. Whether your service provider is your employer or an ISP, the provider should set up a PPP account for you and furnish you with a phone number, a username, and a password. You need this account information to log into the provider's server and eventually to the Internet.

The actual steps required to set up the connection depend on the version of Windows you are using. The latest versions require the phone number and the PPP account information (username and password). In addition, earlier versions require the user to configure the modem (specify its speed) and the server (specify its IP address and enable the TCP/IP protocol). Interested readers should check with their service providers. Follow this sequence if you use Windows XP: `My Computer` => `Control Panel` => `Network Connections` => `Create a new connection` => `Next` => `Connect to the Internet` => `Next` => `Set up my connection manually` => `Next` => `Connect using a dial-up modem` => `Next` => Type ISP name (this becomes the name of the connection after you create it) => `Next` => Type the phone number => `Next` => Type username and password => `Finish`.

This procedure creates a connection icon and places it under the `Dial-up` heading in the `Network Connections` folder of the `Control Panel`. Double-click the icon to connect to the Internet.

1.17.6 Create and Use a Screen Capture (Study Section 1.16)

In this tutorial, we create a screen capture in Windows OS and include it in a Word document. Follow these steps:

1. **Capture the screen.** After you have the desired screen content (e.g., windows or an open file), hit the `Print Screen` key on the keyboard.
2. **Paste the screen capture into a Word document.** Open a Word document. Position the cursor where you want to paste the screen capture, and select `Edit` (on the Word menu bar) => `Paste`. You can also paste the screen capture inside a textbox to scale it down, if required.

Search the Web for more elaborate screen-capture programs. They allow you to control and specify which part of the screen you can capture, such as the active window, multiple windows, or a region, These programs also allow elaborate image editing such as scaling and rotating.

FAQs

Each chapter has a FAQs (frequently asked questions) section. It has answers to previous students' questions as well as to other questions one might ask. If you want to contribute to this section, please e-mail the author at `zeid@coe.neu.edu`.

General

Q: Is the Internet free? Who pays when I am connected to a site in, say, Australia?

A: You pay in the form of an access fee to your ISP.

Q: What is the difference between the Internet and the WWW?

A: The WWW is the part of the Internet that features multimedia capabilities such as images, audio, and video. The WWW is thus a subset of the Internet.

Q: How do I learn more about the chapter topics?

A: Search the Internet itself, using a search engine.

Q: What is a POP?

A: POP is a term that stand for *point of presence*. It is an access point with an IP address to the Internet. ISPs have many POPs in various geographical locations, to allow customers to connect to the Internet via local phone calls. POP also stands for Post Office Protocol. For example, POP3 is a popular e-mail server type. We cover e-mail in more detail in Chapter 3.

Q: How can I find people and companies on the Internet?

A: Use search engines. Try this website: `http://www.switchboard.com`.

Q: Why does a shareware I downloaded and installed not work correctly?

A: Downloading a file could result in its corrupt on because of say, a bad Internet connection. Try to download it again.

URLs and IP Addresses (Sections 1.8–1.11)

Q: What are the different parts of a domain name?

A: Consider the website `www.coe.neu.edu`. `www` is the host name, `coe.neu.edu` is the second-level domain name, and `edu` is the TLD.

Q: What is the difference between a URL, a website, a domain name, and an IP address?

A: Consider the URL `http://www.coe.neu.edu`. `http` is the file protocol, and `www.coe.neu.edu` is the website (also known as the domain name). The IP address is `129.10.32.98`. The website is the name of the IP address. You can use `http://129.10.32.98` as a URL instead of `http://www.coe.neu.edu`.

B l a c k b o x

This section provides a chapter summary in a hands-on fashion. We believe that this approach is beneficial for a couple of reasons. First, readers can use this section as a central location and reminder for the general information provided in this chapter, as well as for review after reading the chapter. Second, readers who prefer to learn by "doing first" before reading the chapter can start with this section.

Sections 1.1–1.3 (the Internet and the WWW): The World Wide Web is the largest section of the Internet. It supports multimedia capabilities.

Sections 1.4–1.7 (communication under the client/server model): This model allows two networked computers to communicate together. Data are transmitted between the two computers as packets via the TCP/IP protocol. Three useful commands that you can use to probe a server are `finger`, `ping`, and `traceroute`. To use them, type them in an OS window. Their syntax is as follows:

`finger` hostname—for example, `finger coe.neu.edu`.
`finger` username@hostname—for example, `finger zeid@coe.neu.edu`.
`ping` hostname—for example, `ping coe.neu.edu`.
`finger` username@hostname—for example, `finger zeid@coe.neu.edu`.
`traceroute` hostname—for example, `traceroute www.mit.edu` (Unix OS).
`tracert` hostname—for example, `tracert www.mit.edu` (Windows OS).

Sections 1.8–1.11 (IP addresses, URLs, domain names e-mail addresses, and file protocols): Consider this URL: `http://www.mit.edu`. `http:` is the file protocol. `www.mit.edu` is the website (also known as the domain name). `www` is the host name. `mit.edu` is the second-level domain. `edu` is the TLD. The IP address corresponds to the domain name. The file protocol is not part of the IP address. The IP address for `www.mit.edu` is `18.181.0.31`. The available file protocols are HTTP, HTTPS, Mailto, NNTP, FTP, Telnet, and File.

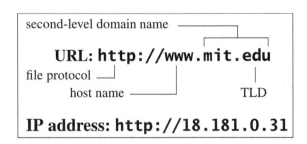

Section 1.12 (compression and decompression of files): We compress (zip) files to reduce their sizes in order to speed up their downloading or uploading. Compressed files must be decompressed (unzipped) before they may be used. The WinZip program for Windows may be used to create zip files and archives. Follow this sequence to create a zip file with the name `testZip`: Right click on your computer's desktop => `New` => `WinZip File` => Type the file name `testZip` and hit `Enter` => Drag and drop file(s) onto the `testZip` icon.

Follow this sequence to create the archive `testFolder`: Start WinZip => Click `New` => Type `testFolder` as the name of the zip archive we want to create => Click `OK` => Select `IZED folder` from the combo box (drop-down list) => Check `Include subfolders` => Click `Add with wildcards`. Unzip `testFolder` to verify its correct creation.

Sections 1.13–1.16 (connecting to the Internet): You need a modem and a PPP account to create a home Internet connection. If you use Windows XP, follow this sequence to create a PPP connection: `My Computer => Control Panel => Network Connections` (see the first of the screen captures shown next) `=> Create a new connection => Next => Connect to the Internet => Next => Set up my connection manually => Next => Connect using a dial-up modem => Next =>` Type the ISP name, say `myPPPConnection` (this becomes the name of the connection after you create it) `=> Next =>` Type `the phone number => Next =>` Type the username and password `=> Finish`.

This procedure creates a connection icon and places it under the `Dial-up` heading in the `Network Connections` folder of the `Control Panel`. (See the second of the screen captures shown next.) Double-click the icon to connect to the Internet.

Check Your Progress

At the end of this chapter, you should be able to

✔   distinguish between the Internet and the WWW (Section 1.2);
✔   describe the client/server model and use its diagnostic commands (Sections 1.4 and 1.5);
✔   explain how data are transmitted across the Internet via the TCP/IP protocol (Section 1.7);

✔ describe URLs, IP addresses, and domain names (Sections 1.8 and 1.9);
✔ recognize the structure of e-mail addresses (Section 1.10);
✔ identify and use file protocols (Section 1.11);
✔ describe and use file compression and decompression (Section 1.12);
✔ understand the difference between the Internet, intranets, and extranets (Section 1.13);
✔ describe the different Internet connections (Section 1.14);
✔ distinguish between the different types of modems (Section 1.15).

Problems

The exercises are designed for a lab setting, while the homework is to be done outside class time.

Exercises

1.1   Use the `ping` and `traceroute` commands to probe the status of `www.amazon.com`.

1.2   Use the `nslookup` command to find the IP address of the website `www.harvard.edu`, and vice versa.

1.3   If you do not have WinZip, download and install it on your computer.

1.4   Use the `Print Screen` button on your keyboard to capture the screen. Include the resulting image in a Word document, and print it.

Homework

1.5   Apply the client/server model of computing to a computer that you use to order books from Amazon.com. Sketch the model, and identify the client and the database servers. Is the model two tier or three tier? Why?

1.6   What is the standard size, in bytes, of the packets that the TCP/IP protocol produces when it breaks down data? If each character is represented by 2 bytes, how many packets are needed to transfer the message, *Our group meeting is next week*?

1.7   Identify the file protocol, the host name, domain name, the second-level domain name, and the TLD for the following URLs:

   a. `http://www.sales.company.com`
   b. `ftp://ftp.gateweay.school.edu`
   c. `telnet://alpha.server.organization.org`
   d. `mailto:brown@seals.navy.mil`

1.8   Write the pattern that a compression program would use to compress the following string: AAAAAAAAAAAAAAZZZZ222222PPPPPPPPPPXXXX . Note that this question oversimplifies compression algorithms. Nevertheless, it serves as a good illustration.

1.9   Using WinZip, follow the directions in Tutorial 1.17.4 to create a zip archive of one of your folders. Use the name `testFolder` for the archive zip file. Unzip the resulting file to ensure its correct creation.

1.10 Example 1.6 shows a home broadband wired network. Adapt it for a wireless network. Sketch the wireless network.

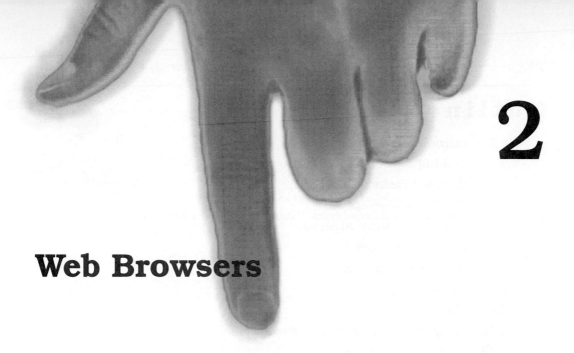

2

Web Browsers

Goal

Understand and master the use of Web browsers, to make surfing the Web a more pleasant and productive experience.

Objectives

- Browser tasks
- Browser window structure
- Microsoft Internet Explorer 6.0
- Netscape Communicator 4.8 and 7.01
- Opera 7 browser and Crazy Browser 1.05
- Managing browsers: cache, plug-ins, and customization
- Managing Web surfing: boomarks, privacy, and security
- Browsers for handhelds

Outline

2.1 Introduction

To access the Web, you need an Internet connection and a browser. A **Web browser** is a computer program that displays the content of Web pages. We use browsers to view Web pages. A **Web page** is a document (file) that typically is richly formatted with fonts, graphics, colors, audio, video, or animation. Browsers originate requests that locate and retrieve Web pages from servers every time you click hyperlinks, or links for short. A **hyperlink** is a word or a collection of words that allows a user to proceed to, and view the content of, another Web page upon clicking the link. A hyperlink in a Web page, thus acts as a pointer to another Web page. Hyperlinks are based on the hypertext concept. Unlike traditional text, **hypertext** is dynamic; it allows a reader of a Web page to jump from one page to another, during reading, by clicking on its link.

A Web-page file stores the code (rules) that defines the presentation format of the page. A Web browser uses this code to render and display the page. If the rendered page is too long to fit in a browser window, the user must scroll it up and down in order to view all of its content.

A browser window is like the window of any other computer application. The user can size it up or down, minimize it, activate it (i.e., bring it to the foreground on the desktop), deactivate it (i.e., send it to the background of the desktop), or close it (i.e., kill, or stop running, the browser application).

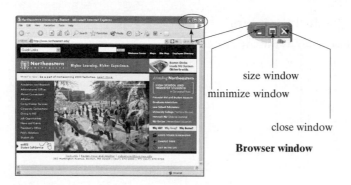

size window

minimize window

close window

Browser window

Many Web browsers exist. We cover four of them in this chapter: Internet Explorer Netscape, Opera, and Crazy Browser.

2.2 Finding a Web Page

The browser fulfills your request of a Web page as follows (Figure 2.1 illustrates this process):

1. The browser receives the request from you when you type the page's URL in its window.
2. The browser sends the URL to the domain name system (DNS) server, which replies with the IP address of the Web-server computer you wish to contact.
3. The TCP/IP packets make their way to the server by passing through some routers.
4. When the Web server receives the packets, it locates the requested file and sends it along with your IP address, as outbound packets to your browser.

2.3 Browser Tasks

The common browser tasks are viewing, navigating, downloading files, and printing. Many browsers have built-in e-mail tools. Viewing and navigation of Web pages are the bedrock of a browser.

The growing popularity of the Web has greatly increased the feasibility of downloading files. After a user finds a particular file on the Web, clicking its associated link will cause it to be downloaded.

Printing is a simple, but useful, task. The user can print a Web page displayed by the browser via the browser's `Print` button.

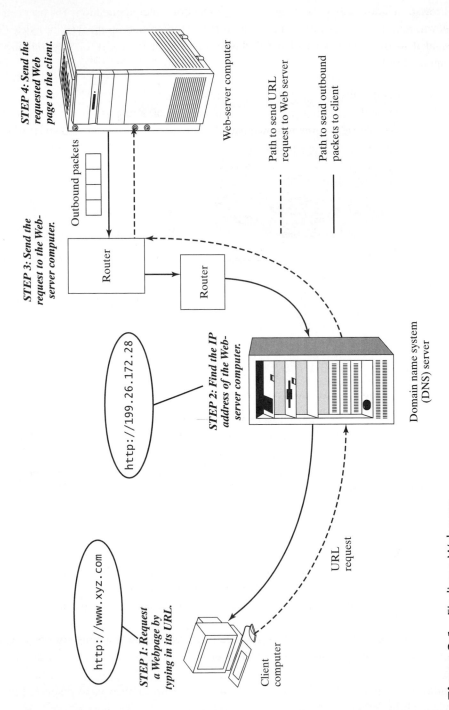

Figure 2.1 Finding a Web page.

2.4   The Two Browsers

Microsoft Internet Explorer (IE) is the major browser that Internet users employ to navigate the Web. Netscape Communicator comes in as a distant second to IE. Both browsers offer similar functionality. Their windows' look and feel are similar. However, there have been debates and studies about the comparative performance, speed, and ease of use of these two browsers.

Downloading and installing a browser software is a straightforward process. Visit `http://www.microsoft.com` to download IE software. Look for the `Downloads` link and then follow the prompts. The version we cover in this chapter is IE 6.0. Double-click the downloaded file and follow the prompts to install IE on your computer.

Visit `http://www.netscape.com` to download Netscape Communicator. Look for the `Downloads` link and then follow the prompts. Double-click the downloaded file and follow the prompts to install Communicator on your computer. Netscape is based on the Mozilla browser of The Mozilla Foundation (`http://www.mozilla.org`). Netscape has two distinct products: Netscape 4.8 and Netscape 7.01. Netscape 4.8 is the older product. It does not support XML (Extensible Markup Language). **XML** is the metalanguage on which XHTML is based. Netscape 7.01 is the newer product. The newer Netscape product originated with version 6.0 and supports XML. Some users of the Netscape browser prefer the older Netscape 4 product. We cover both Netscape 4.8 and 7.01 here. You can download Netscape Communicator 4.8 from the Netscape FTP servers at `ftp://ftp.netscape.com/pub/communicator/english/4.8`. Netscape's website's `Downloads` link directs the user to Netscape 7.01.

Figures 2.2–2.4 illustrate the two browsers' windows. The structure of each window and the use of each browser are covered in detail throughout this chapter. While IE has only one module, Communicator 4.8 consists of five modules: `Navigator`, `Inbox`, `Newsgroups`, `Address Book`, and `Composer`. Figure 2.3 shows icons for the five modules. The `Navigator` is the browser module, whose window is shown in Figure 2.3. The `Inbox` and `Newsgroups` modules enable users to access their e-mail and newsgroup messages, respectively. Users may employ the `Address Book` to save e-mail addresses. The `Composer` is the Netscape XHTML editor that is used to develop Web pages. This chapter covers the details of the `Navigator` only.

Netscape 4.8 provides a `Component` bar that is docked at the bottom right corner of the browser window, as shown in Figure 2.3. The bar has five icons that provide access to the five modules. Clicking any of these icons opens the corresponding module. If, for example, you use Netscape as your e-mail tool, clicking the `Inbox` icon will open the e-mail window. Moving the mouse over each icon displays the icon's name. The user can expand the `Component` bar by clicking the lines at its left edge (as pointed out in Figure 2.3) and can move the expanded bar by dragging its title bar to the desired location. The expanded `Component` bar can be "docked" back at the bottom right corner by clicking the Close box (x). If the user right-clicks on the title bar, a popup menu is displayed, as shown in Figure 2.3. The display of the bar can be changed by choosing any of the menu items. The expanded bar can be displayed horizontally or vertically.

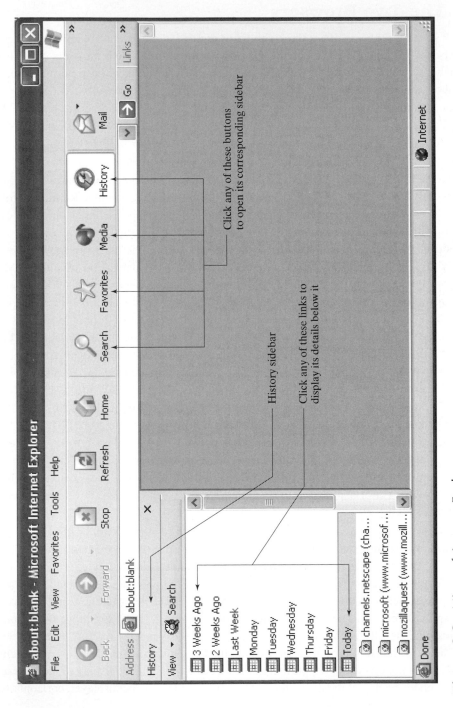

Figure 2.2 Microsoft Internet Explorer.

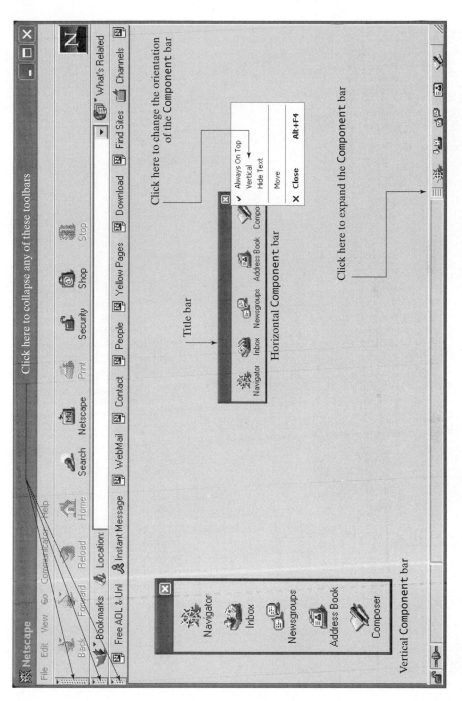

Figure 2.3 Netscape Communicator 4.8.

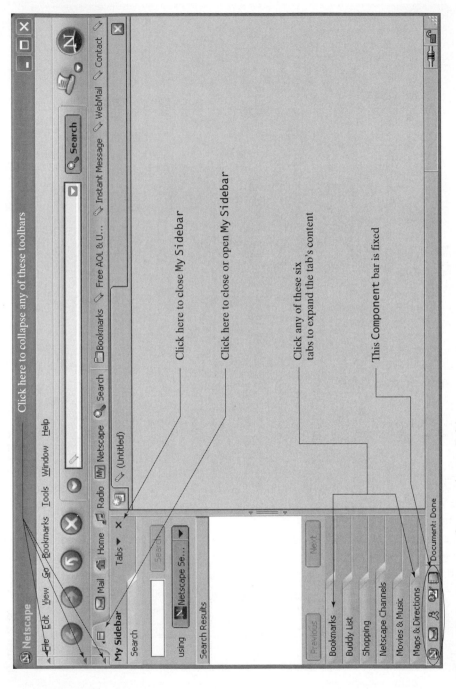

Figure 2.4 Netscape Communicator 7.01.

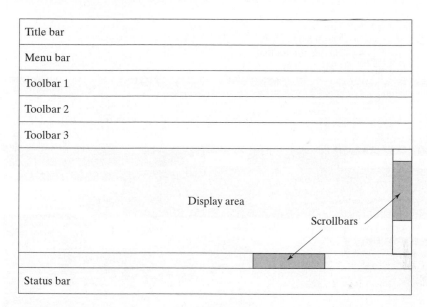

Figure 2.5 Structure of a browser window.

2.5   Browser Window Structure

The generic structure of a browser window is shown in Figure 2.5. The structure consists of several bars on the top of the window and one bar on the bottom, with the display area in between. The **title bar**, at the very top of the window, displays the title of the current Web page being viewed. The **menu bar**, located directly below the title bar, contains the pull-down menus. Following the menu bar are several toolbars, used for navigation, entering URLs, and other activities. The bar at the bottom of the browser window is the **status bar**. This bar displays messages to the users informing them about the progress of the current task. For example, if the current task is the downloading of a Web page, the browser displays a text or other visual message indicating how much of the page has been already downloaded and how much is remaining.

The **display area** of the browser window shows the contents of the current Web page. If the Web page is too big to fit within the display area, the browser creates horizontal or vertical scrollbars automatically, to enable the user to scroll its window to view the page.

Example 2.1 Observe the browser window structure of popular browsers.

Apply the browser window structure shown in Figure 2.5 to both IE and Netscape browsers to point out the various parts of each browser.

Solution 2.1 We use IE version 6.0 and Netscape version 7.01. The window structure for IE browser is shown as follows:

Title bar
Menu bar
Navigation toolbar
URL toolbar

Links toolbar

Status bar   Display area   Scroll bars

2.6 Internet Explorer

2.6.1 Menus

The IE window is shown in Figure 2.2. The figure shows the title bar, the menu bar, three toolbars (`Standard Buttons` (navigation toolbar), `Address` bar (URL toolbar), and `Links`), and the status bar. The title bar displays the title of the current Web page and appends – `Microsoft Internet Explorer` to the title.

The menu bar has six menus: `File`, `Edit`, `View`, `Favorites`, `Tools`, and `Help`. We cover the first three menus and the `Help` menu in this section. Favorites are covered in Sections 2.10 and 2.13. Figure 2.6 shows the four menus we discuss in this section. The `File` menu has

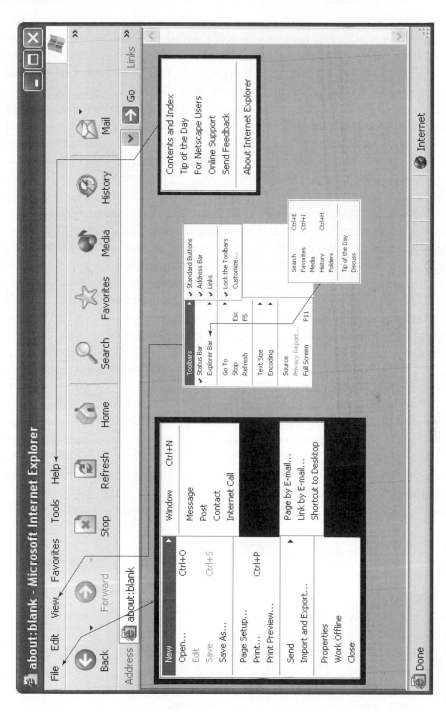

Figure 2.6 Internet Explorer 6.0 menus.

submenus. The `New` submenu allows you to open a new browser (`Window`), open an e-mail window (`Message`), open an Internet connection to post a message to a newsgroup (`Post`), open the address book (`Contact`), or use Microsoft NetMeeting software to communicate with others and use video to see them over the Internet (`Internet Call`). The `Internet Call` is similar to video conferencing on the Internet. The `Open` menu item allows the user to open a file in the browser. While this could be any file, we usually open XHTML files (Web pages), whether they reside on the local hard disk or on the Internet. The `Page Setup` and `Print` menu items act similarly to the corresponding items one finds in a word processor's windows. The `Send` submenu allows the user to send a page or a link by e-mail (`Page By Email` and `Link By Email`, respectively) and to create a shortcut to the currently displayed Web page in the browser window on the desktop (`Shortcut To Desktop`). The `Import and Export` menu item allows the user to import (export) information into (from) IE from (to) other applications or a file on the local disk of the computer on which IE is currently running. The `Properties` menu item lists all the properties of the Web page currently displayed in the browser. The `Work Offline` menu item acts as a toggle that enables use of the browser in an online (can access the Web) or offline (cannot access the Web) mode. The `Close` menu item closes the current browser window.

The `Edit` menu includes items such as `Cut`, `Copy`, `Paste`, and `Select All`. These items work similarly to the menu items one encounters on a word processor's `Edit` menu. The `Find (on This Page)` menu item allows the user to find elements of the currently displayed Web page.

The `View` menu and its items and submenus are shown in Figure 2.6 and in the screen capture on this page. The `Toolbars` submenu can turn on and off the `Standard Buttons`, `Address Bar`, and `Links`. The `Customize` menu item of the `Toolbars` submenu allows the user to replace the `Standard Buttons` by other buttons. This is hardly ever done by most users. The `Status Bar` menu item of the `View` menu toggles on and off the status bar at the bottom of the browser window. The `Explorer Bar` submenu has seven menu items. We discuss some of them here. The `Search` menu item enables the user to search the Internet. The user must be online to use it. The `Favorites` menu item lists the user's bookmarks. The `History` menu item lists the history of the current browser window. The **History** is a list of all visited URLs

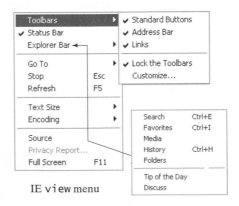

IE `view` menu

recently during a given period of time, such as past 10 days, that the user sets during browser configuration. The `Folders` menu item lists the folders of the computer on which the browser is running. The `Go To` submenu allows the user to navigate the history list. The `Stop` and `Refresh` menu items stop and refresh the current page, respectively. The `Text Size` submenu allows the user to change the size of the text of the current Web page. The `Encoding` submenu allows the user to display a Web page in another language, such as Arabic. The browser will ask the user to download the corresponding language support software if it is not already installed. The `Source` menu item displays the XHTML source (code) of the currently displayed Web page in a Notepad window. **Notepad** is Windows's text editor. The `Full Screen` menu item expands the current IE window to fill the screen.

The last menu on the menu bar of IE is the `Help` menu. Figure 2.6 and the upcoming insert show its items. Some of the menu items, such as `Online Support` and `Send Feedback`, require the user to be online. The other items of the `Help` menu (`Contents and Index`, `Tip of the Day`, `For Netscape Users`, and `About Internet Explorer`) work off-line. The `About Internet Explorer` item displays information about the browser and its version. The `Contents and Index` menu item is quite useful; you can use it to search for details about IE and its use.

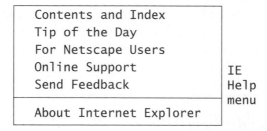

2.6.2   Toolbars

IE has four toolbars, as shown in Figure 2.2 and Example 2.1. (Three are shown in the upcoming insert.) The `Standard Buttons` (navigation) toolbar has several useful buttons. Using the `Back` and `Forward` buttons, the user can cycle through the history list of previously visited websites and reload anyone of them. The browser saves the websites the user visits during a session in its memory cache. These websites make up the history list. The `Stop` button is used to interrupt the current transfer of data from the server to the client and vice versa. The `Refresh`

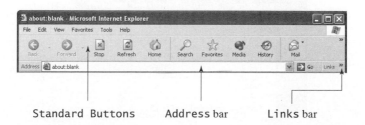

button reloads the current Web page. The Home button loads the home Web page defined in the browser settings. Using the Search button, the user can access search tools to navigate the Web. The Favorites button is similar to the Favorites menu on the menu bar. The History button displays the same results as clicking the sequence View (from the menu bar) => Explorer Bar => History. Clicking the Mail button produces the same menu items as clicking the following sequence Tools (from the menu bar) => Mail and News. Why do the three buttons Favorites, History, and Mail repeat functionality? It is a matter of preference about where to access them. It is more convenient to access them from the Standard Buttons toolbar, where they are directly visible. The Print button (not shown) prints the current Web page as the user sees it on the screen. The Edit button (not shown) invokes an editor to edit the currently displayed Web page.

The Address (URL) toolbar has a text field in which the user types the URL. If the URL is a website, the user does not need to type in the protocol; the browser assumes it is HTTP. Next to the Address bar is the Go button, as shown in the previous insert. After typing the URL in the Address bar, the user clicks the Go button to download the Web page. Alternatively, the user can simply hit the Enter key on the keyboard.

The Links toolbar is located next to the Go button. Some of its links connect the user to the website http://www.microsoft.com.

The Status bar is shown in Figure 2.2 and Example 2.1. On the left, there is an area that displays the status of the loading of Web-page information to the browser. The area on the far right displays a globe next to the word "Internet." If the user double-clicks the globe, a window displaying security settings will popup.

Example 2.2 Use the Edit menu of IE.

Learn when and how to use IE's Edit menu.

Solution 2.2 The Edit menu and its menu items are shown in the upcoming insert. The Cut, Copy, and Paste items apply to the URL of the currently displayed Web page. When you select the URL by highlighting it, these three menu items are activated. If you select text in the Web page itself, you can only copy it and paste it; obviously, you cannot cut it. The Find (on This Page) menu item allows the user to find elements of the currently displayed Web page.

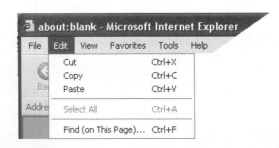

2.7 Netscape Communicator

2.7.1 Menus

Netscape 4.8 and 7.01 windows are shown in Figures 2.3 and 2.4, respectively. Similar to the IE window, each window has a title bar, a menu bar, and four toolbars (`Navigation` toolbar, `Location` (URL) toolbar, `Personal` toolbar, and `Status` bar).

The Communicator for version 4.8 consists of five modules: `Navigator`, `Inbox`, `Newsgroups`, `Address Book`, and `Composer` (Figure 2.3). Version 7.01's modules are `Navigator`, `Mail and Newsgroups`, `Instant Messenger`, `Composer`, and `Address Book` (Figure 2.4). The `Navigator` is the essential module.

Figures 2.7 and 2.8 show the menus and toolbars of Netscape 4.8 and 7.01, respectively. The menus of both versions are somewhat different. Netscape 7.01 employs tabs, a concept that does not exist in Netscape 4.8. The `File` menu in both versions allows the user to open a new Web page or a new browser window, among other things. Netscape 7.01's `New` submenu of the `File` menu opens a `Navigator` tab. A **tab** is a window inside a window. Tabs are convenient to use while surfing the Web. For example, instead of opening four separate browser windows and thereby cluttering the desktop, you open only one window with four tabs.

The following screen capture shows four tabs that holds four separate Web pages.

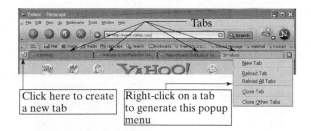

The `Edit` menu in Netscape is similar to that of IE. The most important item of the `Edit` menu is `Preferences`. It allows the user to customize the Netscape browser as needed. This menu item is covered in detail in Section 2.15.

The `View` menu and its items are shown in Figures 2.7 and 2.8. The `Show` submenu for version 4.8 can toggle on and off the `Navigation`, `Location`, and `Personal` toolbars, as well as the `Component` bar. The other menu items are self-explanatory. One item of particular interest is `Page Source`, which, when chosen by the user, causes Netscape to display the XHTML source (code) of the currently displayed Web page in a different window.

The `Go` menu is shown in Figures 2.7 and 2.8. Its menu items `Back`, `Forward`, and `Home` perform the same functions as the corresponding buttons of the `Navigation` toolbar. The last part of the `Go` menu shows the titles of the Web pages that are currently stored in the memory cache, with a check mark in front of the title of the currently displayed page.

The last menu on the menu bar of the Communicator is the `Help` menu. Figures 2.7 and 2.8 show its menu items. Some of the menu items, such as `Software Updates`, require the

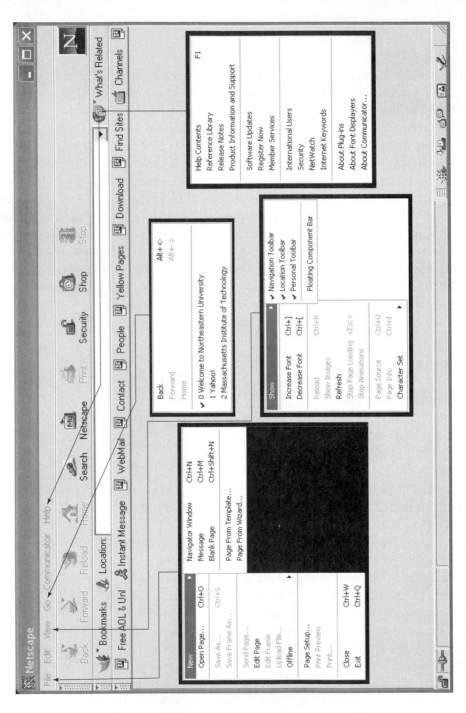

Figure 2.7 Netscape 4.8 menus.

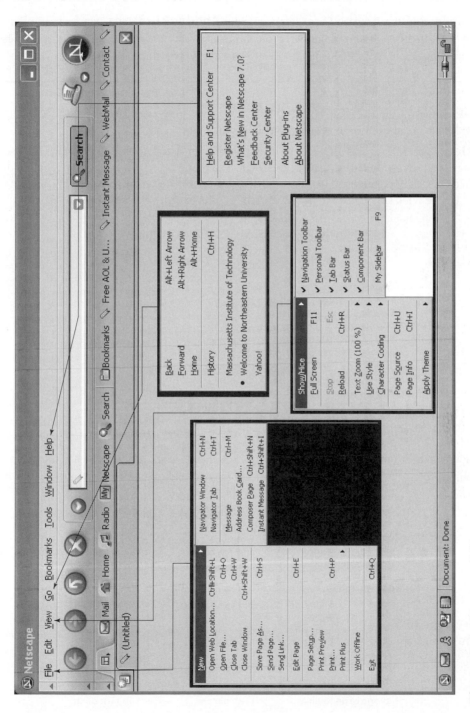

Figure 2.8 Netscape 7.01 menus.

user to connect to the Internet. Other items, such as About Plug-ins can be used off-line. The Help Contents item of the Help menu is quite useful; the user can use it as an online source of help to search for many details about Netscape's operations and use.

Example 2.3 Use Netscape's Help menu.

Use the Help menu to learn more about Netscape 7.0's tabs.

Solution 2.3 Follow this sequence to open the browser search tool: Help (on the browser's menu bar) => Help and Support Center. The Netscape 7.0 Help popup window will open up. Click the Search tab. Type tabbed browsing as the search string, and hit the Enter key or click Go. Click a topic listed in the results in order to learn about it.

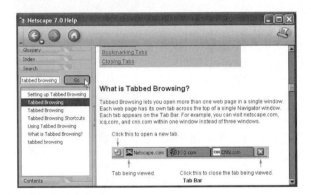

2.7.2   Toolbars

Netscape has four toolbars, as shown in Figures 2.3, 2.4, 2.7, and 2.8. (Three are shown in the following insert.) The Navigation toolbar has several useful buttons. Using the Back and

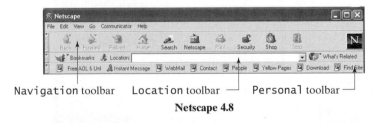

Navigation toolbar   Location toolbar   Personal toolbar

Netscape 4.8

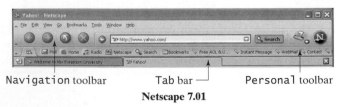

Navigation toolbar   Tab bar   Personal toolbar

Netscape 7.01

Forward buttons, the user can cycle through the history list of previously visited websites and reload any one of them. The Reload button reloads the current Web page. The Print button prints the current Web page. The Stop button stops the current loading of a Web page. It is worth noting that the Back and Forward buttons of the Navigation toolbar are also available as items in the Go menu. However, it is more convenient to access them from the Navigation toolbar, where they are directly visible.

The Personal toolbar includes buttons that provide useful information and services to the user. All of these buttons connect the user to various websites. Therefore, the user must be online to use them.

The Status bar, shown in Figures 2.3, 2.4, 2.7, and 2.8, is divided into five areas. The padlock symbol indicates the security information of the page. Then there is the toggle online/off-line button. The symbol of this button resembles a cable connection. The connection is on by default. Toggling the button forces the browser to go off-line, but it does not disconnect the Internet connection if there is one running at the time the button is clicked. The third area is the Component bar. The last two areas show the status of Web-page loading to the browser.

2.8 Opera

Opera is a Web browser that is similar in nature to both IE and Netscape. It can be downloaded from http://www.opera.com. Its Norwegian developer offers it free of charge, but with banner advertising. When Opera starts, it gives the user the option to continue previous sessions. A **session** is the period starting when a browser window opens until it closes. Opera is fast in downloading Web pages and does not crash very often. It also saves all currently open Web pages of a session and starts the next session where it left off.

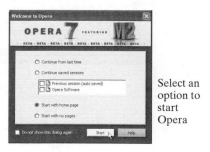

Select an option to start Opera

2.8.1 Menus

The Opera window is shown in Figure 2.9. The figure shows the title bar, the menu bar, and the toolbars. The title bar displays the title of the current Web page.

The menu bar has eight menus: File, Edit, View, Navigation, Bookmarks, Mail, Window, and Help. We cover the File, View, Window, and Help menus here. Figure 2.9 shows the four menus. The New page item of the File menu creates a tab in the current Opera window. The user can display a Web page in the new tab by typing its URL in the Address (URL) bar. The New window menu item, on the other hand, opens a new browser window.

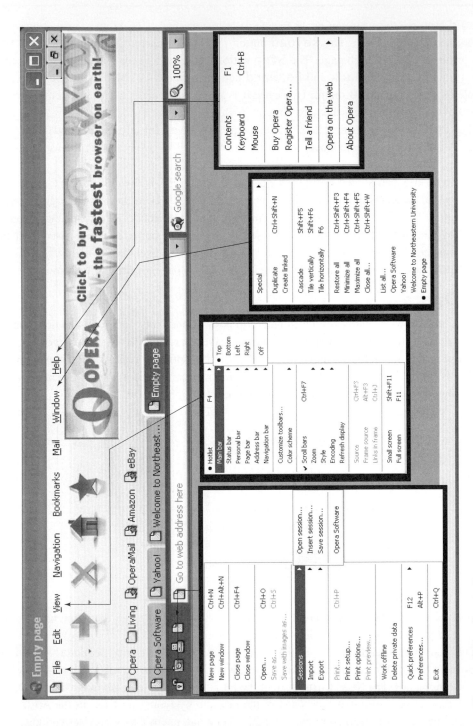

Figure 2.9 Opera 7 menus.

Opera uses the concept of sessions. Figure 2.9 shows the `Sessions` submenu and its items. A user can save sessions and open them later, or even insert a previous session into the current session.

The `View` menu allows the user to control the display and locations of Opera toolbars, among other things, as shown in Figure 2.9. The last two menu items control Opera's window size. If you choose the `Full screen` option, the Opera window will take over the entire desktop. Simply hit the `Esc` or `F11` key on the keyboard to shrink the window size back to its original size, or choose the `Small screen` option.

The `Window` menu enables the user to arrange the Web pages (tabs) of the browser window by cascading them (`Cascade` menu item) or tiling them (`Tile vertically` and `Tile horizontally` menu items). The last portion of the `View` menu lists all the current Web pages of the browser window.

The `Help` menu has two interesting menu items. The `Keyboard` item explains how to use keyboard shortcuts to speed up browsing activities. Similarly, the `Mouse` item shows how to use the mouse with browsing activities.

2.8.2   Toolbars

Opera has six toolbars. They are shown in the screen capture on this page (together with the title and menu bars). Opera allows the user to place any toolbar on the left, right, top, or bottom of the window, as well as turn it off. The `Page` bar is similar to Netscape 7.01's `Tab` bar. The `Main` bar is Opera's navigation toolbar. And its `Navigation` bar provides more navigation activities in addition to those of the `Main` bar.

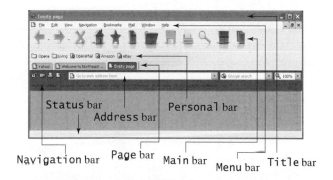

2.9   Crazy Browser

Crazy Browser (CB) looks like a modified IE, as it uses an IE engine to render the Web pages. It can be downloaded from `http://www.crazybrowser.com/download.htm`. CB is a tabbed browser; that is, it has the ability to open multiple Web pages inside a single browser window. It also has a Smart Popup Filter, which blocks all the annoying pop-ups automatically. CB uses the F11 key on the keyboard to toggle the full-screen mode. If you press F11 once, the CB window will fill the entire screen; if you press it again, the window will shrink go back down.

2.9.1   Menus

Figure 2.10 shows CB's window. The figure shows the title bar, the menu bar, and the toolbars. The title bar displays the title of the current Web page.

The menu bar has 10 menus: File, Edit, View, Favorites, History, Groups, Options, Tools, Tabs, and Help. We cover the File, View, Options, and Help menus here. Figure 2.10 shows the four menus. The New submenu of the File menu creates a tab in the current CB window. The user can display a Web page in the new tab by typing its URL in the Address (URL) bar. The URL List submenu of the File menu allows the user to manage and control the URLs the browser has downloaded.

The View menu allows the user to control the display of CB's toolbars, among other things, as shown in Figure 2.10. If you have clicked the Full Screen menu item, you can then hit the F11 key on the keyboard to restore the original window size. The Privacy Report menu item shows whether cookies are restricted or blocked from websites. A **cookie** is a small amount of information (e.g., the client's IP address and its access date of a particular server) that is stored by a Web server in a cookie file on the client computer, for tracking purposes. Web browsers manage cookies.

The Options menu enables the user to control the downloads of images, video, sound, and other elements of a Web page. It also provides control over the browser tabs.

The Help menu has two interesting menu items. The Help Topics item explains how to use CB. The Home Page item connects to CB's website and displays information about CB.

2.9.2   Toolbars

CB has six toolbars (see Figure 2.10); five are shown in the screen capture on this page. The sixth one, the Navigation bar, is shown in Figure 2.10. CB's toolbars are similar to those of IE. The Logo Panel gives the user control of CB's tabs. The Navigation bar opens an area on the left side of the CB window (as shown in the following insert) to allow the user to view information such as navigation history.

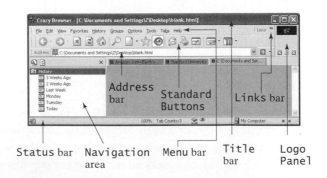

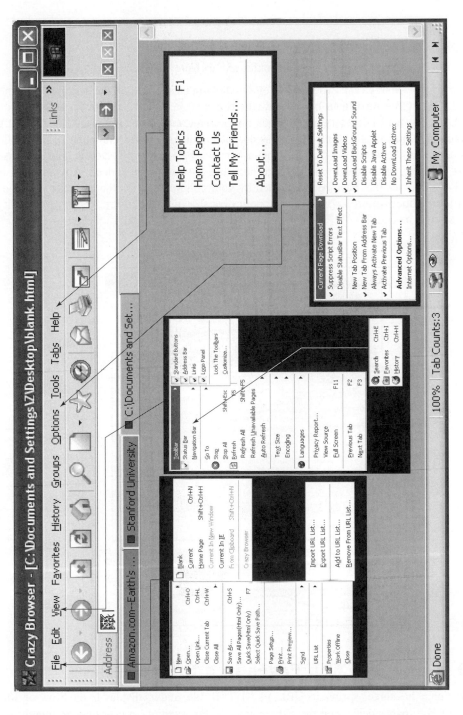

Figure 2.10 Crazy Browser 1.05 menus.

Example 2.4 Find cookies on my computer.

Learn how to use Crazy Browser to find cookies of a website.

Solution 2.4 Start Crazy Browser by double-clicking its shortcut on the desktop. Type these two URLs into CB's `Address` bar to view the two websites: `http://www.amazon.com` and `http://www.fidelity.com`. Click on the `Amazon.com` tab to make it current. We now check if Amazon.com's Web server has dropped cookies into the computer or not. Follow this sequence to check: `View` (in CB's menu bar) => `Privacy Report`. The `Privacy Report` window, shown here on this page pops up. It shows that, indeed, Amazon.com has dropped two cookies that have been accepted by your computer. Click the `Summary` button to find out more about Amazon.com's privacy policy, as shown in the insert. Repeat for Fidelity's website to view its cookies.

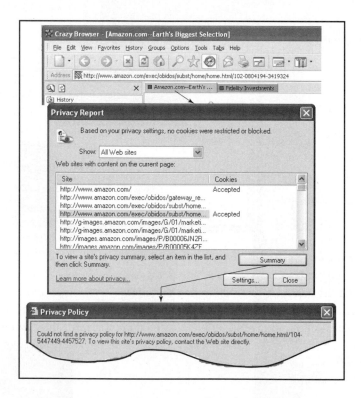

2.10 Managing Web Pages in a Browser

Each Web page has three aspects: its URL, its XHTML file, and its display in the browser. Management of Web pages deals with these three aspects. For example, a user may be interested in saving a page's URL for future revisiting. To save a page's URL, the Web surfer uses the browser to create a favorite (as IE calls it) or a bookmark (as Netscape calls it). Alternatively, the user may want to print the browser's display of a page. To print a page, the Web surfer clicks the browser's `Print` button. A user who is a Web developer may want to save a Webpage's code. To save a page's code to the local (client) hard disk, the Web surfer uses the `Save As` menu item from the browser's `File` menu to save the code for off-line viewing. Use the `htm` or `html` to save Webpage code.

Example 2.5   View a Web page's code.

Learn how to view the code of a Web page that is rendered in a browser window.

Solution 2.5   Display the page in the browser window by entering its URL. Then follow this sequence for IE: `View` (in the menu bar) `=> Source`. The page's code is displayed in a Notepad window. For a Netscape browser, follow this sequence: `View => Page Source`.

2.11 Browser Cache

Browsers use the cache concept to improve the access of Web pages. A **cache** is a temporary storage location. You probably have noticed that, when you return to Web pages you have visited during the current session, the browser displays them faster than it did the first time. After a Web page is downloaded from the Internet during a session, the browser keeps a copy of it in a cache on the client computer. When the user requests a Web page, the browser checks the cache first before downloading a fresh copy from the Internet. If the requested page is found in the cache, the browser displays it without using the Internet again. Keeping visited Web pages in the browser cache improves access dramatically, especially at times of heavy Internet traffic.

A browser uses two types of caching schemes: memory and disk. The **memory cache** is the portion of the computer's RAM that the browser uses to store the most recently downloaded Web pages during the current session of surfing the Internet. A browser typically has a default size for its cache. The user can change this size if needed. If the total size of the Web pages a user has downloaded during one session exceeds the current size of the memory cache being used by the browser, older pages are removed (flushed) from the cache to create space for new pages being downloaded. At the end of a browser session, the memory cache is erased and released back to the computer's available RAM for other applications to use.

The **disk cache** is a portion of the computer's hard disk that the browser uses to store downloaded Web pages from previous sessions. As with memory cache, a browser has a default size for its disk cache that the user can change. The disk cache used by the browser is flushed in a way similar to the memory cache; however, unlike the memory cache, the disk cache retains Web documents between browser sessions.

A browser uses the two types of caches according to the following scenario: A user requests a Web page by typing its URL into the browser's URL toolbar or by using the **Back** and **Forward** buttons of the browser. In either case, the browser checks its memory cache first, followed by its disk cache. If it finds the Web page in either cache, it loads into its window. To guard against old content in its disk cache, the browser usually contacts the Web page's server to verify whether the content of a Web page has been altered since its last retrieval. If it has, the browser downloads the new content. The browser does not perform this check for its memory cache, because content change is highly unlikely within one browser session.

Most browsers allow their users to change the sizes of the memory and disk caches. As the available cache space is filled, old Web pages are replaced with new ones. Decreasing the size of cache will decrease the chances of having previously visited Web pages being available from the cache. A user who does not want to store Web pages between browser sessions should set the disk cache to zero.

Example 2.6 **Change memory and disk caches for IE and Netscape browsers.**

Learn how to control the memory and disk caches of these two browsers.

Solution 2.6 Open both IE and Netscape browsers' windows. Then follow this sequence for IE: `Tools` (in the menu bar) => `Internet Options` => `General` (tab) => `Settings` => Move the slider to the right or left => `OK` => `OK`.

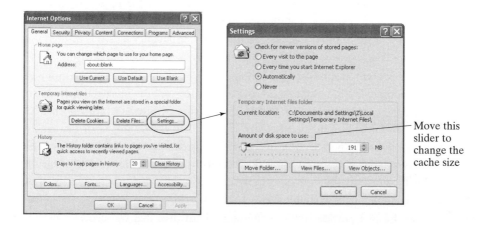

Move this slider to change the cache size

Follow this sequence to change the memory and disk caches for Netscape: `Edit` (in the menu bar) => `Preferences` => `Advanced` => `Cache` => Type new values for the caches => `OK`. The default values are 1024 KB (kilobytes). One KB is equivalent to 1000 bytes.

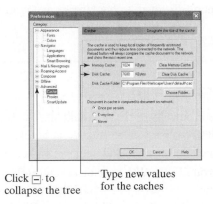

Click ⊟ to   Type new values
collapse the tree   for the caches

As shown in the accompanying inserts, IE allows its users to set the disk cache only, while Netscape allows its users to set both the memory and disk caches. Setting the memory cache to zero prevents the browser from storing Web pages within the same session.

2.12 Plug-Ins

A **plug-in** is a program that, after installation, runs within the browser window, thus extending the browser's capabilities. Even though it is a separate program, a plug-in appears to be part of the browser. Plug-ins are written by third parties, but they are specifically written to an application programming interface (API) exposed by the browser software. As such, they can work more transparently with the browser and are able to display contents directly inside the browser window. Users should be able to install plug-ins easily into their browsers when they need them. The browser informs the user whenever a plug-in application is needed. Adobe Acrobat reader, which displays Portable Document Format (PDF) files; Macromedia Shockwave, which plays animation and sound; and Apple Quicktime, which also plays text, animation, video, and sound, are among the more popular Internet plug-ins.

2.13 Bookmarks

In a Web browser, a **bookmark** is a saved link to a Web page. Browsers allow a user to save the URL of a particular page as a bookmark in order for the user to be able to quickly locate it later. The user may assign a meaningful name to a bookmark, such as "my bank account." Bookmarks created in a browser on one machine are not visible in another browser on the same machine, or in any browser on another machine. For example, IE bookmarks cannot be shared with Netscape on the same computer. Some websites solve this problem by allowing users to save their bookmarks independently of a browser or a machine. Thus, the user can use them anytime.

Management of bookmarks includes adding, deleting, and organizing them. As you save more bookmarks, it will be necessary to organize them in folders. Create the folders, and drag and drop bookmarks into them. IE refers to bookmarks as favorites, and Netscape calls them bookmarks.

Example 2.7 Use bookmarks.

Learn how to use bookmarks in IE, Netscape, Opera, and Crazy Browser.

Solution 2.7 **IE bookmarks:**

The Favorites menu allows you to add, remove, and organize bookmarks:

Add a bookmark. If you like the Web page that is currently displayed by the browser, follow this sequence to bookmark it: Favorites => Add to Favorites (to open the Add Favorite window shown in the insert on this page) => OK. If you open the Favorites menu again, you will notice the new bookmark. You can add the new bookmark to any of the existing folders shown, or to a new one. Click the New Folder button in the Add Favorite popup window a to create a new one. To save a bookmark in a particular folder, click the folder and then click OK.

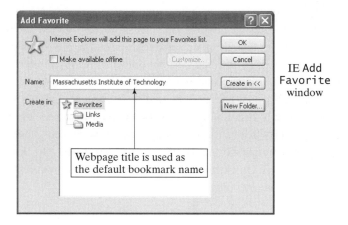

IE Add Favorite window

Delete a bookmark. Click Favorites => Organize Favorites. The Organize Favorites window will popup. Highlight the bookmark or folder you want to delete, and then click Delete in the window. There are three other useful buttons in the popup window that enable you to rename a bookmark, move a bookmark to another folder, or view or change a bookmark's properties, respectively. Click the Properties button to open the Properties window (not shown here). There are four tabs in the popup window that you can use to change the properties of a bookmark. Go ahead and try them. Make sure that the Make available offline checkbox shown here in the insert above and to the right is checked so that you may have access to the Properties button.

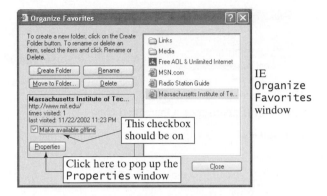

IE
`Organize`
`Favorites`
window

Organize bookmarks. As you save more and more bookmarks, you will need to organize them in folders. Click `Favorites => Organize Favorites` to open the IE `Organize Favorites` window, shown in the foregoing insert. Highlight the bookmark you want to move, and click the `Move to Folder` button. Clicking this button opens the `Browse for Folder` window shown in the upcoming screen capture. Click the folder to which you want to move the bookmark, and then click `OK`. If you want to organize several bookmarks under a new folder, click the `Create Folder` button of the IE `Organize Favorites` window. The browser will create a new folder and wait for you to change its name. After creating the folder, drag the bookmarks one by one and drop them onto the folder icon. The changes you make to your bookmarks are instantly displayed in the `Organize Favorites` window.

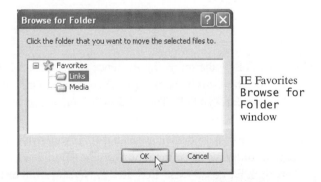

IE Favorites
`Browse for Folder`
window

Netscape Bookmarks:

Add a bookmark. In Netscape 4.8, follow this sequence to bookmark the currently displayed Web page: `Communicator => Bookmarks => Add Bookmark`. (See the upcoming screen capture.) In Netscape 7.01, click `Bookmarks => Bookmark This Page`.

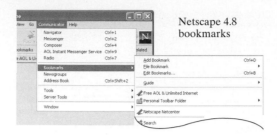

Netscape 4.8
bookmarks

Delete a bookmark. In Netscape 4.8, click `Communicator => Bookmarks => Edit Bookmarks`. In Netscape 7.01, click `Bookmarks => Manage Bookmarks`. The following `Bookmarks` window will be displayed. Highlight the bookmark you want to delete, and click `Edit => Delete`.

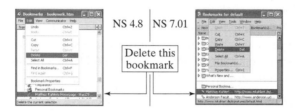

Organize bookmarks. Follow the foregoing sequence to open the `Bookmarks` window. The window shows a tree of the current bookmarks. You can expand or collapse the tree branches by toggling the tree nodes' symbols. The window has menus (Netscape 4.8) or buttons (Netscape 7.01) to allow you to organize your bookmarks.

You can insert a bookmark, a folder, or a separator. If you want to organize several bookmarks under a separate folder, position the mouse where you want to create the folder in the bookmarks tree. Then click `File => New Folder` in Netscape 4.8 or the `New folder` button in Netscape 7.01. The browser will ask you for the name of the folder. After creating the folder, drag the bookmarks one by one and drop them into the folder. You can also order the bookmarks in the tree by dragging and then releasing them. To insert a separator line between bookmarks, position the mouse where you want to insert the separator in the bookmarks tree. Then click `File => New Separator` in Netscape 4.8 or `New Separator` button in Netscape 7.01.

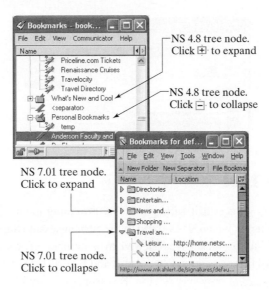

NS 7.01 tree node.
Click to expand

NS 7.01 tree node.
Click to collapse

Opera Bookmarks:

Opera provides the `Bookmarks` menu shown in the accompanying screen capture. You can bookmark a Web page by clicking the `Add page here` menu item. If you click the `Manage Bookmarks` menu item, Opera opens a bookmarks bar on the left side of its window. Opera allows you to manage bookmarks in the same way as Netscape.

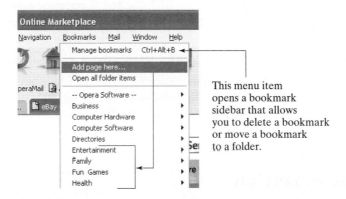

This menu item opens a bookmark sidebar that allows you to delete a bookmark or move a bookmark to a folder.

Crazy Browser Bookmarks:

The CB bookmarks menu is identical to that of IE. Adding, deleting, and managing bookmarks are also the same. Refer to the "IE Bookmarks" section of this example for details. The following screen capture shows CB's bookmarks menu.

2.14 History List

Browsers help their users retrace their surfing steps by providing them with a browsing history. The history can be short term (Web pages viewed in the current session are stored in the browser's memory cache) or long term (Web pages viewed in a number of sessions are stored in the browser's disk cache). All browsers provide the Back and Forward buttons for viewing the previous Web pages of the current browsing session. Browsers also provide a Go or Navigation menu or button, as well as a drop-down list at the right end of the URL toolbar.

Many users employ the CTRL+H keyboard shortcut to display the browser history list. The browser window must be the active window on the desktop for the keyboard shortcut to work. Both the IE and CB browsers provide a History button on the navigation toolbar and the CTRL+H shortcut for opening the history list (sidebar) on the left side of the browser window. Once this list is opened, click any URL in the history list to open it. In both Netscape 4.8 and 7.01, the CTRL+H shortcut opens a separate history window on the desktop. Once this window is opened, double-click any URL in the history list to open it. For the Opera browser, type opera:history in its URL toolbar to open the history list as a Web page inside the Opera browser window. Click any URL in the list to open the corresponding Web page.

We should mention that a browser history list poses a threat to individual privacy. Anyone can display the history list of a browser on a computer and be able to find out all the websites that the user of that computer has visited, for example, in the last 30 days. Investigators use the history list all the time to shed some light on many crimes. To protect their privacy, users can set both the memory and disk cache of their computer to zero.

2.15 Customization

Browsers can be customized to fit the specifications of the user. The user changes their default options and may specify the default Web page the browser displays when invoked. The user can also control the fonts and colors employed by the browser, control the toolbars that the browser displays, enable and disable the displaying of images in Web pages, enable and disable Java and JavaScript (these are Web programming languages), employ style sheets (special sheets that define formats used by browsers to render Web pages), accept and reject cookies, configure mail and newsgroups servers, and change the size of the cache.

Users may choose which skins they would like to frame their browsers. A **skin** is an image that can be overlaid on an area of the browser—say, the browser's navigation toolbar—to change its appearance. The user can change the browser skin as often as desired. Skins can be used as an online advertising tool similar to banners. The skin concept has been used in other areas such as video games, cell phones, and computer desktops. Both the Opera and Mozilla browsers have skins.

Users who use tabbed browsers can choose the colors of the tabs, their locations, and the maximum number of tabs to display.

Example 2.8 Customize browsers.

Learn how to customize the IE, Netscape, Opera, and CB browsers.

Solution 2.8 **IE customization:**

You can customize and set up IE to meet your personal style and surfing needs. For style, you can change the look and feel of the IE window by turning on and off the browser toolbars via its `View` menu. For surfing needs, the `Internet Options` menu item of the `Tools` menu provides the starting point. When you click this item, a window with seven tabs is displayed, as shown in the screen capture on this page. The window allows you to customize just about everything you can imagine, including colors, fonts, the favorites (bookmarks) list, the home page, the history list, languages, toolbars, and privacy options. The `General` tab allows the

user to change the default home page, the temporary internet files, and the History folder. It also provides the user with four buttons to change the colors, fonts, languages, and accessibility, respectively, of the browser. The Security tab allows the user to change the security settings of the browser. The Privacy tab controls the acceptance of cookies. The Content tab provides the user with control over the information and content of Web pages. For example, the user can set up the browser to prevent undesirable Web pages from reaching children, or to save personal information for later use. The Connections tab helps the user establish new connections, edit LAN settings, and edit the current dial-up connections. The Programs tab allows the user to specify which programs Windows automatically uses for such Internet tasks as HTML editing, e-mail, and so forth. The Advanced tab allows the user to control the settings for accessibility, browsing, HTTP settings, multimedia, printing, and security.

Netscape 4.8 and 7.01 Customization:

As in IE, you can use the browser's View menu to turn on and off its toolbars. The Preferences menu item of the Edit menu allows you to configure and customize the browser as needed. The insert displayed next shows the various preferences the may be customized for both Netscape 4.8 and 7.01. The Appearance category allows the user to select the fonts (type and size) and colors of Web-page text and links and the background of choice by overriding the default values. The Navigator category has choices such as Languages, Applications, and Smart Browsing. Clicking Languages, for example, shows that the browser uses English, while clicking Applications shows the helper applications that handle different file types.

Another category in the Preferences window is Advanced. The user can control an important set of preferences via this category, such as the automatic loading of images and the use of Java, JavaScript, and style sheets. The user can also control the handling of cookies that

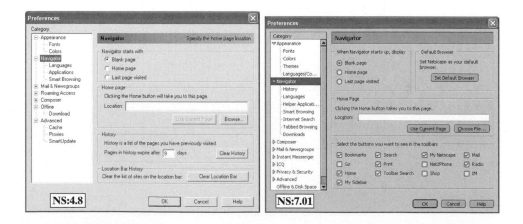

may be dropped by websites onto the user's computer. The user may accept them without knowledge, disable them, or be warned by the browser before receiving a cookie. The `Advanced` category also enables the user to set the sizes of the memory and disk caches.

Opera Customization:

Opera has comprehensive customization capabilities. Its `View` menu enables you to place its toolbars around the sides of its window—top, bottom, left, or right—in addition to turning them on and off. Moreover, it offers two customization tools under its `File` menu. The submenu `Quick preferences` (click `File => Quick preferences`) is shown in the forthcoming screen capture. It allows you to accept or refuse popup windows. It also allows you to hide (mask) the true identity of the browser as Opera to Web servers on the Internet. You can identify Opera as IE or Netscape (Mozilla). This functionality is useful because some Web pages are optimized for IE or Netscape browsers.

The `Preferences` item of the `File` menu (click `File => Preferences`) invokes a popup window (shown in the forthcoming screen capture) that can be used to customize Opera. You can set up Opera to continue browsing from where you left off in the past browsing session, as well as to show the previously saved setup of the browser window.

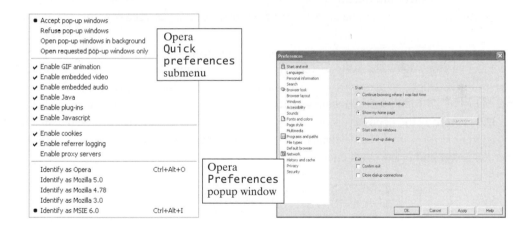

Crazy Browser Customization:

The `Options` menu of CB provides two menu items, `Advanced Options` and `Internet Options`, to customize the browser. Each opens a popup window, shown in the forthcoming insert, full of customization options. The `Internet Options` popup is identical to that of IE. One interesting category in the `Advanced Options` popup is `Browser Tabs`, which allows the user to control the location and color, among other things, of the browser's tabs. Another category is `Popup Filter`, which allows the user to enable or disable pop-ups generated during Web surfing.

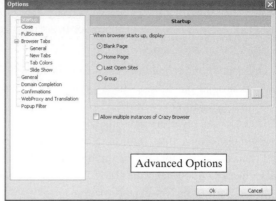

2.16 Security

Security is a major issue in communications, specifically over the Web. Secure Web pages and connections prevent unauthorized access to the information passed between clients and servers. All e-commerce and online applications that require credit card or social security numbers or other personal sensitive information must be secure in order to prevent any misuse of the information. Similarly, sensitive online discussions of company secrets between departments must be kept secure.

Encryption and decryption techniques are commonly used over the Internet to create secure connections between Web servers and client computers whenever they are needed. **Encryption** is defined as the process or method (known as a cipher) of converting data into a form that is very difficult to understand by hackers if they are ever successful in intercepting the data. **Decryption** is the opposite process (known as a decipher); it converts encrypted data back into its original form that is understandable by humans. Encryption and decryption can start at either the server end or the client end.

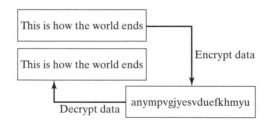

Both encryption and decryption use complex computer and mathematical algorithms, such as RSA, IDEA, and MD5. Simple encryption algorithms may rotate the letters of the data, replace them by numbers, or add frequencies to scramble voice signals. More complex encryption algorithms rearrange the bits of the data in digital signals. The RSA algorithm uses a key pair: a public key *Pbk()* and a private key *Pvk()*. Any data encrypted by one key can be decrypted by the other. Suppose X is a message (data) to be encrypted. X is usually referred to as plaintext and its encryption as ciphertext. If we use the public key to encrypt it, then we use the private key to decrypt it; that is, *Pbk(X)* produces the encryption and *Pvk(Pbk(X))* produces X again. Similarly, *Pvk(X)* is an encryption and *Pbk(Pvk(X))* is the corresponding decryption. The following insert shows an example, and Figure 2.11 illustrates the process.

Example

X = Try to decrypt the two messages that Cambridge don Robert H Thouless encrypted in the late ninteen forties to prove that the dead can communicate with the living

$Pbk()$ = sdfksdfpowirewejsdfskjf
$Pvk()$ = *Pbk()*
    = sdfksdfpowirewejsdfskjf

Pbk(X) =
luddggjrfuxkxdicorrwcbfyhxdzdyroijimzknvrsjy
kjjwmdzrzasoavryvhhwjvswyzhqklhsxbpmvrbsa
lljkdxujraolkfihdmuiwhlsqhgwvzflhklhbxh
dbyihmeaql

Pvk(Pbk(X)) =
trytodecryptthetwomessagesthatcambridgedon
roberththoulessencryptedinthelateninteenforti
estoprovethatthedeadcancommunicatewiththe
living

How is encryption–decryption technology implemented over the Web? Both Web servers and browsers use a technology known as Secure Sockets Layer (SSL) that manages security of data transmission. **SSL** is a communication protocol, like TCP, that securely passes data back and forth between a Web server and a client browser. SSL is a standard technology; it uses the HTTPS protocol. SSL is included in browsers. When a user connects to a Web server that

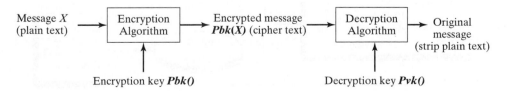

Figure 2.11   Encryption–decryption process.

requires secure communication, the browser notifies the user. The user does not have to do anything other than feel better about the security of the data that are about to be communicated.

SSL technology uses what is known as the public-and-private-key encryption system from RSA Data Security, a subsidiary of Security Dynamics. As shown in Figure 2.11, this system uses two keys. The two keys are generated randomly and come in pairs that are not interchangeable. The private key is never sent over the Internet; the public key is. The private key is used to decrypt data that have been encrypted by the public key. The private key is known only by its owner. To explain the use of these two keys, consider the filling out of a form with a credit card number for online shopping, as illustrated in Figure 2.12. When the user downloads the Web page containing the form from the Web server of the shopping site, the server generates the two keys and sends only the public key with the form. When the user's browser receives the Web page, it checks for a key, finds one, and thereby establishes a secure connection. The user fills out the form and sends it. The browser uses the public key of the page to encrypt the form's data and sends it to the server. When the server receives the code, it uses the corresponding private key to decrypt the data and then processes the form.

Another part of encryption is known as a digital certificate. Digital certificates are used for digital signature. A **digital certificate** is an electronic ID similar to a credit card or driver's license. It is issued by a certification authority and includes the person's name, the expiration date, a public key, and the digital signature of the issuer of the certificate. These certificates are kept in registries, so that their owners can look up their public keys, like the deed of a house. A **digital signature** is an electronic signature that is need to sign messages and documents. It is not a scan of paper signature.

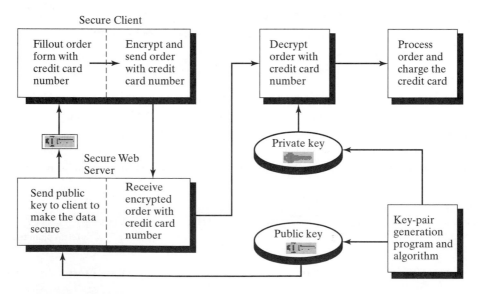

Figure 2.12 Secure exchange of a credit card number.

Example 2.9 Understand security levels in Web browsers.

What are the security levels that browsers can use, and how do we set them up?

Solution 2.9 SSL provides an encrypted TCP connection between a browser and a server. SSL has two versions: SSL 2.0 (developed in 1994) and SSL 3.0 (developed in 1996). SSL was succeeded by TLS 1.0 (Transport Layer Security) in 1999. TLS 1.0 is based on SSL 3.0; it provides improved security because of better cryptographical (encryption–decryption) formulas and better methods used to generate encryption keys. The TLS protocol is the standardization of SSL.

Major browsers support the three versions SSL 2.0, SSL 3.0, and TLS 1.0. The level of security a browser supports depends on the size of the keys used in encryption. The **size of a key** is the number of bits used to represent it. Key sizes range from 40 to 2048 bits. Commonly used sizes are 40 and 128 bits. The larger the key size, the better is the security; that is, more bits mean more security. Forty-bit encryption is known as weak encryption, while 128-bit encryption is known as strong encryption. It will take 2^{128} attempts to crack a message encrypted with a 128-bit key; this figure represents 300 billion trillion as many keys as with 40-bit encryption. Most online applications such as banking are conducted with 128-bit encryption.

Browsers offer their users control over the level of security. Just remember, however, that the Web server you connect to must support your desired level. You can check the default level of security of both IE and Netscape by using the `Help` menu. In IE, click `Help => About Internet Explorer`. In Netscape, click `Help => About Communicator`. In Opera and CB, start with the `Help` menu and search the contents for "security" or "encryption". The four browsers use a padlock symbol (on the `Status` bar in IE, Netscape, and CB and on the `URL` bar in Opera) to indicate the security of Web connections. An open padlock 🔓 means an insecure connection, while a closed padlock 🔒 signifies a secure connection. If you double-click on IE's padlock or click on Netscape's padlock, a popup window will display the security information of the current connection. The four browsers provide users with security options as shown in the following screen captures:

IE browser	NS 7.01 browser	Opera browser	CB browser

```
Tools => Internet      Edit => Preferences =>    File => Preferences =>    Options => Internet
Options => Security    Privacy & Security =>     Security                  Options => Security
                       SSL
```

2.17 Wireless Browsing

Wireless browsing (also known as mobile or handheld browsing) refers to browsing activities on miniature screens of small devices. Handheld devices are mobile, and some are wireless. They include pocket PCs, handheld PCs, cell and smart phones, and PDAs (personal digital assistants) such as Palm Pilots, Handspring Visors, Blackberries, and many organizers. These handhelds are known to be memory starved and power and space constrained, as well as to have small display screens compared with those of desktop computers. Thus, stripped-down versions of desktop Web browsers must be developed to accommodate the limited onboard memory of these devices.

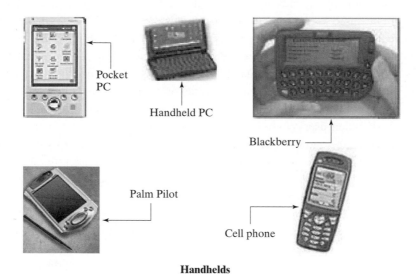

Handhelds

Handheld browsing may be done online or off-line. Handheld online browsing requires a wireless modem and an ISP. Handheld off-line browsing requires the user first to download the desired Web pages from their respective websites to the handheld device itself for later viewing off-line. This process is known as synchronizing (or syncing. for short) the handheld device, and is done by loading the device onto its cradle. The cradle is, in turn, connected to the Internet via a desktop computer during the sync process. Users of handheld devices often sync them in the morning before becoming "mobile" and then browse the Web pages off-line while on the road. The sync process can be used to download new Web pages or replace the old content of already synced Web pages. The downloaded content is mostly text, because of the memory limitations of the handheld devices. Popular content among handheld users includes weather forecasts, news (financial, sports, and otherwise), maps and driving directions, entertainment, travel data, and restaurant information.

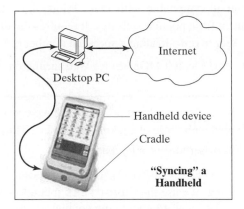

"Syncing" a Handheld

The handheld browsing experience is different from the desktop browsing experience because of the small screens and limited memory size of handhelds. Users confined to viewing small portion of a Web page often lack the overall context and find themselves having to scroll the Web page content extensively. In addition, the user has access to only a few Web pages at any given time. Further, the content may not be current, depending on when the handheld was last synced. Caching Web pages to view them takes up a lot of resources on the handheld.

There are browsers for both off-line and online handheld browsing. Three examples come from Microsoft, AvantGo, and Opera. Microsoft offers Pocket IE (PIE). PIE's a compatible version of Microsoft's desktop IE. PIE runs under Windows CE OS and Pocket PC 2002 OS, both from Microsoft. The user employs desktop IE to sync a Pocket PC for off-line browsing. Desired Web pages are transferred from IE's favorites to PIE's favorites during the sync time. PIE has built-in support for Microsoft Mobile Channels (popular websites) and AvantGo.

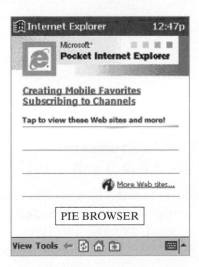

The AvantGo browser is compatible with Palm Pilots and Pocket PCs. The user can employ it to download content from popular websites. It requires the user to have an account on AvantGo. It also limits the user to downloading a specified number of MB at a time.

Opera offers its browser (we call it MOpera) for Web surfing on mobile devices.

Example 2.10 Use IE and PIE.

Learn to use the desktop IE browser to sync a Pocket PC.

Solution 2.10 The `Favorites` and `Tools` menus of desktop IE allow you to sync a Pocket PC for off-line browsing. We use the `Favorites` menu to make Web pages available off-line, and we use the `Tools` menu to update the content of the off-line Web pages. Click this sequence to add an off-line Web page to your favorites: `Favorites => Add to Favorites =>` Check the checkbox in the popup window (see the accompanying insert) => `Customize` (this selection opens the `Offline Favorite Wizard` popup) => `Next` => Follow the instructions to sync. To sync the Web page, click `Tools => Synchronize` and follow the instructions.

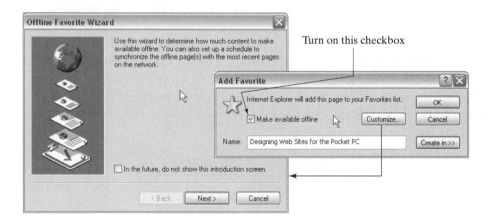

2.18 Tutorials

2.18.1 Manage Cookies in Browsers
(Study Sections 2.6–2.9 and 2.15)

Some websites require your browser to enable cookies. This tutorial illustrates how to change the default and current cookies settings of a browser. In IE, click this sequence (see Figure 2.13): `Tools` (menu on the menu bar) => `Internet Options` => `Privacy` (tab) => Move the slider up and down and observe the change in the status of cookies. Also, you can click the

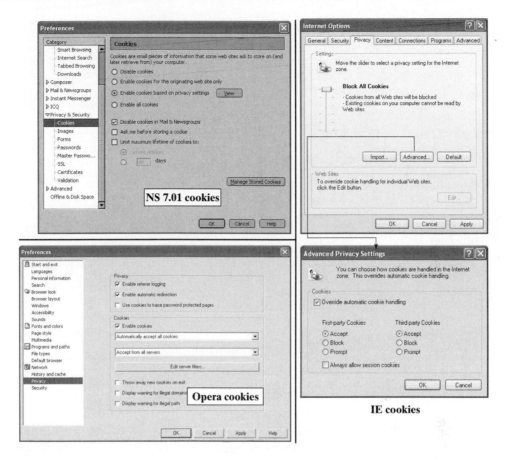

Figure 2.13 Cookies management in browsers.

Advanced button for more control. In Netscape 4.8, click `Edit` (menu on the menu bar) => `Preferences` => `Advanced` (category). In Netscape 7.01, click this sequence (see Figure 2.13): `Edit` => `Preferences` => `Privacy & Security` (category) => `Cookies`. In Opera, click `File` (menu on the menu bar) => `Quick preferences` => `Enable cookies` (see Example 2.8), or, for more control, click `File` => `Preferences` => `Privacy` (category) (see Figure 2.13). Crazy Browser, click the same sequence as in IE, except replace `Tools` by `Options`.

2.18.2 Browser Cache (Study Section 2.11)

Example 2.6 covers how to set the sizes of the memory and disk caches for the IE and Netscape browsers. This tutorial extends the example to the Opera browser and Crazy Browser. In Opera, click `File` => `Preferences` => `History and cache`. (See Figure 2.14.) In Crazy

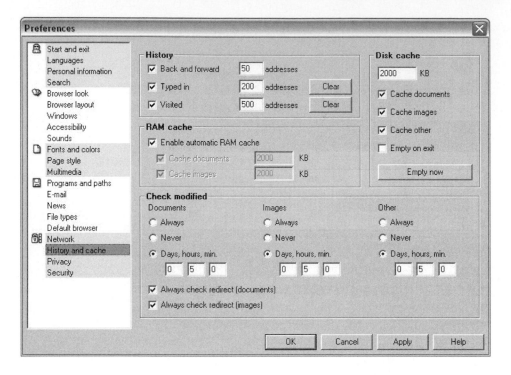

Figure 2.14   Setting caches for the Opera browser.

Browser, click Options (menu on the menu bar) => Internet Options => General (tab) => Settings => Move the slider to the right or left => OK => OK. The foregoing sequence for Crazy Browser pops up the same window that IE uses, which is shown in Example 2.6.

2.18.3   Use Browser Skins (Study Section 2.15)

We illustrate how Opera uses skins in this tutorial. A user can implement images to skin Opera's buttons and toolbars or to skin the background of Opera's windows. The Opera browser comes with some skin images. It also has a skin archive that stores many skins images to choose from; visit http://my.opera.com/customize for more details. When you select an image to skin either Opera's toolbars or the background of its window, Opera tiles that image (repeats the image in a tile pattern) over the background area of the toolbars and the window. Click this sequence to skin Opera: File => Preferences => Browser look. In the Preferences window that pops up (Figure 2.15), you can select a new button set or new skin images. You can also click the Choose button to browse for other files. After selecting the desired files, click the Apply button to display their effect. Figure 2.15 shows a skinned Opera.

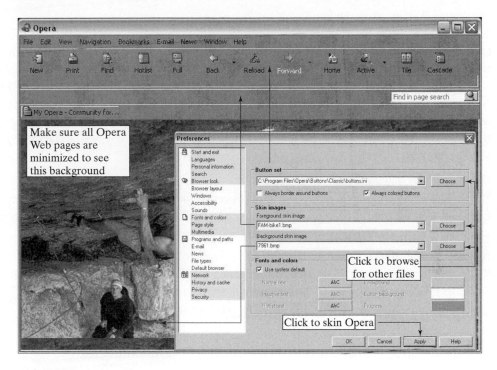

Figure 2.15 Skinned Opera.

FAQs

General

Q: What are the new features of browsers?

A: Browsers' new features include a faster surfing experience (downloading of Web pages as fast as possible), a tabbed interface (to open multiple Web pages within one browser window), popup filters or killers (to block unwanted pop-ups), skins, customized toolbars (to turn them on or off or change their locations within the browser window), and the ability to save full browsing sessions for future continuation and use.

Q: What is Mozilla?

A: Mozilla is an open-source Web browser (the current version is 1.2.1) designed for standards compliance, performance, and portability. **Open source** is a movement supported by software engineers and professionals who believe that software should be free for all and not sold for profit. Mozilla.org coordinates the development and testing of the Mozilla browser by providing discussion forums, software engineering tools, releases, and bug tracking. Visit `http://www.mozilla.org` to learn more. Netscape 7.01 is based on Mozilla 1.0.1.

Q: How many Web browsers are out there?

A: There are many Web browsers in existence. This chapter covers the four major browsers. Other browsers include ActivatorDesk (`http://www.activatordesk.com`), Beonex Communicator (`http://www.beonex.com`), Nubonyx browser (`http://www.nubonyx.com`), Coozilla browser (`http://www.coozilla.com`), OEM-Browser (`http://www.oembrowser.com`), Phoenix browser (`http://www.mozilla.org`), PQBrowser (`http://www.pqbrowser.com`), TouchNet Browser (`http://www.touchingsoft.com`), and Voyager (`http://www.qnx.com/products/photon/internet.html`).

Q: How can I copy and paste parts of a Web page's text?

A: Highlight the text you want to copy. In your browser window, click `Edit` => `Copy` (or press `CTRL + C` in Windows). Then click `Edit` => `Paste` (or `CTRL + V`) in the window where you want to paste. This window could be a text editor or a word processor window.

Q: How can I copy an image from a Web page?

A: Right-click somewhere on the image. In the popup menu, click `Save Image As` or its equivalent. You must be aware of the copyright laws when copying images.

Finding Web pages (Sections 2.1 and 2.2)

Q: How can I find people and companies on the Internet?

A: Use search engines. Try this website: `http://www.switchboard.com`.

Plug-Ins (Section 2.12)

Q: What is Adobe Acrobat Reader? When and why do I need it?

A: Adobe Acrobat Reader is an application written by Adobe that allows you to read and display PDF (Portable Document Format) files. The reader displays the files' formats with great precision. You can download Acrobat Reader by following the links off the main Adobe Web page at `http://www.adobe.com`. The downloaded software is self-extracting and installs itself. Once the reader is installed, Windows associates the PDF file extension to it. Whenever you need to read a PDF file, simply double-click the file, and the reader will open it.

Q: What are the advantages of the PDF format?

A: The PDF format has two advantages. First, a user can view a PDF file and print it out from any computer regardless of the file's its original format (e.g., Word document) and regardless of whether the original program that created it (e.g., Word) exists on the computer being used for printing or viewing. Second, PDF documents are designed to look and print the same on every combination of computer and printer. The Adobe Acrobat software provides powerful features for creating and managing PDF files.

Internet Explorer (Sections 2.6 and 2.13)

Q: How can I import or export bookmarks into or from IE?

A: Follow this sequence: `File` (menu on menu bar) => `Import and Export` => Follow the prompts.

Q: How can I use IE to control and customize the underlining of hyperlinks in Web pages?

A: Follow this sequence: `Tools` (menu on menu bar) => `Internet Options` => `Advanced` (tab) => Scroll down to the `Underline links` section adjust the settings as you desire => `OK` (or `Apply`).

Blackbox

Sections 2.1–2.3 (Viewing Web pages): You need a Web browser to view Web pages, print them, and surf the Web.

Sections 2.4 and 2.5 (The IE browser and other browsers) (Example 2.1): The IE browser is the dominant Web browser now. It comes installed with Windows OS. To download and install the latest version, visit `http://microsoft.com`. Look for the `Downloads` link and follow the prompts. Each browser has a window structure, typically consisting of one menu bar that hold menus and a few toolbars that hold buttons.

Section 2.17 (Wireless browsing) (Example 2.10): You can use handhelds to browse the Web, online or off-line. While handheld online browsing is like desktop online browsing, handheld off-line browsing requires users to sync their handhelds in order to keep the content of their bookmarked Web pages current. Desktop browsers have handheld versions. Microsoft offers PIE, or pocket IE. Opera also has a handheld browser.

Section 2.18 (Tutorials): Three tutorials show how to manage cookies, caches, and skins of browsers.

Quick reference for using the IE 6.0 browser (Sections 2.6 and 2.10–2.16):

1. **Download and install (Examples 2.1 and 2.2):** Visit `http://www.microsoft.com`.
2. **Run multiple copies of the browser:** Click `File` => `New` => `Window`, or use CTRL+N.
3. **Manage Web pages:**
    3.1 **Visit a Web page:** Type the page's URL in the browser's URL toolbar.
    3.2 **View a Web page's source code (Example 2.5):** Click `View` => `Source`.
    3.3 **Print a Web page:** While the page is displayed on the screen, click the `Print` button of the browser, or click `File` (menu on the menu bar) => `Print` => Select the printer and page range, if necessary => `Print`.
    3.4 **Save a Web page:** While the page is displayed on the screen, click `File` => `Save As`.
4. **Open local files in a browsers window:** Click `File` => `Open`.
5. **Control memory and disk caches (Example 2.6):** Click `Tools` (menu on the menu bar) => `Internet Options` => `General` (tab) => `Settings` => move the slider to the right or left => `OK` => `OK`.

6.   **Manage bookmarks (Example 2.7):**
  6.1   **Access bookmarks:** Click `Favorites` (menu on the menu bar).
  6.2   **Add a bookmark for the currently displayed Web page:** Click `Favorites =>`
        `Add to Favorites => OK`.
  6.3   **Delete a bookmark:** Click `Favorites =>` `Organize Favorites =>`
        Highlight the bookmark to be deleted => `Delete` => `Yes`.
  6.4   **Open the bookmarks window:** Click `Favorites =>` `Organize Favorites`.
  6.5   **Rename a bookmark:** Click `Favorites =>` `Organize Favorites =>`
        highlight the bookmark to be renamed => `Rename` => type the new name => Hit
        `Enter` on keyboard.
  6.6   **Create a bookmarks folder:** Click `Favorites =>` `Organize Favorites`
        => `Create Folder`.
  6.7   **Move a bookmark:** Click `Favorites` => `Organize Favorites =>` `Move`
        `to Folder`.
  6.8   **View data for a bookmark or a folder:** click `Favorites =>` `Organize`
        `Favorites =>` Highlight the bookmark or folder => `Properties`.
7.   View the History list: Click the `History` button on the navigation toolbar, or hit the
      CTRL+H shortcut on the keyboard, to open the history list (sidebar) on the left of the
      browser window.
8.   **Customize browser settings (Example 2.8):**
  8.1   **Toolbars:** you can only turn them on or off. Click `View` (menu on the menu bar)
        => `Toolbars`, `Status Bar`, or `Explorer Bar`.
  8.2   **Browser look and feel:** Click `Tools => Internet Options =>`
        `General` (tab).
  8.3   **Security:** Click `Tool => Internet Options => Security` (tab).
  8.4   **Cookies (Tutorial 2.18.1):** Click `Tools => Internet Options =>`
        `Privacy` (tab).
  8.5   **History list:** Click `Tools => Internet Options => General` (tab).
  8.6   **Skins:** Not provided.
9.   **Security (Example 2.9):** Click `Tools => Internet Options => Security`
      (tab).

Quick reference for using Netscape 4.8 (Sections 2.7 and 2.10–2.16):

1.   **Download and install (Example 2.1):** Visit this Netscape FTP server:
      `ftp://ftp.netscape.com/pub/communicator/english/4.8`.
2.   **Run multiple copies of the browser:** Click `File => New => Navigator`
      `Window`, or use CTRL+N.
3.   **Manage Web pages:**
  3.1   **Visit a Web page:** Type the page's URL in the browser's URL toolbar.

3.2 **View a Web page's source code:** Click `View => Page Source`.

3.3 **Print a Web page:** While the page is displayed on the screen, click the `Print` button of the browser.

3.4 **Save a Web page:** While the page is displayed on the screen, click `File => Save As`.

4. **Open local files in a browser window:** Click `File => Open Page`.

5. **Control memory and disk caches (Example 2.6):** Click `Edit` (menu on the menu bar) `=> Preferences => Advanced => Cache =>` Type new values for the caches `=> OK`.

6. **Manage bookmarks (Example 2.7):**

6.1 **Access bookmarks:** Click `Communicator` (menu on the menu bar) `=> Bookmarks`.

6.2 **Add a bookmark for the currently displayed Web page:** Click `Communicator => Bookmarks => Add Bookmark`.

6.3 **Delete a bookmark:** Click `Communicator => Bookmarks => Edit Bookmarks =>` Highlight the bookmark to be deleted `=> Edit => Delete`.

6.4 **Open the bookmarks window:** Click `Communicator => Bookmarks => Edit Bookmarks`.

6.5 **Rename a bookmark:** Click `Communicator => Bookmarks => Edit Bookmarks =>` Highlight the bookmark to be renamed `=> Edit => Bookmark Properties =>` Type the new name `=> OK` (or hit `Enter`).

6.6 **Create a bookmarks folder:** Click `Communicator => Bookmarks => Edit Bookmarks =>` Position the cursor at the desired insertion point `=> File => New Folder =>` Type the folder's name `=> OK`.

6.7 **Move a bookmark:** Click `Communicator => Bookmarks => Edit Bookmarks =>` Drag and drop bookmarks as desired.

6.8 **View data for a bookmark or a folder:** Click `Communicator => Bookmarks => Edit Bookmarks =>` Highlight the bookmark or folder `=> Edit => Bookmark Properties`.

7. **View the history list:** Click `Communicator => Tools => History`, or hit the CTRL+H shortcut on the keyboard to open the `History` window.

8. **Customize browser settings (Example 2.8):**

8.1 **Toolbars:** You can turn them on or off or collapse them. To turn them on or off, click `View` (menu on the menu bar) `=> Show`. To collapse or expand a toolbar, click its left edge.

8.2 **Browser look and feel:** click `Edit => Preferences => Appearance` (`Fonts` or `Colors`).

8.3 **Security:** Click `Edit => Preferences => Advanced` (category).

8.4 **Cookies (Tutorial 2.18.1):** Click `Edit => Preferences => Advanced`.

8.5   **History list:** You cannot customize the history list.

8.6   **Skins:** Not provided.

9.   **Security (Example 2.9):** Not provided.

Quick reference for using Netscape 7.01 (Sections 2.7 and 2.10–2.16):

1.   **Download and install (Example 2.3):** Visit `http://www.netscape.com`.

2.   **Run multiple copies of the browser:** Click `File => New => Navigator Window`, or use `CTRL+N`.

3.   **Manage Web pages:**

    3.1   **Visit a Web page:** Type the page's URL in the browser's URL toolbar.

    3.2   **View a Web page's source code:** Click `View => Page Source`.

    3.3   **Print a Web page:** While the page is displayed on the screen, click the `Print` button of the browser.

    3.4   **Save a Web page:** While the page is displayed on the screen, click `File => Save Page As`.

4.   **Open local files in a browser window:** Click `File => Open File`.

5.   **Control memory and disk caches (Example 2.6):** Click `Edit` (menu on the menu bar) `=> Preferences => Advanced => Cache =>` Type new values for the caches `=> OK`.

6.   **Manage bookmarks (Example 2.7):**

    6.1   **Access bookmarks:** Click `Bookmarks` (menu on the menu bar).

    6.2   **Add a bookmark for the currently displayed Web page:** Click `Bookmarks => Bookmark This Page`.

    6.3   **Delete a bookmark:** Click `Bookmarks => Manage Bookmarks =>` Highlight the bookmark to be deleted `=> Edit => Delete`.

    6.4   **Open the bookmarks window:** Click `Bookmarks => Manage Bookmarks`.

    6.5   **Rename a bookmark:** Click `Bookmarks => Manage Bookmarks =>` Highlight the bookmark to be renamed `=> Edit => Properties =>` Type the new name `=> OK` (or hit `Enter`).

    6.6   **Create a bookmarks folder:** Click `Bookmarks => Manage Bookmarks =>` Position the cursor at the desired insertion point `=> File => New => Folder =>` Type the folder's name `=> OK`.

    6.7   **Move a bookmark:** Click `Bookmarks => Manage Bookmarks =>` Drag and drop bookmarks as desired.

    6.8   **View data for a bookmark or a folder:** Click `Bookmarks => Manage Bookmarks =>` highlight the bookmark or folder `=> Edit => Properties`.

7.   **View the history list:** Click `Go` (menu on the menu bar) `=> History`, or hit the `CTRL+H` shortcut on the keyboard to open the `History` window.

8. **Customize browser settings (Example 2.8):**

   8.1 **Toolbars:** You can turn them on or off or collapse them. To turn them on or off, click View (menu on the menu bar) => Show/Hide. To collapse or expand a toolbar, click its left edge.

   8.2 **Browser look and feel:** Click Edit => Preferences => Appearance (tree node).

   8.3 **Security:** Click Edit => Preferences => Privacy & Security (tree node).

   8.4 **Cookies (Tutorial 2.18.1):** Click Edit => Preferences => Privacy & Security (tree node) => Cookies.

   8.5 **History list:** Edit => Preferences => Navigator (tree node) => History.

   8.6 **Skins:** Not provided.

9. **Security (Example 2.9):** Click Edit => Preferences => Privacy & Security (tree node) => SSL (Certificates or Validation).

Quick reference for using Opera 7 (Sections 2.8 and 2.10–2.16):

1. **Download and install (Example 2.2):** Visit http://www.opera.com.

2. **Run multiple copies of the browser:** Click File => New Window, or use CTRL+ALT+N.

3. **Manage Web pages:**

   3.1 **Visit a Web page:** Type the page's URL in the browser's URL toolbar.

   3.2 **View a Web page's source code:** Not provided.

   3.3 **Print a Web page:** While the page is displayed on the screen, click the Print button of the browser.

   3.4 **Save a Web page:** While the page is displayed on the screen, click File => Save as.

4. **Open local files in a browser window:** Click File => Open.

5. **Control memory and disk caches (Tutorial 2.18.2):** Click File (menu on the menu bar) => Preferences => History and cache=> Type new values for the caches => OK.

6. **Manage bookmarks (Example 2.7):**

   6.1 **Access bookmarks:** Click Bookmarks (menu on the menu bar) => Manage bookmarks.

   6.2 **Add a bookmark for the currently displayed Web page:** Click Bookmarks => Add page here.

   6.3 **Delete a bookmark:** Click Bookmarks => Manage bookmarks => Highlight the bookmark to be deleted => Edit => Delete.

   6.4 **Open the bookmarks window (sidebar):** Click Bookmarks => Manage bookmarks.

6.5   **Rename a bookmark:** Click Bookmarks => Manage bookmarks => Right-click the bookmark to be renamed => Properties => Type the new name => OK (or hit Enter on the keyboard).

6.6   **Create a bookmarks folder:** Click Bookmarks => Manage bookmarks => New folder => Type the folder's name => OK (or hit Enter).

6.7   **Move a bookmark:** Drag the bookmark onto a bookmarks folder.

6.8   **View data for a bookmark or a folder:** click Bookmarks => Manage bookmarks => Right-click the bookmark or folder => Properties.

7.   **View the history list:** The history list cannot be opened.

8.   **Customize browser settings (Example 2.8):**

    8.1   **Toolbars:** You can turn them on or off or relocate them. Click View (menu on the menu bar) => Choose any toolbar to control.

    8.2   **Browser look and feel:** Click File => Preferences => Select any category to customize.

    8.3   **Security:** Click File => Preferences => Security.

    8.4   **Cookies (Tutorial 2.18.1):** Click File => Preferences => Privacy.

    8.5   **History list:** Click File (menu on the menu bar) => Preferences => History and cache=> Type new values => OK.

    8.6   **Skins (Tutorial 2.18.3):** Click File => Preferences => Browser look.

9.   **Security (Example 2.9):** Click File => Preferences => Security.

Quick reference for using Crazy Browser (Sections 2.9 and 2.10–2.16):

1.   **Download and install:** Visit http://www.crazybrowser.com/download.htm.

2.   **Run multiple copies of the browser:** Not provided.

3.   **Manage Web pages:**

    3.1   **Visit a Web page:** Type the page's URL in the browser's URL toolbar.

    3.2   **View a Web page's source code:** Click View => View Source.

    3.3   **Print a Web page:** While the page is displayed on the screen, click the Print button of the browser.

    3.4   **Save a Web page:** While the page is displayed on the screen, click File => Save as.

4.   **Open local files in a browser window:** Click File => Open.

5.   **Control memory and disk caches (Tutorial 2.18.2):** Click Options (menu on the menu bar) => Internet Options => General (tab) => Settings => Move the slider to the right or left => OK => OK.

6.   **Manage bookmarks (Example 2.7):**

    6.1   **Access bookmarks:** Click Favorites (menu on the menu bar).

    6.2   **Add a bookmark for the currently displayed Web page:** Click Favorites => Add to Favorites => OK.

     6.3   **Delete a bookmark:** Click Favorites => Organize Favorites => Highlight the bookmark to be deleted => Delete => Yes.

     6.4   **Open the bookmarks window:** Click Favorites => Organize Favorites.

     6.5   **Rename a bookmark:** Click Favorites => Organize Favorites => Highlight the bookmark to be renamed => Rename => Type the new name => hit Enter on the keyboard.

     6.6   **Create a bookmarks folder:** Click Favorites => Organize Favorites => Create Folder => Type the folder's name => Hit Enter on the keyboard.

     6.7   **Move a bookmark:** Click Favorites => Organize Favorites => Move to Folder.

     6.8   **View data for a bookmark or a folder:** Click Favorites => Organize Favorites => Right-click the bookmark or folder => Properties.

7.   **View the history list:** Click the History button on the navigation toolbar or press the CTRL+H shortcut to open the history list (sidebar) on the left of the browser window.

8.   **Customize browser settings (Example 2.8):**

     8.1   **Toolbars:** You can only turn them on or off. Click View (menu on the menu bar) => Toolbars, Status Bar, or Navigator Bar.

     8.2   **Browser look and feel:** Click Options => Internet Options => General (tab).

     8.3   **Security:** Click Options => Internet Options => Security (tab).

     8.4   **Cookies (Tutorial 2.18.1):** Click Options => Internet Options => Privacy (tab).

     8.5   **History list:** Click Options => Internet Options => General (tab).

     8.6   **Skins:** Not provided.

9.   **Security (Example 2.9):** Click Options => Internet Options => Security (tab).

Check Your Progress

At the end of this chapter, you should

✔   understand the task a browser performs (Sections 2.1–2.3);

✔   understand any browser window's structure (Sections 2.4 and 2.5);

✔   have mastered the use of the IE 6.0 browser (Section 2.6);

✔   have mastered the use of the Netscape 4.8 and 7.01 browsers (Section 2.7);

✔   have mastered the use of Opera 7 browser (Section 2.8);

✔   have mastered the use of Crazy Browser 1.05 (Section 2.9);

✔   understand Web-page management in browsers (Section 2.10);

✔   understand browser cache, plug-ins, bookmarks, the history list, and customization (Sections 2.11–2.16);

✔   understand browser security, encryption, and decryption (Section 2.16);

✔   understand the differences between desktop and handheld browsing (Section 2.17).

Problems

The exercises are designed for a lab setting, while the homework is to be done outside class time.

Exercises

2.1   On a computer with Adobe Acrobat installed, open a local file, such as a Word document, and convert it to a PDF file. The Word program should allow you to do so as follows: `File => Print => Select Acrobat Distiller` (or `PDF Writer`) as the printer name. Input a name for the PDF file. Open the PDF file in your browser. Use the sequence `File => Open`.

2.2   Customize the IE browser to use a blue background color, yellow text, and Arial font for Web pages.

2.3   Repeat Problem 2.2 with the Netscape 4.8 and 7.01 browsers, the Opera browser, and Crazy Browser.

2.4   Customize the IE browser to reject any cookies. Then visit `http://www.fidelity.com`. Click `Accounts & Trade` (tab) `=> Portfolio Summary`. What happens? Correct the problem.

2.5   Repeat Problem 2.4 with the Netscape 4.8 and 7.01 browsers, the Opera browser, and Crazy Browser.

Homework

2.6   Using your favorite browser, visit some websites. Create bookmarks for them. Organize the bookmarks by category. Print the lists of bookmarks and categories and submit them with the rest of your homework.

2.7   Visit your school's website. Refresh (reload the Web page) the browser window. Then set both the memory cache and the disk cache of your browser to zero. Now refresh the browser window again. Does it a little longer to reload the page than it did the first time? Set the caches back to their original values. What is your conclusion?

2.8   Skin the Opera browser with some of your favorite images. Use a new button set, an image for the foreground, and an image for the background. Submit screen captures of your work.

2.9   Associate the HTML file type to the Notepad text editor on your computer. Submit a list of the steps you followed in order to do so and screen captures of these steps.

2.10   Imagine that you are part of an investigative team. Submit a printout of the history lists of all the browsers currently installed on your computer.

E-Mail Tools

3

Goal

Understand and master the essentials of e-mail, such as installation, configuration, the types of e-mail programs, and the effective use of e-mail clients and Web-based e-mail.

Objectives

- Protocols: SMTP, POP3, IMAP, and MIME
- Content, attachments, and netiquette
- Acronyms and emoticons
- The difference between e-mail clients and Web-based e-mail
- Software: Eudora, Outlook Express, Netscape, Opera, Hotmail, and Yahoo! Mail
- E-mail activities: receive, read, send, reply, autoreply, forward, delete, and organize
- Managing e-mail: signature files, vCards, stationery, address book, mailing lists, and spam
- Wireless e-mail

Outline

3.1   Introduction

E-mail (electronic mail) is one method of communication over the Internet. Other methods include instant messaging and newsgroups. **E-mail** is the exchange of computer messages via the Internet. E-mail is widely used by individuals and businesses. It is simple, intuitive, and fast. Different people have different habits of dealing with e-mail messages. Some, such as salespersons, read and respond to them instantly; they even set up their e-mail programs to make an alert sound (such as a beep) when they receive a new message. Others may read and respond to their e-mail less frequently.

E-mail use is based on the client/server model we discussed in Chapter 1. A user must have an e-mail account on an e-mail server, an e-mail address, an e-mail program to manage messages, and an Internet connection in order to be able to send and receive e-mail messages. A server administrator issues accounts and addresses only to valid users. ISPs also issue their customers accounts and addresses. In some cases, the user is able to choose the e-mail programs he or she would like to use, while in other cases the user has no choice. For example, IT (information technology) departments in businesses and other organizations select, install (on an Intranet), and maintain a particular e-mail program, leaving no choice to employees. They also train employees how to use the program. For individual and personal use, there are many choices. Users can set up their favorite e-mail programs at home on their PCs.

3.2 Communication

E-mail client/server communication requires e-mail servers and e-mail clients. To understand e-mail communication, let us compare it to the post office mail system. The mailman delivers your mail to your home mailbox. When you want to send a letter, you can drop it off at a post office. Thus, in the traditional mail system, you have two types of mail (incoming and outgoing) and two mail handlers for your mail (one for incoming mail, and one for outgoing mail). In the e-mail system, e-mail messages are the letters, and e-mail servers and clients are the mail handlers. E-mail servers communicate with the Internet, while e-mail clients communicate with the e-mail servers. These servers send, receive, and store e-mail messages until clients access and read them.

An e-mail system usually has two e-mail servers, as well as an e-mail client to send and receive messages, as shown in Figure 3.1. One server handles incoming mail, and the other handles the outgoing mail. Jones, on `client computer 1`, uses his e-mail client to send a message to Smith, who is on `client computer 2`. Jones's outgoing mail server receives the

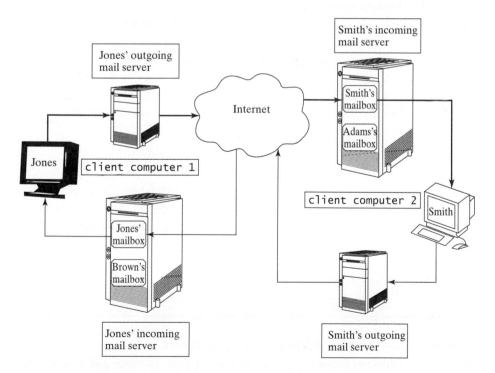

Figure 3.1 Sending and receiving e-mail messages.

message as TCP packets, finds the IP address (via a DNS server) of Smith's incoming mail server, adds the IP address to the TCP packets, and finally delivers them to Smith's mailbox on Smith's incoming mail server. Smith uses her e-mail client to receive and read her e-mail messages, including Jones's, off her incoming e-mail server. Smith may then send a reply to Jones.

ISPs manage and maintain mail servers. An ISP issues each user an e-mail address to send mail and a username and a password to access his or her e-mail account (mailbox). Each mail server holds different accounts for different users. ISPs usually provide two separate servers in order to handle heavy e-mail traffic: one for incoming mail and one for outgoing mail.

How do outgoing and incoming mail servers handle e-mail messages? They both handle mail in a similar fashion to the post office mail system. The outgoing mail server sends e-mail messages as they come. If the recipient's incoming mail server is down, the sender's outgoing mail server holds the messages in a **queue** and tries to send them again later. This holding process is known as **queuing** the messages. The incoming mail server has a queue for the messages that it receives, from which it delivers the messages to the mailboxes of their intended recipients. It also holds the messages in the mailboxes (Figure 3.1) until the recipients check their mail.

A mailbox typically has multiple mail folders, including `Inbox`, `Sent`, `Draft`, and `Trash`. The `Inbox` folder receives and stores the incoming mail. The `Sent` folder holds copies of the outgoing (already sent) mail messages. Users utilize the `Draft` folder to keep their in-progress messages that are not yet ready to be sent. The `Trash` folder keeps the messages to be deleted. A message requires two deletes in order to remove it completely from a mailbox. The first delete removes the message from its current folder, such as `Inbox`, `Sent`, or `Draft`. This delete actually does not delete the message; instead, it moves it to the `Trash` folder. The second delete truly deletes the message. The user must open the `Trash` folder, highlight the message, and delete it.

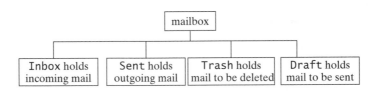

Example 3.1 View the mail folders of some e-mail clients.

Show default mail folders in Eudora, Outlook, Netscape, Opera, Hotmail, and Yahoo!.

Solution 3.1 The following screen captures show the mail folders of these clients:

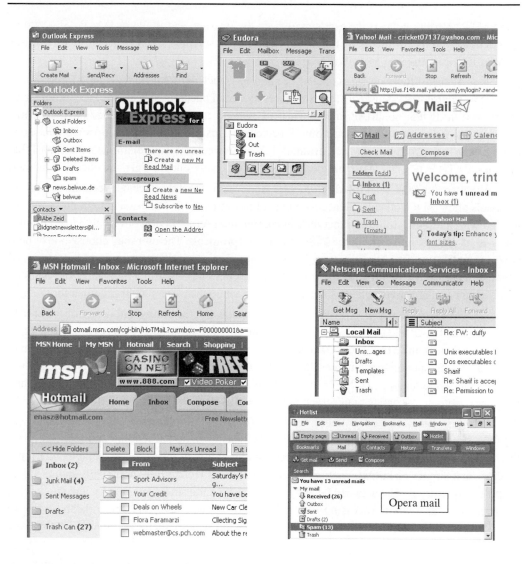

3.3 Protocols

Communication between mail clients and servers is accomplished via three protocols: SMTP (Simple Mail Transfer Protocol), POP3 (Post Office Protocol version 3), and IMAP (Internet Message Access Protocol).

SMTP is the protocol used in transferring (sending and receiving) e-mail over the Internet. At the sending end, the outgoing server uses it. However, because of its limited ability to queue messages at the receiving end, it is usually used with one of the other two protocols: POP3 or IMAP. Either of these two protocols saves the user's e-mail messages in his or her Inbox. Thus, at the receiving end, the incoming mail server uses either SMTP and POP3, or SMTP and IMAP.

The SMTP software collects the user's mail from the Internet, and POP3 or IMAP delivers it to the client to read it. The incoming mail server requires a username and a password from the user in order to access the user's mailbox.

E-mail clients (also known as mailers or programs) such as Eudora and Outlook Express support the three protocols. A user always configures an e-mail client to have an SMTP outgoing mail server and a POP3 or IMAP incoming mail server. `sendmail` (`http://www.send-mail.org`) is the most widely used SMTP server on Unix systems. It is free, open-source software. `Sendmail` (`http://www.sendmail.com`) is a commercial version of `sendmail` that includes SMTP, POP3, and IMAP protocols. It has two versions, one for Unix and one for Windows.

What are the POP3 and IMAP protocols? And what is the difference between the two? Both protocols allow an e-mail client to access and read incoming mail. The e-mail client must be configured with the same protocol as that of its incoming mail server in order to be able to communicate with it. Clients support both the POP3 and IMAP protocols. The user may choose one or both during the client configuration process. The user may also use multiple incoming mail servers of the same type (POP3 or IMAP) or of mixed type (POP3 and IMAP). ISPs control the types of mail servers available to the clients, and they usually set up their users' mail accounts for them.

The difference between POP3 and IMAP boils down to the ability and desire of the user to access e-mail. IMAP allows the user to access e-mail anytime, anywhere (on any computer), while POP3 does not. Both **IMAP** and **POP3** are protocols for receiving and holding (queuing) e-mail on the incoming mail server computer. IMAP allows a user to access e-mail from any client computer connected to the Internet. POP3, on the other hand, allows the user only to download e-mail messages, from the incoming mail server, onto a client computer and then read them.

The last e-mail-related protocol is MIME (Multi-Purpose Internet Mail Extensions). In contrast to the SMTP, POP3, and IMAP protocols, which handle the sending and receipt e-mail, the **MIME** protocol is related to e-mail content. It allows e-mail messages to include other types of data than simple plain text, such as colors, formatting (font, style, and size), audio, video, graphics, and images. The data can be any type of document or file generated by any application program, such as a word-processing files a PowerPoint file, a PDF file, and a database file, to name a few. The MIME protocol makes e-mail a useful way to share files that more than one person wants or needs.

Figure 3.2 extends Figure 3.1 by illustrating the use of these protocols. As in Figure 3.1, Jones sends an e-mail message to Smith. Smith may send a reply. Jones's e-mail addresses is `jones@email1.com`. He uses a POP3 incoming mail server, `pop.email1.com`, and an outgoing SMTP mail server, `smtp.email1.com`. He uses Eudora as his e-mail client (program). Smith's e-mail address is `smith@email2.edu`; she uses an IMAP incoming mail server, `imap.email2.edu`, and an outgoing SMTP server, `smtp.email2.edu`. She uses Outlook Express as her e-mail client. When Jones sends his e-mail message to Smith, Eudora connects to Jones's SMTP server at `smtp.email1.com`, which in turn contacts a DSN server to locate Smith's incoming e-mail server, `imap.email2.edu` and then delivers the message to that server. The SMTP part of `imap.email2.edu` receives Jones' message and puts it on

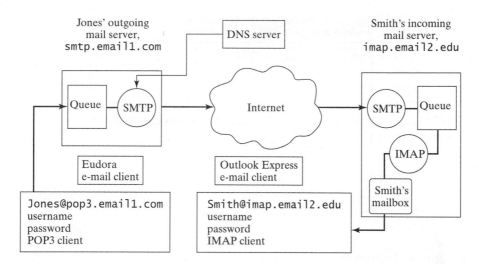

Figure 3.2   Use of SMTP, POP3, and IMAP protocols.

the queue until the IMAP part of `imap.email2.edu` delivers it to (puts it in), Smith's `Inbox` folder of her mailbox. When Smith checks her e-mail, her Outlook Express contacts the `imap.email2.edu` server and allows her to read her new mail, including the message from Jones.

If, for some reason, the SMTP server cannot send a message on the first attempt, the message goes into a queue. The server will periodically try to resend the messages in its queue, say every 15 minutes. After a few hours, it sends a message to the sender informing him or her of the problems it is experiencing. After, for example, five days, the server returns the message to the sender undelivered.

Example 3.2   **Configure some e-mail programs.**

Learn how to set up an e-mail account in Eudora, Outlook Express, Netscape, and Opera.

Solution 3.2   Each browser we covered in Chapter 2 comes with a built-in e-mail module. In this example, we use IE Outlook Express, Netscape, and Opera M2. In addition, we use Eudora, which is a stand-alone e-mail program. See Section 3.7 for information on how to download a copy of Eudora and install it,

   Eudora 5.2:

Start Eudora by double-clicking its shortcut on the desktop. Alternatively, you can use the Windows `Start` menu to open the program. Follow this sequence to set up an e-mail account:

   Right-click `Account` (see the forthcoming screen capture) in Eudora's main window. Then click and follow the prompts in the `New Account Wizard` window. Input the setup information, which includes your name, your e-mail address, your login name, and the domain names of the incoming and outgoing mail servers.

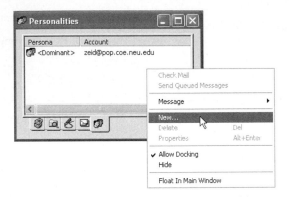

IE Outlook Express 6:

Start Outlook Express by double-clicking its shortcut on the desktop. Alternatively, you can use the Windows `Start` menu to open the program. Click this sequence: `Tools => Accounts => Mail` (tab) `=> Add => Mail`. Follow the prompts in the `Internet Connection Wizard` window. Input the setup information, which includes your name, your e-mail address, your login name (`Account name`, as Outlook calls it), your password, and the domain names of the incoming and outgoing mail servers. Click this sequence to open the following window, which summarizes the account information: `Tools` (menu on the menu bar)

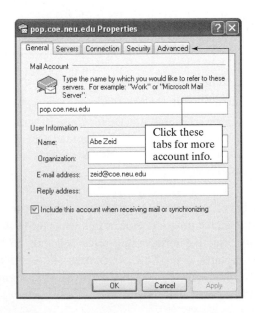

=> `Accounts` => `Mail` (tab) => Highlight the account you just created => `Proper-ties` => Click the tabs (shown in the accompanying insert) to see other account information.

Netscape:

4. 8 Messenger: Start the Netscape 4.8 browser. Click this sequence: `Edit` (menu on the menu bar) => `Preferences` => `Mail & Newsgroups` (tree node) => `Identity` => Input your name and e-mail address => `OK` => `Mail Servers` => `Add` => Input the incoming mail server information => `OK` => Input the domain name of the outgoing mail server => `OK`. (See the forthcoming screen capture.)

7.01 Mailer: Start the Netscape 7.01 browser. Click the `Mail & Newsgroups` icon shown on the left side of the `Status` bar of the browser window. The Netscape `Inbox` window will popup. Click this sequence: `File` (menu on the menu bar of the `Inbox` window) => `New` => `Account`. The `Account Wizard` window will open. Follow the prompts to create an `Email account`. The following screen capture on the right shows the summary of input information:

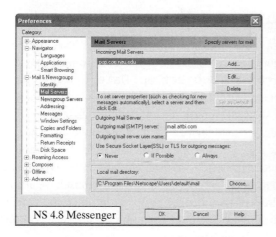

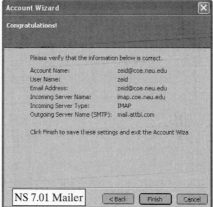

Opera 7 M2:

Start the Opera 7 browser. Click this sequence: `Mail` (menu on the menu bar) => `New account` => Follow the prompts in the `New account wizard` window. Input the setup information, which includes your name (`Real name`, as Opera calls it), your e-mail address (`Mail address`, as Opera calls it), your organization's name, your login name, your password, and the domain names of the incoming and outgoing mail servers. Click this sequence to open the forthcoming window, which summarizes the account information: `Mail` (menu on the menu bar) => `Manage accounts` => Highlight the account you just created => `Edit` => Click the tabs to see the account information.

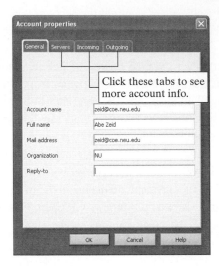

3.4 Content, Attachments, and Etiquette

Similar to a paper memorandum (memo), an e-mail message has four parts: a header, a body (content), a signature, and attachments. Figure 3.3 shows the structure of an e-mail message. The header section includes four headers: From, To, Subject, and Date. E-mail programs provide a "compose" window, where the sender can fill in the To (recipient's e-mail address) and Subject (subject line, which usually states the reason for sending the message) headers. The program adds the From header (the sender's e-mail address) and the Date header (the time stamp, which shows the date and time that the message was sent). It also provides a space for the message body. After writing the message content, the sender signs the message (i.e., types his or her name after the content) and sends it off to the recipient. An e-mail message must have at least the TO header filled out with the e-mail address of the intended recipient in order, to be delivered. If this e-mail address is the only information provided, then sending the message is equivalent to sending someone a blank piece of paper through the mail.

An e-mail message is usually short, informal, timely, and addresses a single topic. It can be a new message or a reply to a previous message. It also can be sent to more than one recipient. The body of the message can be plain or formatted text. Users can implement XHTML to format a message body as a Web page. The "compose" window of an XHTML-enabled e-mail program provides formatting menus and buttons similar to those of word processors. The program also preserves a URL included in a message body. Thus, the message's recipient simply clicks the URL to view the corresponding Web page, instead of copying and pasting it into a browser's URL toolbar.

The body of an e-mail message may contain an e-mail thread. An **e-mail thread** is a sequence of related e-mail messages on a particular topic. The sequence begins with a new (first) message. All the other messages in the thread are responses to each other. It is recommended to

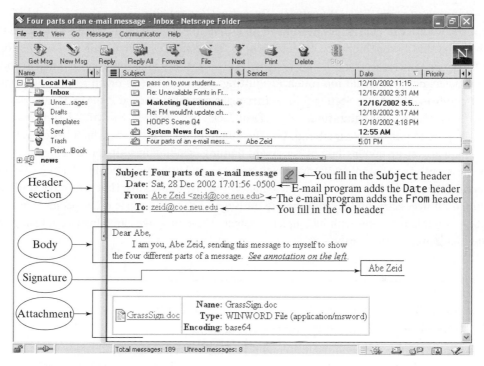

Figure 3.3 Structure of an e-mail message.

include the body of the message to which you are responding as part of your response. This helps the recipient understand your intentions and what you mean when you respond with for example, "OK, that is fine. I'll meet you there." If the thread is long, the message body will be long, too. E-mail threads are typically several exchanges long.

Files (documents) can be added as attachments to e-mail messages. An **attachment** is some data that accompany the body of a message, in the form of a file. The MIME protocol allows the exchange of any file. At the sending end, MIME encodes (converts) both the file and the message body into a plain-text (only characters and numbers) continuous string, so that an e-mail program can send it to its recipient. MIME uses a format known as **Base64** to encode messages and their attachments. At the receiving end, MIME decodes the plain-text string back into the original file and the message body. The recipient can then save or open the attachment file.

Attachments pose a security problem. Almost all computer viruses are spread through e-mail attachments. Users usually run malicious programs unintenionally through attachments. Thus, users need to be aware of the safety issues associated with attachments. The general rule is to be safe rather than sorry. That means that users should not open any attachments from unknown sources, no matter how tempting it is.

E-mail use comes with etiquette that is related to behavior in public places. E-mail etiquette is based on respect and being polite to other people. It is mostly common sense. Here are some etiquette guidelines: **Be concise. Do not use too much punctuation,** as in ! ! ! ! ! !. **Limit the number of characters per line of an e-mail message to 80** by hitting `Enter` on the keyboard at the appropriate place on each line, as the recipient's e-mail tool may not perform word wrap, in which case the message body will become a very long line if not limited to about 80 characters per line. **Avoid too much formatting**; use plain text as much as possible. Don't overuse **abbreviations** (see Section 3.5), as they make messages unclear if the recipient does not know them. **Use proper salutations** (e.g., "Dear Jack" or "Dear Mr. Brown"). **Use threads** to make it easier to follow the e-mail trail. **Use the e-mail quote symbol,** >, which indicates to the recipient that you are quoting him or her. **Avoid flaming** (sending insulting, offending, angry, or rude messages) by not sending offensive mail with the goal of hurting people's feelings. **Do not respond** to flames in order to contain the damage. Finally, **make sure that you have said and included all necessary information in one message** so as not to waste other people's time by sending multiple messages with incomplete content. These messages are always confusing and clutter mailboxes unnecessarily.

Example 3.3 Learn about Base64 encoding and decoding.

See an example of MIME (Base64) encoding and decoding.

Solution 3.3 Let us encode and decode following message. We first encode the message. Then we decode it. Observe that the original and decoded messages are identical, as they should be.

Original message:

Dear Abe

    I am you, Abe Zeid, sending this message to myself to show the four different parts of a message. See annotation on the left.

                                                      Abe Zeid

MIME (Base64) encoded message (continuous string, with no spaces):

RGVhciBBYmUNCiAgICAgICAgSSBhbSB5b3UsIEFiZSBaZWlkLCBzZW5kaW5IH
RoaXMgbWVzc2FnZSB0byBteXNlbGYgdG8gc2hvdw0KdGhlIGZvdXIgZGlmZmVyZW50I
HBhcnRzIG9mIGEgbWVzc2FnZS4gIFNlZSBhbm5vdGF0aW9uIG9uIHRoZSBsZWZ0Lg0KI
CAgICAgICAgICAgICAgICAgICAgICAgICAgICAgICAgICAgICAgICAgICAgICAgICAgI
CAgICAgICAgICAgICAgICAgICAgICAgICAgICAgICAgICAgICAgICAgICAgICAgICAgI
CAgICBBYmUgWmVpZA==

MIME (Base64) decoded message:

Dear Abe

    I am you, Abe Zeid, sending this message to myself to show the four different parts of a message. See annotation on the left.

                                                      Abe Zeid

3.5 Acronyms and Emoticons

Some users include acronyms and emoticons in the text of their e-mail messages. An **acronym** is an abbreviation for a group of words. Acronyms are used to compose a message quickly. An **emoticon** (sometimes referred to as a **smiley**, the name of the original emoticon) is a short sequence of keyboard characters that emulates facial expressions which describe the emotions accompanying parts of an e-mail message. In addition to being used in messages, acronyms and emoticons are used in online chatting. It is recommended not to overuse acronyms and emoticons in e-mail messages, as their recipients may not be aware of them or remember what they mean.

Acronyms TTYL (talk to you later), TTFN (ta-ta for now), B/C (because), ROFL (rolling on the floor laughing), and the ever popular ROFLMAO (rolling on the floor laughing my ass off) include 404 (I have not a clue), 2L8 (too late), AAMOF (as a matter of fact), AFAIK (as far as I know), ASAP (as soon as possible), B4N (bye for now), BAK (back at the keyboard), BRB (be right back), BTA (but then again), BTW (by the way), CRB (come right back), CU (see you), CUL (see you later), CYA (see ya), CYO (see you online), DBA (doing business as), EMSG (e-mail message), EOM (end of message), F2F (face to face), FC (fingers crossed), FOMCL (falling off my chair laughing), FTBOMH (from the bottom of my heart), FYI (for your information), G (grin), GA (go ahead), GF (girlfriend), BF (boyfriend), GL (good luck), H&K (hug and kiss), HAND (have a nice day), HT (hi there), HTH (hope this helps), IAC (in any case), LOL (laugh out loud), IC (I see), IHU (I hear you), ILU or ILY (I love you), IMHO (in my humble opinion), IMO (in my opinion), IMS (I am sorry), IWALU (I will always love you), JIC (just in case), JK (just kidding), KIT (keep in touch), L8R (later), LD (later, dude), LTNS (long time no see), LY (love ya), LY4E (love ya forever), MUSM (miss you so much), NP or N/P (no problem), STW (search the Web), SUP (what's up), SYS (see you soon), TA (thanks again), TAFN (that's all for now), TCOY (take care of yourself), THX (thanks), TIA (thanks in advance), TU or TY (thank you), WFM (works for me), WTG (way to go!), and WU? (what's up?).

Emoticons include :-) (smiley), ;-) (smile with a wink), :-|| (mad), :-((sad), :'-((crying), :-)) (really happy), :-* (a kiss), :-/ (perplexed), =:O (frightened), :-~~~ (drooling), .) (keeping an eye out for you), O:-) (angel),]:-|[(robot), (:V) (duck), 3:-o (cow), :-[(vampire), (_8-(|) (Homer Simpson), C|:-= (Charlie Chaplin), =|:-)= (Abe Lincoln), *<:-) (Santa Claus), (:)-) (scuba diver), :-'| (user has a cold), :-{} (user with heavy lipstick), >:-< (mad), #-) (user partied all night), <:I (dunce), :-| ("Have an ordinary day!" smiley), :}{: (kisses), oooo(O) (O)oooo (toes), (-_-) (secret smile), :-" (oops), and #.-o ("Oh nooooooo, Mr. Bill!")

Japanese emoticons include ^_^ (smile), ^o^;> (excuse me), ^^; (cold sweat), ^o^ (happy), *^o^* (exciting), and (^_^)/ (banzai smiley).

3.6 E-Mail Clients and Web-Based E-Mail

As a client–server application, e-mail messages arrive at a server and a client accesses them. The central question is, How does a client read and manage the messages once they are placed in a designated mailbox on the server? A client may go online, connect to the server, and download all the messages to a local computer at once; the user can read them later off-line. This type of client must use the POP3 protocol. Another client may go online, connect to the server and leave all the messages on it; the user can read them there online. This type of client must use the IMAP protocol. Clients that use IMAP are either stand-alone e-mail programs or Web pages. Clients that use POP3 or IMAP and are stand-alone programs are know as e-mail clients. Clients that are Web pages are known as Web-based e-mail. Thus, a user can utilize either an e-mail client or Web-based e-mail to read and manage e-mail messages. A user can configure an e-mail client to use POP3, IMAP, or both.

There is a distinction between using POP3 and using IMAP. POP3 downloads both the headers and the bodies of all available messages, at the time that e-mail is checked off the incoming mail server. Thus, POP3 is viewed as an e-mail forwarding protocol for off-line reading of e-mail. IMAP, on the other hand, downloads the headers only. The bodies of the messages remain on the incoming e-mail server. The user views the headers and reads a message body online, by clicking the message's header. Thus, IMAP is viewed as an online e-mail reader. Web-based e-mail also requires the user to be online in order to read e-mail messages. E-mail clients that use POP3 can be configured either to delete messages or to leave them on the incoming e-mail server after downloading them. Examples of e-mail clients that use POP3 include Eudora, Outlook Express, Netscape, and Opera. Similarly, e-mail clients that use IMAP can be configured to download copies of messages' bodies in order to allow off-line reading. Eudora is one example.

There are pros and cons for each method of reading e-mail. POP3 works best if the user always reads e-mail from the same computer and if the user has a dial-up connection and pays for connection time. Its con is the unavailability of e-mail on other computers. IMAP is the best solution for those who access their e-mail via different computers. Web-based e-mail allows a user to read e-mail anytime, anywhere. All the user needs is a login account (username and password) and a browser. It does not require any client installation or configuration, as the user accesses the account via a Web page. Its con is that the user must be online in order to read mail. Moreover, it typically is not suitable for people who rely on e-mail for business and crucial communication that cannot be interrupted by banner ads, advertising, and junk mail. To avoid e-mail banners and junk mail, many businesses have Web-based e-mail for employees who travel, and a lot of the time, arrangements are made such, that the employees' access is banner and ad free. In addition, since the Web-based e-mail is just another way of accessing the employees usual business e-mail account, it doesn't cause the employee to receive any junk mail.

Some e-mail programs provide both e-mail clients and Web-based e-mail. Eudora is one of them. The structure of the main window of an e-mail client is somewhat different from the Web page of a Web-based e-mail. Figure 3.4 shows the generic structure for each group. In general, an e-mail client provides more menus and buttons for performing and managing e-mail activities than what Web-based e-mail provides. However, the basic functionality is the same. Both groups provide a mailbox structure with multiple folders, as well as an address book. An **address book** is a file or document that contains e-mail addresses that can be used in sending e-mail messages. A user builds an address book over time by storing e-mail addresses in it. An address book saves the time of retyping e-mail addresses.

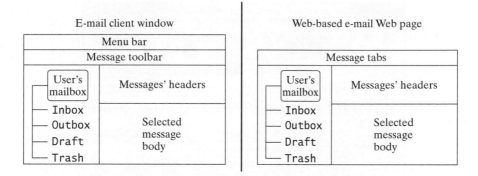

Figure 3.4   Structure of an e-mail client window and a Web-based e-mail Web page.

3.7 Eudora

Eudora is a stand-alone e-mail program. It comes as an e-mail client or as Web-based mail. We illustrate the Eudora 5.2 client here. Download it from `http://www.eudora.com` and install it. Also, visit `http://www.eudoramail.com` to use Eudora Web mail. The two accompanying screen captures show the client window and the Web page, respectively. The client window follows the structure shown in Figure 3.4. When the mouse cursor is moved over a button, the button's name pops up. The right mouse button is very useful in Eudora; try to remember this. After you install the Eudora e-mail client, its Account Wizard will guide you to create the first account. Using Eudora is intuitive. Click `Tools` (menu on the menu bar) => `Options` to set preferences in Eudora. This is the area where Eudora options can be set or changed, including incoming and outgoing e-mail servers.

The Eudora client divides the header of a message into 10 columns as follows (see **❶–❾** in the forthcoming topmost screen capture):

A circle next to a message means that the message has not been read.

Priority: low or high. Attachment.

Label The Label (ranges from 1–7) indicates color; right-click on a message header to change its color (use different colors to indicate message status; for example use red for and end, green for replied to and so forth). Who The sender.

Date The date the message was sent.

The size of the message body, on a scale of 2 (smallest) to 9 (largest).

Indicator: green diamond if the message is left on the server after mail has been downloaded.

Message mood (one, two, or three chili pepper indicate low, high, highest importance of message. User sets the mood when sending the message). Subject Message subject.

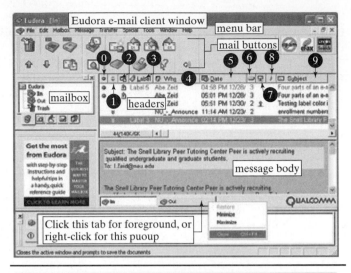

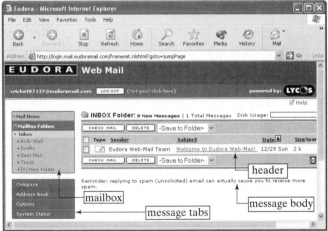

Note that Eudora uses IE to display XHTML-based e-mail; thus, any IE vulnerability is shared by Eudora.

Example 3.4 Use the Eudora e-mail client.

Learn how to set Eudora options and how to download, read, reply to, and forward e-mail.

Solution 3.4 Click this sequence to open Eudora's Options popup window, shown in the accompanying topmost screen capture Tools (menu on the menu bar) => Options. Click any category to change its options. Then click OK. There are several categories that fully control the customization of Eudora. For example, we can change the incoming e-mail server by highlighting its name and typing the new name. Alternatively, we can have more control by clicking the `Incoming Mail` category in order to display the available parameters (not shown here), such as whether to leave messages on the server after downloading them to the Eudora e-mail client or not. You can access and control the outgoing e-mail server's parameters by clicking the `Sending Mail` category.

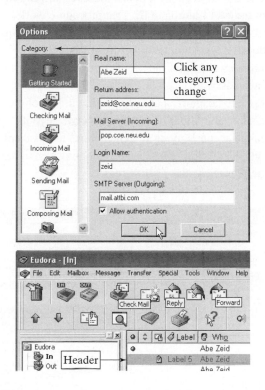

To download mail, click the `Check Mail` button (shown in the foregoing bottom screen capture). To read a message, click its header. To respond to a message, click its header and then click the `Reply` button (shown the in the foregoing bottom screen capture). Type your reply and then click the `Send` button, ⬦ Send (not shown in the screen capture). To forward a message, click its header, click the `Forward` button (shown in the foregoing bottom screen capture), type the recipient's e-mail address in the `To:` section of the `Forward` window, and click the `Send` button.

3.8 Outlook Express

Microsoft offers three e-mail programs: Outlook, Outlook Express, and Hotmail. The first two are e-mail clients, and the third is Web based. Outlook Express is a scaled-down version of Outlook. It comes bundled with IE 6.0; installing IE 6.0 automatically installs Outlook Express 6. Outlook is a stand-alone application, like Eudora. It is intended for business users, while Outlook Express is intended for individual users (personal use). We cover Outlook Express 6 here and Hotmail in Section 3.11. Visit `http://www.microsoft.com` to download and install IE 6.0.

As Outlook Express is a Windows application, click this sequence to start Outlook Express: `Start` (Windows `Start` menu) `=> All Programs => Outlook Express`. Example 3.2 shows how to use IE to create a new e-mail account for Outlook Express. In doing so, it illustrates the use of the `Mail` button in IE. That procedure works only for the first account, however. To add more accounts, start Outlook Express and click this sequence: `Tools` (menu on the menu bar of the Outlook Express window) `=> Accounts => Mail` (tab) `=> Add => Mail =>` Follow the prompts and input the account information (i.e., name, e-mail address, e-mail servers, username, and password).

The accompanying screen capture shows the main window of Outlook Express. Unlike in other e-mail clients, the message toolbar of Outlook has two layouts. The abbreviated one has four buttons (as shown in the accompanying screen capture) and is displayed upon starting Outlook. The extended layout adds five more buttons for handling e-mail messages more effectively and is displayed when the user clicks the `Inbox` folder.

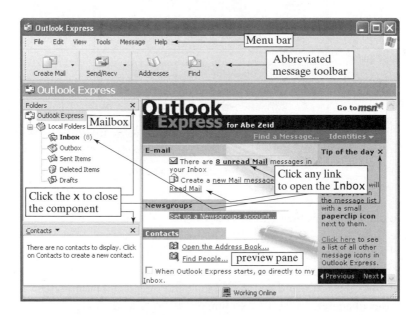

Users of Outlook Express should be aware of its viruses and security problems. A **virus** is a small computer program (macro) that is presented as something harmless, but often causes serious damage to data files, software, and OSs. Viruses can be transmitted via e-mail as attachments. To guard against viruses, do not open an attachment received from a stranger, and always check any attachment with an antivirus software (e.g., Norton or McAfee) before opening it.

Many, if not most, viruses target Outlook Express. Running another e-mail client reduces vulnerability automatically.

Example 3.5 Use the Outlook Express e-mail client.

Learn how to set Outlook Express options and how to download, read, reply to, and forward e-mail.

Solution 3.5 Outlook Express provides three methods for controlling and customizing its options. First, can change the attributes of e-mail accounts. Click this sequence to access e-mail accounts (see the accompanying screen capture): `Tools` (menu on the menu bar) `=>` `Accounts` `=>` Highlight an account `=>` `Properties`. The `General` and `Servers` tabs of the `Properties` window show the username and e-mail server information.

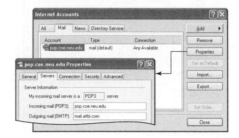

Second, we can customize how e-mail messages are sent, via the use of the `Options` popup window. Click this sequence to open the Outlook Express `Options` window, shown here: `Tools` (menu on the menu bar) `=>` `Options`. Click any tab to change its options. Then click `OK`. There are several tabs that fully control the customization of Outlook Express e-mail messages. For example, the `Security` tab allows us to protect against viruses and create secure e-mail.

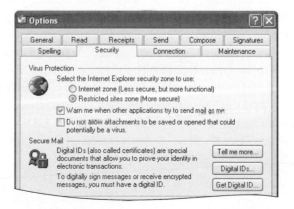

Third, we can customize the Outlook Express window. To do so, follow this sequence (see the forthcoming screen capture): Click the `Inbox` folder and then click `View` (menu on the menu bar) => `Layout`. We now discuss two of the checkboxes shown in this window. The `Contacts` checkbox toggles on and off the `Contacts` component displayed at the bottom left corner of the Outlook Express window. The `Show preview pane` checkbox toggles on and off the pane at the bottom right of the Outlook Express window that displays the bodies of e-mail messages. It is recommended to turn off the preview pane, as doing so guards against viruses that might spread through it.

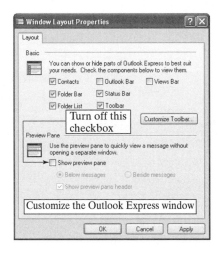

Before dealing with e-mail messages, click the `Inbox` folder in the Outlook Express window to display the extended message toolbar. (See the forthcoming screen capture). To display the abbreviated message toolbar again, click the `Outlook Express` folder in the Outlook Express window. To download e-mail, click the `Send/Recv` button, shown in the forthcoming screen capture. To read a message, click its header once if the preview pane is on; otherwise, double-click it to open it in a new window. To respond to a message, click its header and then the `Reply` button, shown in the forthcoming screen capture. Type your reply and then click the `Send` button (not shown in the screen capture). To forward a message, click its header, click the `Forward` button (see the forthcoming screen capture), type the recipient's e-mail address in the `To:` section of the `Forward` window, and click the `Send` button.

Outlook Express divides the header of a message into 11 fields (columns). The default ones are described as follows (see ❶–❺ on the forthcoming screen capture):

   ! Priority: low, normal, or high.

   ▽ Flag: Flag a message for later reference.

   ∅ Attachment.

   Subject Message subject.

   Received The date the message was received.

To view the others, right-click on any default field and then click `Columns`, as demonstrated in the following screen capture:

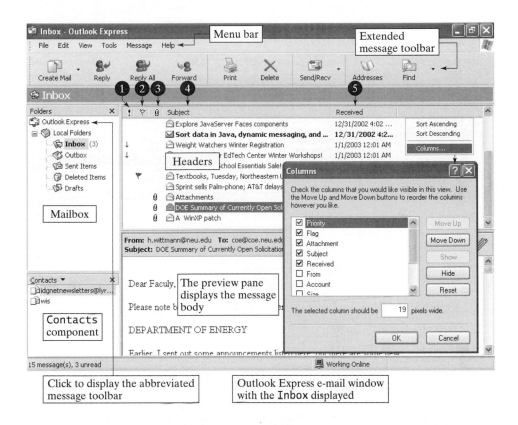

3.9 Netscape Messenger and Mailer

Netscape browser versions 4.8 and 7.01 come with built-in e-mail clients. The name of the version 4.8 client is Netscape Messenger. We choose to refer to the version 7.01 client as Netscape Mailer. Both clients are very similar, and their windows are shown in the forthcoming screen captures. To configure Netscape Messenger, start the Netscape browser and click this sequence: `Edit` (menu on the menu bar) => `Preferences` => `Mails & Newsgroups` => `Identity` (to enter the name, e-mail address, etc.) and then `Mail Servers` (to enter the parameters of the incoming and outgoing e-mail servers). To configure Netscape Mailer, start the mail program and click this sequence: `Edit Mail & Newsgroups Account Settings` (to enter the name, e-mail address, etc.) and then `Server Settings` (to enter the parameters of the incoming and outgoing e-mail servers). Both clients allow you to configure only one POP3 server, but multiple IMAP servers. Neither client permits the configuration of mixed types (POP3 and IMAP) simultaneously. Both clients can remember your e-mail account password if you select this option during configuration.

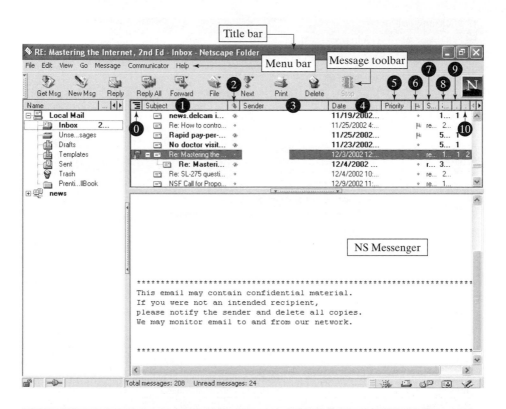

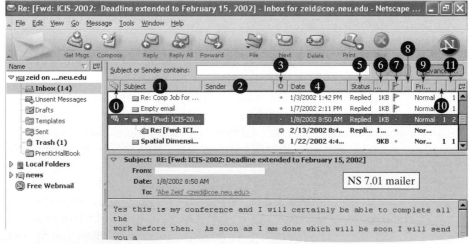

Netscape mail clients divide the header of a message into 11 and 12 columns in Messenger and Mailer, respectively. They are (see ❶–⓫ in the foregoing screen captures):

❶ Thread; groups messages with the same subject together. Click the icon to sort by thread.

❶ Message subject.

❷ (7.01) or ❸ (4.8) Message sender.

❸ (7.01) or ❷ (4.8) Read/unread; unread messages are marked with a bright-green symbol.

❹ The date the message was received.

❺ (7.01) or ❼ (4.8) Status; indicates whether you have read or replied to a message.

❻ (7.01) or ❽ (4.8) Size; the number of KB (kilobytes) of a message.

❼ (7.01) or ❻ (4.8) Flag; click the bullet in this column to flag a message for later reference and handling. To remove the flag off from message, click the flag.

❽ (7.01 only) Label; you can mark a message with a colored label (0–5): Highlight the message and click `Message` (menu on the menu bar) => `Label` => Select a label.

❾ (7.01) or ❺ (4.8) The priority setting the sender applied to the message; low, normal, or high.

❿ (7.01) or ❾ (4.8) Unread; the number of unread messages within a thread.

⓫ (7.01) or ❿ (4.8) Total; the total number of messages within a thread.

Example 3.6 Use the Netscape e-mail client.

Learn how to set Netscape preferences and how to download, read, reply to, and forward e-mail.

Solution 3.6 Example 3.2 has shown how to configure Netscape Messenger and Mailer to create new accounts. The beginning of this section has shown how to change existing settings and preferences.

To download e-mail, click the `Get msg (Messenger)` or `Get Msgs` (Mailer) button on the left of the message toolbar. To read a message, click its header. To respond to a message, click its header and then the `Reply` button on the message toolbar. Type your reply and then click the `Send` button in the `Composition` window. To forward a message, click its header, click the `Forward` button (on the message toolbar), type the recipient's e-mail address in the `Composition` window, and click the `Send` button.

3.10 Opera M2

Opera 7 comes with a built-in e-mail client called M2. As Opera is a tabbed browser, an e-mail window is displayed within the Opera window as a tab, as shown in the forthcoming left screen capture. When a user double-clicks an e-mail folder from the `Hotlist` tab, Opera creates a tab for the folder. To access Opera e-mail folders, click `View` (menu on the menu bar) => `Hotlist` => `Floating`. M2 has a built-in e-mail database and a search engine. The database contains all of the user's e-mail messages. M2 refers to the results of an e-mail search as `access points`. M2's search engine allows searching e-mail by `Subject`, `Sender`, `All headers`, or `Entire mail`, as shown in the forthcoming right screen capture. It also can search for an entire phrase or just words from it.

The M2 e-mail client divides the header of a message into seven columns (see ❶–❼ in the forthcoming screen capture):

❶ Thread; groups messages with the same subject together. Click the icon to sort by thread.

❷ Message sender.

❸ Message subject.

❹ The date the message was sent.

❺ Size; the number of KB (kilobytes) of a message.

❻ Attachments.

❼ Label; you can mark a message with one of seven labels: highlight the message and click a selection from the drop-down list on the right of the e-mail tab window.

Opera also provides Web-based e-mail. Visit `http://www.operamail.com` to sign up. A username and password are required. The use of Opera's Web-based e-mail is easy and intuitive. The Opera browser allows its users to access its Web e-mail from within. Start the Opera browser and click `Mail => New account => Opermail.com Web mail`.

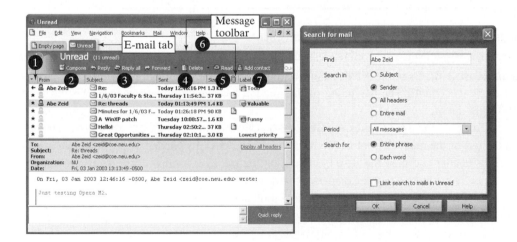

Example 3.7   Use the Opera e-mail client.

Learn how to change M2's settings and how to download, read, reply to, and forward e-mail.

Solution 3.7   Start the Opera 7 browser. Click this sequence to change M2's settings: `Mail` (menu on the menu bar) `=> Manage accounts =>` Highlight the account to edit `=> Edit =>` Use the tabs to change the account's e-mail address or e-mail servers.

To download e-mail, click `Mail => Get => Get all` or select an e-mail address. To read a message, click its header. To respond to a message, click its header and then the `Reply` button on the message toolbar. Type a reply, and then click the `Send` button on the `Compose mail` tab. To forward a message, click its header, click the `Forward` button (on the message toolbar), type the recipient's e-mail address in the `Compose mail` tab, and click the `Send` button.

3.11 Hotmail

Hotmail is a popular Web-based e-mail program. The following screen capture shows a typical screen from a Hotmail session:

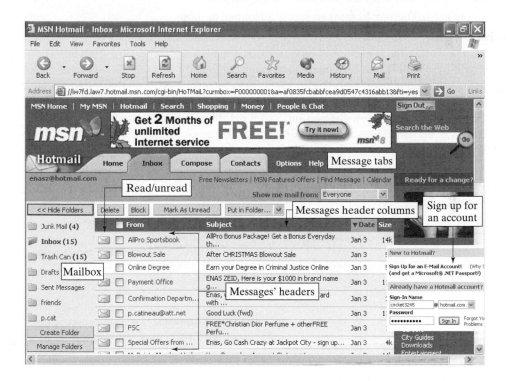

It runs as a Web page in a browser. A user must sign up for an account by visiting `http://www.hotmail.com`. It is Web based, free, and easy to use. However, it has virus and security problems. In addition, at peak times, it may be difficult to sign in and slow to use. Moreover, banner ads always clutter the Hotmail Web page, and junk mail clutters its users' `Inbox` and `Junk Mail` folders. Finally has a limited disk space that restricts the size of a e-mail attachments.

Example 3.8 Use Hotmail.

Learn how to download, read, reply to, and forward e-mail with Hotmail.

Solution 3.8   Start a Web browser. Enter `http://www.hotmail.com` in the URL bar to access Hotmail Web page. Sign in by entering your username and password. To download e-mail, click the `Inbox` tab. To read a message, click its link in the header's `From` column. To respond to a message, click its header and then the `Reply` button. Type a reply and then click the `Send` button. To forward a message, click its header, click the `Forward` button, type the recipient's e-mail address in the `Compose mail` tab, and click the `Send` button.

Example 3.9 Use Hotmail and Outlook Express together.

Learn how to use Outlook Express to access a Hotmail account.

Solution 3.9   Using Outlook Express with Hotmail is a good idea, as Hotmail users get the best of both worlds: the convenience of Web-based e-mail, which accessible from anywhere, and power and the flexibility of an e-mail client such as Outlook Express. If you have a Hotmail account, you can add it to Outlook Express, as we did before. Start Outlook Express and then click this sequence: `Tools` (menu on the menu bar) `=> Accounts => Mail` (tab) `=> Add => Mail =>` Follow the prompts and input the account information. Outlook Express recognizes an e-mail address ending in `@hotmail.com` as a Web-based account. Effectively, you add your Hotmail account as an IMAP account that is appended to your Outlook Express POP3 account, as shown in the following screen capture. Click the `Send/Recv` button to download mail from both the POP3 and Hotmail accounts. Click the `Inbox` for which you would like to review message headers on the right.

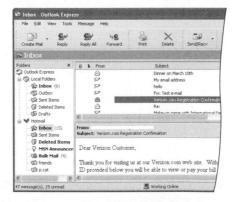

3.12 Yahoo! Mail

Yahoo! Mail is another popular Web-based e-mail program. The forthcoming screen capture shows a typical screen from a Yahoo! Mail session. Visit `http://www.yahoomail.com` (or `http://mail.yahoo.com`) to sign up for an account, which is free. Alternatively, visit `http://www.yahoo.com` and click the `Email` link on the top right corner of the Web page. In addition to being easy to use, Yahoo! Mail is good at blocking unwanted e-mail. It also allows users to access and manage (for a fee) their Yahoo! Mail from an e-mail client such as Eudora or Outlook Express. Moreover, users can set up POP3 accounts (for a fee) to make POP3 mail accessible anytime, anywhere, which is an excellent feature. However, users should be aware of the disk-space limitations imposed by Yahoo!. Some users employ Yahoo! Mail for sign-ups and registration on the Web (that is, so that any junk mail goes to their Yahoo! account) in order to reserve their POP3 accounts for e-mails from family and friends.

Example 3.10   Use Yahoo! Mail.

Learn how to download, read, reply to, and forward e-mail with Yahoo! Mail.

Solution 3.10   Start a Web browser. Enter `http://www.yahoomail.com` in the URL bar to access the Yahoo! Mail Web page. Sign-in by entering your username and password. To download e-mail, click the `Check Mail` button, [Check Mail], on the top left. To read a message, click its link in the `Subject` column. To respond to a message, click its header and then the `Reply` button, [Reply]. Type a reply and then click the `Send` button, [Send]. To forward a message, click its header, click the `Forward` button, [Forward], type the recipient's e-mail address in the `Forward mail` tab, and click the `Send` button.

3.13   S-Mail

S-mail (secure mail) consists of e-mail messages that are sent and received over secure connections, as discussed in Section 2.16. Sending confidential information by s-mail ensures that no one intercepts the e-mail and reads it or alters it in any way. Secure e-mail messages are encrypted and decrypted using public and private keys. A user can configure an e-mail client to provide s-mail.

The encryption and decryption of an s-mail message also requires encrypting and decrypting its attachments, if any. The two available protocols are S/MIME and PGP/MIME. The difference between the two is in the use of different formats and algorithms to encrypt and decrypt the s-mail's content and digital certificates. S/MIME (secure MIME) was originally developed by RSA Data Security, Inc. PGP/MIME is based on PGP, which was developed by individuals. **PGP** (Pretty Good Privacy) is a protocol used to encrypt and decrypt s-mail over the Internet. It can also be used to send encrypted digital signatures.

Example 3.11 Use s-mail.

Learn how to configure e-mail clients and Web mail for s-mail.

Solution 3.11 You can configure e-mail clients to support s-mail. For Web mail, you need to access the Web mail's Web page over a secure connection. Hotmail does not provide s-mail, while Yahoo! provides it for a fee. Here is how to configure some e-mail clients for s-mail:

Eudora: Click `Tools` (menu on the menu bar) => `Options`. To use SSL when receiving e-mail, scroll down and select the `Checking Mail` category. Then select an option from the `Secure Sockets when Receiving` drop-down list. To use SSL when sending e-mail, follow the same procedure, but with the `Sending Mail` category.

Outlook Express: Click `Tools` (menu on the menu bar) => `Options` => `Security` (tab) => Check (turn on) the two checkboxes in the `Secure mail` area.

Netscape 4.8 Messenger: Click `Edit` (menu on the menu bar) => `Preferences` => `Mail Servers` => Select one of the SSL options for outgoing messages; no security is available for incoming messages.

Netscape 7.01 Mailer: To set the security of the incoming e-mail server, click `Edit` (menu on the menu bar) => `Mail & Newsgroups Account Setting` => `Server Settings` => Check `Use secure connection (SSL)` in the `Server Settings` area. To set the security of the outgoing e-mail server, click `Edit` => `Mail & Newsgroups Account Setting` => `Outgoing Server (SMTP)` => Select one of the SSL options in the `Use secure connection (SSL)` area.

Opera M2: Click `Mail` (menu on the menu bar of the Opera browser) => `Manage accounts` => Select an account => `Edit` => `Servers` (tab) => Check `Secure connection (TLS)` in both the incoming server and outgoing server areas.

3.14 E-Mail Activities

We have discussed e-mail clients and Web-based e-mail, how to configure e-mail clients, and how to create e-mail accounts. We have also discussed basic e-mail activities: downloading reading replying to, and forwarding e-mail. This section extends these activities to include printing and sending e-mail, requesting return receipts, enclosing attachments, and using autoreply.

Print e-mail. To print an e-mail message, click its header to display its body. From an e-mail client, click the `Print` button or click `File` (menu on the menu bar) `=> Print`. From a Web-based e-mail Web page, click the `Print` button of the browser. Web-based e-mail provides a `Printer Friendly Version` (Hotmail) or `Printable View` (Yahoo!) link that a user may click to filter out ads before printing.

Send e-mail. We use this activity when we are composing a new e-mail message in order to start an e-mail thread. When a user clicks the `Compose` button or tab, a `Compose` window opens up. The user types in the recipient's e-mail address, the message subject, and the message body and then clicks the `Send` button of the window. While many e-mail programs use the `Compose` button, Outlook Express calls it `Create Mail`. Also, users may use the spell-check tool while composing a message.

Send e-mail to multiple recipients. A user may send a message to both primary and secondary recipients. The e-mail address(es) of primary recipient(s) go(es) in the `To:` field of the outgoing message. The e-mail addresses of secondary recipients go in the `Cc:` (carbon copy) or the `Bcc:` (blind carbon copy) field. The BCC recipients can see the addresses in the To: and Cc: fields, but none of the To and Cc recipients can see the BCC recipients. (And no Bcc recipient can see another Bcc recipient's address.). In order to show the sender's e-mail address to each recipient on the Bcc list in place of other recipients' addresses, the sender must deliberately put his or her e-mail address in the To: field and all recipients' e-mail address in the Bcc: field in order for recipients to see only the sender's address in place of any recipients' addresses. The browser will not do this automatically. Eudora and Opera show the `Cc:` and `Bcc:` fields in the `Compose window` all of the time. To show the `Bcc:` field in Outlook Express, click `View` (menu on the `Compose` window menu bar) => `All Headers`. To show the `Cc:` and `Bcc:` fields in Netscape, click the `To:` button of the `Compose` window, `▼ To:`.

Send e-mail with priority (importance). As part of sending (or replying to or forwarding) a message, the user can set its priority to high or low. The default is normal. When the user receives an e-mail with a priority, the e-mail tool display its priority such as `low`, `high`, or `highest` priority.

Send e-mail with return receipt. The user may request a return receipt, similar to return receipts for post office mail, which acknowledge that the recipient has received the message. However, the recipient may refuse to send a return receipt. A **return receipt** is an e-mail message that is generated and delivered to the sender, stating that the recipient has viewed the e-mail.

Send e-mail with attachments. As discussed in Section 3.4, we can send files with e-mail messages as attachments. E-mail programs provide an `Attach` (or equivalent) button or tab. The user can send multiple files as multiple attachments to the same message or zip them into one zip file and attach this one file only. At the receiving end, the message header shows a symbol in the `Attachment` column (field). The recipient can open the attachment to read it or save it to the disk of the client computer where e-mail is being read.

Autoreply. This is a good activity to use when one plans to be away for a period of time and will not be able to access an e-mail account. The user prepares a message that is sent automatically as a reply to messages received, usually stating that the user is away and when he or she will be coming back. The user can choose to respond to every message received or to respond only to messages coming from a specific domain name.

Example 3.12 Send e-mail attachments.

Learn to send a file as an attachment to an e-mail message.

Solution 3.12 You can send an attachment when you compose, reply to, or forward a message. After you type the message body, you attach the file before clicking the Send button.

    Eudora: Click Message (menu on the menu bar) => Send file => Select the file to attach => Attach => Send.

    Outlook Express: Click Attach (button on the window where you type the message body) => Select file to attach => Attach => Send.

    Netscape 4.8 and 7.01: Click Attach (button on the window where you type the message body) => File (4.8 only) => Select the file to attach => Open => Send.

    Opera M2: Click Attach (button on the window where you type the message body) => Select the file to attach => Open => Send.

    Hotmail: Click Add/Edit Attachments (button on the Compose tab where you type the message body) => Browse => Select the file to attach => Open => Attach => OK => Send.

    Yahoo! Mail: Click Attach Files (link on the tab where you type the message body) => Browse (button) => Select the file to attach => Open => Attach Files => Done => Send.

Example 3.13 Use autoreply to send an e-mail message.

Learn to send an autoreply to an e-mail message.

Solution 3.13 Some e-mail clients and Web e-mail provide autoreply, while others do not. We cover Eudora and Yahoo! Mail here. In general, you type a generic response to a generic recipient and use it to reply to future e-mail. Anytime you receive a message, the generic recipient is replaced by the actual recipient, and the generic message is sent out on your behalf.

    Eudora: Eudora calls the generic response a stationery. To create it, click Tools (menu on the menu bar) => Stationery to open the stationery window (or click its tab) => Right-click in the window => New (to open a composition window for the stationery) => Enter the text for the message body, and fill in the message headers => File (menu on the menu bar) => Save As stationery => Enter the file name => Save => Right-click the stationery tab => Close the stationery.

To create the autoreply, click `Tools` (menu on the menu bar) => `Filters` => Select `<Any Recipient>` for the first `Header` in the `Match` section. In the `Action` section, select `Reply with` in the first drop-down list. In the text field to the right of the first drop-down list, enter the name of the stationery file.

Note that you must delete this filter when you want your autoreply message to stop. Some other e-mail programs allow you to specify a time interval during which autoreply remains in effect.

Yahoo! Mail: Click `Mail` (tab on the top left of the Web page) => `Options` => Scroll down and click the `Vacation Response` link from the `Mail Options` area => Select a duration and type a generic response => `Turn Auto-Response On` (button). When you click the button, it will then read `Turn Auto-Response Off`. If you click it, it will turn the autoreply feature off before the end of the specified duration.

3.15 Managing E-Mail

Over time, mailboxes become cluttered with many forgotten messages. As a matter of fact, as the size of a mailbox increases, it becomes increasingly slow to access e-mail and switch from one e-mail folder to another. In addition, `Inbox` folders usually fill faster than a user can respond to all the messages. Managing e-mail is all about dealing with incoming and outgoing messages. Dealing with incoming messages includes organizing, responding effectively, deleting, archiving, and filtering spam, junk mail, and bulk mail. Dealing with outgoing messages includes creating electronic signatures, vCards, stationeries (templates), mailing lists, aliases, and address books.

Respond to e-mail. Replying to messages can become hard at busy times. A user may label messages according to when to respond to them. We have shown how e-mail clients provide label columns for messages.

Delete e-mail. Highlight a message header and click the `Delete` button to delete the message. To completely remove it, open the `Trash` folder, highlight the message header again, and click `Delete` again.

Archive e-mail. E-Mail folders themselves are files with names and extensions. Their names are the names we see in e-mail clients and Web e-mail. E-mail programs let users import e-mail to them from other programs. But they generally do not let users export e-mail from them. This factor makes it inconvenient to archive and back up e-mail from within an e-mail client. The only way to back up e-mail is to manually copy the files of e-mail folders to backup media such as CDs or floppy disks, or even to another computer.

Filtering. We all are familiar with junk mail, from either the post office or the Internet. We refer to junk e-mail as spam. **Spam** is unsolicited e-mail on the Internet. The sender considers it bulk e-mail to a mailing list. The recipient considers it junk e-mail. Recipients may agree to receive spam when signing up for free Internet services. **Filtering** is a technique that blocks incoming e-mail messages from certain domain names. E-mail programs divert messages received from these addresses into a special `Spam` folder in order to avoid cluttering the recipient's `Inbox` folder.

Signatures. Figure 3.3 shows the signature part of an e-mail message, which is the same for all e-mails sent by a particular user. E-mail clients and Web e-mail allow users to create electronic signatures, either as text within the e-mail or as a file. The text or the file is appended to each outgoing e-mail message automatically. A **signature file** is short text file that the user creates for appendage at the end of e-mail messages. It acts as a stamp. A signature file often includes the user's name, affiliation, and e-mail address; a website; the user's company's motto; and a favorite quote. The user configures the e-mail program to employ the signature file. A signature file is different from digital certificates (see Chapter 2), which are legal documents.

vCards. A **vCard** is an electronic business (or personal) card. It is a file with the `.vcf` extension. vCards are similar to signature files. It is redundant to use both files in one e-mail message. Unlike traditional (paper) business cards, vCards can include images and sound in addition to text. vCards are created according to published industry standards. Thus, a user needs only one vCard for all e-mail programs. vCards are sent as attachments. Click a vCard attachment to view the card. An e-mail program must support vCards in order for its users to view them.

Stationeries. A **stationery** is a template that is useful for formatting messages sent regularly, such as weekly reports. It can include custom margins, text formatting (font and color), and a background image.

Mailing lists. A mailing list has a name (alias) and contains several e-mail addresses of a number of people. Users can create and use mailing lists. Sending a message to a mailing list cause the message to be sent to every address on the list at once.

Aliases. An alias is an alternative name for someone or something. When we create a mailing list, we create an alias for it. For example, the `faculty` alias usually refers to a mailing list of all faculty members in an academic department.

Address book. An address book is a document that stores e-mail addresses and contact information for people to whom a user typically sends e-mail. A user can create and use an address book, add (remove) addresses to (from) it, search it, import it, export it, and creates mailing lists with it.

Example 3.14 Archive e-mail folders.

Learn to back up your e-mail folders.

Solution 3.14 **Eudora:** Using Windows Explorer (Windows) or a terminal window (Unix), go to this directory (or its equivalent, depending on how you installed Eudora) on your system, replacing `Zeid` by your username (see the forthcoming screen capture):

```
C:\Documents and Settings\Zeid\Eudora\Application
    Data\Qualcomm\Eudora
```

Copy all the files with the extension `.toc` (table of contents) and the mailboxes to a new folder, floppy disk, zip disk, or CD. The files composing the default Eudora mailboxes are `In  and In.toc` (Inbox folder), `Out and Out.toc` (Out folder), and `Trash and Trash.toc`

(Trash folder). There are other folders that you may want to back up as well, such as `Filters`, `Sigs`, and `Stationery`.

Outlook Express: Open your Outlook Express `Store` directory in Windows Explorer by clicking `Tools` (menu on the menu bar) `=> Options => Maintenance` (tab) `=> Store Folder`. The full path to this directory looks something like this (see the forthcoming screen capture):

```
C:\Documents and Settings\Zeid\Local Settings\Application
     Data\Identities\{80D6C7A9-B66C-4FE6-B9CC-
     AA6FADD302F1}\Microsoft\Outlook Express
```

Copy this path replacing `Zeid` with your username, and paste it in Windows Explorer (or double-click `My Computer`, paste it to the `Address` bar of the `My Computer` window, and then hit `Enter`) or in a Unix window in order to open the folder. Copy all the files with a `.dbx` extension to a new folder disk, floppy, zip disk, or CD. You should notice the names of the e-mail folders that you see when you use Outlook.

Netscape: Open the Netscape `Mail` folder by using this path (see the forthcoming screen capture):

```
C:\ProgramFiles\Netscape\Users\default\Mail
```

Copy all the files in this folder to a new folder, floppy disk, zip disk, or CD.

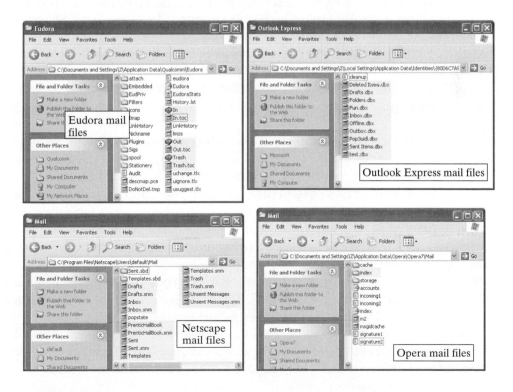

Opera: Open the Opera `Mail` folder by using this path (see the foregoing screen capture):

`C:\Documents and Settings\Zeid\Application Data\Opera\Opera7\Mail`

Copy all the files and folders in this folder, replacing `Zeid` with your username, to a new folder, floppy, zip disk, or CD. The `Index` folder has all the received messages, which have the extension `.idx`.

For Web e-mail accounts, you do not have to worry about e-mail backup, as the companies back up their server computers regularly, including the content of your e-mail account.

Example 3.15 Create and use signature files.

Learn how to create and use a signature file.

Solution 3.15 **Eudora:** Eudora comes with a default signature file called `Standard`. It is an empty file that you fill with text. To access this file, click `Tools` => `Signatures` => Double-click `Standard` => Type the signature text in the window that appears. To create a new signature file, right-click in the `Signatures` panel (on the left) and then click `New` => Enter the name of the signature file => `OK` => Type the signature text in the window that appears. To save the new file, click `File` (menu on the menu bar) => `Save` (to save in the default signature file, `Standard`). To use the signature in outgoing e-mail, click `Tools` => `Personalities` to open the personalities panel. Right-click the desired personality (look at the `Persona` column in the personalities panel) => `Properties` => Select `Standard` from the `Default Signature` drop-down list => `OK`.

Outlook Express: Click `Tools` (menu on the menu bar) => `Options` => `Signatures` (tab) => `New` => Enter the signature text. Alternatively, click `File` and then find the text or HTML file you would like to use => Select (check) `Add signatures to all outgoing messages` checkbox => `OK`. When you send an e-mail, Outlook Express adds the signature.

Netscape: In 4.8, click `Edit` (menu on the menu bar) => `Preferences` => `Mail & Newsgroups` => `Identity` => `Choose` (to locate a signature file you have created) => `OK`. In 7.01, click `Edit` => `Mail & Newsgroups Account Settings` => Select (check) the `Attach this signature` checkbox => `Choose` (to locate a signature file you have created) => `OK`. When you send an e-mail, Netscape appends the signature.

Opera: Click `Mail` => `Manage accounts` => Highlight an account => `Edit` => `Outgoing` (tab) => Type the text in the `Signature` text area => `OK`. When you send an e-mail, Opera appends the signature.

Hotmail: Log into your Hotmail account and click `Options` (tab on the top right side) => `Signature` (link under the `Additional Options` section) => Type the signature text in the text area => `OK`. Hotmail appends the signature to outgoing e-mail.

Yahoo! e-mail: Log into your Yahoo! Mail account and click `Mail` (tab on the left side) => `Options` => `Signature` (link) => Type the signature text in the text area => Select (check) the `Add signature to all outgoing messages` checkbox => `Save`.

Example 3.16 Create and use outgoing vCards, and view incoming vCards.

Learn how to create, use, and view vCards.

Solution 3.16 Eudora: Open the address book. Then click Special (menu on the Eudora menu bar) => Settings => Address Book => Support vCard features in Eudora => OK. Click Window (menu on the Eudora menu bar) => Address Book. Your name is on the top of the Nickname list. Click the Home tab, enter the vCard information, and click File (menu on the menu bar) => Save. To use, the vCard, click the vCard button when you are composing a message. The vCard appears in the message as an attachment with the .vcf extension. To view a vCard attached to an incoming e-mail message, click the attachment.

   Outlook Express: Click Addresses (menu on the menu bar) => New => New Contact => Input the vCard information for yourself in the Properties window that pops up => OK. To attach your vCard to outgoing e-mail, click Tools => Options => Compose (tab) => Select (check) the Mail checkbox (under the Business Cards area) => Select your name from the drop-down list next to Mail => OK. To view a vCard attached to an incoming e-mail message, click its icon, 🖼, while the message is open for reading.

   Netscape 4.8: Click Edit (menu on the menu bar) => Preferences => Mail & Newsgroups => Identity => Select (check) the Attach my personal card to messages (as a vCard) checkbox => Create the card or edit it (if the card already exists).

   While Netscape 7.0 and Opera recognize incoming vCards as attachments, they do not seem to support creating one and sending it with outgoing e-mail.

Example 3.17 Create and use stationeries.

Learn how to create and use e-mail stationeries.

Solution 3.17 Eudora: Example 3.13 shows how to create a stationery. To use it, click Message (menu on the menu bar) => New Message With (or Reply With or Reply to All With) => Select the stationery => Fill the stationery => Send.

   Outlook Express: Click Tools (menu on the menu bar) => Options => Compose (tab) => Create New (in the Stationery area) ➡ Next (in the Stationery Setup Wizard that pops up) => Select the stationery's background picture and color => Next => Select the font, size, color, and style of the stationery's text => Next => Enter the locations of the left and top margins of the stationery => Next => Enter the stationery's name (in order to save it as a file with this name) => Finish. To apply the stationery to all outgoing e-mail, click Tools (menu on the menu bar) => Options => Compose (tab) => Select (check) the Mail checkbox (in the Stationery area) => Select => Select the stationery file from the Select Stationery popup window => OK => OK. To apply the stationery to an individual message, click `Message` (menu on the menu bar) => `New Message Using` => `Select Stationery` => Select the stationery file from the `Select Stationery` popup window => `OK` => Type the message => `Send`. To apply or change stationery after starting a message, click `Format` (menu on the `Compose` window's menu bar) => `Apply Stationery` => Select the stationery from the popup list => Type the message => `Send`.

Netscape: Netscape creates templates by saving the ones of existing messages. Click a message header. Click `File` (menu on the `Mail` window's menu bar) => `Save As` => `Template`. Netscape saves templates in the `Templates` folder of its mailbox. To edit or use a message template, click the `Templates` mail folder then and double-click the template you saved. After editing the message, save it or send it.

Opera: Opera does not offer a direct way to create stationeries. However, you can compose a message and reuse its format by keeping it in the Opera `Drafts` e-mail folder.

Example 3.18 Create and use address books.

Learn how to create and use address books.

Solution 3.18 Eudora: Click `Tools` (menu on the menu bar) => `Address Book` (or click the `Address Book` button) to open the address book. Eudora provides a default address book with the name `Eudora Nicknames`. You cannot delete or rename this book, but you can create new address books. The forthcoming screen capture shows two books. Each book has a name and a list of nicknames (contacts). To open or close a book, double-click its icon, 📖, which appears to the left of its name. To add a name, click the `New` button and fill in the information in the right panel. To delete a name, select it and click the `Del` button. To create a new book, click `New Book` => Enter the book's name in the `New Address Book` window that pops up => `OK`. To send a message to a particular name, click the name and then the `To`, `Cc`, or `Bcc`

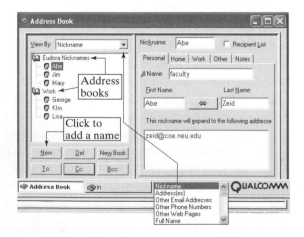

button to open the Compose window. Type the message and then click the Send button of the window. To search a book, click the View By drop-down list and select a search criterion. Eudora does not allow importing or exporting of address books.

Outlook Express: Click Tools (menu on the menu bar) => Address Book (or click the Addresses button) to open the address book. Outlook Express provides a default book with the name Contacts. You cannot delete or rename this book, nor can you create new ones. The forthcoming screen capture shows the Address Book window. The book has a name and a list of contacts. To add a name, click New => New Contact => Input the contact information in the window that pops up => OK. To delete a name, select it and click the Delete button. To send a message to a contact, click the contact's name and then Action => Send Mail to open the Compose window. Type the message and click the Send button of the window. To search a book, click Find People => Type the search information => Find Now. To use the search results, right-click any contact and take the desired action. Close the search window when done. Outlook Express allows importing and exporting of address books. Click File => Import (or Export) to take advantage of this capability.

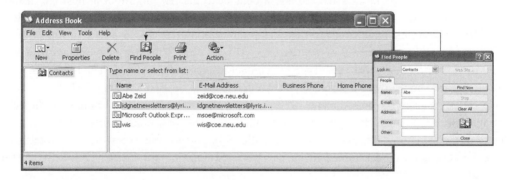

Netscape: Click the Address Book icon on the Status bar of the Netscape browser window to open the Address Book window. Netscape provides multiple default books. You cannot delete or rename these books, but you can create new ones. The forthcoming screen capture shows the Address Book window. Each book has a name and a list of cards (contacts). To add a card, click New Card => Input the card information in the window that pops up => OK. To delete a name, select it and click the Delete button. To create a new book, click File (menu on the menu bar) => New => Address Book => Enter the book's name in the New Address Book window that pops up => OK. To send a message to a card, select the card and click Compose to open the Compose window. Type the message and click the Send button of the window. To search a book, type the search information in the search field. (See the forthcoming screen capture.) Netscape allows importing and exporting of address books. In Netscape 7.0, click Tools => Import (or Export). In Netscape 4.8, click File => Import (or Export).

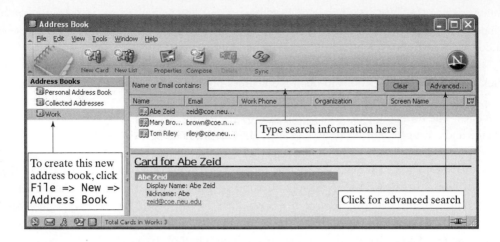

Opera: Opera does not provide an address book per se. Instead, it allows the user to add contacts to its `Contacts` list. To add a contact to the list, highlight a message header and click the `Add contact` button on the `Received` tab window. To display the list, click the `Contacts` button on the `Hotlist` tab window. To add a new list, click `New folder` => Type the name of the list => Hit `Enter`. To add a new contact to a list, select the list and click `Add` => Type the contact information => `OK`. The accompanying screen capture shows a `work` contacts list. To delete a list or a contact, right-click on it and select `Delete` from the popup menu. To send a message to a contact, right-click on the contact and select `Compose` from the popup menu. To search for a contact, use the `Find` field shown in the foregoing screen capture. Opera allows importing and exporting of contact lists. Click `File` (menu on the Opera menu bar) => `Import` (or `Export`) => `Opera contacts`.

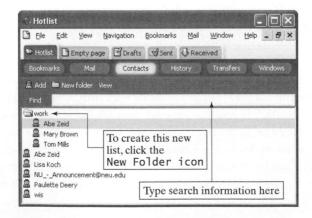

Hotmail and Yahoo! Mail provide contacts and address books. For **Hotmail**, log in and click the `Contacts` tab. (See the forthcoming screen capture.) To add a new contact, click `New Contact` => Type the contact's information => `OK`. To edit, delete, or send mail to an existing contact, select (check) the contact's checkbox and click the `Edit`, `Delete`, or `Send Mail` button, respectively.

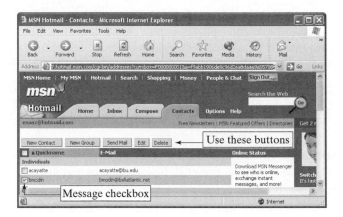

For **Yahoo!**, log in and click the `Addresses` drop-down list. (See the forthcoming screen capture.) To add a new contact, click `Addresses` => `Add Contact` => Type the contact's information => `Save Contact`. To edit or delete an existing contact, select (check) its checkbox and click the `Edit` link or `Delete` button, respectively. To send mail to a contact, click the e-mail address listed underneath it.

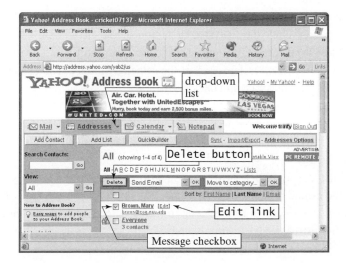

☞ ──

Example 3.19 Create and use mailing lists.

Learn to create and use mailing lists.

Solution 3.19 Users create and manage mailing lists within address books. A mailing list consists of contact entries of these books.

Eudora: Eudora does not allow users to create mailing lists. To send a message to a group of recipients, open the address book and hold down the `Shift` key to select multiple entries in sequence or the `Ctrl` key to make nonconsecutive selections. Click the `To:` button to send a message to all of the selected recipients. The `Recipient List` shown at the top right corner of Eudora window (and in the first screen capture in Example 3.18) only creates a quick list whose recipient members show up when the user clicks `Message` (menu on the menu bar) => `New Message To`. The quick list cannot be used as an alias to send mail to.

Outlook Express: Click `Tools` (menu on the menu bar) => `Address Book` to open the address book. To create a mailing list, click `New` (button on the `Address Book` toolbar) => `New Group` => Type the group's name (alias) in the `Group Name` text field => `Select Members` => Select the contacts to be included in the group => `Select` => OK. To use the list, select (highlight) it in the address book => `Action` => `Send Mail` => Type the message => `Send`.

Netscape: Click the `Address Book` icon on the Netscape window `Status` bar in order to open the address book. To create a mailing list, click `New List` (button on the `Address Book` toolbar) => Type the name of the list and then enter the e-mail addresses to be included in the list or drag them from the `Address Book` => OK. To send a message to the list, select (highlight) the list in the address book => `New Msg` (in 4.8) or `Compose` (in 7.01) => Type the message => `Send`.

Opera: Like Eudora, Opera does not allow users to create mailing lists. To send a message to a group of recipients, click the `Contacts` button of the `Hotlist` tab window and hold down the `Shift` key to select multiple entries in sequence or the `Ctrl` key to make nonconsecutive selections. Right-click on at least one of the selected contacts and select `Compose` from the popup menu. Type the message and click `Send`.

Hotmail: Log in. Click `Contacts` (tab) => `New Group` => Type the name of the group and enter the e-mail addresses to be included in the group => OK. The group is added at the bottom of the `Contacts` tab window. To use it, select (check) its checkbox => `Send Mail` => Type the message => `Send`.

Yahoo! Mail: Log in. Click `Addresses` (drop-down list) => Type the name of the list => Select the e-mail addresses to be included in the list from the `Add Contacts` area => `Add` => `Save`. The list is now added. To use it, select (check) the checkbox on its left => OK (next to the `Send Email` drop-down list) => `Compose` => Type the message => `Send`.

Example 3.20 Filter spam.

Learn to filter unwanted e-mail.

Solution 3.20 **Eudora:** To block a specific e-mail address, click `Tools` (menu on the menu bar) => `Filters` => Follow the prompts. Blocking a message means intercepting the message and moving it to the e-mail folder specified by the filter.

    Outlook Express; To block a specific e-mail address, click `Tools` (menu on the menu bar) => `Message Rules` => `Mail` => Select (check) the rules and actions checkboxes => click the links that show and specify the required data => `OK` => `OK`.

    Netscape: To block a specific e-mail address in Messenger, click `Edit` (menu on the menu bar) => `Message Filters` => `New` => Type the filter name and rules (conditions) => `OK` => `OK`. To block e-mail in Mailer, click `Tools` (menu on the menu bar) => `Message Filters` => `New` => Add filter rules and actions => `OK` => `OK`.

3.16 Wireless E-Mail

Wireless (mobile or handheld) e-mail is an ideal application to use the IMAP protocol for communication, as it avoids the downloading of messages into handheld devices, which have limited storage capacity. IMAP also contributes to keeping e-mail in one location: the incoming e-mail server.

    There are three key issues to wireless, handheld, and mobile e-mail. The first is security. The downloading of e-mail should be done via a secure Internet connection that uses encryption keys. The second issue is a single-mailbox integration. Syncing the handheld device's mailbox with desktop mailboxes could be confusing for users. The third issue is known as a push. **Push** is the process by which e-mail is automatically delivered to the handheld device rather than the user having to initiate the process each time.

3.17 Tutorials

3.17.1 Open and Save E-Mail Attachments
(Study Sections 3.4 and 3.14)

To open an attachment in any e-mail client or Web e-mail, click on the attachment. Some clients, such as Eudora, ask you if you wish to open the attachment. Once opened, you can save it. Other clients, such as Netscape, give you the option to open or save is the attachment. It is recommended that you save the attachment locally and check it with a virus scan program before opening it.

3.17.2   Word Wrap of an E-Mail Message's Text (Study Sections 3.7–3.10)

Sometimes when a user tries to read a downloaded e-mail message, the body of the message appears as one long line of text. This means that the word-wrap option of the e-mail client needs to be turned on. For **Eudora**, select the body of the message and click `Edit` (menu on the menu bar) `=> Wrap Selection`. To unwrap text, hold down the `Shift` key, select the body of the message, and click `Edit` (menu on the menu bar) `=> Wrap Selection`. **Outlook Express** allows word wrap when sending a message. To enable it, follow this sequence: `Tools` (menu on the menu bar) `=> Options => Send` (tab) `=> Plain Text Settings` (button) `=>` Type the number of characters per line in the window that pops up. For **Netscape** 4.8 and 7.01, follow this sequence; `Edit` (menu on the menu bar) `=> Preferences => Mail & Newsgroups => Messages` (4.8) or `Message Display` (7.01) `=>` Turn on the checkbox for text wrapping. The **Opera M2** e-mail client does not provide text wrapping.

3.17.3   Security in Eudora (Study Section 3.7)

Attachments are a big source of security problems and viruses in e-mail. Eudora and other e-mail clients can limit their damage. Eudora offers two options that you can use to restrict the running of any executable file through attachments. To activate the first option click `Tools =>` `Options => Extra Warnings =>` make sure the `(Warn me when I) Launch a` `program from a message` checkbox is checked. (See the accompanying screen capture.) To activate the other option, click `Tools => Options => Viewing Mail =>` Make sure the `Allow executables in HTML content` box is unchecked.

3.17.4   Security in Outlook Express (Study Section 3.8)

Outlook Express allows its users to display the size of attachments and, more importantly, add file-attachment security to prevent files infected with viruses from corrupting and damaging their computers.

To display an attachment's size, we need to add the `Size` column (field) to the message header default fields discussed in Example 3.5. Click `View` (menu on the menu bar) `=> Columns =>` Check (turn on) the `Size` checkbox `=> OK`.

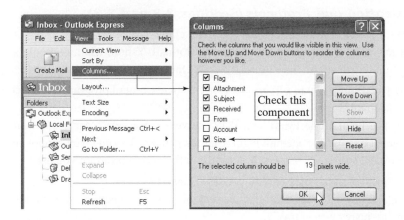

To set file-attachment security, click Tools (menu on the menu bar) => Options => Security (tab) => Check (turn on) this checkbox: ☑ Do not allow attachments to be saved or opened that could potentially be a virus. Be aware that turning on this security option may cause some good files not to open as well.

3.17.5 Import E-Mail Messages and Address Books (Study Section 3.15)

E-mail clients import messages and address books from each other.

Eudora imports Outlook Express and Netscape Messenger e-mail and address books. Click File (menu on the menu bar) => Import => Select one or more accounts => OK.

Outlook Express imports from Eudora, Netscape, Outlook, and Microsoft Exchange. Click File (menu on the menu bar) => Import => Select Address Book or Messages => Follow the prompts.

Netscape imports from Eudora, Outlook Express, and Outlook. In Netscape 4.8, click File (menu on the menu bar) => Import => Follow the prompts. In 7.01, click Tools (menu on the menu bar) => Import => Select Address Book or Messages => Next => Select Eudora or Outlook Express => Next => Finish.

Opera imports from Eudora and Outlook Express. Click: File (menu on menu bar of Opera browser) => Import => Mail => Select Eudora or Outlook Express => Next => Select the account(s) and what you want to import => Next => Finish.

FAQs

Introduction (Section 3.1)

Q: What is an e-mail server?

A: An **e-mail server** is a computer program that sends, receives, and stores e-mail messages.

Communication and Protocols (Sections 3.2 and 3.3)

Q: Is `Inbox` a standard folder name that all e-mail clients use?

A: No. But many clients do use it. For example, Hotmail, Yahoo! Mail, Outlook, and Netscape Mailer use it. However, Eudora uses `In`, while Opera uses `Received`.

Q: How many incoming e-mail servers can I specify in my e-mail program when I configure it to set up an account?

A: You can specify multiple IMAP and POP3 servers. To access your account on any one of them, you need to use the account login (username and password). You cannot always specify multiple IMAP and POP3 servers. It depends on the e-mail program you use.

Q: What are queued e-mail messages on an SMTP server?

A: These are messages that are waiting to be sent, because the receiving server could be down or experiencing heavy e-mail traffic.

Q: What are the standard port numbers used by e-mail servers?

A: SMTP servers listen on port number 25, while POP3 servers listen on port 110 and IMAP servers listen on port 143. When an e-mail client sends a message, the SMTP server receives it through port 25. And when the client checks e-mail, the POP3 (IMAP) server sends it through port 110 (143).

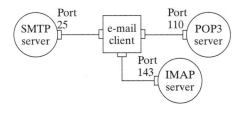

Q: What are some e-mail clients that can be configured to use different types of incoming e-mail servers?

A: The program `Mail.app` that runs on a Macintosh can specify multiple POP3 servers or a mixture of POP3 and IMAP servers. Other e-mail programs that can have multiple servers of mixed type include Pine and Mutt on Unix systems.

Content, Attachments, and Etiquette (Section 3.4)

Q: I received an e-mail message that is only one very long line. Why? How do I read it?

A: Assuming that the sender did not intent to write a very long line, this means that word wrap of your e-mail client did not work for this message. Sometimes this happens when you receive messages from a different OS (e.g., a message sent from Mac to Windows). To read the message, check the setup of your e-mail program and turn the word wrap option on. Alternatively, you can copy and paste the body of the message into Notepad or Word.

Q: How do I use the e-mail quote symbol, >?

A: When you respond to someone's e-mail message, you can quote him or her in order to make communication easier. When you use your e-mail program to respond to the message, it appends the quote symbol to the beginning of each line of the message, in anticipation of your use of quotes. It sometimes also italicizes the body of the message. Simply insert your responses at the proper places in the message. Here is an example:

```
>and can you please tell me the time and place?
3 P.M. in the conference room of the IT department.
```

E-Mail Clients and Web-Based E-Mail (Section 3.6)

Q: What is the difference between the IMAP and POP3 protocols?

A: IMAP keeps your e-mail messages on the incoming e-mail server, allowing you to use any e-mail client anywhere to read them. POP3 requires you to download all your e-mail onto your computer (where your e-mail client resides) before you can read it. Think of IMAP as an online e-mail reader and POP3 as an off-line e-mail reader.

Q: What should I do when I delete a message, but it still shows up with a line through its header instead of going away?

A: This notation means that you are using an IMAP server. Check your e-mail client and make sure that you change its option to remove the message instead of striking its header with a line.

Eudora (Section 3.7)

Q: What is the difference between the `Inbox` and `In` folders of Eudora?

A: Eudora uses the `Inbox` folder to download incoming e-mail when you configure it to use the IMAP protocol. It uses the `In` folder when you configure it to use the POP3 protocol.

Q: My Eudora program does not check my e-mail when I click the `Check Mail` button, even though I am online. What is the problem?

A: Check the incoming e-mail server's setup. If your e-mail server is using POP3 and you check IMAP accidently, this problem occurs.

Hotmail and Yahoo! Mail (Sections 3.11 and 3.12)

Q: Does the `Tab` key on the keyboard work while I am composing messages using Hotmail or Yahoo! Mail?

A: No. If you hit it, the cursor will disappear (it is a mail program issue). Click anywhere in the message area to see it again.

Blackbox

Sections 3.1 and 3.2 (E-mail requirements) (Example 3.1): You need an e-mail account, an ISP, and an e-mail program in order to send and receive messages. You also need to configure the e-mail program with respect to your e-mail account and the domain names of the incoming and outgoing e-mail servers. An e-mail account has a mailbox consisting of e-mail folders.

Section 3.3 (E-mail protocols) (Example 3.2): Four e-mail protocols exist. SMTP connects the sender's server to the Internet to send e-mail connects the receiver's server to the Internet to download e-mail. POP3 and IMAP connect the receiver's client to the receiver's server to download mail. There are differences between POP3 and IMAP. The MIME protocol enables e-mail messages to include attachments (files).

Sections 3.4and 3.5 (Content and etiquette of e-mail) (Example 3.3): An e-mail message has four parts: header, body, signature, and attachments.

Section 3.6 (E-mail clients and Web e-mail): Use e-mail clients when reading messages on one computer in one place. Use Web e-mail when reading messages anywhere, anytime.

Sections 3.13 (S-mail) (Example 3.11): S-mail uses the S/MIME or PGP/MIME protocol for attachments and requires configuration of the e-mail program.

Section 3.14 (E-mail activities) (Examples 3.12 and 3.13): You can send, reply to, delete, and print e-mail.

Section 3.15 (Managing e-mail) (Examples 3.14–3.20): Managing e-mail includes sending e-mail, deleting e-mail, archiving e-mail, filtering spam and junk mail, and creating and using signature files, vCards, stationeries, mailing lists, and address books.

Section 3.16 (Wireless e-mail): Mobile e-mail uses IMAP and secure communication.

Section 3.17 (Tutorials): Five tutorials show how to manage attachments, word-wrap message text, deal with mail security, and import address books.

Quick reference for using Eudora 5.2 (Sections 3.7 and 3.13–3.15):

1. **Type of e-mail program:** Both e-mail client and Web e-mail.
2. **Download and install (Example 3.4):** Visit http://www.eudora.com to download the e-mail client and http://www.eudoramail.com to use Web e-mail.
3. **Default mailbox folders (Example 3.1):** In, Out, and Trash.
4. **Configure (during installation) (Examples 3.2 and 3.4):** Follow the prompts in the New Account Wizard window, and input the name, e-mail address, login name, and the domain names of the incoming and outgoing e-mail servers.
5. **Add account (after installation) (Example 3.2):** Right-click Account (tab in the main window). Then click New => Follow the prompts in the New Account Wizard window.
6. **Configure s-mail (Example 3.11):** Click Tools => Options. Select the Checking Mail category (or the Sending Mail category) and select an SSL option.
7. **Perform e-mail activities (Example 3.4):**
   7.1 **Get e-mail:** Click the Check Mail button on the message toolbar.
   7.2 **Read e-mail:** Click the message header.

7.3 **Reply to e-mail:** Click the message header => `Reply` => Type the reply text => `Send`.

7.4 **Forward e-mail:** Click the message header => `Forward` => Type the recipient's e-mail address in the `Forward` window => `Send`.

7.5 **File e-mail:** Drag a message header from one e-mail folder and drop it onto another.

7.6 **Print e-mail:** Click the message header => `Print`, or click the message header => `File` => `Print`.

7.7 **Delete e-mail:** click the message header => `Delete Message(s)`, or right-click the message header => `Delete Message`. To completely remove the message, open the `Trash` folder, highlight the message header again, and click `Delete Message(s)` again.

7.8 **Send e-mail (Examples 3.11, 3.12, and 3.13; Tutorials 3.17.1 and 3.17.3):** Click `New Message` => Type the recipient's e-mail address, the subject, and the body of the message => `Send`. You can send a message to single or multiple recipients and with priority, return receipt requested, and attachments.

8. **Manage e-mail:**

8.1 **Archive mailbox folders (Example 3.14):** Go to this directory (or its equivalent), making sure to replace `Zeid` by your username:

```
C:\Documents and Settings\Zeid\Eudora\Application
   Data\Qualcomm\Eudora
```

Copy `In and In.toc`, `Out and Out.toc`, and `Trash and Trash.toc` to a new folder, a floppy disk, a zip disk, or a CD.

8.2 **Create and use signature files (Example 3.15):** Click `Tools` => `Signatures` => Double-click `Standard` => Type the signature text. To use the signature file, click `Tools` => `Personalities` => right-click on the desired personality => `Properties` => Select `Standard` from the `Default Signature` drop-down list => `OK`.

8.3 **Create and use vCards (Example 3.16):** Open the address book and click `Special` => `Settings` => `Address Book` => `Support vCard features in Eudora` => `OK`. Then click `Window` => `Address Book`. Your name is on the top of the `Nickname` list. Click the `Home` tab, enter the vCard information, and click `File` (menu on the menu bar) => `Save`. To use the vCard, click the `vCard` button when you are composing a message.

8.4 **Create and use stationeries (Example 3.17):** Click `Tools` => `Stationery` => right-click in the window => `New` => Enter text for the message body, and fill in the message headers => `File` => `Save As stationery`=> Enter the file name => `Save`. To use the stationery, click `Message` => `New Message With` => Select the stationery => Fill in the stationery => `Send`.

8.5 Create and use address books (Example 3.18 and Tutorial 3.17.5): Click New Book => Enter a name for the book => OK. To send a message to a name in the book, click the name => To: => Type the message => Send.

8.6 Create and use mailing lists (Example 3.19): Hold down the Shift key to select multiple entries in sequence or the Ctrl key to make nonconsecutive selections. Click the To: button to send a message to all the selected recipients.

8.7 Create and use spam filters (Example 3.20): To block a specific e-mail address, click Tools=> Filters => Follow the prompts.

Quick reference for using Outlook Express (Sections 3.8 and 3.13–3.15):

1. **Type of e-mail program:** E-mail client.

2. **Download and install (Example 3.5):** Included in the IE browser.

3. **Default mailbox folders (Example 3.1):** Inbox, Outbox, Sent Items, Deleted Items, and Drafts.

4. **Configure (during installation) (Examples 3.2 and 3.5):** Follow the prompts in the Internet Connection Wizard window. Input the name, e-mail address, login name, and the domain names of the incoming and outgoing e-mail servers.

5. **Add account (after installation) (Example 3.2):** Click Tools => Accounts => Mail (tab) => Add => Mail => Follow the prompts in the Internet Connection Wizard window that pops up.

6. **Configure s-mail (Example 3.11 and Tutorial 3.17.4):** Click Tools => Options => Security (tab) => check (turn on) the two checkboxes in the Secure mail area.

7. **Perform e-mail activities (Example 3.5):**

   7.1 Get e-mail: Click the Send/Recv button on the message toolbar.

   7.2 Read e-mail: Click the message header.

   7.3 Reply to e-mail: Click the message header => Reply => type the reply text => Send.

   7.4 Forward e-mail: Click the message header => Forward => Type the recipient's e-mail address in the Forward window => Send.

   7.5 File e-mail: Drag a message header from one e-mail folder and drop it onto another.

   7.6 Print e-mail: Click the message header => Print, or click the message header => File => Print.

   7.7 Delete e-mail: Click the message header => Delete, or right-click the message header => Delete. To completely remove the message, open the Trash folder, highlight the message header again, and click Delete again => Yes.

   7.8 Send e-mail (Examples 3.11, 3.12, and 3.13 and Tutorials 3.17.1 and 3.17.3): Click Create Mail => Type the recipient's e-mail address, the subject, and the body of the message => `Send`. You can send a message to single or multiple recipients and with priority, return receipt requested, and attachments.

8. **Manage e-mail:**

   8.1 **Archive mailbox folders (Example 3.14):** Go to this directory (or its equivalent), making sure to replace `Zeid` by your username:

   ```
   C:\Documents and Settings\Zeid\Local Settings\Application
       Data\Identities\{80D6C7A9-B66C-4FE6-B9CC-
       AA6FADD302F1}\Microsoft\Outlook Express
   ```

   Copy all the files with a `.dbx` extension to a new folder, a floppy disk, a zip disk, or a CD.

   8.2 **Create and use signature files (Example 3.15):** Click `Tools` => `Options` => `Signatures` (tab) => `New` => Enter the signature text. Alternatively, click `File` => find the text or HTML file you would like to use => Select (check) `Add signatures to all outgoing messages` checkbox => `OK`.

   8.3 **Create and use vCards (Example 3.16):** Click `Addresses` => `New` => `New Contact` => Input the vCard information for yourself in the `Properties` window that pops up => `OK`. To attach your vCard to outgoing e-mail, click `Tools` => `Options` => `Compose` (tab) => Select (check) the `Mail` checkbox (under the `Business Cards` area) => Select your name from the drop-down list next to `Mail` => `OK`.

   8.4 **Create and use stationeries (Example 3.17):** Click `Tools` => `Options` => `Compose` (tab) => `Create New` (in the `Stationery` area) => `Next` => select the stationery's background picture and color => `Next` => Select the font, size, color, and style of the stationery's text => `Next` => Enter the values of the left and top margins of the stationery => `Next` => Enter the stationery name (in order to save it as a file with this name) => `Finish`. To apply the stationery to all outgoing e-mail, click `Tools` (menu) => `Options` => `Compose` (tab) => Select (check) the `Mail` checkbox (in the `Stationery` area) => `Select` => Select the stationery file from the `Select Stationery` popup window => `OK` => `OK`.

   8.5 **Create and use address books (Example 3.18 and Tutorial 3.17.5):** Click `Tools` => `Address Book` => `New` => `New Contact` => Input the contact information in the window that pops up => `OK`. To send a message to a contact, click the contact and then click `Action` => `Send Mail` => Type the message => `Send`.

   8.6 **Create and use mailing lists (Example 3.19):** Click `Tools` => `Address Book` => `New` => `New Group` => Type a group name (alias) in the `Group Name` text field => `Select Members` => Select the contacts to be included in the group => `Select` => `OK`. To use the list, select it in the address book and click `Action` => `Send Mail` => Type the message => `Send`.

8.7   Create and use spam filters (Example 3.20): To block a specific e-mail address, click `Tools => Message Rules => Mail =>` Select (check) the rules and actions checkboxes `=>` Click the links that show and specify the required data `=>` OK `=>` OK.

Quick reference for using Netscape
(Sections 3.9 and 3.13–3.15):

1.   Type of e-mail program: Both e-mail client and Web e-mail.

2.   Download and install (Example 3.4): The client is included in the Netscape browser. Visit `http://www.netscape.com` for the Web e-mail.

3.   Default mailbox folders (Example 3.1): `Inbox`, `Unsent Messages`, `Drafts`, `Templates`, `Sent`, and `Trash`.

4.   Configure (during installation) (Examples 3.2 and 3.6): Not applicable.

5.   Add account (after installation) (Examples 3.2 and 3.6): In 4.8 (Messenger), Click `Edit => Preferences => Mail & Newsgroups` (tree node) `=> Identity =>` Input your name and e-mail address `=> OK => Mail Servers => Add =>` input the incoming e-mail server information `=> OK =>` Input the domain name of the outgoing e-mail server => OK. In **7.01 (Mailer)**, click `File` (menu on the menu bar of the `Inbox` window) `=> New => Account =>` follow the prompts.

6.   Configure s-mail (Example 3.11): In **4.8,** click `Edit => Preferences => Mail Servers =>` Select one of the SSL options. For incoming e-mail in 1.01, click `Edit => Mail & Newsgroups Account Setting => Server Settings =>` check the `Use secure connection (SSL)` checkbox. For outgoing e-mail in **7.01,** click `Edit => Mail & Newsgroups Account Setting => Outgoing Server (SMTP) =>` Select one of the SSL options.

7.   Perform e-mail activities (Example 3.6):

    7.1   Get e-mail: Click the `Get Msg` button on the message toolbar.

    7.2   Read e-mail: Click the message header.

    7.3   Reply to e-mail: Click the message header => `Reply` => Type the reply text => `Send`.

    7.4   Forward e-mail: Click the message header => `Forward` => Type the recipient's e-mail address in the `Forward` window => `Send`.

    7.5   File e-mail: Drag a message header from one e-mail folder and drop it onto another.

    7.6   Print e-mail: Click the message header => `Print`, or click the message header => `File => Print`.

    7.7   Delete e-mail: Click the message header => `Delete`, or right-click the message header => `Delete Message`. To completely remove the message, open the `Trash` folder, highlight the message header again, and click `Delete` again.

    7.8   Send e-mail (Examples 3.11, 3.12, and 3.13 and Tutorial 3.17.1): Click `New Msg` (in 4.8) or `Compose` (in **7.01**) `=>` Type the recipient's e-mail address, the subject, and the body of the message => `Send`. You can send a message to single or multiple recipients and with priority, return receipt requested, and attachments.

8. **Manage e-mail:**

   8.1 **Archive mailbox folders (Example 3.14):** Open the Netscape `Mail` folder by using this path:

   `C:\ProgramFiles\Netscape\Users\default\Mail`.

   Copy all the files in this folder to a new folder, a floppy disk, a zip disk, or a CD.

   8.2 **Create and use signature files (Example 3.15):** In **4.8**, click `Edit =>` `Preferences => Mail & Newsgroups => Identity => Choose` `=> OK`. In **7.0**, click `Edit => Mail & Newsgroups Account Settings` `=>` Select the `Attach this signature` checkbox `=> Choose => OK`.

   8.3 **Create and use vCards (Example 3.16):** In **4.8**, click `Edit => Preferences` `=> Mail & Newsgroups => Identity =>` Select the `Attach my` `personal card to messages (as a vCard)` checkbox `=>` Create the card or edit it (if the card already exists). Netscape 7.01 does not support the creation of vCards.

   8.4 **Create and use stationeries (Example 3.17):** Netscape allows you to create templates by saving any existing message in its `Templates` folder. Click a message header `=> File => Save As => Template`.

   8.5 **Create and use address books (Example 3.18 and Tutorial 3.17.5):** Click `File` (menu on the menu bar) `=> New => Address Book =>` Enter the name of the address book `=> OK`. To send the message to the e-mail address on a card, select the card and click `Compose =>` Type the message `=> Send`.

   8.6 **Create and use mailing lists (Example 3.19):** In `Address Book`, click `New` `List =>` Type the name of the list, and type the e-mail addresses of the list or drag them from `Address Book => OK`. To send a message to the list, select the list from `Address Book => New Msg` (**4.8**) or `Compose` (**7.0**) `=>` Type the message `=> Send`.

   8.7 **Create and use spam filters (Example 3.20):** To block a specific e-mail address in **4.8**, click `Edit => Message Filters => New =>` Type the name of the filter and the rules (conditions) `=> OK => OK`. To block e-mail in **7.0**, click `Tools => Message Filters => New =>` Add the filter rules and action `=> OK => OK`.

Quick reference for using Opera M2 (Sections 3.10 and 3.13–3.15):

1. **Type of e-mail program:** Both e-mail client and Web e-mail.
2. **Download and install (Example 3.4):** The client is included in the Opera browser. Visit `http://www.operamail.com` for the Web e-mail.

---

3.   **Default mailbox folders (Example 3.1):** `Received`, `Outbox`, `Sent`, `Drafts`, `Spam`, and `Trash`.

4.   **Configure (during installation) (Examples 3.2 and 3.7):** Not applicable.

5.   **Add account (after installation) (Example 3.2):** Click `Mail` => `New account` => Follow the prompts in the `New account wizard` window, and input the user's name, e-mail address, organization, login name, password, and the domain names of the incoming and outgoing e-mail servers.

6.   **Configure s-mail (Example 3.11):** Click `Mail` => `Manage accounts` => Select an account => `Edit` => `Servers` (tab) => Check `Secure connection (TLS)` in both the incoming and outgoing server areas.

7.   **Perform e-mail activities (Example 3.4):**

   7.1   **Get e-mail:** Click the `Check Mail` button on the message toolbar.

   7.2   **Read e-mail:** Click the message header.

   7.3   **Reply to e-mail:** Click the message header => `Reply` => Type the reply text => `Send`.

   7.4   **Forward e-mail:** Click the message header => `Forward` => Type the recipient's e-mail address in the `Forward` window => `Send`.

   7.5   **File e-mail:** Drag a message header from one e-mail folder and drop it onto another.

   7.6   **Print e-mail:** Click the message header => `Print`, or click the message header => `File` => `Print`.

   7.7   **Delete e-mail:** Click the message header => `Delete Message(s)`, or right-click the message header => `Delete Message`. To completely remove the message, open the `Trash` folder, highlight the message header again, and click `Delete Message(s)` again.

   7.8   **Send e-mail (Examples 3.11, 3.12, and 3.13 and Tutorials 3.17.1 and 3.17.3):** Click `New Message` => Type the recipient's e-mail address, the subject, and the body of the message => `Send`. You can send a message to single or multiple recipients and with priority, return receipt requested, and attachments.

8.   **Manage e-mail:**

   8.1   **Archive mailbox folders (Example 3.14):** Open the Opera `Mail` folder by using this path, making sure to replace *Zeid* by your username.

   `C:\Documents and Settings\Zeid\Application Data\Opera\Opera7\Mail`

   Copy all the files and folders in this folder to a new folder, a floppy disk, a zip disk, or a CD.

   8.2   **Create and use signature files (Example 3.15):** Click `Mail` => `Manage accounts` => Highlight an account => `Edit` => `Outgoing` (tab) => Type the text in the `Signature` text area => `OK`. When you send an e-mail, Opera appends the signature.

   8.3   **Create and use vCards (Example 3.16):** Opera does not support the creation of vCards.

8.4 **Create and use stationeries (Example 3.17):** Opera does not offer a direct way to create stationeries. However, you can compose a message and reuse its format by keeping it in the Opera `Drafts` e-mail folder.

8.5 **Create and use address books (Example 3.18 and Tutorial 3.17.5):** Opera allows the user to add contacts to its `Contacts` list. To add a contact to the list, highlight a message header and click the `Add contact` button on the `Received` tab window. To send a message to a contact, right-click on the contact and select `Compose` from the popup menu.

8.6 **Create and use mailing lists (Example 3.19):** Click the `Contacts` button of the `Hotlist` tab window. Hold down the `Shift` key to select multiple entries in sequence or the `Ctrl` key for nonconsecutive selections. Right-click on the selected contacts and select `Compose` from the popup menu. Type the message and click `Send`.

8.7 **Create and use spam filters (Example 3.20):** Not available.

Quick reference for using Hotmail (Sections 3.11 and 3.13–3.15):

1. **Type of e-mail program:** Web e-mail.

2. **Download and install (Examples 3.8 and 3.9):** Visit `http://www.hotmail.com` to sign up.

3. **Default mailbox folders (Example 3.1):** `Inbox`, `Trash Can`, `Drafts`, and `Sent Messages`.

4. **Configure (during installation) (Example 3.2):** Not applicable.

5. **Add account (after installation) (Example 3.2):** Not applicable.

6. **Configure s-mail (Example 3.11):** Not applicable.

7. **Perform e-mail activities (Example 3.8):**

7.1 **Get e-mail:** Click the `Inbox` tab.

7.2 **Read e-mail:** Click the message header.

7.3 **Reply to e-mail:** Click the message header => `Reply` => Type the reply text => `Send`.

7.4 **Forward e-mail:** Click the message header => `Forward` => Type the recipient's e-mail address in the `Forward` window => `Send`.

7.5 **File e-mail:** Select the message header's checkbox => Select an e-mail folder from the `Put in Folder` drop-down list.

7.6 **Print e-mail:** Click the message header => `Print`, or click the message header => `File` => `Print`.

7.7 **Delete e-mail:** Select the message header's checkbox => `Delete`. To completely remove the message, open the `Trash` folder, select the message header's checkbox again, and click `Delete`.

7.8 **Send e-mail (Examples 3.11, 3.12, and 3.13 and Tutorials 3.17.1 and 3.17.3):** Click Compose => Type the recipient's e-mail address, the subject, and the body of the message => Send. You can send a message to single or multiple recipients and with priority, return receipt requested, and attachments.

8. **Manage e-mail:**

8.1 **Archive mailbox folders (Example 3.14):** Not applicable.

8.2 **Create and use signature files (Example 3.15):** Log into your Hotmail account and click Options (tab on the top right side) => Signature (link under the Additional Options section) => Type the signature text in the text area => OK. Hotmail appends the signature to outgoing e-mail.

8.3 **Create and use vCards (Example 3.16):** Not applicable.

8.4 **Create and use stationeries (Example 3.17):** Not applicable.

8.5 **Create and use address books (Example 3.18 and Tutorial 3.17.5)** log in and click the Contacts tab. To add a new contact, click New Contact => Type the contact's information => OK. To edit, delete, or send mail to an existing contact, select (check) its checkbox and click the Edit, Delete, or Send Mail button, respectively.

8.6 **Create and use mailing lists (Example 3.19):** Log in. Click Contacts (tab) => New Group => Type the group's name and the e-mail addresses of the group => OK. The group is added at the bottom of the Contacts tab window. To use it, select (check) its checkbox => Send Mail => Type the message => Send.

8.7 **Create and use spam filters (Example 3.20):** Not applicable.

Quick reference for using Yahoo! Mail (Sections 3.12 and 3.13–3.15):

1. **Type of e-mail program:** Web e-mail.

2. **Download and install (Examples 3.8 and 3.9):** Visit http://www.yahoomail.com to sign up.

3. **Default mailbox folders (Example 3.1):** Inbox, Draft, Sent, and Trash.

4. **Configure (during installation) (Example 3.2):** Not applicable.

5. **Add account (after installation) (Example 3.2):** Not applicable.

6. **Configure s-mail (Example 3.11):** Not applicable.

7. **Perform e-mail activities (Example 3.10):**

7.1 **Get e-mail:** Click the Check Mail button.

7.2 **Read e-mail:** Click the message header.

7.3 **Reply to e-mail:** Click the message header => Reply => Type the reply text => Send.

7.4 **Forward e-mail:** Click the message header => Forward => Type the recipient's e-mail address in the Forward window => Send.

    7.5   **File e-mail:** Select a message header's checkbox => Select an e-mail folder from the `Move to Folder` drop-down list.

    7.6   **Print e-mail:** Click the message header => `Print`, or click the message header => `File` => `Print`.

    7.7   **Delete e-mail:** Select the message header's checkbox => `Delete`. To completely remove the message, open the `Trash` folder, select the message header's checkbox again, and click `Delete` again.

    7.8   **Send e-mail (Examples 3.11, 3.12, and 3.13 and Tutorials 3.17.1 and 3.17.3):** Click `Compose` => Type the recipient's e-mail address, the subject, and the body of the message => `Send`. You can send a message to single or multiple recipients and with priority, return receipt requested, and attachments.

8.   **Manage e-mail:**

    8.1   **Archive mailbox folders (Example 3.14):** Not applicable.

    8.2   **Create and use signature files (Example 3.15):** Log in to your Yahoo! Mail account and click `Mail` (tab on the left side) => `Options` => `Signature` (link) => Type the signature text in the text area => Select (check) the `Add signature to all outgoing messages` checkbox => `Save`.

    8.3   **Create and use vCards (Example 3.16):** Not applicable.

    8.4   **Create and use stationeries (Example 3.17):** Not applicable.

    8.5   **Create and use address books (Example 3.18 and Tutorial 3.17.5):** Log in and click the `Addresses` drop-down list. To add a new contact, click `Addresses` => `Add Contact` => Type the contact's information => `Save Contact`. To edit or delete an existing contact, select (check) its checkbox and click the `Edit` link or `Delete` button, respectively. To send mail to a contact, click the e-mail address listed underneath it.

    8.6   **Create and use mailing lists (Example 3.19):** Log in. Click `Addresses` (drop-down list) => Type the name of the list => select e-mail addresses for the list from the `Add Contacts` area => `Add` => `Save`. The list is now added. To use it, select (check) its checkbox => `Send Mail` => Type the message => `Send`. To use the list, select (check) its checkbox on its left => `OK` (next to the `Send Email` drop-down list) => `Compose` => Type the message => `Send`.

    8.7   **Create and use spam filters (Example 3.20):** Not applicable.

Check Your Progress

At the end of this chapter, you should

✔   understand the concepts of sending and receiving e-mail messages (Sections 3.1 and 3.2);

✔   understand e-mail protocols (Section 3.3);

✔   know about the content and etiquette of e-mail (Sections 3.4 and 3.5);

✔   be able to identify the differences between e-mail clients and Web-based e-mail (Section 3.6);

✔ have mastered the use of some popular e-mail programs (Sections 3.7–3.12);

✔ understand s-mail (Section 3.13);

✔ have mastered e-mail activities and management (Sections 3.14 and 3.15);

✔ know about some of the issues associated with wireless e-mail (Section 3.16).

Problems

The exercises are designed for a lab setting, while the homework is to be done outside class time.

Exercises

3.1   Add the new folder Fun to the Outlook Express e-mail folders. Move two existing e-mail messages to it.

3.2   Delete the e-mail folder you created in Exercise 3.1.

3.3   Repeat Problems 3.1 and 3.2 in Hotmail.

3.4   Repeat Problems 3.1 and 3.2 in Yahoo! Mail.

3.5   Set your Yahoo! Mail account to autoreply to all your e-mail messages for one day. If you do not have a Yahoo! Mail account, visit http://yahoomail.com and sign up for one.

Homework

3.6   Extend Figure 3.2 to include Jones's incoming e-mail server and Smith's outgoing e-mail server. Follow the display format of the two servers shown in the figure.

3.7   How many top-level e-mail folders would your e-mail client have if you were to use four POP3 e-mail accounts and three IMAP accounts?

3.8   How do you control the displaying/hiding and resizing of columns of messages' headers in the Eudora, Outlook Express, and Netscape e-mail clients?

3.9   List the Label options of the Opera M2 client. Describe the steps involved in labeling your e-mail messages.

3.10   How do you spell check a message that you compose in Hotmail?

Instant Messaging

Goal

Understand and master the use of synchronous communication, such as chatting and instant messaging. Applications include fun (e.g., chatting with family and friends), online meetings, and collaboration among professionals.

Objectives

- Types of synchronous communication
- Types of Web chatting
- BBSs, chat rooms, and IRC channels
- The difference between instant messaging and chat rooms
- IM clients and Web-based IMing
- Popular IMing systems: AIM, Yahoo! Messenger, and MSN Messenger
- Webcasting
- Wireless IMing

Outline

4.1   Introduction

The Web is all about communication in an easy and convenient way, anytime and anywhere. Web communication has two modes: synchronous and asynchronous. **Synchronous communication** is an activity in which the two communicating persons send (receive) messages to (from) each other *simultaneously, in real time*. Examples include instant messaging (IM) and chatting, the subject of this chapter. **Asynchronous communication** is an activity in which the two communicating persons send (receive) messages to (from) each other *independently, at different times*. Examples include e-mail (Chapter 3) and newsgroups (Chapter 5).

Chatting on the Web is fun and easy to do. It is like two friends, family members, or colleagues are in one place at one time. It enables us to stay in touch. In addition to chatting for fun, the uses of Web chatting are unlimited. For example, salespeople who are constantly on the road can use it to talk to their customers and clients. Company executives can hold meetings from remote locations. Professors and instructors can hold office hours with their students online by setting a specific time when students can post questions and ask for help.

Three types of content exist for Web chatting. In text-only chatting, short text messages are exchanged. These messages usually use abbreviations, or acronyms. (See Chapter 3.) In instant messaging, graphics and text content are used such that the text messages are augmented with colors and graphics in the form of emoticons. (See Chapter 3.) The third type of chatting includes both audio and video content. This type is known as Webcasting.

Web chatting is a distributed application that uses the client/server model of communication. (See Chapter 1.) Web-chatting software can be client or Web based. In the client-based type, the user needs to download and install a chatting client. Examples include America Online Instant Messenger (AIM), Yahoo! Messenger (YM), and Microsoft Messenger (MSN Messenger). In Web-based type, users chat through Web pages.

4.2 Text-Only Web Chatting

Web chatting among multiple users is also known as online keyboard chatting. **Chatting** (talking) is the exchange of typed-in messages among two or more users who are all on the Internet at the same time. It requires a chat server, which acts as the repository for the messages. While public chatting is common, a private chat can be arranged between two parties as well. Secure chatting is also available and is used for real-time business communication. Most chats are focused on one topic of interest. Famous people are sometimes invited to join chats in order to increase their popularity. Chats can be ongoing or scheduled at set times. Transcripts of chats may be archived for future use.

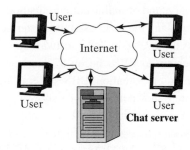

Web chatting, like traditional chatting, spans virtually any aspect of human endeavor and interest. There exist general, kid, teen, movie, food, life, and religion chats, to name a few. Chat servers are organized into chat rooms, with one room per topic. A **chat room** is a chat server or part of a chat server that provides a venue for users with a common interest to communicate in real time. Users join a chat room by registering. By entering a username and a password, a user logs into a room to chat. A chat room usually has a list of its current users, and it alerts the users if another person enters the room. Any user in the chat room can type a message into a text box, and other users can respond. Messages are broadcast immediately to every user in the chat room. Chatting has its own etiqeutte, such as introducing oneself when entering a room, being polite, being clear on whether one is asking a question or responding to a specific user, and not being disruptive.

Chat rooms

Scrolling and lurking are two issues related to chatting. **Scrolling** is monopolizing and disabling a conversation by repeatedly typing the same message or phrase. Scrolling is against chatting protocol. **Lurking** is being a silent participant during a chat, by just reading messages. A user who is lurking does not take an active part in the discussion. Lurking is an accepted chat practice. There are often lurkers in any chat room, and people new to a particular chat are sometimes advised to lurk until they become familiar with the discussion.

4.2.1   Bulletin Board System

Two chatting systems exist: the bulletin board system (BBS; also known as message boards) and Internet relay chat (IRC). We cover IRC in Section 4.2.2. The BBS, the older of the two, was created in 1978. A **BBS** is a computer application dedicated to exchanging messages and files on a network. The BBS was the primary kind of online communication throughout the 1980s. Today's BBS systems are Web based, replacing the text-based user interface of the 1980s. A **Web-based BBS** is essentially a website that is powered by BBS software rather than a Web server.

In the mid-1990s, membership to BBSs began to decrease as the graphics-oriented Web burst onto the scene and grabbed users' attention. BBS systems are free to use. A user needs an account to log in. The screen capture shown in Figure 4.1 show a session of a Web-based BBS. The system show a list of the current users on the right. It also informs current users of who has just joined and who logged off. The system messages that Figure 4.1 shows are, `You have joined`, `***Doomer has joined`, `***Deuce has quit(QUIT:brb.)`, `***Deuece has joined`, and `***DigitalMan is now known as DigitalMan|food`. Each system

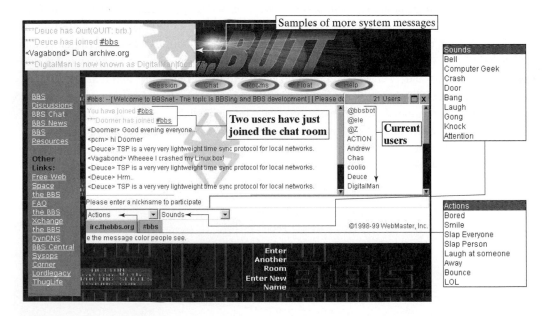

Figure 4.1   A Web-based bulletin board system.

message is preceded by *** and is displayed in green, while users' messages are displayed in black, to make it easier for users to distinguish between system and chat messages. Moreover, this BBS website has two menus—`Actions` and `Sounds`—that users can employ to get attention during chatting.

4.2.2 Internet Relay Chat

An **IRC** network is a communication system, based on BBS technology, that enables forums for discussion and real-time chatting, thus providing a virtual meeting place where people from all over the world can meet and talk. The BBS initially allowed users to post only simple text messages. It was limited. IRC began to develop in 1988. IRC is very popular today, especially among Unix users. It is also available on Windows, MAC, and Linux OSs. The darker side of IRC is that its servers have become a haven for computer hackers with malicious intent.

There are thousands of IRC servers available for users to connect to. Examples include `http://www.efnet.org`, `http://www.undernet.org`, and `http://www.irc-net.org`. Any search engine will turn up many other IRC servers. A user who wishes to communicate with any of these server must download and install an IRC client. `mIRC` is a simple client for Windows and can be downloaded from `http://www.mirc.com`. Other clients include `IRCle` for MAC (`http://www.ircle.com`) and `irc2` for Unix (`http://www.funet.fi/pub/unix/irc/server`). The most common default port for IRC servers is 6667. The IRC protocol uses the TCP protocol.

To utilize an IRC network, a user needs an IRC client, an IRC server to connect to, and a channel to join. A **channel** is a chat room. An IRC network typically has many users, servers, and channels; it is a multiuser and multichannel chat system. The user can start a new channel or join an existing one. The user also needs a login name and password to join a channel, as well as a channel nickname.

Example 4.1 Download, install, and use an IRC client.

Learn how to chat using an IRC network.

Solution 4.1 Download the `mIRC` v6.03 client from `http://www.mirc.com`. Double-click the downloaded self-extracting file and follow the instructions to install it. To run `mIRC`, double-click its shortcut on the desktop, or click `Start` (Windows menu) `=>` `All Programs` `=>` `mIRC` `=>` `mIRC`. In the `mIRC Options` window that pops up (see the forthcoming screen capture), select an IRC network and an IRC server and fill in your name, e-mail address, and nickname. Click the `Connect to IRC Server` button (see the screen capture) to connect to the IRC network and server. Once a connection is established, the `mIRC Channels Folder` window (not shown in the screen capture) pops up. Select a channel to join, and click `Join` to start chatting. (See the screen capture.)

There are many options and menus of the `mIRC` client that are not covered here. Interested readers can pursue them on their own.

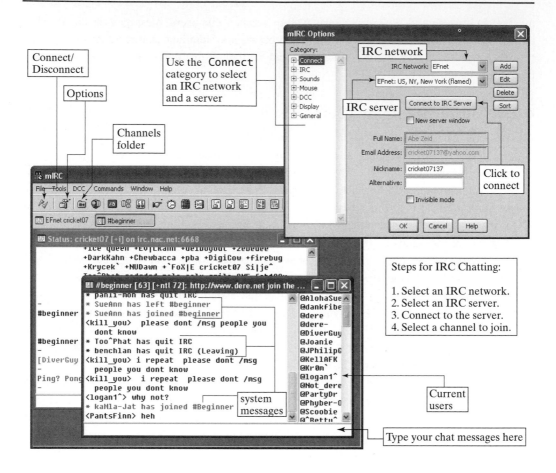

4.3 Instant Messaging

Instant messaging (IM or IMing) is a type of chatting and communication service that enables one person to create a private chat room with another person. Each person creates a list of people (family, friends, colleagues, etc.) with whom he or she wishes to interact, known as a **contact list** or a **buddy list**. The person also maintains this list over time. For two persons to communicate, they must include each other on their lists and must be online at the same time. When a person sends a message to a friend, a small window opens up where the person and the friend can type messages that they both can see. The window is split into two panes. The person types the outgoing messages in the bottom pane, and the friend's (incoming) messages are displayed in the top pane. The top pane also displays the outgoing messages. Typically, the IM system alerts (via a distinctive sound) the user whenever somebody on his or her contact list is online, a capability known as **presence**. Two individuals can initiate a chat session by typing (exchanging) messages to (with) each other.

There is a distinct difference between chat rooms and IM: A chat room typically handles two or more people involved in one or more discussions (see the list of current users in the screen captures of Example 4.1), while IM almost always involves one conversation between two people.

Like IRC, IM has its networks, clients, and servers. An IM user needs to download and install an IM client, create a contacts list on the client, and create an account on the IM server. The account requires a login identity, including a screen name and a password. The contacts list of one user includes the screen names of other users. All the users are able to communicate and chat because all the lists are maintained on the IM server that they all use. Several competing IM systems exist, including America Online IM (AIM), Microsoft IM (MSN Messenger), and Yahoo! Messenger. There are no IM standards that these systems must follow. Thus, two users must use the same IM system. One user, for example, cannot utilize AIM and expect to communicate with another user who utilizes Yahoo! Messenger.

IM systems allow users to do interesting things while chatting. For example, user can record (save) a chat session for future reference. Unlike on BBSs and IRC, users can employ graphics, colors, and text formatting in their chat messages. For example, the IM emoticons are usually available as facial (smiley) icons that the user selects, instead of the text version we covered in Chapter 3. The user can thus select a facial icon to express his or her emotions. The user also can select a color and style (bold, underlined, or italic) for a text message. In addition to exchanging instant messages, users can perform the following activities on an IM system;

- **chat**—create their own chat rooms with friends;
- **share Web links**—share links to their favorite websites;
- **share images**—look at images stored on a friend's computer while IMing;
- **play sounds and music**—play music for a friend;
- **share files**—exchange files directly with a friend while IMing;
- **talk**—use the Internet instead of a phone to actually talk with friends;
- **receive streaming (real-time) content**—receive content such as news and stock quotes.

IM systems and services are available at two levels: personal and enterprise (corporate). While personal IM is simple, enterprise IM services require control (over which groups should use them), management (maintenance, upgrading, and archiving of chat sessions), and security (to protect sensitive chats and company secrets). Many IM systems are available at both levels. While the personal IM system is free, companies pay for their IM systems.

Enterprise IM is used by many companies. The financial industry is a standout example. IM is used routinely by millions of workers to expedite and facilitate all kinds of time-sensitive and fast-paced business transactions. These workers include employees of securities trading firms, stockbrokers, bank employees, and commodity-futures traders.

4.4   AIM

America Online Instant Messenger (AIM) is a popular messaging system. The key AIM features include sending instant messages, seeing who is online in the buddy-list window, starting or joining buddy chats, locating members online, and blocking misbehaving members. Download AIM from `http://www.aim.com` and install it. We cover AIM version 5.1 here. After installation is complete, an AIM shortcut is created on the desktop, and the `Sign On` window (see the forthcoming screen capture) is displayed. The next step is to get an account. Click the `Get a Screen Name` link on the `Sign On` window and follow the prompts.

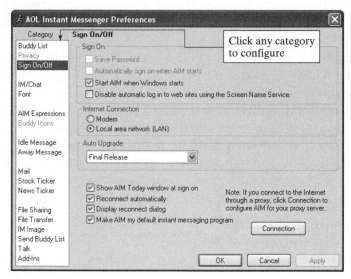 

Now you may want to set up (configure) AIM to suit your personal style. Click the `Setup` icon, ![Setup], on the `Sign On` window to open the `Preferences` window show in the foregoing screen capture. The window provides rich options that the user can set. There are many categories to control, such as the `Font`, `AIM Expressions`, `Idle Message`, `Away Message`, `File Sharing`, `File Transfer`, and `IM image`. Explore them.

The final step before using AIM is to create a buddy list. To do so, you must sign on to access the forthcoming AIM `Buddy List Window` shown on the left. Click the `Setup` icon, ![Setup], to open the `Buddy List Setup` window shown in the forthcoming left screen capture. In this window, click the `Add Buddy` icon. Type a buddy's screen name in the newly created space and hit `Enter`. Repeat to add another buddy to the list. To delete a buddy from the list, highlight the buddy and click `Delete`, as shown in the forthcoming right screen capture. Alternatively, right-click the buddy and select `Delete` from the popup menu.

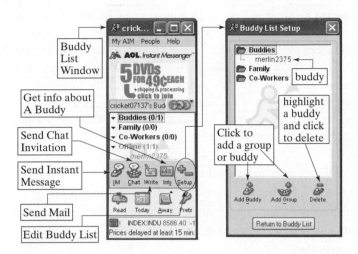

Example 4.2 Use AIM.

Learn how to do IMing, check who is online, locate a member, and block a member.

Solution 4.2 After creating an AIM account and a buddy list, we can start IMing:

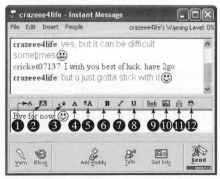

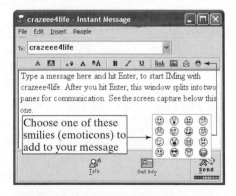

Send an instant message: Click the IM button on the Buddy List Window shown in the foregoing top left screen capture to open the Instant Message window shown in the foregoing bottom screen capture. Type the buddy's screen name in the To text field and a message in the pane. Hit Enter to send the message, and wait for a reply. When you receive a message back, the window splits into two panes, as shown in the foregoing bottom screen capture. You type outgoing messages in the bottom pane. The top pane displays both the incoming and outgoing messages. To jazz up your messages, use the buttons shown on the middle of the strip of the Instant Message window:

❶ Text color: Click and choose a color.

❷ Background color: Click and choose a color.

❸–❺ Smaller, normal, and larger font, respectively.

❻–❽ Bold, italic, and underlined text, respectively.

❾ Create a hyperlink.

❿ Send an IM image.

⓫ Send an IM greeting.

⓬ Insert a smiley.

Check who is online: The Buddy List Window has an Offline group that lists all the buddies who are not online. Any other buddies would be online.

Locate a member: Click this sequence: People (menu on the Buddy List Window) => Find a Buddy => Select a search criterion (By E-mail Address, By Name and Address, or By Common Interest). Click the My Privacy button, [My Privacy], to find out how to protect your privacy.

Block a member: In the Instant Message window where you are communicating with the member, click the Block icon, , and then click Yes. When you block the member, it will show on his or her Instant Message window that you have signed off. In addition, the member's screen name is added to your Offline list, with a red symbol, ⊘ crazeee4life , indicating the block. To unblock the member, right-click the member's name => Unblock Buddy.

☞ ──

Example 4.3 IM with more than one buddy.

Learn how to IM with multiple buddies simultaneously.

Solution 4.3 Click the IM button on the Buddy List Window multiple times to open multiple Instant Message windows. In each window, type a screen name and start IMing. Just be careful to avoid the embarrassment of sending one buddy a message intended for another buddy.

Example 4.4 Create your own AIM chat room.

Learn how to use AIM to create a private chat room.

Solution 4.4 Click this sequence: `Chat` (icon on the `Buddy List Window`) to open the `Chat Invitation` window shown in the accompanying top screen capture => Type the screen names you want to invite to your private chat room (type one name at a time, and hit `Enter` after each one) => `Send` (when done). The `Chat Room window` pops up. (See the accompanying bottom screen capture.) You can invite additional buddies to join after your chat room is open; click `People` (menu on the `Chat Room` window) => `Invite a Buddy` => Type the screen name(s) in the `Screen names to invite` text area => `Send`. After each buddy accepts your invitation, AIM displays the message, `username has entered the room`, in your `Chat Room` window. You can start typing your chat messages in the text area after you receive the notification. Now all the buddies are chatting with each other. This configuration is very similar to the IRC chat rooms discussed in Section 4.2.2. AIM chat rooms are useful for holding a class discussion between the course instructor and the students.

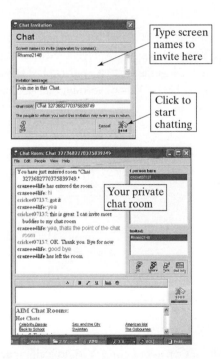

4.5 Yahoo! Messenger

Yahoo! Messenger (YM) is a popular messaging system. The key YM features include sending instant messages, showing who is online, starting or joining friends chats, locating members online, and exploiting its integration with other Yahoo! content and services. YM is also available in a Web version that does not require a client. To use the client, download and install it from `http://messenger.yahoo.com`. We cover YM version 5.5 here.

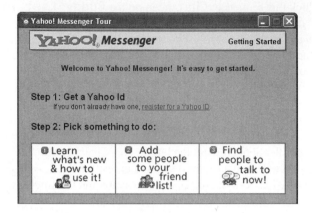

After installation is complete, a YM shortcut is created on the desktop, and the `Yahoo! Messenger Tour` and `Login` windows are displayed. (See the screen captures on this page.) The next step is to get an account. Click the `Get a Yahoo! ID` button on the `Login` window and follow prompts. If you already have a Yahoo! account that you have created for other Yahoo! services, such as Yahoo! Mail, use it.

Now you may want to set up (configure) YM to suit your personal style. Click the `Login` menu on the `Yahoo! Messenger` window (shown in the forthcoming screen capture on the right) to open the `Preferences` window shown in the forthcoming screen capture on the left. The window provides rich options that the user can set. There are many categories to control; click any one and customize.

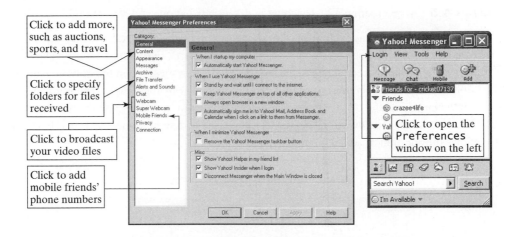

Click to add more, such as auctions, sports, and travel

Click to specify folders for files received

Click to broadcast your video files

Click to add mobile friends' phone numbers

Click to open the **Preferences** window on the left

The final step before using YM is to create a friends list. To do so, you must sign on to access the Yahoo! Messenger window shown on this page. Click the Add button, , to open the Add a Friend window shown on this page. In this window, click the Next button to add a friend by using a Yahoo! ID. Type the friend's ID and a group name (not shown here), and then click the Finish button. Repeat to add another friend to the list. To delete a friend from the list, right-click the friend's screen name and click Delete from the popup menu.

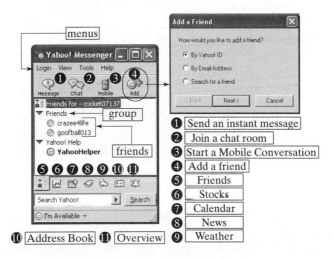

menus

group

friends

❶ Send an instant message
❷ Join a chat room
❸ Start a Mobile Conversation
❹ Add a friend
❺ Friends
❻ Stocks
❼ Calendar
❽ News
❾ Weather
❿ Address Book ⓫ Overview

Example 4.5 Use YM.
Learn how to do IMing, check who is online, locate a member, and block a member.

Solution 4.5   After creating a YM account and a friends list, we can start IMing:

Send an instant message: Click the `Message` button on the `Yahoo! Messenger` window shown in the foregoing screen capture to open the `Instant Message` window shown on this page. Type a friend's screen name in the `To` text field and a message in the bottom pane. Hit `Enter` (or click the `Send` button) to send the message, and wait for a reply. The top pane displays both the incoming and outgoing messages. To jazz up your messages, use the buttons of the `Instant Message` window to format the text messages and add emoticons. The `IMVironment` allows the addition of a background image.

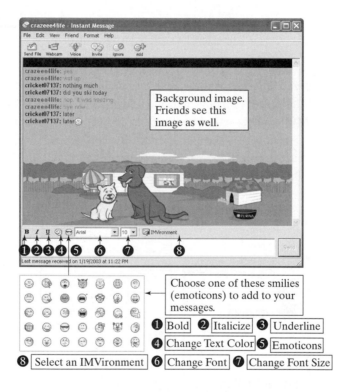

Check who is online: Look at your friends list on the YM window. Those who are online have a yellow emoticon face next to their names. Alternatively, click this sequence: `Tools` (menu on the menu bar) `=> Manage Friend List => Search for a Friend`. The `Search for Friends` window shown in the forthcoming screen capture opens up. Type a keyword (for example, "sports"), a name, or a Yahoo! ID `=> Search`. The first 20 IDs that match the search criterion are displayed in the search window. People on the list who are currently online will have a yellow emoticon face next to their name.

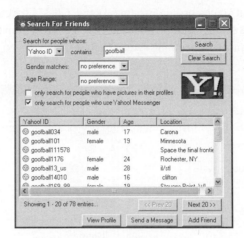

Locate a member: Follow the sequence described in the previous paragraph.

Block a member: This can be done via the YM preferences. Click this sequence: Login (menu on the menu bar) => Preferences => Privacy (category in the Preferences window that pops up) => Add => Type a name to block => Ignore. To remove the block, highlight the name and click Remove.

Example 4.6 IM with more than one friend.

Learn how to IM with multiple friends simultaneously.

Solution 4.6 Highlight a friend's name on the Yahoo! Messenger window and click the Message button to open an Instant Message window. Alternatively, double-click the friend's name. Repeat multiple times to open multiple IMing windows.

Example 4.7 Create your own YM chat room.

Learn how to use YM to create a private chat room.

Solution 4.7 Click this sequence: Chat (button on the YM window) to open the Join Room window => Create a New Room (to configure your room) => Select a category and type a name for your chat room => Create Room. Your new chat room is added to Yahoo's User Rooms under the category you chose. (See the rightmost forthcoming screen capture.) The Chat window of your room pops up. (See the leftmost forthcoming screen capture.) Your friends can join your chat room if you invite them. To do so, in the Chat window, click this sequence: Friend (menu on the menu bar) => Invite to Chat Room => Highlight a friend's name => Add (to Invitation List) => Invite. This sequence alerts your friend to the invitation by displaying a window on his or her computer. If your friend accepts your invitation, YM adds the friend's name to your chat room. Your friends must be online for the invitation to work.

You can change chat rooms or join existing rooms. Click Chat (button on either the YM Chat window or its Messenger window) => Select a chat room from the Join Room window that pops up (see the rightmost forthcoming screen capture) => Go to Room (button).

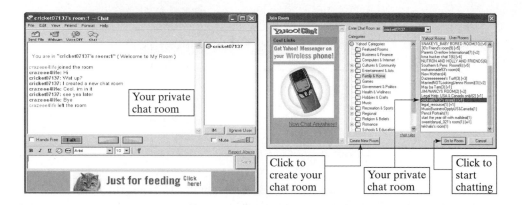

4.6   MSN Messenger

Microsoft (MSN) Messenger (MSNM) is another popular messaging system, like AIM and YM. The key MSNM features include sending instant messages, seeing who is online, starting or joining chat rooms, locating members online, being aware of when someone is typing, and paging a contact's mobile phone. Download MSNM from http://messenger.msn.com and install it. We cover MSNM version 5.0.

After installation is complete, the foregoing MSN Messenger windows is displayed. Alternatively, double-click the program's shortcut to open it. The next step is to get an account. MSNM uses MSN e-mail addresses as default screen names for users. Follow the MSNM prompts to create an account.

Now, you may want to set up (configure) MSNM to suit your style. Log in and click Tools (menu on the MSN Messenger window) => Options. This opens the forthcoming

Options window. The window provides six tabs that the user can use to set options; click any one and customize. The Personal tab allows a user to choose a screen name instead of the MSN e-mail address. The Messages tab provides control over the text and emoticons of IM messages. The General tab provides the Alerts section, which is useful to control Sign In, Alerts, and Sounds options.

The final step before using MSNM is to create contacts and a contact list. To do so, log in to open the MSN Messenger window, shown on the far left. Click Tools (menu on the window) => Add a Contact to open the window shown on the far right. In this window, click the Next button. Type the contact's e-mail address and click the Finish button. Repeat to add another contact. To delete a contact, right-click it and click Delete Contact from the popup menu.

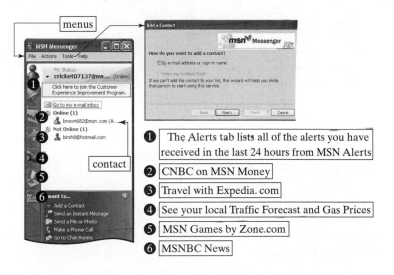

❶ The Alerts tab lists all of the alerts you have received in the last 24 hours from MSN Alerts

❷ CNBC on MSN Money

❸ Travel with Expedia. com

❹ See your local Traffic Forecast and Gas Prices

❺ MSN Games by Zone.com

❻ MSNBC News

Example 4.8 Use MSNM.

Learn how to do IMing, check who is online, locate a member, and block a member.

Solution 4.8 After creating a MSNM account and a contact list, we can start IMing:

   Send an instant message: Double-click a contact (or right-click it => Choose `Send an Instant Message` from the menu that pops up) to open the accompanying `Conversation` window. Type a message in the bottom pane. Hit `Enter` (or click the `Send` button) to send the message, and wait for a reply. The top pane displays both the incoming and outgoing messages. To jazz up your messages, use the buttons shown on the bottom of the `Conversation` window to format the text messages and add emoticons. The `Font` button, **A** Font , controls the font name (e.g., Arial), style (e.g., bold), size (e.g., 10), and color.

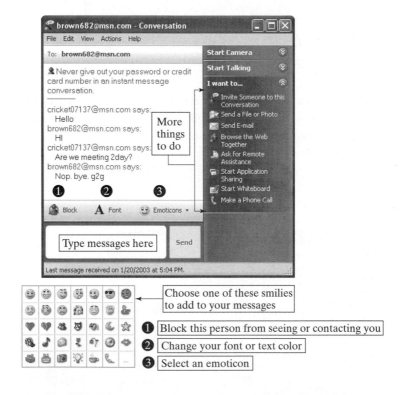

   Check who is online: MSNM shows two groups of contacts in its `MSN Messenger` window: `Online` and `Not Online`.

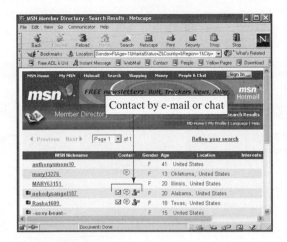

Locate a member: Click this sequence: `Tools => Search for a Contact => Advanced Search`. You will be connected to the `http://www.members.msn.com` website. The Web page of the site opens in a browser. Fill in the member's contact information, including the MSN e-mail address, and click the `Search` button. (See the sample results in the foregoing screen capture.)

Block a member: To block a member, right-click his or her MSN e-mail address or nickname in the `MSN Messenger` window and select `Block` from the menu that pops up. A block stamp, , is posted next to the name. To remove the block, right-click the name again and click `Unblock`.

☞──

Example 4.9 IM with more than one contact.

Learn how to IM with multiple contacts simultaneously.

Solution 4.9 Double-click the contact's name in the `MSN Messenger` window to open an IMing window. Repeat multiple times to open multiple IMing windows.

☞──

Example 4.10 Create your own MSNM chat room.

Learn how to use MSN chat rooms and create a private chat room.

Solution 4.10 Click this sequence: `Actions` (button on the MSNM window) `=> Go to Chat Rooms` (or click the `Go to Chat Rooms` link at the bottom of the window). This sequence opens the `MSN Nickname` window, as you need to create a nickname before chatting. Type a nickname and click the `Save` button. A window opens up and shows a list of all kinds of chat rooms. When you click a chat room, a window opens up asking you to download the MSN chat software. Click `Yes`. After the download is complete, click the smiley face that shows up to enter the chat room you already selected. The forthcoming screen capture shows an example of an MSN chat room. Note that you need to create a nickname and download the MSN chat software only once.

If you want to create your own chat room, open the `MSN Chat` window (shown in the accompanying right screen capture) by clicking the `Go to Chat Rooms` link at the bottom of the `MSN Messenger` window. In this window, click the link that reads `Click Here to Create a Chat Room`. Input information for the room in the form that shows up, such as the room name (e.g., `Wild`), category (e.g., `General`), and language (e.g., `English`). Select (check) the `I accept the Code of Conduct` checkbox and click the `Create` button to finish creating the room. Your friends can start using the room if you give them its name (`Wild`) and category (`General`). The following screen captures show a chatting session in the `Wild` chat room.

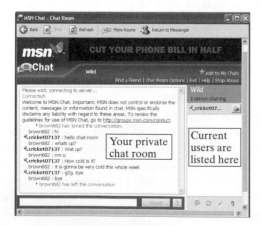

4.7 Opera Instant Messaging

The Opera browser comes with a built-in IM client that provides basic IMing needs. The client is based on the ICQ IMing protocol, icq98. The browser allows the user to establish an IM account. Click `File => Preferences => Programs and paths =>` Enable the IM client. Restart Opera. Then click `Messaging => New Account =>` Enter a password to establish a new IM account. You can create a contact list that allows you to control the receipt of messages from people. You can accept messages only from your list of contacts.

To send IM messages to friends, double-click the contact icon when a friend goes online in order to open the IM window. Type messages in the window and hit `Enter` on the keyboard.

Any personal information entered by users into the Opera IM system becomes available to all users who use the system. Opera displays user's information in Web pages. Users may view and update the Web pages when they need to.

4.8 Webcasting

We have discussed two of the Web-chatting methods: text-based chatting (chat rooms and IRC) and instant messaging. The third method we cover here is Webcasting (also known as netcasting). **Webcasting** is the ability to deliver, via the Web, live or delayed versions of sound and video broadcasts. Webcasting can deliver preview versions of weather reports, news, movies, music videos, radio and television programs, and other information.

Webcasting requires the installation of software on one's computer so that one may receive the digital signals of the broadcasts. The Internet Explorer 6.0 and Netscape 7.01 browsers are examples of such software. Webcasting uses what is called **push technology**, in which the Web server "pushes," or sends, information and news to the user. Webcasting comes to the user in the form of channels to which the user can subscribe.

Example 4.11 Use IE 6.0 and Netscape 7.01 Webcasting channels.

Learn how to use some Webcasting channels.

Solution 4.11 Internet Explorer: IE uses MSN channels located at `http://www.msn.com`. Start the IE browser. Then click this sequence: `Favorites` (menu on the menu bar) => `MSN.com`. (See the forthcoming screen capture.) Select any channel, such as `Movies, Music & TV`. You can also access `MSN.com` in any other browser.

Netscape: The Netscape browser provides Netscape radio, Radio@Netscape, which is integrated into its `Personal` toolbar. (See the forthcoming screen capture.) Radio@Netscape is an easy-to-use player that allows you to choose from dozens of genres of music and over 150 stations. Netscape Radio uses the RealPlayer software to deliver playback of music on a PC. You can customize Radio@Netscape's preset channels by selecting from a wide variety of music, or you can listen to the choices of a guest DJ.

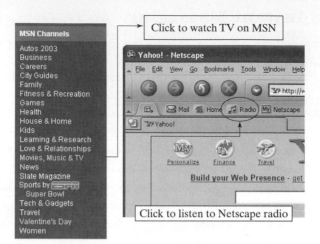

4.9   Wireless Instant Messaging

Wireless IMing is available for handheld devices such as mobile phones, PDAs, and pocket PCs. AIM, Yahoo! Messenger, and MSN Messenger have versions for handheld devices. Another form of messaging on wireless devices is known as short message service (SMS). **SMS** is a service for sending short messages (between 160 and 224 characters long) to mobile phones. SMS is popular in Europe. It is similar to paging, without requiring the mobile phone to be on.

4.10   Tutorials

4.10.1   Use Acronyms and Emoticons in AIM
           (Study Section 4.4)

This tutorial shows an AIM session that uses acronyms and emoticons. (See the forthcoming topmost screen capture.) The IMing language illustrated here is quite common among buddies. We annotate the acronyms here so that we may follow the session's discussion. The annotations are shown in parentheses on the right. We should mention that the annotations are not part of the IMing window. We have added them to make it easier for the reader to understand the IMing session.

4.10.2   Use AIM to Send an Image or a File (Study Section 4.4)

To send any file during chatting, follow this sequence (see the forthcoming bottommost screen captures): Right-click the buddy's screen name in the `Buddy List WIndow` => `Send File` (from the menu that pops up) => `File` (button in the `Send File` window that pops up) => Locate the file on your computer => `Select` => `Send`. AIM contacts and notifies your buddy of the file transfer and waits for acceptance. If your buddy accepts the file, AIM transfers it and displays, on your buddy's `Instant Message` window, the file name, including the full path of the file's location on your buddy's computer.

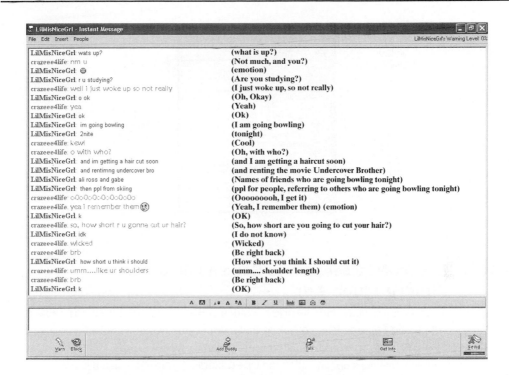

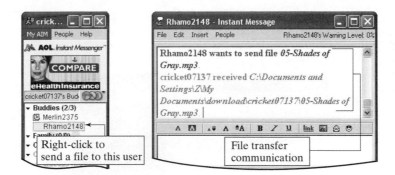

4.10.3   Use Yahoo! Web Messenger (Study Section 4.5)

Yahoo! Web Messenger allows you to IM from anywhere, at anytime. Like Yahoo's Web e-mail it does not require you to install an IM client. It accepts any Yahoo! ID. To access it, visit `http://messenger.yahoo.com` and click the `Web Messenger` link in order to access the login window. After you log in, the forthcoming `Yahoo! Web Messenger` window opens up. The Web Messenger provides only the basic features of the full Yahoo! Messenger. For example, it does not provide all of the content and services that the client provides, such as stock prices, weather reports, and news.

4.10.4 Use MSN Messenger to Send a File or Photo
(Study Section 4.6)

Click File (menu on the MSN Messenger window) => Send a File or Photo, or click the Send a File or Photo link at the bottom of the window. Select a contact in the Send a File or Photo window that pops up, and click the OK button, [OK]. Select a file from the window that pops up, and click the Open button, [Open]. Once the contact accepts the file, the transfer takes place. The Conversation window on the contact's computer shows the full path of the location where the file is saved. The following screen capture shows the communication that takes place in order to transfer the file.

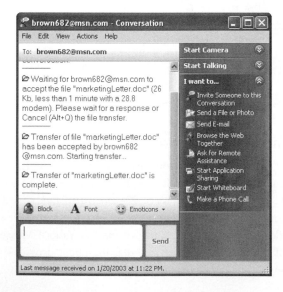

FAQs

General

Q: What is ICQ?

A: ICQ stands for "I seek you." It is an instant messenger, like the others discussed in this chapter. It can be used as a client or as a Web-based application. Visit `http://www.icq.com` to learn more.

Q: What is the difference between a buddy, a friend, and a contact in IM?

A: Nothing. They all refer to a person with whom you do IMing. AIM, YM, and MSNM use the term buddy, friend, and contact, respectively, to refer to that person.

AIM (Section 4.4)

Q: How can I change my chatting profile on AIM?

A: You need to edit your profile. Click `My AIM` (menu on the AIM `Buddy List Window`) `=> Edit Profile =>` Follow the prompts and fill in the required information.

Q: Why is my away message not sent even though I set it up?

A: Because it is not enabled. Click this sequence to enable it: `My AIM => Edit Options => Edit Preferences => Away Message =>` Select (check) the `Auto respond and insert in personal profile` radio button.

Q: Can I sign on using two different screen names on one computer at the same time?

A: No, because AIM would not know how to distribute the incoming messages.

Q: How can I create an away message?

A: Click this sequence: `My AIM` (menu on the `Buddy List Window`) `=> Away Message => New Message =>` Type the message in the window that pops up `=> I'm Away` (button on the window). This command opens the `Default Away Message` window. This window (see the screen capture on this page) will show your away message and the messages you have received while you were away. It also has the `I'm Back` button, which you should click whenever you want to go back online.

Q: How do I save an IMing session?

A: Click `File` (menu on the `Instant Message` window) => `Save` => Choose a folder to save it in, and type a file name for it => `Save`. The IMing session is saved as a Web page that can be opened in a browser for viewing. YM and MSNM do not provide this functionality.

Yahoo! Messenger (Section 4.5)

Q: What is "buzzing a friend" in YM, and why would one use it?

A: This is a way of getting your friend's attention while IMing. Bring the YM window into the foreground on your computer, hold down the CTRL key, and press the G key. Your and your friend's YM windows will make a "ding dong" sound and vibrate. Your friend will also see the word BUZZ in his or her IM window, to let him or her know that an alert was received.

Q: Can I send off-line messages to my friends?

A: Yes. If your friends are not online, but are YM users, they still can receive messages. The off-line messages you send them will popup automatically when they connect to the Internet.

Q: Can I add my own image as a YM IMVironment?

A: No. You can use only the images that come with YM; however, YM provides numerous images. Click this sequence to see all of them: `IMVironment` (button on the YM `Instant Message` window) => `See All IMVironments` => Browse through all the folders. *Me/Q.*

MSN Messenger (Section 4.6)

Q: How do I manage contacts in MSN Messenger?

A: Click `Tools` (menu on the `MSN Messenger` menu bar) => `Manage Contacts` => Select a contact to delete, or view contacts' profile or properties.

Q: How do I create a group?

A: Click `Tools` (menu on the `MSN Messenger` menu bar) => `Manage Groups` => Add, delete, or rename a group.

Blackbox

Section 4.1 (Introduction): Web chatting is a form of synchronous communication, while e-mail is an asynchronous form. The three methods of Web chatting are text-only chatting, instant messaging, and Webcasting.

Section 4.2 (Text-only chatting) (Example 4.1): BBSs and IRC systems provide text-only chatting. IRC has channels (chat rooms) that users can select from and join. A user needs an IRC client (such as `mIRC` for Windows, `IRCle` for MAC, and `irc2` for Unix) in order to join chat rooms.

Section 4.3 (Instant messaging): IMing supports the use of text and graphics during chatting. Users can employ IMing clients or Web-based IMing to chat with friends and family. A user needs to create a buddy list before he or she can chat. IMing systems allow users to create and join chat rooms.

Sections 4.4–4.7 (IMing systems) (Examples 4.2–4.10): The three popular IMing systems are AIM, Yahoo! Messenger, and MSN Messenger. They all require users to create their buddy lists. IMing activities include chatting, sending files, and creating and joining chat rooms.

Section 4.8 (Webcasting) (Example 4.11): Users can watch movies and TV, listen to the radio, and read news via Webcasting.

Section 4.9 (Wireless IMing): AIM, Yahoo! Messenger, and MSN Messenger all have versions that run on handheld devices such as mobile phones, PDAs, and Pocket PCs.

Section 4.10 (Tutorials): Three tutorials show how to use acronyms and emoticons during IMing, how to send a file, and how to use Web-based IMing.

Quick reference for using AIM (Section 4.4):

1. **Download and install:** Visit `http://www.aim.com`.
2. **Configure (set options and preferences):** Click the `Setup` icon, , on the `Sign On` window to open the `Preferences` window.
4. **Create a buddy list:** Sign on to access the AIM `Buddy List Window`. Click the `Setup` icon, => `Add Buddy` => Enter the buddy's screen name => `New` => Follow the prompts in the `New Account Wizard` window.
5. **Perform IMing activities:**
   5.1 **Add a buddy:** Same as the foregoing steps for creating a buddy list.
   5.2 **Delete a buddy from the buddy list:** Highlight the buddy's name and click `Delete`, or right-click the name and select `Delete` from the menu that pops up.
   5.3 **Chat with a buddy (Example 4.2):** Click the `IM` button on the `Buddy List Window` to open the `Instant Message` window. Type the buddy's screen name in the `To` text field and a message in the pane. Hit `Enter` to send the message.
   5.4 **Check who is online (Example 4.2):** The `Buddy List Window` has an `Offline` group that lists all the buddies who are not online. Any other buddies are online.
   5.5 **Locate a buddy (Examples 4.2):** Click `People` (menu on the `Buddy List Window`) => `Find a Buddy` => Select a search criterion.
   5.6 **Block a buddy (Example 4.2):** In the `Instant Message` window where you are communicating with the buddy, click the `Block` icon, , and then click `Yes`.
   5.7 **Unblock a buddy (Example 4.2):** To unblock a blocked buddy, right-click the buddy's name => `Unblock Buddy.`
   5.8 **Send a file (Tutorial 4.10.2):** Right-click the buddy's screen name in the `Buddy List Window` => `Send File` => `File` => Locate the file on your computer => `Select` => `Send`.

5.8 Create a chat room (Example 4.4): Click Chat (icon on the Buddy List Window) to open the Chat Invitation window => Type in the screen names you want to invite to your private chat room (type one name at a time, and hit Enter after each name) => Send. The Chat Room window pops up. You can invite additional buddies; to do so, click People (menu on the Chat Room window) => Invite a Buddy => Type the screen names in the Screen names to invite text area => Send.

Quick reference for using Yahoo! Messenger (Section 4.5):

1. **Download and install:** Visit http://messenger.yahoo.com.
2. **Configure (set options and preferences):** Click the Login menu on the Yahoo! Messenger window to open the Preferences window.
4. **Create a friends list:** Sign on to access the YM Messenger window. Click the Add button, 🖼 => Next => Type in the friend's ID and a group name => Finish.
5. **Perform IMing activities:**
    5.1 **Add a friend:** Same as the foregoing steps for creating a friends list.
    5.2 **Delete a friend from the friends list:** Right-click the friend's name and click Delete.
    5.3 **Chat with a friend (Example 4.5):** Click the Message button on the Yahoo! Messenger window => Type the friend's screen name in the To text field and a message in the bottom pane => Hit Enter (or click the Send button) to send the message.
    5.4 **Check who is online (Example 4.5):** Look at your friends list on YM window. Those who are online have a yellow emoticon face next to their name.
    5.5 **Locate a friend (Examples 4.5):** Click Tools (menu on the menu bar) => Manage Friend List => Search for a Friend => Type in a name or a Yahoo! ID => Search.
    5.6 **Block a friend (Example 4.5):** Click Login (menu on the menu bar) => Preferences => Privacy => Add => Type in a name to ignore => Ignore.
    5.7 **Unblock a friend (Example 4.5):** To remove the block, highlight the name and click Remove.
    5.8 **Send a file:** Right-click a screen name in the Yahoo! Messenger window => Send a File => Enter real name and a file name (browse to choose one) => Send.
    5.8 **Create a chat room (Example 4.7):** Click Chat (button on the Yahoo! Messenger window) => Create a New Room => Select a category and type a name for your chat room => Create Room. The Chat window of your room pops up. Your friends can join your chat room if you invite them. To do so, in the Chat window, click this sequence: Friend (menu on the menu bar) => Invite

to Chat Room => Highlight the friend's name => Add (to Invitation List) => Invite. Your friends must be online for the invitation to work.

Quick reference for using MSN Messenger (Section 4.6):

1. **Download and install:** Visit http://messenger.msn.com.

2. **Configure (set options and preferences):** Log in and click Tools => Options.

4. **Create a contact list:** Log in to open the MSN Messenger window. Click Tools => Next => Type in the contact's e-mail address => Finish.

5. **Perform IMing activities:**

   5.1 **Add a contact:** Same as the foregoing steps for creating a contact list.

   5.2 **Delete a contact from the contact list:** Right-click the contact's name and click Delete Contact.

   5.3 **Chat with a contact (Example 4.8):** Double-click a contact (or right-click it => Send an Instant Message from the menu that pops up), => Type a message in the bottom pane => Hit Enter (or click the Send button) to send the message, and wait for a reply. To jazz up your messages, use the buttons of the Conversation window to format the text messages and add emoticons. The Font button, A Font , controls the font name (e.g., Arial), style (e.g., bold), size (e.g., 10), and color.

   5.4 **Check who is online (Example 4.8):** MSN messenger shows two groups of contacts in its MSN Messenger window: Online and Not Online.

   5.5 **Locate a contact (Example 4.8):** Click Tools => Search for a Contact => Advanced Search, which connects you to http://www.members.msn.com.

   5.6 **Block a contact (Example 4.8):** Right-click the contact's MSN e-mail address or nickname in the MSN Messenger window, and select Block from the menu that pops up. A block stamp, [brown682@msn.com (Bl...], is posted next to the name.

   5.7 **Unblock a contact (Example 4.8):** To remove a block, right-click the contact's name and click Unblock.

   5.8 **Send a file (Tutorial 4.10.4):** Click File (menu on the MSN Messenger window) => Send a File or Photo (or click the Send a File or Photo link at the bottom of the window) => Select a contact => OK => Select a file => Open.

   5.8 **Create a chat room (Example 4.10):** Open the MSN Chat window by clicking the Go to Chat Rooms link at the bottom of the MSN Messenger window => Click Here to Create a Chat Room => Input information for the room => Select (check) the I accept the Code of Conduct checkbox => Create.

Check Your Progress

At the end of this chapter, you should

✔   understand the three methods of Web chatting (Section 4.1);
✔   understand the concepts of the BBS and IRC (Section 4.2);
✔   understand the concept of instant messaging (Section 4.3);
✔   have mastered the use of AIM (Section 4.4);
✔   have mastered the use of Yahoo! Messenger (Section 4.5);
✔   have mastered the use of MSN Messenger (Section 4.6);
✔   understand Opera IMing and Webcasting (Sections 4.7 and 4.8);
✔   understand wireless IMing (Section 4.9).

Problems

The exercises are designed for a lab setting, while the homework is to be done outside class time.

Exercises

4.1   Use AIM to add a new group called `Wild` that has three buddies with these three screen names: `wizard36`, `mystery567`, and `funny109`.

4.2   Use AIM to send a message to your buddy who has a screen name.

4.3   Repeat Problems 4.1 and 4.2 with Yahoo! Messenger.

4.4   Repeat Problems 4.1 and 4.2 with MSN Messenger.

4.5   Use `http://www.msn.com` to watch some TV.

Homework

4.6   Extend Example 4.1 to use the `DCC` (direct connect chat) category of `mIRC`.

4.7   Use AIM to talk to one of your friends.

4.8   Repeat Problem 4.7, with Yahoo! Messenger.

4.9   Repeat Problem 4.7, with MSN Messenger.

4.10 Use `http://www.msn.com` to watch a movie, and use Netscape 7.01 to listen to the radio.

5

Lists and Newsgroups

Goal

Understand and master the use of asynchronous communication, such as mailing lists and Usenet newsgroups. Applications include marketing, advertisement, and asking for help on any subject.

Objectives

- Asynchronous communication
- Mailing lists
- LISTSERV and Majordomo
- Discussion groups
- Yahoo! discussion groups
- Usenet newsgroups
- Google Usenet newsgroups
- Newsreaders: Google, Outlook Express, and Netscape

Outline

5.1   Introduction

E-mail, mailing lists, and newsgroups are forms of asynchronous communication. The latter two are not as prevalent as they once were, because of the recent popularity of instant messaging and chat rooms. However, they still provide a wealth of information that Web surfers can search in order to find answers to about every issue and question you can imagine. Instant messaging and chat rooms do not provide such a permanent record to which we can easily refer.

5.2   Mailing Lists

A **mailing list** is a service that sends information via e-mail to a mailing distribution. The list is composed of a group of people (subscribers) who receieve periodic e-mail messages on a particular topic. There exist many mailing lists today. A mailing list includes the e-mail addresses of its subscribers. Some companies and software vendors use mailing lists to keep in touch with their customers. Some groups use them to distribute announcements and upcoming events.

Two types of mailing lists exist: moderated and unmoderated. A **moderated mailing list** is a mailing list for which a moderator, such as the list owner, reviews the incoming messages before posting them to the list subscribers. Some moderated lists do not accept messages from subscribers. For these lists, the owner posts all the messages and subscribers read them, without any other means of participation. Moderation is often used to increase the "signal-to-noise ratio" of a list—that is, to select meaningful content and filter out uninformative comments and abuse. Moderation requires human intervention, and lists with a high level of activity require more human time. An **unmoderated mailing list** lets one subscriber posts a message to all subscribers without human intervention.

The client/server model of communication applies to mailing lists. A list server hosts a mailing list and its messages, to allow its subscribers (clients) to receive (post) e-mail messages from (to) the server. When the list server receives a message, it automatically broadcasts it to everyone on the list. The result is similar to the services provided by chat rooms and IRC channels, except that the messages are transmitted as e-mail and are therefore available on individual basis.

List servers often support three modes of message delivery to subscribers. With **real-time delivery**, subscribers receive messages from other subscribers as soon as they are sent to the list server. A common alternative, **digest delivery**, summarizes all messages sent to the list over a period of time known as the digest cycle, which can be daily or weekly. When a subscriber requests digest delivery, the list server sends to the subscriber one posting (e-mail message) that contains all messages from the list during the digest cycle. Digest delivery minimizes the number of individual messages received each day or week from the list server. Some list servers provide a mail–no-mail feature to its subscribers to enable them to suspend and resume list message delivery during vacation periods. **Web-based delivery** lets subscribers, or even non-subscribers, view list messages with a browser. Users can navigate the list archives and search for specific content.

Two popular mailing-list servers are LISTSERV and Majordomo. They provide numerous mailing lists that cover many topics. LISTSERV is a commercial product managed by L-Soft International (`http://www.lsoft.com`). LISTSERV is sometimes used incorrectly to refer to any mailing-list server. Majordomo is freeware and can be downloaded from `http://www.greatcircle.com/majordomo`. It works with Unix mailing lists. Both servers provide Web-based services. For example, LISTSERV provides a fully customizable Web interface for site administrators, list owners, and list subscribers. Majordomo provides a Web interface software to its list server, allowing novice list owners to manage their list configuration and subscriber base.

To receieve messages from a mailing list, you subscribe to it, much as you subscribe to a magazine. To stop receiving a messages from a mailing list, you have to unsubscribe from it. Each list server provides two different e-mail addresses. The **server address** is the address to which a person sends commands to subscribe (unsubscribe) to (from) a mailing list that the server offers. The **list address** is the address to which a subscriber submits (posts) messages or shares knowledge with the entire group on the list. To subscribe to a list, send an e-mail message with the command `subscribe list-name@server-address`, or its equivalent—for example, use the command `subscribe pets@someServer.com` to subscribe to the `pets` mailing list offered by `someServer.com`. To unsubscribe, use the command `unsubscribe list-name@server-address`—for example, `unsubscribe pets@someServer`. List servers typically provide their users with instructions and guidance on what information is required in order to subscribe or unsubscribe. Some list servers provides a Web-based subscription–unsubscription service, where the user points and clicks to subscribe or unsubscribe to a list.

Many mailing lists exist. Examples include `crc-request@listserv.classroom.net` (classroom-related list), `listserv@ocmvm.cnyric.org` (list for K–12 educators), and `majordomo@gsn.org` (school foundation). The World Wide Web consortium has a large mailing list, `lists@w3c`, which includes many public archived lists for the benefit of the Web community at large to promote exchange of ideas. Visit `http://www.w3.org/Mail` to access these archives.

In addition to joining an existing mailing list on a list server, you can create a new one. The information required to set up a new list include list name, list owner, list description, type of list (moderated or not), type of subscription and policy (e.g., open to public), and an initial subscriber list. Once approved by the list server, the new list becomes available to people to use.

Using mailing lists is as simple as using e-mail: You receive messages and you respond to them. You can post a reply to a message of an existing thread of a discussion on a topic. Or you can start a new topic and a new thread. There are etiquette rules for using mailing lists, as all responses are posted to all list subscribers. Here some rules: Use a meaningful subject line in your message. Never send e-mail attachments without prior permission from the other list subscribers. Use acronyms and emoticons lightly. Keep your responses brief. When responding to a message, quote part of the message to which you are responding. Stick to the topic of the discussion thread. Be polite in your responses (e.g., don't write in all uppercase; identify yourself). Do not post vague responses such as "I agree." **Avoid** flaming people. Finally, do not criticize other people's messages and postings.

5.3 Discussion Groups

A **discussion group** or **forum** (also known as a **message board**) refers to a group of people who share a common interest and discuss matters relating to that interest amongst themselves. Discussion groups are either Web or e-mail based. Yahoo! provides many Web-based discussion groups. The website to access these groups is `http://groups.yahoo.com`. Figure 5.1 shows the main page for the Yahoo! discussion groups.

Example 5.1 Join a discussion group.

Learn how to join a Yahoo! discussion group.

Solution 5.1 Type `http://groups.yahoo.com` in a browser window in order to access the Yahoo! discussion groups. While you can access all these groups and their postings, you need to join a group in order to receive its e-mail messages. Select a topic. (See Figure 5.1.) These topics have many subtopics. As you select, Yahoo! keeps track of the topic path, for example, `Computers & Internet > Desktop Publishing > Word Processing > Microsoft Word`. Say that we decide to join the `Microsoft Word` group. At this point, the group's postings (e-mail messages) are displayed. Click on one of them to access the Join button, [Join This Group!]. Fillout the form (see the forthcoming screen capture) and click the final Join button, [Join]. The Join form has four sections that use the concepts we have covered in Section 5.2. The first section, `Yahoo! Profile`, enables you to create the identity you will be known by in the discussion-group community. The second section, `Email Address`, is where you input the address to which discussion-group messages are sent. The third section, `Message Delivery`, has you select a delivery cycle. The fourth section, `Message Format`, allows you to choose XHTML format for the messages.

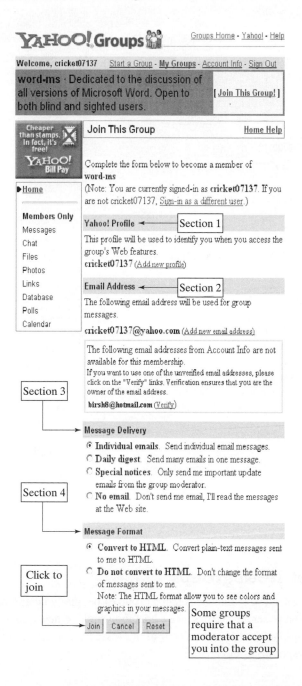

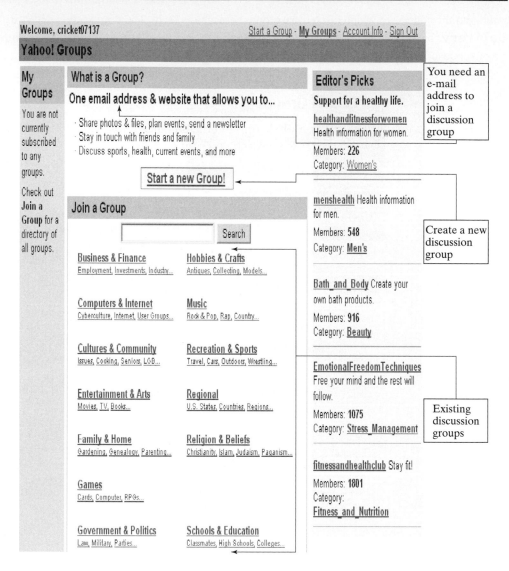

Figure 5.1 Yahoo! discussion groups.

5.4 Usenet Newsgroups

A **newsgroup** is a collection of messages that a group of people (who are interested in a particular topic) posts to a news server. News servers host thousands of newsgroups that are maintained by companies, groups, and individuals. The trail of messages and replies on a specific topic is a thread within a newsgroup.

The collection of news that is posted to servers on a worldwide network is known as **Usenet**. Usenet utilizes software that copies messages that users contribute, so that every participating server has an exact copy of every message contributed to the network. The Usenet software also organizes these messages into newsgroups that people can read and respond to. Newcomers to a newsgroup may want to read its messages for a while before deciding to post messages themselves, a practice know as lurking (see Chapter 4).

Usenet started out as a method of sharing information about Unix computer systems. Users wanted to exchange and organize notes and observations by topic. Further, they wanted the information to be available to many people. Usenet spread widely after its software underwent a major revision during the early 1980s that enabled it to handle a larger volume of messages.

Usenet is intended for technical use, but people also use it to discuss social, political, hobby, entertainment, recreation, and other issues. Usenet is a great resource. Many newsgroups offer intelligent discussions, particularly the moderated ones. One of the best things about Usenet is the FAQs. The FAQs attempt to provide answers to some of the questions people are most likely to ask. There are hundreds of these FAQs, and some of them are among the best sources of information on a topic.

The structure of the Usenet newsgroups is hierarchical. At the top level are some very general topics, and under each of these topics are more and more specific topics. Originally, the Usenet groups were divided into seven subgroups, which are still called the Big Seven. New hierarchies have come into being since then. Listed as follows are some of the newsgroups that are available, with the Big Seven listed first:

1. `comp`: topics related to hardware, computer science, programming languages, and games.
2. `sci`: scientific research and applications topics, such as on physics, biology, and psychology.
3. `rec`: recreational topics, such as sports, music, video making, and cooking.
4. `news`: the hierarchy where Usenet talks about itself; it is very useful for new users.
5. `talk`: loose discussions on unresolved questions; politics and religion are popular topics.
6. `soc`: discussions about social issues relating to countries or regions.
7. `misc`: discussion on other things that do not belong to the foregoing groups, such as job and for-sale postings.
8. `alt`: a bizarre mix of topics from `alt.chinese.computing` to `alt.tv.simpsons`. It is easier to create a new group in the `alt` hierarchy than in other hierarchies. Some `alt` groups are quite useful.
9. `k12`: discussions and groups relating to education from kindergarten through grade 12, for both teachers and students.
10. `fj`: discussions of hundreds of different topics in Japanese.
11. `de`: a hierarchy with the scope and size of `alt`, but all in German.

Some useful newsgroups, especially for new users, include `news.newusers.announce`, `news.newusers.questions`, `news.answers`, `alt.answers`, and `alt.internet.services`.

Users need newsreader software in order to subscribe (unsubscribe) to (from) newsgroups, respond to messages, search for information, and manage (delete and archive) messages. The newsreader also keeps track of which articles a user has already read. The newsreader software reads and manages messages by using the Net News Transport Protocol (NNTP).

A newsreader can be a browser, or a Web page in Web-based newsgroups. One example of a Web-based newsreader is `http://groups.google.com`. The search engine Google has acquired the well-known Deja news website. The URLs `http://www.dejanews.com` and `http://www.deja.com` are directed to `http://groups.google.com`. Figure 5.2 shows the main page for the Google Usenet newsgroups.

Newsreaders use a standard hierarchy to read messages (also known as articles) from a Usenet newsgroup server that is structured with this hierarchy. Each newsgroup server has a set of newsgroups at the top of the hierarchy, one per topic. The topic (and the newsgroup it represents) at this level is very general. It is divided into increasingly specific subtopics (newsgroups) at the subsequent levels of the hierarchy. Under the terminal topic come the topic threads. Each topic thread consists of its messages' headers, which are e-mail messages. The user clicks a header to read its body. Figure 5.3 shows the structure of Usenet newsgroup servers.

Figure 5.2   Google Usenet newsgroups.

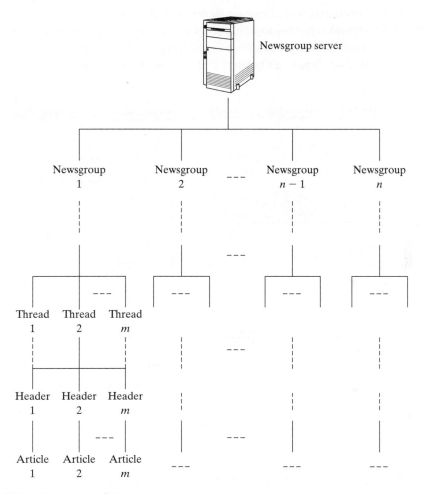

Figure 5.3 Structure of Usenet newsgroups servers.

Example 5.2 Use Newsgroups.

Learn how to use Google to read Usenet newsgroups.

Solution 5.2 Open a browser window, and type `http://groups.google.com` into the URL bar to access the Usenet newsgroups shown in Figure 5.1 Select a group and click it. Select a subgroup. Continue selecting subgroups until you find a group for which you would like to read the postings. Each posting is a thread. (See the leftmost forthcoming screen capture.) When you click any thread, you see all its messages. Click a message header to read its body, similarly to the way in which you read e-mail messages. To post your own response to the message, click the `Post a follow-up to this message` link (not shown in the forthcoming screen captures) underneath the body. You must be a Google member to be able to respond.

The leftmost upcoming screen capture shows the threads of a newsgroup in the left-hand frame. The current thread is the thread whose messages are displayed in the right-hand frame of the window. The rightmost screen capture shows the `Sign in` form. If you are not a member, click the `Sign up for your account now` link to get an account.

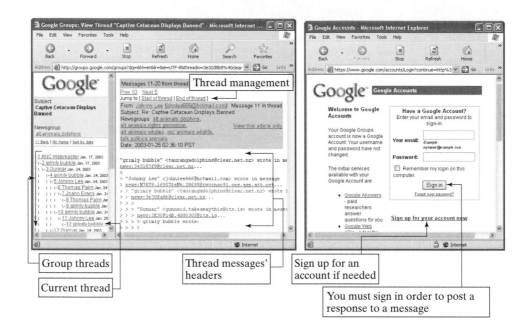

Example 5.3   **Use e-mail clients as newsreaders.**

Learn how to use Outlook Express and Netscape as newsreaders.

Solution 5.3   We need to configure Outlook Express (OE) and Netscape Mailer by supplying the domain name of the Usenet server, downloading the current newsgroup list off the server, and choosing the newsgroups to which we want to subscribe so that we can read their messages. Here are the detailed steps:

Outlook Express:

1. **Install a newsgroups server.** We use the `news.belwue.de` server here. Start OE and click this sequence: `Tools` (menu on the menu bar) => `Accounts` => `News` (tab) => `Add` (button) => `News` => Follow the prompts in the `Internet Connection Wizard` to input your name, e-mail address, and the news (NNTP) server name(`news.belwue.de` in our example) => `Finish` => `Close`. (See the following screen capture.)

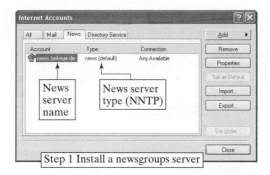

Step 1 Install a newsgroups server

2. **Download newsgroups.** Right-click the newsgroup server's name, `news.belwue.de`, in the OE `Folders` frame on the left of the OE window, and click `Newgroups` from the menu that pops up. Alternatively, click the server's name, `news.belwue.de`, and then click the `Newsgroups` button, [Newsgroups...] on the right of the OE window. The newsgroups on the server are then downloaded to your computer. (See the following screen capture.) This download is done only once.

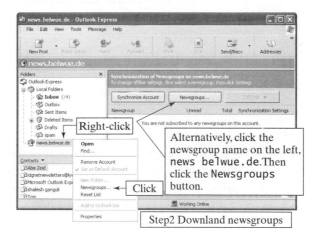

Step2 Downland newsgroups

3. **Subscribe or unsubscribe.** Click `Tools` (menu on the menu bar) => `Newsgroups`, to open the OE `Newsgroup Subscriptions` window. Highlight the newsgroups to which you want to subscribe, and click the `Subscribe` button, [Subscribe]. A subscription symbol, 🕮, is added to the left of the name of each selected newsgroup. To unsubscribe from a group, highlight the group's name and click the `Unsubscribe` button, [Unsubscribe].(See the following screen capture.)

Step 3. Subscribe or unsubscribe

4. Download news articles. After subscribing to the newsgroup `news.belwue.de`, click its name from the `Folders` frame on the left of the OE window (see the following screen capture) to download its latest articles. Repeat this step to download articles from more than one group.

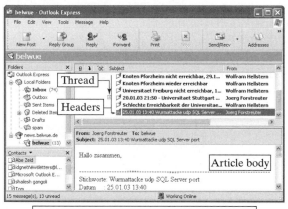

Step 4 and 5: Download and read news articles

5. Read the news articles. To read an article of the newsgroup, click the article's header in the top right frame of the OE window. To reply, click the `Reply` (or `Reply Group`) button => Type a message => `Send`. To start a new thread, click the `New Post` button => Compose your message => `Send`. To redirect a posting to another newsgroup, select the posting and click the `Forward` button. Enter the name of the newsgroup that should receive the posting as the receiving e-mail address.(See the bottommost screen capture on this page.)

Netscape 7.01:

1. Install a newsgroups server. Open the Netscape `Inbox` e-mail mail folder window. Then click Edit (menu on the menu bar) => `Mail & Newsgroups Account Settings` => `news` (tree node) => `Server Settings`. Input the requested information as in Step 1 of the procedure for OE.

2. **Subscribe and download articles.** Click the `Subscribe to newsgroups` link that shows up in the window. Follow the prompts.

3. **Read the news articles.** Same as Step 5 of the procedure for OE.

FAQs

Mailing Lists (Section 5.2)

Q: Will subscribing to a mailing list cause me to receive an increased amount of span

A: Mailing-list servers install spam filters to shield their lists members from spam and unsolicited bulk e-mail.

Q: Can I send an HTML e-mail message to a mailing list?

A: List servers such as LISTSERV support both XHTML and text formats. However, plain text is recommended.

Usenet Newsgroups (Section 5.4)

Q: What port number do NNTP servers use?

A: The standard default port number is 119.

Q: Are there any public news servers that I can use to configure my browser as a newsreader?

A: There are very few today. You have to search hard for them. The one we use in Example 5.3 of this chapter is a German news server. To find others, run a Google search using the string `list of public nntp servers`. Then try one at a time in Step 1 (**Install a newsgroups server**) of Example 5.3 until you hit one that is alive. You cannot access news servers of organizations such as Yahoo! or Google.

Blackbox

Section 5.1 (Introduction): E-mailing, using mailing lists, participating in discussion groups, and subscribing to Usenet newsgroups are asynchronous activities that we perform on the Web.

Section 5.2 (Mailing Lists): There are moderated and unmoderated mailing lists. List servers can deliver messages in three ways: in real time, once every digest cycle, or on demand. The two popular list servers are LISTSERV (`http://www.lsoft.com`) and Majordomo (`http://www.greatcircle.com/majordomo`). Subscribe to one of these servers in order to receive mailing. Each server has two addresses: the **server address** (for subscribe and unsubscribe commands) and the **list address** (for posting messages to a list). Be aware of the etiquette of mailing lists.

Section 5.3 (Discussion Groups) (Examples 5.1): Discussion groups are either Web or e-mail based. Yahoo! has a large collection of discussion groups.

Sections 5.4 (Usenet Newgroups) (Examples 5.2 and 5.3): The Usenet network provides many news servers and newsgroups. New servers use the NNTP protocol and port 119.

A newsreader can be a Web page, such as `http://groups.google.com`, or an e-mail tool, such as Outlook Express to Netscape. Articles on a news server are stored according to the following hierarchy: newsgroup => subnewsgroup => . . . => terminal newsgroup => threads => articles' headers.

Quick reference for using Outlook Express as a newsreader (Section 5.4):

1. **Download and install:** Visit `http://www.microsoft.com`.

2. **Install and configure:** Double- click the executable file and follow prompts.

3. **Install a newsgroup server:** Click `Tools` (menu on the menu bar) => `Accounts` => `News` (tab) => `Add` (button) => `News` => Follow the prompts in the `Internet Connection Wizard` to input your name, e-mail address, and the news (NNTP) server's name => `Finish` => `Close`.

4. **Download newsgroups:** Right-click the news server's name in the OE `Folders` frame on the left of the OE window, and click `Newgroups` from the menu that pops up. The newsgroups on the server are downloaded to your computer.

5. **Subscribe or unsubscribe:** Click `Tools` (menu on the menu bar) => `Newsgroups` to open the OE `Newsgroup Subscription` window. Highlight the newsgroups to which you want to subscribe, and click the `Subscribe` button, ⎡ Subscribe ⎤. A subscription symbol, 📰, is added to the left of the name of each selected newsgroup. To unsubscribe from a group, highlight the group's name and click the `Unsubscribe` button, ⎡ Unsubscribe ⎤.

6. **Download news articles:** After subscribing to a newsgroup, click its name from the `Folders` frame on the left of the OE window in order to download its latest articles.

7. **Read the news articles:** To read an article of a newsgroup, click the article's header in the top right frame of the OE window. To reply, click the `Reply` (or `Reply Group`) button => Type a message => `Send`. To start a new thread, click the `New Post` button => Compose your message => `Send`. To redirect a posting to another newsgroup, select the posting and click the `Forward` button. Enter the name of the newsgroup that should receive the posting as the receiving e-mail address.

Check Your Progress

At the end of this chapter, you should

✔ understand asynchronous Web communication (Section 5.1);

✔ know how to use mailing lists (Section 5.2);

✔ understand discussion groups (Section 5.3);

✔ have mastered the use of Usenet newsgroups (Section 5.4).

Problems

The exercises are designed for a lab setting, while the homework is to be done outside class time.

Exercises

5.1 Follow Example 5.1 to join a Yahoo! discussion group that is of interest to you.

5.2 Follow Example 5.2 to read newsgroups of interest to you, using Google.

5.3 Follow Example 5.3 to configure Outlook Express to become a newsreader.

5.4 Follow Example 5.3 to configure Netscape Mailer to become a newsreader.

5.5 Use Example 5.3 as a guide to configure Opera to become a newsreader.

Homework

5.6 Explain how you can create your own Yahoo! discussion group.

5.7 Follow Example 5.2 to join a newsgroup of interest to you, using Google.

5.8 Follow Example 5.3 to join a newsgroup using Outlook Express as a newsreader.

5.9 Follow Example 5.3 to join a newsgroup using Netscape mailer as a newsreader.

5.10 Use Example 5.3 as a guide to join a newsgroup using Opera as a newsreader.

Security and Privacy

6

Goal

Understand and master the important issues of Web security and privacy, know your online rights, configure browsers for tighter security and better privacy, and find out how to protect the exchange of sensitive data online.

Objectives

- Web security and privacy issues
- Fraud, crackers, and firewalls
- P3P
- Sniffing, stalking, and censorship
- EPIC
- TRUSTe
- .NET Passport
- The Liberty Alliance Project

Outline

6.1   Introduction

Web security is a complex, but important, issue encompassing computer and network security, authentication services, message validation, cryptography, and personal privacy issues. We have already covered some security and privacy issues: firewalls (Section 1.13), cryptography (digital keys, SSL, TLS, digital signatures, and digital certificates; Section 2.16), e-mail security and message validation (s-mail, SHTTP, and PGP; Section 3.13), and e-mail viruses (Chapter 3). In this chapter, we focus on other security and privacy issues.

Web security begins at public Web servers. There are security risks that affect these servers, LANs that host websites, and innocent users of Web browsers. Web servers continue to be attractive targets for hackers seeking to damage them for a variety of reasons, such as personal satisfaction, political motivations, and revenge, to name a few. Security damages can range from corrupting and deleting data files on Web servers to stealing sensitive and private data, or even performing illegal financial transactions. Other damages include denial-of-service attacks, the placement of pornographic material, spreading political messages, and the placement of malicious software.

Both users and Web administrators need to worry about the confidentiality of the data transmitted across the Web. The TCP/IP protocol was not designed with security in mind; hence, it is vulnerable to network snooping and spying. When confidential documents are transmitted from a Web server to a browser, or when a user sends private information back to a server via a form, someone may be listening in.

Web privacy is one of three aspects of Web security; the other two are authentication of the identity of a person using a system and authorization of the operations that the person can do after logging in. Web privacy has to do with protecting personal information, such as credit card numbers, that are transferred across the Web. Many websites use cookies to collect information about users. As discussed in Chapter 2, users can configure Web browsers to accept, selectively accept, or reject cookies.

A website's privacy policy tells users what kind of information the site collects about them, to whom it gives the information, and how the information is used. Users can view privacy policies of websites by using browsers such as IE. Browsers simplify the process of deciding whether and when users disclose personal information to websites. While there are standards (see Section 6.5) for describing privacy practices, there are no standards that Web sites must follow to set privacy rules.

Example 6.1 Managing Web-server security.

What are some of the best security practices?

Solution 6.1 Place the Web server in a firewall. Disallow all remote administration. Keep a log of all users' activities. Remove all unneeded services. Remove all unnecessary programs and files. Apply security patches as soon as they are announced. Scan the server periodically to look for vulnerabilities. Monitor connections to the server.

Example 6.2 Security risks.

What are some of the Web security risks that we should be aware of?

Solution 6.2 Hackers steal confidential documents from Web servers, execute commands on the server that allow them to modify and break into the system, launch denial-of-service attacks that render the machine temporarily unusable, crash users' Web browsers by sending ActiveX content, damage users' systems, breach users' privacy, or merely create an annoyance. **ActiveX** is a technology developed by Microsoft for distributing software over the Internet, similar to Java-Beans from Suns Microsystems.

Example 6.3 Setting Web browsers' security.

Learn how to set up the security level of Internet connections.

Solution 6.3 We covered this issue in Example 2.9, where we showed how to set the level of security with the major four browsers: IE, Netscape, Opera, and Crazy Browser.

6.2 Fraud

Internet fraud and cyberscams are not different from their traditional counterparts. The Internet is just another medium of practicing these unlawful activities. Credit card fraud is a widely known problem. Online credit card frauds occur because online retailers do not check on buyers credit history. Fraud cases are likely to be detected weeks after they have occurred, when cardholders receive their monthly account statements. Who pays for the damage resulting from fraud? Consumers have little to fear. Most credit card companies reimburse cardholders for fraudulent transactions and then write them off as a business loss.

Internet investment scams offer another prime example of Internet fraud. Investment news, whether true or false, can spread very rapidly by posting messages on online bulletin boards, discussing investment opportunities in chat rooms, or sending mass e-mails. It is easy for fraudsters to make their messages look real and creditable. Further, Online investment newsletters may offer false or wrong information or make false claims.

Investment frauds usually fit one of four categories. The *pump-and-dump scam* sends investors messages urging them to buy or sell a company's stock very quickly. Often, the scam perpetrators claim to have inside information from reliable sources. After the fraudsters make their money and the news fades away, innocent investors end up losing money.

The *pyramid scheme* is all about how to make big money from home by working only a few hours a week. The online pyramid scheme is an electronic version of the classic pyramid scheme, where people make money by recruiting others.

The *risk-free fraud* claims to offer investors exciting low-risk investment opportunities in projects and areas such as bank securities. The conventional wisdom holds here: If the deal sound too good to be true, then it is.

The *offshore fraud* capitalizes on investors' lack of knowledge of other countries and their economic systems, as well as currency fluctuations, to convince investors that there are great money-making opportunities waiting for them overseas.

The government and its agencies are tirelessly trying to protect citizens from falling victim to fraud and scams. The *Internet Fraud Complaint Center* (IFCC), working with the FBI, has the mission of addressing fraud committed over the Internet. Victims of Internet fraud can report and alert authorities of suspected activities. The IFCC website is `http://www.ifccfbi.gov`. Another center is the *Internet National Fraud Information Center*; its website is `http://www.fraud.org`. A third free service is the *Fraud Bureau* (FB), which alerts online consumers and investors of prior complaints about online vendors, auction websites, and investment firms. The FB's website is `http://www.fraudbureau.com`.

6.3 Crackers

Crackers are malicious hackers who attack websites and render them dysfunctional, resulting in what is know as **denial-of-service attacks**, such as the attacks that hit Yahoo!, CNN, and other major websites in previous years. The motivations behind these attacks are personal satisfaction and social attention.

Crackers sometimes use automated vulnerability scanners to probe networks in order to find holes in them that they can exploit to deplete the computing resources of the network. While the network computers are busy meeting the demands of the crackers, users cannot access the websites supported by the networks. Crackers may even use holes in one less important network in order to launch and mount attacks on other, major, vital networks. A hole in a network usually leads to one or more routers that crackers can use.

Firewalls are used to prevent crackers from accessing the computers behind them. However, if there is a hole open for a Web server that the public can access, crackers will find it and attack the computers. Having a firewall is not an excuse to leave the machines behind it unsecure.

Web servers are one of the most dangerous services that a network can offer. A Web server gives the entire world access to the inner workings of its file system. Many Web administrators are not experienced enough to handle complex security issues. Moreover, many PC users do not have the knowledge or the time to deal with security issues. This situation creates a haven for crackers.

While system administrators work hard to ensure system security, crackers wait for any slipup they can find. An administrator's job should be to create a cracker-resistant system, and not a crackerproof one, as the latter is a very challenging and costly task. In a cracker-resistant environment, the administrator renders the system as secure as possible, while making provisions such that future successful cracks cause as little damage as possible. An example of such provisions is backing up system data on a regular basis, so that if the data are attacked and corrupted, a near-latest version can be restored from the backup version. Once a cracker has access to a system, he or she can erase data files, sell them to competitors, modify them, or use the system's identity as their own in order to attack other systems.

6.4 Firewalls

We discussed firewalls in Section 1.13. Firewalls are used for security purposes. Firewall software inspects incoming TCP packets before they are transmitted to their final destination. A firewall can implement security rules such as dictating which computers can receive files from outside the company. Such computers would not have any valuable data files on them, in case crackers break through the firewall. Figure 6.1 shows a computer system with a firewall. The firewall keeps the general public from accessing the computers behind it.

Firewalls use at least one of three methods to control traffic flow in and out of networks. The *packet-filtering method* analyzes TCP packets against a set of filters, passing only those that pass the filtering criteria. The *proxy-service method* enables the firewall to receive information coming

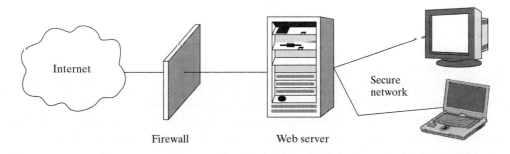

Figure 6.1 Secure system with a firewall.

from the Internet and send it to the requesting source. The net effect is that the outside remote computer hosting the information never comes into contact with any of the computers behind the firewall. The *stateful-inspection method* does not inspect the contents of each TCP packet; instead, it compares key parts of the packet with a database of trusted information. For example, some firewalls do not allow the receipt of e-mail from outsiders unless the outsiders have received prior e-mail messages from addresses inside the firewall.

Firewalls are customizable. A firewall can be set up to block all traffic to or from a given IP address or domain name, to assign one or two computers to accept a specific protocol (only HTTP, for example), to block a certain port number, or to block access to websites that contain specific phrases and words.

A firewall protects against many possible breaches, including unauthorized remote login, exploitation of application holes and operating-system bugs by crackers, and the sending of spam and viruses. The highest level of security a firewall offers is to block everything, which defeats the purpose of an Internet connection. A good system administrator should set up a firewall effectively.

6.5 P3P

Web users and applications have been increasing steadily, at both the professional and personal levels. As a result, large amounts of sensitive and personal information are exchanged via the Internet. This condition has prompted a surge of interest in privacy protection and means of assuring people that their personal information will be collected and used according to their permission and will. The W3C organization has taken the initiative to develop privacy-practice disclosure with respect to data collected through the Internet. The result of this initiative is P3P.

P3P (Platform for Privacy Preferences) is a protocol created by the W3C organization to provide a simple, automated way for users to control the use of their personal information by websites that they visit. P3P is about establishing privacy disclosure technology. For website developers, P3P provides a standard to articulate their privacy policies to their visitors. For Web surfers, P3P provides a set of multiple-choice questions covering the major aspects of a website's privacy policies. The answers a user provides to these questions specify his or her desired level of privacy. Essentially, P3P provides a clear representation of how a website handles personal and private information about its users. P3P-enabled websites make this information available in a machine-readable format. P3P-enabled browsers can automatically retrieve and easily interpret this information and compare it with the user's own set of privacy preferences that he or she specified through the browsers.

P3P allows users to automate the acceptance or the rejection of a website's requests for information (through the use of cookies), based on the privacy preferences they set in their browsers. Users are assured that their privacy is protected without having to read each website's privacy policy. P3P does not give users more privacy; it only allows them to exercise personal data preferences. It makes users better informed about what data are collected and why.

There are commercially available P3P policy editors, with visual development tools and interfaces, to create a website's privacy policy in the P3P protocol. These editors produce

XML-formatted (machine readable by Web browsers) files that describe a website's privacy practices, including the information collected (e.g., names, addresses, bank accounts, and credit card numbers), how it is used, and who has access to it.

Major browsers and websites are P3P enabled and compliant. The four browsers we covered in Chapter 2 (IE, Netscape, Opera, and Crazy Browser) all support P3P protocol. Examples of P3P-enabled websites include the websites of AT&T (`http://www.att.com`), IBM (`http://www.ibm.com`), Lycos (`http://www.lycos.com`), Microsoft (`http://www.microsoft.com`), MSN (`http://www.msn.com`), MSNBC (`http://www.msnbc.com`), TRUSTe (`http://www.truste.org`), the U.S. Department of Commerce (`http://www.commerce.gov`), and W3C (`http://www.w3c.org`).

Cookies are viewed as a precursor to P3P. Before cookies were implemented, the HTTP protocol was "stateless"; that is, a request for a Web page was not linked to any future requests. With cookies, websites can store the browsing history of their visitors; a website can thus tell when a user last accessed the site or how many times the user visited the site. Websites set (drop) cookies on the user's computer. Third parties can also set cookies. For example, third-party banner advertisers can set cookies through the websites that use them (a process known as third-party cookies practice). Cookies are used as a silent tracking mechanism. P3P is designed to change that by allowing the user to set cookies' acceptance options via Web browsers.

The current P3P specification is 1.0. The P3P1.0 specification defines the syntax and semantics (rules) of P3P policies and describes how to associate them with Web resources. P3P1.0 expresses policies as statements that use P3P vocabulary. P3P 1.0 has two goals. First, it enables websites (the server side) to present their data-collection practices in a standardized, machine-readable format by using XML to express P3P statements. Second, it enables Web users (the client side) to view and understand what data will be collected by the websites they visit, how the data will be used, and, more importantly, it gives users the choice of accepting or rejecting the data collection in the first place.

P3P1.0 requires the definition of privacy policies and policy reference files. **P3P policy files** represent the practices of a website. Different parts (Web pages) of the website may require different privacy policies. The P3P **policy reference file** indicates which policies apply to which parts of the website. The file is an XML document that Web browsers can read to find out which policies and cookies apply to the website's parts. A P3P-enabled website must have at least one policy reference file.

The implementation of P3P1.0 must be done on both the server and client sides. Websites can implement P3P1.0 on their servers by translating their human-readable privacy policies into P3P syntax and statements and storing them in one or more files. The website must also develop a policy reference file. The client-side implementation of P3P1.0 is included in the Web browsers. They include a choice of cookies that users can set when they specify the browser preferences.

P3P1.0 is designed to support existing security and privacy efforts, not to replace them. As such, it supports all of the existing encryption techniques covered in Chapter 2. It also supports digital signatures and allows their incorporation, in P3P statements.

Example 6.4   Using P3P.

Examine an example of how P3P can be used.

Solution 6.4   Let us assume that John Doe would like to buy some books from a website. There are three steps to buying the books: Access the website, select the books, and check out. Each step requires John to provide different data; therefore, the website has three different privacy policies, one for each step. In particular, Step 2 requires cookies to keep track of the books that John selects. Let us also assume that the website and John's Web browser have built-in P3P protocol.

When John visits the website, his browser fetches the P3P policy for the Web page and checks it against John's browser preferences. If it matches, the browser proceeds with the page download; otherwise, it pops up a message asking for John's acceptance of the website's privacy policy. At this point, John could refuse and quit.

When John selects books, the website needs to collect more information and stores it in cookies. The Web server provides a separate P3P policy to cover this part of the website, and John's Web browser notifies him. Again, the browser looks to enforce John's privacy on his behalf.

The same scenario is repeated for the last step: checking out. The website needs John's credit card number, phone number, and shipping address in order to complete the transaction. There is a different policy that covers the collection of these data. The browser, again, works on behalf of John.

This example represents an ideal scenario of how to protect a user's privacy. The browser's checking of the privacy policy can be greatly simplified if John is a little more trusting and sets his browser cookies' settings to be more liberal, as shown in the next example.

Example 6.5   Client-side P3P control.

Learn how to set cookies options in browsers.

Solution 6.5   Tutorial 2.18.1 shows how to manage cookies in four browsers: IE, Netscape, Opera, and Crazy Browser. Figure 2.13 shows the different options that each browser offers its users. **IE** and **Crazy Browser** each have six settings that range from blocking all cookies to accepting all cookies. The advanced settings of IE allow its users to control the acceptance of both first-party and third-party cookies. **Netscape** offers similar options to those provided by IE, but it also allows the user to limit the maximum lifetime of cookies. **Opera** provides other privacy settings and filters in addition to cookies.

6.6   Sniffing and Web Bugs

Web sniffing is the act of collecting information about Web surfers without their prior knowledge. A sniffer is a program that collects the information. Sniffing is commonly used by network managers (application programs) to monitor and analyze network traffic to detect bottlenecks and avoid them by routing the traffic through less congested routers. Other sniffers can illegitimately capture data being transmitted through the Web.

Web browsers can sniff out information about their users via JavaScript. For example, a website can use JavaScript to find out the user's browser name and version, as well as the OS running it. Browser sniffing allows websites to send the right version of a Web page, depending on whether the user's browser is IE or Netscape, for example.

Web bugs (beacons) are a form of sniffing. A **Web bug** is a piece invisible code or an invisible file (usually an image file) that is placed on a Web page or in an e-mail message to collect data about Web users (such as the user's name or IP address) and their Web behavior. Web bugs can even install files on a user's computer. An e-mail bug sends information back to its source when the user replies to or forwards the bugged message. Cookies may be considered a form of Web bugs. However, unlike cookies, which a user can decline or accept, as discussed in Section 6.5, Web bugs are invisible; their colors are the same as the background colors of the Web pages on which they appear. Many tracking and advertising Web companies place bugs in their Web pages.

Security and privacy companies provide Web users with tools to track and find Web bugs. They also try to make users aware of these bugs and their potential abuse. Some companies equate bugged e-mail to wiretapping.

Three types of Web bugs can be identified. The simplest bug is an *image file* that works with cookies to send information to third parties about a user. The second type is an *executable bug* that can install a file onto a user's hard drive. The third type is a *script-based executable bug* that can take a document from a user's computer or executes a file on the server to control the client's machine.

Surprisingly enough, there is a good side of Web bugs. They can be used to track copyright violations on the Web and to gather statistics such as the IP address of the computer that fetches a Web page. A Web bug can find the URL of the page of another Web bug or the URL of a Web bug's image.

6.7 Web Stalking

Stalking is harassing someone. **Web stalking** takes the form of spamming, flaming, intrusive IMing, and trolling people. We covered spamming and flaming in Chapter 3 and intrusive IMing in Chapter 4. A **troll** is someone who posts messages intended to insult and provoke. As in real stalking, Web stalking comes from unusual people and causes frightening psychological problems for the stalking victims.

Identity plays a key role in Web stalking. Web stalkers usually hide their true personalities. For example, a stalker may use an alias e-mail address or IM screen name. The disguising of one's identity on the Web makes it difficult to understand and evaluate the interaction with Web stalkers. A stalking victim can identify the IP address and the host of the stalker, but it may still take time and effort to track down the stalker, because stalkers may also be computer hackers hijacking IP addresses and hosts.

There are some good tips on how to fight Web stalking. The best way to track a stalker is to employ team effort, working with different friends and family members. A study of the trail of e-mail messages and IMing sessions (a process known as social engineering) may shed some light on the stalker's psychology. Patience is a good weapon to use against stalkers. Ignore them, and do not respond to their messages. Consider changing ISPs, e-mail addresses, and IM screen names. Avoid meeting strangers online in newsgroups, chat rooms, forums, gaming services, and the like. Last, visit `http://www.cybercrime.gov/reporting.htm` to report the stalking problem.

6.8 Censorship

The Internet is considered one of the best mediums for freedom of speech. All of the synchronous and asynchronous communication methods covered in Chapters 3, 4, and 5 serve as excellent ways of expressing opinions and speaking out freely. The Internet is believed to be empowering and democratizing. Information can be spread very quickly, without facing the traditional barriers of importing and exporting rules and regulations. No smuggling of books and magazines is needed in order to spread sensitive information.

The attempt to ban or regulate access to information is called **censorship**. Internet censorship is a common practice in authoritarian regimes, which crack down on Internet usage and freedom of expression in the name of national security. These regimes rely on many clever techniques to control the spread of information over the Internet. They arrest so-called cyberdissents who speak out against them on the Internet. They introduce tight Internet regulations and laws prohibiting "politically unacceptable" content such as discussion of democracy. Moreover, they block websites considered to be politically or morally objectionable and close Internet cafes (public places that provide Internet access) in order to limit access. Some regimes set up their Internet infrastructure so that they have the capability to monitor e-mail and Web browsing. Other regimes depend on the high cost of Internet access as a method of maintaining control over online information.

Some governments have developed the ability to censor material coming from abroad through the Internet. They force all foreign information to run through government servers that filter and block foreign websites that the government deems potentially dangerous. Some governments lift the ban on foreign websites temporarily when foreign delegates are visiting their countries, as a courtesy to them.

One way to fight censorship is for people from such countries to go into exile and publish their views and criticisms on websites that they build. This practice is referred to as being "virtually in exile." This approach is not very effective in the exiles' home countries, as their websites are blocked there, but it is very useful for educating others about what is happening in oppressive regimes. Another problem with this approach is the declining relevance of the information provided by an exile over time, unless the dissident has reliable underground correspondents who can get information out of the country.

While it appears that traditional censorship techniques work in oppressing the online movement, the spread of the Internet is still hard to stop. The elites in oppressive regimes tend to lead the movement towards change. This group of people is generally wealthy enough to have access to the Internet. Moreover, because of the Internet, it is simply harder today to keep secrets from spreading throughout the world. Breaking news becomes available on the desks of journalists, and on websites, within minutes.

6.9 TRUSTe

TRUSTe (`http://www.truste.org`) is an independent, nonprofit privacy auditing service. It promotes trusting relationships between individuals and organizations, based on respect for personal identity and privacy. Web surfers are assured of identity protection when they visit websites that display the TRUSTe logo. Websites display the logo and list the auditing service in their P3P interaction only if they pass and maintain their auditing requirements, set by TRUSTe through its Privacy Seal Program.

TRUSTe advocates the user's privacy rights. It helps ensure that a user is given a clear notification about what information a website collects and with whom it shares the information. It also ensures that the user has the right to choose whether to share the information with a third party. TRUSTe's website lists *Consumer Privacy Protection Guidelines* that include six tips: Read a website's privacy statement thoroughly; look for seals of approval; know that credit card purchases online are protected by the same consumer laws that apply in the mall; use secure servers for credit card transactions; use common sense on the Web in the same way that you do on the phone; teach children to be "cybersmart" by providing them with Web surfing guidelines. TRUSTe certifies children-oriented websites by issuing the TRUSTe *Children's Privacy Seal*, a seal with expanded safeguards on websites for children.

6.10 EPIC

EPIC (Electronic Privacy Information Center) is a public interest research center (`http://www.epic.org`) that was established to protect privacy, the First Amendment, and constitutional values. EPIC works with various civil-liberties organizations to enforce privacy rights and the Freedom of Information Act (FOIA) on behalf of Web users. It also works with the U.S. Congress and other legal entities to establish new programs and laws that protect users' privacy in cyberspace. EPIC's website lists the latest news on the privacy front.

EPIC has many interesting publications. Its Privacy Law Sourcebook provides many resources to students, attorneys, researchers, and journalists interested in privacy law in the United States and around the world. It lists the full text of major privacy laws such as the Privacy Act, FOIA, the Family Educational Rights and Privacy Act, the Right to Financial Privacy Act, the USA PATRIOT Act, the Privacy Protection Act, the Cable Communications Policy Act, the Video Privacy Protection Act, and the European Union Data Directive for Data Protection and Commerce.

Another publication provided by EPIC is *Filters and Freedom 2.0: Free Speech Perspectives on Internet Content Controls.* This book discusses the pros and cons of content filtering on the Web. While it is viewed as a technological solution that would forestall official censorship, content filtering can pose its own significant threats to free expression on the Internet. The book also discusses the notion that filtering and rating systems can be viewed as a framework that facilitates the suppression of speech. The book discusses the recent efforts within the United States and the European Union to establish a uniform rating regime for online material.

6.11 .NET Passport

.NET Passport is a Microsoft service that allows users to make online purchases and perform other activities across different participating websites and services, with the use of one single login (username and password). The .NET Passport service (`http://www.passport.net`) also includes .NET Passport wallet and .NET Passport express purchase.

The .NET Passport recognizes the user's privacy and the importance of protection of personal information. The website publishes the .NET privacy statements for both adults and children. The statements apply only to the .NET website and its participating websites. They describe the collection, use, and disclosure practices by .NET Passport of personal information. During registration for a .NET Passport, the user must provide certain personal information in order to create a .NET Passport profile: e-mail address, first and last name, country or region, state or territory, zip code or postal code, language, time zone, gender, birth date, and occupation. The .NET Passport service and its participating Web services may require additional personal information during use of their websites, such as telephone number for mobile users, and credit card number and billing and shipping address for the .NET Passport wallet.

Websites associated with .NET Passport require two registrations from the user: one for .NET Passport and one for the participating website. The website may use two registration forms or one form. In the latter case, the .NET Passport information is identified on the form by a .NET Passport icon, ⊞, next each to field.

.NET Passport uses personal information according to its privacy statement. It will not sell or rent the information to third parties. It will not use or share the personal information in a manner different from that stipulated on the privacy statement without prior consent. However, .NET Passport will use the information for maintenance and operation of its accounts. For example, it may send a user an e-mail message in order to verify the e-mail address. Or it may send e-mail about periodic services, recommended security updates, or surveys related to the .NET Passport service.

The .NET Passport service uses cookies. If a cookies-disabled browser attempts to access the service, an error occurs. .NET Passport uses cookies whenever a user signs into a .NET-participating website. A cookie stores a unique identifier, the sign-in time, and other profile information from participating websites. The cookie is stored in an encrypted form on the .NET member's hard disk. The cookie allows the user to move from one page to another within the participating website without having to log in again to each page.

Microsoft in general and .NET Passport in particular are members of the TRUSTe privacy program. As such, the privacy statements of NET Passport websites disclose their privacy practices in accordance with the requirements of the TRUSTe privacy program.

6.12 Liberty Alliance Project

The **Liberty Alliance Project** (LAP) is a collaboration of companies and organizations to develop and deploy an open, federated solution to Internet identity. A **federated identity** is a universal standard for a single sign-on (login). LAP enables consumers and businesses to maintain personal information securely. It also provides an open standard for network identity. It is similar to the .NET Passport service. LAP's website is `http://www.projectliberty.org`.

LAP's specifications focus on interoperability between systems in order to enable simplified sign-on functionality for various Web services. A user may have multiple accounts, one for every website offering a service. LAP's specifications enable the user to have one sign-on for all these accounts. The functionality outlined in version 1.0 of the specifications is opt-in account linking (users link accounts they have with different services), simplified sign-on for linked accounts (signing onto one account provides access to all other accounts), authentication context (companies can limit the access provided by one sign-on to a handful of company accounts), global logout (logging out of the initial website logs the user out of any other websites with live sessions), and LAP client feature (users can employ these clients on desktops or wireless devices in order to access LAP functionality).

The specifications define a set of protocols that provides a solution for identity federation management, cross-domain authentication, and session management. The LAP architecture contains three "actors": principal, identity provider, and service provider. This architecture is based on the scenario that a user signs on in order to buy services from a service provider (a website). The principal acts as an agent between the identity and service providers. The identity providers supply authentication information (username and password) to the principal, who presents the information to the service provider. If the service provider accepts the authentication assertion from the identity provider, an identity federation is said to exist between the two.

The version 1.1 specifications provide maintenance updates to the 1.0 version specifications. Version 1.1 includes editorial changes to clarify the version 1.0 specifications, as well as fixes and enhancements. The version 2.0 specifications will enable organizations to share certain personal information of users according to the users' permissions and preferences.

Examples of entities that can benefit from the LAP concept are plenty. In a business-to-employee example, a business can link the various applications employees use to do their jobs in order to increase their productivity. It can also link applications on its corporate intranet, such as 401K information, health benefits, and travel services. This configuration would enable employees to use one username and password to access all of the different services. In a business-to-business example, a business can have access to multiple suppliers, partners, and vendors on its extranet with the use of a single sign-on. This setup increases operational efficiencies, enhances the business' relationship with suppliers, and reduces IT (information technology) costs. In a business-to-consumer example, companies may partner to create a "circle of trust." A customer can conveniently use one sign-on to access many services of a number of different companies. In the travel industry, for example, one sign-on allows a customer to book airplane tickets, rent cars, and reserve hotel rooms.

FAQs

Introduction (Section 6.1)

Q: How secure are Web servers and operating systems?

A: If two servers are configured correctly, a typical Unix system is more secure than a typical Windows system.

Q: How secure are Web-server software programs?

A: As a rule of thumb, the more features a server offers, the more likely it is to contain security holes.

Q: What should a Web administrator do to ensure better Web security?

A: Write a security policy and implement it. The guidelines of the policy should include who can use the system, when the system can be used, what is allowed to be done, how to grant access (authentication), what constitutes acceptable use of the system, remote and local login methods, and system-monitoring procedures.

Q: Why do IP addresses pose a security threat?

A: A computer connected to the Internet is identified by its IP address. Hackers can use this address to access the computer from anywhere in the world. A fixed (static, or nonchanging) IP address is a larger security risk than a dynamic (changing) address. A dial-up modem connection gets a new IP address every time a connection is established between the computer and the Internet. On the other hand, a cable or DSL connection has a static IP address.

Firewalls (Section 6.4)

Q: What can a firewall protect against? What can it not protect against?

A: A firewall can protect against e-mail traffic and unauthorized remote logins. It cannot protect very well against attacks, poor clients behind the firewall, and viruses.

Q: What is a DMZ, and why do we need one?

A: DMZ stands for demilitarized zone. In the context of firewalls, it means a part of the network that is part of neither the Internet nor the local network. For example, one can install a computer outside a firewall to connect to the Internet. Any software that outside users need to download is put on that computer. The use of a DMZ enhances the security protection offered by firewalls.

P3P (Section 6.5)

Q: What is APPEL?

A: APPEL (A P3P Preference Exchange Language) is a language designed to encode user preferences (received through a Web browser) about privacy. It also permits sharing of a single user preference document across several P3P documents.

Q: What is data privacy, and how is it different from other privacies?

A: Data privacy relates to information about you such as your name, address, age, phone number, bank account, medical records, age, gender, job title, employer, income level, social security number, driver's license number, and habits (eating, buying, spending, and others). It is different from other privacy concerns such as eavesdropping, wiretapping, snooping, and spying. Data privacy means that a website does not share the data about you (that you provide voluntarily) with other websites without your permission. Other privacy concerns deal with someone stealing information about you secretly and using it without your prior concent.

Q: Is privacy a right, like freedom of speech?

A: Surprisingly enough, no. Privacy is not mentioned in the U.S. Constitution.

Q: How long can a website keep personal data?

A: For as long as it wants. P3P does not set a limit on time. Practically, websites should not hold onto the data for too long, as the data can become obsolete.

Sniffing and Web Bugs (Section 6.6)

Q: How do I know if there is a Web bug in a Web page I am surfing?

A: Web bugs are usually included in a page as an image file using the `<img>` XHTML tag. Look at the source code of the Web page. If it has an image loaded from a different Web server than the rest of the page, then the image is a Web bug.

Liberty Alliance Project (Section 6.12)

Q: What is a network identity?

A: It is a set of sign-on information that a user can employ to access different accounts with different service providers.

Q: What is a federated network identity?

A: It is a concept that allows consumers and businesses to use separate specialized companies to manage different sets of identity information for them.

Blackbox

Sections 6.1 (Introduction) (Examples 6.1–6.3): Web security and privacy are very important for a safe Internet. Damages from security breaches can be substantial. Web security includes authentication, authorization, and privacy. Websites usually post their privacy policies.

Section 6.2 (Fraud): Credit card fraud and investment scams are popular on the Internet. Investment scams include the pump-and-dump scam, the pyramid scheme, the risk-free fraud, and the offshore fraud. Websites that help fight and protect against fraud include `http://www.ifccfbi.gov`, `http://www.fraud.org`, and `http://www.fraudbureau.com`.

Sections 6.3 (Crackers): Crackers usually launch denial-of-service attacks on websites, rendering them dysfunctional. Web servers are the most security-sensitive service a network can offer. System administrators should focus on making their systems cracker resistant, not crackerproof.

Section 6.4 (Firewalls): Firewalls implement security rules to protect networks. The three methods firewalls use to control traffic flow through them are packet filtering, proxy service, and stateful inspection. Firewalls are customizable and can protect against unauthorized remote login, crackers, spam, bulk mail, and viruses.

Sections 6.5 (P3P)(Examples 6.4 and 6.5): The P3P protocol simplifies and automates users' acceptances or rejections of cookies in order to help them control their privacy on the Internet. Many Web companies and browsers have embraced P3P. P3P and cookies work together. The current version of P3P is 1.0. P3P1.0 uses two types of files: policy files and policy reference files.

Section 6.6 (Sniffing and Web Bugs): Web sniffers and bugs have bad and good sides. Cookies may be viewed as a form of Web bugs. Types of Web bugs are image files, executable bugs, and script-based executable bugs.

Section 6.7 (Web Stalking): Spamming, flaming, and trolling people is Web stalking. Web stalkers usually hide their identities. Be aware of the tips on how to fight Web stalking.

Section 6.8 (Censorship): The Internet is the best medium to fight censorship, even though oppressive regimes use many techniques to stop online information flow.

Section 6.9 (TRUSTe): The TRUSTe service (`http://www.truste.org`) audits and certifies websites that meet its strict privacy requirements. Certified websites display the TRUSTe seal proudly. On its website, TRUSTe lists its Consumer Privacy Protection Guidelines.

Section 6.10 (EPIC): EPIC performs research work and advocacy efforts to promote and protect Web privacy and enforce the Freedom of Information Act. It publishes its findings in books and reports.

Section 6.11 (.NET Passport): .NET Passport provides one login for use with participating Web services. It uses personal information according to its privacy statements. The .NET Passport service uses cookies to operate.

Section 6.12 (Liberty Alliance Project): The LAP concept (`http://www.projectliberty.org`) enables a business or a consumer to define one identity with which to sign on and use Web services from multiple websites. The LAP specifications versions 1.0 and 1.1 define a set of protocols for identity management, cross-domain authentication, and session management.

Check Your Progress

At the end of this chapter, you should

- ✔ understand Web security and privacy (Section 6.1);
- ✔ know about some online resources to protect against Internet fraud (Section 6.2);
- ✔ know what crackers do to networks (Section 6.3);
- ✔ be able to identify the methods that firewalls use (Section 6.4);
- ✔ have mastered the use of P3P and cookies (Section 6.5);
- ✔ understand the concepts of Web sniffing, Web bugs, Web stalking, and censorship (Sections 6.6–6.8);

✔ be aware of TRUSTe and EPIC (Sections 6.9 and 6.10);

✔ Know about .NET Passport and the Liberty Alliance Project (Sections 6.11 and 6.12).

Problems

The exercises are designed for a lab setting, while the homework is to be done outside class time.

Exercises

6.1   How can you protect confidential documents on a website?

6.2   What are proxy servers, and how do they work?

6.3   Change your IE settings to refuse all cookies. Then use IE to log into `http://www.fidelity.com` or another website that requires cookies. What happens?

6.4   If a website supports three Web pages, each with a different privacy policy, how many P3P policy and policy preference files does it need?

6.5   What are the three types of Web bugs?

Homework

6.6   How can you make SSL work through a firewall?

6.7   How can you make the finger command work through a firewall?

6.8   Change your Netscape and Opera settings to refuse all cookies. Then use them to log into `http://www.fidelity.com` or another website that requires cookies. What happens?

6.9   A website drops cookies onto its surfers' hard drives. It has advertisers who also drop cookies there. What are the types of cookies in this scenario?

6.10 Search the Web and find examples of script-based executable Webbugs.

Searching the Internet

Goal

Understand and master searching the Internet to find relevant information fast, know what information to search for, and know how to search for it.

Objectives

- Subject directories
- The Open Directory Project
- Search and metasearch engines
- Search techniques: words, exact phrase, Boolean operators, title, site, URL, link, and others
- Intelligent agents
- The Visible Web
- The Invisible Web
- Search techniques for the Invisible Web: directories, databases, and search engines

Outline

7.1   Introduction

The Internet is an endless repository of information. Search engines, such as Google, are the primary searching tool that we use to search the Internet. Internet searches can be time consuming. This chapter shows how to formulate a search strategy in order to improve the search results. In order to compose such a search strategy, we must know what to search for and how to search for it. Without these two elements, a search will be difficult to conduct and to bring to a successful conclusion. The result of a search is a list of Web pages. The relevance of these Web pages depends largely on the two aforementioned search elements; the more specific they are, the better the search results will be.

Before we discuss search techniques and methodologies, we need to be aware of the available search tools and the potential and the limitation of each tool. The two main tools are directories and search engines. A **directory** is a subject guide, typically organized by major topics and subtopics. The best-known directory is the one on Yahoo! (`http://www.yahoo.com`). A **search engine** is a piece of software that searches the Internet according to one or more keywords that the user has provided. Each type of tool has a database that users can search for what they want. The difference between the two tools lies in how the database is created: A directory's database is compiled by humans, while search engine's database is generated automatically by the engine's software.

7.2   Directories

A directory organizes information in a hierarchical tree by subject. The subjects are very general at the top of the tree (the root) and become very specialized at its bottom (the leaves). We can search a directory in two ways. First we can search it manually, by browsing its subjects hierarchically. Consider the Yahoo! directory; it lists a set of subjects at the top. If we are in interested in music, we click the `Music` link under the `Entertainment` subject (see the forthcoming screen capture), and continue from there. The second way of searching a directory is to use its search tool, which acts like a search engine. The Yahoo! directory supports this feature. It provides a search field where you type the search words, as shown in the following screen capture.

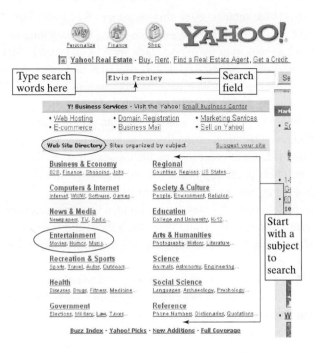

Example 7.1 Search a directory.

Use the Yahoo! directory to find information about travelling to Rome, Italy.

Solution 7.1 Go to Yahoo's website, at `http://www.yahoo.com`. Scroll down to the `Web Site Directory` section shown in the foregoing screen capture. Starting with the

Recreation & Sports subject, click this sequence: Recreation & Sports => Travel. At this point, you can tell that the search is going in the wrong direction, because the subjects under Travel are not what we expect; they are Air Travel, Automotive, and so forth. We expected to find some subjects related to countries and cities. Notice that Yahoo! displays the subject tree at the top of its Web page in order to remind you of the subject path that brought you to where you are. In our example, the path so far is Home > Recreation > Travel > **Air Travel** .

You have two choices to better this search. You can go back and start with another top-level subject and continue searching manually, or you can use the Yahoo! directory's search engine. You should use the latter in order to expedite the search. Type the search words travel to rome in the search field at the top of the Yahoo! Web page and click the Search button, Search . Observe that search engine is case insensitive.

Yahoo! returns some results. The results are divided into four categories. (See the accompanying screen capture.) The top two come from the Yahoo! directory. An abbreviated subject path is listed for each result in the second category. Click a path to expand to the full path. Here is one of the full paths:

Home > Regional > Countries > Italy > Regions > Lazio > Provinces > Rome > **Travel and Transportation**

The third category lists results from searching sponsors, websites, and the fourth one lists results from searching the Web.

This example provides some important concepts:

- Know what to search for. You want to search for Rome. Actually you can be even more specific: Do you want Rome as in Rome, Georgia U.S.A, or Rome as in Rome, Italy? The search produced both results. Your search string should have been travel to rome, italy.
- Know how to search for it. Once you know what to search for, you can search for it manually or by using the Yahoo! directory's search engine. Use the search engine, as it is faster and more comprehensive. Also, search engines are case insensitive.
- Change search words. If you do not like the search results, change the search words and try again.

7.3   Open Directory Project

When users search for information on the Internet by using a directory's search engine, the engine ranks its search results. Different directories use different techniques to develop their ranking systems. For example, Yahoo! and Lycos have an army of paid editors and staff who evaluate websites. Directories are referred to as human-powered search engines.

This approach to create ranking systems faces a monumental challenge. As the number of Web pages on every imaginable subject increases dramatically, directory search engines should try to do more than just list every available page on a given subject. One logical solution is to turn the ranking system over to users. This is the main idea behind a project called the *Open Directory Project* (http://dmoz.org). The project's website offers its own directory and many other interesting facts. The project started in 1998. The project acknowledges that it is impossible for a search service to know everything about anything. Thus, the project turns to users themselves. It invites users to become editors and evaluate sites within their areas of expertise and help create lists of the most useful sites within certain subject areas. For example, experts in the area of child education can create lists of links to pages that they believe offer the best information.

The Open Directory Project provides a way for search engines to get much more content into their services than what editors or freelance writers could provide alone. Search engines that have the most content should get the most traffic and therefore become the leaders. Some websites, such as Lycos, have realized the potential of the project and have joined it.

The Open Directory Project may be compared to the movement of free software that uses the process of peer review to create superior operating systems such as Linux. The project is based on volunteer work by people who love what they do and do it for free. The project should lead to the construction of a superior method to organize the contents of the Web, especially as they become more difficult to manage by just a handful of individuals working for search engines.

7.4 Search Engines

There are many search engines on the Web. Some of these search engines listed in Table 7.1.are:

Table 7.1 Available search engines

Search engine	website that uses the engine	Search engine	website that uses the engine
Google	`http://www.google.com`	AOL Search	`http://search.aol.com`
Yahoo!	`http://www.yahoo.com`	Teoma	`http://www.teoma.com`
AllTheWeb	`http://www.alltheweb.com`	Inktomi	`http://www.inktomi.com`
MSN Search	`http://search.msn.com`	Look Smart	`http://www.looksmart.com`
Lycos	`http://www.lycos.com`	Overture	`http://www.overture.com`
Ask Jeeves	`http://www.askjeeves.com`	AltaVista	`http://www.altavista.com`
Direct Hit	`http://www.directhit.com`	Meta Search	`http://www.metasearch.com`
Dogpile	`http://www.dogpile.com`	Northern Light	`http://www.northernlight.com`
Excite	`http://www.excite.com`	Planet Search	`http://www.planetsearch.com`
HotBot	`http://www.hotbot.com`	Pro Fusion	`http://www.profusion.com`
Infoseek	`http://www.infoseek.com`	Meta Crawler	`http://www.metacrawler.com`
Search	`http://www.search.com`	Web Crawler	`http://www.webcrawler.com`

The most popular search engines are listed at the beginning of Table 7.1 Google's search engine is the most popular by far; it provides both comprehensive coverage of the Web and great relevancy. In addition to searching the Web, Google allows you to search for images and newsgroups and to search the Open Directory. Popular search engines are beneficial for both webmasters and searchers. For webmasters, the popular engines are the most important ones to be listed with, because they provide the heaviest traffic. For searchers, they produce more dependable results, because they are well maintained and upgraded when necessary in order to keep pace with the growing Web.

Search engines provide an easy-to-use user interface. The surfer types a search string in a search field and clicks a search button. A **search string** is one or more keywords that expresses what you want to search for. The Web site `http://www.searchenginewatch.com` offers many tips on search engines and how to use them.

Most search engines are crawler based. That is, they create their listings automatically, as opposed to human-powered directories which depend on people for their listings. Crawler-based search engines have three major software parts that work sequentially. The first part is the spider or crawler. A **spider** or **crawler** is a robot computer program that can find Web pages by following links in the pages they already have in their databases. These pages in turn have other links that the spider follows, and so forth. The spider returns to the websites on a regular basis, such as every month, to look for changes.

The spider passes all the Web pages it finds on to the second part of the search engine, the index or catalog. The index computer program identifies the text, links, and other content in each Web page and stores them in the database files of the search engine.

The third part of the search engine is the search computer program. This program sifts through the millions of Web pages in the engine's index (database) in order to find matches to the search string that a Web surfer types in the search field of the search engine's user interface. The program also ranks the matched Web pages in the order it determine as is most relevant. Each Web pages in the set of matches is known as a **hit**. The search engine displays the hits as links. The Web surfer goes through the hits one by one, by clicking their links' to determine the useful ones. Of course, search engines do not always get it right. Sometimes, irrelevant Web pages are included in the results. But, almost always, search engines do a great job.

How do search engines rank their hits? They use, among other rules, one called the *title–frequency method*. According to this method, search engines first check the titles of the Web pages they have found, to see whether the search keywords appear in them. This approach is similar to searching a traditional library for books on a subject such as golf: Books that have the keyword *golf* in their titles are excellent candidates for the search. In the next step, search engines check to see whether the keywords appear, and with what frequency, in the first several paragraphs of Web pages. This step is based on the notion that any Web page relevant to the topic being searched should mention the keywords right from the start with great frequency. Search engines analyze how often keywords appear relative to other words in the page. A higher frequency quite often indicates higher relevancy. We should mention that the title–frequency method may not work all the time, as some search engines are paid to list certain websites early in the results set.

In light of the foregoing information, the reader may ask two questions. How come search engines do not always return good hits? And, why does the same search, using the same search string and keywords, produce different hits on different search engines? For the first question, search engines should not be the only factor to blame for the failure of a search. Other factors include how the authors of Web pages design their pages and (more importantly) how a surfer formulates a search. If the authors do not select the titles and the content of their pages carefully, search engines may miss them during a search. In addition, if the surfer is careless or vague in defining a search string, search engines will return irrelevant results.

The answer to the second question stems from the fact that each search engine uses its own features to search the Web, and uses the title-frequency method only to a degree. First, some search engines index more Web pages than other search engines and update their index more often. This condition leads to different search engines having different databases to search through. A search engine may also give preference to more popular and heavily visited Web pages over others that are less popular, or it may prefer Web pages reviewed by its own editors. There are many other features that search engines use to make themselves unique. Visit the website `http://www.searchenginewatch.com` for more detail.

7.5 Metasearch Engines

When it comes to building and developing search engines, there are two distinct approaches. The typical, straightforward approach is to develop an engine that searches the Internet. The other, approach, which is less obvious, but very interesting, is to build an engine that searches many other search engines at once for every search request—that is, performs a multiengine search. Search engines that use this latter approach are known as **metasearch engines**. A metasearch engine, therefore, expands an Internet search and makes it more convenient than using multiple search engines. If a search engine is down for some reason, the metasearch engine automatically skips searching it. Metasearch engines do not own a database of Web pages; they send search strings to the databases maintained by other search engines. Examples of metasearch engines include `http://www.dogpile.com`, `http://www.metacrawler.com`, and `http://www.profusion.com`.

7.6 Search Techniques

Most surfers can find satisfactory search results by conducting a basic search using any search engine. A **basic search** implies that a user types a search string in the search field of the search engine. However, most search engines provide users with options (search techniques) to refine searches in order to get better search results. Users can find these options under the `Advanced Search` link located somewhere on the Web page of the search engine.

Keep in mind the following general searching guidelines. Most search engines automatically first list Web pages that include all of your search words and then list Web pages that include only some of your search words. Search engines are case insensitive. Most of the time, a search yields undesirable results because the search string is ill formulated. Change the search string, by using different words. Lastly, search engines treat your search string as keywords, not as a complete sentence as you type it (even when you use the exact-phrase search; See Section 7.6.1). Thus, you may discard articles such as *a*, *in*, *the*, *for*, *to*, and so forth. For example, the search string `travel rome italy` is just as good as `travel to rome in italy`.

7.6.1   Word and Exact-Phrase Searches

These are the basic searches. Search engines provide various levels to which the search can be refined. For example, you can request the search engine to return Web pages that match *any* word in your search string (the widest, but least refined, search), *all* the words (more refined), or the *exact phrase* (most refined). The three levels of search refinements are usually available on the main Web page of the search engine or under its `Advanced Search` link.

When you use the exact-phrase search, you are requesting the search engine to return only the Web pages that match all the words of your search string, in the same order as you type them. You request the exact-phrase search by including the search string in quotation marks.

Usually, the exact-phrase search returns no results (null set), because the odds that a Web page has your exact phrase is very slim. For a successful search, we recommend starting with a search for *any* word. Then keep narrowing the search down via the all-words search and then the exact- phrase search.

Example 7.2 Perform a basic search.

Find information about golf sportswear and equipment.

Solution 7.2 Let us use the Google search engine. Open a browser window and type `http://www.google.com` into the URL bar. Type `golf sportswear and equipment` as the search string and either hit `Enter` or click the search button, Google Search . We can omit the word `and` from the search string. As a matter of fact, Google reminds you that `and` is unnecessary. Google returns thousands of hits. It performs a basic search using all of words in the search string. It bolds all the words that match words of your search string in its results. This is Google's default search technique.

Let us change the search by looking for any word from the search string. Click the `Advanced Search` link next to the search field where you type a search string. Then type `golf sportswear and equipment` in the third search field, as shown in Figure 7.1, and click the `Google Search` button.

As expected, Google returns millions of pages. Note that you must remove and from the search string, as shown in Figure 7.1; otherwise, Google return no hits at all.

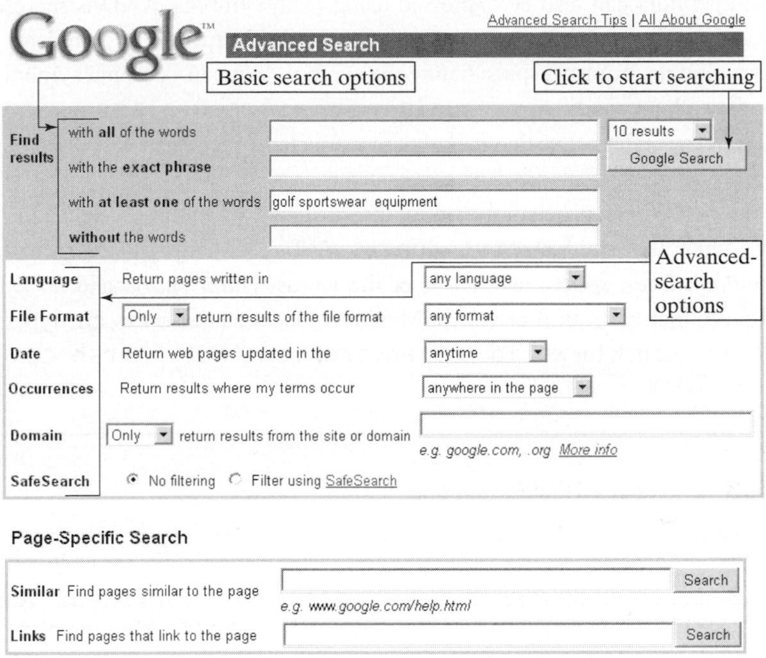

Figure 7.1 Any word Google search.

Let us row use the exact-phrase search. Type the search string shown in Figure 7.1 into the second search field shown in Figure 7.1, and click the search button. Alternatively, you can type `"golf sportswear and equipment"` (including the quotes) into Google's Web page. This search returns no hits.

7.6.2 Boolean Search

A Boolean (also known as math or symbol) search provides users with control over how a search engine uses the words of a search string. There are four operators: AND, OR, NOT, and NEAR. The AND operator requires that all search words be present in the search results, similar to the all-words search described in Section 7.6.1—e.g., *cats* AND *dogs*. The OR operator requires that at least one search word be present, similar to the any-words search described in Section 7.6.2— e.g., *cats* OR *dogs*. The NOT operator is a negation (exclusion) operator. For example, *dogs* AND *breed* NOT *food* returns Web pages that do NOT contain *food*, but contain both *dogs* and *breed*.The NEAR (proximity) operator is used to specify that words should appear close to each other—e.g., *cats* NEAR *dogs*. Search engines provide forms that users can use for simple Boolean searches.

Boolean operators can also be expressed using math symbols. AND is represented by the "+" symbol, and NOT is represented by the "-" symbol. There is no symbol for OR. Search engines such as Google require a space before the symbol. You can combine symbols in any way to control your search precisely — e.g., `world +cup +soccer -last -year`. This search string is used to return Web pages that include the words *world cup soccer*, but do not include the words *last year*.

Users can nest Boolean operators via the use of using parentheses, again for more search control. For example, the search `winter sports AND (skiing OR hockey)` returns Web pages that include *winter*, *sports*, and *skiing* or the words *winter sports* and *hockey*. It will not include Web pages that have all four words. Moreover, users can also mix the types of searches. For example, we can search for `world AND environment NOT "harsh conditions"`.

Example 7.3 Perform a Boolean search.

Use Boolean operators to search for Web pages on golf sportswear and equipment.

Solution 7.3 Let us use these search strings: `golf AND sportswear AND equipment` (same as `golf +sportswear +equipment`) and `golf AND sportswear NOT equipment` (same as `golf +sportswear -equipment`). The first search is expected to yield more hits than the second one, and it does. Use Google and' separately, type both search strings into its search field. Notice that the first search string is the same as using the all-words search `golf sportswear and equipment`. Both search strings produce the same number of hits. You can also use other variations of the search string. For example, try using a nested string like `golf AND (sportswear AND equipment)`.

7.6.3   Other Searches

There are other searches that search engines support to provide more control to their users. The **title search** allows users to search the titles of Web pages for more accurate results. A **page title** is the text that appears in the browser's title bar. If a Web page is designed properly, its title should be an accurate indication of its content, like a book title. The keyword to use to perform a title search depends on the search engine. Use `title:` for AltaVista, Inktomi, and Northern Light; `normal.title:` for AllTheWeb and Lycos; and `allintitle:` or `intitle:` for Google. For example, type `title:solar system` in the search field of the AltaVista search engine, in order to search for Web pages that have the words *solar system in the* title.

The **site search** limits the search to a particular website or host name. That is, the search returns only Web pages found in the specified website in the search. This is a useful feature if the search is to be specific. The host name can be full, in the form `aaa.bbb.ttt`, or a TLD, such as `edu`, `com`, `gov`. The keyword to use to perform a site search depends on the search engine. Use `host:` for AltaVista; `site:` for Excite, Google, and Yahoo!; `url.host:` for AllTheWeb; and `domain:` for Inktomi. For example, type `host:mars.jpl.nasa.gov` into the search field of the AltaVista search engine, in order to find Web pages about Mars that are published only by NASA's Jet Propulsion Laboratory, which is an authority on space programs. (Or type `site:mars.jpl.nasa.gov mars` into Google to find similar results. Google requires a search string after the host name.) In another example, we can search for Web pages about the solar system from U.S. educational institutions by using the search string, `"solar system" + host:edu`. Or we can search for soccer information from England by using `"football teams" + host:uk` as a search string.

The **URL search** offers the ability to search within the text of a URL for information. The keyword to use to perform a url search depends on the search engine. Use `url:` for AltaVista, Excite, and Northern Light; `allinurl:` or `inurl:` for Google; `originurl:` for Inktomi; and `u:` for Yahoo!. For example, type `"football clubs" + inurl:pdf` in the search field of Google in order to search for all URLs that have the word *pdf* in their text.

The **link search** offers the ability to search for all the Web pages linking to a particular Web page or domain. The keyword to use to perform a link search depends on the search engine. Use `link:` for AltaVista, Google, and Northern Light; `linkdomain:` for Inktomi; and `link.all:` for AllTheWeb. For example, type `link:www.google.com` into the search field of Google in order to find the Web pages that link to the Google website.

The **wildcard (*) search** (also known as the **fuzzy search**) is used to expand the search string, or if you do not remember or know the spelling of a word. Use `*` for AltaVista, Inktomi, and Northern Light. For example, type `plant*` into the search field of AltaVista in order to search for words such as *plants*, *plantation*, and so forth. Google does not support this type of search.

The **features search** can be used to filter the search results. Many features are offered by search engines, such as find similar, search with, search by language, porn filter and warning, limit the number of pages displayed, date range, and others. Google support all these features, as shown in Figure 7.1.

Example 7.4   Use refined search techniques.

Show the results of various search strategies in searches for specific information.

Solution 7.4   Let us use Google to perform a search on homeless shelters. Start the Google search engine by entering its URL, `http://www.google.com`, into the URL bar of a browser. Type the following search strings into Google's search field:

- title search: Type `intitle:homeless shelters`; returns hits with only these words in the title.
- site search: Type `"homeless shelters" + site:org`; returns hits with only the `.org` TLD.
- url search: Type `inurl:homeless shelters`; returns hits with one of these words in the URL.

- link search: Type `link:www.pinellascounty.org`; returns hits with links to this website.
- wild search: Type `home*` in AltaVista search field; returns hits containing words such as homes and homeland.
- feature search: Type `homeless shelters` and choose `past 3 months` as a feature.

7.7 Intelligent Agents

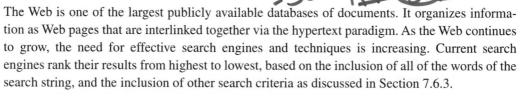

The Web is one of the largest publicly available databases of documents. It organizes information as Web pages that are interlinked together via the hypertext paradigm. As the Web continues to grow, the need for effective search engines and techniques is increasing. Current search engines rank their results from highest to lowest, based on the inclusion of all of the words of the search string, and the inclusion of other search criteria as discussed in Section 7.6.3.

The explosive growth of information is occurring not only on the Web, but also with online databases. These databases are getting larger as well. The searching of databases has different requirements from the searching of the Web. Obstacles facing users searching online databases include finding appropriate search strings, getting a large number of (or zero) hits, and search engines' lack of "understanding" of the types of files and the basic structure of databases.

Searching the Web and online databases is viewed as an information retrieval problem in computer science. Three retrieval paradigms exist: statistical, semantic, and contextual. The first paradigm emphasizes statistical correlations of word counts in documents and document collections. The semantic paradigm uses natural-language processing and artificial intelligence to process search requests. The third paradigm takes advantage of the structural and contextual inferences in documents by use of a thesaurus and encoded relationships among words.

Intelligent agents use the three foregoing retrieval paradigms and other algorithms to search for information. An **intelligent agent** (also known as bot, short for "robot") is a computer program that gathers information or performs services based on human input. The spiders (crawlers) that search engines use, as discussed in Section 7.4, are a form of intelligent agents. Search engines deploy these autonomous mobile and intelligent agents when they need to collect and search for information online.

While intelligent agents are currently deployed within search engines, they can also be launched alone. Users can employ intelligent agents instead of search engines. They can deploy them whenever they need to retrieve new information from the Web. Using intelligent agents when looking for information has advantages over using search engines:

- Intelligent agents can search more effectively via use of a thesaurus, and based on context.
- Intelligent agents can create their own knowledge base (database) and update it when needed.
- Intelligent agents can communicate and cooperate with other agents to perform tasks quicker.

- A user's intelligent agent resides on the user's computer and waits for service orders, day or night.
- A user can customize intelligent agents and adjust them to fit their preferences and wishes.
- Intelligent agents are able to continuously scan the Internet for information.

7.8 Invisible Web   *13 (15)*

As we have discussed in Section 7.7, Web content takes the form of Web pages and online databases. This content is "visible" to us via our personal knowledge of Web pages or databases or via the use of search engines. As search engines cannot find every bit of content, we are bound to miss some content. The **Visible Web** is what we see in the search results from search engines, or the subject directories. The **Invisible Web** (also known as the **Deep Web**) is the hidden Web content. The Invisible Web includes the Web pages and databases that are excluded from search engines results by policy or because spiders cannot access them. The size of the Invisible Web is estimated to be an order of magnitude bigger the Visible Web.

Some search engines exclude some Web pages from their searches because the format of these pages becomes problematic for their spiders. Search engines are optimized for XHTML format. Other types of programming language contain codes and formats that are incompatible with XHTML. Moreover, pages formatted in, for example, PDF, Microsoft Word, and PowerPoint use no XHTML at all; others use little, if any, XHTML text. Some search engines, such as Google, have solved this formatting problem.

Search engines cannot index information that is locked within specialized databases, again because their spiders cannot actually type or think. Spiders find Web pages by following links on other Web pages. Specialized databases, such as library catalogs, that do not require a password are thus invisible.

There are techniques for searching the Invisible Web. Much of the invisible material and content is hidden in directories and databases. The techniques are described as follows:

- **Directories.** Some websites provide Invisible Web catalogs. An **Invisible Webcatalog** is a directory that includes content which will be missed by search engines. The Yahoo! directory is the best example. Other websites have directories as Invisible Web catalogs, such as Lycos.
- **Databases** Invisible databases allow users to search for invisible content. Lycos has an invisible database at `http://dir.lycos.com/reference`. Others include Direct Search (`http://www.freepint.com/gary/direct.htm`), the Invisible Web Catalog (`http://www.invisibleweb.com`), the CompletePlanet (`http://www.completeplanet.com`), Internet (`http://www.internet.com`), and IncyWincy (`http://incywincy.com`). (See the forthcoming screen captures.)
- **Search engines.** Two of the search engines listed in Section 7.4 that can search the Invisible Web are Google and AllTheWeb.

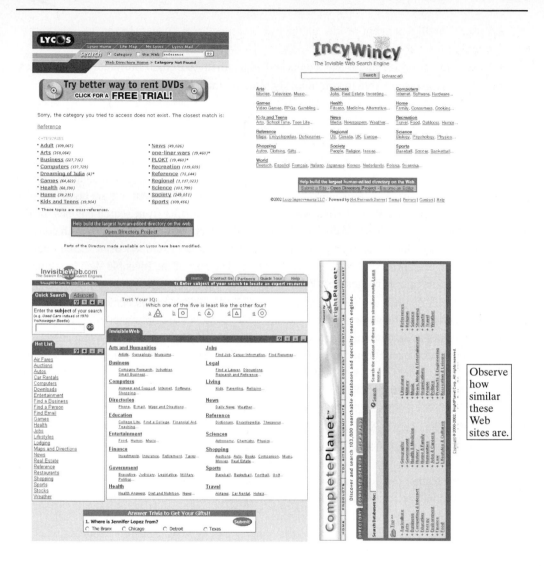

Example 7.5 Search the Invisible Web.

Learn how to use Lycos to search its database for trademarks.

Solution 7.5 Enter `http://dir.lycos.com/reference` into the URL bar in a Web browser window. Type `trademarks` as the search string in its search field. Observe that the search results are links that look like a path or a directory. If you click any of these links, you uncover many other links, as shown in the following screen capture:

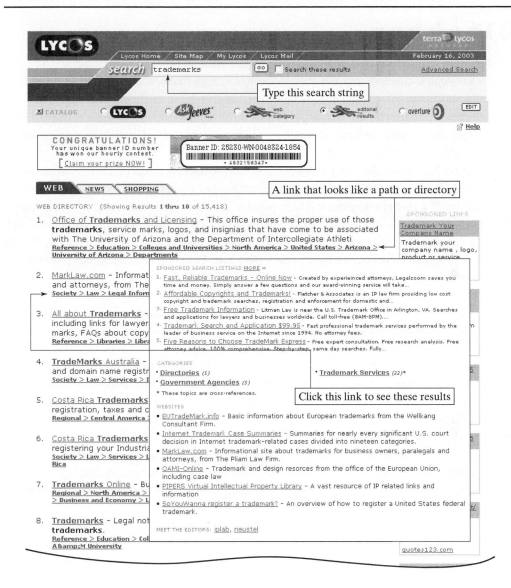

FAQs

Search Techniques (Section 7.6)

Q: When should I use the NEAR Boolean operator?

A: There is no real need to control proximity within your searches. Most search engines try to find words of your search strings within close proximity to each other by default. Exact-phrase searching is what most people need.

Blackbox

Section 7.1 (Introduction): Search the Internet via directories or search engines. The difference between a directory and a search engine lies in how the database of each is created. To perform a successful search, you need to know what to search for and how to search for it.

Section 7.2 (Directories) (Example 7.1): A directory provides a hierarchical tree for each subject. You can search a directory manually or via its search engine. Use the latter approach, as it is faster and more comprehensive.

Section 7.3 (Open Directory Project): The Open Directory Project aims to provide useful search results to users of directories. It relies on the expertise of users to rank the results of a search.

Section 7.4 (Search Engines): Three popular search engines are `http://www.google.com`, `http://alltheweb.com`, and `http://www.yahoo.com`. Feed a search engine a search string. A search engine has three parts: spider, indexer, and searcher. Search engines use the title-frequency method to rank their hits. Different search engines produce different results for the same search.

Section 7.5 (Metasearch Engines): Metasearch engines use other engines to perform a search. Examples are `http://www.dogpile.com`, `http://www.metacrawler.com`, and `http://www.profusion.com`.

Section 7.6 (Search Techniques) (Examples 7.2–7.4): Use the following techniques to search the Internet: words (`homeless shelters`), exact phrase (`"homeless shelters"`), Boolean search (`homeless +shelters`), title search (`title:homeless shelters`), site search (`"homeless shelters" + site:org`), URL search (`link:www.nasa.org`), wildcard (*) search (`home*`), and features search (by dates, language, and others). The Boolean operators are AND (+), OR, NOT (–), and NEAR.

Section 7.7 (Intelligent Agents): The explosive growth of online information and databases requires efficient searching and retrieval techniques such as the use of intelligent agents. These agents use three searching paradigms: statistical, semantic, and contextual. Users may use intelligent agents instead of search engines to search the Internet.

Section 7.8 (Invisible Web) (Example 7.5): The Invisible Web is much larger than the Visible Web. Use directories, databases, and search engines to search the Invisible Web. Some websites that specialize in searching the Invisible Web are Lycos (`http://dir.lycos.com/reference`), Direct Search (`http://www.freepint.com/gary/direct.htm`), the Invisible Web Catalog (`http://www.invisibleweb.com`), the CompletePlanet (`http://www.completeplanet.com`), Internet (`http://www.internet.com`), and IncyWincy (`http://incywincy.com`).

Quick reference for using search techniques in Google (Section 7.4):

1. **One or all words (Example 7.2):** Type the search string into the search field.
2. **Exact phrase (Example 7.2):** Include search phrase in quotes.

3. **Boolean search (Example 7.3)**: Use AND (+), OR, NOT (–), and NEAR.
4. **Title search (Example 7.4):** Type, for example, `inline:homeless shelters`.
5. **Site search (Example 7.4):** Type, for example, `"homeless shelters" + site:org`.
6. **URL search (Example 7.4):** Type, for example, `inurl:homeless shelters`.
7. **Link search (Example 7.4):** Type, for example, type `link:www.pinellascounty.org`.
8. **Wildcard (*) search (Example 7.4):** Not supported.
9. **Feature search (Example 7.4):** Click the `Advanced Search` link => Select a feature.

Check Your Progress

At the end of this chapter, you should

- ✔ understand directories and search engines (Sections 7.1 and 7.2);
- ✔ understand the Open Directory Project (Section 7.3);
- ✔ know how search and metasearch engines work (Sections 7.4 and 7.5);
- ✔ have mastered the various search techniques (Section 7.6);
- ✔ be able to use intelligent agents to search the Internet (Section 7.7);
- ✔ understand and be able to search the Invisible Web (Section 7.8).

Problems

The exercises are designed for a lab setting, while the homework is to be done outside class time.

Exercises

7.1 Use the Yahoo! directory to search for the movie *Gone with the Wind*. Perform a manual search and a directory search-engine search.

7.2 Use any-words, all-words, and exact-phrase to search for the phrase *two door sedan cars*. Compare the numbers of search hits and explain them.

7.3 Run a title search on national security.

7.4 Run a site search on affirmative action.

7.5 Run a URL search on stem-cell research.

Homework

7.6 Use the Yahoo! directory to search for articles on the history of the Civil War. Perform a manual search and a directory search engine search

7.7 Use any-word, all-words, and exact-phrase searches to search for the phrase *dog breed and food*. Compare the number of search hits and explain them.

7.8 Run a Boolean search on overmedication of children.

7.9 Run wildcard search on compensation for war*.

7.10 Run a search to find new developments on sports medicine during the last three months.

FTP and Telnet

Goal

Understand and master electronic file transfer to alleviate the use of media such as floppy disks, zip disks, and CDs, and understand remote login to computer accounts.

Objectives

- Internet downloads
- File types
- FTP
- Telnet

Outline

227

8.1 Introduction

One of the best tools that the Internet offers is electronic file transfer from one computer to another. This transfer requires both computers to be networked, and permissions must be granted to users to transfer files. Internet users download files all the time from Web servers to their local computers. These Internet downloads allow users to transfer files simply by clicking some links.

File transfer across the Internet is very useful in syncing different computers, similar to syncing handheld devices. For example, many of us have files in different locations, primarily at home and at work. It can be confusing at times to remember which location has the latest version of a file. File transfer can solve this problem; after changing a file in one location, the user transfers it across the Internet to the other location.

File transfer can come very handy in many cases. Let us assume that you worked on a file at home and planned to take it to work the next morning. You go to work only to discover that you forgot to bring the files on a floppy disk, zip disk, or CD. If your home computer is accessible via a network, you can access the file from your office and download it. Alternatively, even if you have the file with you on a floppy disk, the floppy disk could get corrupted causing you to be unable to open the file. Here also, you can download it from the home computer instead.

8.2 File Types

We have covered different issues related to files throughout the book thus far. Section 1.11 covered the different file protocols required to exchange files across the Internet. Section 1.12 discussed compressed, or zipped, files and decompression, or unzipping. It also described self-extracting and non-self-extracting files. Section 1.16 covered the two common types of Internet downloads: shareware and freeware. Chapter 2 discussed PDF files and how useful they are.

We extend the previously discussed background about files here. Each file has a type. A **file type** is designated by the extension at the end of the file name. For example, the file `abc.doc` has the name `abc` and the extension `.doc`. The name and extension are separated by a period. File extensions are used by operating systems to launch the appropriate application (program) to open (read) a file when a user clicks a link to it. For example, `abc.doc` can be opened with Word.

OSs such as Windows come with built-in associations of file types and applications. For example, `.txt`, `.ppt`, `.xls`, and `.bmp` files are opened with Notepad, PowerPoint, Excel, and Paint, respectively. If the user clicks a file that has a new type, the OS asks the user to select an application with which to open the file. The user may also change the default associations that an OS offers. For example, a user may associate the `.txt` extension with another text editor instead of the Notepad editor.

Example 8.1 Associate a file type with an application.

Learn how to select a program with which to open a file.

Solution 8.1 We use Windows XP as the OS in this example. Let us create a new file extension, **.myext**, and associate it with the TextPad editor. Double-click My Computer. Then click this sequence: Tools (menu on the My Computer window menu bar) => Folder Options (from the menu that pops up) => File Types (❶ in the forthcoming screen captures) => New (❷; to open the Create New Extension window shown in the screen captures) => Type myext (❸) in the Create New Extension window => OK (❹). So far, we have created the new extension .myext. To associate TextPad with it, click Advanced (❺; to open the Edit File Type window) =>Type the file description (❻) => New (❼; to open the New Action window) => Type open (❽) => Browse (❾; to find the executable program) => OK (❿; twice) => Close (⓫).

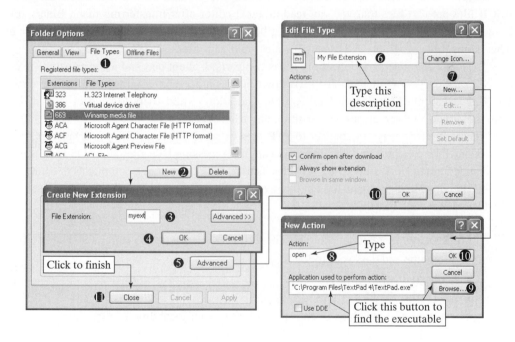

Example 8.2 Show and hide file extensions.

learn how to show and hide file extensions.

Solution 8.2 We use Windows XP as the OS in this example. When you view files in Windows Explorer, file extensions may be hidden. To display them, follow this procedure; Double-click My Computer. Then click this sequence: Tools (menu on the My Computer window menu bar) => Folder Options (from the menu that pops up) => View (tab on the Folder Options window that opens up and is shown in the leftmost foregoing screen capture) => Deselect (uncheck) the ☑ Hide extensions for known file types checkbox => Apply => OK. The default status of this checkbox is on, thus preventing the viewing of file extensions.

8.3 FTP

We have covered different issues related to FTP (File Transfer Protocol) throughout the book thus far. Section 1.2 discussed file downloading and uploading as an Internet activity. Section 1.11 covered FTP as a file protocol. Section 1.12 discussed the need to compress, or zip, files before transferring them in order to reduce their size and consequently to increase the transfer speed and reduce the transfer time. Section 2.3 covered file downloading as one of the essential tasks of browsers.

We extend the previous background about FTP here. **FTP** enables electronic file transfer across networks. FTP lets you download (upload) a copy of a file from (to) a remote host to (from) your local computer. FTP can transfer two types of files: ASCII files and binary files. ASCII files are text files that you can read in a text editor after transferring them. Binary files cannot be opened in a text editor. They must be read by the programs that created them or by other, compatible programs. All executable files are binary files.

FTP is a client/server application. It has two parts: a client part and a server part. The client part runs on your computer. The server part runs as a daemon program on a remote server. The FTP daemon acknowledges FTP requests and allows valid users to send or receive files from the server. FTP servers are set up differently from Web servers.

There are four ways to connect to FTP sites or servers: via an OS, via a browser, via a stand-alone FTP program, and via other applications. Accessing FTP sites at the OS level is popular mainly among Unix users. Unix provides its users with a set of line commands to connect to an FTP site, download files, and log out. For example, the sequence of actions required to access an FTP site may look like this:

`ftp xxx.yyy.zz` (connect to host or server `xxx.yyy.zz` to start an FTP session)
type username and password to log in
`cd sss` (go to subdirectory `sss`)
`ls` or `dir` (list the files in `sss`)
`get myFile1` (download or copy `myFile1` to your local drive)
`put myFile2` (send `myFile2` to host or server `xxx.yyy.zz`)
`quit` (or `bye`) (end the FTP session)

The foregoing terms indicate FTP commands. There are a lot of FTP commands. You can enter `help` or `?` at the `ftp>` command prompt. (When you FTP to a site or a host, you get the `ftp>` prompt.) This command will show you a list of all the available FTP commands. You can then ask for help on a particular one by typing, for example, `help get`, where `get` is the command. If you are a Unix user, type the Unix command `man ftp` for online help.

If these line commands seem displeasing because you are used to graphical user interfaces (GUIs), than you can use a browser to establish an FTP connection to an FTP server by clicking a link to a downloadable file on a Web page. When you click the link, the browser will ask for file name and a folder to save it to. After our input, it downloads the file.

The third method of using FTP is via GUI-based stand-alone FTP programs. You download and install an FTP client on your computer. The client connects to and communicates with an FTP server. The client provides all that you need in order to download and upload files. Some websites have an FTP site that you can access by replacing www with ftp in the site's URL—for example, ftp://ftp.microsoft.com. Also, you must use the FTP, not HTTP, protocol to access the FTP site. You need to be aware of the directory structure of the FTP site you connect to so that you can find the software you need to download.

The fourth method of using FTP is through applications. For example, Dreamweaver allows its users to connect to a Web server via FTP to upload Web pages to the server. These applications hide the FTP procedure and commands from its users.

Two kinds of FTP sites exist. An **anonymous FTP site** is a public site that requires a generic login (the same username, such as anonymous, and password, such as anonymous, for everyone). An **unanonymous FTP site** requires a specific login. FTP sites from which we download shareware and freeware are anonymous sites. Anonymous FTP acts as the underpinning to free the exchange of information on the Internet, because it makes files available to anyone who wants them. Notice in the foregoing set of line commands that you needed a username and a password in order to connect to the host. In anonymous FTP, you use the word anonymous for the username. The password could be guest, your e-mail address, any password, or no password. The FTP host will tell you which username and password to use.

Many FTP servers, particularly those for anonymous FTP, store files in compressed formats. An important fact about compressed files, in addition to their small sizes, is that they can contain multiple files. It is always a good idea to unpack a compressed file in a new directory. Unpacking (unzipping) compressed files requires special programs. The Unix programs for compressing and decompressing files are uuencode and uudecode, respectively. Other programs are gzip, gunzip, zip, and unzip. For Windows, the program WinZip does both compressing and uncompressing, with .zip as the file type (extension).

Example 8.3 Use command-line FTP.

Learn how to use FTP commands in an OS window.

Solution 8.3 We use Windows XP as the OS in this example. Let us assume that you have an FTP account on the ftp.coe.neu.edu server. Start a command (DOS) window; then click a DOS shortcut, or click Start (Windows menu) => Run => cmd => OK). To connect to the server, type ftp ftp.coe.neu.edu at the command line in the DOS window and hit Enter. See the forthcoming screen capture. You can also use the IP address to connect. Input the username and password to log in. At this point, you are connected to your account. The system prompt changes to ftp> to indicate the FTP mode. You can use either OS or FTP commands. For example, if you type dir and hit Enter, you get a list of the files in the current directory of your account. Type help or ? to list the FTP commands. You should recognize all the commands that we listed earlier under the OS FTP method—in particular, the get and put commands. Type quit or bye to end the FTP session.

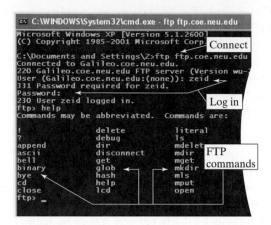

Example 8.4 Use browser FTP.

Learn how to use anonymous FTP in a browser window.

Solution 8.4 Let us download the Netscape 4.8 software from Netscape FTP site. Start a browser and enter: `ftp://ftp.netscape.com` in the browser's URL bar. The folders shown in the upcoming screen capture are displayed. You can navigate your way through the folders. The path is `pub/communicator/english/4.8`. Eventually, you should see the Netscape executable, ⬜ . Double-click it and follow the prompts to download the software. The browser asks you for a file name and a destination.

cc32d48.exe

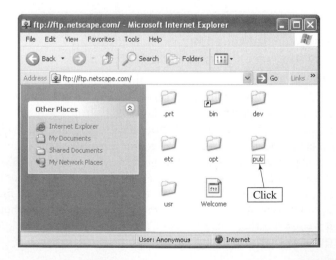

Example 8.5 Use standalone FTP.

Learn how to use a stand-alone FTP program.

Solution 8.5   You need to download and install an FTP client on your computer. You can search the Internet for one. The one we use here is WS_FTP. You can use the client to connect to anonymous and unanonymous FTP sites. Let us redo Example 8.3 here. Start the WS_FTP program via Windows `Start` menu or by double-clicking its shortcut on the desktop. Type the FTP server's name and the login information as shown in the upcoming topmost screen capture. Once you have done this, the program window shows the local system (your computer) on the left and the remote system (the FTP server with your account) on the right. (See the upcoming bottommost screen capture.) Navigate your way to the proper folders on each system as you would normally do

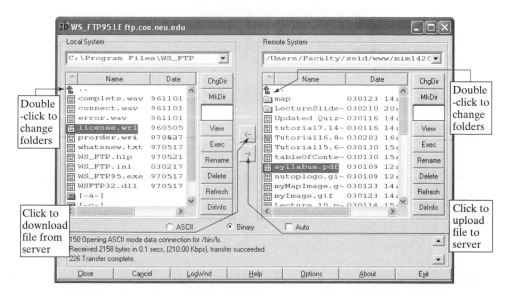

on your computer. To download a file from the server to your computer, select the file in the remote window and click the arrow pointing towards the local system. To upload a file, select it in the local window and click the arrow pointing to the server window. Make sure you select the right folder in both cases before clicking the arrows. One last note: You can use both ASCII and binary transfer. Do not worry about designating which type of transfer you require. The program chooses it for you.

8.4 Telnet

FTP provides a way to obtain files. **Telnet**, on the other hand, provides a way to access computing services from remote hosts or servers. Telnet allows you to log into a remote computer and use it. You must be a valid user and have an account on that computer. When you telnet to a host from a remote location, you are promoted for your username and password. Once logged in, you can use your account to check e-mail, run programs, save files, and so forth.

Telnet is a client/server application. You must run a client program on your local computer in order to start a Telnet session and communicate with a Telnet server. Telnet programs can come bundled with OSs or can be stand-alone. Windows, for example, has a built-in Telnet program. Some stand-alone programs also provide Telnet support.

Multistage Telnet is sometimes useful. Here, you telnet from one host to another and then from that host to yet another, to make connections that otherwise would be impossible. For example, you may be able to connect to one host only via another host, or you may have to connect to a host in order to get access to high-speed modems.

Multisession Telnet happens when you use multiple copies of the Telnet program to access more than one remote host simultaneously. This is different from multistage Telnet. Multisession Telnet is like doing multiple tasks at the same time—for example, telnet to a library to run a search and, while the search is in progress, start another Telnet session to the National Weather Center to check the weather. You can switch back and forth between the sessions.

Anonymous Telnet is available, although it is not as popular as anonymous FTP. Some Internet hosts will let you log in to use Telnet without requiring you to have an individual account.

Telnet requires a set of commands to start, manage, and end sessions. Once you are logged into an account, use the system-level commands to deal with files, or use applications commands to run applications. For example, you can telnet from home to compile a computer program on your computer at school that you forgot to bring home for the weekend.

Example 8.6 Use OS Telnet.

Learn how to use OS Telnet.

Solution 8.6 We use Windows XP as the OS in this example. Let us assume that you have an account on the `gateway.coe.neu.edu` computer, which is running a Telnet server. Start a command (DOS) window. Then click a DOS shortcut, or click `Start` (Windows menu) =>

Run => `telnet` => OK. Type `help` or ? to view the Telnet commands that you can use. To connect to the computer, type `o gateway.coe.neu.edu` at the command line. (See the following screen capture.) You can also use the IP address to connect.

After a Telnet connection is established, log in by typing your username and password. You can now execute any commands remotely, exactly as if you were sitting in the room where the Telnet server computer is. In this example, we are using a computer running Windows to connect to a workstation running Unix. Thus, at the DOS window, we use Unix commands, such as `ls` to list files of current directory (similar to `dir` in DOS) and `pwd` to print the working directory (similar to `path` in DOS). When done, type `q` to close (quit) the Telnet session. The following screen capture shows the commands in use.

8.5   Tutorials

8.5.1   Use FTP and Telnet Sessions Together
(Study Sections 8.3 and 8.4)

This tutorial shows a useful application of both FTP and Telnet sessions together. On the client side (local computer) we use Windows OS, and on the server side (remote computer) we use

Unix OS. We need to create a new directory called `testDir`, on the Unix computer, upload a file called `myFile.txt` from the local computer to it, and list the contents of the `testDir` directory to make sure that the file transfer was successful. The following screen captures show both the Telnet and FTP sessions. Do as follows to use both sessions together:

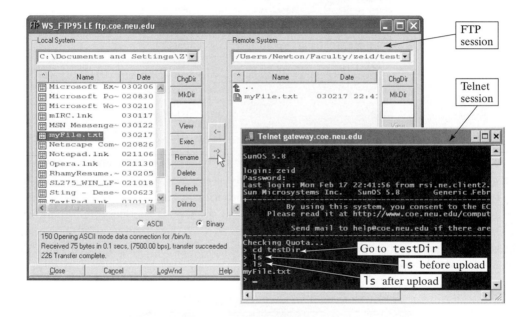

1. **Start a Telnet session on the Windows computer.** Click `Start` (Windows button) => `Run` => `telnet` => `OK`. Type `o gateway.coe.neu.edu` in the DOS window that shows up.
2. **Log into the Unix computer remotely.** Type your username and password.
3. **Create the directory.** Use the Unix command `mkdir testDir`.
4. **Go to this directory.** Use the command `cd testDir`.
5. **List the contents of `testDir`.** Use the command `ls`. Nothing should be there.
6. **Start an FTP session on the Windows computer.** Use a stand-alone FTP program. Log in.
7. **Upload the file `myFile.txt` to the `testDir` directory.** Select it in the FTP local-system window, and click the arrow pointing to the remote-system window. Make sure that the `testDir` is selected in the remote-system window.
8. **Check the contents of `testDir`.** Type `ls` in the Telnet session DOS window. `myFile.txt` should be there, as the prior Telnet screen capture shows.
9. **Close both sessions.** Type `logout` to close Telnet; click `Close` to close FTP WS_FP.

FAQs

File Types (Section 8.2)

Q: How can I convert one file type to another?

A: There are a number of tools. The easiest and quickest way is to find the file formats supported by the program that created the file in the first place. Click `File` (menu on the program's menu bar) => `Save As` or `Export` => Look at the formats the program supports. Choose the desired format and click save.

Q: What file types are returned in a Google search?

A: PDF, XHTML, Lotus, MACWrite, Excel, PowerPoint, Word, and text.

Q: What are the most popular non-XHTML format files on the Web?

A: PDF files are the most popular after XHMTL files. PostScript and Word files are also fairly common. The other file types are relatively uncommon by comparison.

Q: How do I exclude a file type, such as PDF, from an Internet search?

A: If you use the Google search engine, use `-filetype:pdf` in the search string.

Blackbox

Sections 8.1 (Introduction): Electronic file transfer is convenient. It can alleviate many of the annoying problems related to keeping files at home and at work in sync.

Section 8.2 (File Types) (Examples 8.1 and 8.2): A file type is known by its extension. Some extensions are `.txt`, `.ppt`, `.xls.`, and `.bmp` for Notepad, PowerPoint, Excel, and Paint files, respectively.

Section 8.3 (FTP) (Examples 8.3–8.5): FTP enables file downloading and uploading. There are anonymous and unanonymous FTP sites. Four modes exist for FTP use: OS command-line mode, browser mode, stand-alone mode, and applications mode. We recommend the stand-alone mode. You need to download and install an FTP client in order to use the stand-alone mode.

Section 8.4 (Telnet) (Example 8.6): Telnet allows a user with a computer account to log in remotely to that computer from another computer networked to the first one. Telnet is a client/server application. Client Telnet programs can come bundled with OSs or can be stand-alone. Windows, for example, has a built-in Telnet program.

Section 8.5 (Tutorials): One tutorial shows how to use FTP and Telnet sessions to upload a file into a new directory and confirm that the file transfer occurred.

Quick Reference for File Types (Section 8.2):

1. **Create and associate a file type with a program (Example 8.1):** Follow this sequence for Windows XP: Double-click `My Computer`. Then click `Tools` (menu on the `My Computer` window menu bar) => `Folder Options` (from the menu that pops up) => `File Types` (tab on the `Folder Options` window that opens up) => `New` =>

Type the file extension in the window that opens up => OK => Advanced => Type the file description => New => Type open for action => Browse (to select a program from the Open With window) => OK => OK => Close.

2. **Show and hide file extensions (Example 8.2):** To display the file extensions, follow this procedure for Windows XP: Double-click My Computer. Then click this sequence: Tools (menu on the My Computer window menu bar) => Folder Options (from the menu that pops up) => View (tab on the Folder Options window that opens up) => deselect (uncheck) the ☑ Hide extensions for known file types checkbox ......pply => OK. The default status of this checkbox is on, thus preventing the viewing of file extensions.

Check Your Progress

At the end of this chapter, you should

✔   understand the syncing of files (Section 8.1);
✔   understand the concepts of file types and extensions (Section 8.2);
✔   know how to use FTP (Section 8.3);
✔   have mastered the use of Telnet (Section 8.4).

Problems

The exercises are designed for a lab setting, while the homework is to be done outside class time.

Exercises

8.1   Create a new file type mydb and associate it with the Notepad program.
8.2   Show the file extensions in Windows XP.
8.3   Use a stand-alone FTP program to download a file.
8.4   Use a stand-alone FTP program to upload a file.
8.5   Use Telnet to check your computer account from the lab computer.

Homework

8.6   Create a new file type mypic and associate it with the Paint program.
8.7   Hide file extensions in Windows XP.
8.8   Use a stand-alone FTP program to a file from the remote system (computer).
8.9   Use a stand-alone FTP program to rename a file that resides on the remote system (computer).
8.10 Use FTP to upload a file from home to your computer account at work or school. Log into that account using Telnet, and check that the file got transferred successfully.

PART 11

XHTML

This part covers Webpage design, development, and coding. It presents the major design concepts of websites and pages. It also covers XHTML 1.1 in detail. It presents the major XHTML concepts that are needed to write Web pages, covering the 13 elements of XHTML: text, lists, hyperlinks, color, graphics, images, image maps, sound, video, tables, layers, frames, and forms. The goal of this part is to provide a solid and clear understanding of Web page design and XHTML syntax. To achieve this goal, this part stipulates the following objectives:

1. Understand and master the two main concepts of XHTML: markup and hyperlinks, text formatting, creating links, and the use of the AceHTML editor **(Chapter 9)**.
2. Understand and master Web-page design **(Chapter 10)**.
3. Understand and master images and image maps **(Chapter 11)**.
4. Understand and master tables and their use to format Web pages **(Chapter 12)**.
5. Understand and master layers and their use to format Web pages **(Chapter 13)**.
6. Understand and master frames to control the navigation of Web pages **(Chapter 14)**.
7. Understand and master forms and their elements **(Chapter 15)**.
8. Understand and master cascading style sheets (CSS), know why we use them, and comprehend the three levels: CSS1, CSS2, and CSS3 **(Chapter 16)**.
9. Understand and master the use of the three major HTML editors: AceHTML, Microsoft FrontPage, and Netscape Composer **(Chapter 17)**.
10. Understand and master server-side scripting and the use of two servers: Apache HTTP server and Apache Tomcat **(Chapter 18)**.

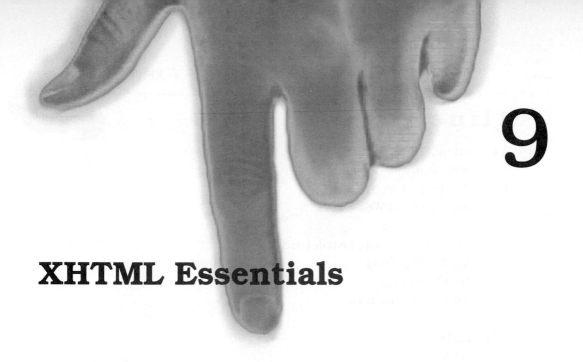

XHTML Essentials

Goal

Understand the difference between HTML and XHTML, master the authoring of Web pages with such content as hyperlinks, and use text and HTML editors to generate XHTML code.

Objectives

- Three views of Web pages: URL, browser display, and document
- Websites and Web pages
- Text formatting: text, lists, colors, hyperlinks, audio, and video
- HTML and XHTML
- Text and HTML editors
- XHTML document structure
- Content of Web pages
- Special characters

Outline

9.1   Introduction

When surfers browse the Web, they are accessing and reading Web pages and other pages that are linked to them. A surfer views a Web page as a URL and a display in a browser. A Web developer views the Web page as a document (file) that must be created according to authoring and development guidelines. A **Web developer** is the person who writes the code for a Web page. Web developers use HTML (HyperText Markup Language) or XHTML (eXtensible HTML) as the authoring language to write the code of the Web page that they save in the page file. Web developers must learn the syntax of the language in which they are writing. The **syntax** is the set of rules or the grammar of writing code. Part II of this book, starting with this chapter, covers all the XHTML syntax.

Web browsers render the HTML file and display its content. A browser has a built-in HTML-rendering engine or an interpreter that reads HTML code and converts it to the visual display in its window. An **interpreter** (**parser**) is a computer program that understands the syntax of the authoring language, executes it, and outputs the results to the browser window.

9.2   Websites and Web Pages

Authors and designers of Web pages generally, keep the pages short in order to avoid content clutter. More often than not, multiple Web pages are needed to provide all the intended content to Web surfers. The collection of these Web pages is known as a **website**. Websites have many

Web pages linked together. How can a Web authors organize the structure and hierarchy of Web pages? Web authors can devise elegant, sophisticated, well-planned structures, but the most natural one is the web structure. A **web structure** suggests that a Web author begins with a home page that includes hyperlinks to other Web pages, which in turn may include other hyperlinks. Some of the hyperlinks may even point back to the home page, if needed. Thus, all the Web pages form a web that begins at the home page. The web structure is not at all restrictive. Web authors can, in the future, add hyperlinks to new Web pages in their existing ones as the need occurs, thereby increasing the size of their webs.

In designing web structures, Web authors may first draw the design on a piece of paper, as shown in Figure 9.1. Each arrow connecting two Web pages represents a hyperlink. The Web page that is at the arrow's tail has the hyperlink in it, while the arrow's head points to the page that is loaded if the hyperlink is clicked by a Web surfer. The **home (index) page** of a website is the first Web page that is loaded when a surfer visits the site. The file name of the page is usually `index.html`.

As Figure 9.1 suggests, it is quite natural and easy to edit and change the web structure. If a Web page becomes obsolete, the corresponding links to it are deleted from all other Web pages that point to it. If a new Web page is added to the web, links are added in the same way. Web authors can add (or delete) hyperlinks in Web pages by editing the corresponding HTML files, using an editor. Moreover, if the website grows out of control, changing its structure could be as simple as shuffling and restructuring its Web pages. For example, Web authors may merge Web pages together and consolidate their content.

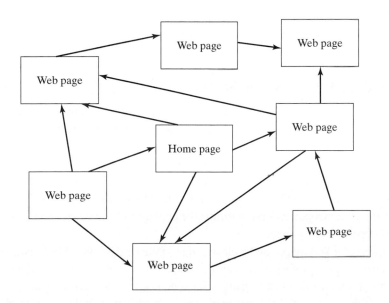

Figure 9.1   The structure of a website.

Example 9.1 Analyze an existing website.

Visit the Northeastern University website at `http://www.neu.edu`, and reverse engineer the site design.

Solution 9.1 The screen capture below shows the Northeastern University website. The URL of its home page is `http://www.neu.edu`. It has a large number of additional pages that are accessible via the hyperlinks shown on the home page. Click any hyperlink.

9.3   Content of Web Pages

As diverse and different as Web pages look at first glance, their contents are assembled from a basic set of elements. Any Web page may contain a combination of 13 standard elements. These elements are text, lists, hyperlinks, color, graphics, images, image maps, sound, video, tables, layers, frames, and forms. We cover all these elements in this book. The designer of a Web page chooses the right combination of elements to build the most attractive and appealing page that will entice Web surfers to want to come back and visit the website frequently. XHTML enables Web authors (programmers or coders) to format the content of Web pages, much like formatting text in a word-processor document.

The content of a Web page can be classified as static or dynamic. **Static content** does not change regularly. Some professional and personal Web pages have this type of content. **Dynamic content**, on the other hand, changes at a much faster rate than static content. Examples include websites that deal with bank accounts, airline bookings, weather reports, stock quotes, news, and traffic reports. Those websites must provide dynamic content in their Web pages in order to accommodate their customers' requests. Web pages that have dynamic content always have static content as well.

The content of Web pages must be updated to stay current. Even the static content needs to be updated over time. Static content is usually updated manually, while dynamic content is updated automatically every time the content changes or a visitor to the Web page makes a new request. Consider, for example, the Web page of a search engine. After a new search, the page updates its content to display its search results. The automatic generation and display of dynamic content is beyond the scope of this book.

Example 9.2 Display static and dynamic content of a Web page.

See an example of a Web page that has both static and dynamic content.

Solution 9.2 The Northeastern University Web page shown in the screen capture of Example 9.1 is an example of a Web page that has both static and dynamic content. Type `http://www.neu.edu` in the URL bar of the browser window. Observe the page's content. Reload the page by clicking the refresh button of the IE browser, ⟳ , or the reload button of Netscape, ⟳ Reload . The image in the middle of the page is the dynamic content. It changes each time you reload the page or refresh the browser window. The Web authors of the page use a random-number generator to pick an image from a large library of images. Each time the page is loaded, the number changes, and so does the image. The content around the image is the static content of the Web page.

9.4   Authoring of Web Pages

Assuming that our Web page's design has been completed, we need to write (author) the HTML code that converts the design into a Web page (HTML document) that can be viewed within a browser. HTML is a descriptive markup language that describes, in a simple way, the formatting of the content of Web pages. It uses special code, known as tags, that instructs Web browsers as to how to display the page's content. This feature allows designers and authors of Web pages to concentrate more on content and structure and less on formatting and presentation.

HTML has evolved over time. It is a subset of Standard Generalized Markup Language (SGML). HTML is defined by Document Type Definition (DTD) within SGML. SGML was developed in the 1960s by IBM to solve the problems of exchanging documents across multiple hardware platforms. Thus, HTML is platform independent and easy to use. That factor contributes to its popularity.

HTML has gone through some revisions, ending with version 4.01, which was released in 1999. The growth and popularity of the Web has far exceeded the limits of HTML and its original intent. This factor forced many developers, especially the browser software companies such as Microsoft and Netscape, to add many extensions to HTML that made it difficult to mange it as a standard. As a result, a new standard known as XML (eXtensible Markup Language) has evolved. One of the goals of XML is to enhance HTML, not replace it. Thus, in early 2000,

HTML 4.01 was modified to conform to the XML syntax standards. The outcome is the XHTML 1.0 standard. HTML has been frozen since then. Any new developments will occur to XHTML. Quite often, we use the terms HTML and XHTML interchangeably.

In 2001, the XHTML 1.1 standard was released. This latest standard eliminates all the legacy and deprecated (see the next section) functionality of HTML 4.01 that was brought forward into XHTML 1.0 in order to ease the transition from HTML to XHTML. All the examples in this book are XHTML 1.1 compliant.

There are fundamental differences between XML and HTML. XML is a metalanguage; that is, it is used to create other languages. XHTML is one of those languages. XML utilizes the concepts of elements and tags, while HTML uses only tags. XML is a data-representation scheme, while HTML is a presentation and formatting language. XHTML and HTML are the same for all practical purposes, except that XHTML must follow the strict syntax of XML, as described in the next section.

The WorldWide Consortium (W3C) controls the development of XML and XHTML, among other standards. Visit the W3C website at `http://www.w3c.org` to learn more about what the W3C does. The W3C organization is a group of companies, small and large, and professionals who develop and approve Web standards. The W3C cannot, however, force its standards on anyone. Companies usually follow these standards in order to gain customer and market satisfaction.

9.5 XHTML Syntax

The fundamental syntactic unit of XHTML is the *tag*. XHTML syntax describes how a Web browser can recognize and interpret the instructions contained in the markup tags. The browser parser reads and executes the tags in order to allow the browser to take the appropriate action. The special control characters that separate XHTML markup from ordinary text are < (left angle bracket) and > (right angle bracket). These brackets enclose the XHTML tags, and the tags enclose the content. The enclosing tags and the content between them form an **XHTML element**. The generic form of an element is

`<start-tag>content goes here<end-tag>`

or, in more detail,

`<tag_name [att1_name="val1" att2_name="val2" ...]>content goes here</tag_name>`

The start tag (opening tag) identifies the beginning of the element, and the end tag (closing tag) indicates the end of the element. The two tags always have the same name. Note the slash (/) in the end tag. For example, the element

`<b>This is bold</b>`

displays the text "This is bold" in bold. A browser would display it as **This is bold**.

The start tag may have optional (indicated by [and]) attribute–value pairs. These pairs provide the tag with more control over the formatting of the element's content. For example, the element

`<img src="myDog.jpg" border="5">`

has two attributes, with the names `src` and `border`, and two corresponding values following the = signs.

Nonempty tags can be nested; a **nonempty tag** has a start and an end. In some cases, a Web author may nest some of the text-formatting tags. For example, some text may be bold and italic. Thus, the `<b>` and `<i>` tags must enclose the text. The XHTML nesting rule of tags is "first open, last closed" (or "last open, first closed")—for example, `<b><i>This is bold and italic text content</i></b>`. Any other nesting is illegal according to the XHTML 1.1 standard — for example, `<b><i>...</b></i>`.

XHTML tags follow much stricter rules than their HTML counterparts. Here are the rules:

1. **XHTML tags must be closed.** Any element that has a starting and ending tag must use both tags. In HTML, there are many tags that we have used without closing them. That would not work in XHTML.

2. **XHTML empty tags must be closed.** An **empty tag** has a start tag, but not an end tag. We close an empty tag by preceding its right angle bracket (`>`) with a slash (`/`) to indicate that the tag is both opening and closing. Examples of empty tags are as follows:

   `<img src="myImage.jpg" />` (insert an image in the `myImage.jpg` file into a Web page) and

   `<br />` (insert a line break; can also be written as `<br></br>`).

3. **XHTML uses lowercase tags.** Unlike in HTML, XHTML starting and ending tags must match perfectly and must be lowercase. In HTML, `<BODY>`, `<Body>`, `<body>`, and `<boDY>` all mean the `<BODY>` tag. In XHTML, however, we must use `<body>` as the start tag and `</body>` as the end tag.

4. **Whitespace matters in XHTML.** In HTML, we casually use whitespaces. Sometimes we use two spaces, tabs, or a carriage return. HTML ignores them all. XHTML, on the other hand, assumes that all whitespaces are important and that they are in the XHTML document for a reason. Thus, XHTML maintains all the whitespaces that it encounters in an XHTML document.

5. **All attribute values must be enclosed in quotes.** While HTML can accept `title="my image"` or `title=red`, XHTML requires the use of quotes to enclose the values of attributes — for example, `title="my image"`.

6. **XHTML tags must not overlap.** When nesting tags, tags that open last must close first.

7. **XHTML allows the use of comments.** Comments are used in XHTML documents in the exact same way as they are used in HTML. A comment has the form `<!-- content -->`. Comments may appear anywhere in the XHTML document.

8. **XHTML uses escaped characters.** This rule is similar to its counterpart HTML. XHTML uses special characters just as HTML does; examples of special characters include #, <, and >. An escaped Character is a Character or symbol that is not alphanumeric, that is, it is not a–z, A–Z, or 0–9.

The release of HTML 4.0 brought some major changes over earlier versions. For example, almost all tags and attributes that specify the presentation of an HTML document, such as alignments, fonts, and colors, have been deprecated and replaced by cascading style sheets (see Chapter 5). A **deprecated tag** is an obsolete tag that must still be supported by browsers for backward-compatibility reasons. Web authors should not use a deprecated tag to develop new Web pages. The `<font>` tag is a deprecated tag; however, it is still being used by many Web pages and is still supported by all Web browsers.

Browsers are very generous and forgiving when it comes to rendering XHTML tags. They usually ignore misspelled tag names, without issuing any prior warning or indication to Web authors that something is wrong, thus forcing them to guess what went wrong. The only indication is visual. Web authors must be clear on how the display of their Web pages should look. When they do not get that display, they should check the tags and their syntax.

Example 9.3 Construct XHTML elements.

Construct the XHTML elements for the following tags and attributes:

- A car has a red color and was built in the year 2004. Write the XHTML element that describes the car. Assume that there is a `<car>` tag.
- There is a dog whose name is Spooky, whose breed is Ainu, who has a height of 20 inches, and who has a weight of 50 pounds. Assume that there is a `<dog>` tag.

Solution 9.3 The `<car>` tag has two attributes. The first is color, with a value "red." The second is year, with a value "2004." The tag should be empty. The first XHTML element is

```
<car color="red" year="2004" />
```

The `<dog>` tag has four attributes. The XHTML element is

```
<dog name="Spooky" breed="Ainu" height="20" weight="50" />
```

9.6 XHTML Document Structure

We begin with the document structure for an HTML document. This structure is quite simple. It begins with a declaration section at the top of the document, followed by a content section. Each section uses HTML tags. The generic HTML document structure is shown as follows:

```
1  <html>
2  <head>
3  <meta name="author" content="Zeid">
4  <title>This is the HTML document structure </title>
5  </head>
6  <body>
7  Web-page content goes here
8  </body>
9  </html>
```

Lines 1–5 define the declaration section. Line 1 tells the browser parser that this is an HTML document, so the browser can render and display the page correctly. Line 2 starts the <head> tag, and line 5 closes it. The <head> tag encloses information about the document such as its title. Line 3 specifies information about the document such as its author. Line 4 specifies the title of the Web page. This title becomes the default bookmark name if the Web surfer bookmarks the page.

Lines 6–8 define the content section. The entire content of the Web page and its markup (tags) go between lines 6 and 8. Line 9 closes the <html> tag.

The structure of an XHTML document is identical to the HTML document structure we just described. The only difference comes in the declaration section. XHTML documents must use additional declarations according to the XHTML 1.1 standard. The generic XHTML document structure is shown as follows:

```
1   <?xml version="1.0" encoding="iso-8859-1"?>
2   <!DOCTYPE html PUBLIC "-//W3C//DTD XHTML 1.1//EN"
    "http://www.w3.org/TR/xhtml11/DTD/xhtml11.dtd">
3   <html xmlns="http://www.w3.org/1999/xhtml ">
4   <head>
5   <meta name="author" content="Zeid" />
6   <title>This is the XHTML document structure </title>
7   </head>
8   <body>
9   Web-page content goes here
10  </body>
11  </html>
```

Lines 1 and 2 are the two extra declarations that an XHTML document uses. In line 3, we add a new attribute to the <html> tag that specifies that the document uses XHTML rules and syntax. Thus, the transition from using HTML to using XHTML is easy. It is also easy to convert an existing HTML document to an XHTML document. Simply add the lines 1 and 2 from the previous XHTML document to the top of the HTML document, modify the existing <html> tag to look like the tag shown in line 3 of the XHTML document, and finally make sure that all of the HTML tags are closed or nested properly.

The remainder of this section explains the concepts behind lines 1–3 of the XHTML document.

Each XHTML document should with an XML declaration (line 1), which specifies the version of XML being used in the XHTML document. This declaration is known as the prolog. A document prolog is written in this form: **<?xml version="1.0"?>**. Notice that all letters are lowercase and that there is no whitespace around the equal (=) sign. This prolog indicates that the XML document conforms to the rules of XML version 1.0. The prolog may also take two more attributes: encoding and stand-alone. The **encoding attribute** specifies the type of language used in the XML document—whether it is the Unicode characters, Japanese, Arabic, and so forth. The **stand-alone** (has a value of yes or no) **declaration** specifies whether the document and its rules are completely self-contained. The prolog may thereby look like this:

```
<?xml version="1.0" encoding="iso-8859-1" standalone="yes"?>
```

The document using this prolog uses Unicode characters and is self-contained.

After this prolog must come the DOCTYPE (document type) declaration (line 2), which specifies the version and the format of XHTML to which the document adheres. XHTML 1.1 defines its formats in a DTD (document type definition) document. The DOCTYPE declaration for XHTML 1.1. is

```
<!DOCTYPE html PUBLIC "-//W3C//DTD XHTML 1.1//EN" "http://
    www.w3.org/TR/xhtml11/DTD/xhtml11.dtd">
```

The document containing this declaration uses XHTML 1.1 and follows the formats specified in the `xhtml11.dtd` DTD document.

After the DOCTYPE declaration must come the root element (line 3), which must be `html` for XHTML documents. The root element is the old `<html>` tag in HTML 4.01. The root element must also specify the XML namespace (`xmlns`) where the XHTML tags come from. In XHTML documents, the namespace is `xhtml`. The root element for XHTML 1.1 documents is

```
<html xmlns="http://www.w3.org/1999/xhtml">
```

After these three declaration elements (`<?xml>`, `<!DOCTYP>`, and `<html>`) comes the rest of the document—that is, the elements that define the document content.

Example 9.4 Write a simple HTML Web page.

Use HTML to write a Web page that displays, "Hello world from HTML".

Solution 9.4 Open a text editor, such as Notepad, and type in the HTML code shown below. Save the file as `example94.html`. View the Web page in a browser by typing its URL into the URL bar, dragging and dropping its file onto the browser window, or double-clicking the file. Alternatively, click this sequence (or its equivalent): `File` (menu on the browser menu bar) `=>` `Open` `=>` Select `example94.html` `=>` `Open`.

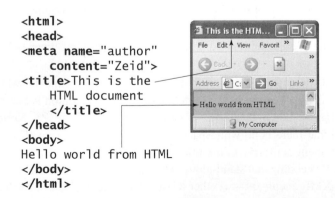

```
<html>
<head>
<meta name="author"
    content="Zeid">
<title>This is the
    HTML document
    </title>
</head>
<body>
Hello world from HTML
</body>
</html>
```

Example 9.5 Write a simple XHTML Web page.

Use XHTML to write a Web page that displays, "Hello world from XHTML".

Solution 9.5 Open a text editor and type in the XHTML code shown below. Save the file as `example95.html`. View the Web page in a browser. Note that we save the file with the `.html` extension, not the `.xhtml` extension. This is the common practice, because there is no real difference between HTML and XHTML other than the syntactic ones.

```
<?xml version="1.0" encoding="iso-8859-1"?>
<!DOCTYPE html PUBLIC "-//W3C//DTD XHTML 1.1//EN"
    "http://www.w3.org/TR/xhtml11/DTD/xhtml11.dtd">
<html xmlns="http://www.w3.org/1999/xhtml">
<meta name="author"content="Zeid">
<title>This is the XHTML document</title>
</head>
<body>
<!-- Add content here -->
Hello world from XHTML
</body>
</html>
```

As we can see from Examples 9.4 and 9.5, HTML and XHTML produce the same results for the same content.

9.7 Authoring Tools

Developing websites and Web pages at the professional level requires a set of tools. Web developers need an editor to write XHTML code, a graphics program to create graphics, digital cameras to create images, scanners to convert existing paper-based documents and photos to digital files, video software to create digital video clips, and audio software to create digital audio clips. After creating the code for the site, developers need a browser to launch their final product: Web pages. We cover these tools throughout the book.

In this chapter, we concern ourselves with editors and browsers only. Two types of editors exist: text and HTML. We used Notepad as a text editor in Examples 9.4 and 9.5. While text editors are simple to use, we must wait until we render the XHTML file in a browser in order to view the resulting Web page. HTML editors solve this problem by allowing Web developers to see the results of their code immediately. HTML editors and translators are the subject of Chapter 17.

Text and HTML editors use opposite approaches to develop XHTML code and Web pages: the bottom-up approach and the top-down approach. There are two outcomes to each approach: the HTML file and the corresponding Web page. In the bottom-up approach, the

HTML file is generated first and the Web page is viewed later. Therefore, the Web page is considered a result of the HTML file. In the top-down approach, the Web page is developed first and the HTML file is generated in the background. Therefore, the HTML file is a result of the Web-page development.

In the bottom-up approach, the Web author writes the XHTML code, using XHTML tags, in a text editor such as Notepad for Windows, Simpletext for Mac, or vi for Unix. After saving the file, the author can review the results of the code by displaying the HTML file in a browser. The Web author obviously needs to know XHTML syntax in order to write the file. The development environment for creating HTML files under this approach uses the following steps:

1. Open a file in a text editor of choice.
2. Enter text and tags.
3. Save the file as text only, and add the extension `.htm` or `.html`. Close the file.
4. Open the file in a Web browser and view the Web page.
5. Edit the HTML file by repeating Steps 1 through 4 as many times as necessary until the Web page takes its final desired form.

To facilitate this approach, the Web author should have a browser window and a text-editor window open at the same time on the screen. The author edits the file, saves it, and opens it in the browser window by using the `Refresh` (for IE) or `Reload` (for Netscape) button or by dragging and dropping the HTML file icon into the browser window.

In the top-down approach, the Web author designs and develops the Web page by using an HTML editor such as FrontPage. These editors provide the author with icons that correspond to XHTML tags. After developing the Web page, the author can review the resulting XHTML code, if needed, by opening the corresponding HTML file in a text editor. The development environment for creating Web pages under this approach uses the following steps:

1. Open an HTML editor of choice.
2. Add elements of the Web page by using the desired HTML icons.
3. Save the automatically generated XHTML code of the page.
4. Use the HTML editor to launch the Web page in a Web browser.
5. Edit the Web page by repeating Steps 1 through 4 as many times as necessary until the Web page takes its final desired form.

Which of these two approaches should Web authors use? We recommend both, as Web authors may have to edit, manually, the code generated automatically by HTML editors. In this

book we use AceHTML, a freeware editor that is a middle ground between the two approaches. This is a good pedagogical idea. The editor provides code templates that we can use. It also allows us to edit the page manually by typing and editing XHTML code. We cover the AceHTML editor again in Chapter 17. Download it from `http://www.visicommedia.com/ace-html`, or just `http://www.acehtml.com`. We use version 5.07 for Windows in this book.

AceHTML has an XHTML template that opens up when we request a new XHTML file. It also has its own internal browser that displays the results of the XHTML code as we write it. Its `View` menu allows us to display its editor and internal browser side by side (see the foregoing screen capture) so that we may view both the code and the Web page simultaneously, or as two separate tabs.

9.8 Text Formatting

One of the main elements of a Web page is text. As in traditional documents, the text of a Web page is structured and organized into basic units of headings and paragraphs. Each paragraph consists of statements and words. XHTML provides tags to format each of these units. There are heading tags, paragraph tags, word tags, and character tags.

XHTML provides six heading elements: `<h1>`–`<h6>`. The `<h1>` tag provides the largest-size heading, while `<h6>` provides the smallest-size heading. Each of these tags has an `align` attribute. The possible values of this attribute are `left` (default), `center`, and `right`. Table 9.1 lists each tag, describes how to use it, and provides the font size it produces.

Paragraphs are created using the `<p>` tag. The effect of the `<p>` tag is to create a line space ahead of the text that defines the paragraph. The `<p>` tag has one attribute: align. The values of the attribute are `left` (default), `center`, and `right`. The attribute aligns the paragraph text. The syntax is `<p align="center">paragraph text goes here</p>`.

XHTML provides a wealth of tags to format words and characters. Many of these tags produce results similar to traditional formatting. Table 9.2 provides a list of some of these tags.

Table 9.1   Heading tags. Syntax example: `<h1 align=value>text content</h1>`.

Tag	Close	Attribute	Value	Font size	Example
`<h1>`	yes	`align`	`left` (default), `center`, or `right`	24	`<h1 align="center">text goes here</h1>`
`<h2>`	yes	`align`	same as `<h1>`	18	`<h2>text goes here</h2>`
`<h3>`	yes	`align`	same as `<h1>`	14	`<h3 align="right">text goes here</h3>`
`<h4>`	yes	`align`	same as `<h1>`	12	`<h4 align="right">text goes here</h4>`
`<h5>`	yes	`align`	same as `<h1>`	10	`<h5>text goes here</h5>`
`<h6>`	yes	`align`	same as `<h1>`	8	`<h6>text goes here</h6>`

Table 9.2   Word and character tags.

Tag	Close	Attribute	Value	Effect	Example
`<b>`	yes	none	none	`bold text`	`<b>text</b>`
`<i>`	yes	none	none	`italic text`	`<i>text</i>`
` `	empty	none	none	`line break`	`text `
`<em>`	yes	none	none	`typographic emphasis`	`<em>text</em>`
`<strong>`	yes	none	none	`typographic emphasis`	`<strong>text goes here</strong>`
`<small>`	yes	none	none	`small-font text`	`<small>text</small>`
`<block- quote>`	yes	none	none	`formats text as a quotation from a specific source`	`<blockquote>text goes here</blockquote>`
`<cite>`	yes	none	none	`a citation reference`	`<cite>text></cite>`
`<kbd>`	yes	none	none	`keyboard font`	`<kbd>text</kbd>`
`<code>`	yes	none	none	`computer-code font`	`<code>text</code>`
`<pre>`	yes	none	none	`display text as is`	`<pre>text</pre>`
`<div>`	yes	none	none	`acts as a line break`	`<div>text</div>`
`<hr>`	empty	`align`	`left`, `center` (default), `right`	`aligns a line in the Web page`	`<hr align="center" />`
		`color`	name or hex code	`specifies the line color; see later for information on hex codes`	`<hr color="red" />` `<hr color="#0000FF" />`
		`noshade`	none	`fades line into the background`	`<hr noshade />`
		`size`	number of pixels	`line thickness`	`<hr size="5" />`
		`width`	number of pixels or %	`length as pixels or as a percent- age of the Web page's width`	`<hr width="200" />` `<hr width="50%" />`

Example 9.6   Use heading tags.

Develop a Web page that uses the <h1>–<h6> tags.

Solution 9.6   Start the AceHTML editor. Click this sequence to open a new XHTML template: File (menu on the AceHTML menu bar) => New => XHTML Document. Use the editor to generate the following XHTML code:

```
1  <! -- filename: example96.html -->
2  <?xml version="1.0" encoding="iso-8859-1"?>
3  <!DOCTYPE html PUBLIC "-//W3C//DTD XHTML 1.1//EN"
4       "http://www.w3.org/TR/xhtml11/DTD/xhtml11.dtd">
5  <html xmlns="http://www.w3.org/1999/xhtml">
6  <! -- Generated by AceHTM http://freeware.acehtml.com -->
7  <head>
8  <meta http-equiv="Content-Type" content="text/html;
   charset=iso-8859-1" />
9  <title>Using headings</title>
10 <meta name="description" content="Heading tags" />
11 <meta name="keywords" content="" />
12 <meta name="author" content="zeid" />
13 <meta name="generator" content="AceHTML 5 Freeware" />
14 </head>
15 <body>
16 <h1>h1 text</h1>
17 <h2>h2 text</h2>
18 <h3>h3 text</h3>
19 <h4>h4 text</h4>
20 <h5>h5 text</h5>
21 <h6>h6 text</h6>
22 </body>
23 </html>
```

Save the code in a file with the name example96.html. AceHTML displays the progress of the Web page in its internal browser as you type the tags. (See the screen capture shown in the foregoing code.) You can also use an external browser, such as IE, to display the page. Drag the file and drop it onto the IE window in order to view it there.

Code explained:

1. Lines 2–5 declare the document as an XHTML document.

2. Line 9 becomes the Web page's title in the browser's title bar, as shown in the screen capture. It also becomes the default bookmark name if the user bookmarks the page in a browser.

3. Lines 16–21 show the use and syntax of heading tags.

Discussion:

The heading tags <h1>–<h6> provide instructions for font size and alignment. They do not provide instructions for font face, such as Arial. You specify the font face by using other tags. The <meta> tags in lines 10–13 are covered later.

Hands-on exercise:

Starting with the foregoing code, add the `align` attribute to lines 16–21. What happens to the text in the Web browser window? Use the different values of the attribute that are shown in Table 9.1. Also, replace the text for each header with different phrases of your choosing.

Example 9.7 Use word and character tags.

Develop a Web page that illustrates the formatting of words and characters.

Solution 9.7 Using the AceHTML editor, generate the following code and save it as `example97.html`:

```
1  <!-- filename: example97.html -->
2  <?xml version="1.0" encoding="iso-8859-1"?>
3  <!DOCTYPE html PUBLIC "-//W3C//DTD XHTML 1.1//EN"
4      "http://www.w3.org/TR/xhtml11/DTD/xhtml11.dtd">
5  <html xmlns="http://www.w3.org/1999/xhtml">
6  <!-- Generated by AceHTM http://freeware.acehtml.com -->
7  <head>
8  <meta http-equiv="Content-Type" content="text/html;
   charset=iso-8859-1" />
9  <title>Formatting text</title>
10 <meta name="description" content="Heading tags" />
11 <meta name="keywords" content="" />
12 <meta name="author" content="zeid" />
13 <meta name="generator" content="AceHTML 5 Freeware" />
14 </head>
15 <body>
16 <em>Typographic emphasis</em><br />
17 <strong>Strong text</strong><br />
18 <small>Small text</small><br />
19 <blockquote>Blocked text<br />
20 Blocked text<br />
21 Blocked text
22 </blockquote>
23 <cite>Cite text</cite><br />
24 <kbd>Keboard text</kbd><br />
25 <code>XHTML Code</code><br />
26 <pre>Pre text</pre>
27 <div>
28 Text formatted using div tag
29 </div>
30 After div
31 <hr align="left" size="6" color="red"
   noshade width="50%" />
32 </body>
33 </html>
```

A browser window titled "Formatting text" displays:

Typographic emphasis
Strong text
Small text

Blocked text
Blocked text
Blocked text

Cite text
Keboard text
XHTML Code

Pre text

Text formatted using div tag
After div

These spaces are the result of the <pre> tag

Also use a browser to render the Web page.

Code explained:

1. Lines 2–13 are explained in Example 9.6.
2. Lines 16–31 use all the word and character formatting shown in Table 9.2.
3. Lines 19–22 result in the indentation of the blockquoted text and the retention of line spaces before and after it.
4. Line 26 results in the retention of line spaces before and after the enclosed text.
5. Lines 27–30 prove that the `<div>` tag produces the same result as the `<br>` tag.
6. Line 31 uses all the attributes of the `<hr>` tag: It creates a red line that is 6 pixels thick, is flush left, and has a length equal to half the width of the browser window. The line changes length as you enlarge or reduce the window.

Discussion:
Some of the foregoing tags are redundant, such as the `<div>` and the `<br>` tags. The `<div>` tag is usually implemented with tables, as we explain later in this book. The effect of the `<strong>` tag is similar to that of the `<b>` tag. Copy the text from the browser window into a word processor, such as Word, and observe its properties in order to understand more about the formatting tags. For example, note that the `<small>` tag produces text of size 10.

Hands-on exercise:
Starting with the foregoing code, delete lines 16–31. Use the `<blockquote>` and `<code>` tags to write some computer code in the C, C++, or Java language. Nest the `<code>` tag inside the `<blockquote>` tag for better formatting. What happens when you remove the `<block-quote>` tag?

9.9 Special Characters

There are a number of special characters, such as Latin characters and Greek symbols. These special characters and symbols are represented by certain XHTML code. A need for special characters also arises when a Web page must use some of the characters reserved by XHTML, such as < or >, as part of its text. If the Web author uses < or >, the browser attempts to render it as part of a tag and therefore renders the XHTML code incorrectly. In such a case, the author must instead use a special character that represents < or >.

Special characters in XHTML are represented by a character entity or a numeric code. The character entity begins with & and ends with ;. The numeric code begins with &# and ends with ;. For example, the copyright symbol is represented by the character entity `&copy;` or by the numeric code `&#169;`. Character entities use words, while numeric codes use numbers. Common practice is to use numeric codes over character entities. When a Web page uses special characters, the browser looks up these symbols and replaces them when equivalent characters when rendering the document.

There are three distinct character sets in XHTML. The ISO 8859-1 (Latin-1) character set contains the Latin characters, including the already commonly used ` ` (nonbreaking space), © (copyright symbol), and ® (registered-mark symbol). The first numeric code in this set is 32, and the last code is 255. Table 9.3 shows a sample of the ISO Latin-1 characters. Each code in the table must be preceded by &# and end with ,.

The second character set is the symbols, including mathematical symbols and Greek letters. These characters are available in the Adobe font Symbols. This set contains all the modern Greek letters. It is not intended for producing Greek text, however, Table 9.4 shows a sample of this character set. Again, each code in the figure must be preceded by &# and ended by ;. We should mention that a browser may not render some of the characters shown in Table 9.4 because it does not implement them. This set has subsets as follows:

1. **Latin extended-B:** The code for this character is ƒ.
2. **Greek characters:** The first code in this set is Α, and the last code is ϖ. The codes in between are incremented by 1. However, the following codes are not present in the sequence: 930, 938–944 inclusive, 970–976 inclusive, and 979–981 inclusive. If a Web page uses any of these codes (say, Ϊ), the browser displays the code as is, because it cannot render it.
3. **General punctuation:** The codes for this subset are • (bullet = small black circle), … (horizontal ellipsis = three-dot leader), ′ (prime for feet, minutes, etc.), ″ (double prime for inches, seconds, etc.), ‾ (spacing overscore or overline), and ⁄ (fraction slash).

Table 9.3 Sample ISO 8859-1 (Latin-1) characters.

Code	Char	Code	Char	Code	Char	Code	Char	Code	Char
32		48	0	64	@	80	P	96	`
33	!	49	1	65	A	81	Q	97	a
34	"	50	2	66	B	82	R	98	b
35	#	51	3	67	C	83	S	99	c
36	$	52	4	68	D	84	T	100	d
37	%	53	5	69	E	85	U	101	e
38	&	54	6	70	F	86	V	102	f
39	'	55	7	71	G	87	W	103	g
40	(	56	8	72	H	88	X	104	h
41	)	57	9	73	I	89	Y	105	i
42	*	58	:	74	J	90	Z	106	j
43	+	59	;	75	K	91	[	107	k
44	,	60	<	76	L	92	\	108	l
45	-	61	=	77	M	93	]	109	m
46	.	62	>	78	N	94	^	110	n
47	/	63	?	79	O	95	_	∃	o

Table 9.4 Sample ISO Greek, math, and other characters.

Code	Char	Code	Char	Code	Char	Code	Char	Code	Char
913	A	929	P	953	ι	969	ω	8954	?
914	B	931	Σ	954	κ	977	ϑ	8595	↓
915	Γ	932	T	955	λ	978	Υ	8596	↔
916	Δ	933	Y	956	μ	982	ϖ	8629	↵
917	E	934	Φ	957	ν	8226	•	8656	⇐
918	Z	935	X	958	ξ	8230	…	8657	⇑
919	H	936	Ψ	959	o	8242	′	8658	⇒
920	Θ	937	Ω	960	π	8243	″	8659	⇓
921	I	945	α	961	ρ	8254	?	8660	⇔
922	K	946	β	962	ς	8260	/	8704	∀
923	Λ	947	γ	963	σ	8465	ℑ	8706	∂
924	M	948	δ	964	τ	8472	℘	8707	∃
925	N	949	ε	965	υ	8476	ℜ	8709	∅
926	Ξ	950	ζ	966	φ	8482	ℵ	8711	∇
927	O	951	η	967	χ	8592	←	8712	∈
928	Π	952	θ	968	ψ	8593	↑	8713	∉

4. **Letterlike symbols:** The codes for this subset are ℑ (blackletter capital *I*), ℘ (script capital *P*), ℜ (blackletter capital *R*), ᴺ (trademark sign), and ℵ (aleph symbol).

5. **Arrows:** The codes for this subset are ← (leftwards arrow), ↑ (upwards arrow), → (rightwards arrow), ↓ (downwards arrow), ↔ (left–right arrow), ↵ (downwards arrow with corner leftwards = carriage return), ⇐ (leftwards double arrow), ⇑ (upwards double arrow), ⇒ (rightwards double arrow), ⇓ (downwards double arrow), and ⇔ (left–right double arrow).

6. **Mathematical operators:** The first code in this subset is ∀, and the last code is ⋅, with several codes missing in between. Interested readers should consult `http://www.w3c.org` for these codes and their meanings.

7. **Geometric shapes:** The only code for this subset is ◊ (lozenge).

8. **Miscellaneous technical:** The codes for this subset are ⌈ (left ceiling), ⌉ (right ceiling), ⌊ (left floor), ⌋ (right floor), 〈 (left-pointing angle bracket), and 〉 (right-pointing angle bracket).

Table 9.5   ISO markup-significant and internationalization characters.

Code	Char	Code	Char	Code	Char	Code	Char
38	&	8206		60	<	8207	‏
62	>	8211	–	338	Œ	8212	—
339	œ	8216	'	352	Š	8217	'
353	š	8218	,	376	Ÿ	8220	"
710	ˆ	8221	"	732	˜	8222	„
8194		8224	†	8195		8225	‡
8201		8240	‰	8204		8249	‹
8205		8250	›				

9. **Miscellaneous symbols:** The codes for this subset are ♠ (black spade suit),
♣ (black club suit), ♥ (black heart suit), and ♦ (black diamond suit).

The third character set is the markup-significant and internationalization characters. These are escaping characters for denoting spaces and dashes. The subsets of characters that make up this set are Controls and Basic Latin, Latin Extended-*A*, Spacing Modifiers, Letters, and General Punctuation. Table 9.5 shows all these characters and their codes. We should mention that a browser may not render some of the characters shown in Table 9.5.

9.10 Hyperlinks

Hyperlinks, or links for short, are one of the two key concepts behind XHTML (the other being markup). A **link** is a connection from one Web source to another. Hyperlinks create hypertext. Hyperlinks link Web pages to each other. This makes it easier for Web surfers to find related information and content. Despite its simplicity, the link has been one of the driving forces behind the Web's success. XHTML provides the <a> tag to create links in Web pages.

9.10.1 Links

A link is the basic hypertext construct. A link has two ends or parts, as shown in Figure 9.2. The link starts at the source, or visible part, and points to the destination, or invisible part. The source may be text, an image, or a list item. The destination may be a Web page, a file, a program, an image, a video clip, a sound bite, an FTP download, a Telnet connection, or an e-mail address. The general structure of the <a> tag is <a invisible part>visible part</a>, as shown in Figure 9.2. The user sees and clicks the visible part of the <a> tag on the Web page. The user goes to the invisible part upon clicking (activating) the visible part.

The <a> tag has several attributes. They are

```
<a href title name charset type hreflang rel rev accesskey shape
    coords tabindex>
```

The first three attributes are the most commonly used ones. The `href` attribute specifies the invisible part of the link, shown in Figure 9.2. All the attributes are described as follows:

- The `href` attribute specifies the destination anchor, or the invisible part. This attribute accepts any Web protocol, such as HTTP, file, FTP, Telnet, or Mailto. Here is an example:

`<a href= "mailto:zeid@coe.neu.edu">Please send us your feedback</a>`

- The `title` attribute specifies a title for the link, which shows when the user moves the mouse over the link.

- The `name` attribute names the current link so that it can be used as the destination of another link. This attribute is typically used to create intradocument links, as discussed in Section 9.10.2.

- The `charset` attribute specifies the character encoding of the destination document (Web page). If a link points to a Web page written in a language that uses characters different from those of the English alphabet (such as the Arabic language), this attribute should be used by the Web author. The browser needs it in order to render the destination Web page correctly.

- The `type` attribute specifies the MIME type of the destination document. The most common type is `text/html`.

- The `hreflang` attribute specifies the language of the destination document, if it is not English. This attribute and the `charset` attribute may be used together. For these two attributes to work, the browser rendering the document must have the proper interpreter. Consider two documents, one in French and the other in Arabic. The `<a>` tag that uses the French document as a destination Web page must use the `hreflang` attribute, as in the following example:

`<a hreflang="fr" href="french.html">Read a French paper</a>`

- The `<a>` tag that uses the Arabic document as a destination Web page must use both the `hreflang` and the `charset` attributes:

`<a hreflang="ar" charset="ISO-8859-6" href="http://aaa.bbb.ccc/`
`    arabic.html>Read an Arabic paper</a>`

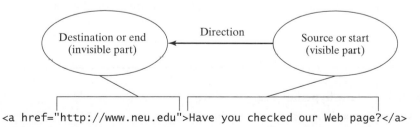

`<a href="http://www.neu.edu">Have you checked our Web page?</a>`

When the user clicks The `HAVE you checked our Web page?` link, the browser fetches the Web page defined by the URL `http://www.neu.edu`.

Figure 9.2   Parts of a link.

- The `rel` (specify forward link), `rev` (specify reverse link), `accesskey` (accessibility-key character), `shape` (used with client-side image maps), `coords` (used with client-side image maps), and `tableindex` (used for tabbing) attributes are not covered here, because they are seldom used with the `<a>` tag.

A link (the source, or visible part) in a Web page may have one of three states: link, active link (alink), or visited link (vlink). If a user has not clicked the link, it is known as just a link. During the time that the user is pressing the mouse button and holding it down while the cursor is on the link, but before releasing it, the link is said to be active (thus the name active link). After the mouse button has been released, the link becomes a visited link. When the user returns to the Web page that holds the link, it remain a visited link. Browsers use three colors to display the three states of links. The default colors are blue for a link, red for an alink, and purple for a vlink. The Web author can override these default colors by using the proper attributes of the `<body>` tag, as shown later in this chapter. Browsers remember link states in the same page for a period of time that can be set by configuring the browser.

The URLs used in conjunction with the `href` attribute of the `<a>` tag may be specified on an absolute or a relative basis. The reference base is the location of the XHTML document using the `<a>` tag. This location could be a Web server on the Internet, a local directory, or a folder. Web authors need to think of an XHTML document as a file name and of its URL as a path to the file. From this point of view, all conventional rules of using path names relative to each other apply here to XHTML documents and their URLs. Three cases exist. The first case is that the location (directory) of the destination HTML file is the same as that of the HTML file using the tag. In the second case, the destination file is in a directory one level above that of the current HTML file. The last case occurs when the destination HTML file is in a directory below that of the current HTML file.

Consider the following example to show how to specify the file path in each of the three cases: Let us assume that an XHTML document with the name `source.html` resides in the directory `http://aaa.bbb.ccc/dir1` and uses an `<a>` tag that links to an HTML file called `destination.html`. If both files reside in the same directory, the Web author uses `<a href="destination.html">`. If `destination.html` resides in a directory, `dir2` one level above that of `source.html`, the Web author specifies the path as `<a href="../dir2/destination.html">`. The two periods (`..`) indicate the directory above the current one. If `destination.html` resides in a directory `dir3`, one level beneath that of `source.html`, the Web author specifies the path as `<a href="dir3/destination.html">`.

Example 9.8 Use the hyperlink tag.

Develop a Web page that illustrates the use of the `<a>` tag.

Solution 9.8 This example creates a Web page with various links. The `href` attribute uses both local files and websites as destination locations. When clicking a link in the page of this example, remember to press and hold the mouse button in order to observe the change of color of the link. Using the AceHTML editor, generate the following code, and save it as `example98.html`:

```
 1  <!-- filename: example98.html -->
 2  <?xml version="1.0" encoding="iso-8859-1"?>
 3  <!DOCTYPE html PUBLIC "-//W3C//DTD XHTML 1.1//EN"
 4      "http://www.w3.org/TR/xhtml11/DTD/xhtml11.dtd">
 5  <html xmlns="http://www.w3.org/1999/xhtml">
 6  <!-- Generated by AceHTM http://freeware.acehtml.com -->
 7  <head>
 8  <meta http-equiv="Content-Type" content="text/html;
    charset=iso-8859-1" />
 9  <title>Linking to different places</title>
10  <meta name="description" content="Heading tags" />
11  <meta name="keywords" content="" />
12  <meta name="author" content="zeid" />
13  <meta name="generator" content="AceHTML 5 Freeware" />
14  </head>
15  <body>
16  <h2 align="center">My Link Store</h2>
17  <!-- Link to a URL -->
18  <a href="http://www.neu.edu">Link to NU URL</a><br />
19  <!-- Use different protocols with href attribute -->
20  <a href=mailto:zeid@coe.neu.edu>Send e-mail to Zeid</a><br />
21  <a href="ftp://ftp.netscape.com">Netscape FTP site</a><br />
22  <a href="telnet://elvis.coe.neu.edu">Telnet to your NU
    account</a><br/>
23  <!-- Use the title and charset attributes of the link tag -->
24  <a href="http://www.neu.edu" title="NU">Move the mouse over
    this link to display its title</a><br />
25  <a href="http://www.w3.org" charset="ISO-8859-1">This link uses
    the charset attribute</a><br />
26  <!-- Link to a local file using the file:// protocol -->
27  <a href="example97.html">Check Example 9.7 Web page</a><br />
28  </body>
29  </html>
```

Also, use a browser to render the Web page.

Code explained:

1. Lines 2–13 are explained in Example 9.6.
2. Lines 18 and 20–22 use, respectively, the HTTP, Mailto, FTP, and telnet protocols.
3. Line 24 uses the `title` attribute.
4. Line 25 uses the `charset` attribute.
5. Line 27 links to a local file; it uses the file protocol implicitly.

Discussion:

When you click any of the links, the browser executes the action specified by the `href` attribute. For example, clicking the `Send e-mail to Zeid` link opens the `Compose` window of your mail tool. Also, line 27 assumes that the `example97.html` file is in the same folder as the `example98.html` file is; Otherwise the link will not work.

Hands-on exercise:

Move the `example97.html` file to a different folder. Run the code. What happens? Fix the problem by using the absolute file path in code line 27.

9.10.2 Anchors

While the `<a>` tag most often is used to link Web pages together, it can also be used to create links within the same page. Links that connect external Web pages to a particular Web page are known as interdocument links, whereas links that connect different sections within the same page are known as intradocument links, or anchors. Thus, the destination anchor for an intradocument link is a tag within the same document that creates the anchor.

There are two useful cases for using anchors. First, a Web author might create a table of contents whose headings link to the corresponding sections in the page. At the end of each section, there should be an anchor that takes the reader back to the table of contents. Using a table of contents allows Web authors to develop long Web pages (typically one to three screens long) to maintain continuity of ideas. Tables of contents with intradocument links have the effect of splitting Web pages, yet maintaining continuity of ideas. This concept is sometimes known as **chunking** an XHTML document. The rule is to chunk the document at the concept level. Chunks that are too large are slow to scroll and render, while chunks that are too small make the concept fuzzy. The design issue here is content stream versus control stream.

The other case when anchors are useful is when specifying a specific location in a Web page that is important for the Web surfer to see as soon as the page is displayed, instead of the user scrolling down to it and running the risk of missing it altogether. For example, if there is a section listing items that are on sale in the Web page and the Web author would like to draw the Web surfer to it, the link to the page would look something like this: `<a href="http://aaa.bbb.ccc/myPage.html#sale">`.

The creation of an anchor requires two `<a>` tags and the `name` attribute. One tag has a name (`<a name="sale">`) and the other refers to it `<a href="#sale">`. The name must be preceded by the # sign when it is used with the `href` attribute.

Example 9.9 Use intradocument links.

Develop a Web page that illustrates the use of anchors.

Solution 9.9 This example creates a Web page that has a table of contents (TOC) and some sections. We link the TOC to the sections via anchors. Using the AceHTML editor, generate the following code, and save it as `example99.html`:

```
1  <! -- filename: example99.html -->
2  <?xml version="1.0" encoding="iso-8859-1"?>
3  <!DOCTYPE html PUBLIC "-//W3C//DTD XHTML 1.1//EN"
4      "http://www.w3.org/TR/xhtml11/DTD/xhtml11.dtd">
5  <html xmlns="http://www.w3.org/1999/xhtml">
6  <!-- Generated by AceHTM http://freeware.acehtml.com -->
7  <head>
8  <meta http-equiv="Content-Type" content="text/html;
   charset=iso-8859-1" />
9  <title>Using intradocument links</title>
10 <meta name="description" content="Heading tags" />
11 <meta name="keywords" content="" />
12 <meta name="author" content="zeid" />
13 <meta name="generator" content="AceHTML 5 Freeware" />
14 </head>
15 <body>
16 <h2 align="center">Using anchors</h2>
17 <! -- Define a destination tag for Toc -->
18 <a name="Contents"><b>Table of contents
   </b></a><br />
19 <! -- Define source tags -->
20 <a href="#Section1">Section 1</a><br />
21 <a href="#Section2">Section 2</a><br />
22 <hr /><p></p>
23
24 <! -- Define destination tag for Section1 source tag -->
25 <a name="Section1"><b><i>Section 1</i></b></a><br />
26 Section1 content goes here<br />
27 <! -- Define a source tag for TOC -->
28 <a href="#Contents">Return to table of contents</a><br />
29 <p></p>
30
31 <! -- Define destination tag for Section2 source tag -->
32 <a name="Section2"><b><i>Section 2</i></b></a><br />
33 Section2 content goes here<br />
34 <! -- Define a source tag for Toc -->
35 <a href="#Contents">Return to table of contents</a>
36 </body>
37 </html>
```

Also, use a browser to render the Web page.

Code explained:

   1. Lines 20 and 25 define the two `<a>` tags of the `Section 1` anchor.
   2. Lines 21 and 32 define the two `<a>` tags of the `Section 2` anchor.
   3. Line 18 and either of lines 28 or 35 define the two `<a>` tags for the `Return to table of contents` anchor.

Discussion:

Pay attention to the URL in the browser window when you load the Web page of this example for the first time. Now click the `Section 1` or `Section 2` link and observe the difference in the URL. To see the effect of the anchors clearly, resize the browser window to reduce its height enough to force scrolling. Scroll all the way up, and try the anchors.

Hands-on exercise:

Add two more anchors to create Section 3 and Section 4.

9.11 Lists

Lists are an essential element of Web-page design. They allow Web authors to distinguish, via indentation and symbols, certain lines of text (known as list items) from other text in a page, such as paragraph text. Thus, a list consists of list items. Browsers perform the indentation when they render list tags. The concept of lists is simple, yet powerful. Much textual information lends itself to list style naturally. For example, lists could be used to describe components of a product, the steps of a procedure, assembly instructions, tasks of a plan, an organizational structure, or a hierarchical structure.

    XHTML supports three types of lists: unordered, ordered, and definition. The unordered list is used to itemize information whose order is insignificant. An example is listing the parts of a car. The ordered list is used to itemize information that has order. An example is listing the steps to tune up a car engine. The definition list is used when we would like to define certain terms. The definition list usually consists of term–definition pairs.

    XHTML provides three tags that implement the three types of lists. They are `<ul>`, `<ol>`, and `<dl>` for unordered list, ordered list, and definition list, respectively. These tags have attributes that allow Web authors to control the symbols of list items. For example, the `type` attribute, while deprecated, can be used at the `<ul>`, `<ol>`, or `<li>` level. If used with the `<ul>` or `<ol>` tag, all the elements of the list assume its value. Local control can be achieved by using the `type` attribute again at the element level. For example, `<ul type="square">` assigns a square symbol to the shape of bullets of all list elements. With `<li type="disc">`, the disc symbol has a solid circle for the shape of bullets.

    Web authors have no control over the amount of indentation in a list. This factor is controlled by the browser displaying the Web page.

9.11.1 Unordered Lists

The `<ul>` tag creates an unordered list. The items (elements) of a list are created via the `<li>` (list item) tag. The `<li>` tag has two deprecated attributes: `type` and `compact`. They are replaced by cascading style sheets. The `type` attribute specifies the symbol (bullet) to be displayed for the list item. The three possible values of the `type` attribute are disc (solid or filled-in circle), square (solid or filled-in square), and circle (hollow or outline circle). The `compact` attribute is a Boolean attribute that tells the browser to render the list in a more compact way.

Example 9.10 Use unordered lists.

Develop a Web page that illustrates the use of unordered lists.

Solution 9.10 Using the AceHTML editor, generate the following code, and save it as `example910.html`:

```
1  <!-- filename: example910.html -->
2  <?xml version="1.0" encoding="iso-8859-1"?>
3  <!DOCTYPE html PUBLIC "-//W3C//DTD XHTML 1.1//EN"
4      "http://www.w3.org/TR/xhtml11/DTD/xhtml11.dtd">
5  <html xmlns="http://www.w3.org/1999/xhtml">
6  <!-- Generated by AceHTM http://freeware.acehtml.com -->
7  <head>
8  <meta http-equiv="Content-Type" content="text/html;
   charset=iso-8859-1" />
9  <title>Unordered lists</title>
10 <meta name="description" content="Heading tags" />
11 <meta name="keywords" content="" />
12 <meta name="author" content="zeid" />
13 <meta name="generator" content="AceHTML 5 Freeware" />
14 </head>
15 <body>
16 <h2 align="center">Web page with two unordered lists</h2>
17 This list uses default list symbols
18 <ul>
19 <li>Tea</li>
20 <li>Coffee</li>
21 <li>Soda</li>
22 <li>Milk</li>
23 </ul>
24 This list controls list symbols
25 <ul>
26 <li type="disc">Tea</li>
27 <li type="circle">Coffee</li>
28 <li type="square">Soda</li>
29 <li>Milk</li>
30 </ul>
31 </body>
32 </html>
```

Also, use a browser to render the Web page.

Code explained:

    1. Lines 18–23 create a list with four items, using the default list symbol, a disc for IE.

    2. Lines 25–30 re-creates the first list, but by specifying list symbols via the `type` attribute.

    3. The list item in line 29 uses no symbol.

Discussion:

Observe how the `<ul>` tag creates two effects: First, it acts as a `<br>` tag. Second, it acts a `<p>` tag.

Hands-on exercise:

Use the IE and Netscape browsers to display the Web page. What happens? Also add the `compact` attribute to lines 19–22 and 26–29. Do you see a difference when you view the Web page? Also use the `type` attribute at the `<ul>` level, and achieve local (element-level) control by using it again at the `<li>` level. What are your conclusions?

9.11.2 Ordered Lists

The `<ol>` tag creates an ordered list. This tag is very similar to the `<ul>` tag. The `<ol>` tag may use the `type` attribute. The elements or items of a list are created via the `<li>` (list item) tag. The `<li>` tag has four deprecated attributes: `type`, `start`, `value`, and `compact`. The `type` attribute specifies the order (numbering) style of the list to be displayed for the list item. The possible values of the `type` attribute are Arabic numbers (1, 2, 3, ...), uppercase or lowercase Latin letters (A, B, C, ..., a, b, c, ...), and uppercase or lowercase Roman numerals (I, II, III, ..., i, ii, iii, ...). The default value is the Arabic numbers.

    The `start` attribute allows the Web author to control the start number of list items. For example, the Web author may want to assign the first item on a list the Arabic number 6. The `value` attribute overrides the numbering sequence. For example, the Web author may want to assign a list item a number out of sequence, such as number 5 following number 3.

    The `compact` attribute is the same as that of the `<ul>` tag. It is a Boolean attribute that tells the browser to render the list in a more compact way. The interpretation of this attribute depends on the browser. In many cases, this attribute does not make a difference in rendering lists, and it is not used often.

Example 9.11 Use ordered lists.

Develop a Web page that illustrates the use of ordered lists.

Solution 9.11 Starting with the AceHTML editor, generate the following code, and save it as `example911.html`:

    Also, use a browser to render the Web page.

Code explained:

    1. Line 1 shows the File name of the program in this example. All the book's source code is on the book's companion website. Visit `http://www.prenhall.com/zeid` and follow the instructions to download any of the code files.

```
 1  <!-- filename: example911.html -->
 2  <?xml version="1.0" encoding="iso-8859-1"?>
 3  <!DOCTYPE html PUBLIC "-//W3C//DTD XHTML 1.1//EN"
 4          "http://www.w3.org/TR/xhtml11/DTD/xhtml11.dtd">
 5  <html xmlns="http://www.w3.org/1999/xhtml">
 6  <!-- Generated by AceHTM http://freeware.acehtml.com -->
 7  <head>
 8  <meta http-equiv="Content-Type" content="text/html;
    charset=iso-8859-1" />
 9  <title>Ordered lists</title>
10  <meta name="description" content="Heading tags" />
11  <meta name="keywords" content="" />
12  <meta name="author" content="zeid" />
13  <meta name="generator" content="AceHTML 5 Freeware" />
14  </head>
15  <body>
16  <h2 align="center">Web page with three ordered lists</h2>
17  This list uses Arabic (default) list numbers
18  <ol>
19  <li>Tea</li>
20  <li>Coffee</li>
21  <li>Soda</li>
22  </ol>
23  This list uses uppercase Latin letters
24  <ol type="A">
25  <li>Tea</li>
26  <li>Coffee</li>
27  <li>Soda</li>
28  </ol>
29  This list uses lowercase Roman numerals
30  <ol type="i">
31  <li>Tea</li>
32  <li>Coffee</li>
33  <li>Soda</li>
34  </ol>
35  </body>
36  </html>
```

2. Lines 18–22 create a list with four items, using the default list numbers.

3. Lines 24–28 re-create the first list, but specifies uppercase Latin numbers.

4. Lines 30–34 re-create the first list, but specifies lowercase Roman numerals.

Discussion:

The `type` attribute behaves in a logical way when it is used with the `<ol>` tag. It can be used only at the `<ol>` tag level. If you use it at the `<ol>` and `<li>` levels at the same time, the browser ignores its value specified at the `<li>` level. If it is used only at the `<li>` level, the browser uses it only for the first `<li>` tag and ignores all the values of the other `<li>` tags.

Hands-on exercise:

Use the `type` attribute at the `<ol>` and `<li>` levels. What happens? Think of the list level and the element level.

9.11.3 Definition Lists

The `<dl>` tag creates a definition list. The `<dl>` tag has no attributes. The definition list differs from the other two types of lists. It consists of term–definition (or term–description) pairs. Thus, two tags are required to build the list. They are the `<dt>` (definition term) tag, which specifies the term to be defined, and the `<dd>` (definition description) tag, which describes the term. Web authors use as many `<dt>`–`<dd>` pairs as they need to create a list.

Example 9.12 Use definition lists.

Develop a Web page that illustrates the use of definition lists.

```
1  <!-- filename: example912.html -->
2  <?xml version="1.0" encoding="iso-8859-1"?>
3  <!DOCTYPE html PUBLIC "-//W3C//DTD XHTML 1.1//EN"
4      "http://www.w3.org/TR/xhtml11/DTD/xhtml11.dtd">
5  <html xmlns="http://www.w3.org/1999/xhtml">
6  <!-- Generated by AceHTM http://freeware.acehtml.com -->
7  <head>
8  <meta http-equiv="Content-Type" content="text/html;
   charset=iso-8859-1" />
9  <title>Definition lists</title>
10 </head>
11 <body>
12 <h2 align="center"><b>Web page with two
   definition lists</b></h2>
13 <!-- List uses DT-DD pairs -->
14 <dl>
15    <dt>XML</dt>
16    <dd>XML is a metalanguage</dd>
17    <dt>XHTML</dt>
18    <dd>XHTML is a strict HTML</dd>
19 </dl>
20 <hr size="5" color="red" />
21
22 <!-- List uses DTs followed by DDs -->
23 <dl>
24    <dt>XML</dt> <dt>XHTML</dt>
25    <dd>XML is a metalanguage</dd>
26    <dd>XHTML is a strict HTML</dd>
27 </dl>
28 </body>
29 </html>
```

Solution 9.12 This example creates a Web page with two definition lists displayed in two styles. The first list uses the `<dt>` and `<dd>` tags in pairs; a `<dt>` tag is followed by a `<dd>` tag. The second style uses a number of `<dt>` tags followed by the same number of `<dd>` tags. Using the AceHTML editor, generate the foregoing code, and save it as `example912.html`:

      Also, use a browser to render the Web page. As the Web page shows, the style of the first list is easier to follow than the style of the second one.

Code explained:

  1. Line 1 shows the file name of the program in this example. All the book's source code is on the book's companion website. Visit `http://www.prenhall.com/zeid` and follow the instructions to download any of the code files.

  2. Lines 14–19 create a definition list using the `<dt>`–`<dd>` pairs.

  3. Line 20 creates a horizontal line to make the Web page easier to follow.

  4. Lines 23–27 create a definition list using two `<dt>`s followed by two `<dd>`s.

Discussion:

We have removed all the `<meta>` tags at the top of the code, except one, in order to make code listing shorter and easier to follow. We indent lines 15–18, and 24–26 to make it easier to read the source code. Any formatting we do in the file is ignored by the browsers. File formatting is strictly a convenience to us, human beings, to make the code somewhat easier to follow. We provide two elements on the line 24. Again, the browser renders them, as long as they are syntactically correct.

Hands-on exercise:

Add a term to define HTML as "a loose authoring language." Use both styles of `<dl>`s.

9.11.4   Nested Lists

Web authors may need to nest lists in order to represent multiple levels of hierarchies. They may nest lists of the same type or of various types. The only rule of nesting is dictated by the web-page design. XHTML allows multiple levels of nesting, but we seldom use more than two or three levels of nesting. When we nest lists, we make one item in a list into an entire new list. Thus, we can think of the first list as the main list. The second list, which makes an item of the main list into a list itself, is viewed as a sublist. The main list and the sublist form two levels of nesting. If we make one item of the sublist another new list, we create a third level of nesting. The main list has a sublist, and the sublist has a sublist in itself.

Example 9.13 Use nested lists.

Develop a Web page that illustrates the nesting of lists.

Solution 9.13 This example creates a Web page with three nested lists, that is, three levels of nesting. None of the lists uses any attributes. The first-level list is an unordered list and has four items. There are two second-level lists. The first of these lists, an ordered list, has four items. The entire ordered list in the second level belongs to the second item of the first unordered list. The second second-level list, a definition list, has two definitions. The entire definition list in the second level belongs to the third item of the first unordered list. The third-level unordered list has three items. This entire list belongs to the third element of the second-level ordered list. Using the AceHTML editor, generate the following code, and save it as `example913.html`:

```
 1  <!-- filename: example913.html -->
 2  <?xml version="1.0" encoding="iso-8859-1"?>
 3  <!DOCTYPE html PUBLIC "-//W3C//DTD XHTML 1.1//EN"
 4       "http://www.w3.org/TR/xhtml11/DTD/xhtml11.dtd">
 5  <html xmlns="http://www.w3.org/1999/xhtml">
 6  <!-- Generated by AceHTM http://freeware.acehtml.com -->
 7  <head>
 8  <meta http-equiv="Content-Type" content="text/html;
    charset=iso-8859-1"/>
 9  <title>Nesting lists</title>
10  </head>
11  <body>
12  <h2 align="center"><b>My Car Assembly</b></h2>
13  <ul>
14    <li>Chassis</li>
15    <li>Engine</li>
16      <ol>
17        <li>Engine block</li>
18        <li>Cylinders</li>
19        <li>Power parts</li>
20        <ul>
21          <li>sparking plugs</li>
22          <li>pistons</li>
23          <li>connecting rods</li>
24        </ul>
25        <li>Timing belt</li>
26      </ol>
27    <li>Transmission</li>
28      <dl>
29        <dt>Clutch</dt>
30        <dd>transmits power from engine</dd>
31        <dt>Universal joint</dt>
32        <dd>transmits power to wheels</dd>
33      </dl>
34    <li>Steering system</li>
35  </ul>
36  </body>
37  </html>
```

First-level list items: 14, 15, 27, 34
Second-level list items: 1, 2, 3, 4,
Clutch, Universal joint,
Third-level list items: ■ elements

Also, use a browser to render the Web page. It is advisable to indent the list tags when typing the code, to make it easier to follow the beginning and end of these tags. As shown in the Web page, the browser alternates the symbols of the unordered lists automatically, without requiring use of the `type` attribute, for better visualization of the lists and the items that belong to them.

Code explained:

1. Line 1 shows the file name of the program in this example. All the book's source code is on the book's companion web-site. Visit `http://www.prenhall.com/zeid`, and follow the instructions to download any of the code files.
2. Lines 14, 15, 27, and 34 create the first-level list items.
3. Lines 17, 18, 19, and 25 create the second-level list items of the ordered list.
4. Lines 29–32 create the second-level list items of the definition list.
5. The unordered list defined by lines 20–24 belongs to the list item defined in line 19.
6. The definition list defined by lines 28–33 belongs to the list item defined in line 27.

Discussion:

We have indented the various tags properly to make it easy to follow and read the code. It is sometimes confusing to keep track of what is nested inside what. We recommend that you write code one nesting level at a time, starting from the first level and working your way in. In this example, we use three passes to write the code. The first pass excludes lines 16–26 and 28–33. Enter the code as we have done and watch the display of the first-level list in the AceHTML internal browser. We also create the definition list by adding lines 28–33. In the second pass, we create the second-level ordered list by adding lines 16–19, and 25–26. Enter this code and watch the results. In the third and final pass, we add lines 20–24 to create the third-level unordered list.

Hands-on exercise:

Add a second-level ordered list to define the steering system's components as the steering wheel, the steering shaft, the shifter, the dashboard panel, and the signals.

9.11.5 Nontext List Items

Items of a list are traditionally composed of text. However, XHTML allows Web authors to use any Web-page element as a list item. This is a powerful concept. A list item could, therefore, be a hyperlink, an image, an audio files, a video files, and so forth. Thus, Web authors are not limited to using only text. In developing a list with nontext items, Web authors simply use the tag that creates the nontext element. For example, we use an `<a>` tag following an `<li>` tag to create a hyperlink for a list item.

Example 9.14 Use links in a list.

Develop a Web page that illustrates the use of links as list items.

Solution 9.14 Using the AceHTML editor, generate the following code, save it as `example914.html`, and display the Web page in a browser:

```
1  <?xml version="1.0" encoding="iso-8859-1"?>
2  <!DOCTYPE html PUBLIC "-//W3C//DTD XHTML 1.1//EN"
3      "http://www.w3.org/TR/xhtml11/DTD/xhtml11.dtd">
4  <html xmlns="http://www.w3.org/1999/xhtml">
5  <!-- Generated by AceHTM http://freeware.acehtml.com -->
6  <head>
7  <meta http-equiv="Content-Type" content="text/html;
   charset=iso-8859-1" />
8  <title>Links in lists</title>
9  </head>
10 <body>
11 <h2 align="center"><b>Links in lists</b></h2>
12 <ul>
13   <li><a href="http://www.neu.edu">Visit NU</a><br /></li>
14   <li><a href="http://www.mit.edu">Visit MIT</a><br /></li>
15   <li><a href="http://www.sun.com">Visit Sun</a><br /></li>
16 </ul>
17 </body>
18 </html>
```

Code explained:

Lines 13–15 create three links as list items.

Discussion:

As shown in lines 13–15, any XHTML content can go between the <li> tags—for example, text, links, and images.

Hands-on exercise:

Add a new <ol> list with three link items to the websites of your school, Dell, and Microsoft.

9.12 Metadata

Web authors have two goals in mind when they design and develop their Web pages: design for surfers and design for search engines. While authors strive to increase the traffic to their websites and increase the number of hits of their pages, they must keep in mind that search engines must find these pages first in order to index them. One of the effective design tools that increases the chances of page indexing is the <meta> tag.

The <meta> tag allows authors to specify metadata of Web pages. **Metadata** refers to data about an XHTML document rather than the document's content. Browsers do not render metadata. Such data are used by search engines for indexing and ranking page hits in a given search. Web authors can define metadata in a variety of ways. For example, metadata could include a brief description of the Web page, some keywords, and the name of the author Examples are <meta name="author" content="zeid"> and <meat name="generator" content="ACEHTML5Freeware">. The <meta> tag has the following attributes: <meta name content http-equiv scheme>. These attributes are described as follows:

- The `name` attribute defines a property in the XHTML document. One `<meta>` tag defines only one property–value pair. Web authors use multiple `<meta>` tags to define multiple property–value pairs, such as author, copyright, date, keywords, and description.
- The `content` attribute defines the value of a property defined by the `name` attribute. Thus, these two attributes come in pairs.
- The `http-equiv` attribute is used by HTTP servers to gather information needed to display the Web page, such as an ISO character set.
- The `scheme` attribute defines a way to interpret the value of a property. The `scheme` attribute is usually found in the URL (metadata profile) defined by the `profile` attribute of the `<head>` tag.

The template of the AceHTML editor we use in this book offers an excellent example of how the `<meta>` tag can be used to define metadata for a Web page.

9.13 Colors

Color is one of the essential elements of a Web page. The design, visualization, and readability of Web pages are greatly improved by the appropriate use of color combinations and contrast. Choosing colors for page background and text that work together enhances the look of a Web page. For example, light-color text displays well against a dark-color background. Web authors should be sensitive to improper use of colors in their Web pages, because some color combinations may cause problems for some people-for example, the use of dark foreground and background colors concurrently makes it hard on the eye to read Web page content. Also, the excessive use of colors may distract viewers from the value and content of a Web page. In addition, the use of unusual colors in a page, such as in an image, may cause browsers to render the page differently on different platforms—for example, PC, Mac, or Unix.

XHTML makes using colors in a Web page easy. Web authors can specify their color choices by setting values of the attributes of some tags. Note that the `<font>` tag, which has a `color` attribute, has been deprecated and replaced by cascading style sheets. We refrain from using it in this book, although many XHTML editors still offer it.

9.13.1 RGB Color Model

The colors used in XHTML are based on traditional color concepts. Existing color models generate colors by mixing primary colors. A **color model** is a three-dimensional space (cube) with three coordinate axes. Each axis represents a primary color. The RGB (red, green, and blue) model, shown in Figure 9.3, is the most commonly used color model. A color in this model is represented by a point inside or on the cube. Any color is obtained by mixing the three RGB primaries. Thus, the model is additive. These three primaries are the primary colors of light. This color model is used in computer monitors, mainly CRTs (cathode ray tubes), as well as television sets, scanners, and digital cameras.

The main diagonal of the RGB cube, shown in Figure 9.3, defines equal amounts of each primary color. It represents the shades of gray. One end point of the diagonal, the origin of the RGB model, represents the color black, while the other end point represents the color white.

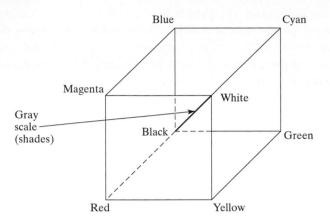

Figure 9.3   The RGB color model.

9.13.2   Hexadecimal Codes

According to the RGB color model, each color is defined by three values, one for each of the primary colors that are mixed together. The values could be specified as decimals or hexadecimals ("hex" for short). A color is expressed as (R, G, B) in decimal and as *#RRGGBB* in hex. Hex values are preceded by a pound (#) sign. Each of the three numbers in a decimal value must be an integer between 0 and 255, and each hex value must consists of numbers between 0 and 9 or letters between A and F. For example, the color red has the decimal value (255, 0, 0) or the hex value #FF0000. The hex or letters between numbers 00 and FF correspond to the decimal numbers 0 and 255, respectively. Thus, the hex value of a color consists of three hex numbers. Each hex number represents the value of a primary color and is between 00 and FF. For example, the color maroon color has the decimal value (176, 48, 96) and the hex value #B03060. Here, the hex numbers B0, 30, and 60 represent the values of the primary colors red, green, and blue, respectively.

Colors are specified in XHTML by using names or hex codes. It is strongly advised that we use hex codes, because they uniquely specify colors. Names are not unique. For example, the name *red* could refer to any one of the many shades of red. The color #FF0000 is red, and the color #FF4500 is orange red. Thus, the name *red* could appear as part of other color names, such as orange red, so it is unclear to the computer which shade is referred to. There are many websites and other publications that provide tables which list both the decimal and hex values of many colors. Table 9.6 shows the names of some sample colors and their corresponding hex codes.

9.13.3   Using Colors in Web Pages

Web authors set and control the colors of the text and the background of Web pages. The text could be simple plain text or hyperlinks. The default text color is black, and the default background color is white. Text colors can be set globally (known as the *foreground* color) or locally

Table 9.6   Color names and their hex codes.

Color name	Hex code	Color name	Hex code	Color name	Hex code
Aqua	#00FFFF	Godzilla	#145F0A	Purple	#800080
Black	#000000	Green	#008000	Red	#FF0000
Blue	#0000FF	Hard Hat	#F6EF31	Scarlet	#8C1717
Blue Violet	#9F5F9F	Hedgehog	#A78424	Silver	#C0C0C0
Braindead	#4566C9	Hunter Green	#215E21	Spicy Pink	#FF1CAE
Brass	#B5A642	Indian Red	#4E2F2F	Spring Green	#00FF7F
Brown	#A62A2A	Khaki	#9F9F5F	Steel Blue	#236B8E
Copper	#B87333	Lime	#00FF00	Succotash	#94BD44
Coral	#FF7F00	Maroon	#800000	Summer Sky	38B0DE
Corn Dog	#F0C373	Navy	#000080	Tan	#DB9370
Dark Brown	#5C4033	Neon Blue	#4D4DFF	Teal	#008080
Dusty Rose	#856363	Neon Pink	#FF6FC7	The Family Rat	#827964
Feldspar	#D19275	Old Gold	#CFB53B	Thistle	#D8BFD8
Firebrick	#8E2323	Olive	#808000	Turquoise	#ADEAEA
Fuchsia	#FF00FF	Orange	#FF7F00	Wheat	#D8D8BF
Full Bladder	#FFC136	Pink	#BC8F8F	White	#FFFFFF
Gray	#808080	Plum	#EAADEA	Yellow	#FFFF00

(known as *spot* colors). Spot colors are assigned to individual characters or words. Spot colors override the foreground color. Depending on design needs, a Web author may set the foreground color to blue. In this case, all of the text on the page is displayed in blue. Whenever the author needs to sprinkle different colors onto the page for some words in the text, such as to attract surfers' attention to them, spot colors are used.

Hyperlink colors are set depending on their state—that is, whether they are links, alinks, or vlinks. Each state is assigned a color. The browser's default colors are blue, red, and purple for links, alinks, and vlinks, respectively. Web authors can override these default colors.

Web authors need XHTML tags or attributes to change and set colors in their Web pages. XHTML does not have separate tags for colors. It has only color attributes. We cover the color attribute of the `<body>` tag here. The `<body>` tag has the following attributes;

```
<body text bgcolor background link alink vlink>
```

These attributes are explained as follows:

- `text` sets the foreground color (the default color of the text on the page). It overrides the default color, which is black.
- `bgcolor` sets the background color of the Web page. It overrides the default color, which is white.
- `background` tiles a Web page with an image. See Chapter 10.
- `link` sets the color of links in a Web page. It overrides the default color, which is blue.
- `alink` sets the color of active links in a Web page. It overrides the default color which is red.
- `vlink` sets the color of visited links in a Web page. It overrides the default color, which is purple.

Example 9.15 Use colors in Web pages.

Develop a Web page that illustrates the use of colors.

Solution 9.15 In this example, we use a gray background and yellow text in a Web page. We also replace the default colors of links, alinks, and vlinks with khaki, brown, and black, respectively. Using the AceHTML editor, generate the following code, save it as `example915.html`, and display the Web page in a browser:

```
1  <?xml version ="1.0" encoding="iso-8859-1"?>
2  <!DOCTYPE html PUBLIC "-//W3C//DTD XHTML 1.1//EN"
3      "http://www.w3.org/TR/xhtml11/DTD/xhtml11.dtd">
4  <html xmlns="http://www.w3.org/1999/xhtml">
5  <!-- Generated by AceHTM http://freeware.acehtml.com -->
6  <head>
7  <meta http-equiv="Content-Type" content="text/html;
   charset=iso-8859-1" />
8  <title>Using colors</title>
9  </head>
10 <body text="#FFFF00" bgcolor="#CCCCCC"
   link="#9F9F5F" alink="#A62A2A" vlink="#000000">
11 <h2 align="center"><b>Using colors</b></h2>
12 <ul>
13   <li><a href="http://www.neu.edu">Visit NU</a><br /></li>
14   <li><a href="http://www.mit.edu">Visit MIT</a><br /></li>
15   <li><a href="http://www.sun.com">Visit Sun</a><br /></li>
16 </ul>
17 </body>
18 </html>
```

Code explained:

    1. Line 10 specifies all the colors of the Web page.

    2. Lines 12–16 create an `<ol>` list with links.

Discussion:

We have modified the code of Example 9.14 by adding colors to the Web page. The choice of colors is not that great. As a matter of fact, you cannot read the yellow heading that says "Using colors" (code line 11).

Hands-on exercise:

Change the colors of the Web page. Use the AceHTML editor to help you. Click the colors icon. Select colors for text, background, links, alinks, and vlinks. Make sure that the colors contrast well together in the page. Also add some text paragraphs to make the page stand out.

9.14 Audio and Video

Audio (sound) and video are XHTML multimedia content that can be included in Web pages in the form of clips (small content that lasts for a short time). Macromedia Flash is typically used to add audio and video to Web pages. Web pages use digital audio and video, as opposed to analog audio and video. Digital audio and video clips are stored in files using certain formats, just as text is saved in a file with a particular text format. The size of an audio clip depends on its duration (how long it lasts), sampling rate (the number of audio samples per second; if the rate is low, the sound seems interrupted), sampling resolution (the number of bits per sample; if the resolution is low, the sound will not be clear and will be hard to understand), and the number of channels (mono sound uses one channel, and stereo sound uses multiple channels; more channels mean better sound effects).

The size of a video clip depends on its duration, frame rate (similar to the sampling rate of sound, it is the number of frames per second to represent the video; if the resolution is low, the video will look unsmooth or discontinuous), frame size (the resolution of each frame; higher resolution means higher quality video), and compression level (to reduce the size of the video clip, similar to compressing or zipping files).

The foregoing audio and video parameters become important if you begin recording your audio and video clips for use in personal Web pages. Even then, you may opt to use the default values offered by the hardware you are using. However, production of professional audio and video clips goes much farther that what we cover here. Our main goal in this section is to discuss the use of existing clips.

There are different audio and video file formats. Some of the existing sound formats are AU, WAV, MIDI, AIFF, and MP3. MP3 and WAV are the most popular formats. Some of the existing video formats are AVI, QuickTime, MPEG, and MJPEG. The QuickTime and MPEG formats are the most widely used. When we embed an audio or video clip in a Web page, the browser uses a plug-in to play it.

For the user to be able to hear sound or watch a video clip (which has sound associated with it) embedded in a Web page, the computer that displays the page must have the right hardware and software. The hardware needed includes a sound card, a video card, and external speakers. The software (known as drivers) must support the cards. Both must be installed on the computer.

A microphone is also required if the computer is used for recording sound. Mics are the only way to record sound on computers. Users can also hook up digital video cameras to their computers. The cameras can be used to generate video clips, which may be played later on the users' computers.

XHTML does not have audio or video tags. Even in HTML, the W3C does not have standards for sound or video tags. The existing tags have evolved over the years from IE and Netscape. The `<embed>` tag is the only tag supported by both IE and Netscape and is used here. It accepts both audio and video clips (files). The `<embed>` tag has the following attributes:

`<embed src width height volume autostart hidden loop>:`

These attributes are explained as follows:

- `src` specifies the name of the file containing the sound or video clip to be included in the Web page. The file and the XHTML file that uses it are usually placed in the same directory.
- `width` and `height` specify the size of the control console, in pixels.
- `volume` determines the volume level (the loudness) of the sound when the browser plays the sound or video clip. It can take a value between 1 and 100. The default value is 50, the middle of the range. Web surfers must also remember to check the volume setting of the external sound speakers. If the volume level of either the speakers or the control console is not set properly, the user will not hear the sound embedded in the Web page.
- `autostart` takes a value of `true` or `false`. If the Web page's author wants the sound or video clip to play automatically when the Web page is loaded, `autostart="true"` is used. The default value is `false`.
- `hidden` takes a value of `true` or `false` (the default). If the Web page's author uses `hidden="true"`, the control console is not displayed in the Web page.
- `loop` allows the browser to play the same clip more than once. It takes a value of `true` or `false`. The default value is `false`, in which case the browser plays the clip only once. If the value is set to `true`, the browser plays the clip repeatedly until the Web surfer stops it.

Example 9.16 Listen to music on Web pages.

Develop a Web page that illustrates the use of an audio clip.

Solution 9.16 Using the AceHTML editor, generate the following code, save it as `example916.html`, and display the Web page in a browser:

```
 1 <?xml version = "1.0" encoding="iso-8859-1"?>
 2 <!DOCTYPE html PUBLIC "-//W3C//DTD XHTML 1.1//EN"
 3     "http://www.w3.org/TR/xhtml11/DTD/xhtml11.dtd">
 4 <html xmlns="http://www.w3.org/1999/xhtml">
 5 <!-- Generated by AceHTM http://freeware.acehtml.com -->
 6 <head>
 7 <meta http-equiv="Content-Type" content="text/html;
   charset=iso-8859-1"  />
 8 <title>Playing sound clips</title>
 9 </head>
10 <body>
11 <h2 align="center"><b>A Web page with music</b></h2>
12 Click the desired button on the control console shown below.
13 <P><embed src="music.mp3" width="145" height="60" volume="70">
   </embed></p>
14 </body>
15 </html>
```

- MP3 music file to play
- The file must reside in the same folder as the example 916.html file

- Control console
- 145 pixels wide
- 60 pixels high
- Volume is set at 70

Progress meter

Play

Pause

Stop

A Web page with music

Click the desired button on the control console shown below.

Fast forward

Rewind

Skip back

Code explained:

Line 13 creates a control console that allows us to play and control the MP3 music file myMusic.mp3.

Discussion:

The <embed> tag creates the control console, using its width and height attributes. To control the playback of the files, you click the buttons shown on the console as you would with a real music player.

Hands-on exercise:

Modify line 13 to use the autostart mode and an infinite playing loop.

Example 9.17 Watch movies on Web pages.

Develop a Web page that illustrates the use of a video clip.

Solution 9.17 Use the AceHTML editor to generate the following code, save it as example917.html, and display the Web page in a browser:

```
1  <?xml version="1.0" encoding="iso-8859-1"?>
2  <!DOCTYPE html PUBLIC "-//W3C//DTD XHTML 1.1//EN"
3     "http://www.w3.org/TR/xhtml11/DTD/xhtml11.dtd">
4  <html xmlns="http://www.w3.org/1999/xhtml">
5  <!-- Generated by AceHTM http://freeware.acehtml.com -->
6  <head>
7  <meta http-equiv="Content-Type" content="text/html;
   charset=iso-8859-1" />
8  <title>Playing video clips</title>
9  </head>
10 <body>
11 <h2 align="center"><b>A Web page with video</b></h2>
12 Click the Play button to start the movie.
13 <p><embed src="movie.mpg" width="400" height="300"
   volume="70"></embed></p>
14 </body><html>
```

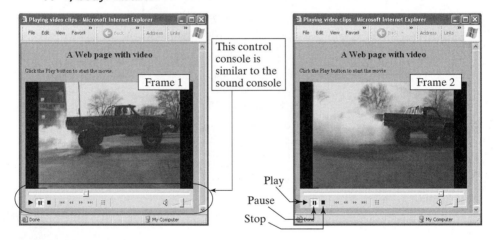

Code explained:

Line 13 creates a control console and a display area that allow us to play and control the MPEG video file, `movie.mpg`.

Discussion:

We show two frames in this example to illustrate the playing of the video clip. We play the clip, freeze (pause) it, and take a screen capture. The `<embed>` tag creates the control console and the display area, using its width and height attributes. You click the buttons shown on the console as you would with a real video player. If the browser cannot find the video file (e.g., if the XHTML file has provided the wrong name, extension, or folder), the control console is displayed, but in a disabled mode. You cannot click any buttons. Make sure the file name and extension are correct and that the file is in the correct folder. For example, the file name `movie.mpeg` uses the wrong extension. The extension should be `.mpg`.

Hands-on exercise:
Modify line 13 to use the `autostart` mode and an infinite playing loop.

9.15 Tutorials

9.15.1 Using Character Sets (Study Section 9.9)

This tutorial demonstrates use of the ISO 8859-1 (Latin-1) and Greek character sets. We use some of the symbols in both sets. Use AceHTML editor to generate the following code, save it as `tutorial9151.html`, and view the page in a browser:

```
1  <?xml version="1.0" encoding="iso-8859-1"?>
2  <!DOCTYPE html PUBLIC "-//W3C//DTD XHTML 1.1//EN"
3      "http://www.w3.org/TR/xhtml11/DTD/xhtml11.dtd">
4  <html xmlns="http://www.w3.org/1999/xhtml">
5  <!-- Generated by AceHTM http://freeware.acehtml.com -->
6  <head>
7  <meta http-equiv="Content-Type" content="text/html;
     charset=iso-8859-1" />
8  <title>Playing video clips</title>
9  </head>
10 <body>
11 <h2 align="center"><b>Using ISO 8859-1
     (Latin-1) and Greek character sets
     </b></h2>
12 54&#62;30
13 <p>5&#60;10</p>
14 <p>You may want to consider joining
     the &#960;&#964;&#931; (Pi Tau Sigma)
     and &#964;&#946;&#960; (Tau Beta Pi) honor societies.</p>
15 </body>
16 </html>
```

Code explained:

1. Lines 12 and 13 use the ISO Latin-1 set.
2. Line 12 prints the inequality 54>30.
3. Line 13 prints the inequality 5<10.
4. Line 14 uses Greek symbols. It prints pi (π), tau (τ), sigma (Σ), tau (τ), beta (β), and pi (π).

Discussion:

We use numeric code to express the special characters.

Hands-on exercise:

Add more special characters for a professional society, or fraternity, or an organization.

9.15.2 Personal Web Site (Study Sections 9.8 and 9.10)

This tutorial creates a personal website. Figure 9.4 shows a possible design for the site. The site has nine Web pages. The home page links to the other eight Web pages. The *Professional* Web page links to the *Resume* Web page, and the *Personal* Web page links to the *Family Tree* Web page. Using the AceHTML editor, generate the upcoming code, which is for the home page, and save it as `tutorial9152.html`. The XHTML code for the other Web pages is not included here, as readers can easily generate it on their own. View the page in a browser.

Code explained:

1. Lines 13–15 create bold text.
2. Lines 19–21 create plain text.
3. Lines 24–31 create interdocument links.

Discussion:

The browser renders lines 19–21 as a long line of text that may wrap around, depending on the size of the browser window, as shown in the foregoing screen capture. You can use `<br />` to break the long line for more control.

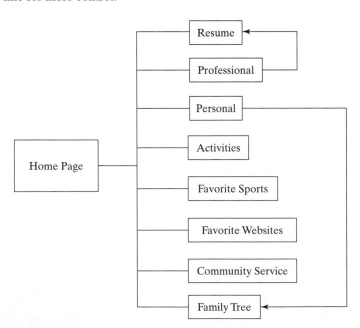

Figure 9.4   Structure of a personal Web site.

```
 1 <?xml version="1.0" encoding="iso-8859-1"?>
 2 <!DOCTYPE html PUBLIC "-//W3C//DTD XHTML 1.1//EN"
 3    "http://www.w3.org/TR/xhtml11/DTD/xhtml11.dtd">
 4 <html xmlns="http://www.w3.org/1999/xhtml">
 5 <!-- Generated by AceHTM http://freeware.acehtml.com -->
 6 <head>
 7 <meta http-equiv="Content-Type" content="text/html;
   charset=iso-8859-1" />
 8 <title>My Website</title>
 9 </head>
10 <body>
11 <h2 align="center"><b>Welcome to my website</b></h2>
12 <hr />
13 <b>Name goes here</b><br />
14 <b>Address goes here</b><br />
15 <b>Phone number goes here</b>
16 <hr />
17 <p>
18 <hr />
19 Let me introduce myself. I have mastered XHTML.
20 I have been working with many people. This is my personal
21 website, in case you want to know more about me.
22 <hr />
23 </p>
24 <a href="resume.html">Resume</a><br />
25 <a href="professional.html">Professional</a><br />
26 <a href="personal.html">
   Personal</a><br />
27 <a href="activities.html">
   Activities</a><br />
28 <a href="favoriteSports.html">
   Favorite Sports</a><br />
29 <a href="favoriteWebsites.html">
   Favorite Websites</a><br />
30 <a href="communityService.html">
   Community Service</a><br />
31 <a href="familyTree.html">
   Family Tree</a>
32 </body>
33 </html>
```

Lines 12–16 create this content

Lines 18–22 create this content

Lines 24–31 create this content

Hands-on exercise:

Write the *Personal* Web page, and link it to the *Family Tree* page, as specified in Figure 9.4.

9.15.3   Create Anchors (Study Section 9.10)

This tutorial shows how to create a personal Web page, using anchors, or intradocument links. We convert some of the hyperlinks developed in Tutorial 9.15.2 into anchors. We only do it for the first three links, however, to keep the page short. This approach to developing a personal Web page results in one XHTML file instead of multiple separate ones. The resulting personal Web page becomes multiple screens long. We make two changes to the XHTML code in Tutorial 9.15.2. First, we replace each HTML file in the three `<a>` tags by a name. Second, we added a heading to each of the anchor sections in order to make it easier to follow the page's structure. Use the Ace-HTML editor to generate the upcoming code, and save it as `tutorial9153.html`.

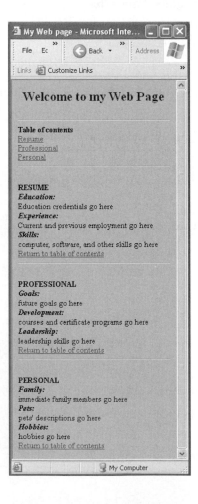

Code explained:

1. Lines 14, 29, 37, and 45 define the TOC links.

2. Lines 16–18 define intradocument links (anchors).

3. Lines 21, 30, and 38 define the links' sections.

Discussion:

We add a `Return to table of content` link at the end of each section of the Web page in order to make page navigation easy.

Hands-on exercise:

Extend the Web page by creating other anchors for the remaining links shown in Tutorial 9.15.2. After you finish, how many screens is the Web page's display? Do you think anchors are a good design idea?

```
1   <?xml version="1.0" encoding="iso-8859-1"?>
2   <!DOCTYPE html PUBLIC "-//W3C//DTD XHTML 1.1//EN"
3       "http://www.w3.org/TR/xhtml11/DTD/xhtml11.dtd ">
4   <html xmlns="http://www.w3.org/1999/xhtml ">
5   <!-- Generated by AceHTM http://freeware.acehtml.com -->
6   <head>
7   <meta http-equiv="Content-Type" content="text/html;
    charset=iso-8859-1" />
8   <title>My Web page</title>
9   </head>
10  <body>
11  <h2 align="center"><b>Welcome to my Web Page </b></h2> <hr />
12
13  <!-- Define a destination tag -->
14  <a name="Contents"><b>Table of contents </b></a><br />
15  <!-- Define source tags -->
16  <a href="#resume">Resume</a><br />
17  <A href="#professional">Professional </a><br />
18  <A href="#personal">Personal </a><br />
19  <hr /> <p></p>
20  <!-- Define destination tag for resume source tag -->
21  <p></p><a name="resume"><b>RESUME</b><br />
22  <b><i>Education: </i></b><br />
23  Education credentials go here <br />
24  <b><i>Experience: </i></b><br />
25  Current and previous employment go here <br />
26  <b><i>Skills: </i></b><br />
27  computer, software, and other skills go here <br />
28  <!-- Define a source tag for TOC -->
```

```
29   <a href="#Contents">Return to table of contents </a><hr />
30   <p><a name="professional"><b>PROFESSIONAL </b><br />
31   <b><i>Goals: </i></b><br />
32   future goals go here<br />
33   <b><i>Development: </i></b><br />
34   courses and certificate programs go here <br />
35   <b><i>Leadership: </i></b><br />
36   leadership skills go here <br />
37   <a href="#Contents">Return to table of contents </a><hr />
38   <p></p><a name="personal"><b>PERSONAL </b><br />
39   <b><i>Family: </i></b><br />
40   immediate family members go here <br />
41   <b><i>Pets: </i></b><br />
42   pets' descriptions go here <br />
43   <b><i>Hobbies: </i></b><br />
44   hobbies go here<br />
45   <a href="#Contents">Return to table of contents </a>
46   </body>
47   </html>
```

9.15.4 Organizational Structure (Study Section 9.11)

This tutorial uses nested lists to describe the structure of a typical college in a university. We use a mix of `<ul>` and `<ol>` lists. Using the AceHTML editor, generate the upcoming code, save it as `tutorial9154.html`, and view the page in a browser:

Code explained:

1. Lines 13 and 40 define a first-level `<ul>` list.
2. Lines 15 and 25 define a second-level `<ul>` list.
3. Lines 27 and 29 define a second-level `<ol>` list.
4. Lines 20–24 define a third-level `<ol>` list.
5. Lines 31 and 35 define a third-level `<ul>` list.

Discussion:

We use the `type` attribute in the lists of lines 15 and 27 in order to use different values than the default, to make it easier to follow the display of the Web page.

Hands-on exercise:

Replace the `type` in line 15 by `circle`, and the `type` in line 27 by `I`. Which bullet shapes changes?

```
1  <?xml version="1.0" encoding="iso-8859-1"?>
2  <!DOCTYPE html PUBLIC "-//W3C//DTD XHTML 1.1//EN"
3         "http://www.w3.org/TR/xhtml11/DTD/xhtml11.dtd">
4  <html xmlns="http://www.w3.org/1999/xhtml">
5  <!-- Generated by AceHTM http://freeware.acehtml.com -->
6  <head>
7  <meta http-equiv="Content-Type" content="text/html;
   charset=iso-8859-1" />
8  <title>Organizational Structure</title>
9  </head>
10 <body>
11 <h2 align="center"><b>College Organizational Structure</b></hr2>
12 <p></p>Here is the structure of a college in a university
13 <ul>
14     <li>Dean's office</li>
15         <ul type = "square">
16             <li>Dean</li>
17             <li>Associate dean</li>
18             <li>Assistant dean</li>
19             <li>Staff</li>
20             <ol>
21                 <li>Staff 1</li>
22                 <li>Staff 2</li>
23                 <li>Staff 3</li>
24             </ol>
25         </ul>
26     <li>Department</li>
27         <ol type="A">
28             <li>Chairman</li>
29             <li>Assoc. chairman</li>
30             <li>Faculty</li>
31             <ul>
32                 <li>Group 1</li>
33                 <li>Group 2</li>
34                 <li>Group 3</li>
35             </ul>
36             <li>Staff</li>
37             <li>Graduate students</li>
38             <li>Undergraduate students</li>
39         </ol>
40 </ul>
41 </body>
42 </html>
```

FAQs

Websites and Web Pages (Section 9.2)

Q: What is the difference between a Web designer and a Web developer?

A: A Web designer designs the layout and content of a website and its Web pages. A Web developer (also known as a Web author, programmer, or coder) implements the design by writing XHMTL code. This difference is similar to that between house architects and builders or contractors.

Authoring of Web Pages (Section 9.4)

Q: Which should I use, HTML or XHTML?

A: Use XHTML. In practice, people mean XHTML when they use the word "HTML."

XHTML Syntax (Section 9.5)

Q: Will deprecated tags ever be completely removed from the Web?

A: No. There are so many Web pages that use these tags. Authoring tools still provide and support them. However, Web authors should refrain from using them in Web pages.

Text Formatting (Section 9.8)

Q: Why does the browser sometimes show the XHTML source code of a Web page in its window instead of showing the actual Web page itself?

A: This means that the XHTML file was inadvertently saved with the extension `.txt` instead of `.html`. In this case, the browser treats the file as a text file's and displays its contents literally. You should resave the file with the `.html` extension or change the existing file's extension from `.txt` to `.html`. Also, if the code is syntactically incorrect, the browser does not how to render it and displays it literally instead.

Q: Does a browser recognize any formatting, such as indenting and spaces, that a Web author uses in the HTML code of a Web page?

A: No. The browser understands and interprets only XHTML tags. It ignores any other formatting that you may use in writing the XHTML code of the page. The manual formatting we have included in our code examples is a convenience to the readers of this volume.

Hyperlinks (Section 9.10)

Q: Can I use no value for the `href` attribute?

A: Yes. Two cases exist for which this attribute can take no value. First if you use `<a href="">`, you get a blank page when the user clicks the link. Second, if you use `<a href="#">`, nothing happens at all when the user clicks the link.

Lists (Section 9.11)

Q: How can I get better control of list formatting—numbering, indenting, and so forth?

A: Cascading style sheets allow better control of list formatting.

Colors (Section 9.13)

Q: Why should a Web-page author not specify colors by names?

A: While many browsers allow the use of color names in XHTML code, there is no list of color names that works the same in all browsers. Specifying colors via hex codes is safer and works consistently in all browsers.

Blackbox

Section 9.1 (Introduction): Web developers write XHTML code for Web pages. A Web browser has an XHTML interpreter that renders the code.

Section 9.2 (Websites and Web Pages) (Example 9.1): A website consists of multiple Web pages, structured as a spider web. The pages are linked together via hyperlinks. Each website has a home page. It is easy to edit and change web structures.

Section 9.3 (Content of Web Pages) (Example 9.2): The content of a Web page is classified into falls among 13 elements: text, lists, color, hyperlinks, sound clips, video clips, graphics, images, image maps, forms, frames, tables, and layers. Web-page content may be static or dynamic. Dynamic content is updated automatically.

Section 9.4 (Authoring of Web Pages): Use XHTML to write Web-page code. It is easy to learn and fun to use. Visit `http://www.w3c.org` to find out about the latest XHTML developments.

Sections 9.5 and 9.6 (XHTML Syntax and HTML Document Structure) (Examples 9.3–9.5): XHTML uses tags and elements. An element consists of its tags and content. An example of an XHTML element is `<b><i>This is a sample</i></b>`. The tags of this element are `<b>` and `<i>`; the content is `This is a sample`. Use lowercase letters for tag names, nest tags properly (first open, last closed), and do not leave blank spaces between tags and the text next to them. Use comments (denoted by `<!-- content -->`) in your code. Avoid using deprecated tags. The generic XHTML document structure is shown as follows:

```
<?xml version="1.0" encoding="iso-8859-1"?>
<!DOCTYPE html PUBLIC "-//W3C//DTD XHTML 1.1//EN"
    "http://www.w3.org/TR/xhtml11/DTD/xhtml11.dtd">
<html xmlns="http://www.w3.org/1999/xhtml ">
<head>
<meta name="author" content="zeid" />
<title>This is the XHTML document structure </title>
</head>
<body>
        Web-page content goes here
</body>
</html>
```

Section 9.7 (Authoring Tools): Web developers need editors and Web browsers to develop and view Web pages, Text and XHTML editors can be used to write XHTML code. We use XHTML editors in this book. Specifically, we use the AceHTML freeware editor. Download it from `http://www.visicommedia.com/acehtml`, or just `http://www.acehtml.com`, and install it. We use version 5.07 for Windows.

Section 9.8 (Text Formatting) (Examples 9.6 and 9.7): XHTML provides the following tags to format text: `<h1>–<h6>`, `<b>`, `<i>`, `<br>`, `<em>`, `<strong>`, `<small>`, `<block-quote>`, `<cite>`, `<kbd>`, `<code>`, `<pre>`, `<div>`, and `<hr>`. The tags with attributes are `<h1` (or h2–h6) `align>` and `<hr align color noshade size width>`.

Section 9.9 (Special Characters): XHTML provides three special-character sets: ISO 8859-1 Latin-1; the symbols, mathematical symbols, and Greek letters; and the markup-significant and internationalization characters. Special characters are represented by a character entity or a numeric code. The character entity begins with & and ends with ;. The numeric code begins with &# and ends with ;. For examples, the copyright symbol is represented by the character entity © or by the numeric code ©.

Section 9.10 (Hyperlinks) (Examples 9.8 and 9.9): The `<a>` tag links Web pages together. Use it to create interdocument or intradocument links. Its syntax and attributes are `<a href title name charset type hreflang rel rev accesskey shape coords tabindex>link text goes here</a>`.

Section 9.11 (Lists) (Examples 9.10–9.14): The three list tags are `<ul>`, `<ol>`, and `<dl>`. Use any of these tags with the `<li>` tag to create lists in Web pages. The syntax and attributes of these tags are `<ul type><li type compact>content</li>...</ul>`, `<ol type><li start value compact>content</li>...</ol>`, and `<dl><dt>...</dt><dd>...</dd>...</dl>`, respectively. Lists can be nested.

Section 9.12 (Metadata): Metadata help search engines find Web pages and return them as search hits. Use the `<meta>` tag. Its syntax and attributes are `<meta name content http-equiv scheme>`.

Section 9.13 (Colors) (Example 9.15): XHTML uses the RGB color model. A color has three signals (R, G, B). Use the hex code to specify color in XHTML tags—for example, #AA96FF. Use the `<body>` tag to specify foreground, background, and hyperlink colors, as well as the tiling of images. Its syntax and attributes are `<body text bgcolor background link alink vlink>`.

Section 9.14 (Audio and Video) (Examples 9.16 and 9.17): Adding sound and video files to Web pages is done mainly with Flash. The `<embed>` tag can be used to add audio and video clips to Web pages. Its syntax and attributes are `<embed src width height volume autostart hidden loop>`.

Section 9.15 (Tutorials): Four tutorials show how to use ISO Latin-1 characters, links, anchors, and lists.

Quick reference for the tags presented in this chapter

Tag	Close	Attribute	Value	Effect	Example
`<!-- -->`	none	none	none	comment statement	`<!-- comment -->`
`<html>`	yes	none	none	begin and end XHTML code	`<html>...</html>`
`<head>`	yes	none	none	defines head section	`<head>...</head>`
`<title>`	yes	none	none	defines page title	`<title>Page</title>`
`<body>`	yes	`text`	hex	foreground color	`<body text="#AA11FF">`
		`bgcolor`	hex	background color	`<body bgcolor="#66BBCC">..</body>`
		`background`	file name	specifies an image file for tiling	`<body background="myFile.jpg">`
		`link`	hex	link color	`<body link="#66BBCC">..</body>`
		`alink`	hex	active-link color	`<body alink="#66BBCC">..</body>`
		`vlink`	hex	visited-link color	`<body vlink="#66BBCC">..</body>`
`<h1>`	yes	`align`	`left` (default), `center`, or `right`	text size is 24	`<h1 align="center">text goes here</h1>`
`<h2>`	yes	`align`	same as `<h1>`	text size is 18	`<h2>text here</h2>`
`<h3>`	yes	`align`	same as `<h1>`	text size is 14	`<h3> text here</h3>`
`<h4>`	yes	`align`	same as `<h1>`	text size is 12	`<h4> text here</h4>`
`<h5>`	yes	`align`	same as `<h1>`	size text is 10	`<h5>text here</h5>`
`<h6>`	yes	`align`	same as `<h1>`	text size is 8	`<h6>text here</h6>`
`<b>`	yes	none	none	bold text	`<b>text</b>`
`<i>`	yes	none	none	italic text	`<i>text</i>`
` `	empty	none	none	line break	`text `

Tag	Close	Attribute	Value	Effect	Example
`<em>`	yes	none	none	typographic emphasis	`<em>text</em>`
`<strong>`	yes	none	none	typographic emphasis	`<strong>text goes here</strong>`
`<small>`	yes	none	none	small-font text	`<small>text</small>`
`<block-quote>`	yes	none	none	formats text as a quotation from a specific source	`<blockquote>text goes here</blockquote>`
`<cite>`	yes	none	none	a citation reference	`<cite>text></cite>`
`<kbd>`	yes	none	none	keyboard font	`<kbd>text</kbd>`
`<code>`	yes	none	none	computer-code font	`<code>text</code>`
`<pre>`	yes	none	none	display text as is	`<pre>text</pre>`
`<div>`	yes	none	none	acts as a line break	`<div>text</div>`
`<hr>`	empty	`align`	`left`, `center` (default), or `right`	aligns a line in the Web page	`<hr align="left" />`
		`color`	name or hex code	specifies the line color	`<hr color="red" />` `<hr color="#0000FF" />`
		`noshade`	none	fades line into the background	`<hr noshade />`
		`size`	number of pixels	line thickness	`<hr size="5" />`
		`width`	number of pixels or %	length as pixels or as a percentage of the Web page's width	`<hr width="200" />` `<hr width="50%" />`
`<a>`	yes	`href`	URL	specifies Web page to link to	`<a href="http://www.neu.edu>...</a>`
		`title`	text	link title	`<a title="My link">`
		`charset`	name	specifies character set	`<a charset="ISO...>`
		`type`	MIME	defines document type	`<a type="text/css">`
		`hreflang`	language	specifies language of page to link to	`<a hreflang="fr">`

Tag	Close	Attribute	Value	Effect	Example
`<ul>`	yes	`type`	`disk`	list disk symbol	`<ul type="disk">`
			`circle`	list circle symbol	`<ul type="circle">`
			`square`	list square symbol	`<ul type="square">`
`<ol>`	yes	`type`	Arabic	Arabic numerals	`<ol type="1">`
			Latin	Latin characters	`<ol type="A">`
			Roman	Roman letters	`<ol type="I">`
`<li>`	yes	`type`	same as `<ul>` and `<ol>`	create list items with symbols	`<li type="disk">`
		`compact`	Boolean	compact list display	`<li compact="true">`
		`start` (for an ordered list)	number	start number	`<li start="4">`
		`value`	number	any number for any list item	`<li value="7">`
`<dl>`	yes	none	none	definition list	`<dl>...</dl>`
`<dt>`	yes	none	none	definition term	`<dt>My term</dt>`
`<dd>`	yes	none	none	definition data	`<dd>definition</dd>`
`<meta>`	empty	`name`	text	specifies keyword	`<meta name="author" />`
		`content`	text	specifies data	`<meta content="zeid" />`
		`http-equiv`	text	specifies keyword	`<meta http-equiv="content-type" />`
		`scheme`	text	specifies keyword	`<meta scheme="ISBN" />`

Check Your Progress

At the end of this chapter, you should

- ✔ understand websites and Web pages (Sections 9.1 and 9.2);
- ✔ understand content elements and types (Section 9.3);
- ✔ understand the difference between HTML and XHMTL (Sections 9.4 and 9.5);
- ✔ be able to identify the structural components of XHTML documents (Section 9.6);
- ✔ be able to use text and XHTML editors (Section 9.7);

✔ have mastered the use of text formatting, special characters, links, lists, and meta data (Sections 9.8–9.12);

✔ have mastered the use of colors in Web pages (Section 9.13);

✔ understand the use of audio and video in Web pages (Section 9.14).

Problems

The exercises are designed for a lab setting, while the homework is to be done outside class time.

Exercises

9.1   Visit the website of your school or organization, and reverse engineer the site design. What is the home page of the site? How many Web pages does it link to?

9.2   Find a Web page that has both static and dynamic content. Identify both types of content in the page.

9.3   Construct the XHTML element for the following tag and attributes: `<house>` with a colonial style, four bedrooms, and 4000 ft^2 of living space.

9.4   Combine the Web pages in Examples 9.6 and 9.7 into one Web page.

9.5   Use the ISO Latin-1 character set to write this statement in a Web page: `Borrowing $5000 @ 10% annual rate costs $500 a year`.

9.6   Use the ISO Greek character set to write this statement in a Web page: `Here are some Greek fraternities:` $\Phi \kappa \varepsilon, \tau \beta \pi$, and $\gamma \alpha \Delta$.

Homework

9.7   Visit your favorite website, and reverse engineer the site design. What is the home page of the site? How many Web pages does it link to?

9.8   Find a Web page that has both static and dynamic content. Identify both types of content in the page.

9.9   Construct the XHTML elements for the following tags and attributes:
   - `<person>` whose first name is Abe, last name is Zeid, and is a professor.
   - A bold and italic `I love` NY text.

9.10   Develop a Web page that uses text heading, text formatting, and horizontal lines.

9.11   Create a Web page for your resume. *Hint*: If you have your resume as an MS Word document, you can simply save it as HTML document: While in Word, click the sequence `File => Save as HTML`.

9.12   Create your personal Web page, using the structure shown in Figure 9.4. Use hyperlinks. Utilize the `title` attribute in all the `<a>` tags you use.

9.13   Convert your personal Web page from Problem 9.12 to use anchors instead of hyperlinks.

9.14   Create a Web page that uses as many of the ISO Latin-1 characters as possible.

9.15   Create a Web page that uses as many of the ISO Greek characters as possible.

9.16   Create a Web page that uses text, hyperlinks, and lists.

9.17   Create a Web page that describes a house. Use the `<a>` tag with its title attribute, the `<hr>` tag with its attributes, and as many of the text tags as necessary.

9.18   Repeat Problem 9.17, but for a car.

9.19   Create an unordered list of the names of 10 people.

9.20   Create an ordered list of the top 10 winners of your favorite competition.

9.21 Create a definition list of the following terms: Internet, intranet, extranet, POP, IP address, TCP/IP, browser, search engine, and metasearch engine.

9.22 Create a nested list of two levels. The first level is an unordered list of three items, and the second level has three ordered lists, one list for each item of the unordered list. The items of the unordered list are winning categories — for example, best design, best effort, and best attitude. Each nested ordered list has the names of three winners—for first, second, and third places.

9.23 Write the HTML code to generate the list shown on the left in Figure 9.5.

9.24 Write the HTML code to generate the list shown on the right in Figure 9.5.

9.25 Write the HTML code to generate the list shown on the left in Figure 9.6.

9.26 Write the HTML code to generate the list shown on the right in Figure 9.6.

9.27 Add text and background colors to the Web pages you created in Problems 9.23–9.26.

9.28 Add text, link, alink, vlink, and background colors to the Web page you created in Problem 9.17.

9.29 Create a Web page that uses your favorite mp3 music clip in the <embed> tag. Try out all the attributes of the tag.

9.30 Create a Web page that uses your favorite video clip in the <embed> tag. Try out all the attributes of the tag.

Building your dream house	**Power PC Instructions**

1. Choose a lot
2. Choose house plan
3. Pour foundation
4. Frame the house
5. Choose bathroom fixtures
    • stick with neural colors, ie white or cream
    • Don't forget to choose countertops and
      vanities for bathrooms
6. Design kitchen layout
    • Choose kitchen cabinets and countertops
    • Choose flooring
        a. Wood
        b. Ceramic tile
        c. Linoleum
7. Choose interior and exterior paint colors
8. Choose flooring for remainder of house
9. Insulate and enclose walls
10. Plaster walls and ceilings
11. Do finish carpentry work
12. Paints walls and mouldings inside house
13. Paint exterior of house
14. Install cabinets   Problem 9.23
15. Install flooring
16. MOVE IN!!!!
	1. Integer Instructions
	    ○ Integer Arithmetic Instructions
	    ○ Integer Compare Instructions
	    ○ Integer Logical Instructions
	    ○ Integer Rotate Instructions
	    ○ Integer Shift Instructions
	2. Floating Point Instructions
	    ○ Floating-Point Arithmetic Instructions
	    ○ Floating-Point Multiply-Add Instructions
	    ○ Floating-Point Rounding and Conversion
	    ○ Instructions
	    ○ Floating-Point Compare Instructions
	3. Load and Store Instructions
	    ○ Integer Load and Store Address Generation
	    ○ Integer Load Instructions
	    ○ Integer Store Instructions
	    ○ Integer Load and Store With Byte Reverse
	    ○ Instructions
	4. Branch and Flow Control Instructions
	    ○ Branch Instructions
	    ○ Trap Instructions
	    ○ System Linkage Instructions Problem 9.24
	5. Processor Control Instructions

Figure 9.5 Problems 9.23 and 9.24.

Using ATM Machines	**To-do list of activities for the busiest week of the month**
There are several transactions you can do an ATM: • Deposits • Withdrawals • Balance Inquiry • And new, to my bank at least, purchase stamps. The steps required for withdrawing money using an ATM machine: 1. Insert card in machine. 2. When prompted, type your secret PIN number. 3. Press ENTER. The machine verifies your PIN and prompts you to choose the amount of money to withdraw. 4. Type or select the amount of money to withdraw. 5. Press ENTER. The ATM display prompts you to confirm that the amount is correct. 6. Press ENTER. IF correct, or click CANCEL and retype or select the correct amount. When you're done, the system prints a receipt, returns your card, and gives you the money requested. *Remember to take your card!* Problem 9.25	1. Monday 　○ NetGravity Meeting 　○ Effective Use of the Internet class 2. Tuesday 　○ Meeting with Joanie 3. Wednesday 　○ Naviplan Meeting 4. Thursday 　○ Internet Systems Architecture class 　○ exam this week! 5. Friday 　○ Unilog Meeting 　○ Valentine's Charity Ball 6. Saturday 　○ Skiing 　○ Go out for dinner with friends 6. Sunday 　○ Visit family 　○ Pay bills Problem 9.26

Figure 9.6   Problems 9.25 and 9.26.

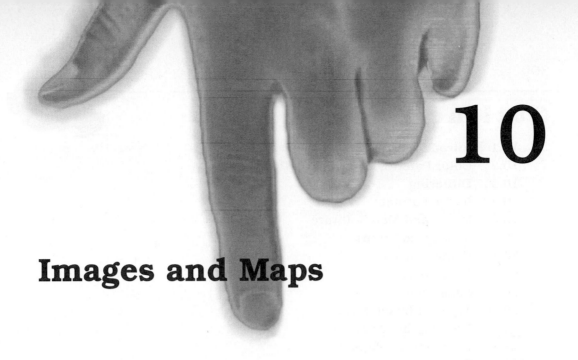

Images and Maps

Goal

Understand images and image maps, know their parameters, recognize the differences between the two, be able to perform image operations effectively, and master the use of images and image maps in Web pages.

Objectives

- Pixels and resolution
- Color palettes and lookup tables
- Browser-safe colors and dithering
- Image formats and software
- Image operations and use
- GIF89a animation
- Tiling a Web page
- Image maps

Outline

10.1 Introduction

Web authors can add icons, logos, and high-impact images to their pages. When working with images, authors need to focus on page content and to use images to enhance it; images in themselves do not add much value to a Web page. The use of images in Web pages brings up two important issues: image complexity and file size. The image complexity usually affects one's first impression of a Web page. The size of the image file affects the length of time required to download it.

There are some common-sense rules that Web authors should follow when it comes to including images in a Web page:

• Use images to enhance page layout and content.
• Keep image complexity low—that is, keep images simple.
• Use thumbnail versions of images in order to reduce the downloading time of Web pages.
• Use icons and logos of organizations as images in order to distinguish the Web page. In many cases, traditional icons, logos, and trademarks are scanned and used by Web authors.

10.2 Color Palettes and Lookup Tables

Images use the RGB color model discussed in Chapter 9. To understand how images use this color model, we present an overview of how computer color monitors display images. These monitors are similar to TV sets. They are called *raster displays*. The display (computer) screen of a raster monitor is divided horizontally and vertically into pixels (picture elements). The numbers of pixels in both directions make up the monitor's resolution. For example, a monitor with a resolution of 800×600 has 800 and 600 pixels in the horizontal and vertical directions, respectively.

The value of each pixel is controlled by a certain number of bits in the computer's memory (known in practice as graphics RAM, adapter, or card). A pixel can hold any one of many values, depending on the number of bits representing it. For example, if the pixel is represented by 8 bits, the pixel can hold 256 distinct values, ranging from 0 to 255. This is because the value of a bit can be 0 or 1 in the computer binary system. Thus, the total number of possible values the pixel can have is $2^8 = 256$.

How are pixel values converted into colors? Pixel values are converted into colors via the display (computer) monitor itself. The hardware design of the monitor performs this conversion. More specifically, the graphics adapter or card of the monitor saves all the possible pixel values and their corresponding colors in its color lookup table. For example, if the display monitor has 8 bits, there are 256 pixel values and therefore 256 available colors. The available colors are usually known as the color palette, and the mappings from pixel values to colors are done via the monitor's color lookup table.

The number of colors in a lookup table does not have to be exactly equal to the number of pixel values. As a matter of fact, many display monitors of computers today have a color palette size of $2^{24} = 16,777,216$ colors, usually referred to as a palette of 16.7 million colors. Thus, their color lookup tables have that many colors available for applications to choose from. However, the number of colors that can be displayed simultaneously by an application on the display monitor can be no more than the number of distinct values of one pixel, which is controlled by the number of bits per pixel. Thus applications running on a monitor with 8 bits/pixel can display only 256 simultaneous colors, which they choose from among the 16.7 million available colors. Applications use the monitor's color lookup table to choose these colors. All Internet applications, including XHTML, support the 24-bit RGB color model. In this model, each primary color is represented by 8 bits and has values from 0 to 255.

Browsers, considered an application, have predefined color tables that they use to display images. An image has multiple colors and therefore has its own color table that browsers use to display it correctly. Actually, displaying an image involves the use of and mapping between three color tables: that of the image, that of the browser, and that of the monitor. The browser reads the image file and its associated color table. It then maps the colors in the image's color table to its own colors, defined in its own color table. Finally, the browser maps its colors to those defined in the color table of the monitor. If, at some time during the mapping, between these three color tables, a color is not found, the browser dithers it, as explained in Section 10.3.

10.3 Dithering

Dithering can be thought of as a method of interpolation to resolve missing colors. The method is used by browsers during the rendering of Web pages. Some of these pages may have images that use colors which are not available in the browser's color table. When faced with this situation, the browser can ignore the colors missing from its table altogether, or it can try to find the closest colors to them by dithering, or mixing, colors from its table. Browsers, by default, dither missing colors. Browsers perform dithering by combining color codes. Browsers analyze the trio of RGB values of a missing color and try to match them with any existing trio. For example, if the missing color is a shade of purple, a browser may change the color values to have more red or more blue.

Dithering colors is not a good practice. The look of a Web page becomes unpredictable from one platform to another when dithering occurs. The same Web page looks different when it is displayed on a PC, a Mac, or a Unix workstation. The main drawback of dithering is that colors do not stand out distinctively, especially when one is viewing high-resolution images. This factor is less noticeable for low-resolution images.

The perfect solution to eliminate dithering is for the browser to have a large color lookup table or palette—one consisting of 16.7 million colors. While this solution seems simple, it fails on account of hardware limitations. Many PCs have color tables of only 256 colors. Moreover, the OS—for example, Windows OS—may reserve some of these colors for its own display management. Thus, browsers have to play it safe when it comes to displaying colors. They have to assume the worst-case scenario. They use what is known as a browser-safe or Web-safe color palette as a minimum palette. This palette is based on the 256 colors that all PCs and Macs support. However, PCs and Macs share only 216 of these 256 colors. Thus, the browser-safe color palette has a size of 216 colors. The remaining 40 colors are platform dependent, or proprietary. As a result, browsers use an RGB color cube of size $6 \times 6 \times 6 = 216$. This cube ensures that images and their Web pages look the same on both PC and Mac monitors. The colors defined by the cube consist of all the hex trio combinations of 00, 33, 66, 99, CC, and FF. The website `http://www.lynda.com/hexh.html` lists the 216 safe colors with their decimal values and hex codes.

Web authors can have control over the color palette for the images they create. Many image-creation and editing tools such Adobe Photoshop allow authors to define an image's color palette. Authors can even read predefined color palettes, save them, and apply them to images. Thus, the author can use the browser-safe color palette in order to ensure consistency in rendering and displaying images. In addition, images created by scanning real photographs should be saved as JPEG files, because this format minimizes the dithering effect on them.

We should mention here that dithering can be done in graphics programs on purpose. And that is not a bad thing, as long as it is done with our knowledge.

10.4 Image Formats

Two important variables of images are resolution and format. Images can be created with high, medium, or low resolution. The higher the resolution, the larger is the size of the image file. For many Web pages, medium-resolution images are satisfactory. Many image formats exist. A list of the most common image formats follows:

- BMP (BitMaP), created by Microsoft (MS);
- JPEG or JPG (Joint Photographic Experts Group), created by the JPEG group;
- GIF (Graphics Interchange Format), created by CompuServe;

- PNG (Portable Network Graphics);
- PCX (PC Paintbrush file), created by Zsoft Corp;
- TIFF (Tagged-Image File Format), created by Aldus, MS, and NeXT.

The JPEG, GIF, and PNG formats are the only three formats supported widely by the major Internet tools, browsers, application programs, and programming languages, such as Java, Java-Script, and XHTML. Any other format is not supported and should not be used. If an image is available in one of the other formats and it must be used in a Web page, the Web author must convert it to either JPEG or GIF. To do so, the Web author uses an image program, such as Photoshop, to read the image with the current format and then saves it in a supported format such as JPEG.

Of the three supported formats, GIF and JPEG are the most popular. The GIF format supports a palette that can consist of 256 (8 bits) colors, each of which is represented in true color. The JPEG format supports 16.7 million (24 bits) colors. These two formats are significantly different from each other in how they compress and store graphics. GIF keeps the original colors of the image, while JPEG may remove some colors. This is why GIF is referred to as a lossless format and JPEG as a lossy format. For Web authors, we offer the following general guideline: The GIF format is typically used for simple drawings from paint programs, screenshot images, images with several distinct colors, and sharp images with borders or text. These images usually have fewer colors than the maximum (256 colors) the GIF format supports. The JPEG format is typically used for high-quality images, photographic images, and scanned photographs. These images have many more than 256 colors. Image software usually allows its users to save JPEG images in low (small-size file) or high (large-size file) resolution.

Images take a long time to load, so the JPEG and GIF formats allow progressive loading of images. In **progressive JPEG** and **interlaced GIF**, the image is loaded with gradually increasing resolution. A low-resolution version of the image loads almost immediately, to keep the attention of the Web-page viewer. The image resolution gets better, and thus the image becomes sharper, progressively with time as the remaining information is received.

There are two GIF formats: 87a and 89a. The 87a format is the original GIF format, designed by CompuServe in 1987. This format was enhanced in 1989, thus the name 89a. The new enhancement features in the 89a format are image interlacing, transparency, and animated GIF. **Transparency** allows the viewer to see the background of a Web page through the part of the image that is transparent. Transparency is used effectively to blend an image with a page's background. With respect to animation, a GIF89a file can contain several images stored in it. When viewed in a browser, these images are displayed one after another, producing the effect of animation.

10.5 Image and Map Software

Images can be created in a variety of ways—for example, via manual creation, scanning of an existing image, and uploading pictures taken by a digital cameras. Web authors can create images and image maps by using graphics and image software. Some existing software packages include Adobe Photoshop, Adobe Illustrator, Paint Shop Pro, and Windows Paint. Some of these packages, such as the Adobe products, provide advanced tools to add realism to images.

Windows Paint is free; it comes with MS Windows. The Paint program creates images in BMP format by default, because this format does not cause loss of colors after the images have been saved. This format is good for creating and editing images, but Web auth ̲ ̲ ̲ ̲ ̲ ̲ ̲ ̲ ̲ to convert the resulting files into JPEG or GIF.

Many image software programs are two-dimensional pixel-based programs. All the coordinates are measured in pixels, and not in inches or other units. No fractional pixels are allowed. The programs use a universal coordinate system, shown in Figure 10.1. The system has its origin, (0, 0), in the top left corner of the drawing window of the software, with the + X-axis going to the right and the +Y-axis going down, as shown in the figure.

Realistic images can be generated by scanning real photographs and saving them as JPEG images. Scanning software allows its users to edit or crop the resulting scans, if needed. Editing an image implies the addition of some visual effects or some text. **Cropping** is a process by which a user can cut out part of an image and save it as a separate image. In addition, images of real objects and people can be generated directly, by using digital cameras to circumvent the scanning process. Digital cameras generate frames and save them as JPEG images, ready for downloading onto a computer's hard disk.

In addition to image creation and editing software, there is another type of software that is just as important. It is image-viewing software, or simply image viewers. Web authors who work with images on regular basis should use image viewers; they simplify the viewing, maintenance, and cataloging of images. Also, image viewers load and open image files faster than image editors. Image viewers are generally used when Web authors just want to look at images; image editors are used to edit and change images and their content.

Image viewers, such as ThumbsPlus, offer cataloging features, such as thumbnails and contact sheets. With thumbnails, an image viewer displays an entire folder of images on the screen side by side, to aid in the sorting and choosing of images for full-size viewing. Contact sheets are pages of thumbnails, either in printed hard copy or as graphics files. Image viewers should allow their users to specify the width and height of thumbnails and their arrangement on a page.

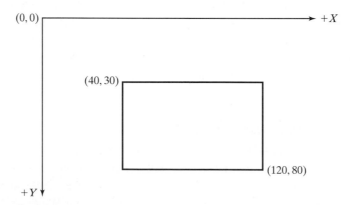

Figure 10.1   Coordinate system for images.

Also, some image viewers generate the thumbnails on the fly, so they take longer to display. Others generate the thumbnails and store them in files, for faster display.

Other features of image viewers include the image formats they support, the ability to customize the size of thumbnails, the ability to link keywords to images, the launching of an external image editor, the viewing of fonts, search tools, and the generation of slide shows.

10.6 Image Operations

Image operations include creating new images and editing and copying existing images. We discuss some of these operations here.

10.6.1 Image Creation

Web authors have three options for generating images for their Web pages: They can create, buy, or capture them. In this section, we focus on using image software to create images. We use the MS Windows Paint program as our image-creation software. To access this program, click the following sequence: `Start` (Windows menu) => `Programs` => `Accessories` => `Paint`. The Paint program is simple and intuitive to use. Figure 10.2 shows the program's GUI. The program is pixel based and uses the coordinate system shown in Figure 10.1.

The GUI consists of the menu bar, the toolbox, the color box, the status bar, and the drawing area. The menu bar has the `File`, `Edit`, `View`, `Image`, `Colors`, and `Help` menus. The `File` menu can be used to open existing image files. The `Edit` menu provides the `Undo` and `Repeat` functions. The `Undo` function can reverse actions taken up to several steps back. This item is sometimes better to use than the eraser (which erases existing graphics), because of the pixel nature of the graphics. For example, erasing a circle intersecting a line may be tricky, because the user may erase part of the line inadvertently. Using the `Undo` function, on the other hand, will remove the circle quite easily. The `Repeat` menu item allows the user to repeat the last construction step.

The `View` menu enables the user to turn on and off the display of the toolbox, the color box, the status bar, and the text toolbar. It also has a `Zoom` submenu, which is particularly useful during construction.

The `Image` menu enables the user to manipulate the image by flipping it, rotating it, or stretching it. The `Attributes` item of the `Image` menu enables the user to set the size of the image by specifying its width and height before or after creating it. The user should set the image size before creating an image. If the size is changed after the image is created, the image may be clipped or skewed, depending on the graphics program. Neither is a good change.

The `Color` menu may be used to change the colors of the Paint program. The `Help` menu provides general help about the program.

The tools provided by the toolbox are shown in the upcoming screen capture. Moving the mouse over each tool displays the tool's name. We can draw a line, a curve, a rectangle, a polygon, an ellipse, or a rounded rectangle with the bottom six tools. The `Pencil` and the `Brush` tools are for drawing shapes. The `Pencil` draws shapes with thin boundaries; the `Brush` draws shapes with thick boundaries. The `Fill With Color` tool fills shapes with colors. The

A tool is the text button. When selected, the text toolbar is displayed, which allows users to control the text size, font, and style.

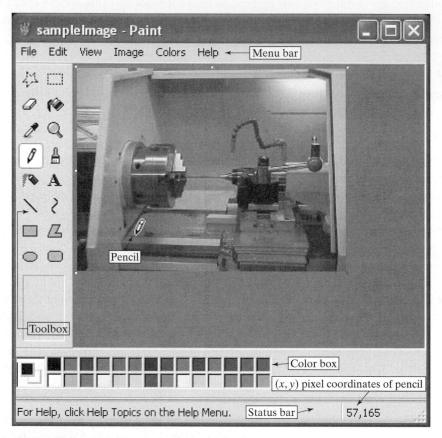

Figure 10.2   Microsoft Windows Paint program.

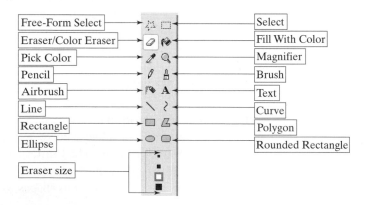

To use Paint, select any tool from the toolbox and click the mouse in the drawing area. To use the `Ellipse` icon to draw a circle, hold down the `Shift` key on the keyboard and click the ellipse icon. To use a color, select it first from the color box before selecting a tool. When you are done drawing, save the image. The default image format is BMP. Paint supports other formats as well, including JPEG, GIF, and PNG.

The color box has many buttons of different colors. The user chooses a color for drawing or filling by clicking the corresponding button. The user should be careful not to choose the background color for foreground construction; otherwise, entities drawn will be invisible.

The status bar displays the (x, y) pixel coordinates of the current location of the mouse cursor. Click the `Pencil` tool, move the mouse cursor in the graphics window of Paint, and watch the status bar; the pixel coordinates change continuously.

10.6.2 Image Editing

Image editing implies that one of two changes are made. First, a Web author can change the image's contents by cropping the image and by adding graphics, color, or text. Image software such as PaintShop Pro provides many image-editing tools that supply capabilities such as zooming in or out of the image (to enlarge it or reduce it, respectively), moving the image, selecting an area in the image to edit, adding new colors, to the image, changing the image's color palette, freehand drawing, copying parts of the image, replacing colors in the image, filling in parts of the image with colors, and adding text to the image.

Second, a Web author may compress (encode) or decompress (decode) an image in order to change its size. An important advantage of GIF is that the image maintains its original (creation) quality even after multiple compressions and decompressions. On the other hand, the JPEG compression scheme reduces the number of colors in the image in order to minimize the space required to save the image's color table. Thus, colors are permanently eliminated from the image, on the assumption that the human eye cannot distinguish very small color variations. Thus, it is not recommended to compress and decompress a JPEG image more than once. Note that a smaller image size means faster downloading of the image.

Because of the JPEG compression scheme, Web authors should not edit original JPEG images and then export them, as exporting compresses them and causes color loss. If a compressed JPEG image suffers enough color loss, it will not look good. Web authors can scale an image down a bit and use antialiasing in order to enhance its look. Other visual enhancements may be provided by image software. Many image editors provide filters that blur or unsharpen, despeckle, reduce image noise, and remove dust and scratches.

10.6.3 Image Capture

On many occasions, surfers of the Internet may have a need to capture and save images they find on Web pages. This practice is legitimate, as long as it does not violate copyright laws. Surfers may need to get permissions from the authors of these images in order to legaly copy and reproduce the images. A Web surfer right-clicks on an image and selects `Save Picture As` (from the popup menu) in IE, or Save Image As in Netscape. The image is now stored on the local hard disk, and the surfer can use it off-line.

10.6.4 Image Scaling

Users can scale images up or down by using an image program or XHTML tags. It is not recommended to scale an image up, as its resolution usually will worsen. What is known as the staircase effect (jaggedness of the image boundaries) then becomes very apparent, especially for nonhorizontal or nonvertical shapes. For example, a horizontal or a vertical line is not affected by scaling up, but a line oriented at any angle or a circle will shows bad jaggedness. This effect is attributed to the fact that pixels are squares with horizontal and vertical borders. Thus, entities that cut across them lose their edge smoothness if the original scale changes.

10.7 Using Images

XHTML provides Web authors with one tag to handle images in Web pages. It is the `<img>` tag, which has enough attributes to provide good control of image insertion in Web pages. Its syntax is `<img src alt border width height align hspace vspace usemap ismap />`. These attributes are described as follows:

- `src` specifies the image's file name. This file must be of type `.jpg` (or `.jpeg`), `.gif`, or `.png` only. Image files can be specified using either the absolute or the relative path.
- `alt` provides alternative text that is rendered in case a browser cannot display the image or does not support the image type (such as BMP). Browsers usually show this text while loading the image as well.
- `border` specifies the width of the border, in pixels, that surrounds an image. When an image is used as a hyperlink, the browser surrounds it with a border automatically.
- `width` and `height` specify a new width and height, respectively, that the browser uses to render the image. These two attributes scale the original image.
- `align` specifies the position of an image with respect to the surrounding text. There are five values of this attribute. They are `top`, `middle`, `bottom`, `left` (default), and `right`. The `top`, `middle`, and `bottom` values align the image vertically (toward the top, middle, and bottom, respectively) with the current text baseline. The `left` and `right` values justify the image to the left or right, respectively of the text on the page.
- `hspace` and `vspace` respectfully specify the amount of horizontal and vertical whitespace, in pixels, around an image. This space is sometimes known as **gutter**.
- `usemap` specifies that the image is used as a client-side image map. Its value is an anchor.
- `ismap` specifies that the image is used as a server-side image map. Its value is an anchor.

Images can be used as hyperlinks. Instead of using text as the link, an image is used. As with text hyperlinks, the mouse cursor changes to a hand when we move it over an image hyperlink. All the attributes of the `<a>` tag are still valid for image hyperlinks; however, unlike text hyperlinks, image hyperlinks do not change colors to reflect whether they are links, active links, or visited links.

To create an image hyperlink, a Web author replaces the text used in the visible part of the `<a>` tag by the `<img>` tag as follows: `<a destination anchor><img /></a>`. A specific example is `<a href= "http://www.neu.edu"><img src= "myImage.gif"></a>`. If we replace the `<img>` tag by text, the link becomes `<a href= "http://www.neu.edu">Check our new offerings</a>`, for example.

Example 10.1 Use images.

Develop a Web page that uses an image.

Solution 10.1 Using the AceHTML editor, generate the following code, save it as `example101.html`, and use a browser to render the Web page:

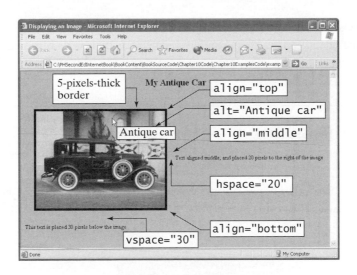

```
1   <?xml version="1.0" encoding="iso-8859-1"?>
2   <!DOCTYPE html PUBLIC "-//W3C//DTD XHTML 1.1//EN"
3      "http://www.w3.org/TR/xhtml11/DTD/xhtml11.dtd ">
4   <html xmlns="http://www.w3.org/1999/xhtml ">
5   <!-- Generated by AceHTM http://freeware.acehtml.com -->
6   <head>
7   <meta http-equiv="Content-Type" content="text/html;
    charset=iso-8859-1" />
8   <title>Displaying an Image</title>
9   </head>
10  <body>
11  <h2 align="center"><b>My Antique Car</b></h2>
12  <!-- Include the image -->
```

```
13   <img src="antiqueCar.jpg" alt="Antique car" border="5"
     align="middle" hspace="20" vspace="30" />Text aligned middle and
     placed 20 pixels to the right of the image <br />
14   This text is placed 30 pixels below the image <br />
15   </body>
16   </html>
```

Code explained:

Line 13 uses the `<img>` tag with the `src`, `alt`, `border`, `align`, `hspace`, and `vspace` attributes to control the image.

Discussion:

The image file `antiqueCar.jpg` must be in the same folder as the HTML file `exampl101.html`. Notice the results of the attributes on the image border and the placement of the text around the image. Also, move the mouse cursor over the image to display the alternative text.

Hands-on exercise:

Starting with the code given in this example, remove the `border`, `hspace`, and `vspace` attributes, and display the Web page. Then move the image file to another folder. What changes do you observe?

Example 10.2 Image scaling.

Use an image twice in a Web page, where the first instance is in the original size and the second instance is scaled by 50%.

Solution 10.2 The `width` and `height` attributes of the `<img>` tag can be used to scale images. Using the AceHTML editor, generate the following code, save it as `example102.html`, and display the Web page in a browser:

```
1   <?xml version="1.0" encoding="iso-8859-1"?>
2   <!DOCTYPE html PUBLIC "-//W3C//DTD XHTML 1.1//EN"
3       "http://www.w3.org/TR/xhtml11/DTD/xhtml11.dtd ">
4   <html xmlns="http://www.w3.org/1999/xhtml ">
5   <!-- Generated by AceHTM http://freeware.acehtml.com -->
6   <head>
7   <meta http-equiv="Content-Type" content="text/html;
    charset=iso-8859-1" />
8   <title>Scaling an Image</title>
9   </head>
10  <body>
11  <h2 align="center"><b>Scaling Down my Dog</b></h2>
12  <!-- Include the image -->
13  <img src="dogScale.jpg" alt="My Dog original size" />
14  <img src="dogScale.jpg" alt="My Dog scaled 50%" width="98"
    height="118" />
15
16  </body>
17  </html>
```

Code explained:

> **1.** Line 13 uses the original size of the image.
> **2.** Line 14 uses the `width` and `height` attributes of the `<img>` tag to scale the image down by 50%.

Discussion:

When scaling down an image, you should maintain its original aspect ratio (width/height) in order to avoid distorting it. To find its original width and height, simply open its file in an image program such as Paint or Photoshop and verify its attributes. The size of the image in this example is 196×236 pixels. Its half-size becomes 98×118 pixels. We purposely display the two images next to each other so that we may see the effect of the 50% scaling.

Hands-on exercise:

Starting with the code given in this example, scale the original width of the image by 25% and the original height by 40%. Did the image get distorted! What should you do if the resulting width or height is a fractional number of pixels such as 135.75?

Example 10.3 Image hyperlinks.

Create an image hyperlink.

Solution 10.3 Using the AceHTML editor, generate the following code, save it as `example103.html`, and display the Web page in a browser:

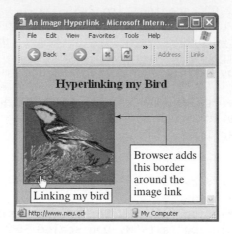

```
1   <?xml version="1.0" encoding="iso-8859-1"?>
2   <!DOCTYPE html PUBLIC "-//W3C//DTD XHTML 1.1//EN"
3       "http://www.w3.org/TR/xhtml11/DTD/xhtml11.dtd ">
4   <html xmlns="http://www.w3.org/1999/xhtml ">
5   <!-- Generated by AceHTM http://freeware.acehtml.com -->
6   <head>
7   <meta http-equiv="Content-Type" content="text/html;
    charset=iso-8859-1" />
8   <title>An Image Hyperlink</title>
9   </head>
10  <body>
11  <h2 align="center"><b>Hyperlinking my Bird</b></h2>
12  <!-- Include the image link -->
13  <a href="http://www.neu.edu"><img src="birdLinking.jpg"
    alt="Linking my bird" /></a>
14
15  </body>
16  </html>
```

Code explained:

Line 13 uses the `<a>` and `<img>` tags to create an image hyperlink.

Discussion:

The image links to `http://www.neu.edu`, as shown in line 13. Without the visual change of the mouse pointer to a hand, we would not know if the image is a link or not. If the image file is not found, the link still works.

Hands-on exercise:

Change the code given in this example to use the wrong file name, and display the Web page in a browser. What do you see? Does the link still work?

Example 10.4 Tiling a Web page.

Develop a Web page that illustrates the use of an image for tiling.

Solution 10.4 An image can be used as a background for a Web page. In this case, the browser uses the image and repeats it horizontally and vertically across the page to create a pattern. This pattern is known as tile, or a tiling effect. Images that are used for tiling a Web page are usually light in color and design, so that they do not overshadow the essential content of the page. Web authors use the `background` attribute of the `<body>` tag to specify an image file for tiling.

Using the AceHTML editor, generate the following code, save it as `example104.html`, and use a browser to display the Web page:

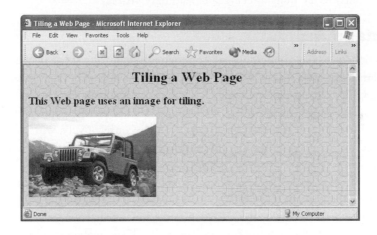

```
1   <?xml version="1.0" encoding="iso-8859-1"?>
2   <!DOCTYPE html PUBLIC "-//W3C//DTD XHTML 1.1//EN"
3       "http://www.w3.org/TR/xhtml11/DTD/xhtml11.dtd ">
4   <html xmlns="http://www.w3.org/1999/xhtml ">
5   <!-- Generated by AceHTM http://freeware.acehtml.com -->
6   <head>
7   <meta http-equiv="Content-Type" content="text/html;
    charset=iso-8859-1" />
8   <title>Tiling a Web Page</title>
9   </head>
10  <body background="tiling.jpg">
11  <h1 align="center"><b>Tiling a Web Page</b></h1>
12  <p>
13  <b><h2>This Web page uses an image for tiling. </h2></b>
14  </p>
15  <img src="jeepCar.jpg" />
16
17  </body>
18  </html>
```

Code explained:

> **1.** Line 10 uses the image file `tiling.jpg` for tiling.
> **2.** Line 15 uses another image file, `jeepCar.jpg`, as content in the page.

Discussion:

The tiling of a Web page enhances its look if the tiled image is designed correctly. A correct design means that the image is composed of light colors and that its edges are hard to identify in the Web page throughout the tiling pattern.

Hands-on exercise:

Change the code given in this example to use tiling image that consists of heavy colors and has strong edges (seams). Is the tiling effect (seams) strongly visible?

10.8 Image Animation

Animation is defined as the consecutive and continuous display of a set of images, one after the other. There are many ways to include animation in Web pages. Web authors may use Java, JavaScript, or GIF89a to display animations. Java allows authors to write Java applets and include them in Web pages via the `<applet>` tag. JavaScript provides functions and methods that can be used to display a sequence of images (frames) consecutively, with time delays, thus creating the effect of animation. **GIF89a animation** is an easy method to create animated GIF image files that can be displayed in Web pages.

GIF89a animation allows a Web author to create a set of image frames in the desired sequence and save them in one GIF file. The file also saves a script that has a set of instructions about how the browser is to display the file, such as the time delay between frames and whether the browser should cycle through the frames repeatedly. Thus, including an animated GIF89a file in a Web page is no different from including a GIF file. The Web author uses the `<img>` tag with all its attributes.

Creating an animated GIF file requires three steps: creating individual frames, using the frames to create the animated GIF file, and making an animated GIF loop. The first step involves creating the sequence of animation. Let us assume that we want to animate a bouncing ball by using five frames. Using image software, we create the five frames as shown in Figure 10.3. The top left corner of the figure shows the animation sequence. After we have created the five frames, the animation software creates the sequence and makes the loop. Once it is done, we save the sequence as a GIF89a file. We then use the file in an `<img>` tag in a Web page in order to display the animation.

It is highly recommended to optimize GIF animation files while creating them, to minimize their sizes. Here are some tips: The fewer the colors, the smaller is the file size. If the animation software permits it, reduce the number of bits per pixels (the pixel depth). Also, save a local color palette with each frame, instead of saving a global palette at the beginning of the file. Finally, use incremental frames, by specifying (x, y) coordinates for each frame. For example, we first create the background frame (the box) for the animation shown in Figure 10.3. Each ball

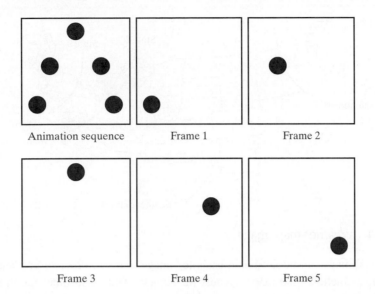

Figure 10.3 Animation sequence of a ball.

then becomes an incremental frame whose (x, y) coordinates are specified relative to the background frame. This approach relieves the animation software from having to redraw the background with each ball frame and thus reduces the size of the final GIF file.

10.9 Image Maps

Images are a valuable addition to a Web page because of their visual appeal. In some applications, we may want to link different parts of an image to different Web pages. Consider the case of an image of a weather map of the United States (shown in Figure 10.4). Different states or cities have different weather and climates. If we link each state (a region) to a weather report, a Web surfer would be able to receive weather information for a particular state by clicking the state on the weather map.

The XHTML concept that allows us to create multiple hyperlinks from a map is known as an image map or clickable map. An **image map** is defined as a single image that links to multiple URLs or XHTML documents. The image is divided into regions, sometimes known as "hot spots" or "hotlinked regions". By clicking on a hot spot, the Web surfer goes to the corresponding URL. Early image maps were server-side maps — that is, they were supported by Web servers only. Today, browsers support both client-side and server-side image maps.

Image maps can be used innovatively and cleverly in many applications. For example, they can be used as GUI buttons or as a geographic menu. To use an image map as buttons, a Web author uses image software to create an image with shapes that have the look and feel of buttons. These shapes form the regions of the image map that can be linked to different URLs.

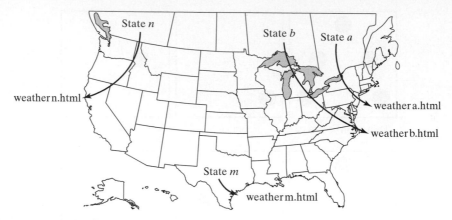

Figure 10.4 Weather-map image.

Traditional maps can be used as a basis for image maps in order to provide geographic menus. Examples include road maps, layouts (of homes, plants, and other facilities), maps of libraries, maps of campuses, and so forth. Here, the traditional map is divided into regions. The map is usually scanned to create the image. Regions or hot spots are then overlaid on the image.

10.10 Types of Image Maps

There are two types of image map: server side and client side. The chief difference between these two types is in the processing (resolving of the coordinates) of a Web surfer's mouse-button click. In the server-side image map, the client browser sends the click to the server, which resolves it and sends the right Web page to the client. This process requires client–server communication twice: once for the browser to send the click, and once for the server to send the Web page. In the client-side image map, the browser resolves the click locally and requests the Web page from the server. This approach eliminates the step of sending the click to the server.

Server-side maps existed before client-side maps. Server-side maps were developed first because Web browsers and HTML were still evolving; neither would have been able to support client-side image maps. This support is available today. Web authors should use the client-side type of image maps in their Web pages. We cover only this type in this book.

10.11 Creating Image Maps

The development of an image map centers around the linking of image areas (sections) to XHTML files (URLs) via geometric regions that we overlay on the image areas, as shown in Figure 10.5. The regions (circles, rectangles, and polygons) are known as virtual shapes, because they are not physically drawn on the image; they are only defined. The coordinates of the regions are defined relative to the image's coordinate system. The virtual shapes act as hyperlinks that link the image areas to the corresponding URLs. The image areas that have virtual shapes overlaid on them are known as hot spots, as stated previously.

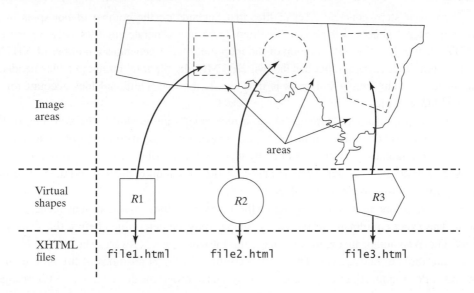

Figure 10.5 Elements of an image map.

Figure 10.5 shows the three elements required to create an image map. They are the image itself, the virtual shapes, and the XHTML files. Use the following four steps to develop an image-map application:

1. **Create the image.** This image is the one that the map uses. The Web author developing the map can draw the image, scan it, or use a digital camera to capture it.
2. **Define the virtual shapes of the map.** The second step is to define the virtual shapes that make up the hot spots of the map. These shapes are not drawn or shown physically on the image of the map. One can think of them as invisible, imaginary (virtual) shapes that overlap with certain areas of the image. A virtual shape does not have to overlap perfectly over the desired region of the image. For example, the rectangle, circle, and polygon shown in Figure 10.5 are within their corresponding areas of the image. However, if the user clicks outside the virtual shapes, nothing will happen; the browser will not load the corresponding XHTML file. If needed, the Web author could use the polygon shape with small sides to follow the boundaries of a complex region accurately.
3. **Configure the image map.** We link the virtual shapes to the corresponding XHTML files via use of the `<area>` tag, which is discussed later.
4. **Create the XHTML files (URLs).** Write the XHTML files that the virtual shapes use, one file per shape. These files are the destinations, as in the case of the `<a>` tag (covered in Chapter 9). The virtual shapes serve as the sources. The shapes do not necessarily have to point to distinct XHTML files; several shapes may point to the same XHTML file. This is strictly a map design issue.

These four steps generate a set of files that depends on the number of hot spots in the image map. Step 1 generates the image file. Step 2 does not generate any files. Step 3 generates one XHTML file. It is the configuration of the map file. Step 4 generates a number of XHTML files. Assuming that each hot spot has its own XHTML file, the total number of files needed to create an image map with n hot spots is thus $n + 2$; the two additional files account for the image and the map files.

XHTML provides three virtual shapes: a rectangle, a circle, and a polygon. Figure 10.6 shows the geometric definitions of these shapes. A rectangle is defined by the two endpoints of one of its two diagonals. A circle is defined by its center and radius. A polygon is defined by its vertices (corner points). The definition of a polygon does not require the first and the last vertices to be the same in order to close the polygon.

Pixel values are allowed only to define these shapes. Other values, such as inches, are not allowed. The exact coordinates of the virtual shapes must be determined before the shapes can be used. The Web author first reads the image file into an image software. The author then uses the software tools to find the coordinates by recording the (x, y) positions of the mouse cursor when on the desired locations on the image. Many image programs display the (x, y) coordinates of the mouse cursor's location in the status bar, (a) the bottom of the program's window). The author selects the virtual shapes that best describe the areas of the image that serve as the map's hot spots.

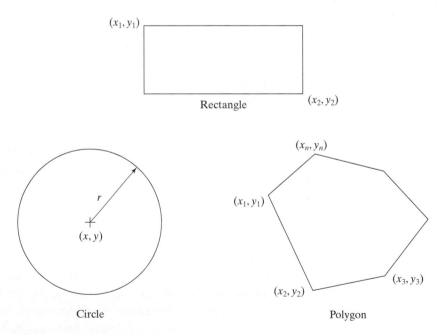

Figure 10.6 Geometric definitions of virtual shapes.

10.12 Using Image Maps

As shown in Figure 10.5, we need to define an image, define the virtual shapes, and write the XHTML files or URLs in order to create an image map. The image is defined by the `<img>` tag. The virtual shapes are defined by using the `<area>` tag. We also need to do something else that is less obvious: We need somehow to associate the coordinates of the virtual shapes and any mouse-button clicks (by map users) with the coordinate system of the map's image. This association tells the browser the context within which the coordinates must be interpreted. In other words, the browser must be told to use the coordinate system of the image to interpret the coordinates of the virtual shapes and clicks. It is the `<map>` tag that defines this association and context.

10.12.1 Define the Image

The use of the `<img>` tag in an image-map application is no different from its use to define an image. All the attributes are still valid; however, the attribute `usemap` or `ismap` must be used if the image is to be used as a map. The former attribute is used for client-side maps and the latter for server-side maps. We use only the `usemap` attribute in this chapter, and we implement it as follows:

```
<img src="myMapImage.gif" alt="My image map" usemap="#myMap" />
```

The value of the `usemap` attribute is a map name that must always be preceded by a pound sign (#). This name must also be used in the `<map>` tag, as shown in Section 10.12.3.

10.12.2 Define the Virtual Shapes

The `<area>` tag is used to define one virtual shape at a time. The syntax of the tag with its attributes is `<area href shape coords alt nohref tabindex accessory>`. The first four attributes are described as follows (the others are hardly used):

- `href` specifies the destination (URL) that is associated with the virtual shape.
- `shape` defines the virtual shape. The possible values are `default`, `rect`, `circle`, and `poly`. The `default` value is used to prompt users when they click outside the map's designated hot spots. This value is seldom used if the map design is logical and good.
- `coords` is the companion to the `shape` attribute. It specifies pixel coordinates of points of shapes according to the scheme illustrated in Figure 10.6. Use the following order to specify coordinates for `rect`, `circle`, and `poly`, respectively: `coords="`x_1,y_1,x_2,y_2`"`; `coords="`x,y,r`"`; `coords="`$x_1,y_1,x_2,y_2,\ldots,x_n,y_n$`"`. The coordinates of the points are separated by commas. The radius of a circle can be calculated by subtracting the x coordinates of two horizontal points, or the y coordinates of two vertical points.
- `alt` specifies alternative text for the virtual shape. It is similar to the `alt` attribute of the `<img>` tag.

10.12.3 Define the Context

The `<map>` tag provides the association and context required to define the map. It encloses all the `<area>` tags of the map. Thus, the `<map>` tag acts as a container for other tags. The only attribute of the `<map>` tag is `name`. The value of this attribute must be the same as the name that is used in the `usemap` attribute of the `<img>` tag. The template for using the `<map>` tag is shown in the following code:

```
1   <?xml version="1.0" encoding="iso-8859-1"?>
2   <!DOCTYPE html PUBLIC "-//W3C//DTD XHTML 1.1//EN"
3       "http://www.w3.org/TR/xhtml11/DTD/xhtml11.dtd ">
4   <html xmlns="http://www.w3.org/1999/xhtml ">
5   <!-- Generated by AceHTM http://freeware.acehtml.com -->
6   <head>
7   <meta http-equiv="Content-Type" content="text/html;
    charset=iso-8859-1" />
8   <title>Image Map Template</title>
9   </head>
10  <body>
11  <h1 align="center"><b>Image Map Template</b></h1>
12  <img src="myMapImage.gif" usemap="#myMap" />
13  <map name="myMap"/>
14  <area href="message file" shape="default" />
15  <area href="value here" shape="rect" coords="your own" />
16  <area href="value here" shape="circle" coords="your own" />
17  <area href="value here" shape="poly" coords="your own" />
18
19  <!--more virtual shapes go here-->
20
21  </map>
22
23  </body>
24  </html>
```

Use the same name

Replace by URLs or local files

Replace by pixel values

Example 10.5 Use image maps.

Develop a Web page that illustrates the use of client-side image maps.

Solution 10.5 Using the AceHTML editor, generate the following code, save it as `example105.html`, and use a browser to render the Web page:

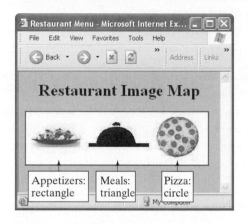

```
1   <?xml version="1.0" encoding="iso-8859-1"?>
2   <!DOCTYPE html PUBLIC "-//W3C//DTD XHTML 1.1//EN"
3       "http://www.w3.org/TR/xhtml11/DTD/xhtml11.dtd ">
4   <html xmlns="http://www.w3.org/1999/xhtml ">
5   <!-- Generated by AceHTM http://freeware.acehtml.com -->
6   <head>
7   <meta http-equiv="Content-Type" content="text/html;
    charset=iso-8859-1" />
8   <title>Restaurant Menu</title>
9   </head>
10  <body>
11  <h1 align="center"><b>Restaurant Image Map</b></h1>
12  <img src="foodMenu.jpg"  usemap="#menuMap" />
13  <map name="menuMap">
14  <area href="http://www.burgerking.com" alt="Appetizers"
    shape="rect" coords="10,25,90,60" />
15  <area href="http://www.legalseafood.com" alt="Meals"
    shape="poly" coords="100,60,210,60,150,10" />
16  <area href="http://www.pizzahut.com" alt="Pizza"
    shape="circle" coords="252,40,35" />
17  </map>
18
19  </body>
20  </html>
```

Code explained:

1. Lines 12–17 use the four steps covered in Section 10.11.

2. Line 12 defines the map image (step 1).

3. Lines 14–16 define virtual shapes (step 2).

4. Lines 13 and 17 define the context (step 3).

5. Lines 14–16 use three URLs (step 4).

Discussion:

This example creates an image map with three hot spots that link to URLs for simplicity, so that we don't have to write our own HTML files. We use a rectangle, a triangle, and a circle as the shapes for the hot spots. The image map resembles a restaurant menu with three categories: Appetizers, Meals, and Pizza. Each item is made to be a hot spot by overlapping a visual shape on top of it. Clicking the Appetizers, Meals, or Pizza hot spot connects the user to the websites of Burger King, Legal Seafood, and Pizza Hut, respectively.

Hands-on exercise:

Extend this example to add a new hot spot for desserts.

10.13 Tutorials

10.13.1 Using Map-Based Buttons (Study Sections 10.9 and 10.12)

This tutorial reverse engineers `http://www.amazon.com` to illustrate its use of image maps. The following screen capture shows the part of the website that is of interest to us here:

Discussion:

Amazon's website uses three image maps, as shown in the foregoing screen capture. We refer to them as Map 1, Tabs, and Map 2. They are shown separately in the upcoming screen capture. Map 1 has four hot spots, and Map 2 has five. The middle map, Tabs, consists of separate images of tabs that are assembled together to make an image that is used in this map.

Hands-on exercise:

Study the corresponding code for Amazon's three image maps. To access the code, click `View` (menu on the IE menu bar) `=> Source`.

10.13.2 Overlapping Hot Spots (Study Section 10.12)

In some image maps, it is unavoidable for a Web author to have overlapping shapes. In these cases, the Web author must be aware of the order of the **\<area>** tags inside the **\<map>** tag: The virtual shape that is created first inside the **\<map>** tag takes precedence. In this tutorial, we create a dartboard. We use three concentric circles to represent three circular hot spots. For these hot spots to work properly, the **\<area>** tag of the smallest circle must come first, followed by the tag of the middle circle. The last \<area> tag is for the largest circle. Create the map image with a size of 300×300 pixels, using Paint, and save it as **overlap.gif**. Save the XHTML files that correspond to the three hot spots in a subdirectory called **board**. Use the AceHTML editor to generate the code shown in this tutorial, and save it as **tutorial10132.html**. View the page in a browser.

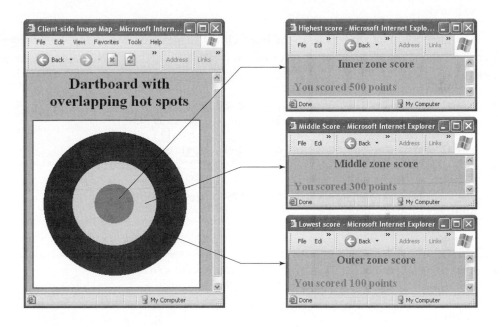

```
1   <?xml version="1.0" encoding="iso-8859-1"?>
2   <!DOCTYPE html PUBLIC "-//W3C//DTD XHTML 1.1//EN"
3       "http://www.w3.org/TR/xhtml11/DTD/xhtml11.dtd ">
4   <html xmlns="http://www.w3.org/1999/xhtml ">
5   <!-- Generated by AceHTM http://freeware.acehtml.com -->
6   <head>
7   <meta http-equiv="Content-Type" content="text/html;
    charset=iso-8859-1" />
8   <title>Client-side Image Map </title>
9   </head>
10  <body>
```

```
11  <h1 align="center"><b>Dartboard with overlapping hot spots </b></h1>
12  <img src="overlap.gif" alt="Image map" usemap="#dartBoard" />
13
14  <!-- Create the hot spots -->
15  <map name="dartBoard">
16  <area shape="circle" coords="145,145,35" alt="Inner zone"
    href="board/innerZone.html" />
17  <area shape="circle" coords="145,145,75" alt="Middle zone"
    href="board/middleZone.html" />
18  <area shape="circle" coords = "145,145,130" alt="Outer Zone"
    href="board/outerZone.html" />
19  </map>
20
21  </body>
22  </html>
```

The three files that correspond to the three virtual shapes are very similar. Following is the code for the inner zone (change the wording to create the other two files, as per the screen captures):

```
1   <?xml version="1.0" encoding="iso-8859-1"?>
2   <!DOCTYPE html PUBLIC "-//W3C//DTD XHTML 1.1//EN"
3       "http://www.w3.org/TR/xhtml11/DTD/xhtml11.dtd ">
4   <html xmlns="http://www.w3.org/1999/xhtml ">
5   <!-- Generated by AceHTM http://freeware.acehtml.com -->
6   <head>
7   <meta http-equiv="Content-Type" content="text/html;
    charset=iso-8859-1" />
8   <title>Highest score</title>
9   </head>
10  <body>
11  <h1 align="center"><b>Inner zone score</b></h1>
12  <h2><b>You scored 500 points </b></h2>
13
14  </body>
15  </html>
```

Code explained:

    1. Lines 12–19 create the image map according to the four steps of Section 10.11.

    2. Lines 16–18 create the three circular virtual shapes.

Discussion:

This example uses the geometry of the three concentric circles to define the virtual shapes. For example, the inner circle has a center at $(x, y) = (145, 145)$ and a radius $r = 35$ pixels. These coordinates are used in code line 16 of the first file. Similarly, the other circular virtual shapes, defined in code lines 17 and 18, respectively, use the coordinates of the other two circles. Also, the radii of the three virtual shapes are 35, 75, and 130 pixels, as shown in code lines 16–18, respectively. As we overlap, we must begin with the circle with the smallest radius.

Hands-on exercise:
Switch the order of code lines 16–18 of the first file to any other sequence. Observe which hot spots work and which do not. Does the order of creating the hot spots attect their functionality?

FAQs

General

Q: Why is the browser not displaying an image in my Web page?

A: The reason is usually unintentional misuse of the `<img>` tag. Quite often, a Web author forgets to close the quotes in the `<img>` tag. Check the `<img>` tag carefully.

Q: How can I turn off the border color that the browser adds around an image map?

A: Use the border attribute of the `<img>` tag with a value of zero—that is, `border="0"`.

Q: How many image maps can a Web author use in one Web page?

A: As many as needed. For example, refer to Amazon's website, discussed in Tutorial 10.13.1.

Image Formats (Section 10.4)

Q: Why is the browser showing a "broken image" icon instead of displaying the actual image?

A: This usually happens because of a problem with one of three factors: the image's file name, the image's file format, or the path to the image file. If the image's file name is wrong, the browser will not be able to find it. If the image's file format is not JPEG, GIF, or PNG, the browser will not be able to display it. If the path or directory to the image file is wrong, the browser will not be able to find the file.

Q: What are the benefits of the PNG image format?

A: The PNG (Portable Network Graphics) format is an image format that combines the best of both the GIF and JPEG formats. More specifically, it combines the 24-bit encoding of JPEG with the lossless compression and transparency of GIF. The PNG format also supports image progression (interlacing). Image progression refers to the gradual (progressive) display of an image on the computer screen. An image is displayed first with a coarse resolution that gets finer progressively. The PNG format should enable Web authors to compress and decompress real-life scanned photographs as many times as needed without any loss of image quality.

Image and Map Software (Section 10.5)

Q: Why am I unable to open an image file that I created by scanning in a photograph?

A: In some cases, an image file created by scanning is corrupt from a bad scan or because of lack of experience in the use of the scanner and its software. Delete the file and scan the photograph again.

Q: What is the difference between painting and drawing programs?

A: Many commercial products exist for creating images. Painting and drawing programs differ in the way they create images. Painting programs create images as a collection of pixels bounded by the image's boundaries. An example of a painting program is the Windows Paint program. Drawing programs, on the other hand, create images as a collection of primitive shapes, such as lines, rectangles, arcs, ellipses, polygons, and splines. These primitives are considered by the drawing program to be distinct objects, instead of just a set of unrelated pixels. An example of a drawing program is Adobe Illustrator. In general, painting programs are easier to learn and use; however, drawing programs produce higher quality results.

Q: How do I create an interlaced image?

A: First, use an image program to create the image. Invoke interlacing only when you save the image. There is a save option that allows you to choose the number of passes. When an image is saved by using one pass, it is not interlaced. When it is saved with, for example, four passes, it becomes interlaced. On each pass, certain scan lines (a **scan line** is a horizontal row of pixels on the computer screen) of the image are saved to the image file. A browser decodes the image file in the same way it is encoded by the save option of the image program. For a four-pass image, the browser starts at scan line 0 and displays every eighth line in the first pass. In the second pass, it starts at scan line 4 and displays every eighth line. In the third pass, the browser starts at scan line 2 and displays every fourth line. In the fourth and final pass, it starts at scan line 1 and displays every other line.

Using Images (Section 10.7)

Q: An image in my Web page does not display in the browser; I get a broken-image icon instead. I checked the `<img>` tag, and everything seems to be correct. The image displays fine by itself. What is the problem, and how do I fix it?

A: The problem is that the image is somehow corrupt. Re-create the image and try again.

Q: How can I control the positioning of text around an image in my Web page?

A: The positioning of text around images in Web pages cannot be controlled without using tables or layers to format the page. The align attribute of the `<img>` tag provided very limited control.

Creating Image Maps (Section 10.11)

Q: How can I define a triangular shape in an image map?

A: XHTML allows three shapes (rectangle, circle, and polygon). We can think of a triangle as a special case of a polygon (i.e., a three-sided polygon). Thus, create a polygon with three sides. This polygon requires three points (vertices). As with any polygon, whether the order of these vertices is clockwise or counterclockwise is not important.

Q: Are the three XHTML shapes enough to define any complex region in an image map?

A: Yes, if we understand why a region is used in the first place in image maps. The purpose of a region in an image map is not to trace the boundaries of a physical image area precisely. Rather, its purpose is to define an area that the map user can click on to invoke the corresponding HTML file. With this in mind, the region could be simple. Figure 10.5 shows the HTML shapes used within the boundaries of three states. While the physical boundaries of the states look complex, the boundaries of the shapes are not following them precisely. If the Web author insists that the boundaries of the shape and the image part be almost identical, an XHTML polygon with multiple small sides can be used.

Q: Where should a Web author place a virtual HTML shape inside an image area, if the former is smaller than the latter?

A: In the center or the middle of the area. Studies of human psychology show that if we are asked to click within an area, we tend to click right in the center of it.

Using Image Maps (Section 10.12)

Q: My image map is not working properly. When I click on one region, it invokes the HTML file of another region. I checked all the tags and the files. Everything seems in order. What is the problem?

A: In many cases, this problem occurs due to the use of the wrong coordinates in defining XHTML virtual shapes. The wrong coordinates may result in one XHTML shape enclosing a neighboring one. Thus, when you click on an area of the map, the browser does not know which shape to use and may invoke the wrong HTML file. This usually happens if the Web author is not using image-map software, but rather image software such as Paint, and is measuring the coordinates of the shapes there manually. Double check the coordinates and correct the wrong ones.

Q: When I move the mouse over a hot spot in my map, I get no links. All the tags and files seem correct. What is the problem, and how do I fix it?

A: The pixel coordinates used to define the hot spot are most likely wrong. For example, using the coordinates (20, 50, 25, 57) for a rectangle defines a 5×7 rectangle. This is a very small rectangle, and the mouse may not detect it. Check and correct the pixel coordinates.

Q: What happens if two or more virtual shapes overlap in an image map?

A: The browser still invokes one of the associated HTML files or URLs, according to the following rule: The virtual shape that appears earlier in the HTML document takes precedence; its associated URL is the one displayed as a response to the user's click.

Q: None of the hot spots in my image map are working. When I move the mouse over any spot, the mouse cursor does not change into a hand. What is the problem? How can I troubleshoot it?

A: This is an indication that there is something wrong related to the image of the map. Perform the following troubleshooting steps: Make sure that the image names used in the `<img>` and the `<map>` tags are the same. Make sure that the pound sign (#) precedes the image's name in the `usemap` attribute. Make sure that the quotes surrounding the image's name in both the `<img>` and the `<map>` tags are closed. Finally, make sure that the `<map>` tag is closed.

Blackbox

Section 10.1 (Introduction): Images and image maps are useful XHTML elements.

Section 10.2 (Color Palettes and Lookup Tables): Computer monitors have a color-palette size of $2^{24} = 16,777,216$ colors, usually referred to as a palette of 16.7 million colors. However, they support only 256 simultaneous colors. They always use color lookup tables.

Section 10.3 (Dithering): Use the browser-safe color palette to prevent the browser from dithering the colors used in your Web pages. This palette has only 216 colors.

Sections 10.4–10.6 (Image Formats, Image and Map Software, and Image Operations): The three image formats that Web browsers support are JPEG, GIF, and PNG. Use JPEG format for images that use many colors, such as scanned photographs. Use GIF format for images with a small set of colors. While PNG format combines the best of JPEG and GIF, it is not very popular. The coordinate system of an image is standard. Its origin is at the top left corner of the image, with the +*X*-axis pointing to the right and the +*Y*-axis pointing down. Image software can be used to create, edit, scan, or scale images.

Section 10.7 (Using Images) (Examples 10.1–10.4): The `<img>` tag supports all image operations. Its syntax and attributes are `<img src alt border width height align hspace vspace usemap ismap />`.

Sections 10.8 (Image Animation): GIF89a animation is the easiest method to add animation to a webpage, as Empared to other methods such as Java or JavaScript.

Sections 10.9 and 10.10 (Image Maps and Types of Image Maps): Use image maps to enable efficient navigation of your Web pages. Use client-side image maps.

Sections 10.11 and 10.12 (Creating Image Maps and Using Image Maps) (Example 10.5): Follow these four steps to create image maps: Define the image file (use the `<img>` tag); define the virtual shapes of the map (use the `<area>` tag); configure the image map (use the `<map>` tag); create the HTML files, or use URLs. The syntax and attributes of the `<area>` tag are `<area href shape coords alt nohref tabindex accessory>`.

Section 10.13 (Tutorials): Two tutorials show how to use image maps.

Quick reference for chapter tags

Tag	Close	Attribute	Value	Effect	Example
`<img>`	empty	`src`	text	image's file name	`<img src="xx.jpg" />`
		`alt`	text	alternative text	`<img alt="xxx" />`
		`border`	pixels	border thickness	`<img border="5" />`
		`width`	pixels	image width	`<img width="100" />`
		`height`	pixels	image height	`<img height="200" />`
		`align`	top	align text with the top of the image	`<img align="top" />`

Tag	Close	Attribute	Value	Effect	Example
			middle	align text with the middle of the image	`<img align="middle" />`
			bottom	align text with the bottom of the image	`<img align="bottom" />`
			left	align text with the left of the image	`<img align="left" />`
			right	align text with the right of the image	`<img align="right"/>`
		`usemap`	anchor	name to be used by the `<map>` tag	`<img usemap="#xx" />`
		`ismap`	anchor	name to be used by the `<map>` tag	`<img ismap="#xx" />`
`<map>`	yes	`name`	text	same name from `<img>`	`<map name="xx">`
`<area>`	empty	`href`	file name	file name to link to	`<area href="URL" />`
		`shape`	rect	rectangular shape	`<area shape="rect" />`
			circle	circular shape	`<area shape="circle" />`
			poly	polygonal shape	`<area shape="poly" />`
			default	used for clicking outside map shapes	`<area shape="default" />`
		`coords`	number of pixels	specify shape coordinates	`<area coords= "x`$_1$`, y`$_1$`,..." />`
		`alt`	text	text to complement virtual shape	`<area alt="xxx" />`

Check Your Progress

At the end of this chapter, you should

- ✔ understand the use of images and image maps (Section 10.1);
- ✔ understand color palettes and dithering (Sections 10.2 and 10.3);
- ✔ know about the various image formats and understand the coordinate system (Sections 10.4 and 10.5);
- ✔ be able to identify the various image operations (Section 10.7);
- ✔ be able to use image animation (Section 10.8);
- ✔ have mastered the use of image maps (Sections 10.9 and 10.10);
- ✔ have mastered the use of virtual shapes (Section 10.11);
- ✔ understand the tags of image maps (Section 10.12).

Problems

The exercises are designed for a lab setting, while the homework is to be done outside class time.

Exercises

10.1   Use a painting program, such as Windows Paint, to create an image that is 400 pixels wide and 200 pixels high. Save the image in GIF format.

10.2   Use the image from Problem 10.1 in a Web page twice: once as is, and a second time scaled down by 50%. Use the `alt`, `border`, `width`, `height`, `align`, `hspace`, and `vspace` attributes of the `<img>` tag.

10.3   Browse the Internet for Web pages with images. Capture and save one image from those pages to the local hard disk of your computer.

10.4   Create a Web page that uses the image from Problem 10.1 as a hyperlink, which in turn uses the image from Problem 10.3 as the destination anchor. Scale the image from Problem 10.1 down by 50%.

10.5   Use the image from Problem 10.3 three times in a Web page, with the following sizes: original size, 50% of original size, and 30% of original size.

10.6   Create a Web page that uses the image from Problem 10.3 to tile a Web page.

10.7   Create an image map for the image shown in the following screen capture:

The football hot spot links to `http://www.nfl.com`. The basketball hot spot links to `http://www.nba.com`. The tennis-racket hot spot links to `http://www.usta.com`. Use `rect`, `circle`, and `poly` virtual shapes for the football, basketball, and tennis racket, respectively.

10.8   Use the upcoming screen capture of the bike to create an image map that explains the three parts of the bike. Use a `circle` virtual shape for the front-wheel hot spot, a `poly` for the frame hot spot, and a `rect` for the seat hot spot. Link each hot spot to an XHTML file that describes the part. Use a subdirectory to house the three XHTML files; call it `parts`.

Homework

10.9 Redesign the personal Web page you developed in Chapter 9 to include three of your favorite images, such as of yourself, your pets, your family, your house, and so forth. Scan your photographs for these images.

10.10 Use a photograph of yourself twice in your personal Web page: once at the top, and once at the bottom. Make the one on the bottom a hyperlink to your personal Web page.

10.11 Develop a Web page that makes good use of images. Use some of the images more than once, with and without scaling, and use some as hyperlinks.

10.12 Search the Web for a GIF89a animation freeware. Use `GIF animation` as a search string. Download the freeware, and create a file that animates a bouncing ball by using seven frames. Display the animation in a Web page.

10.13 Create a GIF89a animation of something interesting to you.

10.14 Create a Web page that uses an image for a tiling effect. Choose your favorite image for tiling. You could draw it or download it.

10.15 Find or scan in an image of your favorite car, and create an image map that uses it.

10.16 Find or scan in an image of the United States, and use it to create an image map that lists statistics about four states of your choosing.

10.17 Find or scan in an image of your college campus, and create an image map that uses it.

10.18 Find or scan in an image of a road map, and create an image map that uses it.

10.19 Find or scan in an image of your family, and create an image map that uses it. Use the face of each family member as the hot spot to access that member's biography or short resume.

10.20 Create an image map for bird-watching lovers. The image should consist of five birds lined up next to each other. Each bird in the map should link to a Web page that shows a larger image of the bird, followed by its description, habitat, and nesting habits.

10.21 Create the image map on dieting shown on the left of the upcoming figure and its related XHTML files. Make up the contents of these files.

10.22 Create the image map on flowers shown on the right of the upcoming figure. Make each flower image in the map link to a bigger image of the same flower.

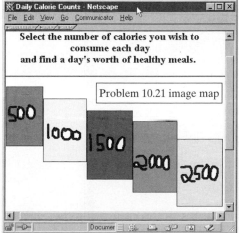

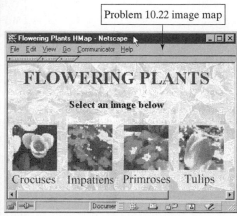

10.23 Create the counting-game image map shown on the left of the upcoming figure and its related XHTML files. Make up the contents of these files.

10.24 Use the screen capture of the tree shown on the right of the upcoming figure to create an image map that explains the three main parts of the tree. Use a `circle` virtual shape for the leaves-and-branches hot spot, a `poly` for the root hot spot, and a `rect` for the trunk hot spot. Link each hot spot to an XHTML file that describes the part. Use a subdirectory to house the three XHTML files; call it `treeAnatomy`.

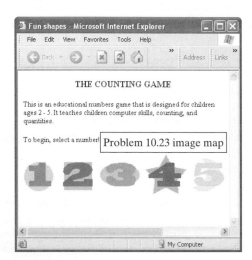

Problem 10.24 image map

Problem 10.23 image map

10.25 Create the office-supplies image map shown in the upcoming figure and its related XHTML files. Make up the contents of these files.

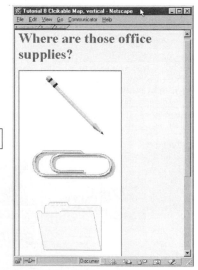

Problem 10.25 image map

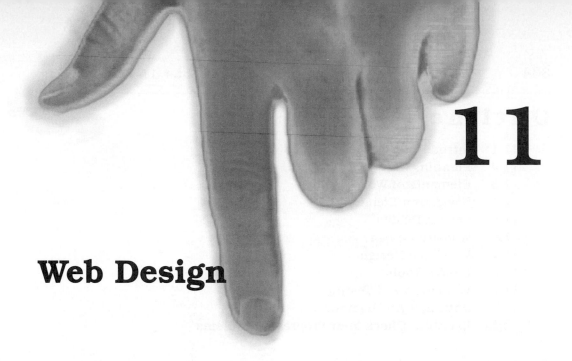

Web Design

Goal

Understand the basic design principles of websites and Web pages, the elements of Web design, the differences between design and coding, and the importance of design in attracting and increasing website traffic.

Objectives

- Website planning
- Elements of Web design
- Navigation elements
- Layout design
- Website and Web page design
- Design tools
- Testing and validation
- Putting all of the elements of Web design together

Outline

11.1 Introduction

Websites and Web pages are products. Like any other products, we first design them, and then we build. Consider cars and houses. Designers and engineers design the cars; then plants produce them. Architects design floor plans of houses; then contractors build them. In the Web field, designers and developers design websites and Web pages; then programmers build them by writing the XHTML code. Each groups excels in what it does. Designers may not be good programmers, and vice versa. In practice, the same individual could do both design and coding, but this is not often a good idea.

The Web offers another method of marketing in addition to the traditional methods such as advertising on television and in newspapers. Companies market their products, and individuals market themselves on the Web. The key question is how to leverage the Web to best serve your needs and goals. It is all in the design. Design is a large field of study. We cannot even attempt to cover it all in one chapter in this book. But we offer some basic principles that serve as a launching pad for those who might be interested in pursuing design further.

The development life cycle of a product, from inception to production, goes through multiple phases, each requiring many details and activities. There are five phases of software development that are applicable to Web design. They are planning, analysis, design, implementation, and support. The planning phase is all about what needs to be accomplished. It results in a road map for what lies ahead. The analysis phase identifies all possible solutions to the problem at hand. It is a synthesis activity that decides on the best final solution to the problem. During the design phase, we perform detailed tasks to determine what hardware to buy, what software to buy off the shelf, what to outsource (hire outside contractors to develop), and what to build in house. The implementation phase is when we acquire hardware, develop software code, assemble both the hardware and software, install the final product, test it, and train users on how to use it. The last phase is the support phase, in which we monitors use of the product and users' feedback.

11.2 Planning

Business wisdom states that you should design for your audience. As such, the first step in designing a successful website is to know the target audience and market that the site will ultimately serve. A website is essentially a marketing and communication tool. It is crucial to learn about markets and consumer behavior as a first step to planning and designing websites.

As part of planning, a few questions need to be raised and answered: How big is the target market? Is it big enough to justify the time and the financial investments spent on the site? Will the company of the intended website use the Web for marketing and sales transactions? More importantly, how do customers hear about and find products in the target market? When it comes to the Web, customers can find companies and products from advertisements containing URLs that they write down and try, by following a link from another site or online ad, by accepting the referral of a friend or acquaintance, or by using a search engine to find websites.

The answers to the foregoing questions translate to a marketing plan and a promotional strategy to reach intended customers or audience. Table 11.1 shows some planning concepts and guidelines for Web design.

Table 11.1   Planning concepts and guidelines for Web design.

Concept	Implementation
URL choice	Choose a domain name and Web host. The choice of the domain name and the URL are important. The URL should be easy to remember, preferably the same name as the company's name. The Web host be could the company itself or a dedicated Web-hosting vendor. This choice depends on whether the company wants to perform all the functions associated with Web testing itself or whether it outsources its entire set of IT needs including hosting and maintaining its website.
Branding	Promote the website and build brand name among potential customers. List the company's URL on heavy-traffic Web portals such as Yahoo!.
E-mailing	Establish communication with customers via e-mail in order to promote the website.
Casting a net	Identify and join discussion groups and special-interest websites relating to the company's line of business, and build storefronts.
Search engines	Submit the website's information repeatedly to search engines, and have a search engine in the website as well.
Online sales	Offer customers online coupons and discounts to entice them to visit and use the website.
E-information	Create an online newsletter, discussion groups, chat rooms, and other promotional material.
Visualization	Visualize and imagine your website as if it is up and running. Consider yourself as a user of the website. Is all the necessary information there? Is the site easy to use (e.g. it take only two or three clicks for you to get what you want), impressively laid out, pleasing to look at, and quick to load?

Table 11.1   Planning concepts and guidelines for Web design. (Continued)

Concept	Implementation
Analysis	Analyze other websites that you visit. Identify elements that you like and use them, and avoid using elements that you do not like.
Reverse engineering	Reverse engineer the websites you admire. Storyboard them—that is, try to understand the flow of the logic behind them, as well as their top-level organization. If needed, look at their code.

11.3 Elements of Web Design

Before we can begin to design websites and Web pages, we need to know the elements that make up the content of the sites and pages and how to navigate through them. This section discusses the elements of Web pages; some of these elements have been covered in the previous chapters of the books while others are covered later. Section 11.4 discusses the navigation elements.

A website consists of a coherent set of Web pages. Web pages are written using XHTML, are rendered by browsers, and have content. In this context, Web design must consider the impact of different XHTML standards, browser compatibility, and content. Website **accessibility** is directly related to the version of the XHTML standard used to write code and supported by Web browsers. It is a measure of how easy it is for browsers to access and read Web pages. There are various versions of HTML and XHTML standards that must be supported by browsers. Some HTML tags have been deprecated in XHTML. Considering accessibility during Web design makes the resulting Web pages usable and viewable by as many people as possible.

Browser compatibility is a measure of which version of HTML or XHTML a browser supports. While browser software is free to download and install and easy to use, assuming that every Web user has the latest version of a browser may be too optimistic. For one, not every user is Internet savvy or computer literate. The reality is that many users will not be using the latest version of a browser. When designing Web pages, we need to consider this compatibility issue and test the pages on different browsers and versions.

While accessibility and compatibility are important design issues, the content of websites and Web pages is also crucial and consumes most of the activities of Web design. We break the content into elements, as shown in Table 11.2. Each element has related design issues that must addressed during Web design. These issues are addressed in Section 11.7.

Table 11.2   Elements of Web design.

Element	Issues
Text	Layout, formatting, spacing, margins, and so forth.
Colors	Best pleasant and readable mix of colors of background, foreground, links, and images.
Links	Ease of forward and backward navigation of the website and its pages.

Table 11.2   Elements of Web design. (Continued)

Element	Issues
Images	Use of the `alt` attribute, and the number of images included in a page.
Image maps	Support for nongraphical browsers must be provided, in case users turn off browser image autoloading.
Animation	Debate over the necessity of animated images, their annoyance to users, and file sizes.
Frames	Browsers have poor implementation of frames, and search engines have hard time indexing Web pages that use frames.
Tables	A most useful feature of XHTML. Make use of it for Web-page formatting and layout.
Forms	A useful element for collecting information and data from users. How many forms should a Web page have?
Cascading Style sheets	A useful concept that separates presentation from content (data). It standardizes the look and feel of a website.
Cookies	Does the website need to track its visitors and their online habits?
JavaScript	How much JavaScript should be used? Sometimes JavaScript crashes browsers.
Java	Used in the form of applets, which are embedded in Web pages. Requires browsers to support it.
Plug-ins	Does the website require them? Browsers have to download and install them on clients.

11.4 Navigation Elements

The goal of navigation is to get around parts (Web pages) of a website or to jump between websites. Web navigation is a mouse-driven activity within the browser window. While the navigation concept is simple, its effective implementation in websites and Web pages is challenging. Navigation design is covered in Sections 11.6 and 11.7.

There are two elements associated with navigating Web pages that Web designers and architects should consider. They are browsers and within-Web-page navigation tools A browser's navigation tools include its `Back` and `Forward` buttons, its URL drop-down menu, its scroll bars (which are present if the Web page is too long to fit in one screen length), the `File` menu, and bookmarks. These tools, however, are out of the control of Web designers.

The within-Web-page navigation tools are part of the Web-page design. They are implemented via XHTML code and therefore are fully controlled by Web designers. These tools are listed in Table 11.3. They are graphics based and provide clear visual appearances.

Table 11.3   Web navigation elements.

Element	Issues
Hyperlinks	Ease of forward and backward navigation.
Buttons [Link 1] [Link 2]	Navigation buttons are popular, but require the use of JavaScript to make them functional.
Menu bars Three versions are shown on the right.	Menu bars are shown on the top or the bottom of a page. The same buttons may appear on many pages of the website in order to provide a consistent user interface for navigation.
Image maps	Similar to buttons, but more efficient.
Bullets and arrows	Used to navigate within a Web page or between website pages.
Tables	Tables do not provide navigation. They are used to highlight links.

11.5 Layout Design

Layouts are what visitors look at first upon visiting a Web page; then they see the page's content. With the proper layout, Web designers can set the tone for their Web pages. Layouts can either add to the viewing experience of visitors or take away from it. Layout design is thus an important first step in effective website and Web page design. Table 11.4 summarizes the major layout concepts and their related issues. The remainder of the section covers them in more details.

Table 11.4   Web-page layout design.

Concept	Issues
Organization scheme	What is content organization within a Web page? Should it be organized by topic, by task, or by type of audience?
Organization structure	This concept relates to the structure of the website and of each Web page. Should it be hierarchical or random? Should a hierarchical structure be narrow and deep, or wide and shallow?
Storyboarding of the site layout	Ensure that the site's visualization, content, and navigation flow as designed and envisioned.
Navigation	Provide a site map, an index, or both.

Table 11.4   Web-page layout design. (Continued)

Concept	Issues
Web-page layout	Decide on one or two types of page layout. Create templates from them, and use them throughout the site.
Tables and layers	Use tables or layers to create formatting patterns within a Web page.
Alignment	Decide on an alignment (horizontal or vertical) within a page and use it.
Proximity	Related items or elements of a Web page should be grouped together.
Repetition	Repetition of layout elements throughout the website is highly desirable. It serves to unify the site and forms a family of related Web pages.
Contrast	This element helps focus and guide visitors' eyes. It also helps create an information hierarchy. Make items that are not exactly the same appear really different.
Mapping of Web pages	Draw the layout of each Web page manually in a freehand sketch on a piece of paper. Indicate sizes (pixels) of the areas (boxes) that hold content.

11.5.1   Organization Schemes

Web designers need to decide on one or two organization schemes to follow for the development a given website. A scheme helps organize content material into related sections (a process known as chunking content). Several types of schemes exist. The **alphabetical scheme** uses names of content as the basis for organization—for example, a list of people. The **chronological scheme** uses a timeline. Content such as events, threaded discussions, and e-mail messages are perfect for this scheme. In a **geographical scheme**, place is the key element for topics such as weather, distribution, and travel. The **topical scheme** organizes content by topics—for example book chapters and departments of a company. The **task-oriented scheme** is best suited for a collection of processes, tasks, or functions. Finally, the **audience-specific scheme** chunks information based on, for example, membership, interests, age groups, gender, and security.

11.5.2   Organization Structures

While organization schemes control the laying out of content within each Web page, organization structures dictate how Web pages are structured relative to each other within the website. There are two types of structures: Web and hierarchical. A Web structure is random; it is based mainly on the navigation of the website. It is flexible and easy to extend in the future. Figure 9.1, shows an example of a Web structure.

The hierarchical structure is similar to a decision tree or a flowchart. It consists of multiple levels, as shown in Figure 11.1. A hierarchical structure can be narrow and deep, or wide and shallow, as illustrated in the figure.

Determining the organization structure is sometimes known as storyboarding, as discussed later in this chapter. The organization sturcture may also suggest or imply the navigation pattern of the website. In this case, each line connecting two nodes (boxes) in Figure 11.1 becomes a hyperlink.

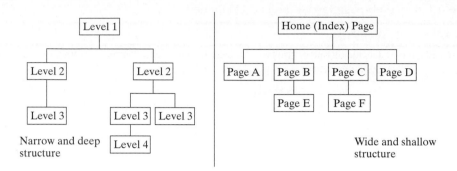

Figure 11.1   Hierarchical structure of a website.

11.5.3   Storyboarding Site Layout

Storyboarding, one of Hollywood's secrets of success, is often applied to the layout design of websites. Hollywood filmmakers leave nothing to chance. They cover walls with pictures of what they want the viewers to see, feel, and know in the right order, before a single scene gets filmed. This same process can be applied to the layout design of websites. Before coding any Web page, Web designers ought to storyboard their layouts from an online customer's point of view, to ensure that the online experience is as easy and pleasant as they have anticipated. Storyboarding makes certain that online customers see, understand, and do exactly what designers intend. It also helps designers figure out and understand the nuances of their websites.

There are a number of ways to create a storyboard, depending on how a Web designer likes to solve problems. In the **top-down approach**, one places the home-page sheet on the top, and all other sheets branch off below it, converging on the checkout (exit) page. Figure 11.2 shows a top-down storyboard, and Figure 11.3 shows a generic layout of a home page. The **bottom-up approach** uses the reverse sequence; it begins with the final (exit) page and works backward until it reaches the home page. The **build-out approach** begins with certain obvious pages (such as order page, confirmation page, and so forth) and builds the site around them.

Storyboarding is like creating the flowcharts we use to plan a computer program before we begin writing the code. Use a sheets of paper (or index card, or Post-it note, as shown in Figure 11.2) to represent each individual Web page. Each sheet describes the page and contains a summary of the page's content and layout. The sheets are arranged in the desired logical order of the online process, with arrows between them. These arrows become the links in the Web pages. The online process could be buying a product, finding information, or applying for a service, for example.

Regardless of the approach taken, each and every sheet in the storyboard must address issues such as what visitors need to know, do, and feel, as well as where they need to go next. Moreover, use the following tips to structure the layout of each sheet and, eventually, of the corresponding Web page: Always place the most important content of a page as close to the top of

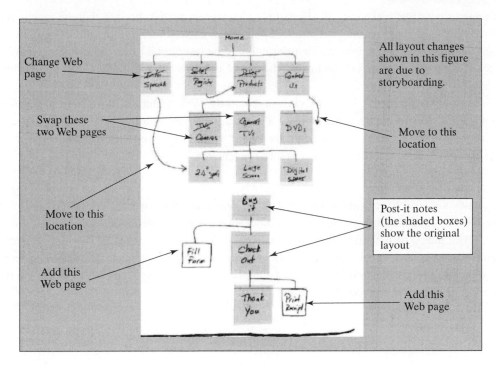

Figure 11.2   Storyboard of a Website.

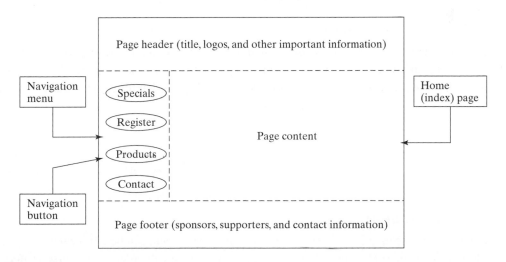

Figure 11.3   A typical Web-page layout.

the page as possible; make sure all sheets have a consistent layout; be sure that the main navigation bars and menus are accessible to site visitors at all times so that the visitors can avoid using the browser's Back button; limit the number of flashing and moving elements on Web pages, as they distract visitors; and avoid the use of pop-ups and pop-unders, as most visitors do not like them.

As websites start to take shape via storyboarding, Web designers move from visualizing organization structure to visualizing navigation and finally to building page content and elements. Rearrange the sheets of paper until the layout works, write your ideas on them, give them titles and file names, and sketch their content and elements.

11.5.4   Navigation

Web navigation can happen at the site level or the page level. We cover the site-level navigation here. Web designers should provide an easy navigation system to site visitors by using an image map, a site index, or both. An image map includes links to all the pages in the site. This map should be repeated in each Web page of the site, in the same location. A site index is a dropdown list of links, as shown in the screen capture below, to the same Web pages included in the site's image map. It should also be repeated in every Web page.

11.5.5   Web Page Layout

It is recommended that Web designers have a uniform page layout for all the pages of a website. They should identify one or two layouts, create templates for them, and use them. If this is not possible, they should at least identify common parts of the layouts. Uniform layout makes it easy for visitors to use the website and navigate it quicker.

11.5.6   Tables and Layers

Tables and layers are an excellent tool for page formatting. They can provide alignment, act as placeholders, group related page elements, create patterns, and establish contrast between background and foreground.

11.5.7   Alignment

Use alignment to line up page elements with each other. Alignment can be left, center, or right. Web designers should stick to one alignment style in a Web page in order to minimize visitors' confusion. If they choose left alignment for text, they should not center headlines.

11.5.8 Proximity

Page items or elements that are related to each other should be placed in close proximity on the page. If information is scattered all over the page, the Web page appears unorganized, and visitors may not be able to access the information quickly. For example, consider the business card shown in the screen capture below. The name and the title are placed in proximity to each others while the address is placed slightly further down. The whitespace between the name and the address makes the different proximities stand out. Also, observe the text alignment and how it makes the eye follow the content easily.

11.5.9 Repetition

Repeat certain items that tie Web pages of a website together. Repetition serves the purpose of unifying the site. Elements that can be used repetitively include navigation tools, images, buttons, layout, and schemes. Repetition is though of as consistency. It helps site visitors anticipate what they will see next.

11.5.10 Contrast

Contrast helps guide visitors around a page. Contrast must be strong to be effective. There are many types of elements that can be contrasted with each other: large text size with small text size; an old-style font with a new-style font; a thick line with a thin line; black color with white color; smooth texture with rough texture; a horizontal line with a vertical line; a small image with a large image;

11.5.11 Mapping Web Pages

This is the last step before writing the XHTML code for each Web page. By now, a Web designer has made all the decisions about the page's content, layout, elements, and so forth. Mapping, as shown in the upcoming screen capture and drawing, helps determine the sizes (in pixels) that the page elements should occupy, how to arrange content, and how to create proximity and alignment. A mapping serves as a container of the Web page.

Mapping provides a start for determining the sizes of page elements and other placements. After the mapping is coded in XHTML and the browser displays the page, the designer gets a better idea of what adjustments need to be done. This is an iterative process that ultimately results in the final and optimum layout.

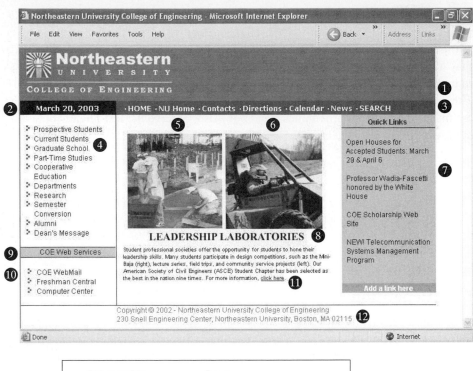

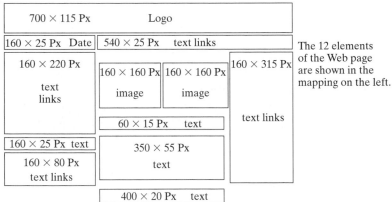

The 12 elements of the Web page are shown in the mapping on the left.

11.6 Website Design

The main premise of website design is to make the site both useful and easy to use. Those factors are what keeps visitors coming back to the site. In addition, making the site look good and load fast should serve as an initial attraction to visitors. Visitors also should be able to tell what a company does by merely viewing its home page.

Table 11.5   Website design.

Concept	Issues
General	Do not force visitors to register before they can use the site's services. This approach may drive visitors away from the site, and to competitors sites. Visitors usually do not like to be pushed. Let them use the site freely until they feel comfortable enough to register. Make registration optional.
Accessibility	Strike a balance between using the latest technology and being accessible to older computers and browsers.
Consistency	• Remember that a meaningful organization scheme and a solid organization structure guide users. • Create and use templates.
Navigability	• A wide and shallow structure is preferred over a narrow and deep structure, as the former reduces scrolling. • Ease of navigating the website is crucial.
Stability	• Stability helps a site meet visitors' expectations. • Limit novelty in order to avoid confusing visitors.
Search-engine optimization	Make liberal use of the website's main keywords in the `<meta>` tag, title, headings, and the `alt` attribute of the `<img>` tag. Also, resubmit the website to search engines periodically. Moreover, submit multiple Web pages of the website so that visitors have "backdrops" to the website.
Conciseness and simplicity	There is nothing more likely to put off site visitors than a site that is confusing and complex to use and navigate.
E-mail reply links	E-mail reply links encourage visitors to become involved with the website, and assure them that the site is backed up by traditional support.
Link to related websites	Links to related websites make the site look more credible and enhance its access and ranking by search engines.
Dynamic and new content	Dynamic content captures visitors attention by providing new information; it engages visitors.

While the layout design discussed in Section 11.5 is applicable to both websites and Web pages, this section adds some more concepts to website design. Table 11.5 summarizes the major website design concepts and their related issues.

11.7 Web Page Design

It is quite easy and fun to create a Web page. The layout design, suggestions in Section 11.5 provide a good start to ensure that the resulting page looks professional. This section presents the fine design details that are needed to produce high-quality Web pages. Table 11.6 summarizes the major Web-Page design concepts and their related issues.

Table 11.6   Web-Page design.

Concept	Issues
General	• Pages should download quickly regardless of whether the visitor's Internet connection is through modem or broadband. Minimize the use of images and graphics in page content. • All pages should fit into a 640×460 –pixel space; this is the ideal size of a browser window on computer screens. • Every Web page in the site should look like it belongs to the site; use the repetition concept. • Avoid page clutter; use the alignment concept to align page elements. • Use the contrast concept (in text, color, and so forth). • Spare visitors from have to scroll pages up, down, or sideways. • Provide one or two focal points in each page; having too many elements confuses visitors and breaks up their focus. • Ensure page accessibility in all browsers, on all platforms, and in all OSs. • Counters on pages are not recommended. • Too much advertising could be a distraction. • The name of the home (index) page of a website is usually `index.html`. (Check the website's server setup.) This is the first page that is served up when a visitor types in the site's URL.
Setup	• Each page should be formatted to have the proper margins, indenting, and columns. Tables are a very effective formatting tool. • Use the `<blockquote>` tag to indent. • Use GIF spacers to add whitespace. A **GIF spacer** is an image file that has, for example, a 2×2 –pixel white (or transparent) square that can be inserted anywhere in the page via the `<img>` tag. GIF spacers are quite effective to use with tables. They can be inserted into any table cell.
Text	• The page's background should not interrupt the text. • Proper text formatting includes using the right size and not employing too much bold, italic, or caps. • Avoid, using underlined text, as it may be mistaken for links. • Avoid using long text that stretches all the way across the page. • Avoid crowding text against the left edge of the page.
Whitespace	Whitespace is more important online than in paper documents. Use paragraphs and list tags or GIF spacers to break up text.
Color	• The color mix (background and foreground) should not strain the eye. • Use nondithering, browser-safe colors only.
Links	• Avoid keeping dead links that do not work anymore. • Coordinate link colors with the rest of the page's color scheme.
Navigation	• Navigation buttons should not overshadow a page's content by being large and visually attractive. They should take a backseat in the page display. • Use the same navigation system (buttons, menu, or links) in all pages of a site.

Table 11.6 Web-Page design. (Continued)

Concept	Issues
Images and graphics	• Minimize the use of images, for faster loading. • Make good use of graphics and images to break up large areas of text. • Tables can be good for placing images relative to each other in a Web page. • Displaying too many small images of awards that your site has won is not recommended. • Use the single-pixel GIF trick, which allows you to control page layout: First, create single-pixel GIF files of different colors, and then use the files to create rectangular regions of any size. This technique is useful, as it allows very small files to cover large regions on the Web page. • USe the `alt` attribute of the `<img>` tag. • Make sure that images on the site fit into the 640×460 –pixel screen size.
Animation	• Animation should run once and then stop. • Minimize the use of animation as much as possible.
Collection of data	• Use e-mail for quick collection of small amounts of data. • Use forms to close online sales and deliver goods.
Printer friendliness	Make sure that the page is printable. It is annoying when visitors print pages only to find that the right edge of text is cut off or that blank pages are printed.

11.8 Design Tools

One of the important factors in designing a website is using the right tools. These tools include an HTML editor, graphics and image software, a validator (see Section 11.9), and a management tool. We have covered graphics and image software in Chapter 10.

HTML editors can be graphical or text based. As we discuss in Chapter 17, text-based editors such as AceHTML, which we use in this book, provide more control to generate cleaner and simpler code than the graphical editors. This is an important issue, as it directly affects site accessibility. Good editors should not rewrite your code without your permission. They should allow you to specify your templates. Be wary of editors offered by browser vendors such as Microsoft (FrontPage) and Netscape (Composer), as they tend to have a bias towards coding for their own browser. Examples of some graphical editors are W3C Amaya, Macromedia Dreamweaver, Microsoft FrontPage, and Netscape Composer. Examples of some text-based editors are AceHTML, EditPlus, and HomeSite.

Site-management tools offer a great deal of help in making accessible sites. For example, we can maintain two versions of the same website (one optimized for the IE browser and one for Netscape) easily. These tools automate the updating of both versions. Manual updating of two versions of the same website is error prone and can lead to some sections of the website not being updated regularly.

Management tools include preprocessors and server-side scripting. Preprocessors use macros and variables to automate information updating. These macros and variables can be used by many Web pages and serve as a center for updating. Changing one of the macros or variables changes the content of all the pages that use it.

Server-side scripting allows the inclusion of dynamic content in Web pages. Server-side code is never sent to the client computer. It is always executed on the server, and only the results are sent to the client with the rest of the Web page.

There are commercial site-management software tools that can be used as well. Interested readers should run an online search using search strings such as `website management tools`, `Website preprocessors`, and `server-side scripting tools`, to name a few.

11.9 Validation and Testing

XHTML **validators** are used to check Web pages against XHTML published specifications for technical errors. Validators are good to use, as they enhance the accessibility of websites. Validators can be stand-alone or embedded in HTML editors. In the latter case, they can be in the form of an XHTML tag menu to choose from, or they can be a separate function that can be applied after the code is developed.

Linting is another method of checking for errors in Web pages. Unlike a validator, a linter does not check specifically against XHTML published specifications and rules. Instead, it looks for common mistakes, such as poor formatting, and points them out. For example, it catches a missing `alt`, `width`, or `height` attributes of an `<img>` tag. If you are interested, search the Web for a lint program.

Testing websites and Web pages is the last activity in Web design. Designers should upload all the Web pages to the intended Web server. Web servers could be Windows or Unix based. In the latter case, knowledge of the Unix commands is required. However, designers can get around this stipulation by using GUI-based FTP software. Get as many people as possible to test the Web pages, particularly all the links. Make sure there are no broken links or images.

11.10 Putting It All Together

The design of websites and Web pages begins with planning and ends with XHTML code and all kinds of files (HTML, image, PDF, and so forth). Table 11.7 shows the four steps that designers need to follow.

Table 11.7   Steps of website and page design.

Step	Advice	Section	Table
1. Planning	• Know your audience and market. • Decide on a URL name.	11.2	11–1
2. Layout	• Select an organization scheme and structure. • Storyboard the website to discover hidden problems, and to understand its exact use.	11.5	11–4

Table 11.7   Steps of website and page design. (Continued)

Step	Advice	Section	Table
3. website design	Make the website accessible, consistent, and easy to use and navigate.	11.6	11–5
4. Web-page design	• The Home page's name should be `index.html`. • Break text by including whitespace, lists, and images. • Test all links to make sure none is broken. • Use the right mix of colors. • Use alignment, proximity, repetition, and contrast.	11.7	11–6

FAQs

General

Q: What are other possible names, besides `index.html`, of the home page of a website?

A: The name depends on what the webmaster decides to use. It could be any name. Another common name is `index.htm`.

Blackbox

Section 11.1 (Introduction): Websites and Web pages require planning and design. The five phases of Web design are planning, analysis, design, implementation, and support.

Section 11.2 (Planning): Effective planning of websites and Web pages requires learning about intended markets and consumer behavior. Planning issues include URL choice, branding, e-mailing, casting a net, search engines, online sales, e-information, visualization, analysis, and reverse engineering.

Section 11.3 (Elements of Web Design): Knowing the elements of websites and Web pages is a prerequisite for good Web design. These elements are website accessibility, browser compatibility, and content. Content is further divided into the following elements: text, colors, links, images, image maps, animation, frames, tables, layers, forms, cascading style sheets, cookies, JavaScript, Java, and plug-ins.

Section 11.4 (Navigation Elements): The navigation tools of websites and Web pages are hyperlinks, buttons, menu bars, image maps, bullets and arrows, and tables. Also provide a site map, an index, or both for each Web page.

Section 11.5 (Layout Design): Use these layout concepts: organization scheme, organization structure, storyboarding of the site layout, navigation, Web-page layout, tables and layers, alignment, proximity, repetition, contrast, and mapping of Web pages.

Section 11.6 (Website Design): Use these website design concepts: accessibility, consistency, navigability, stability, search-engine optimization, conciseness and simplicity, e-mail reply links, link to related websites, and dynamic and new content.

Section 11.7 (Web-Page Design): Use these Web-page concepts: setup, text, whitespace, color, links, navigation, images and graphics, animation, collection of data, printer friendliness.

Section 11.8 (Design Tools): Use these design tools: XHTML editors, graphics and image software, validators, and site-management software.

Section 11.9 (Validation and Testing): Use validators, and linters, and test all Web pages after uploading them.

Section 11.10 (Putting It All Together): All you need are four steps to build websites: planning, layout, website design, and Web-page design.

Check Your Progress

At the end of this chapter, you should

- ✔ understand website planning (Sections 11.1 and 11.2);
- ✔ understand elements of Web design (Section 11.3);
- ✔ know about the various navigation elements (Section 11.4);
- ✔ be able to identify layout principles (Section 11.5);
- ✔ have mastered website design principles (Section 11.6);
- ✔ be able to use Web-page design concepts (Section 11.7);
- ✔ have mastered the use of design tools (Section 11.8);
- ✔ know about the various testing and validation issues (Section 11.9).

Problems

The exercises are designed for a lab setting, while the homework is to be done outside class time.

Exercises

11.1   Identify the elements of Web design in your school's website.

11.2   Identify the navigation elements in your school's website.

11.3   Identify the concepts of layout in your school's website.

11.4   Identify the concepts of website design in your school's website.

11.5   Identify the concepts of Web-page design in your school's website.

Homework

11.6   Identify the elements of Web design in your favorite commercial website.

11.7   Identify the navigation elements in your favorite commercial website.

11.8   Identify the concepts of layout in your favorite commercial website.

11.9   Identify the concepts of website design in your favorite commercial website.

11.10 Identify the concepts of Web-page design in your favorite commercial website.

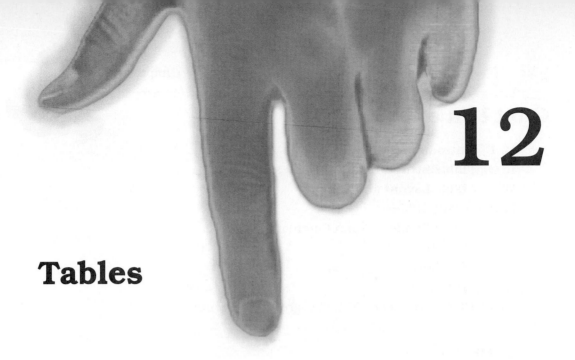

Tables

Goal

Understand the structure, creation, and control of tables; the use of tables for data tabulation and organization; and the use of tables in formatting Web pages and controlling content location in pages.

Objectives

- Table structure and variables
- Table layout design
- Table rows and columns
- Table headings and cells
- Table rendering
- Table nesting
- Tabulating data in tables
- Formatting via tables

Outline

12.1 Introduction

Tables can be used in Web pages to organize and structure page content. In a traditional sense, Web authors can use tables to structure textual data, such as names, IDs, addresses, and so forth. In an XHTML sense, we can use tables to control the positions of XHTML elements, such as images and text, in a Web page. Using tables to format Web pages offer great flexibility in controlling the layout design of Web pages, which was covered in Chapter 11. Without table formatting, the Web page's content becomes concentrated on its left side.

A **table** is defined as a region that has rows and columns of small rectangles, called cells, that are arranged relative to each other in a certain way that makes up the table layout. Each cell holds its own content. Cell content may be textual data or XHTML elements. When the content of all the cells is displayed, the content's layout is recognized.

When tables are used to format Web pages, writing the XHTML code of these pages becomes harder than writing the code for the pages without using tables. The code also becomes more difficult to follow. Web authors need to lay out the design of their Web pages with tables on paper, so that they can refer to it during the writing process of the XHTML code. If the process of writing XHTML code manually while using tables for formatting proves to be difficult for Web authors, they can use XHTML editors. XHTML editors use tables for formatting when they implement the layouts of complex Web pages with many XHTML elements.

12.2 Table Structure and Variables

XHTML provides many variables that allow Web authors to control table structure. This capability is important if tables are to be used for formatting Web pages. For example, rows and columns can be merged together. Another example is that table cells may vary in size to accommodate different types of Web content. Consider the case of a table cell that holds an image. The cell may span multiple rows and columns in order to fit the image's size correctly.

12.2.1 Noncell Variables

The XHTML table variables may be grouped into two categories: noncell and cell. Noncell variables control the properties and structure of the table. They variables specify the table caption, summary, border, header, rows, columns, width, and height. Figure 12.1 shows these variables. The table **caption** is the title of the table. It provides a short description of the table's purpose. It can be placed at the top of the table, as shown in the figure, or at the bottom. The table **summary** provides a longer description that may be employed by people using speech or Braille-based browsers. The table **border** is the table's outside boundary.

The table **header** is the first row in the table. Each cell in this row is a header for the column underneath it; it holds the title of the column. Table **rows** are the horizontal layout of the cells. Similarly, table **columns** are the vertical layout of the cells. The **width** and **height** of a table are a representation of the number of its columns and rows, respectively. XHTML allows Web authors to specify a table width and a height. When Web authors specify a table width, the browser finds the width of a table cell by dividing the width of the page by the number of columns. If no width is specified, the browser uses a default value. Similarly, the browser finds the cell height by dividing the table height by the number of rows. If Web authors do not specify a table height, the browser uses a default value.

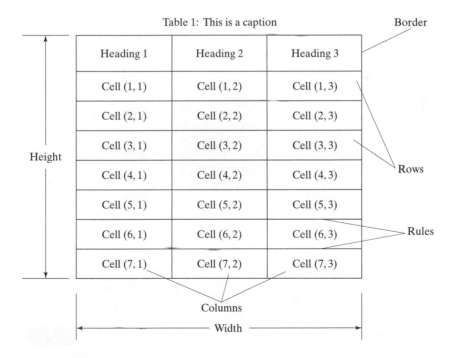

Figure 12.1 Table structure.

12.2.2 Cell Variables

Cells are the basic units that make up a table. Cells are arranged within the table border from top to bottom and left to right. Thus, the cells' layout uses the top left corner of the table as the origin of the grid of cells. As shown in Figure 12.1, each cell location in the layout is defined by two counters to specify its horizontal and vertical position, respectively. The first counter is the number of the cell row. The second counter is the number of the cell column. Thus, cell (i, j) is located at row i and column j. Each cell holds its own content.

The horizontal and vertical lines that separate the cells from each other are known as **rulings** (or **rules**, as XHTML calls them). Web authors can make these rules visible or invisible. They can also remove them for a group of cells in order to create a connected area in the table. The thickness of the rules may be specified as well.

Cell variables control the properties and structure of individual cells. These variables specify the row span, column span, padding, spacing, and alignment of content within the cell. Figure 12.2 shows these variables. This figure shows a large cell in the center that spans four rows and two columns. This cell is surrounded by other cells that span one row and one column. The browser determines the smallest size (width and height) of a table cell by using the table's width and height, together with the number of rows and columns of the table, as described previously. Using this size as a basis, Web authors may specify a larger cell size if needed by using the row and column spans.

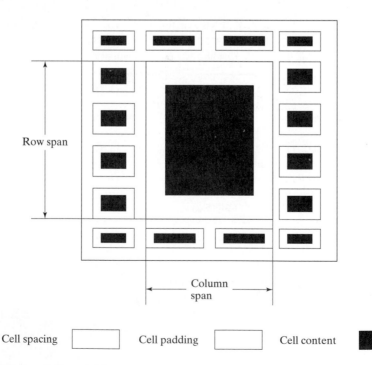

Figure 12.2 Cell variables.

Cell spacing describes the amount of the horizontal and vertical spacing between cells, as in Figure 12.2. Web authors can use cell spacing to control the amount of whitespace (or the background color of the Web page) that is needed to separate cells from each other.

Specifying cell padding is equivalent to specifying top, bottom, left, and right margins for the cell. The padding describes the amount of horizontal and vertical spacing between a cell's content and its border. The color of the cell padding is the color of the cell's background.

Cell content can be aligned within each cell in both the horizontal and vertical directions. Web authors have three choices for aligning content in either direction. Content can be aligned to the left (left justified), middle, or right (right justified) of the cell in the horizontal direction. In the vertical direction, content can be aligned to the top (top justified), middle, or bottom (bottom justified) of the cell. If the cell content fills the entire cell space, no effect of alignment is visible, as the content has no room to move within the cell.

12.3 Table Layout and Design

The purpose of using a table determines the table's layout and design. If the table is used in the traditional way to tabulate data, three styles may be chosen from, depending on the type of table header required. Figure 12.3 shows the three possible styles. The table header could be on the top or on the left side, or the table may have both top and left headers.

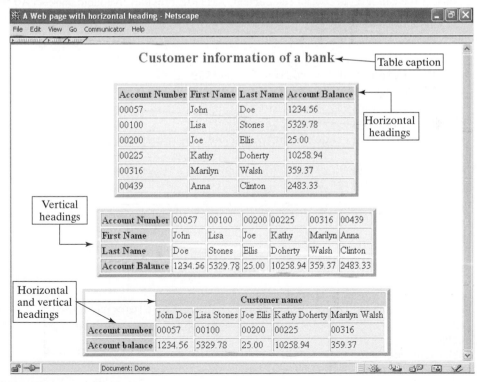

Figure 12.3 Table layout.

Tables used for formatting Web pages have dramatically different layouts from those of tables that display data. In tables used for Web-page formatting, headings are eliminated, as they are not needed. Sizes of cells are also different; some cells may span multiple rows and columns, while other cells are left empty in order to provide spacing between cell content. The table's border and rules are made invisible in order to make the flow of the elements or content of the Web page smooth and seamless. A color may be assigned to the table background. Other, different colors may be assigned to the background of individual cells. Finally, the cells can hold any XHTML elements, including images, lists, and hyperlinks.

Web authors must consider the size of the computer screen when designing tables. As we discussed in Chapter 11, Web pages should fit within a screen size of 640×460 pixels for optimal display. A table with a large width and height forces browsers to create scrollbars so that the full table may be viewed. Such scrolling is a not a good idea, however. In some cases, the tables may be displayed in such a disarray that Web surfers cannot read the Web page.

12.4 Using Tables

XHTML provides all the tags necessary to create tables and control their structures. There are also enough tags at the cell level to control cell content. XHTML provides five table tags: `<table>`, `<caption>`, `<tr>`, `<th>`, and `<td>`. Table 12.1–12.4 show these tags and their attributes. Use the following template to create tables:

```
 1   <?xml version="1.0" encoding="iso-8859-1"?>
 2   <!DOCTYPE html PUBLIC "-//W3C//DTD XHTML 1.1//EN"
 3       "http://www.w3.org/TR/xhtml11/DTD/xhtml11.dtd ">
 4   <html xmlns="http://www.w3.org/1999/xhtml ">
 5   <!-- Generated by AceHTM http://freeware.acehtml.com -->
 6   <head>
 7   <meta http-equiv="Content-Type" content="text/html;
     charset=iso-8859-1" />
 8   <title>Table Template</title>
 9   </head>
10   <body>
11   <table>
12   <caption>caption goes here </caption>
13   <tr>
14   <th>heading goes here</th>
15   <td>cell content goes here</td>
16   </tr>
17   <tr>
18   <th>heading goes here</th>
19   <td>cell content goes here</td>
20   </tr>
```

The `<table>` tags, lines 11 and 22, must enclose the other tags for the table.

The `<caption>` tag, if used, must follow the `<table>` tag immediately.

```
21    ...
22    </table>
23    </body>
24    </html>
```

Add more `<tr>` tags here as needed.

Table 12.1 `<table>` tag—the master tag that encloses all other tags for the table.

Attributes: `<table summary width height border align rules cellspacing cellpadding>`

Attribute	Description
`summary`	Provides a brief description of the table's purpose and structure. A browser uses this attribute when it renders the table to nonvisual media for the disabled.
`width`	Specifies the width of the table. It may be specified in pixels or inches. If table width is not specified, the browser determines it automatically.
`height`	Specifies the height of the table. It may be specified in pixels or inches. If table height is not specified, the browser determines it automatically.
`border`	Specifies the thickness of the table border in pixels.
`align`	Specifies the table's position with respect to the Web page that includes it. Its values are `left` (default), `center`, or `right`.
`rules`	Specifies which rules between cells are visible. Its values are `none`, `groups` (rules appear between row groups and column groups only), `rows` (rules appear between rows only), or `cols` (rules appear between columns only).
`cellspacing`	Specifies the amount of space both between the table cells and between the cells and the table sides. Its value is specified in pixels. Use `cellspacing="0"` to remove all space.
`cellpadding`	Specifies the space between the contents of a cell and its border. Its value is specified in pixels or as a percentage of cell space. For example, `cellpadding = "10%"` means that the top and bottom margins of the cell are each 10% of the cell height, and the left and right margins of the cell are each 10% of the cell width. Use `cellpadding="0"` to remove all space.
Other attributes	There are other attributes that are also used by the `<tr>`, `<th>`, and `<td>` tags. They are `bgcolor`, `cellspacing`, `cellpadding`, `rowspan`, `colspan`, and `valign`. When these attributes are used with the `<table>` tag, they affect all the rows and cells in the table.

Table 12.2 `<caption>` tag—assigns a title to a table and must be used only once.

Attributes: `<caption align>`

Attribute	Description
`align`	Has four possible values. The `top` value places the caption at the top of the table. This is the default value. `bottom`, `left`, and `right` place the caption at the bottom, left, and right of the table, respectively.

Table 12.3   `<tr>` tag—creates a table row, encloses the row cells, and can be used multiple times.

Attributes: `<tr align valign>`	
Attribute	**Description**
`align`	Specifies the horizontal alignment of the cell content (within the cell) for all the cells of the row. Its values are `left` (default), `center`, and `right`.
`valign`	Specifies the vertical alignment of the cell content (within the cell) for all the cells of the row. Its values are `top` (content flush with the top of the cell), `middle` (center content vertically within the cell), and `bottom` (content flush with the bottom of the cell). `middle` is the default value.
Other attributes	There are other attributes that are also used by the `<table>`, `<th>`, and `<td>` tags. They are `bgcolor`, `cellspacing`, `cellpadding`, `rowspan`, and `colspan`. When these attributes are used with the `<tr>` tag, they affect all the cells in the row.

Table 12.4   `<th>` and `<td>` tags—the table heading and data cells.[a]

Attributes: `<th` (or `td`) `abbr headers rowspan colspan nowrap align valign cellpadding>`	
Attribute	**Description**
`abbr`	Provides an abbreviated form of cell content for disabled Web surfers who use speech synthesizers.
`headers`	Used to help Web surfers who use nonvisual browsers. It specifies header information for a cell that is spoken prior to displaying the cell data.
`rowspan`	Specifies the number of rows that the cell spans; the default value is `1`. A value of `0` makes the cell span all rows from the current row to the last row of the table.
`colspan`	The companion to the `rowspan` attribute. It specifies the number of columns that the cell spans. Its value could be any integer, including `1` and `0`, as with `rowspan`.
`nowrap`	A Boolean attribute that tells browsers whether to disable automatic text wrapping for a cell. Disabling automatic text wrapping may result in excessively wide cells.
`align`	Specifies the horizontal alignment of content within the cell. Its values are `left` (default), `center`, and `right`.
`valing`	Specifies the vertical alignment of content within the cell. Its values are `top`, `middle` (default), and `bottom`. It overrides the same attribute of the `<tr>` tag.
`cellpad-ding`	Same as the `cellpadding` attribute of the `<table>` tag. If it is used with the `<th>` or `<td>` tag, it applies locally (i.e., to the cell only). If it is used with the `<table>` tag, it applies globally to all table cells. The local value overrides the global one.
Other attributes	There are other attributes that are also used by the `<table>` and `<tr>` tags. They are `bgcolor` and `cellspacing`. When these attributes are used with the `<th>` or `<td>` tag, they affect the cell only.

a.   The `<th>` tag causes the heading to appear in bold font. Data cells may be left empty in order to provide whitespace for formatting purposes. The `<th>` and `<td>` tags have the same attributes.

Example 12.1 Use tables.

Develop a Web page that illustrates the use of tables.

Solution 12.1 This example creates a Web page that uses the attributes of the `<table>` tag. The example uses five attributes: `align`, `border`, `width`, `height`, and `cellspacing`. Using the AceHTML editor, generate the given code, and save it as `example121.html`. The following screen capture shows the resulting Web page:

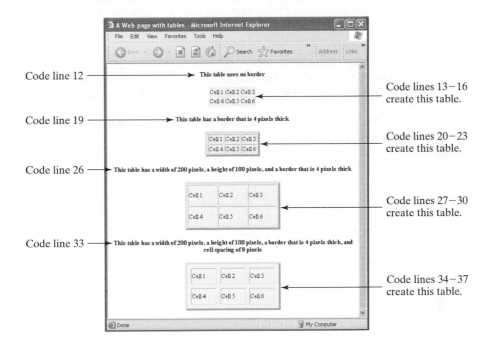

```
1   <?xml version="1.0" encoding="iso-8859-1"?>
2   <!DOCTYPE html PUBLIC "-//W3C//DTD XHTML 1.1//EN"
3       "http://www.w3.org/TR/xhtml11/DTD/xhtml11.dtd ">
4   <html xmlns="http://www.w3.org/1999/xhtml ">
5   <!-- Generated by AceHTM http://freeware.acehtml.com -->
6   <head>
7   <meta http-equiv="Content-Type" content="text/html;
    charset=iso-8859-1" />
8   <title>A Web page with tables</title>
9   </head>
10  <body>
11
12  <h4 align="center">This table uses no border</h4>
13  <table align="center" bgcolor="#FFFF00">
```

```
14   <tr><td>Cell 1</td><td>Cell 2</td><td>Cell 3</td></tr>
15   <tr><td>Cell 4</td><td>Cell 5</td><td>Cell 6</td></tr>
16   </table>
17   <p></p>
18
19   <h4 align="center">This table has a border that is 4 pixels
     thick</h4>
20   <table align="center" border="4" bgcolor="#FFFF00">
21   <tr><td>Cell 1</td><td>Cell 2</td><td>Cell 3</td></tr>
22   <tr><td>Cell 4</td><td>Cell 5</td><td>Cell 6</td></tr>
23   </table>
24   <p></p>
25
26   <h4 align="center">This table has a width of 200 pixels,
     a height of 100 pixels, and a border that is 4 pixels
     thick</h4>
27   <table align="center" border="4" width="200" height="100"
     bgcolor="#FFFF00">
28   <tr><td>Cell 1</td><td>Cell 2</td><td>Cell 3</td></tr>
29   <tr><td>Cell 4</td><td>Cell 5</td><td>Cell 6</td></tr>
30   </table>
31   <p></p>
32
33   <h4 align="center">This table has a width of 200 pixels,
     a height of 100 pixels, a border that is 4 pixels thick,
     and cell spacing of 8 pixels </h4>
34   <table align="center" border="4" width="200" height="100"
     cellspacing="8" bgcolor="#FFFF00">
35   <tr><td>Cell 1</td><td>Cell 2</td><td>Cell 3</td></tr>
36   <tr><td>Cell 4</td><td>Cell 5</td><td>Cell 6</td></tr>
37   </table>
38
39   </body>
40   </html>
```

Code explained:

Refer to the foregoing screen capture of the Web page.

Discussion:

The blank lines 11, 18, 25, 32, and 38 are used to divide the code into four chunks, thus making it easy to follow. Each chunk creates a table. The background color of each table is yellow (bgcolor="FFFF00"). The yellow color is applied to all the cells of each table because the attribute is used at the <table> tag level. Finally, observe the noticeable change in the size of the table, because of the change in the width and height (line 27) and cellspacing (line 34).

Hands-on exercise:

Replace the contents of the cells by XHTML elements such as text, hyperlinks, and images. What happens to the sizes of the cells?

Example 12.2 Use variable-size table cells.

Develop a Web page with a table which contains cells that span multiple rows and columns.

Solution 12.2 This example uses the `rowspan`, `colspan`, and `align` attributes of the `<td>` tags. Using the AceHTML editor, generate the given code, and save it as `example122.html`. The following screen capture shows the resulting Web page:

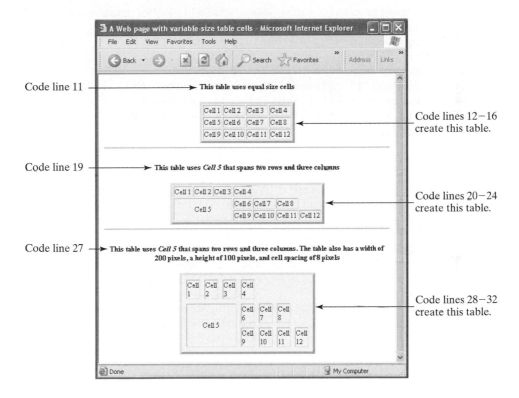

```
1   <?xml version="1.0" encoding="iso-8859-1"?>
2   <!DOCTYPE html PUBLIC "-//W3C//DTD XHTML 1.1//EN"
3       "http://www.w3.org/TR/xhtml11/DTD/xhtml11.dtd ">
4   <html xmlns="http://www.w3.org/1999/xhtml ">
5   <!-- Generated by AceHTM http://freeware.acehtml.com -->
6   <head>
7   <meta http-equiv="Content-Type" content="text/html;
    charset=iso-8859-1" />
8   <title>A Web page with variable-size table cells </title>
```

```
 9   </head>
10   <body>
11   <h4 align="center">This table uses equal size cells </h4>
12   <table align="center" border="4" bgcolor="FFFF00">
13   <tr><td>Cell 1</td><td>Cell 2</td><td>Cell 3</td>
     <td>Cell 4</td></tr>
14   <tr><td>Cell 5</td><td>Cell 6</td><td>Cell 7</td>
     <td>Cell 8</td></tr>
15   <tr><td>Cell 9</td><td>Cell 10</td><td>Cell 11</td>
     <td>Cell 12</td></tr>
16   </table>
17   <hr />
18
19   <h4 align="center">This table uses <i>Cell 5</i> that spans
     two rows and three columns </h4>
20   <table align="center" border="4" bgcolor="FFFF00">
21   <tr><td>Cell 1</td><td>Cell 2</td><td>Cell 3</td>
     <td>Cell 4</td></tr>
22   <tr><td rowspan="2" colspan="3" align="center">Cell 5</td>
     <td>Cell 6</td><td>Cell 7</td><td>Cell 8</td></tr>
23   <tr><td>Cell 9</td><td>Cell 10</td><td>Cell 11</td>
     <td>Cell 12</td></tr>
24   </table>
25   <hr />
26
27   <h4 align="center">This table uses <i>Cell 5</i> that spans
     two rows and three columns. The table also has a width of
     200 pixels, a height of 100 pixels, and cell spacing of 8
     pixels </h4>
28   <table align="center" border="4" bgcolor="FFFF00"
     border="4" width="200" height="100" cellspacing="8">
29   <tr><td>Cell 1</td><td>Cell 2</td><td>Cell 3</td>
     <td>Cell 4</td></tr>
30   <tr><td rowspan="2" colspan="3" align="center">Cell 5</td>
     <td>Cell 6</td><td>Cell 7</td><td>Cell 8</td></tr>
31   <tr><td>Cell 9</td><td>Cell 10</td><td>Cell 11</td>
     <td>Cell 12</td></tr>
32   </table>
33   </body>
34   </html>
```

Code explained:

1. Refer to the foregoing screen capture of the Web page.
2. Lines 17 and 25 create horizontal lines.
3. The blank lines 18 and 26 are used to divide the code into chunks, to make it easy to read. Each chunk creates a table.

Discussion:

Observe that the browser does its best to render each table within the specified constraints. It has to add whitespace at the end of the first two rows of the last two tables. It also has to stretch the cells of the last table to accommodate the specified width and height requirements. This example investigates the effect of the attributes of the `<td>` tag on the rendering of the table. The first table does not use any attributes of the tag. For the second table, the browser must create `Cell 5` with the given size; yet, it must also create the other cells. The only way to meet both constraints is to enlarge the table's width.

If we add one more constraint, the browser must change the way the table looks. The third table is the same as the second table, but has a width and a height of 200 and 100 pixels, respectively. While the two tables have the same general layout, they look different.

The conclusion to make here is that the browser adjusts the size of the cell based on the cell's content, the cell's attributes, and the attributes of the `<table>` tag that affect cells, such as `width` and `height`. Web authors must give careful thought to table rendering during the phase of table design. They may use an iterative approach to design tables. First, they build a simple table. Then they start adding more attributes, to control the size of the table, the sizes of its cells, and the spacing between cells. Also, attention should be paid to cell layout. Usually, all rows or columns of a table have the same number of cells. When Web authors begin using cells that span more than one row or column, they may want to reduce the number of cells in order to avoid having empty spacing in the table, as shown in the screen capture. In this case, the Web author may eliminate cells 7, 8, 10, 11, and 12 in order to remove the empty space in the table.

Hands-on exercise:

Replace the content of the cells by XHTML elements such as text, hyperlinks, and images. What happens to the sizes of the cells?

12.5 Table Rendering and Calculations

As we have discussed in the previous section, there are many conflicting variables and attributes of tables and their tags. There are variables at both the table level (noncell variables) and the cell level. Web authors may specify just rows and columns, in the simplest case, to create a table, or they can specify rows, columns, table width and height, cell spans, and cell padding. In addition to incorporating all of these variables, the browser still must ensure the proper display of cell contents, which can range from simple text to images, lists, hyperlinks, and so forth.

How does a browser resolve all these potential conflicts? What are the basic issues in rendering tables? What are the precedence rules that a browser uses? The main factor in rendering tables is the display of cell contents. The contents of each cell must be displayed properly and correctly. The browser uses all the table and cell variables entered by Web authors via attributes in order to determine the table's layout and the minimum cell size. During this decision process, the browser may ignore some variables, or some variables may override others. Once the minimum cell size is determined, the browser uses it as the common denominator to determine the sizes of other cells. For example, if a cell uses two row spans, its height is double the height of the minimum cell size.

While Web authors are not expected to fully understand the mathematical algorithms a browser uses to perform table calculations, they need to completely comprehend the effect of the tags and attributes they use to develop tables. Such an understanding allows them to control table design and display. The following rules are used by browsers to render and calculate the size of tables:

1. **Calculating table width and height.** Web authors must specify the number of columns and rows in order to create a table. In addition, they may also specify a table width, height, or both, as needed. If no table width or height is specified, the browser determines it. It first receives all the cell data and the number of rows and columns. Using all this information, it calculates the amount of horizontal and vertical space required by the table. Web authors can use one of two methods to specify table width and height: fixed or percentage. Table width and height are specified via the `width` and `height` attributes, respectively, of the `<table>` tag. A fixed specification is given in pixels (e.g., `width="600"` or `height="500"`). A percentage specification is based on the screen width or height at the time that the table is displayed (e.g., `width="70%"` or `height="60%"`).

2. **Calculating the number of columns in a table.** The browser uses the number of cells required by the table rows to calculate the maximum number of columns of the table. This number is equal to the number of columns required by the row with the most columns, including cells that span multiple columns. Once this maximum number is calculated by the browser, it becomes the number of columns for each row in the table. Any row that has fewer than this number of columns is padded by empty cells at its end. Under this method of calculation, there is always at least one row in a table that uses the maximum number of columns. Let us apply this method to the last two tables shown in Example 12.2. The last row has seven columns (cells): one cell that spans three columns and four additional cells. Thus, the maximum number of columns for this table is seven. Any row in the table must therefore have seven columns. As a result, the browser uses three additional empty cells to render the first row and one extra empty cell to render the second row.

3. **Calculating the size of a table cell.** After a browser calculates a table's width and height and its number of columns, it uses these variables, together with cell content (data) and spacing, to determine the minimum cell size (width and height). If the cell data fit within this minimum size, the browser uses it. If the cell data need more space for display, the browser increases the minimum cell size accordingly. The browser must also adjust other cells in the table to accommodate the larger cell size. For instance, consider the second table shown in the screen capture of Example 12.2. All the cells of this table, except `Cell 5`, have an equal size, which is the minimum cell size. The data of each of these cells fit within this size. Let us force the data of, say, `Cell 7` to exceed this minimum size by changing its content to `Cell 7777777777`. The upcoming screen capture shows the results. The browser increases the size of `Cell 7` to accommodate the new cell content.

As a result, all the cells in the same column as `Cell 7` assume the new size as well, to maintain the integrity of the table.

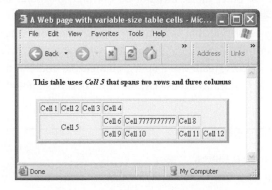

4. **Calculating cell spacing and padding.** Web authors may specify cell spacing and padding in two ways: fixed and percentage. In the percentage specification, the cell spacing is a percentage of the cell width or height. The browser calculates the percentage based on both the width and height and uses the smaller percentage.

5. **Inheritance of alignment specifications.** The alignment of cell content can be specified at three levels: cell, row, or table. Cell content can be aligned horizontally or vertically within the cell via the `align` and `valign` attributes, respectively. If cell-level control is needed, these attributes are used with the `<th>` or `<td>` tag. If row-level control (applies to all cells in a row) is needed, these attributes are used with the `<tr>` tag. If table-level control (applies to all cells in the table) is needed, these attributes are used with the `<table>` tag. If Web authors specify all levels of control at the same time, the browser applies cell-level control only and ignores the other two levels. This is known as the local rule.

12.6 Nesting Tables

Web authors may nest tables in order to achieve certain design goals of their Web pages. When tables are used to format Web pages, table nesting may be used to control the formatting. However, table nesting makes the XHTML code quite complex and difficult to follow and understand.

How do browsers nest tables? The basic unit in a table is the cell. A cell's content could be an entire table, or it could be a combination of a table and other data. For example, a cell could have text followed by a table. Web authors who wish to create a nested table inside a certain cell of an outer table simply add the XHTML code that creates the inner table after the `<td>` tag of the cell. This addition results in nested `<table>` tags in the XHTML code of the Web page. Using this method of nesting, one can implement multiple levels of nesting. For example, a table can be nested inside a table that itself is nested inside a third table, and so forth. These multiple nestings are not uncommon in practice when formatting Web pages.

Nesting tables may produce awkward results, however. The sizes of table cells may vary greatly. In addition, the locations of empty cells may not be acceptable to Web authors. Moreover, the proportions of the outer table may not be optimal; the outer table may be wide and skinny, or tall and thin. We can overcome this problem by specifying the width and height of the outer table. The most general rule that Web authors should follow when dealing with nested tables is to use trial and error. Start by creating the nested-table set as accurately as possible. Use a browser to display the set. Evaluate the display, change the code, and display the set again. Repeat this process as many times as necessary, until the best design and layout of the table set are achieved.

Example 12.3 Use nested tables.

Develop a Web page that nests one table inside another.

Solution 12.3 Using the AceHTML editor, generate the given code, and save it as `example123.html`. Also, use a browser to render the Web page.

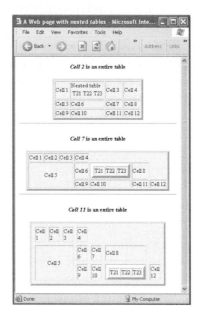

Code explained:

Lines 13, 14, 24–26, 35, and 36 create the three nested tables. Each nested table is a cell content of the outer table. For example, the `<td>` tag that opens in line 35 closes at the end of line 36.

Discussion:

This example uses the Web page of Example 12.2, adding a nested table to each of its three tables. The nested table is 1 × 3 (one row by three columns). The names of the cells of the nested table are T21 (reads as Table 2, Cell 1), T22, and T23. We create the nested table inside Cell 2 of the outside table. As shown in the foregoing screen capture, the content of Cell 2 is text that reads Nested table, followed by the nested table itself. The same table is nested again twice, once inside Cell 7 of the middle table and once inside Cell 11 of the bottom table. In both cases, the text preceding the table has been removed.

Hands-on exercise:

Starting with the code given in this example, add a 2×2 table inside cell T22 of the nested table. What happens to the table display?

```
1   <?xml version="1.0" encoding="iso-8859-1"?>
2   <!DOCTYPE html PUBLIC "-//W3C//DTD XHTML 1.1//EN"
3       "http://www.w3.org/TR/xhtml11/DTD/xhtml11.dtd ">
4   <html xmlns="http://www.w3.org/1999/xhtml ">
5   <!-- Generated by AceHTM http://freeware.acehtml.com -->
6   <head>
7   <meta http-equiv="Content-Type" content="text/html;
    charset=iso-8859-1" />
8   <title>A Web page with nested tables </title>
9   </head>
10  <body>
11  <h4 align="center"><i>Cell 2</i> is an entire table</h4>
12  <table  align="center" border="4" bgcolor="FFFF00">
13  <tr><td>Cell 1</td><td>Nested table<table rows="2" cols="3">
14  <tr><td>T21</td><td>T22</td><td>T23</td></tr></table></td>
15  <td>Cell 3</td><td>Cell 4</td></tr>
16  <tr><td>Cell 5</td><td>Cell 6</td><td>Cell 7</td>
    <td>Cell 8</td></tr>
17  <tr><td>Cell 9</td><td>Cell 10</td><td>Cell 11</td>
    <td>Cell 12</td></tr>
18  </table>
19  <hr />
20
21  <h4 align="center"><i>Cell 7</i> is an entire table</h4>
22  <table align="center" border="4" bgcolor="FFFF00">
23  <tr><td>Cell 1</td><td>Cell 2</td><td>Cell 3</td>
    <td>Cell 4</td></tr>
24  <tr><td rowspan="2" colspan="3" align="center">Cell 5</td>
    <td>Cell 6</td><td><table rows="2" cols="3" border="5">
25  <tr><td>T21</td><td>T22</td><td>T23</td></tr>
26  </table></td><td>Cell 8</td></tr>
27  <tr><td>Cell 9</td><td>Cell 10</td><td>Cell 11</td>
    <td>Cell 12</td></tr>
28  </table>
29  <hr />
30  <h4 align="center"><i>Cell 11</i> is an entire table</h4>
```

```
31  <table align="center" border="4" bgcolor="FFFF00"
    border="4" width="200" height="100" cellspacing="8">
32  <tr><td>Cell 1</td><td>Cell 2</td><td>Cell 3</td>
    <td>Cell 4</td></tr>
33  <tr><td rowspan="2" colspan="3" align="center">Cell 5</td>
    <td>Cell 6</td><td>Cell 7</td><td>Cell 8</td></tr>
34  <tr><td>Cell 9</td><td>Cell 10</td>
35  <td><table rows="2" cols="3" border="5">
36  <tr><td>T21</td><td>T22</td><td>T23</td></table></td>
37  <td>Cell 12</td></tr>
38  </table>
39  </body>
40  </html>
```

12.7 Formatting via Tables

Formatting Web pages by using tables is based on the same idea of nesting tables, covered in the previous section. Each table cell can be viewed as an independent screen that can hold any XHTML content. Thus, we may begin the design of a Web-page layout by dividing the page into regions, where every region holds some of the page's contents. After the design is complete, we substitute a cell or a table for each region. We then create an outer table that holds all these cells and nested tables. We may not use borders for some tables in order to make the layout of the page flow seamlessly.

As we design the Web-page layout, we must keep the table's structure in mind: A table must have rows and columns. As we create the various regions, we make sure that these regions form a grid structure that defines the rows and columns. If finer control over the grid structure is required, we can use nested tables.

Example 12.4 Formatting with tables.

Develop a Web page that is formatted by a table.

Solution 12.4 First, we reverse engineer the layout of Northeastern University's College of Engineering website, `http://www.coe.neu.edu`. We simplify the layout as shown in the upcoming drawing. The upcoming screen capture shows the Web page. The layout is achieved via the use of three tables. The outer *Table 1* has four rows; each row has one cell. The first row, *Row 1*, holds the NU logo image. The second row, *Row 2*, holds *Table 2*, the first nested table. *Table 2* has one row and three cells that hold links the NU image, and quick links respectively. *Row 3* holds the horizontal line. The last row of *Table 1*, *Row 4*, holds *Table 3*, the second nested table. *Table 3* leaves *cells 1* and *3* empty for spacing, and *Cell 2* holds the copyright notice.

Using the AceHTML editor, generate the given code, and save it as `example124.html`. Display the Web page in a browser.

Table 1 (4 × 1)

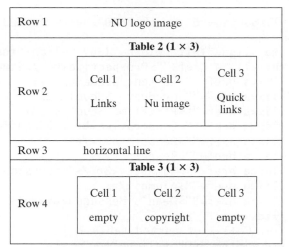

Table 2 (1 × 3)

Table 3 (1 × 3)

```
1   <?xml version="1.0" encoding="iso-8859-1"?>
2   <!DOCTYPE html PUBLIC "-//W3C//DTD XHTML 1.1//EN"
3       "http://www.w3.org/TR/xhtml11/DTD/xhtml11.dtd ">
4   <html xmlns="http://www.w3.org/1999/xhtml ">
5   <!-- Generated by AceHTM http://freeware.acehtml.com -->
6   <head>
7   <meta http-equiv="Content-Type" content="text/html;
    charset=iso-8859-1" />
8   <title>Formatting via Tables</title>
9   </head>
10  <body topmargin="0" leftmargin="0">
11  <table cellspacing="0" cellpadding="0"> <!-- outer table 1 -->
12  <tr> <!-- row 1 of outer table 1 -->
13      <td width="640" height="60">
14      <img src="nulogo.gif" height="60" width="640" />
15      </td>
16  </tr>
```

```
17    <tr> <!-- row 2 of outer table 1 -->
18        <td>
19        <table cellspacing="0" width="640"> <!-- nested table 2 -->
20            <tr>
21                <td align="left" width="150" valign="top">
22                <ul><li><a href="">Prospective<br />Students</a>
23                <li><a href="">Current Students</a>
24                <li><a href="">Graduate School</a>
25                <li><a href="">Part-Time Studies</a>
26                <li><a href="">Cooperative<br />Education</a>
27                <li><a href="">Departments</a>
28                <li><a href="">Research</a>
29                <li><a href="">Semester<br />Conversion</a>
30                <li><a href="">Alumni</a>
31                <li><a href="">Dean's Message</a></ul>
32                </td>
33                <!-- Cell 2 of nested table 2 -->
34                <td width="340" valign="top">
35                <br /><br />
36                <img src="NUImage.jpg">
37                </td>
38                <!-- Cell 3 of nested table 2 -->
39                <td width="150" valign="top" bgcolor="#CCCCCC">
40                <b><h3>Quick links</h3></b>
41                <hr width="150" />
42                <a href="">Open House</a><p></p>
43                <a href="">Scholarship Fund</a><p></p>
44                <a href="">New program
45                </td>
46            </tr>
47        </table> <!-- close nested table 2 -->
48        </td>
49    </tr>
50    <tr><td><hr width="640" align="left"></td></tr><!--row 3-->
51    <tr> <!-- row 4 of outer table 1 -->
52        <td>
53        <table> <!-- begin nested table 3 -->
54            <tr>
55                <td width="150"></td>
56                <td align="center">
57    Copyright © 2002 - Northeastern University College of
      Engineering<br />
58    230 Snell Engineering Center, Northeastern University,
      Boston, MA 02115
59                </td>
60                <td></td>
61            </tr>
62        </table> <!-- close nested table 3 -->
```

```
63          </td>
64      </tr>
65      </table> <!-- close outer table 1 -->
66      </body>
67      </html>
```

Code explained:

1. Line 10 shows the `<body>` tag, which two attributes here.
2. The outer *Table 1* tag opens in line 11 and closes in line 65. The table has cell spacing and padding of zero values in order to make the boundaries of the cells invisible.
3. Lines 13–15 create the content of *Row 1* of outer *Table 1*.
4. Lines 18–48 create the content of *Row 2* of outer *Table 1*.
5. Lines 19–47 create the nested *Table 2*.
6. Line 50 creates the content of *Row 3* of outer *Table 1*.
7. Lines 52–60 create the content of *Row 4* of outer *Table 1*.
8. Lines 53–62 create the nested *Table 3*.

Discussion:

We use an outer-table width of 640 pixels, as we have discussed in Chapter 11. Lines 13, 14, 19, and 50 use this width. Moreover, the widths of the three cells of nested *Table 2* (150 pixels in line 21, 340 pixels in line 34, and 150 pixels in line 39) should add up to 640 pixels. We use two `<br />` tags in line 35 to push the image down for better layout and look. We use the `<hr />` tag to space out the title. We also use the `<p>` tag in lines 42 and 43 to space out the links. We use a width of 150 pixels for the first empty cell of nested *Table 3* (line 55) to push the text (lines 57 and 58) further in. The table cells in lines 21 and 55 should use the same width (155 pixels) in order to line up both cells vertically. Note that line 57 could have used the numeric code of the copyright symbol.

Hands-on exercise:

Starting with the code give in this example, remove *Cell 3* from both nested *Tables 2* and *3*, making each a 1×2 table. Adjust the entire Web page to fit within a width of 640 pixels.

12.8 Tutorials

12.8.1 Creating a Traditional Table (Study Section 12.4)

This tutorial creates three tables that use two different heading layouts: vertical and horizontal–vertical. The two tables have the same content, but the content is presented differently in each table. Use the AceHTML editor to generate the given code, and save it as `tutorial1281.html`. View the Web page in a browser.

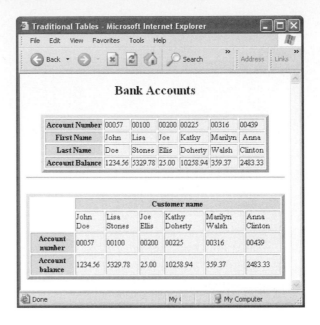

Code explained:

1. Lines 11–49 create the first table.

2. The table's four rows are created by lines 13–21, 22–30, 31–39, and 40–48.

3. Lines 14–20 create five cells for the first row; the first cell of each row is a heading.

4. Lines 53–85 creates the second table.

5. The table's four rows are created by lines 54–57, 58–66, 67–75, and 76–84.

6. Line 55 creates the first cell of the first row of the second table as an empty cell.

7. Line 59 creates the first cell of the second row of the second table as an empty cell. The `<td>` tag uses a white background color to overwrite the row's yellow color set in line 58.

Discussion:

We create two tables with different heading layouts. The first table has a vertical layout. The second table uses dual headings. (See Figure 12.3). Both tables use a border that is 5 pixels thick. We use one caption in the first table. This tag must come after the `<table>` tag. Observe the effect of the `<th>` tag, as makes the text of the cell boldface.

Hands-on exercise:

Starting with the code given in this example, add more code to create the first table (with a horizontal heading) shown in Figure 12.3.

```
1  <?xml version="1.0" encoding="iso-8859-1"?>
2  <!DOCTYPE html PUBLIC "-//W3C//DTD XHTML 1.1//EN"
3       "http://www.w3.org/TR/xhtml11/DTD/xhtml11.dtd ">
```

```
4   <html xmlns="http://www.w3.org/1999/xhtml">
5   <!-- Generated by AceHTM http://freeware.acehtml.com -->
6   <head>
7   <meta http-equiv="Content-Type" content="text/html;
    charset=iso-8859-1" />
8   <title>Traditional Tables</title>
9   </head>
10  <body>
11  <table border="5" align="center">
12  <caption align="center"><h2>Bank Accounts</h2></caption>
13  <tr bgcolor="#FFFF00">
14  <th bgcolor="#33FFFF">Account Number</th>
15  <td>00057</td>
16  <td>00100</td>
17  <td>00200</td>
18  <td>00225</td>
19  <td>00316</td>
20  <td>00439</td>
21  </tr>
22  <tr bgcolor="#FFFF00">
23  <th bgcolor="#33FFFF">First Name</th>
24  <td>John</TD>
25  <td>Lisa</TD>
26  <td>Joe</TD>
27  <td>Kathy</TD>
28  <td>Marilyn</TD>
29  <td align="center" valign="top">Anna</td>
30  </tr>
31  <tr bgcolor="#FFFF00">
32  <th bgcolor="#33FFFF">Last Name</th>
33  <td>Doe</td>
34  <td>Stones</td>
35  <td>Ellis</td>
36  <td>Doherty</td>
37  <td>Walsh</td>
38  <td align="right" valign="bottom">Clinton</td>
39  </tr>
40  <tr bgcolor="#FFFF00">
41  <th bgcolor="#33FFFF">Account Balance</th>
42  <td>1234.56</td>
43  <td>5329.78</td>
44  <td>25.00</td>
45  <td>10258.94</td>
46  <td>359.37</td>
47  <td>2483.33</td>
48  </tr>
```

First Table

Heading

Six cells

Row 1

```
49   </table>
50
51   <!-- Create second table -->
52   <hr /><p></p>
53   <table border="5" align="center">
54   <tr>
55   <td></td>
56   <th bgcolor="#33FFFF" colspan="6">Customer name</th>
57   </tr>
58   <tr bgcolor="#FFFF00">
59   <td bgcolor="#FFFFFF"></td>
60   <td>John Doe</td>
61   <td>Lisa Stones</td>
62   <td>Joe Ellis</td>
63   <td>Kathy Doherty</td>
64   <td>Marilyn Walsh</td>
65   <td>Anna Clinton</td>
66   </tr>
67   <tr bgcolor="#FFFF00">
68   <th bgcolor="#33FFFF">Account number</th>
69   <td>00057</td>
70   <td>00100</td>
71   <td>00200</td>
72   <td>00225</td>
73   <td>00316</td>
74   <td>00439</td>
75   </tr>
76   <tr bgcolor="#FFFF00">
77   <th bgcolor="#33FFFF">Account balance</th>
78   <td>1234.56</td>
79   <td>5329.78</td>
80   <td>25.00</td>
81   <td>10258.94</td>
82   <td>359.37</td>
83   <td>2483.33</td>
84   </tr>
85   </table>
86   </body>
87   </html>
```

Second table

Row 2

Seven cells

12.8.2   Creating a Site Map for Navigation (Study Section 12.7)

In this tutorial, we develop a website that uses tables to create a site map in each of its Web pages. We use the concept of repetition that we have covered in Chapter 11. The map is located on the left side of each Web page of the site. We name the file of the home page of the site as index.html. Let us assume that the URL of the website is http://www.aaa.bbb. When the user types this URL into the URL bar of a browser, the browser fetches the home page, effectively using `http://www.aaa.bbb/index.html`. The website has seven additional Web pages. We show only the code of the home page and the help page in this example. The code of the other pages is very similar. Use the AceHTML editor to generate the given code, and save it as `index.html` for the home page and `help.html` for the help page. View the Web pages in a browser.

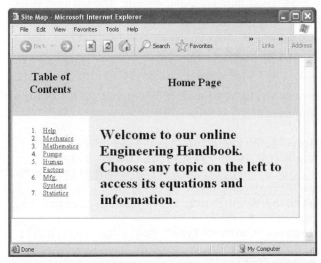

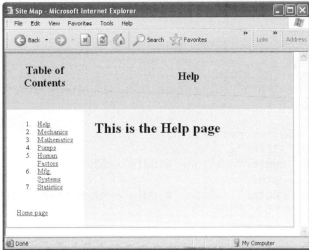

Code explained:

1. Lines 14–43 in file `index.html` create a 2×2 table.

2. Lines 17–20 in file `index.html` create the first row.

3. Lines 23–42 in file `index.html` create the second row.

4. Lines 11–33 in file `help.html` create a 2×2 table.

5. Lines 12–15 in file `help.html` create the first row.

6. Lines 16–32 in file `help.html` create the second row.

7. Line 27 in `help.html` links back to the home page for ease of navigation.

Discussion:

We repeat the same page layout throughout the website. The site map is the same for all of the Web pages. With the exception of the home page itself, every other page links back to the home page. The code block defined by lines 25–35 in `index.html` is used in all the other Web pages. (See lines 17–28 in `help.html`.)

Hands-on exercise:

Follow the code shown in `help.html` to develop the code for the missing Web pages in order to complete the development of the website.

```
1   <?xml version="1.0" encoding="iso-8859-1"?>
2   <!DOCTYPE html PUBLIC "-//W3C//DTD XHTML 1.1//EN"        index.html
3       "http://www.w3.org/TR/xhtml11/DTD/xhtml11.dtd ">
4   <html xmlns="http://www.w3.org/1999/xhtml ">
5   <!-- Generated by AceHTM http://freeware.acehtml.com -->
6   <head>
7   <meta http-equiv="Content-Type" content="text/html;
    charset=iso-8859-1" />
8   <title>Site Map</title>
9   </head>
10  <body>
11  <body topmargin="0" leftmargin="0">
12
13  <!-- Create a 2x2 table -->
14  <table align="left" rules="none" cellpadding="20"
    cellspacing="0">
15
16  <!-- First row has two heading cells -->
17  <tr bgcolor="33FFFF">
18     <th align="center" valign="middle"><h2>Table of
    Contents</h2></th>
19     <th align="center" valign="middle"><h2>Home Page</h2></th>
20  </tr>
21
22  <!-- Second row has two cells -->
23  <tr>
24  <!-- First cell has an ordered list -->
25     <td valign="top">
26     <ol>
27       <li><a href="help.html">Help</a><br />
28       <li><a href="mechanics.html">Mechanics</a><br />
29       <li><a href="math.html">Mathematics</a><br />
30       <li><a href="pumps.html">Pumps</a><br />
```

```
31      <li><a href="humanfactor.html">Human Factors</a><br />
32      <li><a href="mfgsystems.html">Mfg. Systems</a><br />
33      <li><a href="statistics.html">Statistics</a><br />
34    </ol>
35    </td>
36    <!-- Second cell has text -->
37    <td width="500" valign="top" bgcolor="#FFFF00">
38    <h1>Welcome to our online Engineering Handbook.
39    Choose any topic on the left to access its equations
40    and information.
41    </td>
42  </tr>
43  </table>
44  </body>
45  </html>
```

```
1   <?xml version="1.0" encoding="iso-8859-1"?>
2   <!DOCTYPE html PUBLIC "-//W3C//DTD XHTML 1.1//EN"          help.html
3       "http://www.w3.org/TR/xhtml11/DTD/xhtml11.dtd ">
4   <html xmlns="http://www.w3.org/1999/xhtml ">
5   <!-- Generated by AceHTM http://freeware.acehtml.com -->
6   <head>
7   <meta http-equiv="Content-Type" content="text/html;
    charset=iso-8859-1" />
8   <title>Site Map</title>
9   </head>
10  <body topmargin="0" leftmargin="0">
11  <table align="left" rules="none" cellpadding="20"
    cellspacing="0">
12  <tr bgcolor="#33FFFF">
13    <th align="center" valign="middle"><h2>Table of
    Contents</h2></th>
14    <th align="center" valign="middle"><h2>Help</h2></th>
15  </tr>
16  <tr>
17    <td valign="top">
18    <ol>
19      <li><a href="help.html">Help</a><br />
20      <li><a href="mechanics.html">Mechanics</a><br />
21      <li><a href="math.html">Mathematics</a><br />
22      <li><a href="pumps.html">Pumps</a><br />
23      <li><a href="humanfactor.html">Human Factors</a><br />
24      <li><a href="mfgsystems.html">Mfg. Systems</a><br />
25      <li><a href="statistics.html">Statistics</a><br />
26    </ol>
27    <br /><a href="index.html">Home page
28    </td>
29    <td width="500" valign="top" bgcolor="#FFFF00">
```

```
30      <h1>This is the Help page </h1>
31      </td>
32    </tr>
33    </table>
34    </body>
```

FAQs

Using Tables (Section 12.4)

Q: Does the <caption> tag replace the summary attribute of the <table> tag?

A: No. The <caption> tag provides a very brief, one-statement description of a table. The summary attribute of the <table> tag provides much more information about the table's structure and purpose, to help disabled (visually impaired) Web surfers understand the table.

Q: What is a good way to debug HTML code when using tables to format Web pages?

A: Use the border attribute of the <table> tag in order to get an idea of how the browser is creating the table rows, columns, and cells that you have designed. These borders should help you immensely in deciding what to change in order to finalize the formatting. Once you like the final layout of the page, simply set the border attribute to zero.

Q: How do I assign different colors to cell text?

A: You need to use cascading style sheets, which will be explained in Chapter 13.

Blackbox

Section 12.1 (Introduction): XHTML tables are used for organizing data and formatting Web pages.

Section 12.2 (Table Structure and Variables): The XHTML table variables come in two groups: noncell and cell. The non-cell variables specify the table caption, summary, border, header, rows, columns, width, and height. The cell variables specify the rules, row span, column span, padding, spacing, and alignment of content within the cell.

Section 12.3 (Table Layout and Design): If tables are used for formatting Web pages, eliminate table headings, let some cells span multiple rows and columns, make the table border and rules invisible, use different cell colors, and design for a screen size of 640×460 pixels for optimal display.

Section 12.4 and 12.5 (Using Tables, and Table Rendering and Calculations) (Example 12.1 and 12.2): XHTML provides five table tags: <table>, <caption>, <tr>, <th>, and <td>. Their attributes are <table summary width height border align rules cellspacing cellpadding>, <caption align>, <tr align valign cellspacing cellpadding>, and <th (or td) abbr headers rowspan colspan nowrap align valign cellpadding cellspacing cellpadding>, respectively.

Section 12.6 and 12.7 (Nesting Tables and Formatting via Tables) (Example 12.3 and 12.4): Nest an entire table inside a cell of another table. The concept of formatting Web pages by using tables is based on idea of nesting tables. Each table cell can be viewed as an independent Web page that can hold any XHTML content.

Section 12.8 (Tutorials): Two tutorials show how to use tables.

Quick reference for the tags presented in this chapter

Tag	Close	Attribute	Value	Effect	Example
`<table>`	yes	`summary`	text	table summary	`<table summary="abc">`
		`width`	number of pixels	table width	`<table width="200">`
		`height`	number of pixels	table height	`<table height="100">`
		`border`	number of pixels	table border	`<table border="5">`
		`align`	`left`	align text with the left of cells	`<table align="left">`
			`center`	align text with the center of cells	`<table align="center">`
			`right`	align text with the right of cells	`<table align="right">`
		`rules`	none	no rules are displayed	`<table rules="none">`
			`groups`	rules only between groups	`<table rules="groups">`
			`rows`	rules only between rows	`<table rules="rows">`
			`columns`	rules only between columns	`<table rules="columns">`
		`cell-spacing`	number of pixels	spacing between cells	`<table cellspacing="5">`

Tag	Close	Attribute	Value	Effect	Example
		cell-padding	number of pixels	cell margins	`<table cellspad-ding="5">`
		other attributes	There are other attributes that are also used by the `<tr>`, `<th>`, and `<td>` tags. They are `bgcolor`, `cellspacing`, `cellpadding`, `rowspan`, `colspan`, and `valign`. When these attributes are used with the `<table>` tag, they affect all the table's rows and cells.		
`<caption>`	yes	align	top	places the caption at the top of the table	`<caption align="top">`
			bottom	places the caption at the bottom of the table	`<caption align="bottom">`
			left	places the caption at the left of the table	`<caption align="left">`
			right	places the caption at the right of the table	`<caption align="right">`
`<tr>`	yes	align	left	align the text with the left of the cell	`<tr align="left">`
			center	align the text with the center of the cell	`<tr align="center">`
			right	align the text with the right of the cell	`<tr align="right">`
		valign	top	align the text with the top of the cell	`<tr align="top">`
			middle	align the text with the middle of the cell	`<tr align="middle">`

Tag	Close	Attribute	Value	Effect	Example
			bottom	align the text with the bottom of the cell	`<tr align="bottom">`
		other attributes	There are other attributes that are also used by the `<table>`, `<th>`, and `<td>` tags. They are `bgcolor`, `cellspacing`, `cellpadding`, `rowspan`, and `colspan`. When these attributes are used with the `<tr>` tag, they affect all the row's cells.		
`<th>` or `<td>`	yes	abbr	text	table abbreviation	`<td abbr="abc">`
		header	text	table header	`<td header="abc">`
		rowspan	number	specify row span of the cell	`<td rowspan="3">`
		colspan	number	specify column span of the cell	`<td colspna="2">`
		nowrap	Boolean	wrap or don't wrap cell text	`<td nowrap="yes">`
		align	left	align the text with the left of the cell	`<td align="left">`
			center	align the text with the center of the cell	`<td align="center">`
			right	align the text with the right of the cell	`<td align="right">`
		valign	top	align the text with the top of the cell	`<td align="top">`
			middle	align the text with the middle of the cell	`<td align="middle">`

Tag	Close	Attribute	Value	Effect	Example
			bottom	align the text with the bottom of the cell	`<td align="bottom">`
		cell-padding	number of pixels	cell margins	`<td cellpadding="5">`
		other attributes		There are other attributes that are also used by the `<table>` and `<tr>` tags. They are `bgcolor` and `cellspacing`. When these attributes are used with the `<th>` or `<td>` tag, they affect the cell only.	

Check Your Progress

At the end of this chapter, you should

✔ understand the use of tables (Section 12.1);
✔ understand table structure and variables (Section 12.2);
✔ understand table layout and design (Section 12.3);
✔ be able to identify XHTML table tags (Section 12.4);
✔ understand table rendering and calculations (Section 12.5);
✔ have mastered the use of table nesting (Section 12.6);
✔ have mastered the formatting of Web pages and content via tables (Section 12.7);
✔ have practiced using tables (Section 12.8).

Problems

The exercises are designed for a lab setting, while the homework is to be done outside class time.

Exercises

12.1   Create a table containing your class roster. The table should have three columns: student ID, first name, and last name.

12.2   Add one row to the top table in Tutorial 12.8.1.

12.3   Add one column to the top table in Tutorial 12.8.1.

12.4   Add one row to the bottom table in Tutorial 12.8.1.

12.5   Add one column to the bottom table in Tutorial 12.8.1.

Homework

12.6   Create a Web page that uses traditional tables. The table content is left up to you. Be imaginative.

12.7   Create a Web page that uses tables for formatting. The page and table design and layout are left up to you. Be imaginative.

12.8 Create the table shown in the topmost accompanying screen capture. The cells in the last row use bold text and have a background color of #CEEFBD.

12.9 Create the dual-heading table shown in the bottommost accompanying screen capture.

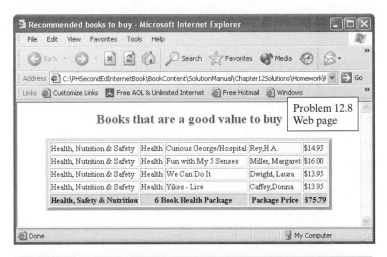

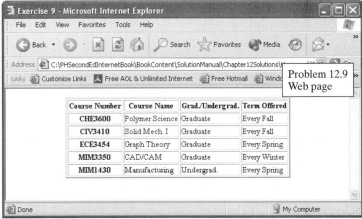

Layers

Goal

Understand layers, their creation and control, their use in formatting and controlling content location in Web pages, and their relationship to tables.

Objectives

- Positioning and the coordinate system of layers
- Creation of layers
- Properties of layers
- Management of layers
- Rendering of layers
- Nesting of layers
- The relationship between layers and tables
- Formatting via layers

Outline

13.1 Introduction

Web designers strive to make the layout of Web pages attractive. XHTML provides them with tables and layers to format Web pages. We cover layers in this chapter. A **layer** is a rectangular container (region) that holds XHTML content and that can be positioned anywhere on a Web page by using the page's x and y pixel coordinates.

Like tables, layers can be used to organize and format Web-page content. We can use layers to control the positions of XHTML elements, such as images and text, in a Web page. Think of layers as sheets of transparencies superimposed on a Web page. Each layer has its own content and positioning. The collective content of all the layers makes up the content of the page. The content of all layers that belong to one Web page must be coherent in order to support the page's context and goal.

We can control the stacking order in which we place layers relative to each other in a Web page. We can also make them transparent or opaque, or visible or hidden, to provide dramatic and pleasing visual effects.

13.2 Layer Positioning

Layers exist in 3D space, occupying regions on the page and stacked up on top of each other as well as on top of the page's content. The appearance of the content of a page's layers depends on the order in which they are stacked; earlier layers get covered by later layers in the same display area. XHTML provides control of the stacking order, as covered in Section 13.4.

XHTML uses a 2D coordinate system, shown in Figure 13.1, to position layers in a Web page. All the coordinates are measured in pixels. The system has its origin, (0, 0), in the top left corner of the Web page, with the +X-axis going to the right and the +Y-axis going down, as shown in the figure.

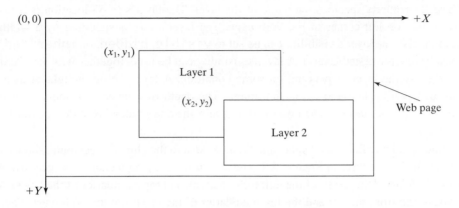

Figure 13.1 Layer positioning.

Figure 13.1 shows a Web page with two layers. Layers 1 and 2 are positioned in the page at locations (x_1, y_1), and (x_2, y_2), respectively. XHTML uses the (*left, top*) designation to refer to the (x, y) location of a layer. This is because the x coordinate shifts the layer's position away from the left edge of the Web page, and the y coordinate shifts the layer's position away from the top edge of the page. Figure 13.1 also shows that Layer 2 is stacked on top of Layer 1, suggesting that Layer 1 was created first, followed by Layer 2.

13.3 Properties of Layers

An XHTML layer has a rich set of properties that, if used cleverly, can create amazing effects. These properties are an ID, (x, y) location, size (width and height), visibility, background color and image, depth (stacking order), clip (definition of the visible area of a layer), and overflow. Figure 13.2 illustrates these properties.

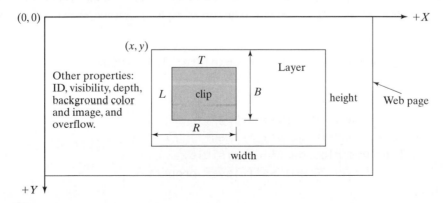

Figure 13.2 Layer properties.

The ID property specifies the name of the layer. The layer's (x, y) location is measured relative to the top left corner of the Web page. The layer's size is specified by a width and height in pixels. The layer's visibility can be set to `visible`, `hidden`, or `inherited` from the parent layer (for nested layers). A layer's visibility can be used, together with JavaScript, to hide or display the layer, depending on some condition. A layer, being thought of as a Web page itself, has a background color and image. The depth of a layer represents its stacking order relative to other layers. When we overlap layers, the one created last hides the one behind it, and so forth.

Clipping a layer limits its displayable (visible) area to the clipping rectangle, shown as the shaded area inside the layer in Figure 13.2. The size of the clipping rectangle is specified by the lengths L, R, B, and T, in pixels, of the left, right, bottom, and top boundaries of the layer respectively, measured from the left and the top boundaries of the layer, not the Web page. Thus, the size of the clipping rectangle is $(R - L) \times (B - T)$.

The overflow property determines what happens if a layer's content exceeds the size of the layer. We can choose to increase the size to enclose the content, leave the size as is and cut the content, or leave both as they are and provide scrollbars.

13.4 Using Layers

XHTML provides the `<div>` and the `<span>` tags to create layers. The `<layer>` and `<ilayer>` tags have been deprecated and should not be used at all, because of browser compatibility problems. IE and Netscape 6 and higher do not recognize the `<layer>` and `<ilayer>` tags. Only Netscape 4*x* still recognizes them. We use the `<div>` tag in this book. All browsers render the tag. However, we use different names for the background color and image attributes in order to overcome some remaining compatibility problems. Browsers simply ignore the attributes that they do not recognize.

The `<div>` tag defines CSS (cascading style sheet) layers, also known as CSS-P (positioning) elements. We cover CSS in Chapter 16. Because of the use of CSS, the syntax of the `<div>` tag is different from what we have covered so far. An example of its use is shown as follows:

```
<div
id="myLayer" style="position:absolute; left:200px;
top:200px; width:300px; height:175px; z-index:1; border:1px;
background-color:#FFFF00; layer-background-color:#FFFF00;
background-image:url(myImage.jpg);
layer-background-image:url(myImage.jpg);
visibility:visible; overflow:visible;
clip: rect(50 30 70 10)">All layer properties
</div>
```

Table 13.1 describes the `<div>` tag and its attributes.

Table 13.1   `<div>` tag.

Attributes: `<div id position left top width height z-index border background-color layer-background-color background-image layer-background-image visibility overflow clip>`

Attribute	Description
`id`	Indicates the name of the layer.
`position`	Indicates that the pixel measurements in the `<div>` tag are referenced from the top left corner, as shown in Figure 13.1. This attribute must be used in order for the `<div>` tag to work in Netscape 4*x*.
`left`	Specifies the *x* position (in pixels, `px`) of the layer relative to the (0, 0) corner of the Web page, as shown in Figure 13.1.
`top`	Specifies the *y* position of the layer relative to the (0, 0) corner of the Web page.
`width`	Specifies the width of the layer, as shown in Figure 13.2.
`height`	Specifies the height of the layer, as shown in Figure 13.2.
`z-index`	Determines the stacking order of the layer. Higher numbered layers appear on top of lower numbered layers.
`border`	Specifies the thickness of the layer's border. This attribute must be used in order for the `<div>` tag to work in Netscape 4*x*.
`background-color`	Specifies the background color of the layer. This attribute must be used in order for the `<div>` tag to work in IE and Netscape 6 and higher. Netscape 4*x* ignores it.
`layer-background-color`	Specifies the background color of the layer. This attribute must be used in order for the `<div>` tag to work in Netscape 4*x*. This attribute is ignored by IE and Netscape 6 and higher.
`background-image`	Specifies the background image of the layer. This attribute must be used in order for the `<div>` tag to work in IE and Netscape 6 and higher. It specifies the image's file name as a URL. This attribute is ignored by Netscape 4*x*.
`layer-background-image`	Specifies the background image of the layer. This attribute must be used in order for the `<div>` tag to work in Netscape 4*x*. It specifies the image's file name as a URL. This attribute is ignored by IE and Netscape 6 and higher.
`visibility`	Determines the initial display status of the layer. It has three values: `visible`, `hidden`, and `inherit`. The `inherit` value uses the visibility properties of the layer's parent. It is applicable to nested layers.
`overflow`	Determines what happens to the layer if its content exceeds its size. It has four values: `visible` (increases the layer's size so that all its content is visible), `hidden` (clips the content to fit into the original size of the layer), `scroll` (adds scrollbars regardless of whether the content exceeds the original size), and `auto` (makes scrollbars appear only when the layer's content exceeds its boundaries).
`clip`	Defines the visible area of the layer, as shown in Figure 13.2. Specify as `clip(L R B T)`.

Example 13.1 Use layers.

Develop a Web page that illustrates the use of layers.

Solution 13.1 This example creates a Web page that uses two layers: one yellow and one red. Using the AceHTML editor, generate the given code, and save it as `example131.html`. The upcoming screen capture shows the resulting Web page.

```
1   <?xml version="1.0" encoding="iso-8859-1"?>
2   <!DOCTYPE html PUBLIC "-//W3C//DTD XHTML 1.1//EN"
3       "http://www.w3.org/TR/xhtml11/DTD/xhtml11.dtd ">
4   <html xmlns="http://www.w3.org/1999/xhtml ">
5   <!-- Generated by AceHTM http://freeware.acehtml.com -->
6   <head>
7   <meta http-equiv="Content-Type" content="text/html;
    charset=iso-8859-1" />
8   <title>A Web page with layers</title>
9   </head>
10  <body>
11  <!-- Create first layer -->
12  <h2 align="center">Using two layers</h2>
13  <div id="layer1" style="position:absolute; width:300px;
    height:175px; left: 54px; top: 45px; background-color:
    #FFFF00; layer-background-color: #FFFF00; border: 1px;
    visibility:visible"><b>This is layer 1</b>
14  </div>
15
16  <!-- Create second layer -->
17  <div id="layer2" style="position:absolute; width:200px;
    height:165px; left: 54px; top: 100px; background-color:
    #33FFFF; layer-background-color: #33FFFF; border: 1px">
    <b>This is layer 2</b></div>
18  </body>
19  </html>
```

Code explained:

Refer to the upcoming screen capture.

Discussion:

Lines 13 and 17 create layers 1 and 2, respectively. They use some of the attributes of the `<div>` tag. Each tag uses the two color attributes so that the Web page will display correctly in IE, Netscape 6 or higher, and Netscape 4x. For Netscape 4x to render the page correctly, we must use these three attributes: `position:absolute; border:1px; layer-background-color: #33FFFF`. Also, if a typo has been made in the tag, the browser will not show any display, nor will it indicate any errors. Look for unclosed quotes or missing semicolons (`;`) when attempting to troubleshoot.

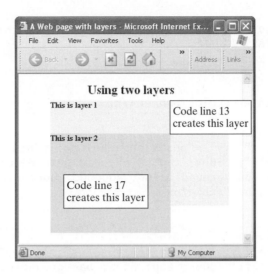

Hands-on exercise:

Starting with the code given in this example, create a third layer that uses the `clip` and the `overflow` attributes.

Example 13.2 Create a color banner.

Use layers to create a color banner.

Solution 13.2 Using the AceHTML editor, generate the given code, and save it as `example132.html`. The following screen capture shows the resulting Web page.

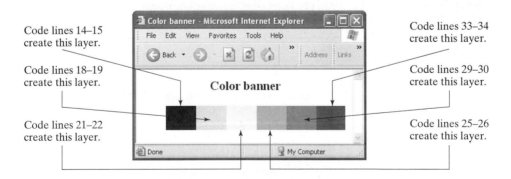

Code lines 14–15 create this layer.

Code lines 18–19 create this layer.

Code lines 21–22 create this layer.

Code lines 33–34 create this layer.

Code lines 29–30 create this layer.

Code lines 25–26 create this layer.

```
1   <?xml version="1.0" encoding="iso-8859-1"?>
2   <!DOCTYPE html PUBLIC "-//W3C//DTD XHTML 1.1//EN"
3       "http://www.w3.org/TR/xhtml11/DTD/xhtml11.dtd">
4   <html xmlns="http://www.w3.org/1999/xhtml">
5   <!-- Generated by AceHTM http://freeware.acehtml.com -->
```

```
 6   <head>
 7   <meta http-equiv="Content-Type" content="text/html;
     charset=iso-8859-1" />
 8   <title>Color banner</title>
 9   </head>
10   <body>
11   <h2 align="center">Color banner</h2>
12
13   <!-- Create layer 1 -->
14   <div id="layer1" style="position:absolute; width:50px;
     height:40px; left: 50px; top: 60px; background-color:
     #000000; layer-background-color: #000000; border: 1px;
     visibility:visible"><b></b>
15   </div>
16
17   <!-- Create layer 2 -->
18   <div id="layer1" style="position:absolute; width:50px;
     height:40px; left: 100px; top: 60px; background-color:
     #33FFFF; layer-background-color: #33FFFF; border: 1px;
     visibility:visible"><b></b>
19   </div>
20   <!-- Create layer 3 -->
21   <div id="layer1" style="position:absolute; width:50px;
     height:40px; left: 150px; top: 60px; background-color:
     #FFFF66; layer-background-color: #FFFF66; border: 1px;
     visibility:visible"><b></b>
22   </div>
23
24   <!-- Create layer 4 -->
25   <div id="layer1" style="position:absolute; width:50px;
     height:40px; left: 200px; top: 60px; background-color:
     #00CC99; layer-background-color: #00CC99; border: 1px;
     visibility:visible"><b></b>
26   </div>
27
28   <!-- Create layer 5 -->
29   <div id="layer1" style="position:absolute; width:50px;
     height:40px; left: 250px; top: 60px; background-color:
     #FF00CC; layer-background-color: #FF00CC; border: 1px;
     visibility:visible"><b></b>
30   </div>
31
32   <!-- Create layer 6 -->
33   <div id="layer1" style="position:absolute; width:50px;
     height:40px; left: 300px; top: 60px; background-color:
     #0000FF; layer-background-color: #0000FF; border: 1px;
     visibility:visible"><b></b>
34   </div>
```

```
35    </body>
36    </html>
```

Code explained:

Refer to the foregoing screen capture of the Web page.

Discussion:

This example uses six layers to create a banner with fading colors from left to right. The fading effect is generated by assigning a lighter color to each layer. All layers have the same width (50 pixels), height (40 pixels), and y coordinate (60 pixels). The x coordinate is incremented by 50 pixels in order to displace each successive layer to the right. The layers do not overlap each other in this example. Instead, they are adjacent to each other. Each layer has a width of 50 pixels, and is displaced by 50 pixels in the horizontal (x) direction.

Hands-on exercise:

Starting with the code given in this example, stack up another six layers by displacing them in the y direction. Use shades of the color yellow.

13.5 Nesting Layers

Web authors may nest layers in order to format and control the layout of their Web pages. A **nested layer** is a layer created inside another layer. A nested layer inherits the visibility of its parent layer. Layer nesting does not complicate XHTML code as much as table nesting does. In addition, nested layers are easier to code than nested tables: Simply nest the <div> tag. Layers are also easier to work with and to change the design of than table cells. If necessary, you can use layers to quickly create complex page designs and then convert them to tables for use by browsers that do not support layers.

Why nest layers if we can position them precisely where we want on the Web page? It is an issue of control more than positioning. If we change the location of a parent (outer) layer, then all its content, including any nested layers, moves with it. This feature is particularly useful if we have multiple levels of nesting. XHTML does not have a limit on the depth (number of levels) of nesting. Here is an example of the tag format for three-level nesting:

```
<div>
   <div>
        <div>
        </div>
   </div>
</div>
```

Example 13.3 Use nested layers.

Use nested layers to design a table layout.

Solution 13.3 Using the AceHTML editor, generate the given code, and save it as example133.html. Use a browser to render the Web page.

Code explained:

1. Line 14 creates the parent (container) layer. This layer has a color that is hidden behind all its nested layers. The `<div>` tag in this line closes at line 41.
2. Line 17 creates layer 1, which simulates `Cell 1` of the table.
3. Lines 21–31 create layer 2 (`Cell 2`). This layer contains three nested layers for the nested table (`Cell 21`, `Cell 22`, and `Cell 23`). The `<div>` tag opens in line 23 and closes in line 31.
4. Lines 23 and 24 create `Cell 21`.
5. Lines 26 and 27 create `Cell 22`.
6. Lines 29 and 30 create `Cell 23`.
7. Lines 34 and 35 create `Cell 3`.
8. Lines 38 and 39 create `Cell 4`.

Discussion:

In this example, we design the layout of a table that is 2×2 (two rows and two columns) and has a nested table. The nested table is 1×3. The design issue here is where we should place the nested table. To investigate this problem, we create a parent layer that has 2×2 layer array. The layers' layouts and sizes are illustrated in the foregoing screen capture. We create a nested layer in place of the nested table and move it around within the parent layer until the layout looks great. This arrangement becomes the final layout, which can be converted to tables if needed. The screen capture shows one possible layout design. This layout can be converted to tables to finalize the page's development.

Hands-on exercise:

Starting with the code given in this example, move the nested table to `Cell 4`'s position.

```
1   <?xml version="1.0" encoding="iso-8859-1"?>
2   <!DOCTYPE html PUBLIC "-//W3C//DTD XHTML 1.1//EN"
3      "http://www.w3.org/TR/xhtml11/DTD/xhtml11.dtd ">
4   <html xmlns="http://www.w3.org/1999/xhtml ">
5   <!-- Generated by AceHTM http://freeware.acehtml.com -->
6   <head>
7   <meta http-equiv="Content-Type" content="text/html;
    charset=iso-8859-1" />
8   <title>Table Design</title>
9   </head>
10  <body>
11  <h2 align="center">Table Design</h2>
12
13  <!-- Create parent layer -->
14  <div id="parentLayer" style="position:absolute; width:400px;
    height:200px; left: 50px; top: 60px; background-color:
    #33FFFF; layer-background-color: 33FFFF; border: 1px;
    visibility:visible"><b></b>
15
16  <!-- Create layer 1 (cell 1) -->
17  <div id="layer1" style="position:absolute; width:100px;
    height:100px; left: 0px; top: 0px; background-color:
    #FFFF66; layer-background-color: #FFFF66; border: 1px;
    visibility:visible"><b>Cell 1</b>
18  </div>
19
20  <!-- begin layer 2 (Cell 2) -->
21  <div
22  <!-- begin layer 21 -->
23  <div id="layer1" style="position:absolute; width:100px;
    height:100px; left: 100px; top: 0px; background-color:
    #00CC99; layer-background-color: #00CC99; border: 1px;
    visibility:visible"><b>Cell 21</b>
24  </div> <!-- close layer 21 -->
25  <!-- begin layer 22 -->
26  <div id="layer1" style="position:absolute; width:100px;
    height:100px; left: 200px; top: 0px; background-color:
    #FFFF66; layer-background-color: #FFFF66; border: 1px;
    visibility:visible"><b>Cell 22</b>
27  </div> <!-- close layer 22 -->
28  <!-- begin layer 23 -->
29  <div id="layer1" style="position:absolute; width:100px;
    height:100px; left: 300px; top: 0px; background-color:
    #00CC99; layer-background-color: #00CC99; border: 1px;
    visibility:visible"><b>Cell 23</b>
30  </div> <!-- close layer 23 -->
31  </div> <!-- close layer 2 -->
32
```

```
33   <!-- create layer 3 (cell 3) -->
34   <div id="layer1" style="position:absolute; width:200px;
     height:100px; left: 0px; top: 100px; background-color:
     #33FFFF; layer-background-color: #33FFFF; border: 1px;
     visibility:visible"><b>Cell 3</b>
35   </div> <!-- close layer 3 -->
36
37   <!-- create layer 4 (cell 4) -->
38   <div id="layer1" style="position:absolute; width:300px;
     height:100px; left: 100px; top: 100px; background-color:
     #33FF66; layer-background-color: #33FF66; border: 1px;
     visibility:visible"><b>Cell 4</b>
39   </div> <!-- close layer 4 -->
40
41   </div> <!-- close parent layer -->
42   </body>
43   </html>
```

13.6 Layers and Tables

Both layers and tables can be used to control layouts and designs of Web pages. Layers have the advantages of being simple to use and less restrictive. The table hierarchical structure (table => rows => cells), on the other hand, makes tables cumbersome and confusing to use. Table nesting further complicates the use of table, in formatting Web pages.

To appreciate the difference between layers and tables, think of a layer and a table each as a container. We create a layer container by using the `<div>` tag, and a table container by using the `<table>` tag. We use the `<div>` tag again to divide the layer container directly into cells; unlike with tables, there is no need for rows. The table container requires that the cell tag (`<th>` or `<td>`) be nested inside a row tag (`<tr>`). With layers, we create the effect of rows by positioning layers horizontally. As a matter of fact, actual rows can be restrictive. We can position layers in a rowlike pattern, or any other pattern, for better control of the layout and formatting.

13.7 Formatting via Layers

Formatting Web pages by using layers is based on the idea of nesting layers. Each layer can be viewed as an independent region that can hold any XHTML content. Thus, we may begin the design of a Web-page layout by dividing the page into regions, where every region holds some contents. After the design is complete, we substitute a layer for each region. We then create an outer layer that holds all the other nested layers.

 ——

Example 13.4 Formatting with layers.

Develop a Web page that is formatted with layers.

Solution 13.4 We convert the table layout of Example 12.4 to layers in this example in order to compare both approaches closely. We use the same layout, as shown in the accompanying drawing. The accompanying screen capture shows the resulting Web page. The layout is achieved via one level-1 layer (*Parent layer 1*), three level-2 layers (*layer 1–layer 4*), and two level-3 layers (*Parent layer 12* and *Parent layer 13*). The number of layers at each level is shown

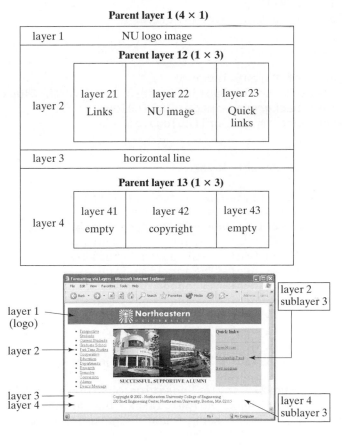

in the top image on this page. *Parent layer 1* has four layers. The first layer, *layer 1*, holds the NU logo image. The second layer, *layer 2*, holds *Parent layer 12*. *layer 2* has three nested layers that hold links, the NU image, and quick links, respectively. *layer 3* holds the horizontal line. The last layer of *Parent layer 1*, *layer 4*, holds *Parent layer 13*. *Parent layer 13* has *layer 41* and *layer 43*, empty for spacing, and *layer 42*, which holds the copyright notice. Using the AceHTML editor, generate the given code, and save it as `example134.html`. Display the Web page in a browser. We need a total of 13 layers: 10 layers and 3 parent (container) layers. While we could do away with the 3 parent layers, we should not, because moving the layers around for any future design changes will then become messy.

```
1    <?xml version="1.0" encoding="iso-8859-1"?>
2    <!DOCTYPE html PUBLIC "-//W3C//DTD XHTML 1.1//EN"
3        "http://www.w3.org/TR/xhtml11/DTD/xhtml11.dtd ">
4    <html xmlns="http://www.w3.org/1999/xhtml">
5    <!-- Generated by AceHTM http://freeware.acehtml.com -->
6    <head>
7    <meta http-equiv="Content-Type" content="text/html;
     charset=iso-8859-1" />
8    <title>Formatting via Layers</title>
9    </head>
10   <body>
11
12   <!-- layer 1 of Parent layer 1 -->
13   <div id="layer1" style="position:absolute; width:640px;
     height:55px; background-image: url(nulogo.gif);
     layer-background-image: url(nulogo.gif)">
14   </div>
15
16   <!-- layer 2 of Parent layer 1 -->
17   <div id="layer2">
18   <div id="layer21" style="position:absolute; top:85px;
     width:150px; height:60px">
19               <ul><li><a href="">Prospective<br />Students</a>
20               <li><a href="">Current Students</a>
21               <li><a href="">Graduate School</a>
22               <li><a href="">Part-Time Studies</a>
23               <li><a href="">Cooperative<br />Education</a>
24               <li><a href="">Departments</a>
25               <li><a href="">Research</a>
26               <li><a href="">Semester<br />Conversion</a>
27               <li><a href="">Alumni</a>
28               <li><a href="">Dean's Message</a></ul>
29       </div>
30       <div id="layer22" style="position:absolute; top:85px;
     left:160px; width:340px; height:185px; background-image:
     url(NUImage.jpg); layer-background-image:url(NUImage.jpg)">
31       </div>
32   <div id="layer23" style="position:absolute; top:85px;
     left:500px; width:150px; height:190px; background-color:
     #CCCCCC; layer-background-color: #CCCCCC">
33               <b><h3>Quick links</h3></b>
34               <hr width="150" />
35               <a href="">Open House</a><p></p>
36               <a href="">Scholarship Fund</a><p></p>
37               <a href="">New program</a>
38       </div>
39   </div> <!-- close layer 2 of Parent layer 1 -->
40   <!-- layer 3 of Parent layer 1 -->
```

```
41  <div id="layer3" style="position:absolute; top:285px;
    width:640px; height:190px">
42      <hr width="640" align="left" />
43  </div>
44  <!-- layer 4 of Parent layer 1 -->
45  <div id="layer4">
46      <div id="layer41" style="position:absolute; top:300px;
    width:150px; height:60px">
47      </div>
48  <div id="layer42" style="position:absolute; top:300px;
    left:160px; width:400px; height:185px">
49  Copyright © 2002 - Northeastern University College of
    Engineering<br />
50  230 Snell Engineering Center, Northeastern University,
    Boston, MA 02115
51      </div>
52  <div id="layer43" style="position:absolute; top:300px;
    left:500px; width:150px; height:190px">
53      </div>
54  </div> <!-- close layer 4 of Parent layer 1 -->
55  </div> <!-- close outer Parent layer 1 -->
56  </body>
57  </html>
```

Code explained:

    1. The outer *Parent layer 1* tag opens in line 13 and closes in line 55.

    2. Lines 13 and 14 create the content of *layer 1* of outer *Parent layer 1*.

    3. Lines 17–39 create the content of *layer 2* of outer *Parent layer 1*.

    4. Lines 18–38 create the nested *Parent layer 12*.

    5. Lines 41–43 create the content of *layer 3* of outer *Parent layer 1*.

    6. Lines 45–54 create the content of *layer 4* of outer *parent layer 1*.

    7. Lines 46–53 create the nested *Parent layer 13*.

Discussion:

We use an outer-layer (*Parent layer 1*) width of 640 pixels, as we discussed in Chapter 11. Lines 13, 18, and 41 use this width. Moreover, the widths of the three layers of nested *Parent layer 12* (150 in line 18, 340 in line 30, and 150 in line 32) should add up to 640 pixels. We use the <p> tag in lines 35 and 36 to space out the links. We use a width of 150 pixels for the first empty layer of nested layer *Parent layer 3* (line 46) in order to push the text (lines 49 and 50) further in. The layers in lines 18 and 46 should use the same width (155 pixels) so that both layers will be lined up vertically. Line 49 could have used the numeric code of the copyright symbol.

Hands-on exercise:

Starting with the code given in the example, remove *layer 3* from both nested *layers 12* and *13*, making each a 1 × 2 layer. Adjust the entire Web page to fit within a width of 640 pixels.

13.8 Tutorials

13.8.1   Creating Embossing Effects (Study Section 13.4)

This tutorial creates embossing effects by displacing two layers with the same text. Use the Ace-HTML editor to generate the given code, and save it as `tutorial1381.html`. View the Web page in a browser. The following screen capture shows the page.

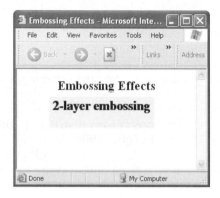

Code explained:

1. Lines 13 and 14 create the first layer.
2. Lines 16 and 17 create the second layer.
3. Lines 13 and 14 use the `z-index` attribute to control the overlapping of the two layers. *layer2* covers *layer1* because the former's `z-index` is higher. We make *layer1* inherit its visibility from its parent layer, while we make *layer2* visible.

Discussion:

We create two layers with the text `2-layer embossing`. The first layer is located at (54, 45), and the second layer is displaced by one pixel in both directions, so it is located at (55, 46). We assign a yellow background color to the first layer and no background color to the second layer. If we assign a background color to the second layer, it blocks the text of the first layer.

Hands-on exercise:

Starting with the code given here, create one more layer and displace it to enhance the embossing effect. Also change the text font from Times New Roman to **Arial**.

```
1   <?xml version="1.0" encoding="iso-8859-1"?>
2   <!DOCTYPE html PUBLIC "-//W3C//DTD XHTML 1.1//EN"
3       "http://www.w3.org/TR/xhtml11/DTD/xhtml11.dtd ">
4   <html xmlns="http://www.w3.org/1999/xhtml">
5   <!-- Generated by AceHTM http://freeware.acehtml.com -->
6   <head>
```

```
 7   <meta http-equiv="Content-Type" content="text/html;
     charset=iso-8859-1" />
 8   <title>Embossing Effects</title>
 9   </head>
10   <body>
11   <!-- Create first layer -->
12   <h2 align="center">Embossing Effects</h2>
13   <div id="layer1" style="position:absolute; width:175px;
     height:50px; left: 54px; top: 45px; background-color:
     #FFFF00; layer-background-color: #FFFF00; border: 1px;
     visibility:inherit; z-index: 1"><h2 align="center">2-layer
     embossing</h2>
14   </div>
15
16   <div id="layer2" style="position:absolute; width:175px;
     height:50px; left: 55px; top: 46px; border: 1px;
     visibility:visible;z-index: 2"><h2 align="center">2-layer
     embossing</h2>
17   </div>
18
19   </body>
20   </html>
```

13.8.2 Creating a Site Map for Navigation (Study Section 13.7)

This tutorial is the same as Tutorial 12.8.2. Instead of using a table to format the website, however, we use layers. We convert the table layout of Tutorial 12.8.2 to layers in this tutorial, so that we may compare both approaches closely. We show only the home page here. Follow the same idea to convert the code of the help page of Tutorial 12.8.2 to use layers instead of tables. Use the AceHTML editor to generate the given code, and save it as `index.html`.

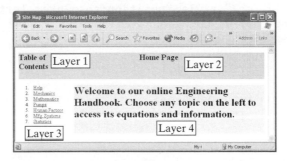

Code explained:

1. Lines 13–19 create the first-row layer, which has two sublayers. Lines 15 and 16 create the first sublayer. Lines 17 and 18 create the second sublayer.
2. Lines 22–39 create the second-row layer, which has two sublayers. Lines 23–33 create the first sublayer. Lines 34–38 create the second sublayer.

Discussion:

The two sublayers of the first-row layer have the same background color, for continuity purposes. The first sublayer of the second-row layer has no background color; it picks up the background color of the browser window. The second sublayer of the second-row layer has a yellow background color. The width and height of each of the four layers are selected to fit the content. Determining the ideal layer size is a matter of trial and error, an easy task in an editor.

Hands-on exercise:

Starting with the code given here, develop the code for the missing Web pages in order to complete the development of the website.

```
1   <?xml version="1.0" encoding="iso-8859-1"?>
2   <!DOCTYPE html PUBLIC "-//W3C//DTD XHTML 1.1//EN"
3       "http://www.w3.org/TR/xhtml11/DTD/xhtml11.dtd ">
4   <html xmlns="http://www.w3.org/1999/xhtml ">
5   <!-- Generated by AceHTM http://freeware.acehtml.com -->
6   <head>
7   <meta http-equiv="Content-Type" content="text/html;
    charset=iso-8859-1" />
8   <title>Site Map</title>
9   </head>
10  <body>
11  <body>
12  <!-- Create a 2x2 outer parent layer -->
13  <div>
14  <!-- First-row two heading layers -->
15      <div id="layer1" style="position:absolute;
    background-color:33FFFF; width:150; height:70"><h2>Table of
    Contents</h2>
16      </div>
17      <div id="layer2" style="position:absolute; left:100;
    width:575; height:70; background-color:33FFFF"><h2
    align="center">Home Page</h2>
18      </div>
19  </div>
20
21  <!-- Second-row two layers -->
22  <div id="layer3" style="position:absolute; top:100;
    width:150">
23      <div>
24    <ol>
25      <li><a href="help.html">Help</a><br />
26      <li><a href="mechanics.html">Mechanics</a><br />
27      <li><a href="math.html">Mathematics</a><br />
28      <li><a href="pumps.html">Pumps</a><br />
29      <li><a href="humanfactor.html">Human Factors</a><br />
30      <li><a href="mfgsystems.html">Mfg. Systems</a><br />
```

```
31        <li><a href="statistics.html">Statistics</a><br />
32     </ol>
33       </div>
34       <div id="layer4" style="position:absolute; top:0;
   left:150;width:515; height:130; background-color:#FFFF00">
35     <h1>Welcome to our online Engineering Handbook.
36     Choose any topic on the left to access its equations
37     and information.
38       </div>
39   </div>
40   </body>
41   </html>
```

FAQs

Using Layers (Section 13.4)

Q: Can I use the `<layer>` and `<ilayer>` tags in my Web pages?

A: No. These tags have been deprecated and replaced by the `<div>` tag. Moreover, neither IE nor Netscape 6 and higher supports them.

Layers and Tables (Section 13.6)

Q: Which is better to use to format Web pages, layers or tables?

A: Layers. They are easier to use and provide better control in positioning content of Web pages. They use pixel coordinates to place the content.

Blackbox

    Sections 13.1 (Introduction): XHTML layers are used for organizing content and formatting Web pages. A **layer** is a rectangular container (region).

    Section 13.2 (Layer Positioning): XHTML positions a layer in a Web page via the pixel coordinates of its top left corner, (x, y). XHTML refers to them in the order (left, top). The x coordinate is positive to the right, and the y coordinate is positive pointing down.

    Section 13.3 (Properties of Layers): The properties of an XHTML layer are ID, (x, y) location, size (width and height), visibility, background color and image, depth (stacking order), clip (definition of the visible area of a layer), and overflow.

    Sections 13.4 (Using Layers) (Example 13.1 and 13.2): XHTML provides the `<div>` tag to define layers. An example of the tags syntax and attributes is shown as follows:

```
<div
id="myLayer" style="position:absolute; left:200px;
top:200px; width:300px; height:175px; z-index:1; border:1px;
background-color:#FFFF00; layer-background-color:#FFFF00;
background-image:url(myImage.jpg);
```

```
layer-background-image:url(myImage.jpg);
visibility:visible; overflow:visible;
clip: rect(50 30 70 10)">All layer properties
</div>
```

Sections 13.5 (Nesting Layers) (Example 13.3): To nest layers simply nest the `<div>`
tag. Layers are easy to work with and to change the design of. If necessary, you can use layers to
quickly create complex page designs and then convert them to tables.

Section 13.6 (Layers and Tables): Both layers and tables can be used to control layouts
and designs of Web pages. Layers have the advantages of being simple to use and less restrictive.

Section 13.7 (Formatting via Layers) (Example 13.4): Formatting Web pages by using
layers is based on the idea of nesting layers. Each layer can be viewed as an independent region
that can hold any XHTML content.

Section 13.8 (Tutorials): Two tutorials show how to use layers.

Quick reference for the tags presented in this chapter

Tag	Close	Attribute	Value	Effect	Example
`<div>`	yes	`id`	text	layer name	`<div id="abc">`
		`position`	`absolute`	use top left corner of layer to measure positions	`<style="position:abso-lute">`
		`left`	number of pixels	x coordinate, layer position	`<style="left:100px">`
		`top`	number of pixels	y coordinate, layer position	`<style="top:50px">`
		`width`	number of pixels	layer width	`<style="width:300px">`
		`height`	number of pixels	layer height	`<style="height:175px">`
		`z-index`	number	layer stacking order	`<style="z-index:2">`
		`back-ground-color`	hex	layer background color; use for IE and Netscape 6 or higher	`<style="background-color:#FFFF33">`
		`layer-back-ground-color`	hex	layer background color; use for Netscape 4x	`<style="layer-back-ground-color:#FFFF33">`

Tag	Close	Attribute	Value	Effect	Example
		back-ground-image	file	layer background image; use for IE and Netscape 6 or higher	`<style="background-image:url(abc.jpg)">`
		layer-back-ground-image	number of pixels	layer background image; use for Netscape 4x	`<style="layer-back-ground-image:url(abc.jpg)">`
		`visibility`	value	determines layer visibility; values are `visible`, `hidden`, and `inherit`	`<style="visibility:hidden">`
		`overflow`	value	adjusts layer size; Values are `visible`, `hidden`, `scroll` and `auto`	`<style="overflow:auto">`
		`clip`	number of pixels	defines visible areas	`<style="clip:rect(L R B T)">`

Check Your Progress

At the end of this chapter, you should

- ✔ understand the use of layers (Section 13.1);
- ✔ understand the coordinate system used by layers (Section 13.2);
- ✔ understand the properties of layers (Section 13.3);
- ✔ be able to identify XHTML layer tags (Section 13.4);
- ✔ understand layer nesting (Section 13.5);
- ✔ understand the differences between layers and tables (Section 13.6);
- ✔ have mastered the formatting of Web pages and content via layers (Section 13.7);
- ✔ have practiced the use of layers (Section 13.8).

Problems

The exercises are designed for a lab setting, while the homework is to be done outside class time.

Exercises

13.1   Use five layers to create a gradual shadow effect. Use this text: Space Man X

13.2   Use five layers to create an outline effect. Use this text: Outline Effects.

13.3 Use four layers to create a spooky glowing-text effect. Use this text: `fox famous box`.

13.4 Use six layers to create a "chilly" effect. Use this text: `SpaceGun Magazine`.

13.5 Use 11 layers to create a bizarre effect. Use this text: `Typography`.

Homework

13.6 Create a Web page that uses layers. The page content is left up to you. Be imaginative.

13.7 Create a Web page that uses layers for formatting. The page and layer design and layout are left up to you. Be imaginative.

13.8 Covert the page shown in the topmost accompanying screen capture to use layers instead of tables. The cells in the last row use bold text and have a background color of #CEEFBD.

13.9 Use layers to create the dual-heading table shown in the bottommost accompanying screen capture.

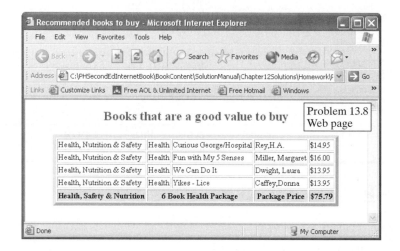

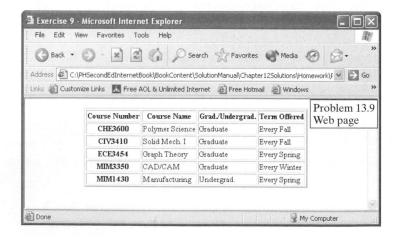

Frames

Goal

Understand frames, their creation and control, their use in navigating Web pages and controlling content location in browser windows, and their relationship to layers.

Objectives

- Positioning and the coordinate system of frames
- Creation of frames
- Layout of frames
- Design of frames
- Management of frames
- Nesting of frames
- Control of frames
- Navigation of frames

Outline

14.1 Introduction

Web pages that do not use layers, tables, or frames in their layout tend to be left-side heavy, or left justified. That means that most of the contents are concentrated on the left. This effect is a direct outcome of the XHTML tags. As a result, the right sides of Web pages are very sparse and are not effectively utilized.

There is another Web-page design issue that we must consider as well. During navigation, an element in a Web page may force the display of a new Web page, thus forcing a Web surfer to use the history (Back) button of the browser to go back to the page originally displayed prior to the navigation. Consider the case of using image maps in Web pages. When a Web surfer clicks a hot spot, the browser displays the corresponding HTML file in a new Web page. The Web page that has the map itself becomes invisible. The surfer must click the browser's Back button to gain access to the map again in order to click another hot spot. This requirement is obviously annoying to the Web surfer. This problem can be solved by using frames. XHTML frames enable Web authors to display Web pages in multiple views in the same browser window. Therefore, frames are used to divide a browser window into regions or areas, with each region having its own Web page.

Frames can be used to provide a table of contents (TOC). A Web author can split a browser window vertically into two frames. The left frame is narrow and holds the TOC. The TOC can also be thought of as a menu. The items of the TOC are either text or image hyperlinks. The right frame is wide and holds Web pages that result from clicking items in the TOC. The contents of the left frame do not change, yet the contents of the right frame keep changing every time a Web surfer clicks a link in the left frame.

In the early days, during the development of Web browsers, earlier versions of the browsers did not support frames. Therefore, Web authors who used frames had to provide alternative, nonframe versions of their Web pages in order to accommodate these earlier versions. This is a much less critical issue today.

14.2 Frame Layout and Design

A **frame** is a rectangle that has a width and height, a location in the browser window, and content (a Web page). Figure 14.1 shows the layout of a Web page with two frames. As shown in the figure, the two frames divide the browser window vertically. The size of each frame is set at the time of the frame's creation. Web surfers can be given the ability to adjust a frame's size; this is very uncommon, though.

What decides the layout and the location of frames inside a browser window? A collection of frames is referred to as a **frame set**. A frame set controls the layout of its frames. For example, Figure 14.1 shows a frame set that has two frames. A frame set is created via the XHTML `<frameset>` tag, and a frame is created via the `<frame>` tag. Once a frame set and its frames are created and displayed on the screen, its layout cannot be changed. Only the contents of each frame in the set can change.

An XHTML document that uses frames must not use the `<body>` tag; the `<frameset>` tag replaces it. The document has a `<head>` section followed by a `<frameset>` section. The `<frameset>` section defines the layout of the frames, such as that in Figure 14.1. In addition, the `<frameset>` section may contain a `<noframes>` tag, to provide alternative content to browsers that do not support frames or are configured not to display frames. In addition, Web authors must never use before the `<frameset>` tag any XHTML tags that normally appear inside the `<body>` tag; otherwise, the browser will ignore the `<frameset>` tag.

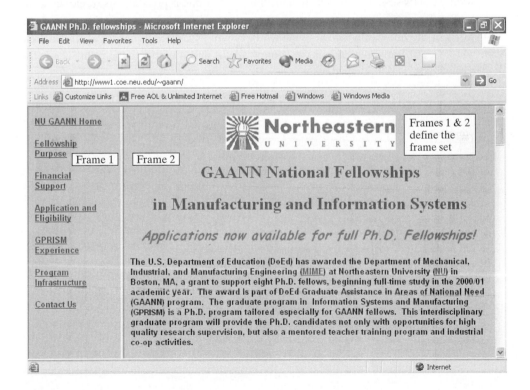

Figure 14.1 A frame set.

There are many useful tips and rules that Web authors usually follow to design XHTML frames: **(1) Keep the frame set simple.** A Web page should not use more than two or three frames. Beyond this number, frames become distracting to Web surfers. **(2) Keep the frame's contents short.** Web authors need to keep Web pages that are displayed in frames short, so that Web surfers do not have to scroll the frames. **(3) Keep the frames organized.** Web authors should clearly distinguish the driver frame from the other frames. The **driver frame** is the frame that holds all the links to the other frames. Examples include the TOC frame and the frame that holds an image map. Web authors may also display messages informing Web surfers how to navigate the frame set.

14.3 Frame Sets and Nesting

A frame set has a width and height, as shown in Figure 14.2. XHTML defines a frame set's width by the number of columns, `cols`, and a frame set's height by the number of rows, `rows`. Figure 14.2 shows a frame with its parameters. The units of `rows` and `cols` are either pixels or a percentage of the browser window. The examples and tutorials in this chapter illustrate some specific cases.

In addition to its size, a frame set contains frames. A frame is placed in its frame set according to the following coordinate-system specifications: The origin of the frame set is located at the top left corner of the browser window, as shown in Figure 14.2. The frame set is effectively the browser window. The horizontal axis is the column's axis, and it points to the right. The vertical axis is the row's axis, and it points downwards.

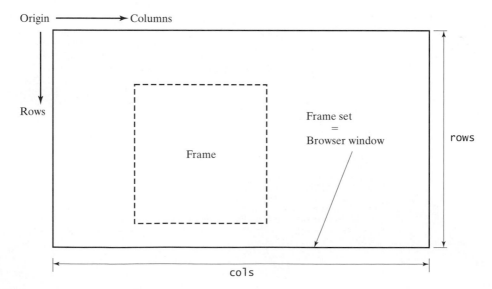

Figure 14.2 A simple frame set.

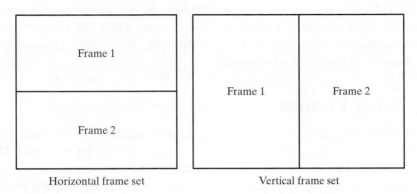

Horizontal frame set   Vertical frame set

Figure 14.3 Simple frame sets.

Using this coordinate system, the browser places frames in their frame set from left to right for columns and from top to bottom for rows. Consider the two frame sets shown in Figure 14.3. The two frames in the horizontal frame set extend to the entire width of the browser window, because no columns are set for the frame set. Similarly, the frames in the vertical frame set extend to the entire height of the browser window, because no rows are specified.

The two frame sets shown in Figure 14.3 are considered simple, because the browser window is divided in one direction only, either horizontally or vertically. Frame sets become complex when the window is divided in both directions multiple times. Such division creates nested frame sets. Nested frame sets are created from left to right in the top row, then from left to right in the second row, and so forth. Consider the two nested frame sets shown in Figure 14.4. The left set is created by nesting columns with a row, the right set is created by nesting rows within a column. To create the left set, the frame set is first divided into two rows. Then the top row is divided into two columns. To create the right set, the frame set is first divided into two columns. Then the left column is divided into two rows. Do not divide a Web page such that it has many small frames; this makes the page too messy and too hard to navigate.

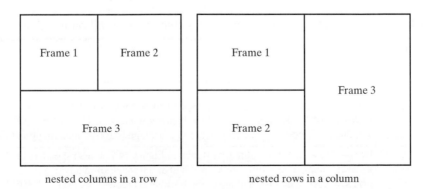

nested columns in a row   nested rows in a column

Figure 14.4 Nested frame sets.

XHTML does not have a limit on the depth of frame nesting. A Web author can nest frames deep enough to divide a browser window into squares, each with a size of $1\,\text{inch} \times 1\,\text{inch}$, to create a checkerboard or a board for the game of Monopoly, for example. However, one or two levels of nesting is all that is needed in practice.

14.4 Using Frames

XHTML provides Web authors with tags for creating and using frames. Web authors control the sizes and locations of frames, initialize the frames, and nest them if needed. Four XHTML tags are available for frames. They are `<frameset>`, `<frame>`, `<iframe>`, and `<noframes>`. The `<frameset>` tag creates the frame set and the layout of frames inside it. It also creates nested frames. Nesting frame sets is equivalent to nesting `<frameset>` tags. The `<frame>` tag creates the contents of each frame. The `<iframe>` tag creates inline frames. The `<noframes>` tag provides alternatives to displaying frame. Tables 14.1–14.3 show these tags and their attributes.

If the `rows` and `cols` attributes of the `<frameset>` tag are set simultaneously, a frame grid is created. For example, the tag `<frameset rows="*, *, *" cols="*, *, *, *">` creates a frame grid of size $3 \text{ rows} \times 4 \text{ columns}$, producing 12 equal frames. The frames in this grid are not nested frames. Nested frames are generated only if the `<frameset>` tag is nested. It is worth mentioning that the `<frameset>` tag cannot be used by itself. It does not produce any visible results on the screen. It must be used with the `<frame>` tag.

The `<iframe>` tag creates inline frames. Inline frames are a special type of frame. An **inline frame** is a frame that is embedded inside the content of a Web page. Unlike with normal frames, no frame sets are required to create inline frames. The concept of inline frames was introduced by Microsoft into its Internet Explorer version 4 and higher. The `<iframe>` tag is part of the HTML 4.0 specification. It is supported by Netscape 6 and higher. Unlike the `<frame>` tag, the `<iframe>` tag is used inside the `<body>` tag of an XHTML document, like any other tag.

If you compare the attributes of the `<iframe>` tag with those of the `<frame>` tag, you find out that the `noresize` attribute is absent in the former. This makes sense, as the size of an

Table 14.1   `<frameset>` tag—the master tag that encloses all other frame tags.

Attributes: `<frameset rows cols>`	
Attribute	Description
rows	Defines the height of the frame, as shown in Figure 14.2. It also specifies the layout of horizontal frames. The height can be specified as a number of pixels (e.g., `rows="200"`), as a percentage of the browser window (e.g., `rows="30%"`), or as a variable (e.g., `rows="*"`). The default percentage is 100%, meaning one full row.
cols	Defines the width of the frame, as shown in Figure 14.2. It also specifies the layout of vertical frames. The width can be specified as a number of pixels (e.g., `cols="200"`), as a percentage of the browser window (e.g., `cols="30%"`), or as a variable (e.g., `cols="*"`). The default percentage is 100%, meaning one full column.

Table 14.2 `<frame>` tag—creates a single frame of a frame set.

Attributes: `<frame name src noresize scrolling frameborder marginwidth marginheight longdesc>`

Attribute	Description
`name`	Assigns a name to the frame. This name may serve as the target of other links.
`src`	Specifies the XHTML document (HTML file) that is displayed in the frame initially upon its creation.
`noresize`	A boolean. When it is used, Web surfers cannot resize the frame by dragging its edges that neighbor other frames in the frame set.
`scrolling`	Specifies, to the browser displaying the frame, whether to provide scrollbars for the frame. It has three values: `auto`, `yes`, and `no`. `auto` is the default value, and it allows the browser to provide scrollbars whenever they are needed. `yes` forces the browser to provide scrollbars, while `no` forbids their provision.
`frameborder`	A binary value: 0 or 1 (the default value). If it takes the value 1, the browser displays a border (separator) between the frame and every frame adjacent to it. A 0 value prevents the browser from displaying borders. However, if an adjacent frame uses borders, the effect of the 0 value is lost.
`marginwidth`	Specifies the left and right margin widths of the frame, in pixels. These margins are the whitespace between the frame's contents and its borders. If this attribute is not used, the browser rendering the frame uses its own default values.
`marginheight`	Specifies the top and bottom margin heights of the frame, in pixels. These margins are the whitespace between the frame's contents and its borders. If this attribute is not used, the browser rendering the frame uses its own default values.
`longdesc`	Specifies a link to a long description of the frame.

Table 14.3 `<iframe>` tag—creates an inline frame.

Attributes: `<iframe name src width height align scrolling frameborder marginwidth marginheight longdesc>`

Attribute	Description
`name`	Assigns a name to the frame. This name may serve as the target of other links.
`src`	Specifies the XHTML document (HTML file) that is displayed in the frame initially upon its creation.
`width`	Specifies the frame's width in pixels.
`height`	Specifies the frame's height in pixels.

Table 14.3   `<iframe>` tag—creates an inline frame. (Continued)

Attributes: `<iframe name src width height align scrolling frameborder marginwidth marginheight longdesc>`

Attribute	Description
`align`	Controls both the placement of the inline frame and the flow of the text surrounding it. For inline alignment, the attribute values are `top`, `middle`, and `bottom`. To allow text to flow around the inline frame, the attribute values are `left` (places the frame to the left edge of the text flow), `center` (the text flows above and below the frame), and `right` (places the frame to the right edge of the text flow).
`scrolling`	Specifies, to the browser displaying the frame, whether to provide scrollbars for the frame. It has three values: `auto`, `yes`, and `no`. `auto` is the default value, and it allows the browser to provide scrollbars whenever they are needed. `yes` forces the browser to provide scrollbars, while `no` forbids their provision.
`frameborder`	A binary value: 0 or 1 (the default value). If it takes the value 1, the browser displays a border (separator) between the frame and every frame adjacent to it. A 0 value prevents the browser from displaying borders. However, if an adjacent frame uses borders, the effect of the 0 value is lost.
`marginwidth`	Specifies the left and right margin widths of the frame, in pixels. These margins are the whitespace between the frame's contents and its borders. If this attribute is not used, the browser rendering the frame uses its own default values.
`marginheight`	Specifies the top and bottom margin heights of the frame, in pixels. These margins are the whitespace between the frame's contents and its borders. If this attribute is not used, the browser rendering the frame uses its own default values.
`longdesc`	Specifies a link to a long description of the frame.

inline frame must be fixed once the frame is inserted in a Web page. In addition, three more attributes are added to control the placement (`align`) and the size (`width` and `height`) of the inline frame. The `align` attribute controls the flow of the text surrounding the inline frame.

Example 14.1 Use frames.

Develop a Web page that illustrates the use of frames.

Solution 14.1 This example creates a Web page with a frame grid. The grid has four frames. We use most of the attributes of the `<frameset>` and the `<frame>` tags. Using the AceHTML editor, generate the given code, and save it as `example141.html`. The upcoming screen capture shows the resulting Web page.

Code explained:

  1. Lines 9 and 14 create a frame set with four equal frames.
  2. Lines 10–14 create Frames 1–4, respectively, as shown in the screen capture.

Discussion:

The four frames have equal sizes. We use the wildcard (*) whenever we need the browser to calculate the size of a frame. For the example, the attribute `rows="*, *"` tells the browser to divide the height of its window equally to create two rows. Similarly, the attribute `cols="50%, *"` produces two equal columns. We could replace the 50% by * and get the same result. Observe the effect of the attributes of the `<frame>` tag on the rendering of each frame in the Web page.

Hands-on exercise:

Starting with the code given in this example, add more attributes and investigate their various values.

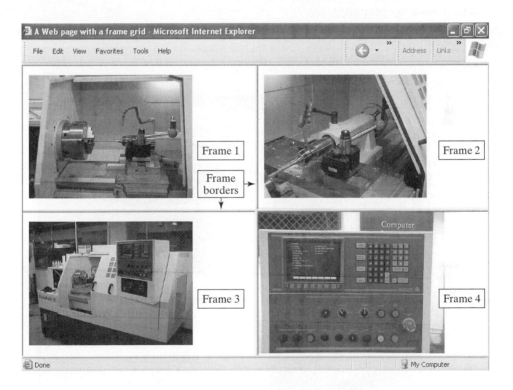

```
1   <?xml version="1.0" encoding="iso-8859-1"?>
2   <!DOCTYPE html PUBLIC "-//W3C//DTD XHTML 1.1//EN"
3       "http://www.w3.org/TR/xhtml11/DTD/xhtml11.dtd">
4   <html xmlns="http://www.w3.org/1999/xhtml">
5   <!-- Generated by AceHTM http://freeware.acehtml.com -->
6   <head>
7   <title>A Web page with a frame grid</title>
8   </head>
9   <frameset rows="*, *" cols="50%, *">
10  <frame src="cncLatheView.jpg" name="myFrame1" frameborder="0"/>
```

Line 10 creates Frame 1

```
11    <frame src="cncLatheView1.jpg" name="myFrame2" />
12    <frame src="cncLatheView2.jpg" scrolling="no" />
13    <frame src="cncLatheController.jpg" noresize marginwidth="0"
      marginheight="0" />
14    </frameset>
15    </html>
```

Line 11 creates Frame 2

Line 12 creates Frame 3

Line 13 creates Frame 4

Example 14.2 Create nested frames.

Use nested frames in a Web page.

Solution 14.2 Using the AceHTML editor, generate the given code, and save it as example142.html. The following screen capture shows the resulting Web page.

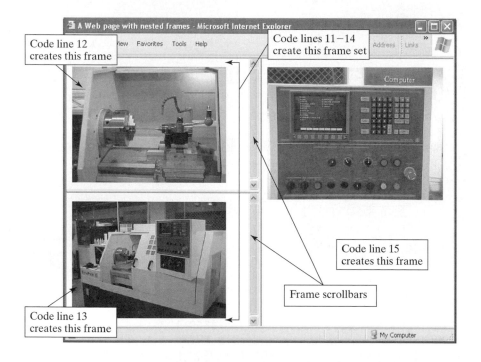

Code line 12 creates this frame

Code lines 11–14 create this frame set

Code line 15 creates this frame

Code line 13 creates this frame

Frame scrollbars

```
1    <?xml version="1.0" encoding="iso-8859-1"?>
2    <!DOCTYPE html PUBLIC "-//W3C//DTD XHTML 1.1//EN"
3        "http://www.w3.org/TR/xhtml11/DTD/xhtml11.dtd">
4    <html xmlns="http://www.w3.org/1999/xhtml">
5    <!-- Generated by AceHTM http://freeware.acehtml.com -->
6    <head>
```

```
 7   <meta http-equiv="Content-Type" content="text/html;
     charset=iso-8859-1" />
 8   <title>A Web page with nested frames</title>
 9   </head>
10   <frameset cols="*, *"> <!-- outer frame set -->
11   <frameset rows="*, *"> <!-- nested frame set -->
12   <frame src="cncLatheView1.jpg" />
13   <frame src="cncLatheView2.jpg" />
14   </frameset> <!-- close tag, line 11 -->
15   <frame src="cncLatheController.jpg" />
16   </frameset> <!-- close tag, line 10 -->
17   </html>
```

Code explained:

1. Lines 10–16 create the outer frame set.
2. Lines 11–14 create the nested (inner) frame set.
3. Lines 12 and 13 create the two frames of the nested frame set.
4. Line 15 creates the right frame of the outer frame set.

Discussion:

This example uses two frame sets and three frames. The outer set has two columns of equal size, as shown in code line 10. The nested set has two rows of equal size, as shown in code line 11. The question now is, Where should the nested set with its two frames go, relative to the outer set? Should it go in the left or the right column of the outer set? It must go in the left column, according to the nesting rule (Place frames top to bottom, left to right starting at top left corner of frame set.) illustrated by the arrows in Figure 14.2. There is another rule that the browser uses. When faced with a choice, the browser looks at the available *empty* frames and uses the rule of Figure 14.2. If a frame has been assigned a source file already, the browser excludes it. Another way to look at this placement issue is that XHTML code is executed from top to bottom and then from left to right.

Hands-on exercise:

Move code line 15 so that it comes after line 10. Save the file and render the Web page. What happens? Why? Apply the foregoing discussion to help you solve the puzzle.

Example 14.3 Use inline frames.

Develop a Web page that illustrates the use of inline frames.

Solution 14.3 Using the AceHTML editor, generate the given code, and save it as example143.html. The upcoming screen capture shows the resulting Web page.

Code explained:

1. Lines 11 and 12 create the inline frame.

2. Lines 14–16 create more content in the Web page.

Discussion:

The content of the inline frame of this example comes from the `statement.html` file shown in the given code. We use the `<p>` tag in line 13 to push the page's content below the border of the inline frame. We use the `<div>` tag in lines 14 and 15 to break the text into two lines. The `<a>` tag in line 16 is used to add more content into the Web page.

Hands-on exercise:

Starting with the code given in this example, add another inline frame after the hyperlink. Use all the attributes of the `<iframe>` tag. How does the resulting frame look?

example143.html

```
1   <?xml version="1.0" encoding="iso-8859-1"?>
2   <!DOCTYPE html PUBLIC "-//W3C//DTD XHTML 1.1//EN"
3       "http://www.w3.org/TR/xhtml11/DTD/xhtml11.dtd">
4   <html xmlns="http://www.w3.org/1999/xhtml">
5   <!-- Generated by AceHTM http://freeware.acehtml.com -->
6   <head>
7   <meta http-equiv="Content-Type" content="text/html;
    charset=iso-8859-1" />
8   <title>A Web page with inline frames</title>
9   </head>
10  <body>
11  <iframe src="statement.html" width="350" height="90">
12  </iframe>
13  <p></p>
```

```
14   <div>This Web page uses inline frames.</div>
15   <div>Text flows around these frames.</div>
16   <a href="http://www.neu.edu">Check the latest programs
     at NU</a>
17   </body>
18   </html>
```

```
statement.html
```

```
1    <?xml version="1.0" encoding="iso-8859-1"?>
2    <!DOCTYPE html PUBLIC "-//W3C//DTD XHTML 1.1//EN"
3        "http://www.w3.org/TR/xhtml11/DTD/xhtml11.dtd">
4    <html xmlns="http://www.w3.org/1999/xhtml">
5    <!-- Generated by AceHTM http://freeware.acehtml.com -->
6    <head>
7    <meta http-equiv="Content-Type" content="text/html;
     charset=iso-8859-1" />
8    <title>A Web page with inline frames</title>
9    </head>
10   <body>
11   <h2 align="center">This is an inline frame created with
     the iframe tag</h2>
12   </body>
13   </html>
```

☞ ───

Example 14.4 Develop Web pages for browsers that may not support frames.

Develop a Web page that illustrates the use of the `<noframes>` tag.

Solution 14.4 The `<noframes>` tag does not have any attributes. The tag specifies alternative contents for a Web page rendered by a browser that does not, or is configured not to, support frames. This tag is enclosed inside the `<frameset>` tag. Thus, browsers that support frames render the `<frameset>` tag and all the other tags that it encloses *except* the `<noframes>` tag and what is inside it. By contrast, browsers that do not support frames render *only* the `<noframes>` tag (and all the other tags that it encloses). In effect, a Web author writes the Web page twice in the same HTML code, once inside the `<frameset>` tag and once inside the `<noframes>` tag.

The following XHTML code modifies the code of Example 14.2 to include the `<noframes>` tag:

```
1    <?xml version="1.0" encoding="iso-8859-1"?>
2    <!DOCTYPE html PUBLIC "-//W3C//DTD XHTML 1.1//EN"
3        "http://www.w3.org/TR/xhtml11/DTD/xhtml11.dtd">
4    <html xmlns="http://www.w3.org/1999/xhtml">
5    <!-- Generated by AceHTM http://freeware.acehtml.com -->
6    <head>
```

```
 7   <meta http-equiv="Content-Type" content="text/html;
     charset=iso-8859-1" />
 8   <title>A Web page with nested frames</title>
 9   </head>
10   <frameset cols="*, *"> <!-- outer frame set -->
11   <frameset rows="*, *"> <!-- nested frame set -->
12   <frame src="cncLatheView1.jpg" />
13   <frame src="cncLatheView2.jpg" />
14   </frameset> <!-- close tag, line 10 -->
15   <frame src="cncLatheController.jpg" />
16   <noframes> <!-- begin noframes code -->
17   Any tags that are normally used inside the BOSY tag go here.
18   </noframes> <!-- end noframes code -->
19   </frameset> <!-- close tag, line 11 -->
20   </html>
```

> Lines 16–18 include the noframes content

14.5 Target Frames and Windows

Frames are typically used to optimize a Web page's layout and to facilitate navigation. For optimum navigation, a Web author may use one frame to hold, for example, hyperlinks and then use another frame to display the results of clicking the hyperlinks. In this case, the contents of the first frame never change, while the contents of the second frame change for each mouse-button click. The advantage to this configuration is that the first frame always displays the site map, for the convenience of the Web surfer.

Frames that receive contents from other frames are known as target frames. Let us refer to frames that hold the TOC as source frames. Figure 14.5 shows the relationship between source

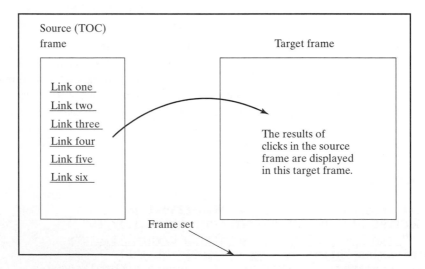

Figure 14.5 Relationship between source and target frames.

frames and target frames. When a Web surfer clicks a hyperlink in a source frame, the contents of the corresponding Web page are displayed in the target frame.

Target frames are not especially different from other frames. The only requirement is that they be named at the time of their creation. Thus, their corresponding `<frame>` tags must use the `name` attribute. Assigning a name to a frame allows other (source) frames to reference it as a target (destination) frame, via use of the `target` attribute. We can think of the `target` attribute as the curved arrow that links two frames in Figure 14.5.

Example 14.5 Use target frames.

Develop a Web page that illustrates the use of target frames.

Solution 14.5 Using the AceHTML editor, generate the given code, and save it as `example145.html`. The following screen capture shows the resulting Web page.

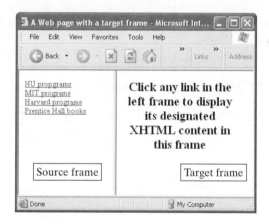

Code explained:

1. Lines 10–13 in the file `example145.html` create a frame set with two frames.

2. Lines 11–14 in the file `toc.html` create four hyperlinks that use the `title` attribute.

Discussion:

This example creates a Web page with two frames. The left frame acts as a TOC. It has four hyperlinks. Each one of them uses the right frame as a target frame. The initial contents of the target frame instruct users on how to utilize the frame set. This example requires three HTML documents. One document is `example145.html`, and it defines the frame set. This document is also the main document, or the driver. The second document is `toc.html`, and it defines the contents of the left frame. The third document is `initialContent.html`, and it defines the initial contents of the right frame.

The source and target frames are connected using the name myTarget. Code line 12 in example145.html uses the name attribute to assign myTarget to the right frame of the frame set. Code lines 11–14 in toc.html use the target attribute to implement myTarget. The use of the name-target pair of attributes connects the frames correctly.

Hands-on exercise:

Starting with the code given in this example, add a link to the website of an organization to which you belong to the frame set. The new link must use the target frame.

example145.html

```
1   <?xml version="1.0" encoding="iso-8859-1"?>
2   <!DOCTYPE html PUBLIC "-//W3C//DTD XHTML 1.1//EN"
3       "http://www.w3.org/TR/xhtml11/DTD/xhtml11.dtd">
4   <html xmlns="http://www.w3.org/1999/xhtml">
5   <!-- Generated by AceHTM http://freeware.acehtml.com -->
6   <head>
7   <meta http-equiv="Content-Type" content="text/html;
    charset=iso-8859-1" />
8   <title>A Web page with a target frame</title>
9   </head>
10  <frameset cols="160, *">
11  <frame src="toc.html" />
12  <frame src="initialContent.html" name="myTarget" />
13  </frameset>
14  </html>
```

initialContent.html

```
1   <?xml version="1.0" encoding="iso-8859-1"?>
2   <!DOCTYPE html PUBLIC "-//W3C//DTD XHTML 1.1//EN"
3       "http://www.w3.org/TR/xhtml11/DTD/xhtml11.dtd">
4   <html xmlns="http://www.w3.org/1999/xhtml">
5   <!-- Generated by AceHTM http://freeware.acehtml.com -->
6   <head>
7   <meta http-equiv="Content-Type" content="text/html;
    charset=iso-8859-1" />
8   <title>A Web page with a target frame</title>
9   </head>
10  <body>
11  <h2 align="center">Click any link in the left frame to
    display its designated XHTML content in this frame</h2>
12  </body>
13  </html>
```

```
toc.html
1   <?xml version="1.0" encoding="iso-8859-1"?>
2   <!DOCTYPE html PUBLIC "-//W3C//DTD XHTML 1.1//EN"
3       "http://www.w3.org/TR/xhtml11/DTD/xhtml11.dtd">
4   <html xmlns="http://www.w3.org/1999/xhtml">
5   <!-- Generated by AceHTM http://freeware.acehtml.com -->
6   <head>
7   <meta http-equiv="Content-Type" content="text/html;
    charset=iso-8859-1" />
8   <title>A Web page with a target frame</title>
9   </head>
10  <body>
11  <a href="http://www.neu.edu" target="myTarget"
    title="NU Web page">NU propgrams</a><br />
12  <a href="http://www.mit.edu" target="myTarget"
    title="MIT Web page">MIT programs</a><br />
13  <a href= "http://www.harvard.edu" target="myTarget"
    title="Harvard Web page">Harvard programs</a><br />
14  <a href="http://www.prenhall.com" target="myTarget"
    title="Prentice Hall Web page">Prentice Hall books</a>
15  </body>
16  </html>
```

Example 14.6 Use frames to open a new browser window for linked pages.

Develop a Web page that displays content of linked pages in a new browser window.

Solution 14.6 We rewrite the XHTML code of Example 14.5 so that it uses new browser windows to open linked pages. Using the AceHTML editor, edit the code of `example145.html` to generate the code given here, and save it as `example146.html`.

Code explained:

Code lines 12 and 13 create a new browser window for each link.

Discussion:

We modify the `target` attribute of code lines 12 and 13 of `example145.html` to specify a target name that has not been defined by the `name` attribute of any frame. We use the name `new`; any other name could be used, however. This name is not defined in `example145.html`; it defines the `myTarget` name only. When a user clicks the first or the fourth link, the browser displays the corresponding XHTML contents in the `myTarget` frame. However, if the user clicks the second or third link, the browser opens a new window and displays the content of the corresponding Web page in it. This new window is now called `new`.

Hands-on exercise:

Starting with the code given in this example, add two more links that open a new browser window when a user clicks them.

```
1   <?xml version="1.0" encoding="iso-8859-1"?>
2   <!DOCTYPE html PUBLIC "-//W3C//DTD XHTML 1.1//EN"
3       "http://www.w3.org/TR/xhtml11/DTD/xhtml11.dtd">
4   <html xmlns="http://www.w3.org/1999/xhtml">
5   <!-- Generated by AceHTM http://freeware.acehtml.com -->
6   <head>
7   <meta http-equiv="Content-Type" content="text/html;
    charset=iso-8859-1" />
8   <title>A Web page with a target frame</title>
9   </head>
10  <body>
11  <a href="http://www.neu.edu" target="myTarget"
    title="NU Web page">NU propgrams</a><br />
12  <a href="http://www.mit.edu" target="new"
    title="MIT Web page">MIT programs</a><br />
13  <a href= "http://www.harvard.edu" target="new"
    title="Harvard Web page">Harvard programs</a><br />
14  <a href="http://www.prenhall.com" target="myTarget"
    title="Prentice Hall Web page">Prentice Hall books</a>
15  </body>
16  </html>
```

14.6 Tutorials

14.6.1 Using Ordered Lists in a TOC Frame
(Study Section 14.5)

Using the AceHTML editor, generate the given code, and save it under the given file names.

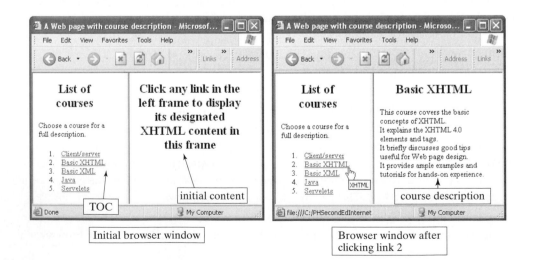

Initial browser window

Browser window after clicking link 2

tutorial1461.html

```
1   <?xml version="1.0" encoding="iso-8859-1"?>
2   <!DOCTYPE html PUBLIC "-//W3C//DTD XHTML 1.1//EN"
3       "http://www.w3.org/TR/xhtml11/DTD/xhtml11.dtd">
4   <html xmlns="http://www.w3.org/1999/xhtml">
5   <!-- Generated by AceHTM http://freeware.acehtml.com -->
6   <head>
7   <meta http-equiv="Content-Type" content="text/html;
    charset=iso-8859-1" />
8   <title>A Web page with course description</title>
9   </head>
10  <frameset cols="165, *">
11  <frame src="toc.html" />
12  <frame src="initialContent.html" name="myTarget" />
13  </frameset>
14  </html>
```

toc.html

```
1   <?xml version="1.0" encoding="iso-8859-1"?>
2   <!DOCTYPE html PUBLIC "-//W3C//DTD XHTML 1.1//EN"
3       "http://www.w3.org/TR/xhtml11/DTD/xhtml11.dtd">
4   <html xmlns="http://www.w3.org/1999/xhtml">
5   <!-- Generated by AceHTM http://freeware.acehtml.com -->
6   <head>
7   <meta http-equiv="Content-Type" content="text/html;
    charset=iso-8859-1" />
8   <title>A Web page with a target frame</title>
9   </head>
10  <body>
11  <h2 align="center">List of courses</h2>
12  Choose a course for a full description.
13  <ol>
14  <li><a href="clientServerCourse.html" target="myTarget"
    title="client/server">Client/server</a>
15  <li><a href="xhtmlCourse.html" target="myTarget"
    title="XHTML">Basic XHTML</a>
16  <li><a href="xmlCourse.html" target="myTarget"
    title="XML">Basic XML</a>
17  <li><a href="javaCourse.html" target="myTarget"
    title="Java">Java</a>
18  <li><a href="ServletsCourse.html" target="myTarget"
    title="Servelts">Servelets</a>
19  </ol>
```

```
20   </body>
21   </html>
```

initialContent.html

```
1    <?xml version="1.0" encoding="iso-8859-1"?>
2    <!DOCTYPE html PUBLIC "-//W3C//DTD XHTML 1.1//EN"
3        "http://www.w3.org/TR/xhtml11/DTD/xhtml11.dtd">
4    <html xmlns="http://www.w3.org/1999/xhtml">
5    <!-- Generated by AceHTM http://freeware.acehtml.com -->
6    <head>
7    <meta http-equiv="Content-Type" content="text/html;
8    charset=iso-8859-1" />
9    <title>A Web page with a target frame</title>
10   </head>
11   <body>
12   <h2 align="center">Click any link in the left frame to
     display its designated XHTML content in this frame</h2>
13   </body>
14   </html>
```

xhtmlCourse.html

```
1    <?xml version="1.0" encoding="iso-8859-1"?>
2    <!DOCTYPE html PUBLIC "-//W3C//DTD XHTML 1.1//EN"
3        "http://www.w3.org/TR/xhtml11/DTD/xhtml11.dtd">
4    <html xmlns="http://www.w3.org/1999/xhtml">
5    <!-- Generated by AceHTM http://freeware.acehtml.com -->
6    <head>
7    <meta http-equiv="Content-Type" content="text/html;
     charset=iso-8859-1" />
8    <title>Basic XHTML Course Description</title>
9    </head>
10   <body>
11   <h2 align="center">Basic XHTML</h2>
12   <div>This course covers the basic concepts of XHTML.</div>
13   <div>It explains the XHTML 4.0 elements and tags.</div>
14   <div>It briefly discusses good tips useful for Web page
     design.</div>
15   <div>It provides ample examples and tutorials for hands-on
     experience.</div>
16   </body>
17   </html>
```

Code explained:

1. Lines 10 –13 in the file `tutorial1461.html` create a frame set with two frames.
2. Lines 14 –18 in the file `toc.html` create five hyperlinks that use the `title` attribute.
3. Line 11 in the file `initialContent.html` creates the right frame's initial text.
4. Lines 12–15 in the file `xhtmlCourse.html` create the course description.

Discussion:

This tutorial creates a TOC as an ordered list with hyperlink items. We create a Web page that provides a course description. The page has a frame set that consists of two vertical frames. The left frame holds the course links that make up the items of the ordered list. The right frame displays the description of the course selected in the left frame.

Hands-on exercise:

Starting with the code given in this tutorial, add two more courses and their corresponding descriptions to the Web page.

14.6.2   Using Image Maps with Frames (Study Section 14.5)

Using the AceHTML editor, generate the given code, and save it under the given file names.

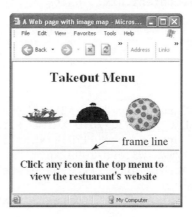

Code explained:

1. Lines 10–13 in the file `tutorial1462.html` create a frame set with two frames.
2. Line 12 in the file `toc.html` uses the `border` attribute, so the browser does not add an image border.
3. Line 11 in the file `initialContent.html` creates the initial text of the page.

Discussion:

This tutorial creates a TOC as an image map. When the user clicks an icon of the map, a Web page is displayed in the bottom frame. Initially, this frame instructs Web visitors on how to use the website. We use the `name` attribute in code line 12 of `tutorial1462.html`. We also use the `target` attribute in code lines 14–16 in `toc.html` to complete the navigation design of the website.

Hands-on exercise:

Remove the `border` attribute. Also, add two more food items to the current menu.

```
tutorial1462.html
```

```
1   <?xml version="1.0" encoding="iso-8859-1"?>
2   <!DOCTYPE html PUBLIC "-//W3C//DTD XHTML 1.1//EN"
3       "http://www.w3.org/TR/xhtml11/DTD/xhtml11.dtd">
4   <html xmlns="http://www.w3.org/1999/xhtml">
5   <!-- Generated by AceHTM http://freeware.acehtml.com -->
6   <head>
7   <meta http-equiv="Content-Type" content="text/html;
    charset=iso-8859-1" />
8   <title>A Web page with image map</title>
9   </head>
10  <frameset rows="173, *">
11  <frame src="toc.html" />
12  <frame src="initialContent.html" name="myTarget" />
13  </frameset>
14  </html>
```

```
toc.html
```

```
1   <?xml version="1.0" encoding="iso-8859-1"?>
2   <!DOCTYPE html PUBLIC "-//W3C//DTD XHTML 1.1//EN"
3       "http://www.w3.org/TR/xhtml11/DTD/xhtml11.dtd">
4   <html xmlns="http://www.w3.org/1999/xhtml">
5   <!-- Generated by AceHTM http://freeware.acehtml.com -->
6   <head>
7   <meta http-equiv="Content-Type" content="text/html;
    charset=iso-8859-1" />
8   <title>Restaurant Menu</title>
9   </head>
10  <body>
11  <h1 align="center"><b>Takeout Menu</b></h1>
12  <img src="foodMenu.jpg" border="0" usemap="#menuMap" />
13  <map name="menuMap">
14  <area href="http://www.burgerking.com" alt="Appetizers"
    shape="rect" coords="10,25,90,60" target="myTarget" />
15  <area href="http://www.legalseafood.com" alt="Meals"
    shape="poly" coords="100,60,210,60,150,10" target="myTarget" />
16  <area href="http://www.pizzahut.com" alt="Pizza"
    shape="circle" coords="252,40,35" target="myTarget" />
```

```
17   </map>
18
19   </body>
20   </html>
```

┌─────────────────────┐
│ initalContent.html │
└─────────────────────┘

```
1    <?xml version="1.0" encoding="iso-8859-1"?>
2    <!DOCTYPE html PUBLIC "-//W3C//DTD XHTML 1.1//EN"
3        "http://www.w3.org/TR/xhtml11/DTD/xhtml11.dtd">
4    <html xmlns="http://www.w3.org/1999/xhtml">
5    <!-- Generated by AceHTM http://freeware.acehtml.com -->
6    <head>
7    <meta http-equiv="Content-Type" content="text/html;
     charset=iso-8859-1" />
8    <title>Using Image Maps and Frames</title>
9    </head>
10   <body>
11   <h2 align="center">Click any icon in the top menu to
     view the restaurant's website</h2>
12   </body>
13   </html>
```

FAQs

Using Frames (Section 14.4)

Q: What happens if I create a frame without using the rows and cols attributes?

A: The browser creates a frame that takes up its entire window. In effect, you do not need a frame.

Q: I am trying to create three horizontal frames with a heading that reads A horizontal frame set. The browser displays the heading only; it ignores the frame set all together. What is wrong with my code, given as follows?

```
<html>
<head>
<title>A Web page with a horizontal frame set</title>
</head>
A horizontal frame set
<frameset rows="100, 40%, *">
<frame src="#" />
<frame src="#" />
<frame src="#" />
</frameset>
</html>
```

A: You cannot use any XHTML tags or text before the `<frameset>` tag. If you do, as in this case, the browser renders "A horizontal frame set" and ignores the `<frameset>` tag.

Q: I am trying to create a frame container with three empty frames. The browser does not display any frames in its window. What is wrong with my code, given as follows?

```
<html>
<head>
<title>A Web page with a horizontal frame set</title>
</head>
<frameset rows="100, 40%, *">
</frameset>
</html>
```

A: There is nothing wrong with the code syntax. Unless you use the three expected `<frame>` tags, the browser does not show any frames. Add the three expected `<frame>` tags, and the browser will display them.

Q: Why is the browser unable to display the latest changes I just made to an HTML file, although I made sure to save the code a couple of times? I use the browser's `Reload` button to display the file.

A: The problem is not yours; it's the browser's. When you use the `Reload` button, the browser loads the file version it has saved in its cache, instead of loading the latest version you have just saved on your hard disk. To force the browser to load from the hard disk, drag the HTML file and drop it in the browser; use the browser's `File => Open` sequence; simply place the mouse cursor in the browser's URL bar, click it to bring the focus to the bar, and hit `Enter` on your keyboard; or hold down the `Shift` key on the keyboard and click the browser's `Reload` button simultaneously.

Q: What does the following frame-set definition mean? `<frameset rows="4*, 300, 1*">`

A: The browser window is divided into three rows. The middle row has a fixed height of 300 pixels. The first row receives 80% of the remaining space, and the last row receives 20% of the remaining space. The fixed-height frame could be useful for holding an image of a known size.

Q: What does the following frame-set definition mean for a browser window that is 1000 pixels wide? `<frameset cols="30%, 400, 2*, *">`

A: The first frame is allotted 300 pixels. The width of the second frame is already specified to be exactly 400 pixels. That leaves 300 pixels for the remaining two frames. The width of the third frame is twice that of the last frame. Thus, the third frame becomes 200 pixels wide, and the last frame receives 100 pixels for its width.

Q: What happens if a Web author underspecifies or overspecifies the allocation of a browser window's height or width when defining a frame set?

A: The browser should adjust the heights and widths of the set's frames to match exactly its window's height and width, respectively. When the set is underspecified (or overspecified), remaining (or lacking) space should be allotted (or reduced) proportionally for each frame.

Q: Why does my browser not display all the frames I expect, although the code of the frame set is correct?

A: This is an issue of space allocation that depends on the size of the currently displayed browser window. Let us assume that the size of the window is 300 pixels wide by 200 pixels high. If you request two rows of frames, and the first is 400 pixels high, you will not see the second row in this window size. If you enlarge the browser window to fill the entire screen, you should see all the frames, unless you are using very large sizes. It is usually recommended to use the wildcard (`*`) to describe the sizes of frames, to give the browser full freedom at display time.

Blackbox

Section 14.1 (Introduction): XHTML frames are used for organizing content and formatting Web pages. A **frame** is a rectangular container (region).

Section 14.2 (Frame Layout and Design): A frame set decides the layout of its frames. An XHTML document that uses frames must not use the `<body>` tag. The `<frameset>` tag replaces it. Keep the layout design of a frame set simple.

Section 14.3 (Frame Sets and Nesting): An XHTML frame set has a width and height. The width and height are specified by the number of rows and columns, respectively. The units of `rows` and `cols` are either pixels or a percentage of the browser window. The browser uses the top left corner of its window as the origin of a coordinate system for placing frames in the frame set. The horizontal axis is the columns' axis, and it points to the right. The vertical axis is the rows' axis, and it points downwards. Frames are nested using this coordinate system.

Section 14.4 (Using Frames) (Examples 14.1–14.4): XHTML provides the `<frameset>`, `<frame>`, `<iframe>`, and `<noframes>` tags to define frame sets and frames. The `<noframes>` tag has no attributes. The attributes of the other tags are `<frameset rows cols>`, `<frame name src noresize scrolling frameborder marginwidth marginheight longdesc>`, and `<iframe name src width height align scrolling frameborder marginwidth marginheight longdesc>`.

Section 14.5 (Target Frames and Windows) (Examples 14.5 and 14.6): Target frames are used to optimize navigation. Use the `name` attribute to specify a target frame and the `target` attribute to refer to it.

Section 14.6 (Tutorials): Two tutorials show how to use frames.

Quick reference for the tags presented in this chapter

Tag	Close	Attribute	Value	Effect	Example
`<frameset>`	yes	`rows`	number of pixels, %, or *	defines frame height	`<frameset rows="200">` `<frameset rows="30%">`
		`cols`	number of pixels, %, or *	defines frame width	`<frameset cols="200">` `<frameset cols="30%">`
`<frame>`	empty	`name`	text	assigns a name to the frame	`<frame name="abc" />`
		`src`	file	specifies the frame's content	`<frame src="abc.html">`
		`nore-size`	none	disables resizing of the frame's window	`<frame noresize />`
		`scroll-ing`	auto	browser decides whether scrollbars should appear	`<frame scroll-ing="auto" />`
			yes	create scrollbars for the frame	`<frame scroll-ing="yes" />`
			no	do not create scrollbars for the frame	`<frame scrolling="no" />`
		`frame-border`	1 (default)	creates borders between frames	`<frame framebor-der="1" />`
			0	no borders are created	`<frame framebor-der="0" />`
		`margin-width`	number of pixels	left–right margin	`<frame margin-width="10" />`
		`margin-height`	number of pixels	top–bottom margin	`<frame margin-height="10"/>`

Tag	Close	Attribute	Value	Effect	Example
`<iframe>`	yes	`name`	text	assigns a name to the frame	`<iframe name="abc">`
		`src`	file	specifies the frame's content	`<iframe src="abc.html">`
		`width`	number of pixels	specifies the frame's width	`<iframe width="300">`
		`height`	number of pixels	specifies the frame's height	`<iframe height="400">`
		`align`	top	places the frame at the top of the page	`<iframe align="top">`
			middle	places the frame in the middle of the page	`<iframe align="middle">`
			bottom	places the frame at the bottom of the page	`<iframe align="bottom">`
			left	places the frame to the left of the text	`<iframe align="left">`
			center	places the text around the frame	`<iframe align="center">`
			right	places the frame to the right of the text	`<iframe align="bottom">`
		`scroll-ing`	auto	browser decides whether scroll-bars should appear	`<iframe scroll-ing="auto">`
			yes	create scroll-bars for the frame	`<iframe scroll-ing="yes">`
			no	do not create scrollbars for the frame	`<iframe scroll-ing="no">`

Tag	Close	Attribute	Value	Effect	Example
		`frame-border`	1 (default)	create borders between frames	`<iframe framebor-der="1">`
			0	do not create borders between frames	`<iframe framebor-der="0">`
		`margin-width`	number of pixels	left–right frame margin	`<iframe margin-width="10">`
		`margin-height`	number of pixels	top–bottom frame margin	`<iframe margin-height="10">`
`<noframes>`	yes	none			

Check Your Progress

At the end of this chapter, you should

- ✔ understand frames (Section 14.1);
- ✔ understand frame layout and design (Section 14.2);
- ✔ have mastered the use of frame sets and their nesting (Section 14.3);
- ✔ have mastered the use of XHTML frame tags (Section 14.4);
- ✔ understand target frames (Section 14.5);
- ✔ be able to make links open in a new browser window, using the `target` attribute (Section 14.5);
- ✔ be able to use frames to format Web pages (Section 14.6);
- ✔ have practiced using frames (Section 14.6).

Problems

The exercises are designed for a lab setting, while the homework is to be done outside class time.

Exercises

14.1   Create the two frame sets shown in Figure 14.3. The ratio between the frame sizes for the horizontal set is 1:2 and for the vertical set is 2:1. All of the frames are empty (i.e., hold no contents). Use all the attributes of the `<frame>` tag, with different values.

14.2   Create the nested frame sets shown in Figure 14.4. The two rows and columns are of equal size for the set shown on the top of the figure. For the bottom set, use the following sizes: The width of Frame 1 is 40% of the width of the browser window. The height of Frame 1 is 30% of the height of the browser window. All of the frames are empty (i.e., hold no contents). Use all the attributes of the `<frame>` tag, with different values.

14.3   Rewrite the HTML code for Example 14.5 so that a top frame is the TOC frame and a bottom frame is the target frame.

Homework

14.4 Create a Web page that uses nested and target frames to facilitate navigation of the page. The page's design and layout are left up to you. Be imaginative.

14.5 Create a Web page that uses frames and uses unordered lists in its TOC frame.

14.6 Create a Web page that uses frames and uses image maps in its TOC frame.

14.7 Create a two-frame set that displays food recipes. The TOC frame should list the names of the recipes, while the other frame displays their details.

14.8 Rewrite the XHTML code for Tutorial 14.6.1 so that it uses an unordered list instead of an ordered one.

14.9 Rewrite the XHTML code for Tutorial 14.6.2 so that it uses two vertical frames.

14.10 Create a Web page that uses inline frames. Be imaginative.

Forms

Goal

Understand forms, their structure, their communication cycle, their elements, and formatting their layouts via the use of tables and layers.

Objectives

- Data collection over the Web
- Name–value pairs
- Front and back ends
- The communication cycle of a form
- Elements of forms
- Using forms
- Formatting forms with tables
- Formatting forms with layers

Outline

15.1 Introduction

Many online activities and services require the use of forms. Consider e-commerce or online purchases and ordering. A Web surfer browses through a website, selects products, and buys them, which requires the use of forms. Taking and participating in online surveys and polls require the use of forms as well. Other online activities that utilize forms include taking exams, filling in applications, registering, creating computer accounts, and changing login information.

Websites that have forms requiring personal information such as credit card numbers usually use secure Internet connections. These connections use the HTTPS protocol, which encrypts the form's data before sending the data across the Internet, from the client to the server. The encryption protects the privacy of the Web surfers and prevents the hacking of personal data.

Sending the information collected via a form to a Web server is easy and automatic. The information is bundled (encoded) by the browser into what are known as name–value pairs, according to a Common Gateway Interface (CGI) protocol (format). These pairs are sent to the Web server hosting the form, for processing. Chapter 18 discusses the various methods that are used to process the name–value pairs of form data.

Information collected from a form can be processed in different ways. For example, it can be written to a database; this is the case when the form is used for surveying or feedback purposes. Another way is to process the information for online purchases and e-commerce; this is the case when the form is used by Web surfers to order products. A third way is for the form's input to be e-mailed someone.

15.2 Structure and Communication

A form has two distinct parts: the front end and the back end. The front end is included in a Web page; it is the visible part. A Web surfer sees this part in a Web page on the client computer, fills in its fields, and interacts with it. The back end is not visible to Web surfers, and they do not interact with it at all. This part is the computer program that is responsible for processing form information and data, once they are submitted by a Web surfer.

All forms available on the Web obviously have both ends; however, during the early stages of development or when learning forms and their tags, Web authors may focus only the front end. It is much simpler to develop the front end of a form than to develop the back end. A form's front end requires only XHTML tags. Its back end, on the other hand, requires a knowledge of a programming language (such as Perl, PHP, C, C++, or Java) as well as the structure of the name–value pairs.

What exactly does the back end of a form do? A computer program processing form data has two main functions. First, it extracts the form's input. Second, it processes the input and sends a response. Consider the case of ordering a book over the Internet. First, the program extracts the book's name from the name–value pairs in the form and locates the book in the database on the Web server handling the order. Second, it sends a response to the Web surfer who has submitted the order. The response is typically a Web page that the computer program develops and sends over the Internet to the client computer.

What is the communication cycle from the time a Web surfer fills in a form until he or she receives a response back? Figure 15.1 shows the cycle. The two client computers shown in the figure represent the same user and the same client computer. The client computer is shown twice for ease of illustration. As the figure shows, the cycle begins by the Web surfer filling in the form. When the user clicks the submit button on the form, the client browser encodes the name–value pairs according to the CGI formats and sends them across the Internet to the Web server. The server has a computer program that reads the name–value pairs and extracts the user's input.

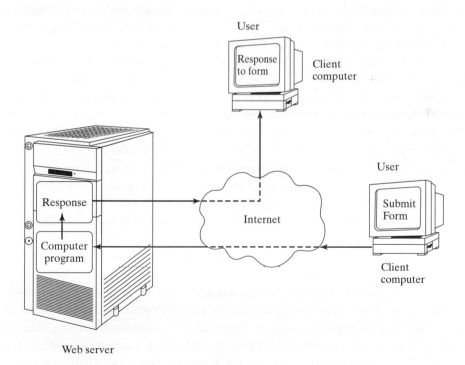

Figure 15.1 Communication cycle of a form.

The program uses the input to make decisions. The decisions result in the generation of a response, in the form of a Web page that is sent to the user across the Internet. If there is any follow-up action that needs to be taken, such as sending merchandise, the server administrator takes care of it.

How do the front end and back end of a form recognize each other? The link between a form and its computer program is established in the `<form>` tag. The tag has an `action` attribute that specifies the name of the program and its directory on the server that is supposed to handle the form's input.

The remainder of this chapter focuses on the front end of forms and how to build forms. It covers all the possible elements of a form, form layout and design, and the form tags. Chapter 18 discusses the details of server-side scripting.

15.3 Elements

XHTML provides a comprehensive set of form elements that is guaranteed to meet all of the design needs of XHTML forms. These elements are text fields, radio buttons, checkboxes, menus, text areas, submit buttons, and reset buttons. Figure 15.2 shows the shapes of these elements. As the figure shows, some of these elements, such as text fields and text areas, have certain parameters.

The text-field element is typically used when one line of text is needed as input. According to XHTML, each text field is displayed as a rectangle, as shown in Figure 15.2, and has two parameters that define it: size and maximum length. Each parameter is specified as a number of characters. The maximum length defines the maximum number of characters, m, that the text field can hold. Out of this number, only the number of characters specified by the size parameter, n, is displayed (visible) in the text field. If the user types more characters in the text field than n, the text scrolls to display only the last n characters typed. If the user inputs more characters than m, the extra characters are ignored by the browser.

Whenever Web authors have a need to present potential users of their Web pages with multiple (nonexclusive) choices, they use checkboxes. Users can select the checkboxes with a click of the mouse button. Checkboxes are displayed in a Web page as squares, as shown in Figure 15.2. Checkboxes that have already been selected (checked) by a Web user are shown with a checkmark inside them. Two of the checkboxes shown in Figure 15.2 are checked, while the others are not. Checkboxes act as on–off, or toggle, switches. When a user clicks inside a checkbox, its state reverses itself from checked (on, or true) to unchecked (off, or false), or vice versa. Checkboxes are mutually inclusive: A user can have more than one checkbox selected at the same time.

Whenever Web authors have a need to present potential users of their Web pages with multiple choices of which only one must be selected, they use radio buttons. Radio buttons are displayed in a Web page as circles, as shown in Figure 15.2. Radio buttons that have already been selected by a Web user are shown with a filled circle inside them. The first radio button shown in Figure 15.2 is selected, while the other two are not. Like checkboxes, radio buttons act as on–off, or toggle, switches. When a user clicks inside a radio button, its state reverses itself from selected

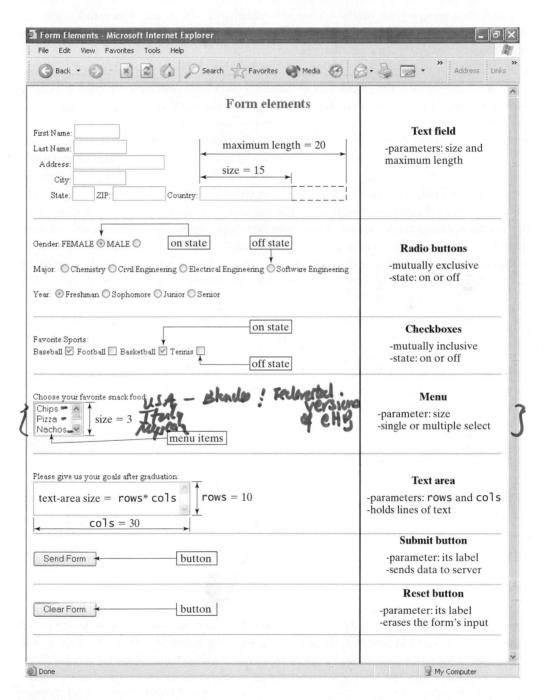

Figure 15.2   Form elements.

to unselected, or vice versa. Radio buttons are mutually exclusive; this means that a user can select only one radio button, from one group of buttons, at any one time. Examples of when radio buttons might be used include presenting a user with choices of gender (male or female) college year (freshman, sophomore, junior, or senior), answer's to a question, (yes or no), and so forth.

A menu is a useful form element. Web authors present users with menus of choices. A menu may be defined to allow its users to choose either at most one menu item or multiple items at the same time. Checkboxes and radio buttons perform the same function as menus, but menus are usually employed whenever there are many choices whose descriptions are verbose. In such cases, the use of checkboxes or radio buttons becomes very cumbersome and inefficient. A menu may display only one of its items at a time, or it may display multiple items; the latter case is shown in Figure 15.2. XHTML provides a size parameter in order to control the display of a menu. This parameter defines the number of menu items that can be displayed on the screen at one time. Thus, the size parameter controls the size of the menu box. If the menu has a larger number of menu items than that specified by the size parameter, scrollbars are added automatically (by the browser) to the menu display. If no size is specified, only one item is displayed at a times, and the menu acts as drop-down menu. A menu is also known as a list. Other names that are frequently used for an XHTML menu are option list or menu, select list or menu, and drop-down list or menu.

Unlike the text-field element, the text-area element provides multiple lines of text. Text areas are useful if Web authors need to display many lines of text to users. For example, Web authors can use text areas to display recipes or instructions on how to fill in forms. Users who fill in the forms can employ text areas to send their feedback to Web authors. XHTML defines two parameters for a text area—width and height, as shown in figure 15.2. Both parameters are specified as numbers of characters. Furthermore, the width and the height are referred to as the number of columns and the number of rows, respectively. Each column is a character wide, and each row is a line of text. The text area shown in Figure 15.2 is 30 characters wide by 10 characters (lines) high; thus, this text area can hold 300 characters.

The submit button and the reset button, shown in Figure 15.2, are two other elements of a form. These buttons act globally, that is, at the form level. After filling out a form, the user clicks the submit button in order to send the form's data to the designated Web server. Clicking the submit button triggers the browser to collect the form's input, encodes the input as name–value pairs according to the CGI formats, and sends the pairs to the Web server. The label of the submit button is known as its value. The default value is `Submit Query`. Web authors can also use different values, such as `Send it`, `Send this form`, and `Send Entry`.

The reset button performs the opposite function to that provided by the submit button: It erases or clears the form's input. For example, if the user is not satisfied with his or her responses a form or decides not to submit it, the user clicks the reset button. All the user's input is then erased and replaced by the default values of the form. These default values are defined in the form's XHTML code. The label of the reset button is known as its value. The default value is `Reset`. Web authors can use different values, such as `Erase`, `Clear Form and Start Over`, and `Reset all Values and Start Over`.

There are other form elements that are provided by XHTML, but are less frequently used. They are the hidden element and the password element. Hidden elements are never displayed on the screen as form elements. Thus, form users never see them. Hidden elements are used by Web authors to track information between clients and servers. To find out whether a Web page uses hidden elements, simply view the page's source code and look for them. The password element allows Web authors to request passwords from users before allowing them to access secure Web pages or documents. Examples include accessing a stock market account or reading a magazine online. Hidden and password elements are typically used in Web pages that use JavaScript code in addition to XHTML code.

15.4 Layout and Design

When Web authors need to create forms, they think in terms of the form elements covered in Section 15.3. The design and layout of a form are what distinguish it from other forms. However, there is a common theme for form layout and design. First, each form must have a submit button and a reset button. Second, each form must have an `action` attribute, to tell the browser how to process the name–value pairs. Third, each form must have a `method` attribute, to tell the browser how to send the name–value pairs to the Web server that hosts the form-processing computer program. Beyond this common theme, each form has a different body that contains the proper form elements. Figure 15.3 shows the generic layout of a form. As shown in the figure, the form's body represents the top part of the form. The submit and reset buttons represent the bottom part of the form and are usually placed at the end of the form.

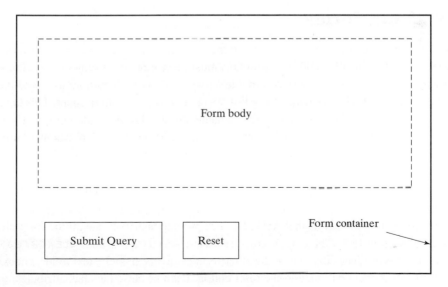

Figure 15.3   Form layout.

There are many useful tips and rules that Web authors usually follow to design XHTML forms. They are mostly simple and logical and follow common sense. Here is a partial list of these tips:

1. **Keep the form short.** A form should not be more than one computer screen long. A half-screen-long form is ideal. We have learned this rule from tradition: Long paper forms tend to discourage us from filling them out. XHTML forms are no exception.

2. **Keep the form simple.** A simple form goes hand in hand with a short form. Web authors should ask for only the information they need, in order to keep forms short and simple. Web authors generally receive many more responses from a short, simple form than from a long, complicated one.

3. **Keep the form organized.** Web authors should group related fields together. The form's body should be divided into logical sections or groups. Let us consider the design of a form for ordering books online. We can divide the form's body into three sections. The first section could be for collecting shipping information, such as a person's name, a shipping address, and a phone number. The second section could be a list of books from which to choose. The third section could be for choosing a method of shipping. It is also beneficial to add headings that stand out at the beginning of each section, to alert the user to the type of information needed in the section.

4. **Use tables or layers to arrange form elements.** Forms look more appealing when their elements are organized in an easy-to-follow pattern. For example, the text fields shown in Figure 15.2 are flush left. Web authors can use tables or layers to format a form's layout.

15.5 Using Forms

XHTML provides the necessary tags to create the front end of a form that Web surfers see on the screen and interact with. XHTML form tags must meet three requirements in order to successfully create forms. First, they must provide a way to allow Web authors to create the form layout they design. XHTML provides the `<form>` tag to meet this requirement. This tag acts as a container of the form elements. The form elements are displayed on the computer screen in the order of their use inside the `<form>` tag. The `<form>` tag also has two important attributes. One is the `action` attribute, which specifies the name and the location of the computer program that should parse the name–value pairs in order to make use of them. The other attribute is the `method` attribute, which specifies the way the name–value pairs are sent to the Web server.

The second requirement is that XHTML must provide tags to create all the form elements discussed in Section 15.3. These tags are `<input>`, `<select>`, and `<textarea>`. The `<input>` tag has attributes that create the other form elements, namely, text fields, checkboxes, radio buttons, the submit button, and the reset button. Each of these tags has attributes to allow Web authors more control over their outcomes.

The third requirement is that XHTML must provide a way to initialize form elements as needed—that is, the ability to specify initial values. For example, we may want to display text fields or text areas with initial text, or we may want to display a set or group of radio buttons or checkboxes with one of them already selected or checked. Each tag that creates a form element has the ability to specify an initial value. These values appear in the form when it is initially displayed in the Web page. Web surfers may replace these initial values with their specific values. These values become the current values. However, the initial values of form elements do not change. Therefore, when a form is reset via the reset button, each element's current value is reset to its initial value. If an element does not have an initial value, resetting it causes its initial state to be blank (text fields and text areas), unselected (radio buttons), or unchecked (checkboxes). Tables 15.1–15.5 list all the form tags and their attributes.

As Table 15.1 states, the `method` attribute has two values: `get` and `post`. The difference between the two values lies in how form data are sent to a Web server, as well as the size limit on

Table 15.1   `<form>` tag—the master tag that encloses all other tags of a form.

Attributes: `<form name method action enctype accept-charset accept>`	
Attribute	Description
`name`	Specifies the form's name. This attribute is useful if we need to reference the form by name in a computer program that processes the form's input.
`method`	Specifies the method that the browser uses to send the form's data to the Web server. This attribute has two values: `get` and `post`. The former is the default. We recommend using `post` over `get`. `post` can send both ASCII and non-ASCII data, and it places no limit on the amount (number of bytes) of data it can send. Read more about the difference between `get` and `post` in the discussion following this table.
`action`	Specifies the name and location of the computer program that processes the form's data. When a Web surfer clicks the form's submit button, the browser encodes the form's data into name–value pairs and sends them according to the information provided by the `action` attribute. This attribute can specify a computer program, an e-mail address to which the form's data should be sent, or any other protocol, such as that for opening a file in which the data are to be placed.
`enctype`	Specifies the content type used to submit the form's data to the Web server. This attribute is used only with the `post` method. Its default value is `application/x-www-form-urlencoded`. If a Web author uses the value `file` for the `type` attribute of the `<input>` tag, the value of the `enctype` should be `multipart/form-data`.
`accept-charset`	Specifies the list of character codes for the input data that the Web server processing the form's data should accept. We seldom utilize-this attribute, and when we do, we let the browser use its default value.
`accept`	Specifies the content types that the Web server processing the form can handle correctly. Again, we seldom use this attribute, and when we do, we let the browser use its default value.

Table 15.2　　`<input>` tag—creates 10 form elements: text, checkbox, radio button, password element, submit button, reset button, hidden element, image, button, and file.

Attributes: `<input type name value size maxlength checked>`	
Attribute	**Description**
`type`	Specifies the type of form element to create. The values for this attribute are `text`, `checkbox`, `radio`, `password`, `submit`, `reset`, `hidden`, `image`, `button`, and `file`. The default value is `text`. This value creates text fields. It should be mentioned that the password element acts in the usual way, hiding the actual characters and replacing them by an echo character (such as an asterisk); however, it provides only minimal security protection. Applications that require higher levels of security should use additional (encryption) techniques.
`name`	Assigns a name to a form element. This name is used by the browser to create the name–value pairs before sending them to the Web server. The computer program that parses the pairs also uses these names.
`value`	Specifies the initial value of the form element. This value serves as the default value for the element. The value of this attribute takes on different meanings, depending on the form element with which is used. It is the initial text when it is used with a text field. It is the name of a checkbox when it is used with checkboxes. It is the name of the group of radio buttons when it is used with radio buttons. (Radio buttons do not work properly—that is, mutually exclusively—unless the same group name is used for all of them.) It is the label of the submit or reset button if it is used with either one.
`size`	Specifies the visible width of the text field, as shown in Figure 15.2. Its value is given as a number of characters.
`maxlength`	Specifies the maximum number of characters that the user can enter. The default value of this attribute is infinity.
`checked`	Used only with checkboxes and radio buttons. It is a Boolean attribute whose default value is `on`. When it is used in a form, the checkbox(es) or the radio button using it is displayed as being selected. It can be used more than once with checkboxes, but only once with radio buttons.
`src`	Used only with the image element. As in the `<img>` tag, it specifies the image's file name. This attribute can be used to create a decorated graphical submit button only. It cannot be used to create a decorated reset button. It is seldom used in practice.

the data. In the case of `get`, form data are sent in the environment variable `QUERY_STRING`. In the case of `post`, form data are sent through `STDIN` (standard input), from which the form's computer program should read. (The number of bytes to read is given by the `content-length` header.) In both cases, the `content type` is identical for both `get` and `post`. Refer to Chapter 18 for more details.

In practice, post is preferred over get. get can send only ASCII data and is limited to a size of 1 KB for both the URL the parameter's while post can send both ASCII and non-ASCII data and does not have a size limit.

If a form uses the get method, the browser extracts all the name–value pairs of the form, appends them to the URL specified by the action attribute, and sends the resulting string to the Web server. The URL is separated from all the name–value pairs by a question mark (?) that the browser adds, as required by the CGI protocol.

If a form uses the post methods, the browser sends the form's data set to the Web server, instead of appending it to the URL as a string as in the get method. Once the Web server has received a request from a form using the post method, it knows to continue "listening" for the rest of the information.

The get method is typically used when a form does not cause any changes or side effects, such as the searching of databases. If the form is expected to cause side effects, such as the modification of a database or subscription to a service, the post method should be used. The get method may run the risk of losing form data if the string of name–value pairs is too long. Some operating systems, such as Unix, have a limit on how long a single string can be. The Unix limit is 255 characters.

Table 15.3   <select> tag—creates a menu (also known as drop-down list or select list).

Attributes: <select name size multiple>	
Attribute	Description
name	Specifies the name of the select list. This attribute is useful if the Web page employs JavaScript in addition to XHTML.
size	Specifies the number of visible rows of the list on the computer screen. The default value of this attribute is one.
multiple	Allows multiple selections from the select list. The default is a single selection. The Web surfer must hold down the CTRL or SHIFT key on the keyboard and click the desired rows to achieve multiple selections.

Table 15.4   <option> tag—creates menu items for the <select> tag.

Attributes: <option selected value label>	
Attribute	Description
selected	Specifies whether the option is the preselected option of the menu. It is a Boolean attribute. If it is not specified for any of the options in a list, the default is the first option in the <select> tag.
value	Specifies the value of the menu item.
label	Allows Web authors to specify a shorter label for an item than its actual content.

Table 15.5   `<textarea>` tag—creates a text area.

Attributes: `<textarea name rows cols wrap>`

Attribute	Description
`name`	Specifies the name of the text area. This attribute is useful if the Web page employs JavaScript in addition to XHTML.
`rows`	Specifies the height of the text area as a number of lines of text, as shown in Figure 15.2. This attribute does not stop users of a text area from typing more lines of text than the value of `rows`.
`cols`	Specifies the width of the text area as a number of characters per line, as shown in Figure 15.2. Thus, the maximum number of characters a text area can hold is equal to `rows` × `cols`.
`wrap`	Specifies to the browser how to wrap the text typed in a text area. If this attribute is not used by Web authors, the text input continues on one line, scrolling to the right, until the user presses the `Enter` key on the keyboard to start a new line. The values of this attribute are `soft` and `hard`. The `hard` wrap forces a carriage return at the end of each line of text in the text area. The length of each line of text is equal to the value of the `cols` attribute of the text area. The `soft` wrap forces a new line of text without physically placing a carriage return at the end of each line of text. The choice of either value depends on the computer program written to process the name–value pairs of the form. If the `hard` value is used, the program must strip the carriage returns at the ends of the lines of text.

A menu provides Web surfers with many options from which to choose. Whenever the choices become too many, the use of checkboxes or radio buttons becomes impractical. The menu is the perfect alternative. The `<select>` tag by itself is useless; it does not create any list items. The `<option>` tag is always used inside it to create the list items.

The XHTML `<textarea>` element is used to input multiple lines of text. Text fields, on the other hand, allow the input of one line of text only. A text field is suitable for input such as names and phone numbers. In some cases, such as when soliciting the user's feedback, a multiline text input is usually needed, in a "free form." The `<textarea>` element serves this purpose. Text areas can be created with initial text or can be blank. If initial text is used, users who fill in the text area simply delete the initial text and replace it by their text input.

Example 15.1 Use text fields.

Develop a Web page that illustrates the use of text fields.

Solution 15.1 Using the AceHTML editor, generate the given code, and save it as `example151.html`. Render the Web page in a browser.

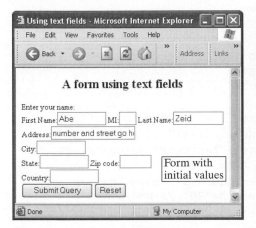
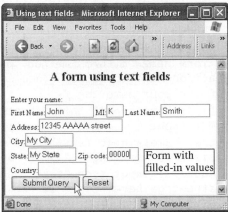

Code explained:

1. Line 11 creates a form with the name `myForm`. It uses the Mailto protocol.
2. Lines 13–15 create the first line of text fields shown in the screen capture.
3. Lines 16–20 respectively create the address, city, state, zip code, and country text fields.
4. Line 21 creates the form's submit button.
5. Line 22 creates the form's reset button.

Discussion:

This example creates a form that uses text fields, which are defined in lines 13–20. We use different attributes in each code line. Each text field has a name. You will not be able to appreciate the use of these names until you begin checking form input with JavaScript, as shown later in the book, or when you begin processing form input, as discussed in Chapter 18. Lines 13 and 15 use default values. The submit and reset buttons created in lines 21 and 22, respectively, use the XHTML default label names, as shown in the foregoing screen capture. When you click the submit button, the browser executes the `action` attribute used in code line 11; thus, it e-mails the form's input to `zeid@coe.neu.edu`.

Hands-on exercise:

Starting with the code given in this example, add three more text fields. Also, use `Send` and `Clear` as the labels of the submit and reset buttons, respectively.

```
1  <?xml version="1.0" encoding="iso-8859-1"?>
2  <!DOCTYPE html PUBLIC "-//W3C//DTD XHTML 1.1//EN"
3      "http://www.w3.org/TR/xhtml11/DTD/xhtml11.dtd">
4  <html xmlns="http://www.w3.org/1999/xhtml">
5  <!-- Generated by AceHTM http://freeware.acehtml.com -->
6  <head>
```

```
 7   <title>Using text fields</title>
 8   </head>
 9   <body>
10   <h2 align="center">A form using text fields</h2>
11   <form name="myForm" method="post"
     action="mailto:zeid@coe.neu.edu">
12   Enter your name:<br />
13   First Name:<input name="firstName" value="Abe" size="10" />
14   MI:<input type="text" name="middleInitial" size="1" />
15   Last Name:<input type="text" name="lastName" value="Zeid"
     size="10" maxlength="15" /><br />
16   Address:<input type="text" name="address" value="number and
     street go here" size="22" maxlength="30" /><br />
17   City:<input type="text" name="city" size="10"
     maxlength="15" /><br />
18   State:<input type="text" name="state" size="10"
     maxlength="15" />
19   Zip code:<input type="text" name="zipCode" size="5"
     maxlength="10" /><br />
20   Country:<input type="text" name="country" size="10"
     maxlength="15" /><br />
21   <input type="submit" name="submitButton" />
22   <input type="reset" name="resetButton" />
23   </form>
24   </body>
25   </html>
```

Example 15.2 Use checkboxes.

Develop a Web page that illustrates the use of checkboxes.

Solution 15.2 Using the AceHTML editor, generate the given code, and save it as
`example152.html`. Render the Web page in a browser.

Code explained:

Lines 11–13, 15–17, and 19–21 create checkboxes.

Discussion:

We create three groups of checkboxes. Their names are `food`, `sports`, and `books`. Each
group has three checkboxes. One of them is checked via `checked`. The label (name) of each
checkbox is not part of the `<input>` tag. It is text we add before (code lines 19–21) or after
(code lines 11–13 and 15–17) the checkbox's square. We use the ` ` (nonbreaking space)
element in lines 19 and 20 to align the three checkboxes vertically, as shown in the following
screen capture.

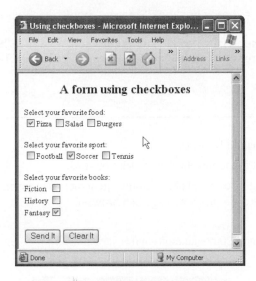

Hands-on exercise:

Starting with the code given in this example, add a group of four checkboxes. Call it `movies`. Also, set two checkboxes to be checked initially.

```
1   <?xml version="1.0" encoding="iso-8859-1"?>
2   <!DOCTYPE html PUBLIC "-//W3C//DTD XHTML 1.1//EN"
3       "http://www.w3.org/TR/xhtml11/DTD/xhtml11.dtd">
4   <html xmlns="http://www.w3.org/1999/xhtml">
5   <!-- Generated by AceHTM http://freeware.acehtml.com -->
6   <head><title>Using checkboxes</title>
7   </head><body>
8   <h2 align="center">A form using checkboxes</h2>
9   <form name="myForm" method="post"
    action="mailto:zeid@coe.neu.edu">
10  <div>Select your favorite food:</div>
11  <input type="checkbox" name="food" value="pizza" checked />
    Pizza
12  <input type="checkbox" name="food" value="salad" />Salad
13  <input type="checkbox" name="food" value="burgers" />
    Burgers<br /><p></p>
14  <div>Select your favorite sport:</div>
15  <input type="checkbox" name="sports" />Football
16  <input type="checkbox" name="sports" checked />Soccer
17  <input type="checkbox" name="sports" />Tennis<p></p>
18  <div>Select your favorite books:</div>
19  Fiction  <input type="checkbox" name="books" /><br />
20  History <input type="checkbox" name="books" /><br />
```

```
21   Fantasy<input type="checkbox" name="books" checked /><br />
     <p></p>
22   <input type="submit" name="submitButton" value="Send It" />
23   <input type="reset" name="resetButton" value="Clear It" />
24   </form>
25   </body></html>
```

Example 15.3 Use radio buttons.

Develop a Web page that illustrates the use of radio buttons.

Solution 15.3 Using the AceHTML editor, generate the given code, and save it as example153.html. Render the Web page in a browser.

Code explained:

Lines 10,11, 14–17, 19, and 20 create radio buttons.

Discussion:

We create three groups of radio buttons. Their names are gender, year, and gradSchool. The label (name) of each radio button is not part of the <input> tag. Adding it before or after the radio symbol is a design issue. We use labels for the submit and reset buttons via the value attribute (code lines 21 and 22).

Hands-on exercise:

Starting with the code given in this example, add a four-radio-button group. Call it gpa. Also, set one radio button to be selected initially.

```
1   <?xml version="1.0" encoding="iso-8859-1"?>
2   <!DOCTYPE html PUBLIC "-//W3C//DTD XHTML 1.1//EN"
3      "http://www.w3.org/TR/xhtml11/DTD/xhtml11.dtd">
```

```
4   <html xmlns="http://www.w3.org/1999/xhtml">
5   <!-- Generated by AceHTM http://freeware.acehtml.com -->
6   <head><title>Using checkboxes</title></head><body>
7   <h2 align="center">A form using radio buttons</h2>
8   <form name="myForm" method="post"
    action="mailto:zeid@coe.neu.edu">
9   <div>Check your gender:</div>
10  <input type="radio" name="gender" value="male" /> Male
11  <input type="radio" name="gender" value="female" />Female
12  <p></p>
13  <div>Check your current college year:</div>
14  <input type="radio" name="year" value="first" />Freshman
15  <input type="radio" name="year" value="second" />Sophomore
16  <input type="radio" name="year" value="third" />Junior
17  <input type="radio" name="year" value="fourth" />Senior<p></p>
18  <div>Do you plan to go to grad school?</div>
19  <input type="radio" name="gradSchool" value="go" />Yes
20  <input type="radio" name="gradSchool" value="nogo" />No<p></p>
21  <input type="submit" name="submitButton" value="Send" />
22  <input type="reset" name="resetButton" value="Erase" />
23  </form></body></html>
```

☞ ───

Example 15.4 Use images, passwords, and hidden fields.

Develop a Web page that illustrates the use of images, passwords, and hidden fields.

Solution 15.4 Using AceHTML editor, generate the code that follows, and save it as `example154.html`. Render the Web page in a browser.

Code explained:

  1. Line 9 creates a hidden field.
  2. Line 11 creates a password.
  3. Line 13 creates a button that uses an image stored in the file `submitButton.jpg`.

Discussion:

In this example, we use a hidden element (code line 9) to track the effectiveness of the e-mail marketing technique. The value of a hidden element could be anything of interest to us. The Web surfer never sees the hidden element, unless he or she views the page's source code. The example also uses a password field in code line 11. In addition, we use an image (code line 13), as a submit button. However, an image cannot be used as a reset button. All attributes of the `<img>` tag can be used with the image.

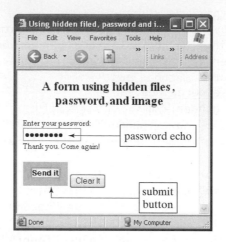

Hands-on exercise:

Change the `type` in code line 14 to `image`. What happens when you click the button?

```
1   <?xml version="1.0" encoding="iso-8859-1"?>
2   <!DOCTYPE html PUBLIC "-//W3C//DTD XHTML 1.1//EN"
3        "http://www.w3.org/TR/xhtml11/DTD/xhtml11.dtd">
4   <html xmlns="http://www.w3.org/1999/xhtml">
5   <!-- Generated by AceHTM http://freeware.acehtml.com -->
6   <head><title>Using hidden files, password, and image</title>
7   </head><body><h2 align="center">A form using hidden files,
    password, and image</h2>
8   <form name="myForm" method="post"
    action="mailto:zeid@coe.neu.edu">
9   <input type="hidden" name="tracking" value="e-mailMarketing" />
10  <div>Enter your password:</div>
11  <input type="password" name="pass" size="12" />
12  <div>Thank you. Come again!</div><p></p>
13  <input type="image" value="submit" src="submitButton.jpg"
    alt="Send It" />
14  <input type="reset" name="resetButton" value="Clear It" />
15  </form>
16  </body></html>
```

☞──

Example 15.5 Use files in a form.

Develop a Web page that illustrates the use of files in a form.

Solution 15.5 Using the AceHTML editor, generate the given code, and save it as `example155.html`. Render the Web page in a browser.

Code explained:

1. Line 11 uses the `enctype` attribute because a file is being sent with the form.
2. Line 13 creates a field in which a file name is specified.

Discussion:

In this example, we transfer a file with a form. We create a form element of type `file` in code line 13. The browser renders this element as a field, as shown in the foregoing screen capture, and places a `Browse` button next to it. The user clicks the button to browse local files in order to choose the right one to send with the form. We also must use the `enctype` attribute of the form tag, as shown in code line 11, to ensure that the file transfer occurs properly.

Hands-on exercise:

How can you send multiple files? Can you select multiple files via the `Browse` button? If not, add another button and try again.

```
1    <?xml version="1.0" encoding="iso-8859-1"?>
2    <!DOCTYPE html PUBLIC "-//W3C//DTD XHTML 1.1//EN"
3        "http://www.w3.org/TR/xhtml11/DTD/xhtml11.dtd">
4    <html xmlns="http://www.w3.org/1999/xhtml">
5    <!-- Generated by AceHTM http://freeware.acehtml.com -->
6    <head>
7    <title>Using files in a form</title>
8    </head>
9    <body>
10   <h2 align="center">A form using files</h2>
11   <form name="myForm" method="post"enctype="multipart/form-data"
     action="mailto:zeid@coe.neu.edu">
12   <div>Select the file you like to send with this form:</div>
```

```
13  <input type="file" name="myFile" size="32" />
14  <p></p>
15  <div>Thank you. Come again!</div><p></p>
16  <input type="submit" value="Send It" />
17  <input type="reset" value="Clear It" />
18  </form></body></html>
```

Example 15.6 Use buttons.

Develop a Web page that illustrates the use of buttons.

Solution 15.6 Using the AceHTML editor, generate the given code, and save it as `example156.html`. Render the Web page in a browser.

Code explained:

Lines 10–13 and 15–17 create buttons.

Discussion:

We create seven buttons in two groups: one group for the four seasons, and one group for office furniture. The browser adjusts each button's size to fit its label. A Web surfer clicks a button to make a selection. The buttons are dysfunctional in this example. To make them functional, we must add JavaScript code to handle their clicks. Each button click generates a unique event that can be handled in JavaScript, as covered later in the book. Without event handling, Web surfers cannot use the buttons.

Hands-on exercise:

Add one group of four buttons for selecting a car make: Toyota, Honda, Ford, or Jeep.

```
1  <?xml version="1.0" encoding="iso-8859-1"?>
2  <!DOCTYPE html PUBLIC "-//W3C//DTD XHTML 1.1//EN"
```

```
3        "http://www.w3.org/TR/xhtml11/DTD/xhtml11.dtd">
4   <html xmlns="http://www.w3.org/1999/xhtml">
5   <!-- Generated by AceHTM http://freeware.acehtml.com -->
6   <head><title>A form using buttons</title></head>
7   <body><h2 align="center">A form using buttons</h2>
8   <form name="myForm" method="post"
    action="mailto:zeid@coe.neu.edu">
9   <div>Select your favorite season:</div>
10  <input type="button" name="button1" value="Fall" />
11  <input type="button" name="button2" value="Winter" />
12  <input type="button" name="button3" value="Spring" />
13  <input type="button" name="button4" value="Summer" /><p></p>
14  <div>Select the furniture you need for your office:</div>
15  <input type="button" name="button5" value="Desks" />
16  <input type="button" name="button6" value="Chairs" />
17  <input type="button" name="button7" value="Book Cases"/><p></p>
18  <div>Thank you. Come again!</div>
19  <input type="submit" value="Send It" />
20  <input type="reset" value="Clear It" />
21  </form></body></html>
```

☞

Example 15.7 Use menus.

Develop a Web page that illustrates the use of drop-down lists.

Solution 15.7 Using the AceHTML editor, generate the given code, and save it as `example157.html`. Render the Web page in a browser.

Code explained:

Lines 10–16 create a menu with the for multiple selection (line 10).

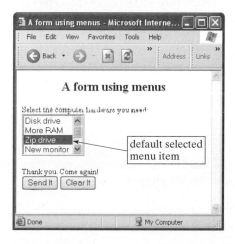

Discussion:

We create a menu with six items. The foregoing screen capture shows the menu. The default selected menu item is shown highlighted. The browser does its best to render the menu if we do not use the `size` attribute of the `<select>` tag. The size of the menu affects the amount of Web-page space allocated to the menu. We use `size="1"` for very long menus, such as for months of the year or U.S. states. The one initially visible menu item tells the Web surfer what to do—e.g., `Select a month`.

Hands-on exercise:

Create a four-item menu of software programs that allows single selection only, uses no default, and has a size of one. The displayed item should read `Select software`.

```
1   <?xml version="1.0" encoding="iso-8859-1"?>
2   <!DOCTYPE html PUBLIC "-//W3C//DTD XHTML 1.1//EN"
3       "http://www.w3.org/TR/xhtml11/DTD/xhtml11.dtd">
4   <html xmlns="http://www.w3.org/1999/xhtml">
5   <!-- Generated by AceHTM http://freeware.acehtml.com -->
6   <head><title>A form using menus</title></head>
7   <body><h2 align="center">A form using menus</h2>
8   <form name="myForm" method="post"
        action="mailto:zeid@coe.neu.edu">
9   <div>Select the computer hardware you need:</div>
10  <select name="compHardware" multiple>
11  <option>Disk drive</option>
12  <option>More RAM</option>
13  <option selected>Zip drive</option>
14  <option>New monitor</option>
15  <option>Faster printer</option>
16  <option>New mouse</option></select><p></p>
17  <div>Thank you. Come again!</div>
18  <input type="submit" value="Send It" />
19  <input type="reset" value="Clear It" /></form></body></html>
```

Example 15.8 Use a text area.

Develop a Web page that illustrates the use of text areas.

Solution 15.8 Using the AceHTML editor, generate the given code, and save it as `example158.html`. Render the Web page in a browser.

Code explained:

Lines 11–13 create a text area that holds $7 \times 35 = 245$ characters.

Discussion:

We create a text area that has seven rows and 35 columns. The text area is seeded with instructions to users of the Web page on sending their feedback. A user needs to highlight this initial text, delete it, and type the feedback text. The soft wrap stops the length of each row at 35 characters, after which it forces text wrapping. Without this attribute, the feedback becomes one very long line of text.

Hands-on exercise:

Remove the wrap attribute, and render the page. Type some feedback text that is at least 40 characters long. What do you see? Also try using the hard wrap instead of the soft one. Do you see a difference? Where does the difference show up?

```
1   <?xml version="1.0" encoding="iso-8859-1"?>
2   <!DOCTYPE html PUBLIC "-//W3C//DTD XHTML 1.1//EN"
3       "http://www.w3.org/TR/xhtml11/DTD/xhtml11.dtd">
4   <html xmlns="http://www.w3.org/1999/xhtml">
5   <!-- Generated by AceHTM http://freeware.acehtml.com -->
6   <head><title>A form using text areas</title></head>
7   <body>
8   <h2 align="center">A form using text areas</h2>
9   <form name="myForm" method="post"
    action="mailto:zeid@coe.neu.edu">
10  <div>We love to hear from you:</div>
11  <textarea name="myTextArea" rows="7" cols="35" wrap="soft">
12  Please input up to 7 lines of text as your feedback and
    comments. Any additional lines beyond the first ten are
    ignored by our database. Thank you for your cooperation!
13  </textarea><p></p>
14  <div>Thank you. Come again!</div>
15  <input type="submit" value="Send It" />
16  <input type="reset" value="Clear It" />
17  </form></body></html>
```

15.6 Formatting Forms

A typical form has multiple elements that should be organized to make it easier for Web surfers to recognize the elements and fill them in. We used some   elements in Example 15.2 to align some checkboxes.

Tables and layers are typically used to format forms, control their layout, and space their elements out in a quest for the most attractive layout. If a table is used, the table encompasses the form, and the form elements occupy cells. Some cells can be empty, while others can span multiple rows and columns. The <table> tag encloses the <form> tag. The use of tables to format forms require advance planning of the table design and layout to accommodate the form.

If using layers to format forms, we have more flexibility, as we are no longer restricted by rigid row and cell structure of tables. We place a form element in a layer and position it where we want. We can nest layers in order to control the relative locations of the form elements to each other.

Example 15.9 Use tables to format forms.

Develop a Web page that uses a table-formatted form.

Solution 15.9 Using the AceHTML editor, generate the given code, and save it as example159.html. Render the Web page in a browser.

Code explained:

Lines 9–36 create the table that formats the form. It has 11 rows, each with six cells.

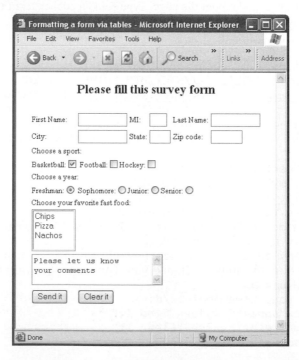

Discussion:

The common theme in formatting a form via a table is that each form element is a data cell. Begin by enclosing each form element tag in a `<td>` tag. Use a browser to display the form. If some form element wraps around even though there is still enough space left on a line, use the `colspan` attribute of the `<td>` tag. As a common rule, a group of checkboxes or radio buttons can fit on one line if their enclosing `<td>` tag has a large `colspan` value.

Hands-on exercise:

Redo this example with a different formatting scheme.

```
1   <?xml version="1.0" encoding="iso-8859-1"?>
2   <!DOCTYPE html PUBLIC "-//W3C//DTD XHTML 1.1//EN"
3       "http://www.w3.org/TR/xhtml11/DTD/xhtml11.dtd">
4   <html xmlns="http://www.w3.org/1999/xhtml">
5   <!-- Generated by AceHTM http://freeware.acehtml.com -->
6   <head><title>Formatting a form via tables</title>
7   </head>
8   <body>
9   <table align="center">
10  <caption><h2 align="center">Please fill this survey
    form</h2></caption>
11  <form name="myForm" method="post"
    action="mailto:zeid@coe.neu.edu">
12  <tr>
13  <td>First Name:</td><td><input type="text" name="first"
    size="10" maxlength="15"></td>
14  <td>MI:</td><td><input type="text" name= "mi" size="1"></td>
15  <td>Last Name:</td><td><input type="text" name="last"
    size="10" maxlength="18"></td>
16  </tr><tr>
17  <td>City:</td><td><input type="text" name="city" size="10"
    maxlength="13"></td>
18  <td>State:</td><td><input type="text" name="state" size="2">
    </td>
19  <td>Zip code:</td><td><input type="text" name="code" size="5">
    </td></tr><tr>
20  <td colspan="2">Choose a sport:</td>
21  </tr><tr>
22  <td colspan="4">Basketball:<input type="checkbox" checked>
    Football:<input type="checkbox">Hockey:<input type="checkbox">
    </td></tr><tr>
23  <td colspan="2">Choose a year:</td>
24  </tr><tr>
25  <td colspan="6">Freshman:<input type="radio" name="year"
    checked> Sophomore:<input type="radio">Junior:<input type=
    "radio" name="year">Senior:<input type="radio" name="year">
    </td></tr><tr>
```

```
26  <td colspan="3">Choose your favorite fast food:</td>
27  </tr><tr>
28  <td><select multiple> <option>Chips</option><option>Pizza
    </option><option>Nachos</option></select></td>
29  </tr><tr>
30  <td colspan="5">
31  <textarea rows="3" cols="25" wrap="soft">Please let us know
32  your comments</textarea></td>
33  </tr><tr></tr><tr>
34  <td><input type="submit" value="Send it"></td>
35  <td><input type="reset" value="Clear it"></td></tr>
36  </form></table></body></html>
```

Example 15.10 Use layers to forms.

Develop a Web page that uses a layer-formatted form.

Solution 15.10 Using the AceHTML editor, generate the given code, and save it as example1510.html. Render the Web page in a browser.

Code explained:

1. Lines 12–18 create six layers for the names.
2. Lines 19–27 create six layers for the address.
3. Lines 28–38 create an outer layer that encloses the layers for the rest of the form.

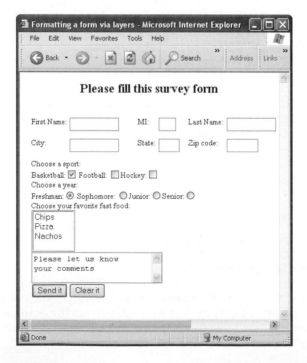

Discussion:

This example uses layers to format the form in Example 15.9. The common theme in formatting a form via layers is that each form element is placed in a layer. Begin by placing each form element tag in a <div> tag. If some form elements overlap, adjust their left and top coordinates. We format the names with six separate layers, as shown in code lines 12–18. We also formatted the address with six separate layers, as shown in code lines 19–27. We then use a layer that opens in code line 28 and closes in line 38 to format the rest of the form. Inside this layer, we enclose five layers in lines 28, 30, 32, 33, and 35. We use an empty layer in line 33 to space out the submit and reset buttons.

Hands-on exercise:

Redo this example with a different formatting scheme. Study the coordinates of the layers given in the example first.

```
1   <?xml version="1.0" encoding="iso-8859-1"?>
2   <!DOCTYPE html PUBLIC "-//W3C//DTD XHTML 1.1//EN"
3       "http://www.w3.org/TR/xhtml11/DTD/xhtml11.dtd">
4   <html xmlns="http://www.w3.org/1999/xhtml">
5   <!-- Generated by AceHTM http://freeware.acehtml.com -->
6   <head><title>Formatting a form via layers</title>
7   </head>
8   <body>
9   <div>
10  <form name="myForm" method="post"
    action="mailto:zeid@coe.neu.edu">
11  <div style="position:absolute; left:20px; top:75px;
    width:400px; height:200px">First Name:</div>
12  <div style="position:absolute; left:85px; top:75px;
    width:300px; height:200px"><input type="text"
    name="first"size="10" maxlength="15"></div>
13  <div style="position:absolute; left:200px; top:75px;
    width:300px; height:200px">MI:</div>
14  <div style="position:absolute; left:235px; top:75px;
    width:300px; height:200px">
15  <input type="text" name= "mi" size="1"></div>
16  <div style="position:absolute; left:285px; top:75px;
    width:300px; height:200px">Last Name:</div>
17  <div style="position:absolute; left:350px; top:75px;
    width:300px; height:200px">
18  <input type="text" name="last" size="10" maxlength="18"></div>
19  <div style="position:absolute; left:20px; top:110px;
    width:300px; height:200px">City:</div>
20  <div style="position:absolute; left:85px; top:110px;
    width:300px; height:200px">
21  <input type="text" name="city" size="10" maxlength="13"></div>
22  <div style="position:absolute; left:200px; top:110px;
    width:300px; height:200px">State:</div>
```

```
23   <div style="position:absolute; left:235px; top:110px;
     width:300px; height:200px">
24   <input type="text" name="state" size="2"></div>
25   <div style="position:absolute; left:285px; top:110px;
     width:300px; height:200px">Zip code:</div>
26   <div style="position:absolute; left:350px; top:110px;
     width:300px; height:200px">
27   <input type="text" name="code" size="5"></div></div>
28   <div style="position:absolute; left:20px; top:145px;
     width:300px; height:200px"><div>Choose a sport:</div>
29   Basketball:<input type="checkbox" checked> Football:
     <input type="checkbox">Hockey:<input type="checkbox">
30   <div>Choose a year:</div>
31   Freshman:<input type="radio" name="year" checked> Sophomore:
     <input type="radio">Junior:<input type="radio"
     name="year">Senior:<input type="radio" name="year">
32   <div>Choose your favorite fast food:</div><select multiple>
33   <option>Chips</option><option>Pizza
     </option><option>Nachos</option></select><div></div>
34   <textarea rows="3" cols="25" wrap="soft">Please let us know
35   your comments</textarea><div>
36   <input type="submit" value="Send it">
37   <input type="reset" value="Clear it"></div>
38   </form></div></body></html>
```

15.7 Tutorials

15.7.1 Performing E-Commerce (Study Section 15.5)

The most popular use of a form is for ordering products online. Web surfers find order forms in almost every website they visit. In this tutorial, we create an order form for buying bikes. The form uses many of the form elements. Using the AceHTML editor, generate the given code, and save it as `tutorial1571.html`. Render the Web page in a browser.

Code explained:

1. Line 8 starts the form, and line 39 closes it.
2. Lines 10–12 create three radio buttons.
3. Lines 14–16 create three checkboxes.
4. Lines 18–23 create a select list.
5. Lines 25–30 create text fields.
6. Line 32 creates a text area.
7. Lines 35 and 36 create text fields.
8. Lines 37 and 38 create the form's submit and reset buttons, respectively.
9. Some lines use the <p> and <div> tag to space out the form elements and force new lines.

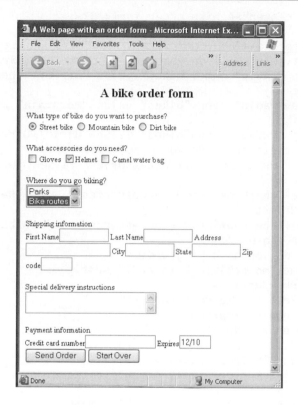

Discussion:

The `<form>` tag uses the HTTP protocol in its `action` attribute. When the Web surfer submits the form, the encoded name–value pairs are sent to the server `aaa.bbb.ccc`, where the CGI script `bikeOrder` processes them. The server has a directory called `cgi-bin`. It is quite common to find a directory with this name on Web servers. The select list shows two items, because we use the `size="2"` attribute in the `<select>` tag. The default selected item is shown highlighted. The Web surfer can scroll the list up and down to read its items. The Web server of this form must establish a secure connection with the client computer using this form in order to ensure that the credit card information of the customer is protected.

Hands-on exercise:

Redo this tutorial to format the form's `shipping information` text fields with layers.

```
1    <?xml version="1.0" encoding="iso-8859-1"?>
2    <!DOCTYPE html PUBLIC "-//W3C//DTD XHTML 1.1//EN"
3        "http://www.w3.org/TR/xhtml11/DTD/xhtml11.dtd">
4    <html xmlns="http://www.w3.org/1999/xhtml">
5    <!-- Generated by AceHTM http://freeware.acehtml.com -->
6    <head><title>A Web page with an order form</title></head><body>
```

```
 7    <h2 align="center">A bike order form</h2>
 8    <form name="myForm" method="post"
      action="http://aaa.bbb.ccc/cgi-bin/bikecgi/bikeOrder">
 9    <div>What type of bike do you want to purchase?</div>
10    <input type="radio" name="bikes" value="street" checked />
      Street bike
11    <input type="radio" name="bikes" value="mountain" />
      Mountain bike
12    <input type="radio" name="bikes" value="dirt"/>Dirt bike<p></p>
13    </div>What accessories do you need?</div>
14    <input type="checkbox" name="accessories" value="gloves" />
      Gloves
15    <input type="checkbox" name="accessories" value="helmet"
      checked />Helmet
16    <input type="checkbox" name="accessories" value="bag" />
      Camel water bag<p></p>
17    <div>Where do you go biking?</div>
18    <select name="mountBiking" size="2" multiple>
19    <option>Parks</option>
20    <option selected>Bike routes</option>
21    <option>Mountains</option>
22    <option>Races</option>
23    <option>Streets</option></select><p></p>
24    <div>Shipping information</div>
25    First Name<input type="text" name="firstName" size="10"
      maxlength="13" />
26    Last Name<input type="text" name="lastName" size="10"
      maxlength="15" />
27    Address <input type="text" name="address" size="20" />
28    City<input type="text" name="city" size="10" />
29    State<input type="text" name="state" size="10" />
30    Zip code<input type="text" name="zipCode" size="5" /><p></p>
31    <div>Special delivery instructions</div>
32    <textarea name="myTextArea" rows="2" cols="25" wrap="soft">
33    </textarea><p></p>
34    <div>Payment information</div>
35    Credit card number<input type="text" name="cardNumber"
      size="16" />
36    Expires<input type="text" name="expires" value="12/10"
      size="5" /><p></p>
37    <input type="submit" name="submitButton" value="Send Order" />
38    <input type="reset" name="resetButton" value="Start Over" />
39    </form></body></html>
```

15.7.2   Guest and Alumni Books (Study Section 15.5)

Some websites use forms to create what is known as guest and alumni books. For example, a university may create a form to collect information about its alumni in order to keep up with them.

The form uses a computer program that creates a database of alumni information from form entries. The university can use the database for mailing event letters, newsletters, and so forth. Use the AceHTML editor to generate the given code, and save it as `tutorial1572.html`. View the Web page in a browser.

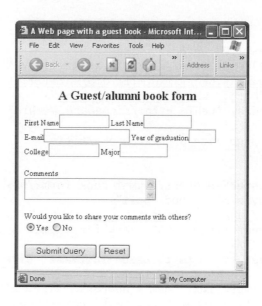

Code explained:

1. Line 11 begins the form, and line 31 ends it.
2. Lines 12 and 13 create the name text fields. They both use a size of 10 characters for the fields.
3. Line 14 acts a line break.
4. Line 15 create the e-mail address text field, which is 20 characters long.
5. Line 16 uses 4 characters for the year of graduation.
6. Line 17 acts as a line break.
7. Lines 18 and 19 use 10 characters for their text fields.
8. Line 20 acts as a spacer.
9. Line 21 uses the `<div>` tag as a line break.
10. Lines 22 and 23 create a text area that has two rows and 25 columns. It uses a soft wrap.
11. Line 25 uses the `<div>` tag as a line break.
12. Lines 26 and 27 create two radio buttons that belong to a group with the name `share`.
13. Line 28 acts a spacer.
14. Lines 29 and 30 create the form's submit and reset buttons, respectively.

Discussion:

This tutorial uses a form with text fields, a text area, and radio buttons. The form must have a submit button in order to function properly. Clicking this button triggers the execution of the `action` attribute in line 11.

Hands-on exercise:

Redo this tutorial to format the form's text fields via layers.

```
1    <?xml version="1.0" encoding="iso-8859-1"?>
2    <!DOCTYPE html PUBLIC "-//W3C//DTD XHTML 1.1//EN"
3        "http://www.w3.org/TR/xhtml11/DTD/xhtml11.dtd">
4    <html xmlns="http://www.w3.org/1999/xhtml">
5    <!-- Generated by AceHTM http://freeware.acehtml.com -->
6    <head>
7    <title>A Web page with a guest book</title>
8    </head>
9    <body>
10   <h2 align="center">A Guest/alumni book form</h2>
11   <form name="myForm" method="post"
     action="http://aaa.bbb.ccc/cgi-bin/guestbook">
12   First Name<input type="text" name="firstName" size="10"
     maxlength="13" />
13   Last Name<input type="text" name="lastName" size="10" />
14   <div></div>
15   E-mail<input type="text" name="address" size="20" />
16   Year of graduation<input type="text" name= "year" size="4" />
17   <div></div>
18   College<input type="text" name="college" size="10" />
19   Major<input type="text" name="major" size="10" />
20   <p></p>
21   <div>Comments</div>
22   <textarea name="myTextArea" rows="2" cols="25" wrap="soft">
23   </textarea>
24   <p></p>
25   <div>Would you like to share your comments with others?</div>
26   <input type="radio" name="share" vlaue="yes" checked>Yes
27   <input type="radio" name="share" value="no">No
28   <p></p>
29   <input type="submit" name="submitButton" value="Send Entry" />
30   <input type="reset" name="resetButton" value="Clear Form"
31   </form>
32   </body>
33   </html>
```

15.7.3 Customer Survey (Study Section 15.5)

This tutorial shows how we can use a form for an online customer survey. It is advisable to keep such survey forms short, to encourage Web surfers to fill them out. Use the AceHTML editor to generate the given code, and save it as `tutorial1573.html`. View the Web page in a browser.

Code explained:

1. Line 11 begins the form, and line 48 ends it.
2. Lines 13–34 create radio buttons.
3. Lines 37–40 create checkboxes, and lines 43 and 44 create a text area.

Discussion:

This tutorial uses a form with radio buttons, checkboxes, and a text area. The form must have a submit button in order to function properly. Clicking this button triggers the execution of the `action` attribute in line 11.

Hands-on exercise:

Add a section to the survey that collects personal information such as name and address.

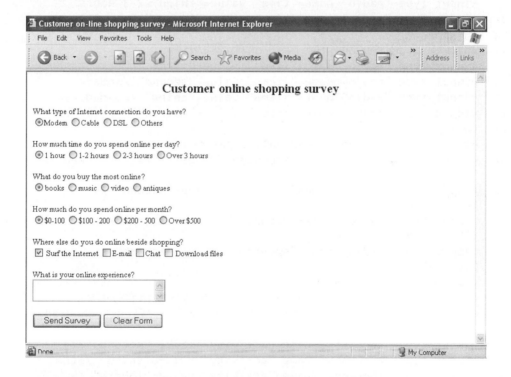

```
1   <?xml version="1.0" encoding="iso-8859-1"?>
2   <!DOCTYPE html PUBLIC "-//W3C//DTD XHTML 1.1//EN"
3       "http://www.w3.org/TR/xhtml11/DTD/xhtml11.dtd">
4   <html xmlns="http://www.w3.org/1999/xhtml">
5   <!-- Generated by AceHTM http://freeware.acehtml.com -->
```

```
6    <head>
7    <title>Customer online shopping survey</title>
8    </head>
9    <body>
10   <h2 align="center">Customer online shopping survey</h2>
11   <form name="myForm" method="post"
     action="http://aaa.bbb.ccc/cgi-bin/guestbook">
12   <div>What type of Internet connection do you have?</div>
13   <input type="radio" name="connect" value="one" checked />Modem
14   <input type="radio" name="connect" value="two" />Cable
15   <input type="radio" name="connect" value="three" />DSL
16   <input type="radio" name="connect" value="two" />Others
17   <p></p>
18   <div>How much time do you spend online per day?</div>
19   <input type="radio" name="time" value="first" CHECKED>1 hour
20   <input type="radio" name="time" value="second">1-2 hours
21   <input type="radio" name="time" value="third">2-3 hours
22   <input type="radio" name="time" value="fourth">Over 3 hours
23   <p></p>
24   <div>What do you buy the most online?</div>
25   <input type="radio" name="items" value="first" checked />books
26   <input type="radio" name="items" value="second" />music
27   <input type="radio" name="items" value="third" />video
28   <input type="radio" name="items" value="fourth" />antiques
29   <p></p>
30   <div>How much do you spend online per month?</div>
31   <input type="radio" name="spending" value="first" checked />
     $0-100
32   <input type="radio" name="spending" value="second" />
     $100 - 200
33   <input type="radio" name="spending" value="third" />
     $200 - 500
34   <input type="radio" name="spending" value="fourth" />
     Over $500
35   <p></p>
36   <div>Where else do you do online beside shopping?</div>
37   <input type="checkbox" name="activity" value="first" checked />
     Surf the Internet
38   <input type="checkbox" name="activity" value="second" />E-mail
39   <input type="checkbox" name="activity" value="third" />Chat
40   <input type="checkbox" name="activity" value="fourth" />
     Download files
41   <p></p>
42   <div>What is your online experience?</div>
43   <textarea name="myTextArea" rows="2" cols="25" wrap="soft">
44   </textarea>
```

```
45   <p></p>
46   <input type="submit" name="submitButton" value="Send Survey"/>
47   <input type="reset" name="resetButton" value="Clear Form" />
48   </form>
49   </body>
50   </html>
```

FAQs

Introduction (Section 15.1)

Q: What is an XHTML form?

A: An XHTML form is simply a Web-page element with special HTML tags that instruct Web browsers about how to display the various elements, such as text fields, radio buttons, and checkboxes.

Layout and Design (Section 15.4)

Q: In the `action` attribute of a form, I used the Mailto protocol to send the form's name–value pairs to myself. However, when I clicked the submit button on the form, the browser opened an e-mail composition window instead of e-mailing the pairs. What is the problem? How can I fix it?

A: The problem is that you forgot to use the `method` attribute of the `<form>` tag. In such a case, the browser does not know how to send the information, and it instead opens the e-mail composition window. When you add the `method` attribute, the form's submission works fine. Thus, the syntax should look like this:

```
<form action="mailto:zeid@coe.neu.edu" method="post">
```

Q: Can I use more than one submit button in my form?

A: Yes, you can. However, it is not advisable to do so, as you may confuse the users of your Web page.

Q: What are the risks of including forms in Web pages?

A: We can identify four potential problems. First, Web pages with forms can bog down the Web server by draining its computational power and memory resources. Second, the processing computer program can pose security problems to the website if the program has undiscovered flaws in it. Third, forms are confusing to create. Fourth, formatting forms via tables and layers is a challenge, even when using an HTML editor.

Using Forms (Section 15.5)

Q: What are the types of buttons that XHTML can create?

A: XHTML allows the creation of three types of buttons: submit, reset, and push. The submit and reset buttons are always used with forms. The push buttons are typically used in Web pages that employ JavaScript to process their clicks. Clicking push buttons does not cause any name–value pairs to be generated; thus, the processing program has no way of telling which push button the user clicks. However, the clicks can be handled via what are called event handlers in JavaScript.

Q: What is a good example of the use of a hidden element in a form?

A: Hidden elements are a way of passing information to a Web server. The information is usually not relevant to the Web surfer who fills out the form. However, it is not a secret either, because the surfer can view the page's source code and thereby see hidden elements. The processing computer program decodes the hidden information and then takes relevant actions. Let us assume that we need to send an e-mail message to thank a Web surfer who fills in a form. We use the following hidden elements:

```
<input type="hidden" name= "SendTo" value="zeid@coe.neu.edu" />
<input type="hidden" name= "Subject" value="Thank you for your
    time" />
<input type="hidden" name="Message" value="http://www.neu.edu/
    thankYou.html" />
```

The computer program can decode the three name–value pairs that correspond to these three hidden fields and send an automatic e-mail message to the foregoing e-mail address, with the foregoing subject and with the body defined in the `thankYou.html` file.

Blackbox

Section 15.1 (Introduction): Many online activities require the use of forms. Forms that request personal information use secure Internet connections. Form data are encoded into name–value pairs before they are sent to a Web server for processing.

Section 15.2 (Structure and Communication): A form has two distinct parts: the front end and the back end. The front end is the form itself, and the back end is the computer program that processes the form's data and input. When a user fills in a form and clicks the submit button, the browser sends the name–value pairs to the server. The computer program processes the input and sends a response back to the user.

Section 15.3 (Elements): The elements of a form are text fields, radio buttons, buttons, checkboxes, menus, text areas, submit buttons, and reset buttons.

Section 15.4 (Layout and Design): Each form must have a submit button and should have a reset button, must have an `action` attribute, and must have a `method` attribute. Keep forms simple, short, and easy to follow.

Section 15.5 (Using Forms) (Examples 15.1–15.8): XHTML provides the `<form>`, `<input>`, `<select>`, `<option>`, and `<textarea>` tags to define forms and elements. The attributes of these tags are `<form name method action enctype accept-charset accept>`, `<input type name value size maxlength checked>`, `<select name size multiple>`, `<option selected value label>`, and `<textarea name rows cols wrap>`, respectively.

Section 15.6 (Formatting Forms) (Examples 15.9 and 15.10): Both layers and tables can be used to control layouts and designs of forms. Layers have the advantages of being simpler to use and less restrictive.

Section 15.7 (Tutorials): Three tutorials show how to use forms.

Quick reference for the tags presented in this chapter

Tag	Close	Attribute	Value	Effect	Example
`<form>`	yes	`name`	text	form name	`<form name="abc">`
		`method`	`get`	encode form data	`<form method="get">`
			`post`	encode form data	`<form method="post">`
		`action`	text	sends name–value pairs	`<form action="program">`
		`enctype`	text	content type in which to send the form's data to the server	`<form enctype="multi-part/form-data">`
		`accept-charset`	text	character encoding	`<form accept-charset="set goes here">`
		`accept`	text	content type	`<form accept="type here">`
`<input>`	empty	`type`	`text`	create text element	`<input type="text">`
			`check-box`	create checkbox	`<input type="checkbox">`
			`radio`	create radio button	`<input type="radio">`
			`pass-word`	create password element	`<input type="password">`
			`submit`	create submit button	`<input type="submit">`
			`reset`	create reset button	`<input type="reset">`
			`hidden`	create hidden element	`<input type="hidden">`
			`button`	create push button	`<input type="button">`
		`name`	text	element name	`<input name="abc">`

Tag	Close	Attribute	Value	Effect	Example
		`value`	text	element value	`<input value="abc">`
		`size`	number	size of the text field	`<input size="5">`
		`max-length`	number	maximum size of text field	`<input max-length="10">`
		`checked`	Boolean	set state of a check-box or radio button	`<input checked>`
`<select>`	yes	`name`	text	menu name	`<select name="abc">`
		`size`	number	number of menu elements displayed at one time	`<select size="5">`
		`multiple`	Boolean	allows multiple selection	`<select multiple>`
`<option>`	yes	`selected`	Boolean	default selection	`<option selected>`
		`value`	text	element name	`<option value="abc">`
		`label`	text	element label	`<option label="abc">`
`<tex-tarea>`	yes	`name`	text	name of the text area	`<textarea name="abc">`
		`rows`	number	width of the text area	`<textarea rows="5">`
		`cols`	number	height of the text area	`<textarea cols="20">`
		`wrap`	`soft`	no carriage return added	`<textarea wrap="soft">`
			`hard`	carriage return added	`<textarea wrap="hard">`

Check Your Progress

At the end of this chapter, you should

- ✔ understand the use of forms (Section 15.1);
- ✔ understand form structure and processing (Section 15.2);
- ✔ know the form elements (Section 15.3);

✔ understand form layout and design (Section 15.4);
✔ have mastered the use of forms (Section 15.5);
✔ have mastered the formatting of forms (Section 15.6);
✔ have practiced the use of forms (Section 15.7).

Problems

The exercises are designed for a lab setting, while the homework is to be done outside class time.

Exercises

15.1 Combine Examples 15.1 and 15.2 to create a book order form.

15.2 Combine Examples 15.1 and 15.3 to create a college survey form that collects information such as student gender, year and graduation plans.

15.3 Write the XHTML code to generate the pizza order form shown in the corresponding screen capture.

15.4 Write the XHTML code to generate the bug report form shown in the corresponding screen capture.

15.5 Write the XHTML code to generate the evaluation form shown in the corresponding screen capture. The items for the select list shown in the figure are `Doctorate`, `Master`, `Bachelor`, `High school`, and `None of the above`.

Homework

In Problems 15.6–15.12, write an XHTML document and save it in an HTML file.

15.6 Write a Web page to create a survey form about the stocks the user owns.

15.7 Write a Web page to create a car service form. The form should help a mechanic to take an order from a customer to service a car.

15.8 Users of databases may have to use Structured Query Language (SQL) in order to query the databases. They use SQL commands to receive results from the database. Many applications develop very easy-to-use GUIs that novice customers can use in order to shield them from using SQL. Write a Web page to create a bank-database query form. The form can request such data as customer information (name, address, account number, etc.), deposits, withdrawals, and balances.

15.9 Write the XHTML code to generate the college survey form shown in the corresponding screen capture.

15.10 Write the XHTML code to generate the file access form shown in the corresponding screen capture.

15.11 Write the XHTML code to generate the survey shown in the corresponding screen capture.

15.12 Write the XHTML code to generate the dog adoption form shown in the corresponding screen capture. The two select lists allow multiple selections. The list of available breeds has the items shown, plus the following ones: `Golden Retriever`, `Wire-haired Fox Terrier`, `Malamute`, `Dalmatian`, `Pug`, `Mixed breed (large)`, and `Mixed breed (small)`. The list for dog age has the items shown, plus the following ones: `1 to 2 years`, `3 to 4 years`, `5 to 6 years`, `7 to 8 years`, and `over 8 years`.

15.13 Write the XHTML code to generate the pizza order form shown in the corresponding screen capture. Use tables to format the form as shown.

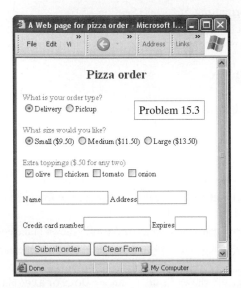

Problem 15.3

Problem 15.4

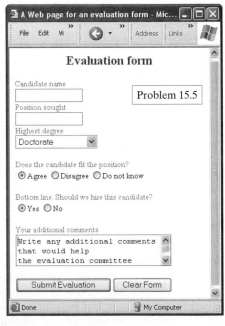

Problem 15.5

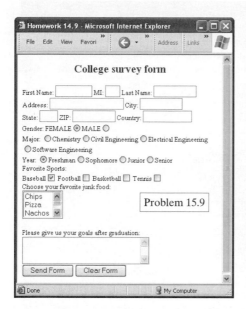

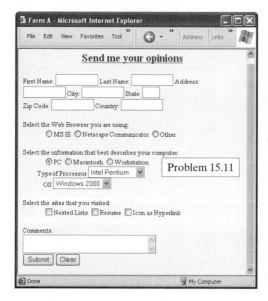

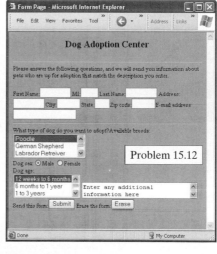

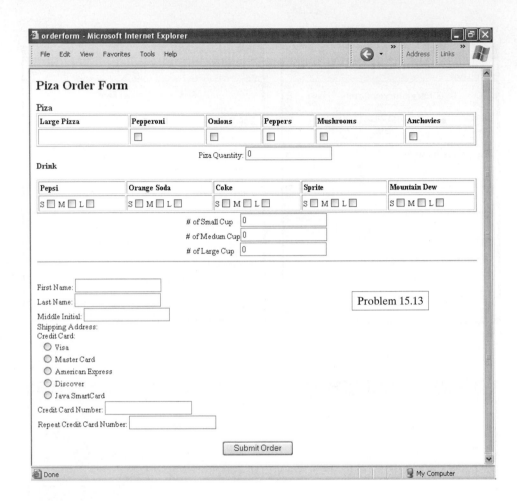

Cascading Style Sheets

Goal

Understand CSS; their syntax, properties, and use in formatting Web pages and controlling content location in Web pages; how style sheets cascade; and how they inherit from each other.

Objectives

- Separation of Web page content and formatting
- CSS syntax
- Linking CSS and XHTML
- Inheritance and cascading order
- The box model
- Font properties
- Text properties
- Content positioning

Outline

16.1 Introduction

A closer look at many Web page's shows that their content is formatted via XHTML tags. When we mix both content and formatting together, it becomes difficult to edit and change the content. Keeping the two parts separate provides Web authors with more freedom and control over each part.

Cascading style sheets (CSS) is a language for describing the rendering of XHTML and XML documents on screen, on paper, in speech, on printers, and on other devices (e.g., handhelds). The CSS concept separates content from presentation. It allows Web authors to create content first and format it later. Consider the following example of the deprecated `<font>` tag:

```
<font face="arial" size="3" color="#FF0000">Formatted text</font>
```

The browser displays `Formatted text` in size-2, red Arial font. The content here is the text itself, and the presentation (formatting) is the `<font>` tag. CSS allows us to define a text style separately as follows:

```
body {font-family: arial; font-size: 12pt; color:#FF0000}
```

We can apply this style to any text in Web page, as shown later in this chapter. The separation of content and presentation makes it easy to change the content and helps create a consistent look and feel throughout a website, making site maintenance much easier.

CSS is easy to use. Its syntax is also easy to learn. However, the concept itself is powerful. CSS has been extended to XML. The main premise behind XML is the separation of content and presentation. XML provides XSL (eXtensible Style Sheets) and XSLT (XSL Transformations). XSL is to XML as CSS is to XHTML. Simply put, XSL is CSS written in XML syntax. XML documents use XSL for formatting, just as XHTML documents use CSS. Actually, XML documents can use either XSL or CSS for formatting. XSLT is a language that is used to transform one XML document into other XML documents; that is, XSLT changes the formatting of XML documents from one style to another.

CSS has gone through three major revisions, known as levels: CSS1, CSS2, and CSS3. The CSS1 (Cascading Style Sheets, level 1) specifications were released by the W3C in December 1996. CSS2 came out in May 1998. CSS2 builds on CSS1. It extends CSS1 to support the display Web pages in visual browsers, via aural devices (which employ a combination of speech synthesis and sound effects and are useful for visually disabled people), via braille devices, on printers, and on handheld devices. It also supports positioning, downloadable fonts, table layout, features for internationalization, automatic counters and numbering and device-independent colors. CSS3 was introduced in April 2001. CSS3 extends CSS2 by adding background colors and images. It also modularizes the CSS specification to help clarify the relationship between the different parts of the specification and to make it easy to maintain the specification in the future. We cover CSS3 here.

CSS authoring tools exist either as stand-alone editors or as part of HTML editors. Some comprehensive CSS documents for a website could be quite long, thus necessitating the use of an authoring tool. CSS authoring tools enable Web authors to create CSS documents and save them. They also support the previewing, editing, changing, copying, or deleting of them. CSS files are text files. All file operations are applied to them whether the Web author is using a CSS editor or just a text editor. Web authors who use HTML editors should find it quite easy to use CSS editors.

16.2 CSS Syntax

The fundamental syntactic unit of CSS is the *rule*. A **CSS rule** is a statement that follows a specific syntax. A **CSS style sheet** consists of a list (sequence) of rules (statements). There are two types of statements: *at-rules* and *rule sets*. The **at-rule** begins with an @ character followed immediately by an identifier—for example, `@import` or `@page`. Following the identifier comes the rule definition, terminated by a semicolon — for example, `@import "printPage.css";`.

An example of a **rule set** (or just a rule) is `h1, h2 {color:blue; font-weight:bold}`. This rule sets the color of the `<h1>` and `<h2>` tags to red and their font weight to bold. Any text that uses them is rendered by a browser as red bold text—for example, `<h1>text with CSS</h1>`.

The rule set has the following general syntax:

```
selectors {declaration block}
```

This syntax means that a rule set is defined by one or more selector, followed by a declaration block. The declaration block starts with a { and ends with a }. We write the foregoing syntax in more details as follows:

```
selector1[, selector2, .., selectorn ]{declaration1[;
    declaration2; .., declarationn]},
```

where the [and] indicate optional content. A rule set may have more than one selector or more than one declaration. Selectors are separated by commas (,), and declarations are separated by semicolons (;). The last declaration does not require a semicolon. Applying this definition to the foregoing rule for `<h1>` and `<h2>` tags, we conclude that `h1` and `h2` are the selectors. The selectors are the XHTML tags. They act as the link between XHTML and the style. The rule uses two declarations: `color:red` and `font-weight:bold`.

A declaration consists of a `property:value` pair separated by a colon (`:`). The rule for `<h1>` and `<h2>` tags uses the two pairs `color:red` and `font-weight:bold`. The two properties are `color` and `font-weight`, and the two values are `red` and `bold`.

The properties are keywords. They are the XHTML tags without the `<` and `>`. The values may be strings, integers, real (decimal) numbers, lengths, counters, colors, angles, times, frequencies, or URLs. Table 16.1 gives some examples.

Table 16.1   Possible values for CSS properties.

Values may be strings, integers, real (decimal) numbers, frequencies, URLs, lengths, counters, colors, angles, or times.

Value Type	Example
string	`"This is a string"`. Use single or double quotes.
integer	`4`.
real number	`2.5`.
frequency	Used with aural style sheets. Frequency is measured in Hertz (Hz or hz) or kiloHertz (kHz or khz). Example include: `{pitch: 200hz} /* Hertz */` and `{pitch: 10khz} /* kilo Hertz */`.
URL	Used to specify URLs. Here is an example: `body {background: url(http://aaa.bbb.ccc/myImage.gif)}`
length	A length can be specified in pixels (`px`); as the same size as the font size used (em space); as the same *x*-height as that of the font used (`ex`), which is the same size as a lowercase *x*; or as a percentage (`%`) of another length, such as font size. Here are some examples: `h1 {margin: 0.5 em} /* em */` `h1 {margin: 1ex} /* ex */` `p {font-size: 12px} /* px */` `p {font-size: 10 pt} p {line-height: 150%} /* 150% of font size */`
	Lengths can be specified as absolute lengths. This approach is useful only when the physical properties of the output medium are known. The absolute units are inches (`in`), centimeters (`cm`), millimeters (`mm`), points (`pt`; 1 point is equal to $1/72$ of an inch, and pica (`pc`; 1 pica is equal to 12 points). Here are some examples: `h1 {margin: 0.5 in} /* inches */` `h2 {line-height: 3 cm} /* centimeters */` `h3 {word-spacing: 4 mm} /* millimeters */` `h3 {font-size: 12 pt} /* points */` `h4 {font-size: 1pc} /* picas */`

Table 16.1   Possible values for CSS properties. (Continued)

Values may be strings, integers, real (decimal) numbers, frequencies, URLs, lengths, counters, colors, angles, or times.

Value Type	Example

counter	Counters are specified by identifiers. Examples include the following:
	
	`p {counter-increment: par-num}`
	`h1 {counter-reset: par-num}`

color	`h1 {color: #FF0000}`

angle	Used with aural style sheets. Angle can be specified in degrees (`deg`), gradients (`grad`), or radians (`rad`). Here are some examples:
	
	`h1 {azimuth: 30deg} /* degrees */`
	`h1 {azimuth: 100grad} /* gradients */`
	`h1 {azimuth: 0.26rad} /* radians */`

time	Used with aural style sheets. Time is measured in seconds (`s`) or milliseconds (`ms`). Examples include the following:
	
	`{pause: 5s}`
	`{pause: 2000ms}`

CSS syntax provides comment statements. Comments begin with `/*` and end with `*/`, as shown in Table 16.1—for example, `/* comments here */`. CSS also allows the XHTML comments, `<!-- .. -->`.

Example 16.1 Use a simple style sheet.

Develop a Web page that uses CSS to specify blue text and yellow background color.

Solution 16.1 Using the AceHTML editor, generate the given code, and save it as `example161.html`. Use a browser to render the Web page.

```
1   <?xml version="1.0" encoding="iso-8859-1"?>
2   <!DOCTYPE html PUBLIC "-//W3C//DTD XHTML 1.1//EN"
3       "http://www.w3.org/TR/xhtml11/DTD/xhtml11.dtd">
4   <html xmlns="http://www.w3.org/1999/xhtml">
5   <!-- Generated by AceHTM http://freeware.acehtml.com -->
6   <head>
7   <meta http-equiv="Content-Type" content="text/html;
    charset=iso-8859-1" />
8   <title>Inline CSS</title>
9   <style type="text/css">
10  body {color: #0000FF; background: #FFFF00}
11  </style>
12  </head>
13  <body>
14  <h2 align="center">Hello World!</h2>
15  </body>
16  </html>
```

Code explained:

1. Lines 9–11 create a style sheet. The `<style>` tag opens in line 9 and closes in line 11.

2. Line 10 defines the desired style.

Discussion:

The `<style>` tag is included inside the `<head>` tag. The `<style>` tag in line 9 defines the `type` attribute that defines a style sheet. Line 10 defines the foreground and background colors for the Web page as blue and yellow, respectively. We use the hex codes to specify the colors. The `color` property defines the foreground color.

Hands-on exercise:

Use different colors and text. Move the `<style>` tag to the inside of the `<body>` tag. Does it still work? How else can you achieve the same result without using CSS?

16.3 Linking CSS to XHTML

The main premise of style sheets is that they can be used across Web pages. How do we make one style sheet available to more than one Web page? The main issue here is linking CSS to Web pages. Five options exist. They range from inlining and embedding CSS code into XHTML code, to saving it independently from XHTML code (known as external CSS). Embedded and inline CSS can be used only by the Web page that includes it. Table 16.2 summarizes the linking options. The remainder of the section explains them in details.

Table 16.2   Options for linking CSS to XHTML.

The five options are inline, embedded, external, imported, and attributes and tags.

Option	Description
inline CSS	Use to apply a style to one XHTML tag only. Use the `style` attribute inside the tag itself. Here is an example: `<b style="color: blue; font-size:10">text goes here</b>`
embedded CSS	Use to apply a style to an entire Web page. The style applies only to the page that defines it. Use the `<style>` tag inside the page's `<head>` section. See Example 16.1.
external CSS	Use to apply a style to an entire website (one Web page at a time). Save the CSS code in its own (external) file. Use the `<link>` tag inside the `<head>` section of the Web page to be styled with the external CSS file. Here is an example: `<link rel="stylesheet" type="text/css" href="css-File.css"  media="screen, print" />`
imported CSS	Works the same way as external CSS. Use the `@import` statement inside the `<style>` tag or in a CSS file. Here is an example: `@import url("myStyle.css");`
attributes and tags	Two attributes (`class` and `id`) and two tags (`span` and `div`) exist to allow fine control of style.

16.3.1   Inline CSS

CSS code is included (inlined) in an XHTML tag via the `style` attribute. The style is applicable only to this tag, thus making it a local style. The `style` attribute may be applied to any tag inside the `<body>` tag (including `<body>` itself). The `style` attribute takes any number of CSS declarations. Here is an example (use the `<meta>` tag in the `<head>` section as shown):

```
<head>
<title>Inline CSS</title>
<meta http-equiv="content-style-type" content="text/css">
</head>
<h1 style="color:blue; font-weight:bold">CSS inline style</h1>
```

Inline style suffers from two problems. First, it mixes content with presentation. Second, it implicitly applies to all media such as screens and printers, as there is no `media` attribute for the `<style>` tag to specify media. Inline styles should thus be used infrequently. If a style should be applied to a single tag, use the `id` attribute instead of `style`.

16.3.2   Embedded CSS

CSS code is included in the XHTML code of a Web page via the `<style>` tag. The style sheet is visible only within the page and cannot be used by other Web pages. An embedded style sheet should be used when a single document has a unique style. If the same style sheet is used by multiple documents, an external style sheet is more appropriate. Include the `<style>` tag inside the `<head>` section. Example 16.1 shows the embedding of a style sheet.

16.3.3 External CSS

CSS code is stored in its own file that the XHTML code of any Web page can reference and use. External CSS should not contain any XHTML tags such as `<style>` or `<head>`. The style sheet should consist only of style rules and statements. The CSS file has the `.css` extension. Use the `<link>` tag in the `<head>` section of a Web page to access the external CSS stored in the `.css` file. Here is an example:

```
<head>
...
<link rel="stylesheet" type="text/css" href="cssFile.css"  />
</head>
```

Other examples are as follows:

```
<link rel="stylesheet" type="text/css" href="cssFile.css"
    media="screen, print" />
<link rel="stylesheet" type="text/css" href="cssFile.css"
    media="aural" />
```

The full set of attributes of the `<link>` tag is described in Table 16.3. External CSS are ideal for applying a style to numerous pages. A Web author can thereby change the look and feel of an entire website by changing one file.

Table 16.3   `<link>` tag—allows the use of external CSS files in Web pages.

Attributes: `<link rel type href media title rev charset hreflang lang />`	
Attribute	Description
`rel`	Defines the relationship between the linked CSS file and the Web page. The possible values are `stylesheet`, `alternate stylesheet`, and `persistent`. For example, use `rel=stylesheet`.
`type`	Specifies the type of media storing the external CSS code. For example use `type="text/css"`.
`href`	Specifies the URL (path and file name) of the CSS file.
`media`	Specifies the output medium to which the style sheet should be applied. The possible values are `screen` (default), `print` (printer), `projection` (projected presentations), `aural` (speech synthesizers), `braille` (braille devices), `tty` (typewriter font), `tv` (television), and `all` (all output devices).

Table 16.3   `<link>` tag—allows the use of external CSS files in
Web pages. (Continued)

Attributes: `<link rel type href media title rev charset hreflang lang />`	
Attribute	Description

`title`	Combines multiple style sheets into a single style. Here is an example:
	
	`<link rel="stylesheet" type="text/css"`
	`    href="cssFile1.css" title="classic" />`
	`<link rel="stylesheet" type="text/css"`
	`    href="cssFile2.css" title="classic" />`
	`<link rel="stylesheet" type="text/css"`
	`    href="cssFile3.css" title="classic" />`

`rev`	Specifies a reverse link.
`charset`	Specifies character encoding set for Web pages written in non-English languages.
`hreflang`	Specifies the language of non-English Web pages. This attribute is usually used with the `charset` attribute.
`lang`	Specifies a rendering language of the Web page that is different from the language in which it is written.

16.3.4 Imported CSS

A style sheet may be imported with the at-rule. The `@import` statement may be used inside the `<style>` tag or in a CSS file. Here is an example:

```
<head>
<title>Importing CSS</title>
<style type="text/css">
@import url("myStyle.css");
@import url("http://www.aaa.bbb/ddd.css");
body {color: #FF0000; background: yellow}
</style>
</head>
```

If used, the `@import` statement(s) must be the first line(s) inside the `<style>` tag, followed by other rules as shown in the previous code. Conflicting rules are resolved using the local scope; that is, any rules specified inside the `<style>` tag override those specified in the `@import` statements. Moreover, the order of the `@import` statements determines how the imported style sheets cascade. Also, if no rules are used after the `@import` statements, the `<link>` tag can be used in place of the `@import` statement. Imported style sheets are useful for the purpose of modularity. For example, we can create three style sheets, one for each specific set of tags.

16.3.5 Attributes and Tags

Two attributes are class and id, and two tags are span and div. They provide fine control of style. The attributes are used with XHTML tags. The class attribute specifies a style class. Let us define these two classes respectively as follows:

```
.shine {color:FF0000; background:#FFFF00} /* may apply to all XHTML
    tags */
p.flag {color:#FF0000; font-weight:bold; font-size:16pt} /* may
    apply only to <p> tags */
```

A class definition begins with a dot (.). We may specify an XHTML tag to the left of the dot, to associate the class with the tag. We refer to this notation as *dot notation*. Here is how we use the two foregoing classes:

```
<h1 class="shine">Text goes here</h1>
<p class="flag">Warning goes here</p>
```

The id attribute specifies a style for one tag. Its function is similar to that of the inline <style> tag, with one difference: The id attribute uses a style that is defined in an external CSS file, making it applicable to multiple Web pages. Here is an example:

```
#greeting {color: #0000FF; font-size: 15 pt; font-weight: bold} /*
    define in a CSS file */
<h1 id="greeting">Greeting text goes here</h1>
```

The greeting style rule is defined in an external CSS file and must begin with a pound sign (#) to indicate that it may apply individually to XHTML tags in multiple Web pages. When it is used as a value of the id attribute in a tag, we drop the pound sign, as shown in the second line of the foregoing code example.

The <span> tag specifies a style for structured XHTML elements such as tables and layers. It may also apply to elements such as text, links, and so forth. It provides inline style. The <span> tag accepts the style, class, and id attributes. The <span> tag defines a block to which it applies the inline style. Here is an example:

```
#greeting {color: #0000FF; font-size: 15pt; font-weight: bold} /*
    define in a CSS file */
<h1>Greeting text goes here. <span id="greeting">This text is
    different</span></h1>
```

The <div> tag is similar to the <span> tag. We have used it already with layers in Chapter 13. The <div> and <span> tags are used interchangeably. Here is the foregoing example, but with the <div> tag substituted for the <span> tag:

```
#greeting {color: #0000FF; font-size: 15 pt; font-weight: bold} /*
    define in a CSS file */
<h1>Greeting text goes here. <div id="greeting">This text is
    different</div></h1>
```

Example 16.2 Link style sheets to XHTML.

Develop a Web page that illustrates the use of the different ways to link style sheets.

Solution 16.2 Using the AceHTML editor, generate the given code, and save it as `example162.html`. Use a browser to render the Web page.

Code explained:

1. Line 10 specifies an external CSS file: `cssFile.css`.
2. Lines 11–18 use the `<style>` tag to define embedded CSS.
3. Line 12 uses the `import` statement to specify the external CSS file `myStyle.css`.
4. Lines 15 and 17 define two classes: `shine` and `flag`.
5. Line 22 uses the `style` attribute with the `<h2>` tag.
6. Lines 24 and 25 use the `class` attribute.
7. Lines 29 and 32 use the `<div>` and `<span>` tags, respectively, with the `id` attribute.

Discussion:

This example uses one HTML file and two CSS files. We use the AceHTML CSS template to create CSS files. When we save a CSS file, AceHTML uses the `.css` extension. The example shows the various methods of linking CSS to XHTML that we have discussed in this section. The order in which the two CSS files are specified affects the rendering of the Web page, as discussed in the next section. The file `cssFile.css` defines a yellow background for the Web page. The file `myStyle.css` defines the font, style, and size of any text (see code line 3 in the `myStyle.css` listing given in this example) that is used inside the `<body>` tag of a Web page. The file also defines an individual style rule (`greeting`) in code line 4. This rule uses a background color (white) that is attached to each piece of text that uses the rule. The `shine` and `flag` classes also use background colors that apply only to the text. This is an interesting design tool we can use to make Web pages look attractive. As shown in the foregoing screen capture, the classes and the `<div>` tag apply their background colors to the entire width of the browser window along the text strip. In contrast, the `<span>` tag limits the color to the text only.

Hands-on exercise:

Use different colors and text in the Web page in this example. Also, apply the CSS styles to new text.

example162.html

```
1   <?xml version="1.0" encoding="iso-8859-1"?>
2   <!DOCTYPE html PUBLIC "-//W3C//DTD XHTML 1.1//EN"
3       "http://www.w3.org/TR/xhtml11/DTD/xhtml11.dtd">
4   <html xmlns="http://www.w3.org/1999/xhtml">
5   <!-- Generated by AceHTM http://freeware.acehtml.com -->
6   <head>
7   <meta http-equiv="Content-Type" content="text/html;
    charset=iso-8859-1" />
8   <title>Linking CSS to XHTML</title>
9   <!-- Use external CSS file -->
10  <link rel="stylesheet" type="text/css" href="cssFile.css"  />
11  <style type="text/css">
12  @import url("myStyle.css");
13
14  /* may apply to all XHTML tags */
15  .shine {color:FF0000; background:#AABBCC}
16  /* may apply only to <p> tags */
17  p.flag {color:#00FF00; font-weight:bold; font-size: 16pt;
    background:#000000}
18  </style>
19  </head>
20  <body>
21  <!-- Use inline style -->
22  <h2 align="center" style="color:blue; font-weight:bold">
    Hello World!</h2>
23  <!-- Use class attribute -->
24  <h1 class="shine">This is the way it is</h1>
25  <p class="flag">We have a problem</p>
26  Greeting text goes here.
27  <p></p>
28  <!-- Use id and <div> attribute -->
29  <div id="greeting">This text is different</div>
30  <p></p>
31  <!-- Use id and <span> attribute -->
32  <span id="greeting">This is not the same text</span>
33  </body>
34  </html>
```

cssFile.css

```
1  @charset "iso-8859-1";
2  /* Generated by AceHTML Freeware http://freeware.acehtml.com */
3  body {background:#FFFF00}
```

myStyle.css

```
1  @charset "iso-8859-1";
2  /* Generated by AceHTML Freeware http://freeware.acehtml.com */
3  body {font-size:12; font-weight:bold; font-family: arial}
4  #greeting {color:#0000FF; font-size: 15pt; font-weight:bold;
5  background:#FFFFFF}
```

16.4 Inheritance and Cascading Order

Like XHTML tags, CSS tags and selectors may be nested. This approach generates a tree structure that raises the issue of inheritance: How do the nested tags and selectors inherit styles from each other? The inheritance rule is simple and logical: Children inherit from parents, unless they override the parents' styles. Consider a <p> tag inside a <body> tag. If the <body> tag uses a style sheet that specifies a red color for the text, all text inside it becomes red, unless the <p> tag specifies another color, such as blue, for its text.

When multiple style sheets are used, they cascade. When they cascade, conflicts may arise among them. For example, one sheet may set the background color to blue, while another sheet may set it to red. Cascading order is used to resolve this conflict according to the following general rule: Style sheets that are specified last in Web pages override the style sheets specified before them. Consider this example:

```
<link rel="stylesheet" type="text/css" href="cssFile1.css" />
<link rel="stylesheet" type="text/css" href="cssFile2.css" />
```

If both files specify a background color, the color used in cssFile2.css prevails. If the order of the two <link> tags is reversed, the color used in cssFile1.css prevails.

The aforementioned cascading order is the default order, which assumes that all the styles specified have the same weight. However, be aware of the following cases:

1. **!important.** Rules can be designated as important by using the !important keyword. A style that is designated as important prevails over contradictory styles of otherwise equal weight. Here is an example:

   body {color:#FF0000; background:#0000FF !important}

2. **Authors versus browsers.** Web browsers use their own style sheets to render Web pages. When Web authors use their own style sheets that conflict with those of the browsers, the authors' sheets take precedence.

3. Specificity prevails. Style sheets that specify a large number of `class` and `id` attributes, as well as use many XHTML tags in their selectors, win out over less specific ones. Compute the specificity of a selector as follows:

a. Count the number of `id` attributes in the selector—for example, *a*=0.
b. Count the number of `class` attributes in the selector—for example, *b*=3.
c. Count the number of XHTML tag names in the selector—for example, *c*=1.
d. Write the three numbers in the foregoing order, with no spaces or commas between them, to obtain a three-digit weight number—for example; specificity = 031. The leftmost digits are more significant than the others; for example, 100 is a higher specificity than 035. Here are some examples:

```
#id1             {...} /* a=1 b=0 c=0 -> specificity = 100 */
h1 h2 h3 p.flag {...} /* a=0 b=1 c=4 -> specificity = 014 */
h1.shine         {...} /* a=0 b=1 c=1 -> specificity = 011 */
b                {...} /* a=0 b=0 c=1 -> specificity = 001 */
```

16.5 The Box Model

CSS uses a simple box model for formatting, as shown in Figure 16.1. Each piece of formatted content or formatting tag results in a rectangular box that surrounds other resulting boxes, with the content centered inside the core box. The width of the outer box is the sum of the widths of the content, the padding, the border, and the margin.

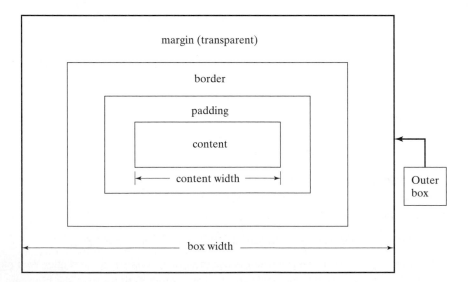

Figure 16.1 CSS box model.

The sizes of the margin, border, and padding are set with the margin, border, and padding properties, respectively. The background color of the padding area is the same as that for the tag itself. The border has a color and style that are set with the border property. The margins are always transparent, allowing the background to show through.

16.6 Font Properties

Setting font properties for text is among the most common activities in CSS. CSS specifies the font of text according to the font properties shown in Table 16.4, which lists each property and its permissible values.

16.7 Text Properties

CSS provides a rich set of text-formatting properties. Among others, CSS specifies the text properties shown in Table 16.5, which lists some properties and their permissible values.

Table 16.4   CSS font properties.

CSS font properties are `font-family`, `font-style`, `font-size`, `font-weight`, `font-variant`, and `font-stretch`.

Property	Values
`font-family`	Specifies text font. The following is an example: `{font-family: Arial, Times, Courier}`
`font-style`	Specifies text style. The allowed values are `normal`, `italic`, or `oblique`. The following is an example: `{font-style: italic}`
`font-size`	Specifies text size. The following is an example: `{font-size: 12pt}`
`font-weight`	Specifies the degree of boldness of text. The allowed values are `normal` (corresponds to 400), `bold`, `bolder`, `lighter`, 100, 200, 300, 400, 500, 600, 700, 800, and 900. The following is an example: `{font-weight: bold}`
`font-variant`	Specifies small-caps text. The only value is `small-caps`: `{font-variant: small-caps}`
`font-stretch`	Specifies the degree to which text should be stretched horizontally. The allowed values are `normal`, `wider`, `narrower`, `ultra-condensed`, `extra-condensed`, `condensed`, `semi-condensed`, `semi-expanded`, `expanded`, `extra-expanded`, and `ultra-expanded`. The following is an Example: `{font-stretch: wider}`

Table 16.5   CSS text properties.

Some CSS text properties are `text-align`, `text-justify`, `text-align-last`, `min-font-size`, `max-font-size`, `vertical-align`, `text-indent`, `line-break`, `text-space`, `text-wrap`, `white-space`, `text-spacing`, `word-spacing`, and `text-transform`.

Property	Values
`text-align`	Specifies how text is aligned in a block. The allowed values are `start`, `end`, `left`, `center`, and `justify`. The following is an example: `{text-align: center}`
`text-justify`	Specifies text justification. The allowed values are `auto`, `inter-word`, `inter-ideograph`, `distribute`, `newspaper`, `inter-cluster`, and `kashida`. The following is an example: `{text-justify: auto}`
`text-align-last`	Specifies how the last line of text in a block is aligned. The allowed values are `auto`, `start`, `end`, `center`, `justify`, and `size`. An example is as follows: `{text-align-last: center}`

`min-font-size` and `max-font-size`	Specify the minimum and maximum font size of text, respectively. An example of each is as follows:
	
	`{min-font-size: 10pt}`
	`{max-font-size: 20pt}`

`vertical-align`	Specifies the vertical alignment of text with respect to the text's baseline. The allowed values are `auto`, `auto-script`, `baseline`, `sub`, `super`, `top`, `text-top`, `central`, `middle`, `bottom`, `text-bottom`, `<percentage>`, and `<length>`. The following are some examples:
	
	`{vertical-align: sub}`
	`{vertical-align: 30%}`
	`{vertical-align: 5mm} /* raise text by 5 mm from baseline */`
	`{vertical-align: -5mm} /* lower text by 5 mm from baseline */`

`text-indent`	Specifies text indentation. The allowed values are `<length>` and `<percentage>`. The following are some examples:
	
	`p {text-indent: 5em}`
	`p {text-indent: 10%} /* indent paragraph by 10% of text block width */`

`line-break`	Specifies a line break. The allowed values are `normal` and `strict`. The following is an example: `p {line-break: strict}`
`text-space`	Controls whether whitespace in a text stream is collapsed or kept as is. The Allowed values are `normal` (collapse whitespace) and `honor` (keep whitespace). The following is an example: `{text-space: honor}`

Table 16.5 CSS text properties. (Continued)

Some CSS text properties are `text-align`, `text-justify`, `text-align-last`, `min-font-size`, `max-font-size`, `vertical-align`, `text-indent`, `line-break`, `text-space`, `text-wrap`, `white-space`, `text-spacing`, `word-spacing`, and `text-transform`.

Property	Values
`text-wrap`	Controls whether to wrap text at the end of a line. The allowed values are `normal` (wrap text) and `none` (do not wrap text). The following is an example: `{text-wrap: normal}`

`white-space`	Specifies how to handle whitespace inside tags. The allowed values are `normal`, `pre`, and `nowrap`. The following are some examples:
	
	`pre {white-space: pre}`
	`p {white-space: normal}`
	`td {white-space: nowrap}`

`text-spacing`	Specifies spacing between text characters. The allowed values are `normal` and `<length>`. The following is an example: `blockquote{letter-spacing: 0.1em}`
`word-spacing`	Specifies spacing between words. The allowed values are `normal`, `none`, and `<length>`. The following is an example: `h1 {word-spacing: 1.5em}`
`text-transform`	Controls the capitalization of text. The allowed values are `capitalize`, `uppercase`, `lowercase`, and `none`. The following is an example: `h1 {text-transform: uppercase}`

16.8 Color Properties

CSS specifies colors according to the color properties shown in Table 16.6, which lists each property and its permissible values.

Table 16.6 CSS color properties.

CSS color properties are `color`, `background`, `background-repeat`, `opacity`, `color-profile`, and `rendering-intent`.

Property	Values

`color`	Specifies text (foreground) color. A color can be specified by name, hex code, or RGB signals. The following are some examples:
	
	`h1 {color: red}`
	`p {color: #FF0000}`
	`h2 {color: rgb(255, 0, 0} /* RGB range 0 - 255 */`

Table 16.6   CSS color properties. (Continued)

CSS color properties are `color`, `background`, `background-repeat`, `opacity`, `color-profile`, and `rendering-intent`.

Property	Values
background	Specifies the background color of the Web page. A background color can be specified by name, hex code, or RGB signals. The following are some examples:

```
body {background: red}
h1 {background: #FF0000}
p {background: rgb(255, 0, 0} /* RGB range
   0 - 255 */
```

background-repeat	Creates a tiling effect if an image is used. The allowed values are `repeat`, `repeat-x`, `repeat-y`, and `no-repeat`. The following are some example:

```
body {background: url (myImage.jpg); background-
   repeat: repeat}
body {background: url (myImage.jpg); background-
   repeat: repeat-x}
body {background: url (myImage.jpg); background-
   repeat: repeat-y}
body {background: url (myImage.jpg); background-
   repeat: repeat-x repeat-y}
body {background: url (myImage.jpg); background-
   repeat: no-repeat}
```

opacity	Specifies how transparent an XHTML element is to be. The allowed values are numbers between 0.0 (fully transparent) and 1.0 (fully opaque). The following is an example:

```
img {opacity: 0.5}
```

color-profile	Specifies the color model to be used. The allowed values are `auto` (RGB model), `sRGB` (standardized RGB model, which provides device-independent colors), and URL. The following are some examples:

```
img {color-profile: sRGB}
img {color-profile: "http://www.aaa.ccc/images/
   profiles/profile1.icm"}
```

rendering-intent	Specifies a color profile (model) for rendering intent. The allowed values are `auto`, `perceptual`, `relative-colorimetric`, `saturation`, and `absolute-colorimetric`. The following is an example:

```
img {rendering-intent: auto}
```

16.9 Content Positioning

CSS offers excellent control of the placement of elements in Web pages via the `position` property, as we discussed in Chapter 13. Positioning in CSS uses the coordinates system shown in Figures 13.1 and 13.2, where the system origin is placed in the top left corner of the Web page, with the +*X*-axis pointing to the right and the +*Y*- axis pointing down. The `position` property takes one of two values: `absolute` or `relative`. It allows Web authors to place the elements by using the absolute or relative coordinates, respectively. Absolute positioning measures coordinates by using the top left corner as the reference point. Relative positioning measures coordinates relative to the position of the last placed (inserted) page element. This approach allows the elements of the page's content to flow well together. It also is sometimes easier to use relative positioning than absolute positioning.

Web authors use other placement properties in addition to `position` in order to have full control. These properties are `top` (*y* coordinate of position), `left` (*x* coordinate of position), `bottom`, `top`, and `z-index`. The `z-index` controls element overlapping as discussed in Chapter 13 for layers. Here are some examples that use placement properties:

```
{position: absolute; top: 20px; left:30px, z-index: 2}
.super {position: relative; top: -1ex}
.shiftright {position: relative; right: 2em}
```

16.10 Tutorials

16.10.1 Using External CSS (Study Sections 16.6–16.8)

This tutorial renders the Web page of Example 9.14, using an external style sheet. Use the Ace-HTML editor to generate the given code, and save it as `tutorial16101.html`. View the page in a browser. Also, generate the given CSS code, and save it as `style.css`. The following screen capture shows the web page.

Code Explained (`style.css file`):

 1. Line 4 specifies the text properties and the background color.
 2. Lines 6–8 specify the colors of hyperlinks.
 3. Line 10 specifies the size and style of list items.
 4. Lines 12–14 specify rules for `<h1>` and `<h2>` tags.

Discussion:

We specify all the rendering requirements for our Web page in the style sheet. First think of the elements of the Web page, such as text, links, lists, and so forth. Then write the required rules in the style sheet. We import the external style sheet in line 10 in the `tutorial16101.html` file.

Hands-on exercise:

Add an image to the page, and extend the CSS file `style.css` to include rules to render it.

```
1   <?xml version="1.0" encoding="iso-8859-1"?>
2   <!DOCTYPE html PUBLIC "-//W3C//DTD XHTML 1.1//EN"
3       "http://www.w3.org/TR/xhtml11/DTD/xhtml11.dtd">
4   <html xmlns="http://www.w3.org/1999/xhtml">
5   <!-- Generated by AceHTM http://freeware.acehtml.com -->
6   <head>
7   <meta http-equiv="Content-Type" content="text/html;
    charset=iso-8859-1" />
8   <title>Linking CSS to XHTML</title>          tutorial16101.html
9   <!-- Use external CSS file -->
10  <link rel="stylesheet" type="text/css" href="style.css"  />
11  </head><body>
12  <h2 align="center">Links in lists</h2>
13  <ul>
14    <li><a href="http://www.neu.edu">Vist NU</a></li>
15    <li><a href="http://www.mit.edu">Visit MIT</a></li>
16    <li><a href="http://www.sun.com">Visit Sun</a></li>
17  </ul></body>
18  </html>
```

```
1   @charset "iso-8859-1";
2   /* Generated by AceHTML Freeware http://freeware.acejtml.com */
3   /* foreground and background colors */
4   body {color: #0000FF; font-size:14; font-family: arial;
    background:#FFFF00}
5   /* hyperlink colors */                          style.html
6   a:link {color: #00FFFF}
7   a:active {color: #FF0000}
8   a:visited {color: #FF00FF}
9   /* list items' colors */
10  li {font-size: 14; font-style: italic}
11  /* header tags */
12  h1 h2 {font-weight: bold}
13  h1 {font-size: 24pt}
14  h2 {font-size: 18pt}
```

16.10.2 Styling Using Images (Study Sections 16.6–16.8)

This tutorial is the same as Example 10.4. Here, however, we tile the Web page by using CSS rules. Use the AceHTML editor to generate the given code, and save it as `tutorial16102.html`. View the pages in a browser. In this example, we use embedded CSS.

Code explained:

Lines 10–12 create the embedded CSS. Line 11 uses the tiling image.

Discussion:

We could also have used `background-image` in line 11 instead of `background`.

Hands-on exercise:

Add the `repeat` property to line 11. Use its three possible values: `repeat`, `repeat-x`, and `repeat-y`. Use one at a time. What do you see? Also, replace the embedded CSS by an external CSS file, and render the page.

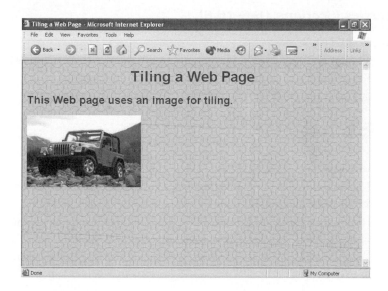

```
1   <?xml version="1.0" encoding="iso-8859-1"?>
2   <!DOCTYPE html PUBLIC "-//W3C//DTD XHTML 1.1//EN"
3       "http://www.w3.org/TR/xhtml11/DTD/xhtml11.dtd">
4   <html xmlns="http://www.w3.org/1999/xhtml">
5   <!-- Generated by AceHTM http://freeware.acehtml.com -->
6   <head>
7   <meta http-equiv="Content-Type" content="text/html;
    charset=iso-8859-1" />
8   <title>Tiling a Web Page</title>
9   <!-- Use embedded CSS -->
10  <style>
```

```
11   body {background: url(tiling.jpg)}
12   </style>
13   </head>
14   <body>
15   <h1 align="center">Tiling a Web Page</h1>
16   <p>
17   <h2>This Web page uses an image for tiling.</h2>
18   </p>
19   <img src="jeepCar.jpg" />
20   </body>
21   </html>
```

FAQs

CSS Properties (Sections 16.6–16.8)

Q: What is the best way to master CSS?

A: Practice. Apply the properties and values discussed in Sections 16.6–16.8 to Web pages. Use one or two properties at a time. Use embedded styles for quick results.

Blackbox

Section 16.1 (Introduction): CSS separates content from presentation. It allows Web authors to have better control over the look and feel of websites and Web pages. CSS has three levels: 1, 2, and 3. It is simple, easy, and fun to learn.

Section 16.2 (CSS Syntax) (Example 16.1): The fundamental syntactic unit of CSS is the *rule* (statement). There are two types of statements: *at-rules* and *rule sets*. A rule set has the following general syntax: `selectors {declaration block}`. We write this rule in more detail as follows:

```
selector1[, selector2, .., selectorn ]{declaration1[;
    declaration2; .., declarationn]}
```

A declaration consists of a `property:value` pair. Some examples are `h1 {color: #FF0000; font-weight: bold}` and `body {color:#0000FF; background: url(myImage.jpg}`. Possible values for properties are strings, integers, real (decimal) numbers, frequencies, URLs, lengths, counters, colors, angles, and times.

CSS syntax provides comment statements. Comments begin with /* and ends with */.

Section 16.3 (Linking CSS to XHTML) (Example 16.2): Five options exist for using CSS in XHTML: inline, embedded, external, imported, and attributes and tags. Here is an example for each option:

inline: Use the `style` attribute in the tag: `<h1 style="font-weight: bold">CSS inline style</h1>`

embedded: Use the `<style>` tag in the `<head>` section:

```
<style>
body {color:#0000FF; background: AABBFF}
</style>
```

external: Create CSS files and link to them in XHTML code as follows:

```
<link rel="stylesheet" type="text/css" href="style.css"  />
```

import: An example is as follows: `@import url("myStyle.css");`

`class` attribute:

Create a class and then use it:

```
.shine {color:FF0000; background:#FFFF00} /* may apply to all XHTML
    tags */
p.flag {color: #FF0000; font-weight: bold; font-size: 16pt} /* may
    apply to <p> tags */
<h1 class="shine">Text goes here</h1>
<p class="flag">Warning goes here</p>
```

`id` attribute: Create an attribute and then use it:

```
#greeting {color: #0000FF; font-size: 15 pt; font-weight: bold} /*
    define in a CSS file */
<h1 id="greeting">Greeting text goes here</h1>
<span> or <div> tag: each tag accepts the style, class and id
    attributes.
#greeting {color: #0000FF; font-size: 15pt; font-weight: bold} /*
    define in a CSS file */
<h1>Greeting text goes here. <span id="greeting">This text is
    different</span></h1>
```

Section 16.4 (Inheritance and Cascading Order) (Examples 16.1 and 16.2): The inheritance rule is simple and logical: Children inherit from parents, unless they override the parents' styles. When multiple style sheets are used, they cascade. The cascading order is determined according to this rule. Style sheets that are specified last in Web pages override the ones specified before them.

Section 16.5 (The Box Model): CSS uses a box model for formatting. The box has margins, border, padding, and content (centered inside the box). The sizes of the margin, a border, and padding are set with the margin, border, and padding properties, respectively. The background color of the padding area is the same as that for the tag itself. The border has a color and style that are set with the border property.

Section 16.6 (Font Properties): The CSS font properties are `font-family`, `font-style`, `font-size`, `font-weight`, `font-variant`, and `font-stretch`.

Section 16.7 (Text Properties): Some CSS text properties are `text-align`, `text-justify`, `text-align-last`, `min-font-size`, `max-font-size`, `vertical-align`, `text-indent`, `line-break`, `text-space`, `text-wrap`, `white-space`, `text-spacing`, `word-spacing`, and `text-transform`.

Section 16.8 (Color Properties): The CSS color properties are `color`, `background`, `background-repeat`, `opacity`, `color-profile`, and `rendering-intent`.

Section 16.9 (Content Positioning): CSS controls the placement of elements in Web pages via the `position` property. Positioning in CSS uses a coordinate system where the system origin is placed in the top left corner of the Web page, with the +X-axis pointing to the right and the +Y-axis pointing down. The `position` property takes one of two values: absolute or relative.

Section 16.10 (Tutorials): Two tutorials show how to use CSS.

Quick reference for the tags presented in this chapter

Tag	Close	Attribute	Value	Effect	Example
`<link>`	empty	`rel`	`stylesheet`	specifies stylesheet type	`<link rel="stylesheet">`
		`type`	`text/css`	specifies the media type that stores the external CSS code	`<link type="text/css" />`.
		`href`	text	specifies the CSS file	`< link href="style.css" />`
		`media`	value	specifies the output medium	`<link media="screen" />`
		`title`	text	combines multiple style sheets into a single style sheet	`<link title="multiple" />`
		`rev`	text	specifies a reverse link	`<link rev="URL" />`
		`charset`	value	specifies the encoding set	`<link charset="iso-8859-1">`
		`hreflang`	text	specifies the language	`<link hreflang="fr" />`
		`lang`	text	specifies the language	`<link lang="de" />`

Check Your Progress

At the end of this chapter, you should

- ✔ understand the uses of style sheets (Section 16.1);
- ✔ understand CSS syntax (Section 16.2);
- ✔ know how to link CSS to XHTML (Section 16.3);
- ✔ be able to predict inheritance and cascading order (Section 16.4);
- ✔ understand the CSS box (formatting) model (Section 16.5);
- ✔ have mastered the use of font, text, and color properties (Sections 16.6–16.8);
- ✔ have mastered content positioning in CSS (Section 16.9);
- ✔ have practiced the use of CSS (Section 16.10).

Problems

The exercises are designed for a lab setting, while the homework is to be done outside class time.

Exercises

16.1 Modify Example 16.1 to use inline styles.

16.2 Modify Example 16.1 to use imported styles.

16.3 Modify Example 16.1 to use external styles.

16.4 Modify Example 16.1 to use the `class` and `id` attributes.

16.5 Modify Example 16.1 to use the `<span>` and `<div>` tags.

Homework

16.6 Create two different style sheets that include formatting of text and colors. Apply them to the same Web page. Be imaginative.

16.7 Extend the style sheets from Problem 16.6 to include lists and links. Apply them to the same Web page. Be imaginative.

16.8 Extend the style sheets from Problem 16.7 to include images. Apply them to the same Web page. Be imaginative.

16.9 Extend the style sheets from Problem 16.8 to include tiling of images. Apply them to the same Web page. Be imaginative.

16.10 Extend the style sheets from Problem 16.9 to include positioning of Web-page elements. Apply them to the same Web page. Be imaginative.

HTML Editors

Goal

Understand HTML editors, their benefits, their use in developing websites and Web pages, the tasks they support, and how to use them effectively to increase productivity.

Objectives

- Why we need HTML editors
- The difference between editors, translators, and converters
- The tasks performed by editors
- WYSIWYG (pronounced "wiz-e-wig") editors
- How editors work
- The FrontPage editor
- AceHTML editor
- Netscape Composer

505

Outline

17.1 Introduction

We have covered all the XHTML concepts, elements, tags, and syntax that Web authors need in order to write XHTML code to implement the design and layout of their Web pages. The central question now is, What is the best way to generate code? Should we write code manually, semi-manually, or use automatic code generators? Code generation, be it XHTML, Java, C, C++, or other languages, has always been a topic of debate with respect to automation. We believe that the best answer is to generate code manually first to understand the basic concepts and then use code automation tools to increase productivity and reduce product development cycles.

Many programming languages, such as Java, C++, and Visual Basic, have what is known as an IDE (integrated development environment). These IDEs are tools that allow programmers to write, compile, test, and debug programs in an efficient way. The tools make this development cycle faster and more productive. For example, the tools report the compilation errors in a friendly and easy-to-understand way. They also make the code easy to follow by using different colors for code parentheses and keywords.

The idea of using IDEs for programming languages has been applied to HTML in the form of HTML editors. An **HTML editor** is a tool (in this case, a computer program) that allows the author to choose the XHTML element (e.g., a hyperlink or an image) to be created, from among the editor's GUI icons. The editor guides the author to create the element by presenting a series of requests for the data required to define the element. After the author inputs the data, the editor creates the elements in the Web page and generates its XHTML code. Now the author evaluates the element as it looks on the Web page. If not satisfied, the author can delete it and then either create it again or create a new element.

There are also HTML translators and converters. An **HTML translator** is a tool that can convert a text file into an HTML file. Some Word processors can perform this function as well. For example, Word allows its users to save documents in HTML format if they click `File =>` `Save as Web Page`. An **HTML converter** is the exact opposite of a translator: It converts an HTML document into a text file.

HTML editors hide the XHTML code from Web authors during the development phase, allowing them to focus on the layout and design of their Web pages. The author builds the XHTML elements of the page one by one. While doing so, the author uses the menus, icons, and other tools provided by the editor. Every time the author creates an element in the page, the editor generates the corresponding XHTML code and places it in an HTML file specified by the author. At the end, the Web page is fully displayed in the editor's window, and the XHTML code is stored in the HTML file.

In contrast, the manual approach works opposite to the editor's approach: In the former, we start with XHTML code and end with the Web page. In the latter, we start with the Web page and end with XHTML code. The net outcome of both approaches is, however, the same: A Web page and an HTML file. Some Web authors may prefer not to get involved with XHTML code; they argue that their main goal is the look and appeal of their Web pages and websites to their potential online customers, not the writing of XHTML code. In such a case, they use HTML editors. Other Web authors use a hybrid approach They use editors to develop the bulk of their Web pages and websites and then use the manual approach to fine-tune and finalize the development.

Is the XHTML code generated by editors for a Web page the same as or close to what the manual code would be? In general, the editor's code is more complex and cumbersome than manually written code. The editor's code is often full of tags that may not be necessary. Editors act as an automation tool for code generation, so they use and apply the same algorithms equally to the same problems. Thus, editors, like any other automation tool, cannot precisely generate the most compact code; they use the approach of "one size fits all." In addition, editors always use tables to format Web pages according to the pages' design and layout needs.

17.2 Editors' Tasks

The main goal of using an HTML editor is to speed up and automate the creation process of Web pages. This approach reduces the cycle time (the time elapsed from designing a page to posting it on the Web). Using an editor should also make page creation easier, especially if the user of the editor knows XHTML. Knowledge of XHTML enables users to understand all the editor's functions.

The use of an HTML editor is an iterative process. The process begins with a blank Web page or a template and ends with a filled page that has all the required XHTML elements. During the process, Web authors add elements, evaluate the page, make adjustments, change the design, and so forth. This loop of adding elements and evaluating the resulting Web page continues until the Web author is satisfied with the final page design and layout.

During the process of generating Web pages, Web authors can use all the functions an HTML editor provides them with. When using editors, authors can drag and drop HTML building blocks to construct the page. Such building blocks can include hyperlinks, forms, and tables. Some editors provide *split-view editing*, where authors write and edit HTML code in one window and view the resulting Web page in another window. While the functions and tasks of various editors may be different, there is a common set that all editors support and provide. Here is a list of common editor tasks:

1. **Design and write Web pages.** This is the core, essential task of an editor. Editors provide Web authors with either blank pages or default templates. The templates may be used to jump-start page design and layout. Authors may also design and save their own customized templates. There are many activities provided by editors in order to support this task. These activities support the creation of all the XHTML elements covered in this book. Using editors, Web authors create text, links, images, forms, frames, tables, layers, and so forth. They can also import existing images into their Web pages. They may use different fonts, colors, clip-art work, backgrounds, and special characters in their Web pages as well.

2. **Upload and download pages.** After authors finish their Web pages, editors enable them to use FTP to upload or download them for distribution on the Web. In this task, an editor guides authors to define the URL of the hosting server and of the server directory to store the pages. Some editors allow Web authors to publish their Web pages on free Internet hosts and servers or on any ISP where they have accounts.

3. **Save code for reuse.** Web authors, like other programmers, quite often reuse the same code many times. Towards this goal, editors allow them to save snippets of their generated code separately from Web pages, for reuse in the future.

4. **Provide code components.** The software industry promotes the concept of software components. The idea here is to provide off-the-shelf software components that can be reused while developing new software products. This concept is similar to buying standard auto parts in the automotive industry. HTML editors provide canned (prewritten) code and scripts to enhance and activate Web pages.

5. **Provide e-mail links.** Some editors provide wizards that Web authors can use to add e-mail links to their Web pages. Web authors and webmasters use them to receive feedback from Web surfers.

6. **Provide time and date stamp.** This function is very useful when a Web page is frequently updated. Editors provide an automatically updated stamp for time and date that is normally displayed as part of a page's footer.

7. **Enable of use directory structures.** Editors allow the use of the directory structure found on Web servers. This feature helps authors to place their pages in the space allowed for them.

8. **Provide a help function.** As with any software programs online help provides Web authors with instant access to an editor's documentation. Web authors can read about any command or function provided by an editor.

9. **Provide spell checking.** This is a useful function, as many of us overlook wrong spelling, no matter how hard we check. Editors also allow their users to customize the spell checking by adding their own words and acronyms to the editor's dictionary.

10. **Highlight HTML errors.** Editors usually use color codes to highlight XHTML tags, attributes, text, and so forth. They also highlight errors associated with XHTML tags and attributes, to make it easier for Web authors to spot the errors and correct them.

11. **Support *redo* and *undo* functions.** These are useful universal functions supported by many HTML editors.

12. Search for words and strings. Some of the common search-text functions are offered by editors for Web authors. They include the `Find`, `Find Again`, and `Find/Change` functions.

13. Perform concurrent page development. Some editors allow their users to work on and test multiple pages at the same time. This feature is particularly useful when Web authors want to compare different design ideas for the same page. Contrasting the different designs on the screen side by side offers the best comparison methodology.

14. Import code files. Some editors support the importation of files into the code of Web pages. A Web author can define an insertion point in the XHTML code and import the file.

17.3 Overview of Editors

There are many HTML editors in existence. Some are more sophisticated than others. HTML editors may be categorized in three groups. The first group is known as *What You See Is What You Get* (WYSIWYG) *editors*. This group includes Microsoft `FrontPage`, Netscape `Composer`, and Macromedia `Flash` and `Dreamweaver`. Any editor that belongs to the WYSI-WYG group allows Web authors to set up and insert the elements of a Web page in the editor, which, in turn, generates the XHTML code automatically.

The second group is known as *XHTML tag editors*. Web authors who use editors in this group still use XHTML tags and their attributes. HTML editors in this group provide authors with menus of tags. When the authors choose a tag, editors display the tag's attributes and insert the code for the tag in the Web page's code.

The third group is known as *hybrid* or *semi-WYSIWYG editors*. This group includes the AceHTML editor we use in this book. These editors provide Web authors with XHTML tags. When authors select a tag, the editor inserts it in the Web page's code and displays its result immediately. The final product of the editors of this group, like that of the other groups, is the Web page and its XHTML code.

An HTML editor has a general structure for its user interface, regardless of its type. Figures 17.1–17.3 show three editors: FrontPage 2002, Netscape Composer (which comes with Netscape Communicator 7.01), and AceHTML 5. Any editor provides three distinctive tools: the word-processing-like functions to format text; the XHTML menus and icons to insert any XHTML element in a Web page; and menus such as `File`, `Edit`, `View`, and `Insert`.

AceHTML is free and can be downloaded and installed, as we discussed in Chapter 9, from `http://download.visicommedia.com`. Netscape Composer is installed automatically when you install Communicator browser. FrontPage is part of Microsoft Office; it is installed when Office is installed. Both the AceHTML and FrontPage editors can be invoked from the Windows `Start` menu or by clicking their shortcuts on the desktop. Netscape Composer is invoked by clicking its icon at the docking position, as we discussed in Section 2.7.

Using any HTML editor should help you learn how to use others. They all employ the same XHTML concepts. We cover three editors in this chapter—AceHTML, FrontPage, and

Netscape Composer—so that we may gain experience in using them. Composer, however, does not provide all the XHTML elements. For example, it does not create forms or frames.

Figure 17.1 shows the AceHTML editor configured to show its XHTML-code and internal-browser windows next to each other. They can float or be configured in other ways as well. We use this configuration so that we can view the results of the XHTML code instantly. Make sure that the browser refreshes each time a new XHTML tag is typed. The GUI shown in Figure 17.1 is full of icons and menus, but they are easy to use. Besides the icons of some basic XHTML elements, there is a `tags` icon, as shown. Clicking this icon opens the tags window shown in the bottom right corner of Figure 17.1. To use it, click the alphabet character corresponding to the first letter of the tag to insert; for example click H to insert an `<h1>` tag. Then place the cursor in the code window, and double-click the `<h1>` tag in the tags window.

Multiple files can be opened at the same time. The editor creates a tabbed window for each file. Thus, AceHTML is a tabbed editor. A user clicks the corresponding tab in order to activate the desired window. AceHTML supports many languages and provides templates for them. The languages it supports are HTML, XHTML, XML, CSS, JavaScript, PHP, WML, Perl, and ASP. Simply click `File => New` to find all these templates. It also allows the creation of custom templates.

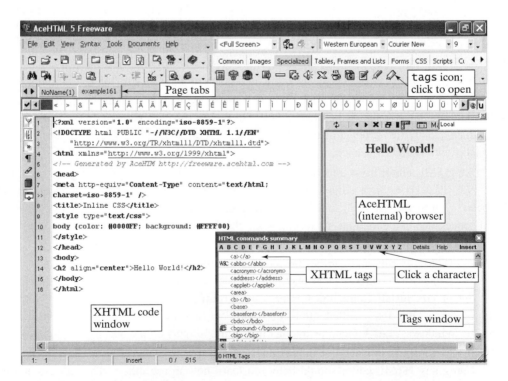

Figure 17.1 AceHTML editor.

Figure 17.2 shows the FrontPage window. FrontPage was designed with website design in mind. Its `File => New` menu has two menu items: `Page` (for a single Web page) and `Web` (for a website). Clicking `Web` and selecting a project opens a tree of Web documents that can be customized and developed. FrontPage offers all the XHTML elements we have covered. Its menu bar offers the `Table` and `Frames` menus. Its `Insert` menu offers horizontal lines, forms, breaks, and images (pictures). Its other icons (see Figure 17.2) offer headings, text formatting, unordered and ordered lists, colors, and indentations.

FrontPage has three panes at the bottom of its window, as shown in Figure 17.2. The `Normal` pane displays the Web page as the editor renders it. The `HTML` pane shows the generated XHTML code. The `Preview` pane renders the Web page as a browser displays it. These panes are similar to what the AceHTML editor offers. A Web author works with the `Normal` pane all the time. The `Preview` pane disables all XHTML elements and makes them unselectable.

FrontPage allows authors to insert raw XHTML tags. Click `Insert => Advanced => HTML`. A window opens up in which you may type XHTML code. The code is inserted into the generated HTML code. However, the results are visible only in the `Preview` window.

Figure 17.3 shows the Composer window. Composer allows Web authors to create single Web pages, one at a time. It does not offer all the XHTML elements we have covered. It cannot create a form, frame, or image map. Its menu bar offers the `Table` menus. Its `Insert` menu

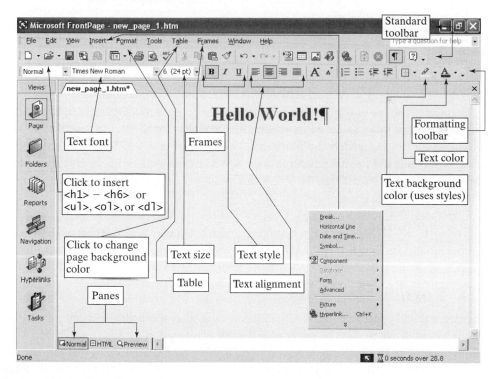

Figure 17.2 FrontPage editor.

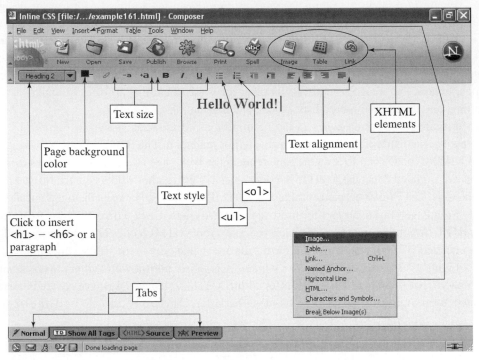

Figure 17.3   Composer editor.

offers horizontal lines, links, anchors, breaks, and images. Its other icons (see Figure 17.3) offer headings, text formatting, unordered and ordered lists, colors, and indentations.

Composer has four tabs at the bottom of its window, as shown in Figure 17.3. The `Normal` tab displays the Web page as the editor renders it. The `HTML` tab shows the generated XHTML code. The `Preview` tab renders the Web page as a browser displays it. These tabs are similar to what the AceHTML and FrontPage editors offer. A Web author works with the `Normal` window all the time. Unlike in FrontPage, the `Preview` window does not disable XHTML elements; only the HTML window does.

Like AceHTML and FrontPage, Composer allows authors to insert raw XHTML tags. Click `Insert => HTML`. A window opens up in which you may type XHTML code. The code is inserted into the generated HTML code, and the results are displayed in the `Normal` window instantly.

17.4 Formatting Text

Formatting text and paragraphs in HTML editors is as easy as formatting text and paragraphs in word processors. It can be done before or after the text is inserted in the Web page. If you want to set the formatting before inserting text, select and activate all required styles and formats. Then begin typing. If you prefer to format text after it has been inserted, highlight the text to select it, and apply the desired styles and formats. Following are the menus for text formatting in the three editors:

AceHTML:

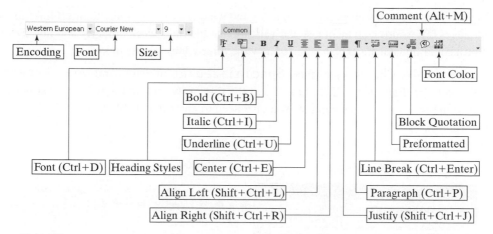

FrontPage:

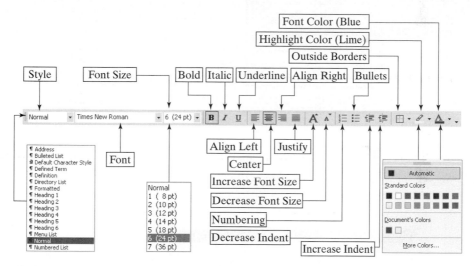

Composer:

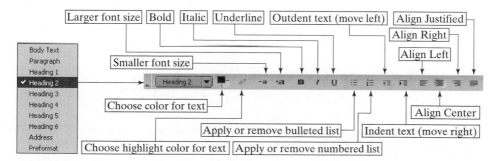

17.5 Creating Hyperlinks

HTML editors provide Web authors with icons and windows to allow them to insert links in their Web pages. They also help them test and validate that the links work properly and that they are not broken. Following are explanations of how the three editors create links:

AceHTML: Click this sequence: `Specialized` (tab in main window) => `External Link` (icon) => Enter the URL to link to and the title of the link in the window that pops up. Refer to the following screen capture. You also need to enter the visible text for the link in the code window.

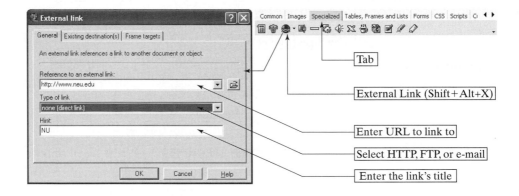

FrontPage: Click `Insert` (menu) => `Hyperlink` to open the window shown in the following screen capture:

Composer: Click the `Link` icon (in the Composer window) to open window shown in the following screen capture:

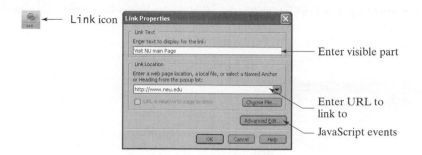

17.6 Inserting Images

HTML editors support the insertion of images and image maps in Web pages. They provide GUI
windows based on the attributes of the `<img>` tag. The three editors support images as follows:

AceHTML: Click `Images` (tab) => `Insert an Image` (icon) => Fill in the information for the image, as shown in the corresponding screen capture. To insert an image map,
click the `Image Map` icon shown in the screen capture.

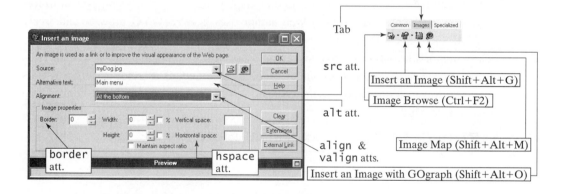

FrontPage: Click `Insert` (menu) => `Picture` => `From File` => Select the file
=> `OK`. See the following screen capture:

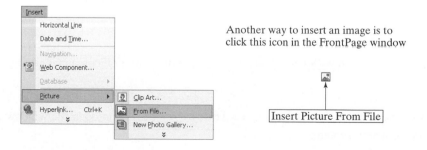

Composer: Click `Insert` (menu) => `Image` => Select the file => OK. See the following screen capture:

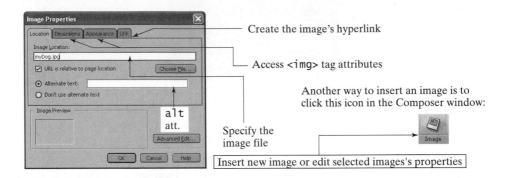

17.7 Creating Tables

HTML editors can create tables that can be used to display information in Web pages or to format the Web pages themselves. When a Web author uses a WYSIWYG browser and freely places XHTML elements in the browser window, the browser uses tables in the background to keep track of author's layout. FrontPage and Composer operate in this manner. The AceHTML editor, on the other hands, does not use tables in the background, as it is not exactly a WYSIWYG editor. However, it does allow users to create tables. Here is how the three editors help Web authors create tables:

AceHTML: Click the `Tables` tab shown in the following screen capture:

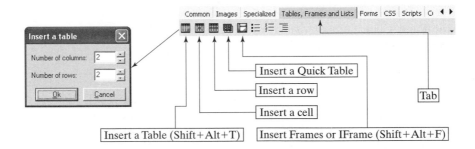

FrontPage: Click `Table` (menu) => `Insert` => `Table` to open the window shown in the following screen capture:

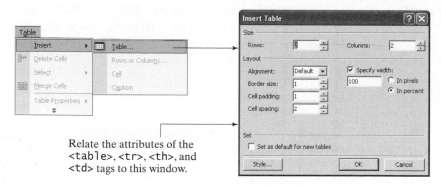

Relate the attributes of the
`<table>`, `<tr>`, `<th>`, and
`<td>` tags to this window.

Composer: Click `Table` (menu) => `Insert` => `Table` to open the window shown in
the following screen capture:

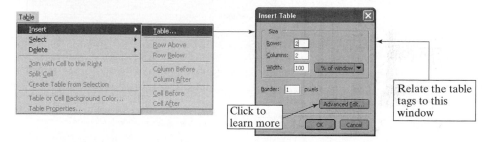

17.8 Creating Frames and Forms

Composer does not create frames and forms. The AceHTML and FrontPage editors support both
of them as follows:

AceHTML: To create a frame, refer to the first screen capture shown in Section 17.7. To
create a form, click the `Forms` tab shown in the following screen capture:

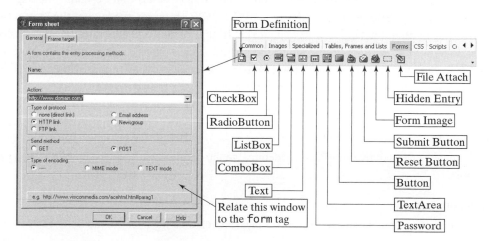

FrontPage: To create a frame, click `File` (menu) => `New` => `Page` => `Frames Pages` (tab). To create a form, click `Insert` (menu) => `Form` => `Form`. This sequence creates a form with only the submit and reset buttons, [Submit] [Reset] . Add elements to the form as needed, using the form elements shown in the following screen capture:

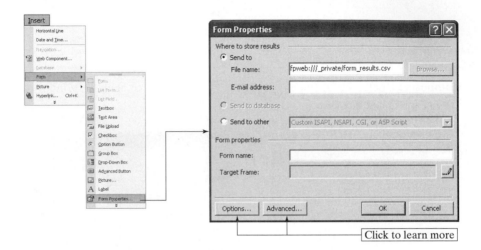

17.9 Tutorials

17.9.1 Creating Text and Links (Study Sections 17.4 and 17.5)

In this tutorial, we use FrontPage to create a Web page that has some text and links. One link connects to `http://ww.neu.edu`, and the other sends an e-mail message to `zeid@coe.neu.edu`. Since FrontPage is a WYSIWYG browser, we lay out the elements of the Web page without having to worry about HTML tags. FrontPage generates the HTML code in the background. We show the code in the second screen capture in this tutorial. Note that FrontPage generates HTML code, not XHTML. Click the editor's three tabs (`Normal`, `HTML`, and `Preview`) to view the page in different manners.

Save the generated HTML code as `tutorial1791.html`.

Discussion:

The code, as generated by FrontPage, is identical to the handwritten code, because the Web page is simple.

Hands-on exercise:

Edit the code to delete the unnecessary `<p>` tags, and change the background color to #FFFF00.

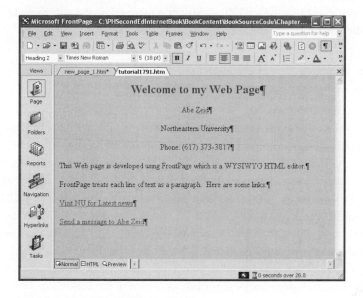

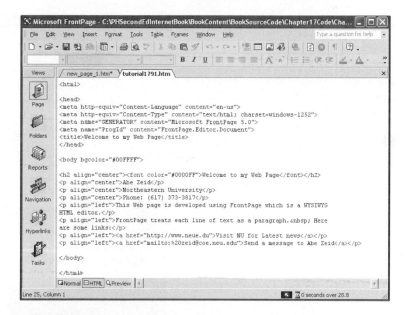

17.9.2   Creating Images and Tables
(Study Sections 17.6 and 17.7)

In this tutorial, we use Composer to create a 1×2 table. We insert an unordered list and an ordered list in the first cell and an image in the second cell. Save the file as `tutorial1792.html`. Click the Show All Tags tab to see the tags that Composer has created. Also, you may click the <HTML> Source tab to view the source code. These two tabs are shown in the bottom left of the accompanying screen captures.

Discussion:

Examining the generated code, Composer uses the <div> tag to format the Web page, while FrontPage uses the <p> tag for formatting, as shown in tutorial 19.7.1.

Hands-on exercise:

Add a two-cell second row to the table. Add some text in the first cell and a form in the second cell.

The accompanying bottommost screen capture shows all the tags of the Web page in a very clear and useful manner. Each HTML element is a <div>. Starting from the top, the <body> tag contains all the pages content. There are <div> tags for the <h1>, text, and <table> elements. There is no <div> tag for the <hr> tags because the <hr> tag itself acts as a <div> tag. Within the <table> tag, there are two <td> tags for the table's two cells. The first <td> tag contains the <ul> and <ol> tags. The second <td> tag contains the <img> tag. We have edited the HTML code of the resulting table to remove the table's border by changing the size of the border from one to zero pixels. Composer created the table with a one-pixel- thick border. We remove the border in order to make the Web page looks seamless, as shown in the following screen capture. Also,

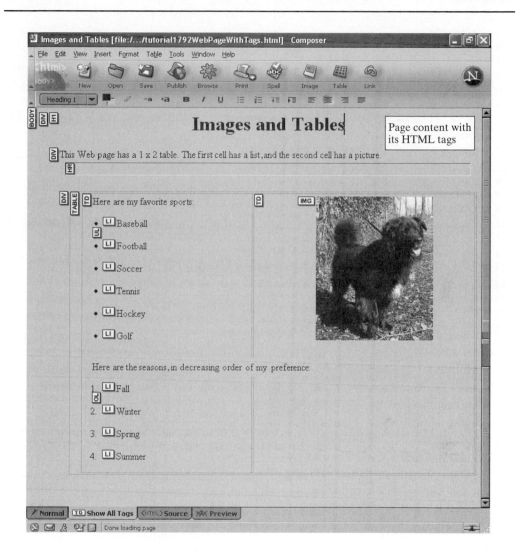

note that Composer uses the full path to specify image files. We have edited the code to use the relative path instead. (See line 47.) The final HTML code is as follows:

```
1   <!DOCTYPE html PUBLIC "-//W3C//DTD HTML 4.01 Transitional//EN">
2   <html>
3   <head>
4     <title>Images and Tables</title>
5
6     <meta http-equiv="content-type"
7   content="text/html; charset=ISO-8859-1">
8     <meta name="author" content="Abe Zeid">
```

```
 9  </head>
10  <body>
11
12  <div align="center">
13  <h1>Images and Tables</h1>
14
15  <div align="left">This Web page has a 1 x 2 table. The first cell
    has a list, and
16  the second cell has a picture.<br>
17
18  <hr width="100%" size="2"><br>
19
20  <div align="center">
21  <table cellpadding="2" cellspacing="2" border="1" width="100%">
22     <tbody>
23       <tr>
24         <td valign="top">Here are my favorite sports:<br>
25
26       <ul>
27          <li>Baseball</li>
28          <li>Football</li>
29          <li>Soccer</li>
30          <li>Tennis</li>
31          <li>Hockey</li>
32          <li>Golf</li>
33
34       </ul>
35   Here are the seasons, in decreasing order of my preference:<br>
36
37       <ol>
38          <li>Fall</li>
39          <li>Winter</li>
40          <li>Spring</li>
41          <li>Summer<br>
42          </li>
43
44       </ol>
45        </td>
46        <td valign="top" align="center"><img
47  src="dogScale.JPG" alt="My Dog" width="196" height="236">
48             <br>
49          </td>
50       </tr>
51
52     </tbody>
53  </table>
54    <br>
55    </div>
```

```
56    </div>
57    <br>
58    </div>
59
60    </body>
61    </html>
```

FAQs

Introduction (Section 17.1)

Q: How do I know whether a Web page was developed manually or by using an HTML editor?

A: View the page's source code in a browser. In Netscape, use `View => Page Source`. In IE, use `View => Source`. There are two clues you should look for when you view the page's source code. Assess the codes complexity, and check the `<meta>` tag. If the code looks complex and uses tables for formatting, most likely the page was developed by using an editor. To double-check, inspect the `<meta>` tag at the top of the page. If it shows a generator's name, version, date, and other information, then the stated editor was used to create the page.

Overview of Editors (Section 17.3)

Q: Can I use MS Word to create HTML documents?

A: Yes. MS Word allows you to take a Word document and save it as an HTML document. Use this sequence: `File => Save as Web Page =>` Input the file name. Word inserts all the required tags into the document automatically and assigns the `.html` extension to the file. You can then view the document in a browser. Thus, you can have two versions of the same document: Word and HTML. This approach is useful if you have existing Word documents that you need to convert into HTML or embed in other HTML documents. An example is your resume.

Q: How can I create forms when using Composer?

A: Composer does not have a direct way to create forms. One way is to use tables and raw HTML tags to create forms.

Blackbox

Section 17.1 (Introduction): HTML editors are useful in developing websites and Web pages. They free Web designers and programmers from having to write XHTML syntax, allowing them to focus on Web design. Editor-generated XHTML code is usually more complex and harder to read than manually written code.

Section 17.2 (Editors' Tasks): The main task of an HTML editor is to generate XHTML code automatically while Web designers use the editor to insert or create Web-page content and elements such as text, links, and images.

Section 17.3 (Overview of Editors): Three types of HTML editors exist. The WYSIWYG (What You See is What You Get) type lets Web designers insert or create Web-page content while generating the XHTML code in the background. Examples include Microsoft FrontPage and Netscape Composer. The second type lets designers insert raw XHTML tags. Examples include AceHTML. The third type is a middle ground between the first two types. It is called a semi-WYSIWYG editor. AceHTML can be considered an example.

Section 17.4 (Formatting Text): Formatting text and paragraphs in HTML editors is as easy as formatting text and paragraphs in word processors. It can be done before or after the text is inserted in the Web page. If you want to set the formatting before insertion, select and activate all required styles and formats. Then begin typing. If you prefer to format text after it has been inserted, highlight the text to select it, and apply the desired styles and formats.

Section 17.5 (Creating Hyperlinks): HTML editors provide Web authors with icons and windows to allow them to insert links in their Web pages.

Section 17.6 (Inserting Images): HTML editors support the creation of images and image maps in Web pages. They provide GUI windows based on the attributes of the `<img>` tag.

Section 17.7 (Creating Tables): HTML editors can create tables that can be used to display information in Web pages or to format the Web pages themselves.

Section 17.8 (Creating Frames and Forms): HTML editors can create frames and forms. Forms can be formatted more easily in editors than manually.

Section 17.9 (Tutorials): Two tutorials show how to use editors.

Check Your Progress

At the end of this chapter, you should

- ✔ understand the use of HTML editors (Section 17.1);
- ✔ understand the tasks performed by HTML editors (Section 17.2);
- ✔ know about WYSIWYG editors and the other types of HTML editors (Section 17.3);
- ✔ have mastered the use of HTML editors to create Web-page content (Sections 17.4–17.9).

Problems

The exercises are designed for a lob setting, while the homework is to be done outside class time.

Use an HTML editor such as FrontPage or Netscape Composer to create the given Web pages, each of which we have created in previous chapters of this book. Compare the editor's HTML code with the manually written code from the previous chapter.

Exercises

17.1   Create the Web page of Example 9.8 (hyperlinks).

17.2   Create the Web page of Example 9.10 (unordered lists).

17.3   Create the Web page of Example 9.11 (ordered lists).

17.4   Create the Web page of Example 9.12 (definition lists).

17.5   Create the Web page of Example 10.3 (image hyperlinks).

Homework

17.6   Create the Web page of Example 9.9 (anchors).

17.7   Create the Web page of Example 9.13 (nested lists).

17.8   Use an HTML editor to create the table shown in the first of the three screen captures given next. The cells in the last row use bold text and have a background color of #CEEFBD.

17.9   Use an HTML editor to create the dual-heading table shown in the second of the three screen captures given next.

17.10 Use an HTML editor to create the Web page shown in the third of the three screen captures given next.

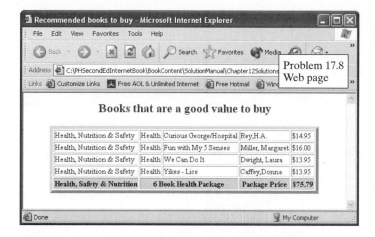

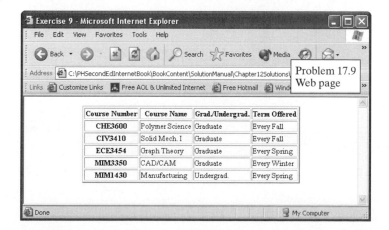

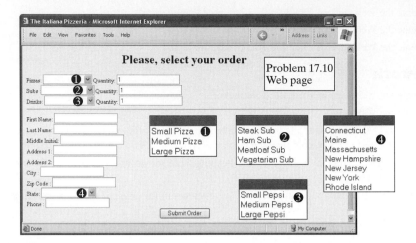

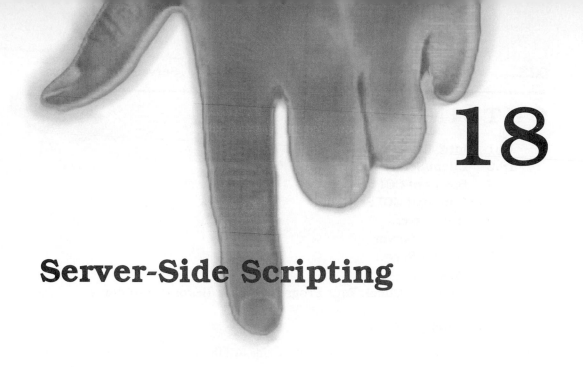

Server-Side Scripting

Goal

Understand data communication between clients and servers, CGI protocol, name/value pairs, pairs encoding and decoding, processing form data, and installing and using the Apache and Tomcat servers.

Objectives

- Processing Web-page data
- Client/server architecture
- Basics of CGI protocol and scripting
- Structure of CGI scripts
- Standard environment variables
- Output structure
- Web servers
- Apache and Tomcat servers

OUTLINE

18.1 Introduction

Thus far, this book has concentrated on the client side. All the Web pages and their XHTML code have been tested on a client computer without the computer having to be online or connected to a server. We were even able to test forms without having to be online, because we ignored their data-processing computer programs. In this chapter, we move from the client side to the server side and show how CGI (Common Gateway Interface) facilitates the communication between both sides. We also show how we can install and set up Apache and Tomcat Web servers on the same client computer, to allow us to practice this chapter's server-side concepts.

The interaction between clients and servers is accomplished via browsers that run on the client side. Web surfers send a request through a browser to a server by clicking buttons or hyperlinks that they see on a Web page. This server hosts the website and its Web pages. The browser bundles (encodes) the information of the request as name/value pairs, according to the rules of CGI, and sends it across the Internet to the server. The server usually holds many CGI scripts (also known as CGI computer programs). The script requested by the Web page is automatically executed as part of the CGI rules. When this CGI script runs, it reads all the encoded name/value pairs, decodes them, extracts the data from them, processes the data, and finally sends the results to the browser, according to the CGI rules. As soon as the browser receives the results, it displays them on the screen for the Web surfer. CGI scripts can send back Web pages, files, or any other type of MIME document. Figure 18.1 shows this loop of communication.

The aforementioned communication loop is necessary in order to make Web pages interactive. Interactivity is the key to performing all transactions on the Web. Selling goods and services online requires Web surfers first to place their orders by filling in forms. Upon the submission of a form to the Web server that hosts the Web page of the form, the CGI script of the form processes the name/value pairs. It then sends a confirmation to the surfer that the order has been received and informs the user of when the product is to be shipped for delivery.

What is a CGI script? A **CGI script** is a computer program that a Web author writes to process the data and input of an interactive element in a Web page. This element is usually a form.

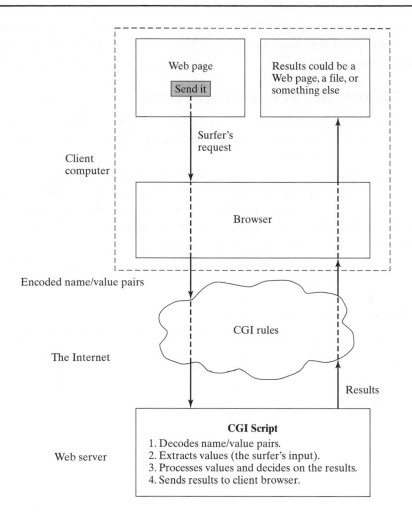

Figure 18.1   CGI communication loop.

It is known ahead of time that the data and input are sent to the Web server of the page as name/value pairs, so the CGI script is written accordingly. It performs three main functions. First, it parses and decodes the name/value pairs and extracts the data that were input by a Web surfer. Second, it makes a decision based on the data. Third, it sends a response back to the surfer based on its processing of the data.

Which programming language should we use to write CGI scripts? Any programming language is acceptable, although some are more popular than others. For example, CGI scripts are written in Perl, C, C++, Java, Java servlets, JSP (Java Server Pages), ASP (Active Server Pages), Visual Basic, and PHP. PHP is derived from "Personal Home Page Tools," an actual set of tools to build Web pages. PHP stands for "PHP: Hypertext Preprocessor," a term that is sometimes described as a "recursive acronym." The choice of a scripting language depends on the server's setup and configuration. Web authors tend to use the programming languages they already know to write CGI scripts.

18.2 Client/Server Architecture

One of the most important commercial applications of the Internet is the access of databases of companies by customers, clients, and suppliers. Many CGI scripts access these databases. These CGI scripts serve as a front end to the databases.

There are three types of client/server architecture. They are the single-tier, the two-tier, and the three-tier models. All three models access a database stored on a server via an application program, such as a CGI script. The difference between these three models depends on how many layers there are between the database and the application. If both the database and the application reside on the same computer, we have a single-tier model. Thus, one computer serves as the client and the server at the same time. Figure 18.2(A) shows a single-tier model. We use this model in Sections 18.6 and 18.7 when we set up the Apache and Tomcat servers, respectively.

If the application resides on a client, while the database resides on a server, we have a two-tier model, as shown in Figure 18.2(B). Client applications send requests to the database server. The server returns the results to the client. The three-tier model uses a middle layer (tier) to separate the database from the client application, as shown in Figure 18.2(C). This middle layer resides on an intermediate server. This layer can handle multiple client requests and can manage the connection to one or more database servers.

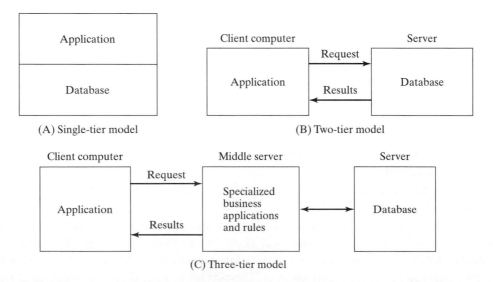

Figure 18.2 Layer positioning.

18.3 Basics of CGI Scripting

The CGI protocol determines how CGI scripts should be written. The scripts follow a certain structure, perform certain tasks, and use certain standard environment variables and server set-ups, regardless of their programming languages. A CGI script receives input from the browser through the Web server in the form of name/value pairs, processes the input, and then produces output that can go back to the Web surfer or to a file.

18.3.1 Script Structure and Tasks

The general structure of a CGI script has three main parts. The first part receives, checks, and parses the name/value pairs from the client. This part uses standard environment variables that are discussed later in this section. The second part decodes the name/value pairs and extracts the values. These values are the Web surfer's input in, for example, a form. Using these values, the script does further processing to find what the Web surfer needs. The third part of the script prepares the output that should be sent to the Web surfer as a response. The output could be a Web page, a file, an image, or any other MIME type. The script sends the output to the client browser, which, in turn, formats it and displays it on the screen for the surfer's review.

We can identify four generic tasks that any CGI script may perform. They are initialization, parsing, decoding, and output. During the initialization task, the script may set initial values of its variables, determine how it is invoked by the client's request, and read the client's input. The variables that the script may initialize include loop counters and strings, for example. The method of invoking the script determines how the client data are read, as will be discussed in Section 18.3.3. Once the script knows this method, it reads the client's input by using a standard environment variable.

The parsing and the decoding tasks form the heart of the script. The client's input comes to the script as name/value pairs that are encoded according to the standard rules of CGI (covered in Section 18.3.2). The script separates and isolates the name/value pairs from each other. Finishing this step ends the parsing task. The decoding task extracts all the values of all the names. These are the values that the Web surfer has submitted. The script now knows the value for each name or variable of the form. It uses these values to make decisions about how to process the surfer's input or request.

The last task of a CGI script is producing its output. The output is based on the decisions that the script makes in the previous task. The type of output is determined by the design of the original Web page that has originated the request that the script just processed. This output may be another Web page, an image, a file, and so forth. The script has to format the output in such a way that the client browser can understand it. The browser needs to know what type of MIME output it is receiving from the script, so that it can display it on the client screen. There is a standard generic structure that CGI scripts use to format their output. Section 18.3.4 covers the details of this structure and format.

Once the script sends its output to the browser, it cleans up after itself, such as by releasing system and memory resources, before it terminates.

18.3.2 Encoding and Decoding Name/Value Pairs

CGI is a standard method of communication between clients and Web servers which ensures that both understand each other in a clear, unambiguous manner. Thus, when the client sends information, the server knows what to do with it. When the server sends back a response, the client handles it correctly. A CGI script executes in real time. It outputs dynamic information based on user input. CGI scripts allow Web surfers to query Web servers all the time, as long as the servers are up and running.

Part of CGI is format that a client browser uses to send user input or a request to a Web server. The browser uses this format to encode the input as name/value pairs before sending it to a CGI script on the server for processing. The following string is an example of name/value pairs generated by a browser:

```
firstName=John&middleInitial=K&lastName=Smith&address=12345+AAAAA+
    street&city=My+City&state=My+State&zipCode=00000&coun-
    try=My+Country&submitButton=Submit+Query
```

A close investigation of this string reveals a pattern. There are equal signs (=), plus signs (+), and ampersands (&). The CGI format separates the name/value pairs by ampersands. It separates each name from its value by an equal sign. It replaces each space in the user input by a plus sign. It also does one more thing that is not shown in this string (because it is not needed in these case): It replaces special characters (non-Unicode characters) by their hexadecimal values. A hex value **xx** is represented by **%xx** in the CGI format. The format uses the hex value for any character that is not part of a–z, A–Z, and 0–9. For example, if the user input includes a question mark (?) or a hyphen(-), the format replaces that character by its hex value. Script programmers do not have to know the hex code for every character, as scripting languages have functions that enable them to convert between Unicode (formerly known as ASCII code) and hex code. Converting a character from Unicode to hex code is known as *escaping the character*. The opposite process (converting a character from hex code to unicode) is known as *unescaping the character.* Many programming languages have two functions, `escape()` and `unescape()`, for these two conversions.

Knowing the aforementioned format makes the implementation of parsing and decoding name/value pairs by a CGI script simple. The CGI programmer has a loop in the CGI script that scans the string containing the name/value pairs and dissects it at the & signs to collect the pairs. Thus, the result of the parsing task for the foregoing string is the following   pairs: `first-Name=John`, `middleInitial=K`, `lastName=Smith`, `address=12345+AAAAA+street`, `city=My+City`, `state=My+State`, `zipCode=00000`, `country=My+Country`, and `submitButton=Submit+Query`.

The decoding task of the CGI script starts with the foregoing pairs. The CGI programmer provides another loop that scans each pair and splits it at the equal sign (=), in order to separate the name from the value. The loop also replaces each plus sign (+) by a space. If there are percent signs (%), the loop converts the hex codes of the values that follow the percent signs to Unicode. Thus, the result of the decoding task is all the values that the Web surfer used to fill in the form. The result of the task of decoding the foregoing pairs is as follows: The names are `Name`, `middleInitial`, `lastName`, `address`, `city`, `state`, `zipCode`, `country`, and `submitButton`. The values, are respectively, `John`, `K`, `Smith`, `12345 AAAAA street`, `My City`, `My State`, `00000`, `My Country`, and `Submit Query`.

Now that all the mystery has been removed from the string of the name/value pairs, the CGI programmer and the script know exactly how to process the input, make the right decisions, and send the right response to the surfer.

The names in the name/value pairs are the names that are assigned to the elements of the form as attributes of the `<input>` tags during the creation of the form. Thus, the Web author who is also the CGI programmer has control over both the front end and the back end of a form. The Web author uses the names of the form's input elements in the CGI script, knowing ahead of time what to expect.

18.3.3 Standard Environment Variables

In addition to defining the encoding format for the name/value pairs, CGI defines a standard set of environment variables in order to provide a standard method of communication between the client browser and the Web server. All that is left now is for the CGI programmers to use these variables in their scripts to establish client/server communications. The communication is simply a request from a client to a server. Therefore, there are three groups of variables: server, request, and client.

The server variables identify the server parameters. These variables are `GATEWAY_INTERFACE`, `SERVER_NAME`, `SERVER_PORT`, `SERVER_PROTOCOL`, and `SERVER_SOFTWARE`. The `GATEWAY_INTERFACE` shows the CGI version with which the Web server complies. The format is `CGI/version`. The `SERVER_NAME` is the server's IP address, such as `www.xxx.yyy`. The `SERVER_PORT` is the server port that receives HTTP requests. It is port 80 for most servers. The `SERVER_PROTOCOL` is the name and version of the protocol that the server uses to process user requests. The format is `protocol/version`. The `SERVER_SOFTWARE` provides the name and version of the software of the Web server. The server information specified by these variables rarely changes, unless a new version of the software is installed.

The request variables hold all the information in a request. These variables are `AUTH_TYPE`, `CONTENT_FILE`, `CONTENT_LENGTH`, `CONTENT_TYPE`, `OUTPUT_FILE`, `PATH_INFO`, `PATH_TRANSLATED`, `QUERY_STRING`, `REMOTE_ADDR`, `REMOTE_USER`, `REQUEST_LINE`, `REQUEST_METHOD`, and `SCRIPT_NAME`. The `AUTH_TYPE` shows the authentication type used by the server. The `CONTENT_FILE` specifies a file name, if the CGI script needs one. The `CONTENT_LENGTH` holds the length of the string of name/value pairs, if a form uses the POST method in the `<form>` tag. The `CONTENT_LENGTH` is set to the number of URL-encoded bytes being sent to the standard input (`STDIN`) stream. The `CONTENT_TYPE` describes the type (e.g., `text/plain`) of data being sent to the server. In the case of form data, its value is `application/x-www-form-urlencoded`. The `OUTPUT_FILE` specifies the name of an output file, if the script needs one. The PATH_INFO holds additional path information. The PATH_TRANSLATED provides the absolute path of the relative path specified in PATH_INFO. The QUERY_STRING holds name/value pairs if the get method is used in the <form> tag or in any other tag. As we have discussed in Chapter 15, use of the get method is not recommended, as data may get lost or truncated. The REMOTE_ADDR is the IP address of the client originating the request. The REMOTE_USER is the username, if one was used, of the person originating the request. The REQUEST_LINE shows the full request line provided to the server by the client. The REQUEST_METHOD specifies whether the post or the get method is used in the request. The SCRIPT_NAME specifies the name of the script that is used to process the request.

Out of all the foregoing request variables, there are three variables that are very important to any CGI script: REQUEST_METHOD, CONTENT_LENGTH, and QUERY_STRING. The CGI script reads the value of the REQUEST_METHOD variable. If it is post, the script uses the CONTENT_LENGTH to read all the user input and data that are stored in it. If the value is get, the script uses the QUERY_STRING instead to read the user input and data.

The client variables hold all the information about the client. They are ACCEPT, REFERER, and USER_AGENT. The ACCEPT variable specifies the MIME type that is accepted as a response by this request. The REFERER specifies the URL of the document that has the link which triggered the current document requesting information from the script. The USER_AGENT specifies the client browser's software name and version. This is a very important variable. Web pages usually display best on only one browser. There are also some XHTML tags that are specific to one browser. When using these tags, Web authors develop, say, two versions of the same page. When a Web surfer requests the page, a CGI script can check for the name of the browser sending the request by reading the value of the USER_AGENT variable. Depending on whether it is Netscape Communicator or Microsoft IE, the script sends the correct page to the surfer.

18.3.4   Output Structure

The ultimate goal of a CGI script is to send its response or results to fulfill the original request of the Web surfer. There are three different types of outputs (also known as the content type) that a script can send: a document, a location, or a status. The script must tell, the browser what type of output it is sending, so that the browser can format the output and display it accordingly.

The output of a script has a specific structure. It has two main sections: the output header and the output data. The two sections must be separated by an empty line. The output header specifies to the browser what type of output data to expect. It specifies only one of the three aforementioned types. Thus, the first line in the script's output is the header statement. The second line is empty. The third line and all lines thereafter are the output data, if there are any.

If the output is a document, the output header looks something like this: Content-type: text/html. This line tells both the Web server and the client browser that the CGI script is sending an HTML file with MIME content. The type of the MIME content is what comes after the colon in the output header. The Content-type for the common MIME types are text/html, text/plain, image/gif, image/jpeg, application/postscript, and video/mpeg for XHTML, text, GIF, JPEG, PostScript, and MPEG documents, respectively.

The output-data section must match the content type specified in the output-header section. For example, the header specifies an HTML type, then the output data should be XHTML code. The following sample pseudocode shows the structure of a CGI script that sends an HTML document as its response:

```
Content-type: text/html

<head>
<title>CGI script output</title>
</head>
<body>
<h1>Output from a CGI script</h1>
...
</body>
```

Notice the empty line separating the header from the data. This code looks exactly like XHTML code. The difference is that this code is not stored in any file. It is part of the CGI script code. The script sends it, as its response, to the client browser for display. Thus, this process is like writing and displaying a Web page on the fly.

How is the CGI script going to send this XHTML code to the client browser? The idea here is to let the script pretend to print this code as an output stream to the screen. The Web server intercepts this stream with the code in it and sends it to the browser, which displays the corresponding page. Thus, the script prints anything it needs to send to the client browser. The syntax of the `print` statement that the script uses depends on its programming language. In all languages, the `print` statement requires that the string which is to be printed be enclosed in single or double quotes. Thus, the foregoing XHTML code is used, as is, in the `print` statements of the script. For example, let us assume that a language uses `print()` as its statement. The foregoing code is therefore written as follows:

```
print ("Content-type: text/html");
print ("");
print ("<head>");
print ("<title>CGI script output</title>");
print ("</head>");
print ("<body>");
print ("<h1>Output from a CGI script</h1>");
...
print ("</body>");
```

The output of the CGI script does not have to be a stream of data. It could also be a remote or a local location. In this case, the script header specifies a location, followed by an empty line, as follows:

```
Location: http://www.xxx.yyy
```
When this header is sent to the browser, the browser displays the corresponding URL (a document).

In some cases, the script does not have to send a response to the client. In this case, the script simply reports the status of the client's request. There are standard status codes defined by XHTML standards. These codes can be found in the document `http://www.w3.org/Protocols/HTTP/HTRESP.html`. One common response is `204 No Response`. This response occurs when the server is down or has ceased to exist. The output header to send such a status is the following line, followed by an empty line:

```
Status: 204 No Response
```

18.4 Universal CGI Scripts

CGI scripts can be thought of as universal tools that can be used over and over. The tasks that these scripts perform and the environment variables that they use are standard. Thus, we expect to write a script only once and then use it in many Web pages. For example, we need to write a script that processes form input by parsing and decoding name/value pairs only once. Every Web author who needs it can use it. Other example scripts include page-hit counters, scripts that automatically send e-mails, and so forth. In these section, we present the pseudocode of the CGI script for a form. Section 18.6 shows the implementation of this script in some programming languages.

The script is based on the concepts discussed Section 18.3. Let us assume that we use the post method in the <form> tag. Let us also assume that the script sends its output to the client as an HTML document that displays the name/value pairs as items of an unordered list. Let us further assume that the script's name is pageQuery. Here is the pseudocode of the pageQuery script:

```
declare and initialize variables;
print ("Content-type: text/html");
if the environment variable REQUEST_METHOD is NOT equal to POST,
    then
        print ("This script should be referenced with a METHOD of
        POST");
exit script;
if the environment variable CONTENT_TYPE is NOT equal to
        application/x-www-form-urlencoded, then
        print ("This script can only be used to decode form
        results");
exit script;
retrieve the value of the environment variable CONTENT_LENGTH;
        if CONTENT_LENGTH is greater than zero, then read
        CONTENT_LENGTH bytes from STDIN stream;
        parse and decode the name/value pairs;
        print ("<h1>Query Results</h1>");
        print ("You submitted the following name/value pairs");
        print ("<ul>");
        loop over all the pairs
```

```
            print ("<li>" name of form element " = " value of form
         element);
      end loop
      print ("</ul>");
   end script
```

The statements describing the parsing and decoding of the name/value pairs shown in the foregoing pseudocode will require a bit of work to implement. One or more functions will need to be written. We need to break the CONTENT_LENGTH variable at the ampersand (&) in order to separate the name/value pairs. Then we need to break each name/value pair at the equal sign (=) in order to extract the value. Finally, we need to unescape any hex code. These details are shown in Section 18.6.

18.5 Web Servers

There are many types of Web servers. Each type is related directly to the tasks for which the server is intended to be used. There are HTTP, e-mail, newsgroup, application, proxy, FTP, and Telnet servers. Each type of these servers uses the corresponding protocol: for the example's HTTP server use the HTTP protocol. HTTP servers are the most common type of server's and they serve websites Web pages. E-mail servers are set up to handle a very large number of e-mail messages. They are also set up to respond to some messages automatically. Some of the busiest e-mail servers may handle hundreds of millions of e-mail messages daily. Newsgroup servers are set up to handle multiple newsgroups, with many threads within each group. Application servers are typically used to support database applications. A server hosts the database and responds to client requests to access the database. An example is a bank server that allows bank customers to access their accounts online to perform different transactions.

A proxy server is an intermediary between an enterprise network (and its workstations) and the Internet. Thus, a proxy server could be part of the enterprise's intranet or extranet. The proxy server allows the enterprise to ensure the security and administrative control of its network. A proxy server receives requests from the Internet. Each request must pass filtering requirements, set up by the webmaster, before the server can respond to the request. Proxy servers are invisible to Web clients.

FTP and Telnet servers allow clients to establish sessions. FTP servers have files and shareware that Web surfers can download. Most FTP servers allow anonymous login. Telnet servers allow users to connect to them so that the users perform certain tasks. Most Telnet servers require users to have accounts. Refer to Chapter 8 for examples.

A Web server typically runs on a stand-alone dedicated computer, for efficiency, speed, and security. A Web server, regardless of its type and what it does, needs to be set up. Some Web servers are set up to be secure. The setup of a Web server includes tasks such as configuring it and optimizing its utilization. HTTP services handled by Web servers are not CPU intensive, but frequency intensive. There are many hits, or requests, that a server receives per minute, and they come randomly. Thus, the load on a server is of a variable nature. All Web servers have peaks, which occur when the number of hits reaches a maximum. Other setup tasks of a Web server include creating a firewall, if one is needed; setting up e-mail accounts; creating directories for different websites and Web pages; creating user accounts; installing software; and creating directories for CGI scripts.

Web servers typically house and run CGI scripts. Each Web server may have a designated directory in which CGI scripts are stored, for security reasons. This directory is usually known as the `cgi-bin` directory. CGI scripts could be a drain on a server's resources, especially if it has heavy traffic. Every time a server executes a CGI script, it must spawn a new task or a process. The server must both monitor all these tasks and listen for new tasks or requests at the same time. The server has an HTTP daemon that enables it to listen to requests from different clients concurrently. Spawning a task usually takes system resources specifically, memory and disk space and processor time. These resources are usually minimal for a single spawning task, but they add up very quickly if the server attempts to handle dozens of hits or tasks simultaneously. The result could be a very slow server. This is why it is very crucial for a Web server of a website to be configured properly to handle its peak load. Otherwise, Web surfers will shy away from using the site.

There are many Web servers in existence. Some are free, while others charge for use. The majority of them support all major OSs, such as Unix (in all its varieties), Windows, Macintosh, and IBM OS/2. The Unix varieties include Sun Solaris, IBM AIX, HP-UX, SGI IRIX, Linux, FreeBSD (Berkeley Software Distribution, or Berkeley Software Design—a form of Unix OS), and NetBSD. Servers are offered by Apache, Sun Microsystems, Microsoft, and Oracle, for example.

Web servers are supported by system administrators and webmasters in companies and organizations. These individuals maintain these servers and upgrade them over time. One important task they perform is daily backups of the servers. These backups are important if a server crashes, loses its data, or is hacked into by outsiders. Backed-up data can be retrieved if needed.

18.6 Apache Server

The Apache server is one of the most widely used Web servers on the Internet. It offers a customizable approach and comes with the source code. Apache is a Unix-based server, but Windows-based and Mac-based versions are available as well. In this chapter, we install and use Apache under Windows XP to allow us to develop, run, and test CGI scripts. Webmasters who use Apache must be very experienced with Unix in order to be able to customize it and fine-tune it; however, the Windows version can be used as an out-of-the-box product. Its installation is easy. Readers who need to customize the Apache server further are encouraged to read the documentation that comes with the software.

Apache was originally based on the HTTP server of the National Center for Supercomputing Applications (NCSA) at the University of Illinois at Urbana–Champaign; however, it is a far different system today, one that can compete easily against other existing Unix-based servers. Apache was created by a nonprofit organization called the Apache Software Foundation. It is based on the volunteer work of software engineers and programmers who simply wanted a server that can behave well and is easy to customize. Apache has been tested thoroughly by both its developers and its users.

The name Apache comes from "A PAtCHy server"—to reflect its start as some patches and existing code that were put together. It is also a name of a native American tribe that has adapted with time. This adaptability reflects the nature of Apache software as well. The Apache Software Foundation does not offer official support for Apache. There are three newsgroups, one for each of the three OSs (Unix, Windows, and Mac), that offer help. Apache also has extensive documentation. In addition, the Apache website (`www.apache.org`) provides links to Apache-specific articles and books.

The remainder of this section covers downloading, installing, and using Apache to run CGI scripts. We show how and where to install and use these scripts. This section does not, homework, provide in-depth coverage of how to customize Apache. Such in-depth coverage is beyond the scope of this book.

18.6.1 Downloading and Installing Apache

To download the latest version of the Apache server, access the Web page of the Apache Software Foundation, `http://www.apache.org`. We use version 2.0.45 in this chapter. Once the Web page is up, look for the `HTTP Server` link on the left side of the page, and click it. Look for a `Download` link towards the bottom of the Web page. Click it and follow the instructions to download the Windows version.

The installation procedure for the Apache server is simple; the Apache download is a self-extracting file. Double-click it and follow the instructions. Accept all default values, for ease of installation.

During installation, Apache configures itself for the current OS by using the files in its `conf` directory. The root folder (directory) for Apache is `Apache Group`. The next folder underneath the root is `Apache2`. This folder includes all the remaining subfolders of the Apache server, as shown in Figure 18.3. Three folders of particular interest to users are `cgi-bin` (holds the CGI Scripts), `htdocs` (holds the HTML files), and `conf`. We use the first two folders to run CGI scripts. The `conf` folder has configuration files that can be edited to customize Apache. The `Apache` folder also has the executable. It is an icon with the shape of a feather and the name `Apache`. Double-clicking this icon starts the server.

18.6.2 Running and Using Apache

The TCP/IP protocol must be set up and running on the intended computer in order to run Apache. A quick test to find out whether this protocol is up to `ping` some IP address, or you can just `ping` yourself. The IP address of a PC (local computer or client) is `127.0.0.1`. Thus, type `ping 127.0.0.1` in a DOS window. If TCP/IP is installed and working, you will receive a message, as we have discussed in Chapter 1, slating that packets have been sent and received.

To run Apache in Windows, click the following sequence: `Start` (Windows `Start` menu) => `Programs` => `Apache HTTP Server 2.0.45` => `Control Apache Server` => `Start`. Alternatively, double-click the shortcut for the executable. Apache opens a temporary DOS window and starts running. The DOS window disappears quickly and leaves no visible signs that Apache is running.

To stop Apache, click `Start` (Windows `Start` menu) => `Programs` => `Apache HTTP Server 2.0.45` => `Control Apache Server` => `Stop`.

While running, the Apache daemon is listening to port 80 (unless Apache is configured to use a different port), in real time, for any requests from a client through the HTTP protocol. Port 80 is the default port that Apache uses. In order to establish a client/server communication session, open a browser window. In the browser's URL bar, type `http://localhost`, or `http://127.0.0.1`. (`localhost` is the same as the `127.0.0.1` IP address.) If Apache is running, it sends a Web page, shown in Figure 18.4, to the browser, indicating that communication has been established. Now we are running a Web server (Apache) and a client (a browser) on the same computer. This is all that we need to develop and test CGI scripts.

Once an Apache/browser connection is established, we begin running CGI scripts as described next. The Apache server has two default folders (directories) for this purpose. They are `cgi-bin` and `htdocs`, as shown in Figure 18.3. The `cgi-bin` folder holds the CGI scripts we intend to use and run. The `htdocs` folder holds the HTML files (documents) of the Web pages we intend to load into the browser. Let us consider running a Web page with a form.

Figure 18.3 Apache directory structure.

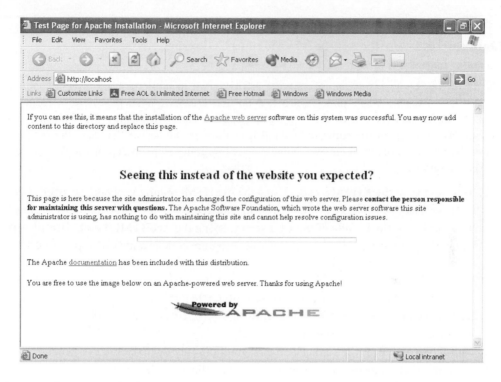

Figure 18.4 Apache/browser communication.

The `<form>` tag uses a CGI script `myScript.exe` in its `action` attribute. Here are the steps we need to run the form's CGI script from's the same computer when running Apache:

1. Place the HTML file of the page in the Apache `htdocs` folder. Assume that the name of the HTML file is `myForm.html`.
2. Place the CGI script `myScript.exe` in the Apache `cgi-bin` folder.
3. Run the Apache server.
4. Invoke a browser window.
5. Download (request) the Web page from the Apache server by typing this URL in the browser's URL bar: `http://localhost/myForm.html`.
6. Fill in the form. When done, click the form's submit button.

After step 6 is complete, the browser encodes the form's data as name/value pairs and sends them to the Apache server. Apache looks in its `cgi-bin` directory, finds the CGI script `myScript.exe` specified in the `action` attribute of the `<form>` tag, and runs it. After the script finishes running, Apache sends its results to the browser, which displays them in its window. This cycle simulates client/server communication and allows us to test CGI scripts.

Example 18.1 Use the Apache server to run a CGI script.

Use the Apache server to write and deploy a Web page.

Solution 18.1 In this example, we write a C program to implement the pseudocode from Section 18.4. We also write some XHTML code that creates a Web page with a form. The `<form>` tag in this page uses the C program as its script. We display the Web page in a browser. We then fill in the form and submit it to the Apache server that runs the script and returns the results to the browser. We follow the six foregoing steps to deploy the Web page via the Apache server:

1. **Type and save the XHTML code.** Using the AceHTML editor, generate the given code, and save it as `example181.html`. This file must reside in the `htdocs` folder of Apache.

2. **Type and save the C code of the CGI script.** Using the AceHTML `text Document` template, type the given C program. Save the program code in a file called `posttest.c`. Compile this program, and create an executable with the name `posttest.exe`. This executable must reside in the `cgi-bin` folder of Apache.

3. **Run the Apache server on the client computer.** Click this sequence: `Start` (Windows `Start` menu) => `Programs` => `Apache HTTP Server 2.0.45` => `Control Apache Server` => `Start`.

4. **Run the browser on the same client computer.** Simply open the browser window.

5. **Load the Web page into the browser.** Type the following URL into the browser's URL bar: `http://localhost/example181.html`.

6. **Fill in and send the form.** Fill in all the form elements and then click the `Place Order` button.

The following screen captures show the Web page and the data processed by the CGI script.

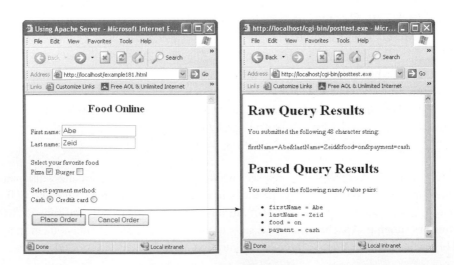

```
1   <?xml version="1.0" encoding="iso-8859-1"?>
2   <!DOCTYPE html PUBLIC "-//W3C//DTD XHTML 1.1//EN"
3       "http://www.w3.org/TR/xhtml11/DTD/xhtml11.dtd">
4   <html xmlns="http://www.w3.org/1999/xhtml">
5   <!-- Generated by AceHTM http://freeware.acehtml.com -->
6   <head>
7   <meta http-equiv="Content-Type" content="text/html;
    charset=iso-8859-1" />
8   <title>Using Apache Server</title>
9   </head><body>                                    example181.html
10  <h2 align="center">Food Online</h2>
11  <form action="../cgi-bin/posttest.exe" method="post">
12  First name: <input type="text" name="firstName" /><br />
13  Last name: <input type="text" name="lastName" /><br />
14  <p></p>
15  Select your favorite food<br />
16  Pizza<input type="checkbox" name="food" />
17  Burger<input type="checkbox" name="food" /><br /><p><p/>
18  Select payment method:<br />
19  Cash<input type="radio" name="payment" value="cash" />
20  Credtit card<input type="radio" name="payment"
    value="creditCard" /><br /><p></p>
21  <input type="submit" value="Place Order" />
22  <input type="reset" value="Cancel Order" />
23  </form>
24  </body>
25  </html>
```

```
1   #include <stdio.h>
2   #include <stdlib.h>
3   #include <string.h>                              posttest.c
4
5   #define PAIR_DELIM_STRING "&"
6   #define VALUE_DELIM_CHAR '='
7
8   char hex2char (char *what);
9   void RemoveEscapeSequences (char *url);
10  void plus2space (char *str);
11
12  /////////////////////////////////////////////////////////
13  // Purpose of this program is to simply parse the query
    // string that is passed from a POST operation.
14  // The program will output a page to the client that shows:
15  // 1. the original query string
16  // 2. a list of the name/value pairs that were submitted
17  /////////////////////////////////////////////////////////
18  void main(int argc, char *argv[])
```

```
19   {
20       int     cl;         // length of the query string
21       char    *buf;       // pointer to the query string buffer
22       char    *name;      // pointers used to parse query string
23       char    *value;     //   and extract name/value pairs
24
25   // start by sending the html header string
26       printf ("Content-type: text/html\n\n");
27
28   // check to make sure that the page that is being received
29   // from the client is in the correct format
30       if( (!getenv ("REQUEST_METHOD")) ||
31           (strcmp (getenv("REQUEST_METHOD"), "POST")))
32       {
33           printf("This script should be referenced with a
     METHOD of POST.\n");
34           exit (1);
35       }
36       if( (!getenv("CONTENT_TYPE")) ||
37           (strcmp(getenv("CONTENT_TYPE"), "application/x-www-
     form-urlencoded")))
38       {
39           printf("This script can only be used to decode form
     results.\n");
40           exit(1);
41       }
42
43   // get length of query string
44       cl = atoi (getenv("CONTENT_LENGTH"));
45   // alloc an input buffer and read the query string
46       buf = (char *) malloc(sizeof(char) * (cl + 1));
47       if (cl != (signed)fread(buf, sizeof (char), cl, stdin))
48       {
49           printf("Read of query data failed.\n");
50           exit(1);
51       }
52       buf[cl] = '\0';
53
54   // let the client know what the original query string was
55   // and write heading for parsed section of page
56       printf("<H1>Raw Query Results</H1>");
57       printf("You submitted the following %i character
     string:<br><br>%s",cl, buf);
58       printf("<H1>Parsed Query Results</H1>");
59       printf("You submitted the following name/value pairs:<p>\n"
60       printf("<ul>\n");
61
62   // let's start processing the query string by putting in
```

```
63   // blanks where the +'s have been used plus2space (buf);
64   // the parsing of the query string involves:
65   // 1. finding a name/value pair - delimited by "&"
66   // 2. removing any escape sequences in this string - %xx
67   // 3. splitting the name and value - delimited by "="
68   // 4. printing the name and value
69   // 5. and then repeating until we run out of pairs
70       name = strtok(buf, PAIR_DELIM_STRING);
71       while(name)
72       {
73           RemoveEscapeSequences(name);
74           value = strchr(name, VALUE_DELIM_CHAR);
75           *value = '\0';        // terminate the name string
76           value++;              // point to start of value string
77           printf ("<li> <code>%s = %s</code>\n", name, value);
78           name = strtok (NULL, PAIR_DELIM_STRING);
79       }
80
81   // finish up the page and cleanup
82       printf("</ul>\n");
83       free (buf);
84   }
85   /////////////////////////////////////////////////////////
86   // Utility routine that takes the next 2 hex characters from
     // the input character string and converts them to binary
     // characters. The routine assumes that the characters are either
     // 0-9, A-F, or a-f.
87   /////////////////////////////////////////////////////////
88   char hex2char (char *what)
89   {
90       char digit;
91   // convert the first hex character
92   // if it's >='A' then it's either A-F or a-f
93   // so convert to uppercase (mask of 0xdf),
94   // subtract 'A', and add result to 10
95   // if digit is 0-9, then just subtract '0'
96       digit = (what[0] >= 'A' ? ((what[0] & 0xdf) - 'A')+10 :
     (what[0] - '0'));
97   // shift hex digit to upper nibble of result
98       digit *= 16;
99   // convert the second hex digit and place it in the lower nibble
100      digit += (what[1] >= 'A' ? ((what[1] & 0xdf) - 'A')+10 :
     (what[1] - '0'));
101      return(digit);
102  }
103
104  /////////////////////////////////////////////////////////
105  // Utility routine that searches the input character string
```

```
106   // for hex escape sequences and replaces them with binary
      // characters
107   /////////////////////////////////////////////////////////////
108   void RemoveEscapeSequences (char *url)
109   {
110       int x,y;
111   // iterate through the character string
112       for (x=0, y=0;url[y];++x,++y) {
113   // if we find an escape character then
114   // then replace it with the binary representation
115   // of the next 2 hex digits and adjust the pointers
116           if((url[x] = url [y]) == '%') {
117               url[x] = hex2char(&url[y+1]);
118               y+=2;
119           }
120       }
121   // append the null termination, since we never moved it
122       url[x] = '\0';
123   }
124   /////////////////////////////////////////////////////////////
125   // Utility routine that replaces all the +'s in the input
126   // string with blanks
127   /////////////////////////////////////////////////////////////
128   void plus2space (char *str) {
129       int x;
130   // simply iterate over the string and replace all +'s
131       for (x=0;str[x];x++)
132           if(str[x] == '+')
133               str[x] = ' ';
134   }
```

Code explained:

`example181.html`:

1. Line 11 specifies the C executable `posttest.exe` as the CGI script that processes the form's data.
2. Lines 12 and 13 create two text fields.
3. Line 14 uses the <p> tag to space out the page's content.
4. Lines 16 and 17 create two checkboxes. While we use the same name, `food`, for both of them, this practicse is not a requirement for checkboxes.
5. Lines 19 and 20 create two radio buttons. The names of both buttons must be the same— `payment` in this case. Each button, however, has a unique value.
6. Lines 21 and 22 create the submit and reset form buttons, respectively.

`posttest.c`:

1. Lines 54–61 and 77 print the output of the CGI script.
2. Lines 74 and 78 decode the name/value pairs.

Discussion:

The `action` attribute of the `<form>` tag uses `posttest.exe` as the CGI script. This script must reside in the Apache `cgi-bin` folder. The `../` in front of `cgi-bin` tells the browser to go one level up in the directory's tree structure to find `cgi-bin` relative to the directory of the `example181.html` file, which is `htdocs`. Both `cgi-bin` and `htdocs` reside inside the `Apache` directory. The C program `posttest.c` must be compiled, and the executable be placed in Apache `cgi-bin` directory.

The Apache server is running and listening to any HTTP requests that might come its way from port 80. The CGI script needed to process the form's data, `posttest.exe`, is waiting to be invoked by the server. When the user clicks the `Place Order` button of the form, Apache invokes `posttest.exe`, which processes the form's data and sends the results to the browser.

The name of each name/value pair comes from the names we assign to the form elements in lines 12, 13, 16, 17, 19, and 20 in `example181.html`. The values of the text fields (lines 12 and 13) are what the user types into these fields. The value of the checkbox (line 16) is `on`. If we had assigned the checkbox a value in its tag by using the `value` attribute, then this value would have been printed. The value of the selected radio button is `cash`.

Hands-on exercise:

Add the `<value>` attribute to both lines 16 and 17 of `example 181.html`. Use `value="pizza"` and `value="burger"`, respectively. Fill in the form and check the script's output. What has changed? Compare your result with the screen captures in this example. Explain your results.

18.7 Tomcat Server

The Apache server is an HTTP server that allows its users to connect to the Internet and that serves Web pages which have XHTML code only. The Apache Software Foundation has another server, Tomcat, that renders Java Server Pages (JSPs), servlets, and Web pages that have XHTML code only. The Apache Tomcat server is the result of the Apache Jakarta project. It has a JSP engine that compiles JSPs and generates Java servlets that are used in turn to render JSPs. In this chapter, we install and use Tomcat under Windows XP to allow us to develop, run, and test JSPs. We use the Windows version as an out-of-the-box product. Its installation is easy. Readers who need to customize Tomcat are encouraged to read the documentation that comes with the software.

18.7.1 Downloading and Installing Tomcat

To download the latest version of the Tomcat server, access the Web page of the Apache Group, `http://www.apache.org`. We use version 4.1.24 in this chapter. Once the Web page is up, click this sequence: `Jakarta` (link on the left side of the page) => `Binaries` (under the `Downloads` section) => `Tomcat 4.1.24` => `tomcat-4.1.24.zip`.

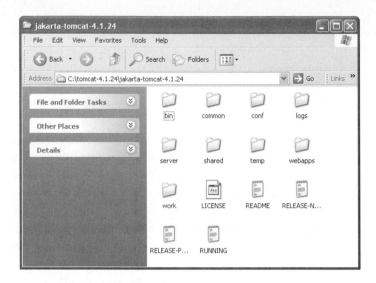

Figure 18.5   Tomcat directory structure.

The installation procedure for the Tomcat server is simple. The Tomcat download is a zip file. Double-click the file to unzip its contents into a folder `tomcat-4.1.24` (the default name).

The root folder (directory) for Tomcat is `tomcat-4.1.24`. The next folder underneath the root is `jakarta-tomcat-4.1.24`. This folder includes all other remaining subfolders of the Tomcat server, as shown in Figure 18.5. Two folders of particular interest to users are `webapps` and `conf`. We use the first folder to run JSPs. The `conf` folder has configuration files that can be edited to customize Tomcat.

18.7.2   Running and Using Tomcat

As with the Apache server, the TCP/IP protocol must be set up and running on the intended computer in order to run Tomcat. Type `ping 127.0.0.1` in a DOS window. If TCP/IP is installed and working, you will receive a message, as we have discussed in Chapter 1.

To run Tomcat in Windows, follow these four steps:

1. **Set the JAVA_HOME system variable.** Set this variable to point to the directory of the currently installed JVM (Java Virtual Machine) on the computer where Tomcat will run. Click this sequence to open a DOS window: `Start` (Windows `Start` menu) => `Run` => Type `cmd` in the window that pops up => `OK`. Type this DOS command in the DOS window: `set JAVA_HOME=c:\j2sdk1.4.1`.
2. **Set the current directory to the Tomcat bin directory.** Type this command in the DOS window from step 1: `cd \tomcat-4.1.24\jakarta-tomcat-4.1.24\bin`.

3. Start the Tomcat server. Type this command in the DOS window from steps 1 and 2: `startup`.

4. Load up a test Web page. Open a browser window and type this URL into the browser's URL bar. `http://localhost:8080`. Tomcat uses port 8080 (not 80) for communication with the client (browser).

Figures 18.6 and 18.7 show the results.

Once a Tomcat–browser connection is established, we begin running Web pages as described next. The Tomcat server has two default folders (directories) for this purpose. They are

> `C:\tomcat-4.1.24\jakarta-tomcat-4.1.24\webapps\examples\jsp`

and

> `C:\tomcat-4.1.24\jakarta-tomcat-4.1.24\webapps\examples\WEB-INF\classes.`

The `jsp` folder holds the Web page that we intend to load into the browser window. It also holds any JSPs. The `classes` folder holds the Java classes, if any, that process requests from the Web page. A request can be processed by a JSP, as shown in Example 18.2, or by a Java class. Let us consider running a Web page with a form. The `<form>` tag uses a Java class `myClass` in its

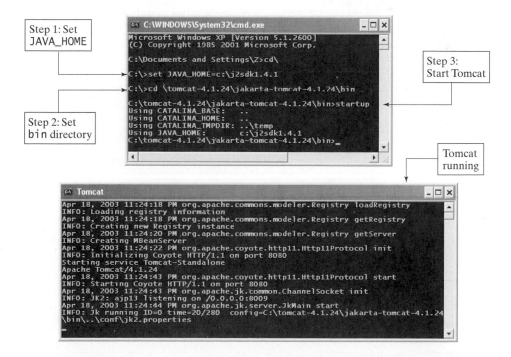

Figure 18.6 Setting up and running the Tomcat server.

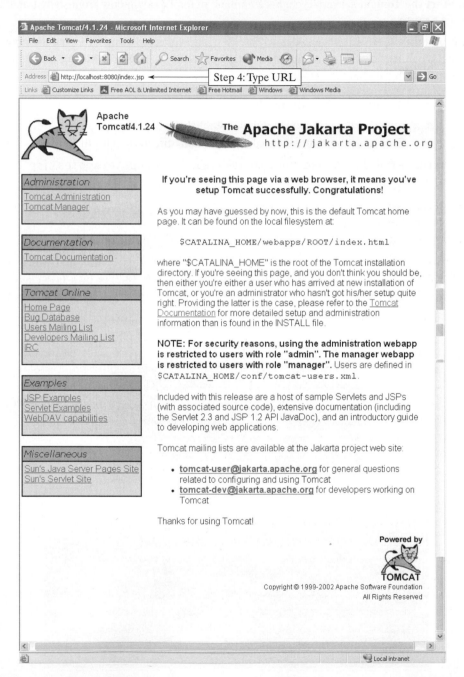

Figure 18.7   Tomcat/browser communication.

`action` attribute. Here are the steps we need to run the form's Java class from the same computer when running Tomcat:

1. Place the Web-page file in Tomcat's `jsp` folder. Assume that the name of the file is `myForm.html`.
2. Place the Java class `myClass` in Tomcat's `classes` folder.
3. Run the Tomcat server.
4. Invoke a browser window.
5. Download (request) the Web page from the Tomcat server by typing this URL into the browser's URL bar: `http://localhost:8080/examples/jsp/myForm.html`.
6. Fill in the form. When done, click the form's submit button.

After step 6 is complete, the browser encodes the form's data as name/value pairs and sends them to Tomcat. Tomcat looks in its `classes` directory, finds the `myClass` class that is specified in the `action` attribute of the `<form>` tag, and executes it. After the class finishes running, Tomcat sends its results to the browser, which displays them in its window. The code for the class should be written in Java. This cycle simulates client/server communication and allows us to test JSPs.

Example 18.2 Use the Tomcat server to run a Web page.

Use the Tomcat server to write and deploy a Web page.

Solution 18.2 In this example, we write a JSP, `processFormInput.jsp`, to replace the C program of Example 18.1. The JSP processes the form's input (data) received from a user. It retrieves the names of the form's elements as specified in the XHTML code of the Web page that uses the JSP, `example182.html`. It also retrieves the value of each element as input by the user. The `<form>` tag of the page uses the JSP in its `action` attribute. We display the Web page in a browser. We then fill in the form and submit it to the Tomcat server that runs the JSP and returns the results to the browser. We follow the six foregoing steps to deploy the Web page via the Tomcat server:

1. **Type and save the XHTML code.** Using the AceHTML editor, generate the given code, and save it as `example182.html`. This file must reside in the `C:\tomcat-4.1.24\jakarta-tomcat-4.1.24\webapps\examples\jsp` folder of Tomcat.
2. **Type and save the Java code of the JSP.** Using the AceHTML `text Document` template, type the given Java code. Save the code in a file called `processFormInput.jsp`. This file must reside in the
   `C:\tomcat-4.1.24\jakarta-tomcat-4.1.24\webapps\examples\jsp folder of Tomcat.`
3. **Run the Tomcat server on the client computer.** Follow steps 1–3 listed at the beginning of this (Section 18.7.2.)

4. **Run the browser on the same client computer.** Simply open the browser window.
5. **Load the Web page into the browser.** Type the following URL into the browser's URL bar: `http://localhost:8080/examples/jsp/example182.html`.
6. **Fill in and send the form.** Fill in all the form elements and then click the `Place Order` button. The given screen captures show the Web page and data processed by the JSP.

Code explained:

`example182.html`: This file is identical to `example181.html`, with the following exception:

Line 11 specifies the JSP `processFormInput.jsp` as the handler of the form's data.

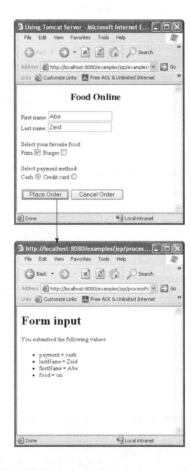

`processFormInput.jsp`:

1. Line 1 imports the classes into two Java libraries.
2. Lines 3–5, 9, and 13 print the output of the JSP.

3. Line 6 retrieves the names of the form's elements, and line 12 retrieves the value for each name.

Discussion:

The `action` attribute of the `<form>` tag uses `processFormInput.jsp`. The Tomcat server is running and listening to any HTTP requests that might come its way from port 8080. The JSP `processFormInput.jsp` needed to process the form's data is waiting to be invoked by the server. When the user clicks the `Place Order` button of the form, Tomcat invokes the JSP, which processes the form's data and sends the results to the browser. The processing is similar to that in Example 18.1.

Hands-on exercise:

Add the `value` attribute to both lines 16 and 17 of `example182.html`. Use `value="pizza"` and `value= "burger"`, respectively. Fill in the form and check the script's output. What has changed? Compare your results with the screen captures in this example. Explain the results.

```
1   <?xml version="1.0" encoding="iso-8859-1"?>
2   <!DOCTYPE html PUBLIC "-//W3C//DTD XHTML 1.1//EN"
3       "http://www.w3.org/TR/xhtml11/DTD/xhtml11.dtd">
4   <html xmlns="http://www.w3.org/1999/xhtml">
5   <!-- Generated by AceHTM http://freeware.acehtml.com -->
6   <head>
7   <meta http-equiv="Content-Type" content="text/html;
    charset=iso-8859-1" />
8   <title>Using Apache Server</title>              example182.html
9   </head><body>
10  <h2 align="center">Food Online</h2>
11  <form action="processFormInput.jsp" method="post">
12  First name: <input type="text" name="firstName" /><br />
13  Last name: <input type="text" name="lastName" /><br />
14  <p></p>
15  Select your favorite food<br />
16  Pizza<input type="checkbox" name="food" />
17  Burger<input type="checkbox" name="food" /><br /><p><p/>
18  Select payment method:<br />
19  Cash<input type="radio" name="payment" value="cash" />
20  Credit card<input type="radio" name="payment"
    value="creditCard" /><br /><p></p>
21  <input type="submit" value="Place Order" />
22  <input type="reset" value="Cancel Order" />
23  </form>
24  </body>
25  </html>
```

```
1   <%@ page import=" java.io.*, java.util.*" %>
2   <%
3       out.print ( "<h1>Form input</h1>" +
4                       "You submitted the following values"
5                       + "<ul>");
6       Enumeration paramNames = request.getParameterNames ();
7       while (paramNames.hasMoreElements ()) {
8         String name = (String) paramNames.nextElement () ;
9         out.print ("<li>" + name + " = ");
10        String[] value =                        processFormInput.jsp
11          request.getParameterValues (name);
12        String inputValue = value [0];
13            out.println (inputValue);
14        }
15        out.print("</ul>");
16  %>
```

18.8 Tutorials

18.8.1 Accessing Environment Variables
(Study Section 18.3.3)

In this tutorial, we write a C program that displays all the environment variables that we have discussed in Section 18.3.3. The program accesses and prints the three sets of variables (server, request, and client variables). After we compile the code, we use the executable as the CGI script in a form. The upcoming screen captures show the results. Here are the detailed steps:

1. **Type and save the XHTML code.** Copy example181.html and save it as tutorial1881.html. Change the action attribute, to read action= "../cgi-bin/envvar.exe". This file must reside in the Apache htdocs folder.
2. **Type and save the C code of the CGI script.** Using the AceHTML text Document template, type the given C program. Save the program code in a file called envvar.c. Compile this program, and create an executable with the name envvar.exe. This executable must reside in the cgi-bin folder of Apache.
3. **Run the Apache server on the client computer.** Click this sequence: Start (Windows Start menu) => Programs => Apache HTTP Server 2.0.45 => Control Apache Server => Start.
4. **Run the browser on the same client computer.** Simply open the browser window.
5. **Load the Web page into the browser.** Type the following URL into the browser's URL bar: http://localhost/tutorial1881.html.
6. **Fill in and send the form.** Fill in all form elements and then click the Place Order button.

Code explained:

`tutorial1881.html`:

Line 7 specifies the C executable `envvar.exe` as the CGI script that processes the form's data. `envvar.c`:

Lines 59, 67, 78, 80, and 85 print the CGI script's output.

Discussion:

The screen captures in this tutorial show the three sets of CGI variables. Only the server variables have values, because the script is running on the server side. The server variables show the expected values about the server. The request variables have values only for the variables that apply to the submitted form. For example, the value of the CONTENT_LENGTH variable is 48. This value is equal to the length (including spaces) of the string that holds the submitted name/value pairs and is the same here as in Example 18.1, as shown in the second screen capture of both examples. The value of the QUERY_STRING is null, because the method used in the form is post, not get. The value of the CONTENT_TYPE is what is expected from a form, as was explained in Section 18.3.3. The REMOTE_ADDR variable is the address of the server. This address corresponds to the name localhost that we have been using in the URLs. The values of REQUEST_METHOD and SCRIPT_NAME are what we expect.

None of the client variables have values. If we need them, we need to run a client script to find these values and send them to the server. This task is outside the scope of this chapter.

Hands-on exercise:

Change the form's input and resubmit the form. What happens to CONTENT_LENGTH?

```
1   <?xml version="1.0" encoding="iso-8859-1"?>        tutorial1881.html
2   <!DOCTYPE html PUBLIC "-//W3C//DTD XHTML 1.1//EN"
3       "http://www.w3.org/TR/xhtml11/DTD/xhtml11.dtd">
4   <html xmlns="http://www.w3.org/1999/xhtml">
5   <head><title>Using Apache Server</title></head><body>
6   <h2 align="center">Food Online</h2>
7   <form action="../cgi-bin/envvar.exe" method="post">
8   First name: <input type="text" name="firstName" /><br />
9   Last name: <input type="text" name="lastName" /><br />
10  <p></p>Select your favorite food:<br />
11  Pizza<input type="checkbox" name="food" />
12  Burger<input type="checkbox" name="food" /><br /><p><p/>
13  Select payment method:<br />
14  Cash<input type="radio" name="payment" value="cash" />
15  Credit card<input type="radio" name="payment"
    value="creditCard" /><br /><p></p>
16  <input type="submit" value="Place Order" />
17  <input type="reset" value="Cancel Order" /></form></body></html>
```

```
1   #include <stdio.h>
2   #include <stdlib.h>                                envvar.c
3
4   ////////////////////////////////////////////////////////////////
5   // Purpose of this program is to print the values of the
6   // environment variables established by the Apache server
```

```
7     // when it launches this program
8     ////////////////////////////////////////////////////////////
9     void main (int argc, char *argv[])
10    {
11        int     indx1 = 0;         // a couple of indexes for the
12        int     indx2 = 0;         // array processing
13
14    // the list of server variables to be displayed
15        char    *sv[] = {"GATEWAY_INTERFACE",
16                         "SERVER_NAME",
17                         "SERVER_PORT",
18                         "SERVER_PROTOCOL",
19                         "SERVER_SOFTWARE",
20                         NULL };
21
22    // the list of request variables to be displayed
23        char    *rv[] = {"AUTH_TYPE",
24                         "CONTENT_FILE",
25                         "CONTENT_LENGTH",
26                         "CONTENT_TYPE",
27                         "OUTPUT_FILE",
28                         "PATH_INFO",
29                         "PATH_TRANSLATED",
30                         "QUERY_STRING",
31                         "REMOTE_ADDR",
32                         "REMOTE_USER",
33                         "REQUEST_LINE",
34                         "REQUEST_METHOD",
35                         "SCRIPT_NAME",
36                         NULL};
37
38    // the list of client variables to be displayed
39        char    *cv[] = {"ACCEPT",
40                         "REFERER",
41                         "USER_AGENT",
42                         NULL};
43
44    // one more list
45    // containing the title to display on the page
46    // and the address of the list that follows
47        struct LIST
48        {
49            char *title;
50            char **envVarName;
51        };
52        struct LIST list[] = {"SERVER VARIABLES", sv,
```

```
53                                 "REQUEST VARIABLES", rv,
54                                 "CLIENT VARIABLES", cv,
55                                 NULL, NULL};
56
57      // ok, all that setup is done. . .
58      // start by sending the HTML header string
59          printf("Content-type: text/html\n\n");
60
61      // now loop through all the groups until we hit the NULL
62          while (list[indx1].title)
63          {
64              char **varNames;
65              char *value;
66      // print each heading with a little flair
67              printf("<br /><b>%s"
68                  "</b><br />-----------------------------",
69                      list[indx1].title);
70      // get the address of the list of variables
71      // and loop through the list until we hit NULL
72              varNames = list[indx1].envVarName;
73              while (varNames[indx2])
74              {
75      // print the variable we're looking for and
76      // if the variable has been set, print the value
77      // then go to the next entry in the variable list
78                  printf("<br />%s = ", varNames[indx2]);
79                  if (value = getenv(varNames[indx2]))
80                      printf("%s", value);
81                  indx2++;
82              }
83      // print one extra blank line between groups
84      // and set up the indexes for the next group and variable list
85              printf("<br />\n");
86              indx2 = 0;
87              indx1++;
88          }
89      }
```

18.8.2   Processing a Hyperlink Click (Study Section 18.7)

This tutorial uses two files. tutorial1882.html has XHTML code that creates a hyperlink. processLinkClick.jsp has JSP code that processes the click of the link by displaying some text in the browser window. Use the AceHTML editor to generate the code of both files. These two files must reside in the Tomcat jsp directory. Follow the steps in Example 18.2 to deploy this tutorial in Tomcat.

Code explained:

1. Line 12 in `tutorial1882.html` uses the JSP file as the value for the `href` attribute.

2. Lines 3–9 in `processLinkClick.jsp` print some text to the browser window.

Discussion:

When the user clicks the link in the Web page, Tomcat runs the JSP and displays its output.

Hands-on exercise:

Change the output of the JSP. Use as many XHTML tags as possible in the JSP code.

```
1    <?xml version="1.0" encoding="iso-8859-1"?>    tutorial1882.html
2    <!DOCTYPE html PUBLIC "-//W3C//DTD XHTML 1.1//EN"
3        "http://www.w3.org/TR/xhtml11/DTD/xhtml11.dtd">
4    <html xmlns="http://www.w3.org/1999/xhtml">
5    <!-- Generated by AceHTM http://freeware.acehtml.com -->
6    <head>
7    <meta http-equiv="Content-Type" content="text/html;
     charset=iso-8859-1" />
8    <title>Using Tomcat Server</title>
9    </head>
10   <body>
11   <h2 align="center">Link Processing</h2>
12   <a href="processLinkClick.jsp" title="JSP link processing">
13   Check JSP processing</a>
14   </body>
15   </html>
```

```
1    <%@ page import=" java.io.*, java.util.*" %>
2    <%                                          processLinkClick.jsp
3        out.print( "<h1>Hello World!</h1>" +
4                    "Here are some lucky numbers:"
```

```
5                    + "<ul>");
6        for (int i=1; i<6; i++) {
7          out.print ("<li>Number " + i + " is great");
8        }//for
9         out.print("<\ul>");
10   %>
```

FAQs

Introduction (Section 18.1)

Q: What are some of the tasks that CGI scripts can perform?

A: CGI scripts can be written for various reasons. They can be viewed as small application programs. CGI scripts let users communicate with Web servers in order to allow users to obtain customized information, to build interactivity between clients and servers, to enable users to search databases, to provide feedback to users, and to be able to send replies to users that are based on their requests.

Q: When I use CGI scripts written in a given programming language, do I need to have the language's compiler and runtime environment on my computer?

A: Not necessarily. It all depends on the language you use. For example, if you use already existing executables written in C or another compiled language, you do not need to install anything on your computer. The executables are machine code and should run fine. If you use classes and JSPs written in Java, you need to install the Java virtual machine (VM). You can download the J2SDK from the Sun website, `http://java.sun.com`. If you write and compile your own scripts, you need the language's compiler and runtime environment.

Basics of CGI Scripting (Section 18.3)

Q: Why do Web servers use the `cgi-bin` directory for CGI scripts?

A: A CGI script is an executable running on a Web server. This configuration is equivalent to letting the entire world, including hackers, run a program on your Web server, which, of course, raises security issues. A webmaster must therefore implement precautions when it comes to using CGI scripts. Webmasters designate a special directory, usually with the name `cgi-bin`, that stores all CGI scripts. They set up all types of security restrictions on this directory. These restrictions prevent the average user from creating CGI programs in it. As a result, CGI programmers must first give webmasters their scripts in order to post them. The outside world is allowed only "execute" access to this directory on the Web server and thus cannot sneak into any other resources of the Web server.

Apache Server (Section 18.6)

Q: Can I run more than one invocation of Apache on Windows simultaneously?

A: No. An error that port 80 is being used will be generated. There is no need for two Apache servers to be running on the same machine.

Blackbox

Section 18.1 (Introduction): Server-side scripting uses the rules established by the CGI protocol. CGI programs can be written in any programming language.

Section 18.2 (Client/Server Architecture): Three types of client/server architectures exist: single-tier, two-tier, and three-tier models.

Section 18.3 (Basics of CGI Scripting): CGI scripts receive, check, and parse the name/value pairs from the client: First, they decode the encoded name/value pairs they receive from the browser. Second, they parse the pairs to separate the names and values. Last, they process the values and send a response to the user.

Section 18.4 (Universal CGI Scripts): Universal CGI scripts are readily available for use. For example, use the CGI scripts in this chapter to process any input to a form.

Section 18.5 (Web Servers): Many Web servers exist. The two most popular ones are the Apache server (processes HTTP requests and Web pages) and the Apache Jakarta Tomcat server (processes JSPs, servlets, and Web pages).

Section 18.6 (Apache Server) (Example 18.1): Download and install Apache from `http://www.apache.org`. Here are the steps we need to run a Web page containing a form in Apache:

1. Place the HTML file of the page in the Apache `htdocs` folder. Assume that the name of the HTML file is `myForm.html`.
2. Place the CGI script in the Apache `cgi-bin` folder.
3. Run the Apache server.
4. Invoke a browser window.
5. Download (request) the Web page from the Apache server by typing this URL into the browser's URL bar: `http://localhost/myForm.html`.
6. Fill in the form. When done, click the form's submit button.

Section 18.7 (Tomcat Server) (Example 18.2): Download and install Tomcat from `http://www.apache.org`. To run Tomcat in Windows, follow these four steps:

1. Set the JAVA_HOME system variable to point to the directory of the currently installed JVM on the computer where Tomcat will run. Click this sequence to open a DOS window; `Start` (Windows `Start` menu) => `Run` => Type `cmd` in the window that pops up => OK. Type this command in the DOS window: `set JAVA_HOME=c:\j2sdk1.4.1`.
2. Set the current directory to the Tomcat `bin` directory. Type this command in the same window of step 1: `cd \tomcat4.1.24\jakarta-tomcat-4.1.24\bin`.
3. Start the Tomcat server. Type this command in the DOS window of steps 1 and 2: `startup`.
4. Load up a test Web page. Open a browser window and type this URL into the browser's URL bar: `http://localhost:8080`. Tomcat uses port 8080 for communication with the client (browser).

Here are the steps we need to run a Web page with a form in Tomcat:

1. Place the HTML file of the page in the Tomcat `jsp` folder
   `C:\tomcat-4.1.24\jakarta-tomcat-4.1.24\webapps\exam-ples\jsphtdocs`. Assume that the name of the HTML file is `myForm.html`.

2. Place the JSP file in the Tomcat `jsp` folder. (The full path is shown in step 1.)

3. Run the Tomcat server.

4. Invoke a browser window.

5. Download (request) the Web page from the Apache server by typing this URL into the browser's URL bar: `http://localhost:8080/examples/jsp/myForm.html`.

6. Fill in the form. When done, click the form's submit button.

Section 18.8 (Tutorials): Two tutorials show how to use the Apache and Tomcat servers.

Check Your Progress

At the end of this chapter, you should

✔ understand server-side scripting (Section 18.1);
✔ understand the different tiers of the client/server model (Section 18.2);
✔ know the standard variables of the CGI protocol (Section 18.3);
✔ be able to write and use universal CGI scripts (Section 18.4);
✔ Understand Web servers (Section 18.5);
✔ have mastered the use of the Apache server (Section 18.6);
✔ have mastered the use of the Apache Tomcat server (Section 18.7);
✔ have practiced using the Apache and Tomcat servers (Section 18.8).

Problems

The exercises are designed for a lab setting, while the homework is to be done outside class time.

Exercises

18.1 Fill in the form of Example 15.6. Use `posttest.exe` as its CGI script. Capture the screen that displays the results of the script.

18.2 Repeat Problem 18.1 for Example 15.7.

18.3 Repeat Problem 18.1 for Example 15.8.

18.4 Repeat Problem 18.1 for Example 15.9.

18.5 Repeat Problem 18.1 for Example 15.10.

Homework

18.6 Repeat Problem 18.1 for Tutorial 15.7.1.

18.7 Repeat Problem 18.1 for Tutorial 15.7.2.

18.8 Repeat Problem 18.1 for Tutorial 15.7.3.

18.9 Repeat Problem 18.1 for Problem 15.4.

18.10 Repeat Problem 18.1 for Problem 15.13.

PART III

JavaScript

This part covers the major concepts of client-side JavaScripts that are used by Web pages. It employs JavaScript 1.5, which is fully compatible with ECMA-262 Edition 3. The chapters in this part show how JavaScript "thinks." The goal of this part is to provide a solid and clear understanding of JavaScript syntax and its DOM model. To achieve this goal, we accomplish the following objectives:

1. Understand and master JavaScript syntax and how JavaScript and XHTML are combined in the same Web-page code **(Chapter 19)**.
2. Understand and master JavaScript functions and arrays **(Chapter 20)**.
3. Understand and master the JavaScript event model, the different types of events, and how to handle events **(Chapter 21)**.
4. Understand and master Javascript objects **(Chapter 22)**.
5. Understand and master popup windows and frames **(Chapter 23)**.
6. Understand and master form processing, and the validation of form input on the client side before sending the input to the server for processing **(Chapter 24)**.
7. Understand and master JavaScript temporal control, including animation and its use in certain applications **(Chapter 25)**.
8. Understand and master cookies **(Chapter 26)**.

JavaScript Syntax

Goal

Understand the basics of JavaScript; its syntax; the development environment; the order of code execution, debugging and testing; the inclusion of JavaScript in XHTML and Web pages; and the reasons for including JavaScript in Web pages.

Objectives

- Why JavaScript should be used?
- JavaScript and Java
- JavaScript Variables
- JavaScript Statements
- JavaScript Operators
- JavaScript Control structures
- JavaScript Input and output

Outline

19.1 Introduction

XHTML is limited in what it offers Web surfers in terms of interactivity: Web surfers can either click a hyperlink or fill in a form. JavaScript makes Web pages more dynamic by generating events that can results in many actions. **JavaScript** is a cross-platform, object-based scripting language that is simple to comprehend, easy to use, and powerful. When used in conjunction with the Document Object Model (DOM), it produces useful DHTML (dynamic HTML) applications.

The two main reasons that we use JavaScript in Web pages are dynamics and client-side execution. JavaScript dynamic and visual effects include intercepting and processing mouse clicks, opening popup windows upon loading and unloading of Web pages, and producing animation. Client-side execution includes validating form input and processing client requests that do not require server processing.

Client-side processing minimizes client/server communication and traffic. When a client requests a Web page through a Web browser, the XHTML code, along with the embedded JavaScript, is sent to the client. The Web browser interprets the XHTML document, executes the JavaScript code, and finally displays the Web page. It is important to understand that JavaScript is executed on the client side, not the server side.

Like XHTML, JavaScript is an interpretive language, not a compiled language. The browser has an interpreter that scans the JavaScript code and interprets it. If it finds syntax errors, it flags them and stops executing the code. All that is needed to execute JavaScript code is a Web browser; there is no need for compilers or runtime environments.

JavaScript was developed by Netscape and became successful because of its simplicity and power. Microsoft has a clone of JavaScript, called JScript, that is designed to run inside the IE browser. With a few exceptions, JScript is a carbon copy of JavaScript. We cover JavaScript only in this book, as it is universal and runs in any browser.

JavaScript has gone through a number of revisions since its first release. The latest version is 1.5. We cover this version in this book. This version is fully compliant with the European Computer Manufacturing Association (ECMA) language specification known as ECMA-262 Edition 3 (also known as ECMAScript). **ECMA** is the international standards association for information and communication systems. Different version of browsers support different versions of JavaScript. For example, Netscape 6 and higher and IE 6 and higher support JavaScript 1.5.

Two types of JavaScript exist: client side and server side. **Client-side JavaScript** is the code that is sent to the browser along with the XHTML code of a Web page and is executed on the client by the browser. **Server-side JavaScript** stays on the server and can be executed only by the server. Web browsers cannot execute it. The client never sees it; they see only its results as part of the Web page's content. We cover only client-side JavaScript in this book.

19.2 JavaScript and Java

JavaScript and Java are similar in some ways, but fundamentally different in other ways.Unlike Java, JavaScript does not use explicit variable types. However, it supports most Java expression syntax and Java's basic control structure.

While Java's class definitions are built by declarations, JavaScript uses implicit data types representing numbers, Booleans, and strings. Java uses the more common class-based object model, while JavaScript uses a prototype-based model that provides dynamic inheritance: What is inherited can vary for individual objects. In class-based objects, on the other hand, every object inherits from a root object. Unlike Java, JavaScript supports functions without any special declarative requirements. In JavaScript, functions can serve as behaviors of objects, executing as loosely defined methods.

Compared with Java, JavaScript is a very free-form language; there is no need to declare classes, methods, or variables, and there is no need to declare public or private variables. This factor makes JavaScript a smaller, dynamically typed language, such as HyperTalk and dBASE. JavaScript offers tools to a much wider, less sophisticated audience, such as novice Web developers and programmers, because of its easy syntax, specialized built-in functionality, and minimum requirements to create objects.

However, JavaScript cannot automatically read from or write to the hard disk of a client computer, which poses a security issue. JavaScript scripts that are downloaded by a browser as part of a Web-page request are thus considered untrusted scripts, similar to Java applets or any other Web application. These applications should not access the client's hard disk without permission. Client data must be protected against malevolent forces on the Web.

19.3 Embedding JavaScript in XHTML

JavaScript is designed to work inside Web pages and within Web browsers. With this spirit, it extends the XHTML philosophy of using tags. We use the `<script>` tag to embed JavaScript code in XHTML code of a Web page. The `<script>` tag must be closed. All the JavaScript code goes inside the `<script>` tags. Here is a generic template that uses both XHTML and JavaScript code:

```
<?xml version="1.0" encoding="iso-8859-1"?>
<!DOCTYPE html PUBLIC "-//W3C//DTD XHTML 1.1//EN"
    "http://www.w3.org/TR/xhtml11/DTD/xhtml11.dtd">
<html xmlns="http://www.w3.org/1999/xhtml">
<!-- Generated by AceHTM http://freeware.acehtml.com -->
<head>
<title>JavaScript template</title>
<script language="javascript">
JavaScript code goes here
</script>
</head>
<body>
XHTML code goes here
</body>
</html>
```

JavaScript section

JavaScript template:
Embed the `<script>` tag inside the `<head>` tag.

Where do we embed the JavaScript code in the XHTML code of a Web page? While it can be inserted anywhere in the code, we prefer embedding it right before (or after) the `<head>` tag closes, as shown in the foregoing template. This preference is strictly for organization purposes only. Many pages on the Web follow the same format. Sometimes, JavaScript is included within the `<body>` section.

There are no limits on how many `<script>` tags can be embedded in the XHTML code of a Web page. However, again for simplicity, one `<script>` tag is enough. HTML editors tend to generate more than one `<script>` tag; some within the `<head>` section and others within the `<body>` section. Macromedia Dreamweaver does this, for example. Nesting `<script>` tags is prohibited; the nesting generates a syntax error.

19.4 Development Environment

The JavaScript development environment is no different from that of XHTML. We need an editor to write the JavaScript source code, and we need a browser to run and test the code, along with the XHTML code. We may use a text editor or an HTML editor. We use the AceHTML editor in this book. It has a JavaScript template, a `Scripts` tab, and `JavaScript commands Summary` button (under the `Specialized` tab). It also enables us to write JavaScript code manually, but view the results in its internal browser immediately.

The WYSIWYG editors, such as Dreamweaver, generate JavaScript automatically in the background as users add JavaScript functionality to their Web pages. We refrain from using this approach here until we learn the JavaScript syntax and concepts well. Neither FrontPage nor Composer can generate JavaScript code automatically without add-ons.

Writing JavaScript code can, and does, generate syntax errors. Unlike when we make errors in XHTML, where partial display of the Web page still happens, an error in JavaScript results in blockage of the rendering of the entire content of the Web page still including XHTML elements. This leaves us wondering where the errors are, and without a debugger it is time consuming trying to guess.

Due to the simplicity of JavaScript, a full-fledged debugger is not really necessary or required here, to avoid the overhead associated with learning how to use one. The JavaScript interpreter does a good job in reporting syntax errors; it shows the error and the source-code line number where the error occurs. Most of the time, fixing the error is easy, once we know where it is in the code. Note that one JavaScript error can generate others. JavaScript reports one error at a time. The first error blocks the others from being reported. Fixing one error causes the next one in line to be displayed, and so forth.

If a JavaScript error occurs while using AceHTML, the editor displays the error message in the `Script Error` window shown in the upcoming set of screen captures. Netscape Composer comes with its own built-in JavaScript console window that catches the errors. To invoke this debugger, type `java script:` in Netscape's URL toolbar. This debugger is a protocol, like `http:`. This debugger window is also shown in the upcoming set of screen captures, for both versions of Netscape. IE does not have a debugger, and it does not recognize the `javascript:` protocol. This leaves one option: Use the AceHTML editor or Netscape browser to test and develop JavaScript code. Once the development is complete, use IE to test again before the full deployment of the Web page into the Web for the intended users.

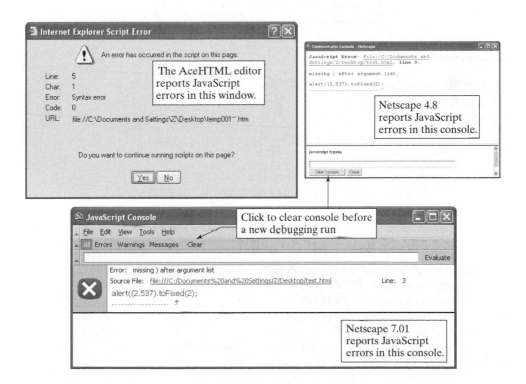

Example 19.1 Create a Hello World! JavaScript program

Write a first JavaScript program (script).

Solution 19.1 This example creates a Web page that uses JavaScript code. Using the Ace-HTML editor, generate the given code, and save it as `example191.html`. The following screen capture shows the resulting Web page.

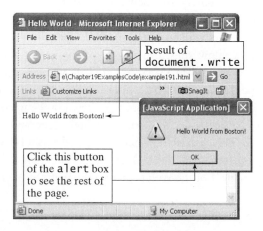

Code explained:

1. Lines 9–12 define the JavaScript code block.

2. Line 9 begins the script block.

3. Line 10 creates the `alert` box shown in the foregoing screen capture.

4. Line 11 creates the text shown in the Web page in the foregoing screen capture.

```
1   <?xml version="1.0" encoding="iso-8859-1"?>
2   <!DOCTYPE html PUBLIC "-//W3C//DTD XHTML 1.1//EN"
3       "http://www.w3.org/TR/xhtml11/DTD/xhtml11.dtd">
4   <html xmlns="http://www.w3.org/1999/xhtml">
5   <!-- Generated by AceHTM http://freeware.acehtml.com -->
6   <head>
7   <meta http-equiv="Content-Type" content="text/html;
    charset=iso-8859-1" />
8   <title>Hello World</title>
9   <script language="javascript">
10  alert ("Hello World from Boston!");
11  document.write ("Hello World from Boston!");
12  </script>
```

```
13    </head>
14    <body>
15    </body>
16    </html>
```

Discussion:

The Web page of this example does not have XHTML content, only a script. (We use the words *script*, *program*, and *application* interchangeably throughout the book.) As shown in code lines 10 and 11, each JavaScript statement ends with a semicolon (;). While the semicolon is not mandatory, it is recommended; it becomes mandatory if we include more than one JavaScript statement on the same line.

The JavaScript code outputs the Hello World from Boston! text twice in two different ways. Code line 10 uses the JavaScript built-in alert function. This function produces the alert box shown in the foregoing screen capture. This box blocks further execution of JavaScript code or rendering of the Web page until the user clicks its OK button. Once the button has been clicked, line 11 executes and writes the text in the Web page.

Had we had errors in our JavaScript, none of the text would have shown, which signals to us that there are JavaScript errors. The error window of AceHTML (if used) would have been displayed immediately, or we could have invoked the JavaScript console of Netscape (if used). Always remember to clear the console of Netscape before a fresh run of the Web page after fixing errors, for better management and tracking of errors.

Observe that Netscape 4.79 has a problem refreshing its window when the alert box is active and has not been cleared yet (by the user clicking its OK button): Dragging the alert box around the screen leaves a trace of the box. Once the box is cleared, the problem goes away. This refresh problem does not happen with AceHTML, IE, or Netscape 7.01.

Hands-on exercise:

Starting with the code given in this example, change the text and render the Web page again.

19.5 Variables

JavaScript begins with variables. A **variable** is a symbolic name that can store a value; the script that defines the variable can change or reset its value. For example, $x = 5$ assigns the value of 5 to the variable x. The variable's name is x, and its value is 5. We can change the value to -10, for example, by using $x = -10$.

19.5.1 Identifiers

As stated previously, variable has a name and a value. The name is known as an identifier. An **identifier** is simply a group of characters. JavaScript identifiers conform to certain rules: An identifier must begin with a letter (lowercase or uppercase), underscore (_), or dollar sign ($). It must not begin with a number. Subsequent characters can be digits, however. JavaScript is case sensitive; for example sum and Sum are two different variables. Some examples of valid identifiers are test, Test, jam234, _best, $abc, and a_12$4. Some illegal identifiers are 3abc, -abc, &sam, and 8west.

We recommend using long names for variables, in the spirit of current practice in the object-oriented field. For example, use a variable called carMaintenance, not carMain or cm.

19.5.2 Types

JavaScript does not declare variable types explicitly, thus making it a dynamically typed language. In JavaScripts, Data types are implicit. Moreover, data types are converted automatically during script execution. The context of the first use of a variable declares (defines) its type. The implicit data types that JavaScript recognizes are numbers, logical (Boolean), and strings.

Numbers in JavaScript can be integers (for example, 3, 40, and 29) or real numbers (for example, 2.459, -10.5, and 8.0). Unlike other languages, JavaScript does not have different types of integers (such as int or long) or real numbers (such as double or float). This aspect makes it simple to use.

Logical values in JavaScript are true or false. These are reserved identifiers. They are typically used to check on logical expressions and control statements.

Strings are sets of characters enclosed in single or double quotes (for example, "Abe Zeid" and 'sunshine'). A string can be as short as one character long. There are no restrictions on the first character of a string. Thus, we can use numbers; For example, "9abc" is a valid string.

While it is possible, we do not recommend changing the implicit data type of a variable in a JavaScript program after that variable has been initialized. This practice makes it easy to read and reuse the program. For example, using x = 10 and later x = true changes the data type of x from a number (integer) to a Boolean, which is not good practice.

When we use x = 10, we implicitly declare x as an integer and initialize it to 10. What happens if we just want to declare a variable without assigning an initial value to it? JavaScript provides the keyword var for this purpose. For example, var y. var does not assign a type or a value to y; it simply flags it as a variable that will be assigned a value later in the JavaScript program. y assumes the default value of undefined, another JavaScript keyword. This value is the default for all JavaScript variables that are not initialized. We may also assign the value null, yet another JavaScript keyword, to a variable in order to stop JavaScript from using undefined.

The only good reason to use var is if you want to group all the variables of a JavaScript program at its beginning for ease of following the program. Do not forget, however, that JavaScript is not designed for very long programs, just small scripts. In this context, var might not even be needed. It is good to be aware of it, however, as it is in many Web pages.

Example 19.2 Create JavaScript variables.

Write a JavaScript program that uses some variables.

Solution 19.2 Using the AceHTML editor, generate the given code, and save it as `example192.html`. Render the Web page in a browser.

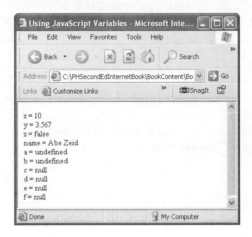

Code explained:

1. Line 10 defines an implicit integer.
2. Line 11 defines an implicit real number.
3. Line 12 defines an implicit Boolean.
4. Line 13 defines an implicit string.
5. Lines 14–16 declare a, b, c, d, e, and f as variables.
6. lines 20–29 print the variables' values.

Discussion:

Lines 10–19 show the various ways to declare and initialize variables in JavaScript. Lines 10–13 use the three data types of number (lines 10 and 11), Boolean (line 12), and string (line 13). Line 14 uses var to declare a and b as variables. The values of these variables are undefined (which is a valid value in JavaScript), as shown in the screen capture. Line 15 is similar to line 14, but uses null to initialize the variables.

Line 16 is similar to line 15, but shows that var is not required. Line 18 shows that an error occurs; we must use var with a variable that does not have an initial value, as we do in line 14. JavaScript would issue an error message for g and stop execution there; it would not report the error for h yet. However we include line 18 inside a comment block (lines 17 and 19) to allow the program to continue execution.

Lines 20–29 mix strings with variables to print onto the Web page. Notice how we include XHTML tags, <br /> in this example, inside the double quotes. This part of the code introduces an important concept in JavaScript: We can embed XHTML tags anywhere inside JavaScript code by enclosing them in double quotes; that is, we use them as strings. This capability is useful, as it allows us to format JavaScript output easily.

Hands-on exercise:

Remove lines 17 and 19. Fix line 18, using two different ways. Test both methods, one at a time.

```
1   <?xml version="1.0" encoding="iso-8859-1"?>
2   <!DOCTYPE html PUBLIC "-//W3C//DTD XHTML 1.1//EN"
3       "http://www.w3.org/TR/xhtml11/DTD/xhtml11.dtd">
4   <html xmlns="http://www.w3.org/1999/xhtml">
5   <!-- Generated by AceHTM http://freeware.acehtml.com -->
6   <head>
7   <meta http-equiv="Content-Type" content="text/html;
    charset=iso-8859-1" />
8   <title>Using JavaScript Variables</title>
9   <script language="javascript">
10  x = 10;
11  y = 3.567;
12  z = false;
13  name = "Abe Zeid";
14  var a, b;
15  var c = null, d = null;
16  e = null, f = null;
17  /*
18  g, h;  //Error: g is not defined
19  */
20  document.write ("x = " + x + "<br />");
21  document.write ("y = " + y + "<br />");
22  document.write ("z = " + z + "<br />");
23  document.write ("name = " + name + "<br />");
24  document.write ("a = " + a + "<br />");
25  document.write ("b = " + b + "<br />");
26  document.write ("c = " + c + "<br />");
27  document.write ("d = " + d + "<br />");
28  document.write ("e = " + e + "<br />");
29  document.write ("f = " + f + "<br />");
30  </script>
31  </head>
32  <body>
33  </body>
34  </html>
```

19.5.3 Scope

The **scope** of a variable is defined as the code block within which the variable is visible, or available for use. JavaScript variables may be global or local. A **global variable** is available everywhere within the <script> tag. A **local variable** is visible only inside a code block such as a function. A variable that is declared without var is a global variable. When it comes to variable scope, we recommend that you use different variable names inside and outside functions that you do and not use the `var` keyword. This approach makes all variables global and accessible throughout the `<script>` tag, which makes it simple to manage and track variables.

19.5.4   Constants

Constants are read-only variables and are defined with the `const` keyword—for example, `const x = 35`. A constant cannot change value through assignment or be redeclared to take a different implicit type—for example, `x = "hello"`—while a script is running. JavaScript ignores any reassignment of a constant in a script, and a reassignment does not produce an error. Only Netscape 7.01 recognizes the `const` keyword. IE and Netscape 4.79 produce errors and do not render the Web page. All rules of variable identifiers and scope apply to constants.

19.5.5   Literals

Literals are fixed values in JavaScript. They are not variables. We *literally* provide them in the JavaScript program. They are also known as hard-coded values. Examples of number, Boolean, and string literals are respectively `3.5`, `false`, and `"Hello"`.

Nesting literal strings requires extra care to avoid creating syntax errors when we run a script. We must toggle the types of quotes we use—for example, from double to single quotes or vice versa. Consider this example: `str = "Our teacher said, 'We must study for the exam' last week"`. The literal string `We must study for the exam` is nested inside the outer literal string via single quotes. If we had used double quotes instead, a syntax error would have occurred, because JavaScript would have paired the quotes incorrectly. As a general rule, use a different type of quotes (single or double) for each level of nesting. We seldom go beyond two levels of nesting in practice.

19.5.6   Data-Type Conversion

In addition to not declaring variable types explicitly, JavaScript converts data types automatically as needed during script execution. This is because JavaScript is dynamically typed. Theoretically, then, we can write `answer=true` and then change it to `answer=35`—effectively converting the variable `answer` from Boolean to number. Practically, however, we should not do this, so as to avoid confusion.

JavaScript bestows the addition operator, +, with a dual meaning. An **operator** is a special procedure that takes input and produces output. The + operator can be used to add numbers arithmetically (e.g., `3 + 4.6`) or to add strings and numbers (e.g., `"Answer is " + 45`). In the latter case, it is used as a concatenation operator. When concatenating, the + operator converts numbers to strings (e.g., `Answer is 45`).

19.5.7   Escaping and Special Characters

JavaScript uses the backslash (\) as an escaping character. An **escaping character** is an instruction to the JavaScript interpreter to ignore what follows the character, and not to execute it according the JavaScript syntax rules. For example, we can insert a quotation mark inside a string by preceding the quotation mark by a backslash—for example, `str = "Our teacher`

Table 19.1   JavaScript special characters.

Special characters: \b, \f, \n, \r, \t, \v, \', \", \\, \XXX, \xXX, and \uXXXX	
Character	Meaning
\b	Backspace.
\f	Form feed.
\n	New line.
\r	Carriage return.
\t	Tab.
\v	Vertical line.
\'	Single quote.
\"	Double quote.
\\	Backslash character (\).
\XXX	Latin-1 character specified in octal value *XXX* between 0 and 377. For example, \251 is the octal sequence for the copyright symbol (©).
\xXX	Latin-1 character specified in hex values *XX* between 00 and FF. For example, \xA9 is the hex sequence for the copyright symbol(©).
\uXXXX	A Unicode character specified by four hex digits *XXXX*. For example, \u00A9 is the Unicode sequence for the copyright symbol(©).
	Note: Unicode uses 16 bits/character, as opposed to the 8 bits/character used by ASCII.

said \"We must study for the exam\" last week". To include a literal backslash inside a string, we must escape it; for example, "cd c:\\temp" produces c:\temp.

JavaScript uses the escaping character, \, to define its own special characters. A **special character** is a character that produces a certain result when the JavaScript interpreter executes it. Table 19.1 shows some special characters. We believe that none of the browsers has implemented these special characters as we show in Example 19.3.

Example 19.3 Use JavaScript variables.

Write a JavaScript program that uses constants, literals, data-type conversion, and escaping and special characters.

Solution 19.3 Using the AceHTML editor, generate the given code, and save it as example193.html. Render the Web page in a browser.

Code explained:

   1. Line 12 uses the const keyword to create a constant.
   2. Lines 18–20 create different types of literals.

3. Line 24 uses a literal string in a `write` statement.

4. Lines 31–33 use escape characters.

5. Lines 36–38 use special characters.

Discussion:

This example illustrates all the concepts covered in Sections 19.5.4–19.5.7. Code line 14 attempts to change the value of x, which is defined as a constant in code line 12. Printing the value of x before (line 13) and after (line15) line 14 produces the same original value, 35. This proves that the JavaScript interpreter ignores line 14. However, the script runs only in Netscape 7.01; it does not run in either IE 6.0 or Netscape 4.79, because those browsers do not recognize the `const` keywords.

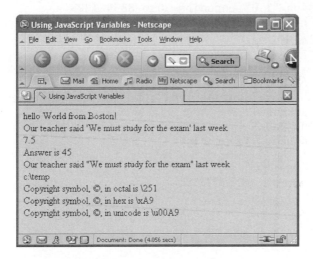

We use the `<br />` tag in many code lines of this example in order to force a new line, because none of the special characters shown in Table 19.1 works in any browser. When we use \n (new line) or \r (carriage return), for instance, nothing happens. The syntax we use, for example, in line 20 is

```
str = "hello World from Boston <br />";
```

Code lines 24 and 31 show two different ways of nesting string literals. Line 24 uses the idea of toggling the quotes from double to single. Line 31 uses the escaping character (\); it precedes each of the two internal double quotes ("), with the backslash.

Code lines 27 and 28 show the overloading nature of the + operator. Its two operands decide which mode to use. If they are numbers, as in line 27, it adds them arithmetically. If one of the two operands is a string, it converts the number (the other operand) to a string and concatenates (combines) it with the other string. Thus, note that 45 in the output of line 28 in the browser window is not a number; it is a string.

Code line 32 shows that `document.write()` can take a string variable (`str`) instead of a string literal as in line 24 or 28. We can use the literal string of line 31 in place of `str` in line 32 and still get the same result.

Lines 36–38 use special-characters. Each special character code must be used as a string literal. We use the escaping character (\) in each line so that we can print the code for the special character. The three lines use the codes for the copyright symbol in octal, hex, and unicode.

Hands-on exercise:

Add more statements to each section of the code given in this example. Use Latin-1 characters (discussed in Chapter 9). Also, turn off AceHTML's internal browser in order to disaple the AceHTML JavaScript error window temporarily, to stop it from popping up any time. To do so, click `View => Display Internal Browser`.

```
1    <?xml version="1.0" encoding="iso-8859-1"?>
2    <!DOCTYPE html PUBLIC "-//W3C//DTD XHTML 1.1//EN"
3        "http://www.w3.org/TR/xhtml11/DTD/xhtml11.dtd">
4    <html xmlns="http://www.w3.org/1999/xhtml">
5    <!-- Generated by AceHTM http://freeware.acehtml.com -->
6    <head>
7    <meta http-equiv="Content-Type" content="text/html;
     charset=iso-8859-1" />
8    <title>Using JavaScript Variables</title>
9    <script language="javascript">
10
11   //constants
12   const x = 35;
13   alert (x);  //prints 35
14   x = 45;  //no error; interpreter ignores this statement.
15   alert (x);  //still prints 35
16
17   //literals
18   alert (3.5);  //number literal
19   alert (true);  //boolean literal
20   str = "hello World from Boston<br />";  //string literal
21   document.write(str);
22
23   //nesting literal strings
24   document.write ("Our teacher said 'We must study for the exam'
     last week" + "<br />");
25
26   //data-type conversion
27   document.write (3 + 4.5 + "<br />");//7.5
28   document.write ("Answer is " + 45 + "<br />");//Answer is 45
29
30   //escaping characters
31   str = ("Our teacher said \"We must study for the exam\"
     last week");
```

```
32   document.write (str + "<br />");
33   document.write ("c:\\temp" + "<br />");//c:\temp
34
35   //special characters
36   document.write ("Copyright symbol, \251, in octal is \\251
     <br />");
37   document.write ("Copyright symbol, \xA9, in hex is \\xA9
     <br />");
38   document.write ("Copyright symbol, \u00A9, in unicode is
     \\u00A9");
39
40   </script>
41   </head>
42   <body></body></html>
```

19.6 Statements

A **statement** is a line of JavaScript code that uses the assignment operator, the equal sign (=). The assignment operator has two operands, one on each side. The value of the right operand is assigned to the left one. Consider this example: x = y. In this statement, the value of y is assigned to x. The values of all the variables used in the right operand must be known; otherwise, the JavaScript interpreter generates a syntax error of `... is not defined`, where `...` is a variable name.

JavaScript does not allow a statement to be broken into two lines. Each statement must be one line long, no matter how long it is. Breaking a statement by entering a carriage return results in a syntax error. A statement may end with a semicolon (;). We use this syntax consistently in this book. We must use the semicolon to separate statements if they are written on the same line.

The use of whitespace in statements has no effect on the statement's results. We use it for the purpose of code readability. The only time whitespace matters is when we use it in literal strings.

JavaScript provides comment statements to help in code documentation for future reference. A one-line comment statement takes this form: `//this is an inline comment`. Use two forward slashes to begin the comment statement. A multiple-line (block) comment statement uses this form:

```
/*
Begin comments
...
end comments
*/
```

Begin the comment block with /* and end it with */. The block may span multiple lines, or it could be confined to one line, such as follows: `/* this is a one-line comment */`. Nesting comment blocks is illegal and is not permitted; doing so produces errors. Use as many comments as possible to make reverse engineering of JavaScript code easy. Refer to Examples 19.2 and 19.3.

19.7 Expressions and Operators

An **expression** is any valid set of variables, literals, operators, and other expressions that evaluates to a single value; the value could be a number, a Boolean, or a string. Think of expressions as the right-hand operands of statements. The types of expressions are arithmetic (evaluates to an number), Boolean (evaluates to `true` or `false`), or a string (evaluates to a character string).

JavaScript has a rich set of operators. We cover some in the upcoming subsections. We do not cover bitwise operators, bitwise logical operators, or bitwise shift operators. These operators are used to manipulate bit data.

19.7.1 Assignment Operators

The equal sign (=) is the main assignment operator. Other assignment operators are shorthand for certain standard operators. For example, we can write `x = x + y` or use `x += y` (the shorthand version). Here, we add `y` to `x` and store the result back in `x`. Other shorthand operators include `x -= y (x = x - y)`, `x *= y (x = x * y)`, and `x /= y (x = x/y)`.

19.7.2 Comparison Operators

A **comparison operator** compares its operands, based on given set of criteria (conditions), and returns a Boolean (true or false). The operands can be of any data type: number, Boolean, or string. Table 19.2 shows the comparison operators.

Table 19.2   Comparison operators.

Comparison operators are ==, !=, ===, !==, >, >=, <, and <=		
Operator	Description	Example
==	**Equal.** Returns true if operands are equal, or false if they are not equal. The operands of the == operator do not have to be of the same type in order to be equal.	`if (x == y) alert ("equal")` `else alert ("not equal");`
!=	**Not equal.** The opposite to (negation of) ==; it returns true if operands are *not* equal, or false if they are equal.	`if (x != y) alert ("not equal")` `else alert ("equal");`
===	**Strict equal.** Returns true if the operands are equal and of the same type. Note that the operands of the == operator do not have to be of the same type in order to be equal.	`if (x === y) alert ("strict equal")` `else alert ("not strict equal");`
!==	**Strict not equal.** Returns true if the operands are *not* equal and are *not* of the same type.	`if (x !== y) alert ("not strict equal")` `else alert ("strict equal");`

Table 19.2 Comparison operators. (Continued)

Comparison operators are ==, !=, ===, !==, >, >=, <, and <=		
Operator	Description	Example
>	**Greater than.** Returns true if the left operand is greater than the right operand.	`if (x > y) alert ("x is greater than y")` `else alert ("x is smaller than y");`
>=	**Greater than or equal.** Returns true if the left operand is greater than or equal to the right operand.	`if (x >= y) alert ("x greater than or equal to y")` `else alert ("x smaller than or equal to y");`
<	**Less than.** Returns true if the left operand is less than the right operand.	`if (x < y) alert ("x is smaller than y")` `else alert ("x is greater than y");`
<=	**Less than or equal.** Returns true if the left operand is less than or equal to the right operand.	`if (x <= y) alert ("x smaller than or equal to y")` `else alert ("x greater than or equal to y");`

19.7.3 Arithmetic Operators

These operators work on numbers. Their operands and results are numbers. Many of these operators are familiar to all of us. One operator of interest is the division operator, $/$. Unlike the division operators in other programming languages such as Java, C++ and C, the JavaScript division operator does not perform integer division; that is, it returns a floating-point (decimal number) result, not a truncated result. For example, $2/4$ produces 0.5 in JavaScript, but 0 in Java, C++, and C. Table 19.3 lists JavaScript's arithmetic operators.

Table 19.3 Arithmetic operators.

Arithmetic operators are +, −, *, /, %, ++, −−, and −		
Operator	Description	Example
+	**Addition.** Returns the algebraic sum of two numbers (its operands).	`x + y (3 + 5.5 = 8.5)`
−	**Subtraction.** Returns the algebraic difference of two numbers (its operands).	`x - y (7 - 9 = -2)`
*	**Multiplication.** Multiplies two numbers and returns the result.	`x * y (7 * 4 = 28)`

Table 19.3   Arithmetic operators. (Continued)

Arithmetic operators are +, -, *, /, %, ++, --, and -

Operator	Description	Example
/	**Division.** Divides two numbers and returns a floating-point number.	x / y (5 / 4 = 1.25)
%	**Modulus** (binary operator). Returns the integer remainder of dividing two integers.	x % y (5 % 3 = 2)

++	**Increment.** Adds one to its operand. If used as a prefix (++x), it returns the value of the operand after adding one (x + 1). If used as a postfix (x++), it returns the value of the operand before adding one (x).	x = 10;
		alert (++x) ; //prints 11 and sets x to 11
		alert (x++); //prints 10 and sets x to 11

--	**Decrement.** Subtracts one from its operand. It behaves in the same way as the increment operator.	x = 10;
		alert (--x); //prints 9 and sets x to 9
		alert (x--);//prints 10 and sets x to 9

-	**Unary negation.** Changes the sign of a number from positive to negative and vice-versa.	x = 10; y = -7;
		-x; //returns -10
		-y; //returns 7

Operator precedence in JavaScript is the same as in other languages. For the arithmetic operators, * and / are of equal precedence and with respect to each other and are of higher precedence than + and - which are of equal precedence with respect to each other. Parentheses override this default precedence. We interpret the operator precedence within the context of the flow of code execution. JavaScript statements are executed from top to bottom and from left to right. That is, top statements are executed before the bottom ones, and each statement is executed from left to right. Consider these examples:

```
12/2 * 3 + 4 - 1 = 21.0
12/(2 * 3) + 4 - 1 = 5.0
12/2 * (3 + 4 -1) = 36.0
12/(2 * 3 + 4) -1 = 0.2
```

19.7.4 Logical Operators

Logical operators allow us to combine and check for multiple conditions simultaneously. Table 19.4 shows the three logical operators.

Table 19.4 Logical operators.

Logical operators are &&, ||, !		
Operator	Description	Example

&&	**Logical AND.** Returns true if both operands are true, or false if either is false. The truth table is as follows:
	
	true **&&** true returns true
	true **&&** false returns false
	false **&&** true returns false
	false **&&** false returns false
		`if (x && y) ...`
		`if (x/y && (w + z)) ...`
		`if (x && y && z) ...`

||	**Logical OR.** Returns true if either operand is true, or false if both are false. The truth table is as follows:
	
	true | | true returns true
	true | | false returns true
	false | | true returns true
	false | | false returns false
		`if (x || y) ...`
		`if (x/y ||(w + z)) ...`
		`if (x || y ||z) ...`

!	**Logical NOT.** Also known as the negation operator. It takes one operand. Its truth table is as follows: ! true returns false ! false returns true.	`if (!x) ...` `if (!x && !y || y) ...`

We can use the logical operators in assignment statements as follows:

```
x = true && false; //return false; x becomes false
x = true || false; //return true; x becomes true
x = !false; //return true; x becomes true
x = !(true && false); //return true; x becomes true
```

Example 19.4 Use JavaScript operators.

Write a JavaScript program that uses different operators.

Solution 19.4 Using the AceHTML editor, generate the given code, and save it as `example194.html`. Render the Web page in a browser.

```
1  <?xml version="1.0" encoding="iso-8859-1"?>
2  <!DOCTYPE html PUBLIC "-//W3C//DTD XHTML 1.1//EN"
3     "http://www.w3.org/TR/xhtml11/DTD/xhtml11.dtd">
4  <html xmlns="http://www.w3.org/1999/xhtml">
5  <!-- Generated by AceHTM http://freeware.acehtml.com -->
```

```
 6   <head>
 7   <meta http-equiv="Content-Type" content="text/html;
     charset=iso-8859-1" />
 8   <title>Using JavaScript Operators</title>
 9   <script language="javascript">
10
11   //comparison operators
12   document.write ((3 == 5) + "<br />");          //returns false
13   document.write ((3 != 5) + "<br />");          //returns true
14   document.write (("abe" == 5)  + "<br />");     //returns false
15   document.write (("5" == 5)  + "<br />");       //returns true
16   document.write (("5" != 5)  + "<br />");       //returns false
17   document.write (("5" === 5)  + "<br />");      //returns false
18   document.write (("5" !== 5)  + "<br />");      //returns true
19   document.write ((3 > 5) + "<br />");           //returns false
20   document.write ((5 >= 5) + "<br />");          //returns true
21   document.write ((3 < 5) + "<br />");           //returns true
22   document.write ((7 <= 5) + "<br />");          //returns false
23
24   //arithmetic operators
25   document.write ((3 + 5)  + "<br />");          //returns 8
26   document.write ((3 - 5)  + "<br />");          //returns -2
27   document.write ((3 * 5)  + "<br />");          //returns 15
28   document.write ((3 / 5)  + "<br />");          //returns 0.6
29   document.write ((3 % 5)  + "<br />");          //returns 3
30   document.write ((3.0 % 5.0)  + "<br />");      //returns 3
31   document.write ((3 % 5.0) + "<br />");         //returns 3
32
33   x = 4;
34   document.write ((++x)  + "<br />");            //returns 5
35   document.write ((x++)  + "<br />");            //returns 5
36   document.write (x + "<br />");                 //returns 6
37   document.write ((--x)  + "<br />");            //returns 5
38   document.write ((x--)  + "<br />");            //returns 5
39   document.write (x + "<br />");                 //returns 4
40   document.write (-x + "<br />");                //returns -4
41
42   //logical operators
43   w = 20;
44   x = 10;
45   y = -5;
46   z = 0;
47   document.write ((w == x && y != z)+"<br />");  //returns false
48   document.write ((w == x || y != z)+"<br />");  //returns true
49   document.write (!(w == (x + z)) +  "<br />");  //returns true
50
51   </script>
52   </head>
```

```
53   <body>
54   </body>
55   </html>
```

Code explained:

    1. Lines 12–22 use comparison operators. The XHTML `<br />` tag forces a new line.

    2. Lines 25–40 use arithmetic operators.

    3. Lines 43–46 initialize four variables.

    4. Lines 47–49 use logical operators.

Discussion:

Lines 14–18 show the difference between the equal and strict-equal operators. Lines 29–31 show that using integer float (decimal) numbers does not change the results of the modulus operator (%). We define a variable `x` in line 33 to use in lines 34–40. We print the value of `x` in lines 36 and 39 to show the effect of the increment and decrement operators. Line 40 uses the unary-negation operator.

Hands-on exercise:

Add more statements to each section of the code given in this example.

19.8 Control Structures

A **control structure** is defined as a group (block) of statements that controls code execution according to certain criteria. JavaScript provides conditional (`if` and `switch`) and loop (`for`, `while`, and `do while`) statements. We cover each statement in this section.

19.8.1 Conditional Statements

A conditional statement executes if a specified condition in the statement is met. JavaScript supports `if` and `switch` statements. The `if` statement has two structures:

    a. `if (condition) {...}`. Here are two examples:

```
if (x == 5) z = 34; //no need for curly brackets (braces)
 for one statement
if (x != 3 && y =="test") {
  str = "pass first test"; result = 2 * a;}
```

    b. `if (condition) {true block}`
        `else {false block}`

    Here is an example:

```
1   <script language="javascript">
2   x = 1;                        //initialize x
3   y = 0;                        //initialize y
4   z = 20;                       //initialize z
5   a = 10;                       //initialize a
```

```
6    if (x != 3 && y == 50) {       //begin if block
7    str = "pass first test";
8    result = 2 * a; }              //close if block
9    else {                         //begin else block
10   x = y + z;
11   d = a;
12   }                              //close else block
13   </script>
```

The switch statement has this syntax;

```
1    <script language="javascript">
2    switch (expression) {
3    case label1:                   //begin first case (action)
4    statement(s);
5    break;                         //skip executing code that follows
6    case label2:                   //begin second case (action)
7    statement(s);
8    break;                         //skip executing code that follows
9    ...                            //ditto
10   default:                       //set default case (action)
11   statement(s);
12   }                              //close switch statement
13   </script>
```

The switch statement evaluates an expression (code line 2) and attempts to match the value of the expression to a case label (line 3, 6, or 10). The expression may evaluate to a number, Boolean, or string. If a match is found, the corresponding case code block (line 4 or 7) is executed. If no match is found, the default code block (line 11) is executed. The default case (lines 10 and 11) is optional and may be eliminated all together. The break statement (line 5 or 8) forces the program to break out of the switch statement and continue execution after line 12. The break statement is optional; if it is omitted, the code executes at the next statement in the switch statement.

Example 19.5 Use conditional statements.

Write a JavaScript program that uses if and switch statements.

Solution 19.5 Using the AceHTML editor, generate the given code, and save it as example195.html. Render the Web page in a browser.

Code explained:

   1. Lines 17–22 create two nested if statements. The XHTML <br /> tag forces a new line.
   2. Lines 25–40 use a switch statement with five cases, including the default case.

Discussion:

The output of the given JavaScript program comes from lines 21, 36, and 41, as shown in the foregoing screen capture. The `if` statement of lines 20–22 is nested into the `else` block of the outer `if` statement (lines 17–19). The `switch` statement (lines 25–40) uses the expression `x*x`. This expression evaluates to 4, thus executing `case 4`. The program then jumps (because of the `break` statement) from line 37 to execute line 41 and then stops.

Hands-on exercise:

Change the values used in lines 12–14 to generate different results for the program. Also, add more `if` and `switch` statements.

```
1   <?xml version="1.0" encoding="iso-8859-1"?>
2   <!DOCTYPE html PUBLIC "-//W3C//DTD XHTML 1.1//EN"
3       "http://www.w3.org/TR/xhtml11/DTD/xhtml11.dtd">
4   <html xmlns="http://www.w3.org/1999/xhtml">
5   <!-- Generated by AceHTM http://freeware.acehtml.com -->
6   <head>
7   <meta http-equiv="Content-Type" content="text/html;
    charset=iso-8859-1" />
8   <title>Using JavaScript if and switch statements</title>
9   <script language="javascript">
10
11  //initialize variables
12  x = 2;
13  y = 3;
14  z = 4;
15
16  //if statement
17  if (x == y)
18      document.write ("x and y are equal<br />");
19  else
20      if ((x * x) == z)
21          document.write ("x*x and z are equal<br />");
```

```
22          else document.write ("they are not equal");
23
24   //switch statement
25   switch (x*x){
26          case 1:
27              document.write ("This is case 1<br />");
28              break;
29          case 2:
30              document.write ("This is case 2<br />");
31              break;
32          case 3:
33              document.write ("This is case 3<br />");
34              break;
35          case 4:
36              document.write ("This is case 4<br />");
37              break;
38          default:
39              document.write ("This is the default case<br />");
40   }
41   document.write ("Script execution continues here");
42
43   </script>
44   </head>
45   <body>
46   </body>
47   </html>
```

19.8.2 Loop Statements

A loop statement executes repeatedly until a specific condition is met. Looping can be achieved via a `for`, `while`, or `do  while` statement. `break` and `continue` statements can be used with loop statements to control the flow of execution. `break` exits the loop all together, while `continue` skips the current iteration.

The syntax of a `for` loop is as follows:

```
for (initial value of a counter; ending value; increment){
   for block (body)
}
```

An example is

```
for (i=0; i<=10; i++) {alert ("value of i is " + i + "<br />");}
```
The `while` loop has this syntax:
```
while (condition) {
   statements
}
```

The `condition` evaluates to a Boolean: `true` or `false`. The `while` loop executes as long as it evaluates to `true`. The execution stops the first time it evaluates to `false`.

Table 19.5   Passes of a `while` loop.

i = 0; sum = 0; sum = sum + 3*i;				
Pass	i at loop start	i < 3?	sum = sum + 3*i	i at loop end
One	0	yes	sum = 0 + 3*0 = 0	1
Two	1	yes	sum = 0 + 3*1 = 3	2
Three	2	yes	sum = 3+ 3*2 = 9	3
	3	no	Exit `while` loop	

Here is an example:

```
i = 0;
sum = 0;
while (i < 3){
    sum = sum + 3*i;
    document.write ("Sum is " + sum);
    i++;
}
```

The foregoing `while` loop has three passes, as detailed in Table 19.5.
The `do while` loop has this syntax:

```
do {
   statements
} while (condition)
```

The `condition` evaluates to a boolean: `true` or `false`. The `do while` loop executes as long as it evaluates to `true`. The execution stops the first time it evaluates to `false`.

Here is an example:

```
i = 0;
sum = 0;
do {
    sum = sum + 3*i;
    document.write ("Sum is " + sum);
    i++;
} while (i < 3)
```

This `do while` statement executes in the same way as the `while` loop.

Which loop statement should we use, `for`, `while`, or `do while`? There is no definite answer. One statement may be more efficient than the others, depending on the problem at hand. It depends on how easy it is to formulate the condition. For example, the `for` statement is not an ideal choice if there is no upper limit for the loop counter, but there is a loop termination condition. In this case, a `while` loop would be better to use.

Example 19.6 Use loop statements.

The Fibonacci sequence is defined as 0, 1, 1, 2, 3, 5, . . ., where each element in the sequence is the sum of the two immediate previous elements.

Write a JavaScript program that prints the sequence for the 10 elements starting at the third element, 1.

Solution 19.6 Using the AceHTML editor, generate the given code, and save it as `example196.html`. The following screen capture shows the resulting Web page.

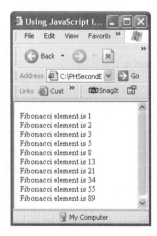

Code explained:

Lines 11 and 12 initialize x and y, respectively.

Discussion:

This example uses a `for` loop to create the Fibonacci sequence. Any element in the sequence is the sum of the two immediate previous elements. Therefore, we must provide the first two elements of the sequence in order to jump-start the algorithm. These elements are defined as 0 and 1. The foregoing screen capture shows the results. Take, for example, the last element, 89. It is equal to 34 + 55. We can extend the `for` loop counter, i, to any number we want in order to increase the number of elements provided.

Hands-on exercise:

Change the code given in this example to stop the algorithm when the value of the last element in the sequence exceeds 150.

```
1   <?xml version="1.0" encoding="iso-8859-1"?>
2   <!DOCTYPE html PUBLIC "-//W3C//DTD XHTML 1.1//EN"
3       "http://www.w3.org/TR/xhtml11/DTD/xhtml11.dtd">
```

```
4    <html xmlns="http://www.w3.org/1999/xhtml">
5    <!-- Generated by AceHTM http://freeware.acehtml.com -->
6    <head>
7    <meta http-equiv="Content-Type" content="text/html;
     charset=iso-8859-1" />
8    <title>Using JavaScript loop statements</title>
9    <script language="javascript">
10
11   x = 0;            //jump-start Fibonacci sequence
12   y = 1;            //jump-start Fibonacci sequence
13   //calculate elements in the sequence
14   for (i=1; i<=10; i++) {
15       z = x + y;              //calculate next element
16       x = y;                  //move element i to i-1
17       y = z;                  //move element i + 1 to element i
18       document.write("Fibonacci element is " + z + "<br />");
19   }//for
20
21   </script>
22   </head><body></body></html>
```

Example 19.7 Sort numbers.

Write a JavaScript program that finds all the numbers between 1 and 50 that are

   a. divisible by 5,
   b. odd and divisible by 7, and
   c. even and divisible by 9.

Solution 19.7 Using the AceHTML editor, generate the given code, and save it as `example197.html`. The upcoming screen capture shows the resulting Web page.

Code explained:

   1. Lines 12–14, 18–20, and 24–26 create three `for` loops.
   2. Line 13 finds numbers that are divisible by 5 and prints them.
   3. Line 19 finds numbers that are divisible by 7 & odd and prints them.
   4. Line 25 finds numbers that are divisible by 9 & even and prints them.

Discussion:

This example uses different conditions in three `for` loops to sort numbers between 1 and 50. We avoid using numerals in the first part of each statement for ease of following the output. We also use lines 15, 21, and 27 to separate the results of the three `for` loops. We use the modulus operator (%) to determine whether a number is odd or even. This test analyzes the remainder of dividing the number by 2. If there is no remainder, the number is even; otherwise, it is odd.

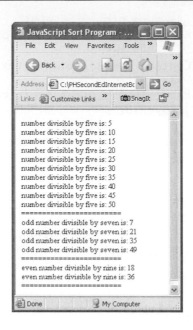

Hands-on exercise:

Combine the three for loops into one, yet maintain the three tests of lines 13, 19, and 25.

```
1   <?xml version="1.0" encoding="iso-8859-1"?>
2   <!DOCTYPE html PUBLIC "-//W3C//DTD XHTML 1.1//EN"
3       "http://www.w3.org/TR/xhtml11/DTD/xhtml11.dtd">
4   <html xmlns="http://www.w3.org/1999/xhtml">
5   <!-- Generated by AceHTM http://freeware.acehtml.com -->
6   <head>
7   <meta http-equiv="Content-Type" content="text/html;
    charset=iso-8859-1" />
8   <title>JavaScript Sort Program</title>
9   <script language="javascript">
10
11  //numbers divisible by 5
12  for (i=1; i<=50; i++) {
13      if (i%5 == 0) document.write ("number divisible by five is:
    "       + i + "<br />");
14  } //for
15  document.write ("=========================<br />");  //separator
16
17  //odd numbers divisible by 7
18  for (i=1; i<=50; i++) {
19      if (i%7==0 && i%2!=0) document.write ("odd number divisible
    by seven is: "    + i + "<br />");
```

```
20    } //for
21    document.write ("=========================<br />");  //separator
22
23    //even numbers divisible by 9
24    for (i=1; i<=50; i++) {
25        if (i%9==0 && i%2==0) document.write ("even number
      divisible by nine is: "    + i + "<br />");
26    } //for
27    document.write ("========================");  //separator
28
29    </script>
30    </head>
31    <body>
32    </body>
33    </html>
```

19.9 Code Execution

JavaScript uses functions, a topic we cover in Chapter 20. A function is a block of code. We must first define a function before we can use (call) it. Functions are defined within the <script> tag along with other statements. Thus a JavaScript code shell looks like this:

```
<script language="javascript">
function definition code
function definition code
function definition code
statements
function calls
statements
function calls
</script>
```

The JavaScript interpreter executes statements from top to bottom and from left to right, with the exception of function definitions. The interpreter does not execute them unless they are called by the JavaScript program that defines them. This factor is important to remember when debugging code.

19.10 Input and Output

Client-side JavaScript has limited input–output utilities, because of security reasons. As a result, it cannot open, read from, write to, or close files. The only input functions available are prompt() and confirm(). The prompt() function has the following syntax: prompt (message, default). The message is a string that informs the user of what to input. The default is a value that the user can accept instead of inputting a value. The prompt() function preserves the type of input no matter whether it is a number, Boolean, or string. prompt() returns the input value and makes it available to the JavaScript program.

The `confirm()` function is used to ask the user to confirm an input value. It return a Boolean whose value depends on the user's confirmation or lack thereof. If the user confirms the input value, it returns `true`; otherwise, it returns `false`. A JavaScript program can use the return value to make decisions. Its syntax is `confirm (question)`, where `question` is a string.

The output functions in JavaScript are `document.write(string)` and `alert (string)`. Each of these functions takes a string. We have been using both of them to output results into Web pages. When neither one is used, a JavaScript program will not display any results, even if it runs perfectly.

Example 19.8 Use input functions.
Write a JavaScript program that uses the `prompt()` and `confirm()` functions.

Solution 19.8 Using the AceHTML editor, generate the given code, and save it as `example198.html`. Also, use a browser to render the Web page.

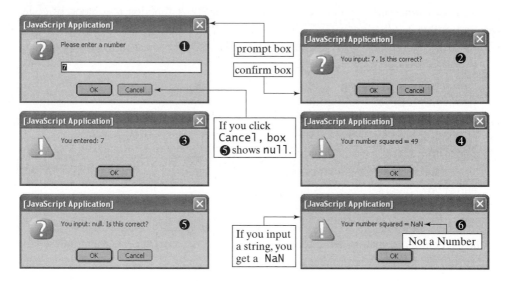

Code explained:

1. Line 11 uses the `prompt()` function and displays box ❶ shown in the foregoing screen captures.
2. Line 12 uses the `confirm()` function and displays box ❷ shown in the foregoing screen captures.
3. Line 13 uses the `alert()` function and displays box ❸ shown in the foregoing screen captures.
4. Line 14 uses the `alert()` function and displays box ❹ shown in the foregoing screen captures.

```
1   <?xml version="1.0" encoding="iso-8859-1"?>
2   <!DOCTYPE html PUBLIC "-//W3C//DTD XHTML 1.1//EN"
3       "http://www.w3.org/TR/xhtml11/DTD/xhtml11.dtd">
4   <html xmlns="http://www.w3.org/1999/xhtml">
5   <!-- Generated by AceHTM http://freeware.acehtml.com -->
6   <head>
7   <meta http-equiv="Content-Type" content="text/html;
    charset=iso-8859-1" />
8   <title>JavaScript Sort Program</title>
9   <script language="javascript">
10
11  got = prompt ("Please enter a number", 7);
12  answer = confirm ("You input: " + got + ". Is this correct?");
13  alert ("You entered: " + got);
14  alert ("Your number squared = " + got*got);
15  </script>
16
17  </head>
18  <body>
19  </body>
20  </html>
```

Discussion:

This JavaScript program uses the two input mechanisms provided by client-side JavaScript: prompt() and confirm(). The program asks the user to input a number. The prompt box ❶ shows a default value of 7. The program stores the user's input value in the got variable shown in code line 11. Code line 12 displays the user's input value back in a confirm box ❷ and asks for confirmation. If the user clicks the OK button, answer becomes true. Currently, the program does not do anything with the Boolean answer. Line 14 squares the user's input and displays the result in box ❹. If the user clicks the Cancel button of the prompt box ❶, got takes the null value, as shown in box ❺. In this case, the square becomes zero. If the user inputs a string (nonnumber) value, the square becomes NaN, as shown in box ❻.

Hands-on exercise:

Modify the program to accept a person's first and last names as two separate inputs. Concatenate them, and print the person's full name in an alert box.

19.11 Tutorials

19.11.1 Integer Division (Study Section 19.7)

This tutorial shows how to divide integers in JavaScript. For example dividing $2/4$ gives 0 and not 0.5. Use the AceHTML editor to generate the given code, and save it as tutorial19111.html. Render the Web page in a browser. See the following screen captures.

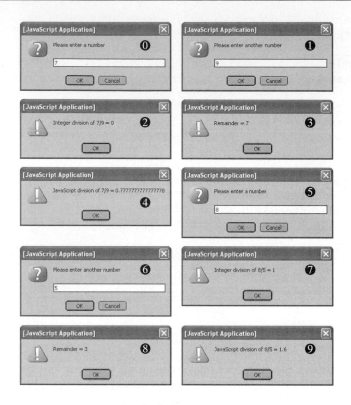

Code explained:

1. Lines 12 and 14 read two numbers from the keyboard.
2. Line 15 uses the modulus operator.
3. Line16 calculates the quotient.
4. Lines 17 and 18 print the results of integer division.
5. Line 19 prints the JavaScript result of dividing two integers.

Discussion:

We run the program twice to perform two divisions. The windows ❶–❾ shown in the screen captures illustrate the divisions of 7/9 and 8/5. Windows ❶, ❶, ❺, and ❻ show the keyboard input. Windows ❹ and ❾ show the floating-point division performed by JavaScript. Windows ❷ and ❼ show the integer division.

Hands-on exercise:

Modify the code to use a `for` loop to execute the division of four pairs of integers.

```
1   <?xml version="1.0" encoding="iso-8859-1"?>
2   <!DOCTYPE html PUBLIC "-//W3C//DTD XHTML 1.1//EN"
3       "http://www.w3.org/TR/xhtml11/DTD/xhtml11.dtd">
4   <html xmlns="http://www.w3.org/1999/xhtml">
```

```
5   <!-- Generated by AceHTM http://freeware.acehtml.com -->
6   <head>
7   <meta http-equiv="Content-Type" content="text/html;
    charset=iso-8859-1" />
8   <title>Integer Division</title>
9   <script language="javascript">
10
11  //get numerator
12  numerator = prompt ("Please enter a number", 7);
13  //get denominator
14  denominator = prompt ("Please enter another number", 9);
15  remainder = numerator % denominator;
16  quotient = (numerator - remainder) / denominator;
17  alert ("Integer division of " + numerator + "/" + denominator + "
    = " + quotient);
18  alert ("Remainder = " + remainder);
19  alert ("JavaScript division of " + numerator + "/" + denominator +
    " = " + numerator/denominator);
20
21  </script>
22  </head>
23  <body>
24  </body>
25  </html>
```

19.11.2 Dollars and Cents (Study Section 19.7)

This tutorial shows how to round off money to the nearest cent. JavaScript division produces many unnecessary digits after the decimal point. This tutorial is particularly important because JavaScript is used to verify online orders and provides online shoppers with the total cost of their orders. Use the AceHTML editor to generate the given code, and save it as `tutorial19112.html`. View the pages in a browser.

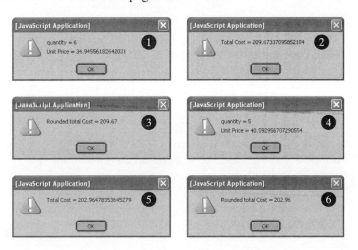

Code explained:

1. Line 12 starts a `for` loop for two iterations.
2. Lines 13, 14, and 18 use the `Math` object of JavaScript.
3. Line 21 uses the `toFixed()` method of JavaScript.
4. Lines 19 and 21 print the results of the program.

Discussion:

The `Math.random()` method used in code line 13 generates a random number between 0 and 1, exclusive. We multiply the number by 10 to scale it up. The `Math.round()` method rounds the resulting number to the nearest integer. In code line 14, we scale up the random number by a factor of 100. Code line 16 calculates the total cost. Code lines 18 and 21 round the total cost to the nearest cent in two different ways. Line 18 multiplies the total cost by 100, rounds the results, and divides back by 100 to restore the result to the scale of the original value. Line 21 uses the `toFixed()` built-in method of JavaScript. This method takes the desired number of decimal places as its argument. Windows ❶–❻ in the foregoing screen capture show the results for two iterations.

Hands-on exercise:

Other JavaScript methods are `toPrecision()` and `toExponential()`. Follow code line 21 with these two methods, using 2 and 4 as the arguments, respectively. What do they do?

```
1   <?xml version="1.0" encoding="iso-8859-1"?>
2   <!DOCTYPE html PUBLIC "-//W3C//DTD XHTML 1.1//EN"
3       "http://www.w3.org/TR/xhtml11/DTD/xhtml11.dtd">
4   <html xmlns="http://www.w3.org/1999/xhtml">
5   <!-- Generated by AceHTM http://freeware.acehtml.com -->
6   <head>
7   <meta http-equiv="Content-Type" content="text/html ;
    charset=iso-8859-1" />
8   <title>Dollars and Cents</title>
9   <script language="javascript">
10
11  //Buy two products
12  for (i=0; i<2; i++) {
13  quantity = Math.round(Math.random ()*10);
14  unitPrice = Math.random()*100;
15  alert ("quantity = " + quantity + "\n" + "Unit Price = " +
    unitPrice);
16  totalCost = quantity * unitPrice;
17  alert ("Total Cost = " + totalCost);
18  totalCostRounded = Math.round(totalCost * 100)/100;
19  alert ("Rounded total Cost = " + totalCostRounded);
20  //use toFixed() method
21  alert ("Rounded total Cost = " + totalCost.toFixed (2));
22  }  //for
23
24  //Try totalCost.toPrecision(2). See hands-on exercise of tutorial
```

```
25    //Try totalCost.toExponential(4). See hands-on exercise of
      tutorial
26
27    </script>
28    </head>
29    <body>
30    </body>
31    </html>
```

FAQs

Introduction (Section 19.1)

Q: Can I use JavaScript as a stand-alone language?

A: No. JavaScript is a small, lightweight language that is designed for easy embedding in Web browsers.

Development Environment (Section 19.3)

Q: Do I need stand-alone JavaScript debuggers? If so, where can I find them?

A: JavaScript is a simple language; thus, it is easy to debug and fix JavaScript code. There is no need for full-scale debuggers. However, you can use a search engine to find a JavaScript debugger.

Q: Can I nest `<script>` tags?

A: No. Nesting would take this form:

```
<script>
...
<script>
...
</script>
...
</script>
```

A syntax error would occur, however, because the interpreter would attempt to treat the nested tag as a JavaScript syntax.

Q: If I use two or more `<script>` tags, are variables and functions visible across the tags?

A: Yes. The following example is an: `<script langauge="javascript">x=5;
y=6;</script>`

```
<script langauge="javascript">
z=z+y;alert(z); //prints 11</script>
```

Q: Can I format text in an `alert()` function by using tags such as `<h1>`—for example, `alert("<h1 align='center'>Hello World!</h1>`?

A: No. The browser ignores all the tags; it does not render them. The alert `box` is not designed to hold a full page; it is a quick way to display text messages to Web surfers.

Blackbox

Section 19.1 (Introduction): JavaScript provides dynamics in Web pages, as well as client-side execution and verification. It is an interpretive language that runs within a Web browser. JavaScript 1.5 is the latest version. We use client-side JavaScript because it is more useful and more widely used than server-side JavaScript.

Section 19.2 (JavaScript and Java): JavaScript supports most Java expression syntax and control structures. Unlike Java, it does not declare variable types or functions and cannot read from or write to the hard disk of a client computer.

Section 19.3 (Embedding JavaScript in XHTML): Use the `<script>` tag to embed JavaScript code in XHTML code of a Web page. Use this template to include both XHTML and JavaScript code:

```
<html><head><title>title goes here</title>
<script language="javascript">script code goes here</script>
</head><body>content goes here</body></html>
```

Section 19.4 (Development Environment) (Example 19.1): As with XHTML, an editor (text or WYSIWYG) and a browser are required in order to develop JavaScript code. In addition, a JavaScript console is needed to in order debug code during development. AceHTML and the Netscape browser have a built-in console. IE does not. Use AceHTML or Netscape to develop code and IE to deploy it.

Section 19.5 (Variables) (Examples 19.2 and 19.3): Names of variables must begin with a letter (lowercase or uppercase), underscore (_), or dollar sign ($). There is no need to declare data types. Use global scope for variables in order to keep code simple. Use the `const` keyword to declare constants. Literals can be numbers (`e.g., x=3.5`), Booleans (e.g., `answer=true`), or strings (e.g., `name="abe"`). Nesting literal strings requires toggling the quote type (e.g., single (`'`) to double (`"`)) or escaping the internal quote (`\"`).

Section 19.6 (Statements): A statement must be written on one line. Breaking a long statement over multiple lines produce syntax errors. Use comment statements in code in order to make the code more readable. Use inline comments (e.g., `//This is an inline comment`) or block comments, which span multiple lines (`/* ... */`).

Section 19.7 (Expressions and Operators) (Example 19.4): The JavaScript operators are assignment (=), comparison (==, !=, ===, !==, >, >=, <, and <=), arithmetic (+, -, *, /, %, ++, --, -), and logical (&&, ||, !). The arithmetic operators *, /, and % precede + and -. Parentheses override this default precedence.

Section 19.8 (Control Structures) (Examples 19.5–19.7): The JavaScript control structures are as follows:

`if` statement — examples: `if (x<5) alert("I am here");`
`if (x<5) alert("Great") else alert ("Too bad");`
`for` loop — example: `for (i=0; i<=10; i++) {x = y; z = a;}`

`while` loop — example: x=0; `while (x<5) {a=b; d=e; x++;}`
`do while` loop — example: x=0; `do {a=b; d=e; x++;} while (x<5)`

Section 19.9 (Code Execution): The JavaScript interpreter executes statements from top to bottom, and from left to right, with the exception of function definitions. The interpreter does not execute function definitions unless they are called by the JavaScript program that defines them. This aspect is important to remember when debugging code.

Section 19.10 (Input and Output) (Example 19.8): Client-side JavaScript provides `alert()` and `document.write()` functions for output, and `prompt()` and `confirm()` functions for input.

Section 19.11 (Tutorials): Two tutorials show how to use JavaScript syntax.

Quick reference for the syntax presented in this chapter

Topic	Subtopic	Syntax	Example
Embed JavaScript in XHTML	None	`<html>` `<head>` `<title>...</title>` `<script language = "javascript">` `...` `</script>` `</head>` `<body>...</body>` `</html>`	`<html>` `<head>` `<title>...</title> <script language = "javascript">` `alert("Hello");` `</script>` `</head>` `<body>content</body>` `</html>`
Variables	Identifiers (names)	Must begin with a letter (lowercase or uppercase), underscore (_), or dollar sign ($).	`test, Test, jam234, _best, $abc,` and `a_12$4`
	Data types	Number, Boolean, and string.	`x = 5; y=3.5;` (number) `answer=true;` (Boolean) `name="Abe";` (string)
	Declaration	Not required. Just use variables.	See the foregoing cell.
	Scope	Local or global. Use global to keep code simple.	Writing `x=5;` makes `x` global.
	Constants	`const` identifier.	`const x = 10;`
	Literals	number = a value; boolean = `true` or `false`; string = `"..."` or `'...'`.	`x = 3; y = 9.3;` (number) `answer = false;` (Boolean) `name = "Abe";` (value)
	Nesting strings	Toggle quote types, or escape inside quotes.	`"this is a 'quick quiz'";` `"this is a \"quick quiz\"";`

Topic	Subtopic	Syntax	Example
Comment statements	One-line comment	`//comment here`	`//this is a comment on one line.` `//it is known as inline comment`

	Comment block	`/* comment block begins`
		`*/`
			`/********************`
			`* comments go here`
			`* over multiple lines`
			`*********************/`

Operators	Assignment	`left operand = right operand`	x = y + z;
	Comparison	`left operand <op> right operand`	`x == y;` (equal) `x!=y;` (not equal) `x=== y;` (strict equal) `x!==y;` (strict not equal) `x>y;` (greater than) `x>=y;` (greater than or equal) `x<y;` (less than) `x<=y` (less than or equal)
	Arithmetic	`left operand <op> right operand`	`x+y` (add) `x-y` (subtract) `x*y` (multiply) `x/y` (divide) `x%y` (modulus) `++x` or `x++` (increment) `--x` or `x--` (decrement) `-x` (negation)
	Logical	`left operand <op> right operand`	`x&&y` (logical AND) `x||y` (logical OR) `!x` (logical NOT)

Control structures	`if` statement	two styles:
		`if (condition) {true block}`
		`if (condition) {true block}`
		`else {false block}`
			`if (x<5) alert ("You win");`
			`if (x<5) alert ("You win")`
			`else alert("Try again later");`

	`for` loop	`for (counter values) {...}`	`for (i=0; i<9; i++) {x +=i;}`

Topic	Subtopic	Syntax	Example
	while loop	while (condition) {...}	x=0;while(x<5){a=b;c=d;x++;}
	do while loop	do {...} while (condition)	x=0;do{a=b;c=d;x++;}while(x<5)

Check Your Progress

At the end of this chapter, you should

✔   understand the nature of JavaScript (Section 19.1);
✔   understand the difference between JavaScript and Java (Section 19.2);
✔   know how to embed JavaScript in XHTML (Section 19.3);
✔   understand the JavaScript development environment (Section 19.4);
✔   have mastered JavaScript syntax (Section 19.5–19.8);
✔   understand JavaScript code execution (Section 19.9);
✔   have mastered JavaScript input and output (Section 19.10);
✔   have practiced using JavaScript syntax (Section 19.11).

Problems

The exercises are designed for a lab setting, while the homework is to be done outside class time.

Exercises

19.1   Write a JavaScript program that finds the sum of the numbers from 1 to 10, inclusive. Print the numbers and the sum.

19.2   Write a JavaScript program that finds the sum of the odd numbers between 1 to 10, inclusive. Print the numbers and the sum.

19.3   Write a JavaScript program that finds the sum of the even numbers between 1 to 10, inclusive. Print the numbers and the sum.

Homework

19.4   Write a JavaScript program that reads a number from the keyboard, squares it, and prints the result.

19.5   Write a JavaScript program that reads two literal strings from the keyboard, concatenates them, and prints the results.

19.6   Write a JavaScript program that converts an angle in degrees to radians, according to this equation: $r = \theta \times \pi / 180$. Define π as a constant with a value of 3.14159. The program should read θ from the keyboard.

19.7   Write a JavaScript program that calculates the area and perimeter of a square.

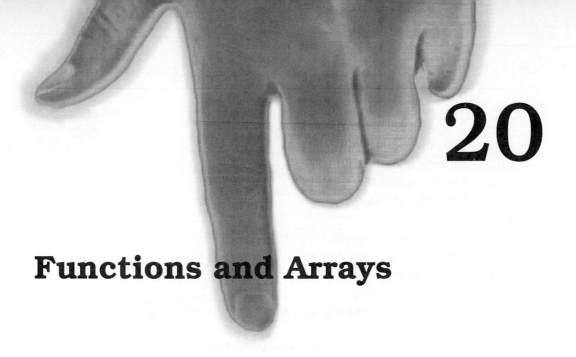

Functions and Arrays

Goal

Understand the basics of JavaScript functions and arrays, their definitions, their use, their role in automating repetitive tasks, their algorithms, their input, their output, and the use of predefined (built-in) JavaScript functions.

Objectives

- The importance of functions and arrays
- Function definition and calling
- Recursion
- Array definition and use
- Array dimensionality
- Array manipulation
- Objects and associative arrays

Outline

20.1 Introduction

As in real life, there are many repetitive tasks that we encounter in the computer field and in programming languages. We refer to these tasks as algorithms. An **algorithm** is a finite set of instructions that are general (can be applied to any problem that the algorithm is intended to solve), unique (produce the same output for the same input all the time), finite (the algorithm does not run forever), precise (well defined), and take input and produce output.

Consider the example of a recipe for apple pie. The recipe's steps are the algorithm. The input to the algorithm is the ingredients (flour, butter, apples, and so forth). The output of the algorithm is the pie itself. On a more academic note, the procedure for sorting a set of numbers is also an algorithm. The sorting steps define the finite set of instructions of the algorithm. The input is the set of unsorted numbers, and the output is the set of sorted numbers.

A **function** is defined as a set of statements that takes an input, uses an algorithm, and produces an output. While the input can change, the algorithm does not. The output changes when the input changes. Figure 20.1 shows a function that uses an algorithm for making a phone call from a cell phone. When you dial a number, the phone's circuitry uses an embedded algorithm in the phone to connect you. The algorithm reads the dialed number, converts it into packets, bundles the packets, and sends them through wireless networks.

Functions are useful in programming, as they make programs modular and more portable. If we need to use a function in multiple programs, we can copy its code into each program, or we can store it in a library and call it from there.

Functions and arrays provide a useful combination in programming. An **array** can be viewed as a complex variable that can hold multiple values at the same time. We can pass arrays to functions as input. We can also generate multiple output values from a function via an output array.

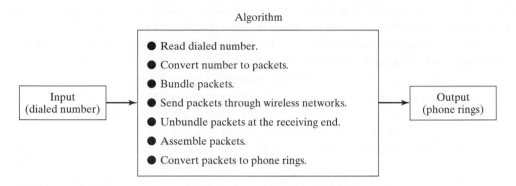

Figure 20.1 A phone call function.

Arrays allow us to index a variable that may have or take multiple values concurrently. JavaScript uses arrays in a unique way when it associates them with objects, as we explain later in this chapter. As with functions, we must define arrays before using them. This chapter covers the details of defining and using functions and arrays.

20.2 Function Definition

A function must be defined before it can be used. A function is defined as follows:

```
1   <meta http-equiv="Content-Type" content="text/html;
    charset=iso-8859-1">
2   <script language="javascript">
3
4   //function definition
5   function functionName ([param1, param2, param3, ...]) {
6   ...
7   ... body goes here
8   ...
9   return something;   //optional; may be used to return true or false
10  alert("hello");   //will never be reached or executed
11  } //close functionName
```

A function definition has two parts: a signature (header) and a body. The signature, shown in code line 5 of the foregoing definition, specifies the function name and the function's input parameters. The keyword `function` declares the function. The JavaScript interpreter therefore treats lines 5–11 as a function definition. Following the `function` keyword must come the function name, `functionName`, as one word with no spaces. For example, the name `function Name` (with a space between the two words) produces a syntax error. Every function signature must end with parentheses; they differentiate between variables and functions. Inside the parentheses comes an optional list of parameters, separated by commas, as shown in line 5. The brackets, [ ] indicate that the material is optional. Do not actually enter the brackets into the code. These parameters are the input the function needs in order to execute the algorithm defined in its body.

The function body is included between two braces (curly brackets), as shown in lines 5–11. The body includes any legal JavaScript statements. A `return` statement, such as in line 8, may be used in the body. If so, it should be the last statement in the body (unless it is used with a conditional statement), as any code after the `return` statement, such as in line 10, is never executed. JavaScript ignores such code; it does not issue a syntax error. Only one `return` statement (or conditional multiple `return` statements) is allowed in a function.

In the spirit of keeping JavaScript simple, there is seldom a need to use `return` statements in functions. Remember that all variables are global, as long as we do not use the `var` keyword. As a result, any variables used inside a function are visible (and thus accessible) outside of it as well and can be readily used without being `returned` by the function. One case where a `return` statement is needed is shown in line 9; we return from the function a Boolean that is used later in event handling, which we cover in Chapter 21. We should mention that a few of JavaScript's predefined functions return values.

A function definition is not executed until the function is called. So, in this example, the JavaScript interpreter skips lines 5–11. Whenever it encounter a call that uses the name in line 5, it execute lines 6–9. (Again, line 10 is never executed.)

20.3 Function Calls

Defining a function does not cause the function to be called. After we define a function, we can call (invoke) it in order to execute it. The following code sample shows how to call a function:

```
1   <meta http-equiv="Content-Type" content="text/html;
    charset=iso-8859-1">
2   <script language="javascript">
3   returnValue = functionName(1,2,3,...);  //call function before
    definition
4
5   //function definition
6   function functionName ([param1, param2, param3, ...]) {
7   ...
8   ... body goes here
9   ...
10  return something;  //optional; may be used to return true or false
11  alert("hello");   //will never be reached or executed
12  } //close functionName
13
14  returnValue = functionName(1,2,3,...); //call function after
    definition
```

Code lines 3 and 14 calls the function `functionName()`, which we define in lines 6–12. The call consists of the function name and values that are passed as the parameters, if the function has any. These values are known as arguments. The arguments must be of the same data type as their corresponding parameters. For example, lines 3 and 14 pass numbers in the function call for `param1`, `param2`, and `param3`. We assume that the function uses them in its body.

A function call can be placed before (line 3) or after (line 14) the function definition. We recommend defining functions before using them, as we have demonstrated in Section 19.9. This method is possible because JavaScript has a *double-pass interpreter*. In the first pass, it scans all the code of the script to know what is there; it peeks ahead. In the second pass, it executes the code from top to bottom and from left to right.

There are two ways to call functions. If the function does not return a value, we call it by using its name and passing arguments to it, if needed. If the function returns a value, we call it in an assignment statement, as shown in lines 3 and 14. The assignment operator captures the function's return value and stores it in its left operand—`returnValue` in lines 3 and 14. The left operand assumes the same data type as that of the return value. If we do not use an assignment statement, the return value is lost and cannot be used in the code that follows the call. Other examples of functions that return values are JavaScript's `prompt()` and `confirm()` functions, which we used in Chapter 19.

We can nest function calls; that is, we can call a function inside another function definition. For example, line 11 in the foregoing code calls JavaScript's `alert()` function inside `functionName()`. There is no limit on the number or level of nested function calls.

___

Example 20.1 Define and call functions.

Write a JavaScript program that defines and uses a function which takes an integer as input and finds and prints all the numbers divisible by it in the range of 1 to 25, inclusive.

Solution 20.1 Using the AceHTML editor, generate the given code, and save it as `example201.html`. The following screen capture shows the Web page.

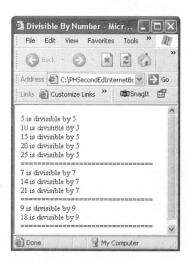

Code explained:

1. Lines 12–16 define the function `divisibleByNumber()`.
2. Line 13 begins the `for` loop.
3. Line 14 uses the `num` parameter to check for divisibility.
4. Lines 19, 21, and 23 call the function with argument values of 5, 7, and 9, respectively.
5. Lines 20, 22, and 24 print dividers to separate the results of the three function calls.

Discussion:

The program defines the `divideByNumber()` function, which has one parameter, `num`. The signature of the function is `function divisibleByNumber(num)`. The function name follows the long-name convention commonly used in object-oriented programming. The name should always begin with a lowercase letter and must follow the rules of JavaScript identifiers. The three function calls come after the function definition. We could have also written them following line 10 instead.

Hands-on exercise:

Add another parameter, `num1`, to the function definition. Then print the numbers between 1 and 50, inclusive, that are divisible by both `num` and `num1`. Make three function calls.

```
1    <?xml version="1.0" encoding="iso-8859-1"?>
2    <!DOCTYPE html PUBLIC "-//W3C//DTD XHTML 1.1//EN"
3        "http://www.w3.org/TR/xhtml11/DTD/xhtml11.dtd">
4    <html xmlns="http://www.w3.org/1999/xhtml">
5    <!-- Generated by AceHTM http://freeware.acehtml.com -->
6    <head>
7    <meta http-equiv="Content-Type" content="text/html;
     charset=iso-8859-1" />
8    <title>Divisible By Number</title>
9    <script language="javascript">
10
11   //define function
12   function divisibleByNumber (num) {
13       for (i=1; i<=25; i++) {
14           if(i%num == 0)document.write(i+"isdivisibleby"
     + num + "<br />");
15       } //for
16   } //divisibleByNumber()
17
18   //call function
19   divisibleByNumber (5);
20   document.write ("================================<br />");
21   divisibleByNumber (7);
22   document.write ("================================<br />");
23   divisibleByNumber (9);
24   document.write ("================================");
```

```
25
26    </script>
27    </head>
28    <body>
29    </body>
```

Example 20.2 Define and call functions.

Write a JavaScript program that simulates bank account transactions. The program should use a function that takes an item's price as input and calculates the current balance after a payment for that item has been deducted.

Solution 20.2 Using the AceHTML editor, generate the given code, and save it as example202.html. The following screen capture shows the resulting Web page.

Code explained:

1. Line 12 initializes the bank account's balance to $2000.00.

2. Lines 15–21 define the buyItem() function.

3. Line 16 does not allow a negative balance.

4. Line 17 reduces the current balance by the price of an item.

5. Lines 18 and 19 print the results. A <br /> tag is used to force line breaks in order to format the output.

6. Lines 24, 26, and 28 call the function to calculate the balance after purchases of a TV, stove, and a refrigerator, respectively.

Discussion:

The program defines the buyItem() function, which has two parameters: item and price. The signature of the function is function buyItem(item, price). The function name follows the long-name convention commonly used in object-oriented programming. The function first checks the current balance (code line 16) to ensure that it is enough to cover the current purchase. If it is, it executes the purchase and reduces the balance by the purchase price (line 17).

Hands-on exercise:

How can you solve the problem of the printed balance containing too many decimal places, as shown in the last calculation in the screen capture? Modify the code to fix it.

```
1    <?xml version="1.0" encoding="iso-8859-1"?>
2    <!DOCTYPE html PUBLIC "-//W3C//DTD XHTML 1.1//EN"
3        "http://www.w3.org/TR/xhtml11/DTD/xhtml11.dtd">
4    <html xmlns="http://www.w3.org/1999/xhtml">
5    <!-- Generated by AceHTM http://freeware.acehtml.com -->
6    <head>
7    <meta http-equiv="Content-Type" content="text/html;
     charset=iso-8859-1" />
8    <title>Define and Call Functions</title>
9    <script language="javascript">
10
11   //define account starting balance
12   balance = 2000.00;
13
14   //define function
15   function buyItem (item, price) {
16       if (balance > price) {
17           balance -= price;
18           document.write ("You bought a " + item + " for $" + price +
     "<br />");
19           document.write (" Current balance is $" + balance +
     "<br />");
20       } //if
21   } //buyItem()
22
23   //call function
24   buyItem ("TV", 150.75);
25   document.write ("==============================<br />");
26   buyItem ("stove", 538.97);
27   document.write ("==============================<br />");
28   buyItem ("refrigerator", 985.32);
29   document.write ("==============================");
30
31   </script>
32   </head>
33   <body></body></html>
```

Example 20.3 Include XHTML tags in functions.

Write a JavaScript program that uses XHTML tags inside a function in order to format the function's output.

Solution 20.3 Using the AceHTML editor, generate the given code, and save it as `example203.html`. The accompanying screen capture shows the resulting Web page.

Code explained:

1. Lines 13–31 define the `namesList()` function.
2. Line 15 requests the number of people (`peopleNumber`) on the list from the user, this variable has a default value of 5.
3. The `for` loop (lines 16–29) reads the first and last names from the keyboard and prints them in a table format.
4. Line 19 checks whether `i` is even.
5. Lines 33–35 call the `namesList()` function.

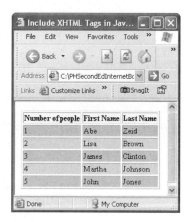

Discussion:

The program defines the `namesList()` function with no parameters. The signature of the function is `function namesList()`. The function creates an $n \times 3$ table; see the foregoing screen capture. The number of rows, n, is a variable that the user inputs. The number of columns is fixed at three, as shown. The function embeds the XHTML table tags in its `document.write()` statements. This embedding of the tags is an important concept, as it allows JavaScript output to be easily formatted. Code lines 19 and 24 allow the function to alternate the background color of the table rows, as shown in the screen capture. One color is used for even rows, and a different color is used for odd rows. Code lines 11 and 36 hide the JavaScript code away from browsers that do not support JavaScript. They makes the code appear as a comment to those browsers. Browsers that support JavaScript ignore the comment and execute the code.

Hands-on exercise:

What does the second argument of the prompt() function, " ", in code lines 17 and 18 do? To find out, remove the argument, run the code, and observe. What is your conclusion?

```
1   <?xml version="1.0" encoding="iso-8859-1"?>
2   <!DOCTYPE html PUBLIC "-//W3C//DTD XHTML 1.1//EN"
3      "http://www.w3.org/TR/xhtml11/DTD/xhtml11.dtd">
4   <html xmlns="http://www.w3.org/1999/xhtml">
5   <!-- Generated by AceHTM http://freeware.acehtml.com -->
6   <head>
7   <meta http-equiv="Content-Type" content="text/html;
    charset=iso-8859-1" />
8   <title>Include XHTML Tags in JavaScript</title>
9   <script language="javascript">
10
11  <!-- hide script away from browsers
12  //list of people provided in table
13  function namesList() {
14      document.write('<table border=1><tr bgcolor=#FFFFCC><th>' +
    'Number of people' + '</th><th>' + 'First Name' + '</th><th>' +
    'Last Name' + '</th>');
15      peopleNumber = prompt("Enter number of people",5)
16      for (i = 1; i <= peopleNumber; i++){
17          firstName = prompt("Enter first name for person number
    i + "on the list", " ");
18          lastName = prompt("Enter last name for person number
    "+ "on the list", " ");
19          if (i%2==0){
    //changing color of table rows
20              document.write ('<tr bgcolor=#DDDDDD><td>' + i);
21              document.write ('<td>' + firstName);
22              document.write ('<td>' + lastName + '</tr>');
23          }//if
24          else {
25              document.write ('<tr bgcolor=#CCCC99><td>' + i);
26              document.write ('<td>' + firstName);
27              document.write ('<td>' + lastName + '</tr>');
28          }//else
29      }//for
30      document.write ('</table>');
31  }//namesList()
32
33  peopleList = confirm ("Would you like to create a list of
    people?");
34  if(peopleList) namesList()
```

```
35   else alert ("Maybe next time");
36   -->
37
38   </script>
39   </head>
40   <body>
41   </body>
42   </html>
```

20.4 Predefined Functions

JavaScript has several predefined functions. We discuss some of them here. The `eval(string)` function takes a string and evaluates it. The string can be any JavaScript statement or a sequence of statements. The function is useful for analyzing small chunks of code quickly. Here is an example: `eval("if (5%2==0) alert ('Even number'); else alert ('odd number');")`. The Netscape console has a text field where we can type an `eval ()` function and see the result; see the screen capture that shows the `Evaluate` text filed in Section 19.4.

The two parse functions are `parseFloat(string)` and `parseInt(string)`. They convert the string representation of a number to a true number. Note, however, that the string must be convertible to a number. Each function takes a string and returns a numeric value. Examples are `num1 = parseInt("4");` and `num2 = parseFloat("8.96");`.

The `escape(string)` and `unescape(string)` functions allow us to encode and decode strings, respectively. They should be used with ASCII characters only, as they do not work properly otherwise. Character encoding means converting a character to its equivalent ASCII (or Unicode which uses 16 bits/character, enabling if to support international characters, as opposed to ASCII, which uses only 8 bits/characters) code. For example, the ASCII code for $ is `%24`. All ASCII codes begin with the % sign. Character decoding, the opposite of encoding, converts an ASCII code to its equivalent character. Examples are `escape("A")` and `unescape("%20")`. The ASCII codes for A–Z, a–z, and 0–9 are the same as the respective characters themselves. For example, `escape("P")` gives P. All other characters use the format `%xx`. The code for whitespace is `%20`. To find out any character's code, use the `eval()` function in the Netscape console—for example, `alert(eval("escape('#');"))`.

20.5 Recursion

Recursion is a natural and powerful way to solve a large class of problems. **Recursion** is the decomposition of a problem into subproblems of the same type as the original problem. Each subproblem, in turn, can be decomposed further until we reach one or more final subproblems that can be solved in a straightforward manner. The solution of the original problem is the assembly of the solutions of all the subproblems.

Recursive functions support recursion. A **recursive function** is a function that calls itself. JavaScript supports recursive functions.

Example 20.4 Use recursive functions.

Write a JavaScript program that calculates the factorial of a number.

Solution 20.4 The factorial of a number is defined by the following equation:

$$n! = n \times (n-1)! = n \times (n-1) \times (n-2)!$$

This equation evaluates to

$$n! = n \times (n-1) \times (n-2) \times (n-3) \ldots \times 3 \times 2 \times 1$$

Note that $1! = 1$ and $0! = 1$, by definition. Using the AceHTML editor, generate the given code, and save it as `example204.html`. Render the Web page in a browser.

Code explained:

    1. Lines 13–18 define the recursive function `factorial(num)`.
    2. Line 14 defines the exit condition.
    3. `factorial()` calls itself repeatedly in line 17, with different arguments.
    4. Line 20 requests a number from the user.
    5. Lines 21, 23, and 25 calculate the factorials of three numbers derived from the input value.
    6. Lines 27–29 print the factorials of the three numbers.

Discussion:

Line 17 reduces the current `num` by `1` and makes the recursive call. In each call, `num-1` is passed as the argument, replacing the `num` parameter. The result from each call is kept by the interpreter until `factorial()` exits itself in lines 14 and 15. The interpreter multiplies all the values and returns the result.

Hands-on exercise:

Change the code to read in two numbers and calculate the factorial of their difference.

```
1    <?xml version="1.0" encoding="iso-8859-1"?>
2    <!DOCTYPE html PUBLIC "-//W3C//DTD XHTML 1.1//EN"
```

```
3          "http://www.w3.org/TR/xhtml11/DTD/xhtml11.dtd">
4     <html xmlns="http://www.w3.org/1999/xhtml">
5     <!-- Generated by AceHTM http://freeware.acehtml.com -->
6     <head>
7     <meta http-equiv="Content-Type" content="text/html;
      charset=iso-8859-1" />
8     <title>Factorials</title>
9     <script language="javascript">
10
11    <!-- hide script away from browsers
12    //define function
13    function factorial (num){
14         if (num <= 1)//final subproblem; exit factorial()
15              return 1;
16         //recursive call
17         return num*factorial (num-1);
18    }  //factorial()
19    //call function
20    input = prompt("Please enter an integer", 5);
21    result1 = factorial(input);
22    //double input
23    result2 = factorial(2*input);
24    //triple input
25    result3 = factorial(3*input);
26    //print results
27    document.write(input + "! = " + result1 +        "<br />");
28    document.write(2*input + "! = " + result2 +       "<br />");
29    document.write(3*input + "! = " + result3 +       "<br />");
30    -->
31
32    </script>
33    </head>
34    <body></body></html>
```

20.6 Array Definition and Properties

Arrays are useful in many applications. Say we want to define and implement four color values: red, green, blue and yellow. One option is to use four variables, one for each value, with names like `color1`, `color2`, `color3`, and `color4`. This approach is repetitive, however, and there is a better way: arrays.

An **array** is an ordered set of values associated with a single variable name. An **array** is also defined as an indexed collection of items, all of which have the same variable type. It is considered a data structure. A **data structure** is a predefined pattern that holds data in an organized way. Arrays eliminate repetition among variables of the same type and almost the same name. For our color example, we can use an array structure like this one: `colorArray=(red, green, blue, yellow)`.

We define arrays in the same way that we define variables. An array may be defined as follows:

    myArray = new Array(4); //similar to var x;, where x is a variable

Each array has an implicit data type (number, Boolean, or string) and must have a name. Unlike a variable, an array must have a size that specifies the number of its elements. The foregoing statement defines an array with the name myArray that has a size of 4—that is, four elements. Each element has an undefined value. The new operator indicates that arrays are objects; Array is a predefined (built-in) JavaScript object. We cover objects in detail in later chapters.

As with variables, we can define and initialize arrays at the same time, such as in the following examples:

    myArray = new Array ("red", "green", "blue", "yellow"); //similar
        to x = 5;
    myArray = ["red", "green", "blue", "yellow"]; //similar to x = 5;

Either of these two statements defines myArray with four elements and four values, one value per element.

The size of an array should be specified when the array is defined; for example, myArray2 = new Array() defines myArray2 as an empty array with no elements.

How do we access array elements? Each array element has an index and a value. The **index** is a counter that locates the element in its array. JavaScript uses zero-based arrays, meaning that the index of the first element in the array is zero (0). Thus the index of the last element in the array is one less than the size of the array. The indexes and values of the elements of myArray are shown as follows:

Element value	red	green	blue	yellow
Element index	0	1	2	3

Use the square brackets ([]) to access an array element. For example, myArray[2] accesses the third element of the foregoing array. The first element is myArray[0], and the last element is myArray[3]. The values of the first and last elements are red and yellow, respectively.

Use the length property of an array in dot notation in order to find the size of the array. For example, the dot notation myArray.length returns the value 4, this array's size. We defer discussion of dot notation until we cover objects. If we must cycle through all the elements of an array, the most effective way is to use the length property in a loop statement, such as the for loop.

The size of an array defines its bounds. Unlike other programming languages, JavaScript allows access to out-of-bound elements, effectively allowing arrays with dynamic sizes. After an array has been given an initial size, the program can add new elements to the original array, thus increasing its size. For example, we can use myArray[4]="purple"; to add a fifth element to myArray.

Example 20.5 Use arrays.

Write a JavaScript program that calculates the sum of the squares of the following elements of an array: 2, 5, 6, –3, 0, –7, 9, and 4.

Solution 20.5 Using the AceHTML editor, generate the given code, and save it as example205.html. Render the Web page in a browser.

Code explained:

    1. Line 13 defines and initializes numArray to have eight elements.

    2. The for loop in lines 15–17 calculates the sum of the elements' squares.

    3. Lines 20–24 print the array and the sum of the elements' squares.

Discussion:

Line 14 defines and initializes sumSquares to store the sum of the elements' squares. Lines 15 and 21 hard code the array's size, 8, in the for loops. We could use numArray.length instead to make the code more general. Line 16 accesses each array element, squares it, and adds it to the sum. Line 20 uses the array's length property to print the array size. We could have used a hard value of 8 instead, but it is preferable to avoid hard coding.

Hands-on exercise:

Change code line 13 to use [] to define the array. Also, change the code to create a new array that contains the elements' squares; call it squaresArray. Print the elements of this new array.

```
1   <?xml version="1.0" encoding="iso-8859-1"?>
2   <!DOCTYPE html PUBLIC "-//W3C//DTD XHTML 1.1//EN"
3       "http://www.w3.org/TR/xhtml11/DTD/xhtml11.dtd">
4   <html xmlns="http://www.w3.org/1999/xhtml">
5   <!-- Generated by AceHTM http://freeware.acehtml.com -->
6   <head>
```

```
 7   <meta http-equiv="Content-Type" content="text/html;
     charset=iso-8859-1" />
 8   <title>Using Arrays</title>
 9   <script language="javascript">
10
11   <!-- hide script away from browsers
12   //define array and calculate sum of element squares
13   numArray = new Array (2, 5, 6, -3, 0, -7, 9, 4);
14   sumSquares = 0;
15   for (i=0; i<8; i++) {
16       sumSquares += numArray[i]*numArray[i];
17   }//for
18
19   //print results
20   document.write("The sum of the squares of the " + numArray.length
     + " numbers<br />");
21   for (i=0; i<8; i++) {
22       document.write(numArray[i] + ", ");
23   }//for
24   document.write("is <h2>" + sumSquares + "</h2>");
25   -->
26
27   </script>
28   </head>
29   <body>
30   </body>
31   </html>
```

20.7 Multidimensional Arrays

The number of indexes used in an array definition determines the array's **dimensionality**. Thus far, we have used only one dimensional (1D) arrays. However, we can define two-dimensional (2D), three-dimensional (3D), ..., n-dimensional (nD) arrays. 2D arrays can be viewed as a matrix (grid). 3D arrays can be viewed as a cube (box). Beyond 3D arrays, we cannot visualize an array in space, but we can still define it. Each dimension of an array corresponds to an index that allows us to scan the array along that dimension. 1D, 2D, 3D, and nD arrays use, respectively, one, two, three, and n indexes. Figure 20.2 shows the indices for 1D, 2D, and 3D arrays.

We nest array definitions in order to create multidimensional arrays (also known as arrays of arrays). The following definition creates a 2×3 array (two rows by three columns):

```
arr = new Array(new Array(2), new Array(3));
```

Any element can be accessed by two indexes—for example, `arr[i][j]`. The following definition creates and initializes a 2×3 array:

```
arr = new Array(new Array(3, 9, 2), new Array(5, 1, 7));
```

it is easier to use `arr = [[[3, 9, 2], [5, 1, 7]];`.

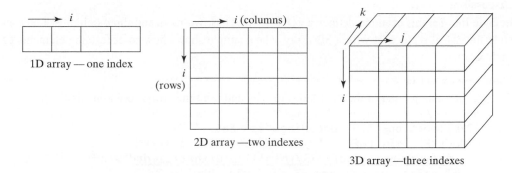

Figure 20.2   Multidimensional arrays.

The following definition creates a $1 \times 2 \times 3$ array:

```
arr = new Array(new Array (new Array(2), new Array(3)));
```

Any element is accessed by three indexes—for example, `arr[i][j][k]`. The following definition creates and initializes a $1 \times 2 \times 3$ array:

```
arr=new Array(new Array(new Array(3, 9, 2), new Array(5, 1, 7)));
```

Alternatively, it is easier to use arr = [[[3, 9, 2], [5, 1, 7]]];

Example 20.6   Use multidimensional arrays.

Write a JavaScript program that uses multidimensional arrays

Solution 20.6   Using the AceHTML editor, generate the given code, and save it as `example206.html`. Render the Web page in a browser.

Code explained:

1. Lines 13 and 24 define a 2D and a 3D array, respectively.
2. The two `for` loops in lines 16 and 17 cycle through all the elements of the 2D array `arr`.
3. The three `for` loops in lines 27–29 cycle through all the elements of the 3D array `arr`.

Discussion:

In code line 13, this example defines a 2D array that has two rows and three columns. Later, in code line 24, it replaces it with a 3D array. The example shows how to access the elements of each array.

Hands-on exercise:

Change the nesting order of the for loops to scan and print the arrays' columns first.

```
1   <?xml version="1.0" encoding="iso-8859-1"?>
2   <!DOCTYPE html PUBLIC "-//W3C//DTD XHTML 1.1//EN"
3       "http://www.w3.org/TR/xhtml11/DTD/xhtml11.dtd">
4   <html xmlns="http://www.w3.org/1999/xhtml">
5   <!-- Generated by AceHTM http://freeware.acehtml.com -->
6   <head>
7   <meta http-equiv="Content-Type" content="text/html;
    charset=iso-8859-1" />
8   <title>Using Multidimensional Arrays</title>
9   <script language="javascript">
10
11  <!-- hide script away from browsers
12  //define 2D array squares
13  arr = [[3, 9, 2], [5, 1, 7]];
14  document.write("Here is a 2D array (matrix)<br />");
15  //print array elements
16  for (i=0; i<2; i++) {          //loop over rows
17      for (j=0; j<3; j++) {      //loop over columns
18      document.write (arr[i][j] + " ");
19      }//inner for loop
20  document.write("<br />");
21  }//outer for loop
22
23  //define 3D array squares
24  arr = [[[3, 9, 2], [5, 1, 7]]];
25  document.write("Here is a 3D array<br />");
26  //print array elements
27  for (i=0; i<1; i++) {              //loop over i
28      for (j=0; j<2; j++) {          //loop over j
29          for (k=0; k<3; k++) {      //loop over k
30          document.write (arr[i][j][k] + " ");
31          }//k for loop
32      document.write("<br />");
33      }//j for loop
34  document.write("<br />");
35  }//i for loop
36  -->
37
38  </script>
```

```
39   </head>
40   <body>
41   </body>
42   </html>
```

20.8 Array Manipulations

Once we create arrays, we can manipulate them in various ways. For example, we can resize, copy, and sort arrays. JavaScript provides many predefined functions for array manipulation. Table 20.1 lists some of them.

Example 20.7 Sorting arrays.

Write a JavaScript program that sorts arrays of strings and numbers.

Solution 20.7 Using the AceHTML editor, generate the given code, and save it as example207.html. Render the Web page in a browser.

Table 20.1 JavaScript functions to manipulate arrays.

Functions are `reverse()`, `sort()`, `concat()`, and `slice()`

Function	Description	Example

reverse()	Reverses the order of array elements.	`arr=[1,2,3,4]; //define array`
		`arr.reverse(); //gives`
		`arr=[4,3,2,1]`

sort()	Sorts array elements in an ascending order. If the array elements are strings, they are sorted in alphabetical order.	`arr=[13,-4,0,9]; //define array`
		`arr.sort(); //gives`
		`arr=[-4,0,9,13]`

concat()	Combines the elements of two arrays. If we have arrays of arrays, as in the case of 2D and 3D arrays, `concat()` does not flatten the arrays of arrays recursively.	`a=[1,2,3,4]; //first array`
		`b=[5,6,7]; //second array`
		`a.concat(b); //gives`
		`[1,2,3,4,5,6,7]`
		`b.concat(a); //gives`
		`[5,6,7,1,2,3,4]`

slice()	Slices an array and returns a subarray of it. It has various formats, as shown in the examples in the cell in the right-hand column.	`a=[1,2,3,4,5,6] //define array`
		`a.slice(0, 4) //returns [1,2,3,4]`
		`a.slice(4) //returns [5,6]`
		`a.slice(2, -1) //returns [3,4,5]`

Code explained:

1. Lines 13–17 define a function that takes two strings, converts them to numbers, and returns their difference.
2. Line 20 defines a string array, and line 26 defines a number array.
3. Lines 21 and 22 sort the string array in ascending and descending order, respectively.
4. Lines 27 and 28 use the default behavior of the `sort()` function.
5. Lines 30 and 31 use a modified behavior of the `sort()` function.

Discussion:

This example shows how to sort string and number arrays. Sorting string arrays is easy. The `sort()` function (code line 21) sorts a string array in ascending order. Code line 22 uses a double-dot notation to sort the array in descending order.

Sorting a number array is less intuitive. If we use the methods in code lines 27 and 28, we get wrong results, as shown in the accompanying screen capture. The reason is that `sort()` converts the numbers into strings. To override this behavior we supply the `ascendingOrder()` function which converts the strings to numbers. We then use the function as an argument to `sort()`.

Hands-on exercise:

Change the values of the elements of the array in code line 26 in many ways until you fully understand what the `ascendingOrder()` function does.

```
1   <?xml version="1.0" encoding="iso-8859-1"?>
2   <!DOCTYPE html PUBLIC "-//W3C//DTD XHTML 1.1//EN"
3       "http://www.w3.org/TR/xhtml11/DTD/xhtml11.dtd">
4   <html xmlns="http://www.w3.org/1999/xhtml">
```

```
5   <!-- Generated by AceHTM http://freeware.acehtml.com -->
6   <head>
7   <meta http-equiv="Content-Type" content="text/html;
    charset=iso-8859-1" />
8   <title>Using Multidimensional Arrays</title>
9   <script language="javascript">
10
11  <!-- hide script away from browsers
12  //need this function for numbers
13  function ascendingOrder(a, b) {
14      num1 = parseInt(a);
15      num2 = parseInt(b);
16      return num1 - num2;
17  }//ascendingOrder()
18
19  //define a string array and sort it
20  someStates = ["MA", "AZ", "RI", "NH"];
21  document.write("States sorted in ascending order:<br />" +
    someStates.sort());
22  document.write("<br />States sorted in descending order:<br />" +
    someStates.sort().reverse());
23  document.write("<br />==============================");
24
25  //define a number array and sort it
26  someNumbers  = [25, -10, 3, 0, 56, 78, 90];
27  document.write("<br />Numbers sorted in an ascending order<br />"
    +  someNumbers.sort());
28  document.write("<br />Numbers sorted in a descending order<br />"
    +  someNumbers.sort().reverse());
29  document.write("<br />==============================");
30  document.write("<br />Numbers sorted in an ascending order<br />"
    +  someNumbers.sort(ascendingOrder));
31  document.write("<br />Numbers sorted in a descending order<br />"
    +  someNumbers.sort(ascendingOrder).reverse());
32  -->
33
34  </script>
35  </head>
36  <body>
37  </body></html>
```

20.9 Associative Arrays

The associative array is an interesting concept in JavaScript. It allows us to associate implicit arrays with objects in order to save the object's properties and variables. We will cover it in more detail in Chapter 22, as it requires a thorough understanding of objects and the concepts related to them.

20.10 Combining Functions and Arrays

Functions can use arrays in two ways: They can use arrays in their bodies or arrays can be passed to functions as arguments for manipulation and processing. Once an array is inside a function, we use the array's `length` property in loop statements to cycle through the array's elements and manipulate them.

Example 20.8 Pass arrays to functions.

Write a JavaScript program that uses functions and arrays.

Solution 20.8 We modify Example 20.5 to define a function and pass an array to it. Using the AceHTML editor, generate the given code, and save it as `example208.html`. Render the Web page in a browser.

Code explained:

1. Lines 12–25 define a function that takes an array as input.
2. Line 14 saves the array's length in a variable for later use in lines 15, 20, and 21.
3. Line 28 defines a number array.
4. Line 31 calls the function.

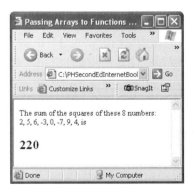

Discussion:

The code of this example is almost identical to that of Example 20.5, illustrating how easy it is to convert the code. We use code line 14 to save computing time: Instead of calculating `numAr-ray.length` three times in lines 15, 20 and 21, we do it once in line 14 and use the result later. As shown in code lines 12 and 31, passing an array to a function is the same as passing a single variable to a function.

Hands-on exercise:

Change `squares()` so that it accepts two arrays as input, calculates the squares of their elements, and adds them together. *Hint*: Do this exercise in two ways: using the arrays individually, and by using the concat() function. Using the arrays individually means repeating the code given in this example, more or less. Using the concat() function means combining the two arrays, calculating the length of the new array, and then using the code given in this example almost as is.

Also, create a new array that saves the squares of the elements and then sorts them in an ascending and descending order.

```
1   <?xml version="1.0" encoding="iso-8859-1"?>
2   <!DOCTYPE html PUBLIC "-//W3C//DTD XHTML 1.1//EN"
3       "http://www.w3.org/TR/xhtml11/DTD/xhtml11.dtd">
4   <html xmlns="http://www.w3.org/1999/xhtml">
5   <!-- Generated by AceHTM http://freeware.acehtml.com -->
6   <head>
7   <meta http-equiv="Content-Type" content="text/html;
    charset=iso-8859-1" />
8   <title>Passing Arrays to Functions</title>
9   <script language="javascript">
10
11  <!-- hide script away from browsers
12  function squares(numArray) {
13      sumSquares = 0;
14      len = numArray.length;
15      for (i=0; i<len; i++) {
16          sumSquares += numArray[i]*numArray[i];
17      }//for
18
19      //print results
20      document.write("The sum of the squares of these " + len
    + " numbers:<br />");
21      for (i=0; i<len; i++) {
22          document.write(numArray[i] + ", ");
23      }//for
24      document.write("is <h2>" + sumSquares + "</h2>");
25  }//squares()
26
27  //define an array and pass to function
28  arr = new Array (2, 5, 6, -3, 0, -7, 9, 4);
29
30  //call function and pass array as an argument
31  squares(arr);
32  -->
33
34  </script>
35  </head>
36  <body></body></html>
```

20.11 Tutorials

20.11.1 Flying from Boston (Study Section 20.10)

This tutorial shows how to synchronize multiple arrays in order to search them for related information. We simulate the provision of flight information to a traveler in Boston's Logan Airport. Given a flight number, the JavaScript program displays the airline, terminal, and gate number. Table 20.2 shows the flight data. Using the AceHTML editor, generate the given code, and save it as `tutorial20111.html`. Render the Web page in a browser.

Code explained:

1. Lines 12–24 define the `flightInfo()` function.
2. Lines 27–30 define and initialize the four required arrays.
3. Line 33 receives input from the keyboard.
4. Line 34 calls the `flightInfo()` function.

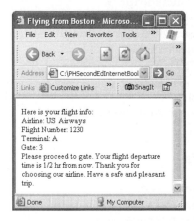

Table 20.2   Boston Logan airport flight data.

Airline	Departure data		
	Flight number	Terminal	Gate
Lufthansa	356	E	5
Swiss Air	89	D	10
US Airways	1230	A	3
Northwest Airlines	952	C	7
British Airways	513	B	1
Air France	910	F	8

Discussion:

The four arrays defined in lines 27–30 are synchronized together; the elements of the four arrays in a particular index belong to each other according to the relationships shown Table 20.2. For example, at index 1, the flight information matches the second row of Table 20.2.

We take advantage of this observation in processing the flight number in the function. The for loop in code lines 14–15 breaks out of the loop once a flight match occurs. We use the value of the counter i, where the match occurs, as an index to access the corresponding elements from the four arrays and print the flight information.

All the variables in the program are global as long as we do not use the var keyword. This practice simplifies code management a great deal.

Hands-on exercise:

Run the code, and hit Enter without entering a flight number. What happens to the program's output? Explain the result. Also, modify the code around line 14 to check if the user has input a valid flight number; if not, display an alert box saying, Sorry! Wrong flight number. Try again.

```
1   <?xml version="1.0" encoding="iso-8859-1"?>
2   <!DOCTYPE html PUBLIC "-//W3C//DTD XHTML 1.1//EN"
3       "http://www.w3.org/TR/xhtml11/DTD/xhtml11.dtd">
4   <html xmlns="http://www.w3.org/1999/xhtml">
5   <!-- Generated by AceHTM http://freeware.acehtml.com -->
6   <head>
7   <meta http-equiv="Content-Type" content="text/html;
    charset=iso-8859-1" />
8   <title>Flying from Boston</title>
9   <script language="javascript">
10
11  <!-- hide script away from browsers
12  function flightInfo(got) {
13      //obtain flight info
14      for (i=0; i<6; i++) {
15          if (got == flightNumber[i]) break;
16      }//for
17          //print results
18          document.write("Here is your flight info:<br />");
19          document.write("Airline: " + airline[i] + "<br />");
20          document.write("Flight Number: " + flightNumber[i] +
    "<br />");
21          document.write("Terminal: " + terminal[i] + "<br />");
22          document.write("Gate: " + gate[i] + "<br />");
23          document.write("Please proceed to gate. Your flight
    departure time is 1/2 hr from now. Thank you for choosing our
    airline.  Have a safe and pleasant trip.");
24  }//flightInof()
25
```

```
26   //define flight data
27   airline = ["Lufthansa", "Swiss Air", "US Airways", "Northwest
     Airlines", "British Airways", "Air France"];
28   flightNumber = [356, 89, 1230, 952, 513, 910];
29   terminal = ["E", "D", "A", "C", "B", "F"];
30   gate = [5, 10, 3, 7, 1, 8];
31
32   //obtain traveler's flight number
33   input = prompt("Please, select your flight number", "356, 89,
     1230, 952, 513, or 910");
34   flightInfo(input);
35   -->
36
37   </script>
38   </head>
39   <body>
40   </body>
41   </html>
```

FAQs

Function Definition (Section 20.2)

Q: Should I use the `var` keyword?

A: Only if you want to group all the variables of a script at the beginning of the script. Keep in mind that JavaScript is used within the context of Web pages and XHTML, so it should be kept simple.

Q: Should I return values from functions?

A: Only on occasion. The problem will present itself then. What allows us to avoid returning values is that we usually do not use `var`; thus, all variables are global.

Blackbox

Section 20.1 (Introduction): Functions and arrays provide a powerful combination for developing useful and efficient JavaScript code.

Section 20.2 (Function Definition): A function has a signature (header) and a body. Follow this template to define a function:

```
<script language="javascript">
//function definition
function functionName ([param1, param2, param3, ...]) {
...
... body goes here
...
```

```
return something; //optional; may use to return true or false
} //close functionName
</script>
```

Section 20.3 (Function Calls) (Examples 20.1–20.3): Call a function above or below its definition as follows:

```
<script language="javascript">
returnValue = functionName(1,2,3,...);//call here
//function definition
function functionName ([param1, param2, param3, ...]) {
... body goes here
return something;  //optional
} //close functionName
returnValue = functionName(1,2,3,...);//call here
</script>
```

Section 20.4 (Predefined Functions): JavaScript has many predefined functions, including `eval(string)`, `parseInt(string)`, `parseFloat(string)`, `escape(string)`, and `unescape(string)`.

Sections 20.5 (Recursion) (Example 20.4): A recursive function calls itself repeatedly until an exit condition (Boolean) becomes true.

Section 20.6 (Array Definition and Properties) (Example 20.5): An array has elements. Each element has a value and an index. The properties of an array are its elements, index, and size (length). We define and initialize arrays as follows, respectively:

```
arr1 = new Array(3); //define an array with three elements
arr2 = [1, 5, 7, 9, 5]; //define and initialize an integer array
     with five elements
```

Section 20.7 (Multidimensional Arrays) (Example 20.6): JavaScript provides 1D, 2D, 3D, ..., nD arrays. Each of these arrays has 1, 2, 3, ..., n indexes, respectively. 2D arrays consist of rows (along the horizontal direction) and columns (along the vertical direction). The following definition creates a 2×3 2D array (two rows by three columns):

```
arr = new Array(new Array(2), new Array(3));
```

Any element is accessed by two indexes—for example, `arr[i][j]`. The following definition creates and initializes a 2×3 array:

```
arr = [[3, 9, 2], [5, 1, 7]];
```

The following definition creates a $1 \times 2 \times 3$ 3D array:

```
arr = new Array(new Array (new Array(2), new Array(3)));
```

Any element is accessed by three indexes—for example, `arr[i][j][k]`. The following definition creates and initializes a $1 \times 2 \times 3$ array:

```
arr = [[[3, 9, 2], [5, 1, 7]]];
```

Section 20.8 (Array Manipulations) (Example 20.7): Once we create arrays, we can manipulate them in various ways. For example, we can resize, copy, and sort arrays. JavaScript provides many predefined functions for array manipulation, including `reverse()`, `sort()`, `concat()`, and `slice()`.

Section 20.9 (Associative Arrays): Associative arrays allow us to associate implicit arrays with objects in order to save the objects' properties and variables. We will cover them in more detail in Chapter 22.

Section 20.10 (Combining Functions and Arrays) (Example 20.8): Use arrays inside a function body, or pass them to functions as arguments.

Section 20.11 (Tutorials): One tutorial shows how to synchronize related arrays.

Quick reference for the syntax presented in this chapter

Topic	Subtopic	Syntax	Example

Functions	Definition	`function`
		`name([params]) {`
		`body`
		`}//name()`
			`function hello() {`
			`alert ("Hello World!");`
			`}//hello()`

	Calls	`name([args]); //use`	`hello();`

	Predefined	`eval(string),`
		`parseInt(string),`
		`parseFloat(string),`
		`escape(string),` and
		`unescape(string)`
			`eval("x=5");`
			`num = parseInt("3");`
			`num = parseFloat("4.5");`
			`hex = escape("$");`
			`character =`
			`unescape("%54");`

	Recursion	`function`
		`name([params]) {`
		`condition;`
		`name([params]);`
		`}//name()`
			`i=15;`
			`function sum(i) {`
			`if (==0) return;`
			`i--;`
			`return i*sum(i-1);`
			`}//sum()`

Arrays	Definition and properties	`arr = new Array(5);`
		`//define`
		`arr = [3, 6, 8, 1];`
		`//initialize`
		`arr = new Array();`
		`//define`
			`arr = new Array(5);`
			`//define`
			`arr = [3, 6, 8, 1];`
			`//initialize`
			`arr = new Array();`
			`//define`

	Multidimensional	`1D: arr = [a, b, c];`
		`2D: arr = [[2, 5],`
		`[1, 9]];`
		`3D arr = [[[2, 5],`
		`[1, 9]]];`
			`arr = [a, b, c]; //1D`
			`arr = [[2, 5], [1, 9]];`
			`//2D`
			`arr = [[[2, 5], [1, 9]]];`

Topic	Subtopic	Syntax	Example

	Manipulation	`reverse()`, `sort()`, `concat()`, and `slice()`.	`a = [2, 3, 6, 7, 9];`
			`b = [1, 4, 5];`
			`a.reverse();`
			`a.sort();`
			`a.concat(b);`
			`a.slice(2);`

	Associativity	See Chapter 22	See Chapter 22
	Combining functions and arrays	`function abc(arr){` `process array}`	`function sort (arr) {` `arr.sort();}`

Check Your Progress

At the end of this chapter, you should

- ✔ understand the need for functions and arrays (Section 20.1);
- ✔ understand how to define functions (Section 20.2);
- ✔ know how to call functions (Section 20.3);
- ✔ be able to identify JavaScript's predefined functions (Section 20.4);
- ✔ have mastered resursion (Section 20.5);
- ✔ understand array definition and types (Sections 20.6 and 20.7);
- ✔ have mastered array manipulation (Sections 20.8–20.10);
- ✔ have practiced using functions and arrays (Section 20.11).

Problems

The exercises are designed for a lab setting, while the homework is to be done outside class time.

Exercises

20.1 Write a JavaScript function with no parameters that multiplies 10 numbers by 10.

20.2 Write a JavaScript function that takes two numbers and divides them. Pass a zero value as the divisor in the function. What happens?

20.3 Write a JavaScript program that defines a string array and a number array and adds the respective elements of the two arrays together. Print the results.

Homework

20.4 Write a JavaScript program that uses a function which takes an array as input and calculates the square roots of its elements.

20.5   Write a JavaScript program that uses a function which takes an array as input and calculates the third power of each of its elements.

20.6   Write a JavaScript program that uses a function which takes an array of decimal elements as input and rounds up each of its elements, to the nearest integer.

20.7   Write a JavaScript program that uses a function which creates an array of size 10, using a random-number generator.

Handling Events

Goal

Understand how JavaScript makes it possible to interact with Web pages, minimizes client/ server traffic, enables verification of user input, and processes events generated by the <body> and <a> tags.

Objectives

- The importance of events in Web-page control
- Event model
- Events
- Event handling
- Handling of <body> and <a> events
- On-the-fly Web pages
- Disabling of XHTML actions

Outline

21.1 Introduction

The key to JavaScript's ability to interact with Web surfers is its events. JavaScript is largely an event-driven language. An **event** is an action that usually occurs as a result of an interaction between the Web surfer and a Web page, such as when the surfer clicks a hyperlink or button, moves the mouse cursor over a hyperlink, or fills out a form.

JavaScript events increase the interactivity of Web pages dramatically. Without them, the only interaction with Web pages occurs when a Web surfer clicks a hyperlink, clicks a hot spot of an image map, or fills out a form. Even with filling out a form, there would be potential problems in the absence of JavaScript events. The main problem is input validation. How can we tell if a form has been filled out properly at the client side, so that we do not send wrong data to the server? JavaScript localizes the form validation process by keeping it on the client side, and it sends only the correct and complete form data and input to the server.

JavaScript events minimize client/server traffic considerably. With them, processing of Web-page requests may be done locally at the client side. For example, after the form validation process, a *Thank You* Web page could be sent to the Web surfer to acknowledge the correct input and notify the surfer of the delivery date of goods and services. There is no need to go to the server to get the *Thank You* page. It is shipped with the Web page that has the form. Section 21.6 covers this concept in more detail.

JavaScript interacts with Web surfers through events and event handlers. An **event handler** is the tool that processes an event in order to make decisions. Event processing is usually done via a function call, as we discuss in Section 21.4. For example, JavaScript can intercept a value that a Web surfer enters in a form field and then check it against a set of criteria.

This chapter covers all the events that JavaScript provides. It also covers the contexts in which these events may arise. Moreover, it shows how to use event handlers to process events.

21.2 Event Model

The JavaScript event model is based on interaction between a Web surfer and a Web page. Printing a Web page or highlighting text in a Web page does not generate interaction and therefore is not considered a JavaScript event. There are only two groups of actions that generate interaction:

1. **Navigation.** Navigation means clicking a hyperlink in order to jump from one Web page to another or to go to a different section within the same page.
2. **Filling out a form.** A Web surfer may select form elements, such as checkboxes or radio buttons, or input text in text fields or areas.

At the core of the JavaScript event model is the `event` object, which connects an event source to an event handler, as shown in Figure 21.1. An **event source** is an XHTML element that is used in the two aforementioned groups of actions (navigation and filling out a form). Valid event sources are a window (of a browser), a document (the Web page itself), a hyperlink (text and image), an image, an image map, a layer, a form (itself), and all form elements (text fields, checkboxes, radio buttons, buttons, select lists, passwords, hidden fields, files, the submit button, and the reset button).

JavaScript associates a unique `event` object with each event source. The `event` object provides all the relevant information about the event that is necessary to process the event. When an event occurs, and if an event handler has been written to handle it, JavaScript's event manager sends the `event` object as an argument to the event handler. The handler can extract all or part of the event information that it encapsulates and process it.

While the `event` object is passed to every event handler, its properties vary from one type of event to another. Some of these properties use pixel measurements, as shown in Figure 21.2. Table 21.1 shows the full set of event properties that JavaScript uses. Not all of these properties are relevant to each event type.

Let us consider the example of clicking a link, in order to show how the JavaScript event model works. When the user clicks a hyperlink, the `event` object contains the type of event (a click in this case), the (x, y) position of the mouse cursor at the time of the event, and some other information. The event handler can then print the (x, y) location of the click or display a message in an `alert` box.

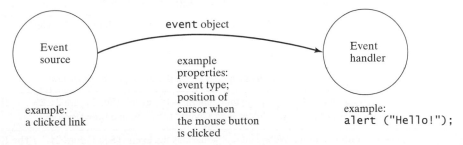

Figure 21.1   JavaScript event model.

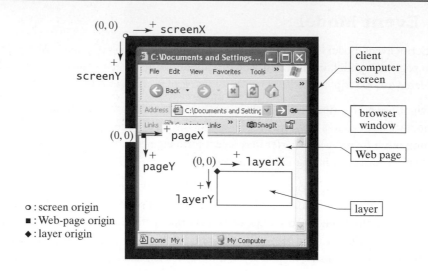

Figure 21.2   Pixel measurements used by the JavaScript `event` object.

Table 21.1   Full set of properties of the JavaScript `event` object.

Full set of properties: `type`, `target`, `width`, `height`, `layerX`, `layerY`, `pageX`, `pageY`, `screenX`, `screenY`, `data`, `modifiers`, and `which`

Property	Meaning
`type`	A string representing the event type (all events).
`target`	A string representing what received the event—typically the Web page that generated it. The IE browser does not recognize this property, while the Netscape browser does.
`width`	The width of the browser window (or frame) that generates the event. The IE browser does not recognize this property, while the Netscape browser does.
`height`	The height of the browser window (or frame) that generates the event. The IE browser does not recognize this property, while the Netscape browser does.
`layerX`	The *x* coordinate of the layer that generates the event. (See Figure 21.2.) The IE browser does not recognize this property, while the Netscape browser does.
`layerY`	The *y* coordinate of the layer that generates the event. (See Figure 21.2.) The IE browser does not recognize this property, while the Netscape browser does.
`pageX`	The *x* coordinate of the Web page that generates the event. (See Figure 21.2.) The IE browser does not recognize this property, while the Netscape browser does.
`pageY`	The *y* coordinate of the Web page that generates the event. (See Figure 21.2.) The IE browser does not recognize this property, while the Netscape browser does.

Table 21.1 Full set of properties of the JavaScript **event** object. (Continued)

Full set of properties: `type`, `target`, `width`, `height`, `layerX`, `layerY`, `pageX`, `pageY`, `screenX`, `screenY`, `data`, `modifiers`, and `which`

Property	Meaning
`screenX`	The x coordinate of the client screen that generates the event. (See Figure 21.2.)
`screenY`	The y coordinate of the client screen that generates the event. (See Figure 21.2.)
`data`	Returns a string array of the dropped objects. The IE browser does not recognize this property, while the Netscape browser does.
`modifiers`	A string specifying the modifier keys used with a mouse-button or key event. The values are ALT_MASK, CONTROL_MASK, SHIFT_MASK, and META_MASK. The IE browser does not recognize this property, while the Netscape browser does.
`which`	A number specifying either the mouse button that was pressed or the ASCII value of a pressed key on the keyboard. For a mouse, 1, 2, and 3 represent, respectively, the left, middle, and right button. The IE browser does not recognize this property, while the Netscape browser does.

Example 21.1 Understand all the properties of a JavaScript **event** object.

Write a JavaScript program that prints all the properties of a JavaScript **event** object.

Solution 21.1 Using the AceHTML editor, generate the given code, and save it as `example211.html`. The following screen capture shows the Web page.

Code explained:

1. Line 32 creates a hyperlink that has an event-handler name, `onClick`, and an event-handler function, `listAllProprs(event)`.
2. Lines 12–27 define the event-handler function.
3. Lines 13–25 build the string `str` that the `alert()` function prints in line 26.

Discussion:

This example prints all the properties of the JavaScript `event` object. While we will cover the concepts behind code line 32 in more detail later, note that clicking the hyperlink calls the `listAllProps()` function, which takes the `event` object as its argument. When a Web surfer clicks the link, the browser encapsulates all the properties of the click in `event` and makes it available to any set of JavaScript code that wants it. In this case, `listAllProps()` intercepts the `event` object and uses it as an argument in code line 32. If no function or Java-Script code intercepts the event immediately after it is generated, it gets lost.

Not all browsers understand all the properties of the `event` object. The Netscape browser understands all of them, while IE understands only three, as demonstrated in the next set of screen captures. The Netscape 7.01 and 4.8 browsers produce slightly different results, as shown in the screen captures.

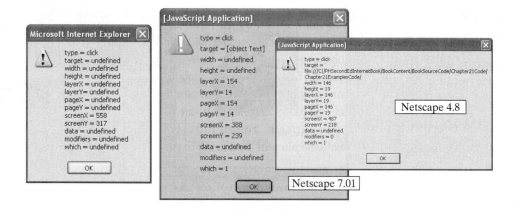

The foregoing screen captures show that some properties are undefined. This is because they are not applicable to a mouse click, such as `width` and `height`. All the shown coordinates are measured according to the three coordinate systems presented in Figure 21.2. Observe that the Web-page and layer coordinate systems are coincident, because the Web page does not use any layers. This is why `layerX` = `pageX` = 154 `px`, and `layerY` = `pageY` = 14 `px`. The `which` property is equal to 1, which means that we clicked the mouse's left button to generate the event.

Hands-on exercise:

Remove the argument of the `listAllProps()` function and run the code. What happens. Does the result make sense? Why?

```
1   <?xml version="1.0" encoding="iso-8859-1"?>
2   <!DOCTYPE html PUBLIC "-//W3C//DTD XHTML 1.1//EN"
3        "http://www.w3.org/TR/xhtml11/DTD/xhtml11.dtd">
4   <html xmlns="http://www.w3.org/1999/xhtml">
5   <!-- Generated by AceHTM http://freeware.acehtml.com -->
6   <head>
7   <meta http-equiv="Content-Type" content="text/html;
    charset=iso-8859-1" />
8   <title>Divisible By Number</title>
9   <script language="javascript">
10
11  //define event handler
12  function listAllProps(evt) {
13  str = "type = " +        evt.type    + "\n";
14  str += "target = " +     evt.target   + "\n";
15  str += "width = " +      evt.width   + "\n";
16  str += "height = " +     evt.height  + "\n";
17  str += "layerX = " +     evt.layerX  + "\n";
18  str += "layerY= "+       evt.layerY   + "\n";
19  str += "pageX = " +      evt.pageX   + "\n";
20  str += "pageY = " +      evt.pageY   + "\n";
21  str += "screenX = " +    evt.screenX   + "\n";
22  str += "screenY = " +    evt.screenY  + "\n";
23  str += "data = " +       evt.data   + "\n";
24  str += "modifiers = " +  evt.modifiers + "\n";
25  str += "which = " +      evt.which;
26  alert (str);
27  } //listAllProps()
28
29  </script>
30  </head>
31  <body>
32  <a href="#" onClick="listAllProps(event)">List all properties of
    Javascript <b><i>event</i></b> object</a>
33  </body>
34  </html>
```

21.3 Events

JavaScript has a unique event for each event source discussed in Section 21.2. Table 21.2 and 21.3 list all the events that JavaScript supports. Table 21.2 lists the events in alphabetical order, while Table 21.3 lists them by the event source. This dual listing makes it easy and fast for the reader to find an event.

Table 21.2 JavaScript events listed alphabetically.

All events: `abort`, `blur`, `change`, `click`, `dragDrop`, `error`, `focus`, `keyDown`, `keyPress`, `keyUp`, `load`, `mouseDown`, `mouseMove`, `mouseOut`, `mouseOver`, `mouseUp`, `move`, `reset`, `resize`, `select`, `submit`, and `unload`

Event name (type)	Generated by (event source)	When event is generated	Event-handler name
`abort`	image	image loading is aborted	`onAbort`
`blur`	windows and all form elements	focus is removed from a window or element	`onBlur`
`change`	text field, text area, and select list	value of an element is changed	`onChange`
`click`	checkbox, radio button, submit button, reset button, button, and link	a form element or link is clicked	`onClick`
`dragDrop`	window	an object (such as a file) is dragged or dropped in a window	`onDragDrop`
`error`	image and window	an error occurs in loading a document or image	`onError`
`focus`	window and all form elements	a window or element is clicked on	`onFocus`
`keyDown`	document, image, link, and text area	a key on keyboard is pressed	`onKeyDown`
`keyPress`	document, image, link, and text area	a key is pressed or held down	`onKeyPress`
`keyUp`	document, image, link, and text area	a key is released	`onKeyUp`
`load`	document	a Web page is loaded into a browser	`onLoad`
`mouseDown`	document, button, and link	a mouse button is pressed	`onMouseDown`
`mouseMove`	nothing	the mouse cursor is moved	`onMouseMove`
`mouseOut`	link and image map	the mouse cursor is moved off hyperlink or image map	`onMouseOut`
`mouseOver`	link and image map	the mouse cursor is moved over a hyperlink or image map	`onMouseOver`
`mouseUp`	document, button, and link	a mouse button is released	`onMouseUp`
`move`	window	a window is moved	`onMove`
`reset`	reset button of a form	the reset button of a form is clicked	`onReset`
`resize`	window	a window is resized	`onResize`

Table 21.2   JavaScript events listed alphabetically. (Continued)

All events: `abort`, `blur`, `change`, `click`, `dragDrop`, `error`, `focus`, `keyDown`, `keyPress`, `keyUp`, `load`, `mouseDown`, `mouseMove`, `mouseOut`, `mouseOver`, `mouseUp`, `move`, `reset`, `resize`, `select`, `submit`, and `unload`

Event name (type)	Generated by (event source)	When event is generated	Event-handler name
`select`	text field, text area, and select list	an element is selected	`onSelect`
`submit`	submit button of a form	the submit button of a form is clicked	`onSubmit`
`unload`	document	a Web page is exited	`onUnload`

Table 21.3   JavaScript events listed by event source.

All event sources: `window`, `document`, `hyperlink`, `image`, `image map`, `layer`, `form`, `text field`, `checkbox`, `radio button`, `button`, `select list`, `password`, `hidden field`, `file`, `submit button`, and `reset button`.

Event source	Event name (type)	When event is generated	Event-handler name
`window`	`blur`	an area outside a window is clicked	`onBlur`
	`focus`	an area inside a window is clicked	`onFocus`
	`load`	a Web page is loaded	`onLoad`
	`unload`	a Web page is unloaded	`onUnload`
`document`	`load`	a Web page is loaded in a browser	`onLoad`
	`unload`	a page is unloaded from a browser	`onUnload`
`hyperlink`	`click`	a link is clicked	`onClick`
	`mouseOver`	the mouse cursor is moved over a link	`onMouseOver`
	`mouseOut`	the mouse cursor is moved off a link	`onMouseOut`
`image`	`load`	an image is loaded	`onLoad`
	`abort`	the loading of image files is stopped	`onAbort`
	`error`	there is an error in loading an image	`onError`
`image map`	`click`	a hot spot is clicked	`onClick`
	`mouseOver`	the move cursor is moved over a hot spot	`onMouseOver`
	`mouseOut`	the move cursor is moved off of a hot spot	`onMouseOut`

Table 21.3   JavaScript events listed by event source. (Continued)

All event sources: `window`, `document`, `hyperlink`, `image`, `image map`, `layer`, `form`, `text field`, `checkbox`, `radio button`, `button`, `select list`, `password`, `hidden field`, `file`, `submit button`, and `reset button`.

Event source	Event name (type)	When event is generated	Event-handler name
`layer`	`load`	a layer is loaded into a Web page	`onLoad`
	`mouseOver`	the move cursor is moved over a layer	`onMouseOver`
	`mouseOut`	the move cursor is moved off of a layer	`onMouseOut`
`form`	`reset`	a form's reset button is clicked	`onReset`
	`submit`	a form's submit button is clicked	`onSubmit`
`text field`	`blur`	an area outside a text field is clicked	`onBlur`
	`change`	a text field's text is changed	`onChange`
	`focus`	an area inside a text field is clicked	`onFocus`
	`select`	an text in a text field is highlighted	`onSelect`
`checkbox`	`click`	a checkbox is clicked	`onClick`
`radio button`	`click`	a radio button is clicked	`onClick`
`button`	`click`	a button is clicked	`onClick`
`select list`	`blur`	an area outside a select list is clicked	`onBlur`
	`change`	selected items are changed	`onChange`
	`focus`	an area inside a select list is clicked	`onFocus`
`password`	`blur`	an area outside a password field is clicked	`onBlur`
	`change`	password text is changed	`onChange`
	`focus`	an area inside a password field is clicked	`onFocus`
	`select`	text in a password field is selected	`onSelect`
`hidden field`	`none`	a call to an event handler is forced	none
`file`	`blur`	an area away from a file is clicked	`onBlur`
	`focus`	a file name is clicked	`onFocus`
	`select`	a file is selected	`onSelect`
`submit button`	`click`	the submit button is clicked	`onClick`
`reset button`	`click`	the reset button is clicked	`onClick`

21.4 Event Handling

We define event handlers to handle and process events. Event handlers "glue" XHTML and JavaScript together. The event handler is included as an attribute in the tag of the XHTML element that generates the event. The event-handler name is the event name preceded by `on`. The general syntax for an event handler is

```
<tag_name onEventName="eventHandler1, eventHandler2, …">
```

For example, when a Web surfer click a hyperlink, the following tag handles it:

```
<a href="http://www.neu.edu" onClick="alert('Hello!')">
```

Be sure to alternate (toggle) double quotes with single quotes. As shown, event handlers must be enclosed in quotation marks in XHTML. When a Web surfer clicks the link, two actions happen: First, the event handler is executed and prints `Hello!`. Second, the Web page specified in the `href` attribute is loaded. This loading does not start until the Web surfer clicks the `OK` button of the `alert` box. This is the general rule when we include event handlers in XHTML tags. Handlers are executed first, and then XHTML content is rendered.

Two styles exist for writing event handlers: the inline script and the function call. If we use the inline script style, we include the JavaScript code inside the XHTML tag, as shown in the foregoing example. If we must use multiple JavaScript statements, we must separate them with semicolons (;). The inline style is not recommended, as it makes the XHTML code hard to read and less modular. In the second style, we write one or more functions as the event handler. We place the function(s) inside the `<script>` tags as we did in Chapter 20. We include the function call in the XHTML tag. Using this style, we write the foregoing example as

```
<a href="http://www.neu.edu" onClick="processIt()">
```

where `processIt()` is the event-handler function. This function call is executed only when the Web surfer clicks the link. Using functions make the code modular, as we can use the same function for many different XHTML elements.

21.5 Navigation Events

In the navigation group of actions, a Web surfer may perform one or more of the following interactions: click a hyperlink, open a new URL, and quit the browser window.

Clicking a hyperlink generates a click event. Also, when we move the mouse cursor over the link, a `mouseOver` event is generated. This event can be used to alert Web surfers by changing the color of the link or by displaying a popup window. The `mouseOut` event is generated as the mouse moves away from the link.

In many cases, the current page is unloaded and a new page is loaded, perhaps in a new window. Thus, loading and unloading a Web page are two separate events that can be intercepted by JavaScript programs. JavaScript can check if the loading of a page is successful or not (the later typically occurring when the Web-page server is down or the URL is obsolete). The loading and unloading events happen at the document level; their event handlers are used in the <body> tag.

The innovation and excitement of JavaScript events come in their handling. There are many clever ideas for handling events on the Web. Surf a number of pages to discover some of these methods on your own. The main theme among all these tricks is in how to grab the attention of Web surfers as they are visiting Web pages. Static content may go by us without noticing it, while any dynamic action (e.g., a popup, a flashing image, or a sound that is played) is sure to get our attention. All these clever ideas are implemented in the event handlers of the XHTML elements of Web pages.

Example 21.2 **Handle the click event of the <a> tag.**

Write a JavaScript event handler for the click event of the <a> tag.

Solution 21.2 Using the AceHTML editor, generate the given code, and save it as `example212.html`. Render the Web page in a browser.

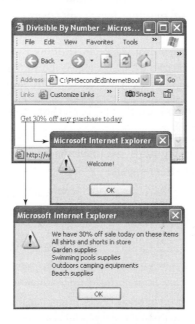

Code explained:

1. Line 25 creates a hyperlink with two event handlers.
2. Lines 12–20 define the `sale()` function.

Discussion:

When we combine XHTML and JavaScript code in one Web page, errors are likely to occur in both during the development phase. We therefore recommend that you develop the code in two phases. In the first phase, develop the XHTML content of the page with no JavaScript. After this phase is complete, implement the second phase by adding the JavaScript code. Thus, you focus on one type of code (either XHTML or JavaScript) in each phase.

We use two event handlers in code line 25: `alert()` and `sale()`. These handlers are both invoked (called) by the browser for each click of the link. Each time a Web surfer clicks the link shown in the first of the accompanying screen captures, the `alert()` function is called and executed first. (This function prints an `alert` box with the text `Welcome!`). When the Web surfer clicks the `OK` button of the `alert` box, the `sale()` function is called and executed and prints the second `alert` box shown in the accompanying screen captures. After the event handlers finish running, the browser executes the `href` attribute of the `<a>` tag and displays the `http://www.amazon.com` website.

This example uses the two methods of writing event handlers: inline JavaScript (`alert()`) and function calls (`sale()`). We recommend using functions, to keep code modular and to promote code reuse.

Hands-on exercise:

Add a third event handler, a function called `moreDiscount()` that is associated with a new link called "More Discount". The function gives the customer an extra 5% on the purchase amount. Use the `prompt()` function to receive the customer purchase amount, and `document.write()` to output the results.

```
1   <?xml version="1.0" encoding="iso-8859-1"?>
2   <!DOCTYPE html PUBLIC "-//W3C//DTD XHTML 1.1//EN"
3       "http://www.w3.org/TR/xhtml11/DTD/xhtml11.dtd">
4   <html xmlns="http://www.w3.org/1999/xhtml">
5   <!-- Generated by AceHTM http://freeware.acehtml.com -->
6   <head>
7   <meta http-equiv="Content-Type" content="text/html; charset=iso-
    8859-1" />
8   <title>Handle the Click Event</title>
9   <script language="javascript">
10
11  //define event handler
12  function sale() {
13  str = "We have a 30% off sale today on these items" + "\n";
14  str += "All shirts and shorts in store" + "\n";
15  str += "Garden supplies" + "\n";
16  str += "Swimming pool supplies" + "\n";
17  str += "Outdoor camping equipment" + "\n";
18  str += "Beach supplies" + "\n";
19  alert (str);
```

```
20   } //sale()
21
22   </script>
23   </head>
24   <body>
25   <a href="http://www.amazon.com" onClick="alert('Welcome!'),
     sale()">Get 30% off any purchase today</a>
26   </body>
27   </html>
```

Example 21.3 Handle the mouse events of the <a> tag.

Write a JavaScript application that swaps images.

Solution 21.3 We use the mouseOver and mouseOut events of the <a> tag to swap images. Using the AceHTML editor, generate the given code, and save it as example213.html. Render the Web page in a browser.

Code explained:

1. Line 24 creates a hyperlink with two event handlers.

2. Lines 12–14 and 17–19 define two functions.

3. Line 24 uses the pound sign (#) to disable the href attribute for now.

Discussion:

The idea in this example is that one image is swapped for another when a Web surfer moves the mouse cursor in and out of an image hyperlink. The two images alternate. Their files must reside in the same directory as the example213.html file. As per code line 24, image1() (code lines 12–14) and image2() (code lines 17–19) handle the onMouseOver and onMouseOut events, respectively.

Code lines 13 and 18 will be covered later, in Chapter 22. They use the associate array, `images[]`, of the `document` object. For now, each line displays the image file shown on the right of the equal sign (=) sign of its statement.

Hands-on exercise:

Use the `border="0"` attribute of the `<img>` tag to remove the border of the image hyperlink. Also, add a click event and handler to the `<a>` tag.

```
1   <?xml version="1.0" encoding="iso-8859-1"?>
2   <!DOCTYPE html PUBLIC "-//W3C//DTD XHTML 1.1//EN"
3       "http://www.w3.org/TR/xhtml11/DTD/xhtml11.dtd">
4   <html xmlns="http://www.w3.org/1999/xhtml">
5   <!-- Generated by AceHTM http://freeware.acehtml.com -->
6   <head>
7   <meta http-equiv="Content-Type" content="text/html;
    charset=iso-8859-1" />
8   <title>Handle Mouse Events</title>
9   <script language="j avascript">
10
11  //define event handler
12  function image1() {
13  document.images[0].src = "image1.jpg";
14  } //image1()
15
16  //define event handler
17  function image2() {
18  document.images[0].src = "image2.jpg";
19  } //image2()
20
21  </script>
22  </head>
23  <body>
24  <a href="#" onMouseOver="image1()" onMouseOut="image2()"><img
    src="image1.jpg" title="image swap"></a>
25  </body>
26  </html>
```

☞───

Example 21.4 Handle some of the `<body>` tag events.

Write a JavaScript event handler for the load and unload events of the `<body>` tag.

Solution 21.4 Using the AceHTML editor, generate the given code, and save it as `example214.html`. Render the Web page in a browser.

Code explained:

  1. Line 28 use the load and unload events.
  2. Lines 12–24 define two functions.
  3. Line 23 uses the `\n` special character to create new lines in the `alert` box.

Discussion:

The load event is triggered after the Web page is fully loaded. This is why the page is rendered before the event handler (`sale()` function) is executed. We first see the Web page shown in the foregoing screen capture and then the `alert` box.

The load event is triggered when we display the Web page in a browser. The unload event is triggered when we exit the Web page, by loading another one or by using the `Back` or `Forward` button of the browser. Remember, if no event has been triggered, the event handler will not execute. So, do not expect the unload `alert` box to show up automatically, as the load `alert` box did. The load event executed because we triggered it by loading the Web page in the browser.

The load event is responsible for all the pop-ups, containing all kind of ads, that show up when you open a browser window or load a Web page. Chapter 23 covers how to open a new popup window upon the loading of a browser window.

Hands-on exercise:

Add an event that detects movement of the browser window on the computer screen. The event-handler name is `onMove`.

```
1   <?xml version="1.0" encoding="iso-8859-1"?>
2   <!DOCTYPE html PUBLIC "-//W3C//DTD XHTML 1.1//EN"
3       "http://www.w3.org/TR/xhtml11/DTD/xhtml11.dtd">
4   <html xmlns="http://www.w3.org/1999/xhtml">
5   <!-- Generated by AceHTM http://freeware.acehtml.com -->
6   <head>
7   <meta http-equiv="Content-Type" content="text/html;
    charset=iso-8859-1" />
8   <title>Handle Body Tag Event</title>
9   <script language="javascript">
10
11  //define event handler
12  function sale() {
13  str = "We have a 30% off sale today on these items" + "\n";
14  str += "All shirts and shorts in store" + "\n";
15  str += "Garden supplies" + "\n";
16  str += "Swimming pool supplies" + "\n";
17  str += "Outdoor camping equipment" + "\n";
18  str += "Beach supplies" + "\n";
19  alert (str);
20  } //sale()
21
22  function comeBack() {
23  alert ("Please be sure to come back.\n We always have great
    bargains.\n We sure appreciate your business.");
24  } //comeBack()
25
26  </script>
27  </head>
28  <body onLoad="sale()" onunLoad="comeBack()">
29  <h1 align="center">Welcome to our online store</h1>
30  </body>
31  </html>
```

21.6 On-the-Fly Web Pages

Consider this scenario: A Web page has a form. A Web surfer fills out the form and clicks the form's submit button. We verify the form's input. How do we send the verification results to the surfer? We have two solutions: one using the server, and the other using the client. The server solution is not recommended, because it increases the server traffic for no reason. Moreover, it is not necessary to go to the server, because all the form's data are generated by the client, so we can verify them right there.

The client-side solution uses the concept of building Web pages on the fly. What this means is that we send two pages to the Web surfer upon his or her request for the Web page that has the form. In addition to that Web page containing the form that the surfer fills out, we include another, "hidden" Web page in a JavaScript function. When the user clicks the submit button, the function is called, and it sends the "hidden" Web page to the browser for rendering.

On-the-fly Web pages can be used as part of any event handler, be it a form or a hyperlink handler. Use of on-the-fly Web pages with forms is covered in Chapter 24. Here, we use them with hyperlinks.

Example 21.5   Use on-the-fly Web pages.

Write a JavaScript program that creates on-the-fly Web pages.

Solution 21.5   Using the AceHTML editor, generate the given code, and save it as `example215.html`. Render the Web page in a browser.

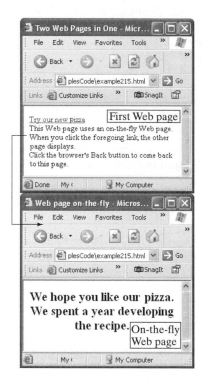

Code explained:

  1. Line 27 creates a hyperlink with a click event handler that uses the `newCooking()` function.

  2. Lines 12–22 define the `newCooking()` function.

  3. Lines 13–20 create the on-the-fly Web page.

  4. Line 21 sends the Web page to the browser for rendering.

Discussion:

When the Web surfer clicks the hyperlink, the `newCooking()` function is executed. The string variable `page` has all the XHTML code for the on-the-fly Web page. The `document.write()` function sends it to the browser that displays it.

The two Web pages in this example are `example215.html` and the one defined by code lines 13–20. This page does not have a file that stores its XHTML code. This is why we call it an on-the-fly Web page. Observe that when we load the `example215.html` page into the browser, code lines 13–20 are also loaded and await execution. While the `example215.html` page is displayed in the browser, click `View => Source`. You should see code lines 13–20 displayed with the others. After the on-the-fly Web page is displayed, view its source. You should see code lines 13–20 only. In the code given in this example, we use the `<div>` tag to force line breaks in order to keep the lines of text short.

When we examine code lines 13–20 closely, we conclude that writing an on-the-fly Web page is identical to writing other Web pages. However, we need to convert all the tags of an on-the-fly Web page into a literal string, by enclosing them in quotes, and assign them to a string variable (`page` in this example). The string variable is the equivalent of an explicit XHTML file. We include the string in a JavaScript function (`newCooking()` in this example). Whenever we need to render the page in a browser, we invoke the event handler that uses it at will.

Hands-on exercise:

Add `<img>` and `<a>` tags to the on-the-fly Web page. The `<a>` tag should link back to `example215.html`.

```
1   <?xml version="1.0" encoding="iso-8859-1"?>
2   <!DOCTYPE html PUBLIC "-//W3C//DTD XHTML 1.1//EN"
3       "http://www.w3.org/TR/xhtml11/DTD/xhtml11.dtd">
4   <html xmlns="http://www.w3.org/1999/xhtml">
5   <!-- Generated by AceHTM http://freeware.acehtml.com -->
6   <head>
7   <meta http-equiv="Content-Type" content="text/html;
    charset=iso-8859-1" />
8   <title>Two Web Pages in One</title>
9   <script language="javascript">
10
11  //create an on-the-fly Web page
12  function newCooking () {
13  page = "<html>";
14  page += "<head>";
15  page += "<title>On-the-fly Web page</title>";
16  page += "</head>";
17  page += "<body>";
18  page += "<h2 align='center'><div>We hope you like our pizza.</
    div><div>We spent a year developing the recipe.</div><h2>";
19  page += "</body>";
20  page += "</html>";
```

```
21   document.write (page);
22   } //newCooking()
23
24   </script>
25   </head>
26   <body>
27   <a href="#" onClick="newCooking()">Try our new pizza</a>
28   <div>This Web page uses an on-the-fly Web page.</div>
29   <div>When you click the forgoing link, the other page displays.</div>
30   <div>Click the browser's Back button to come back to this page.</div>
31   </body>
32   </html>
```

21.7 Web-Page Context

A Web browser can have only one active Web page at a time. An **active Web page** is the current page that the browser displays in its window. Any XHTML, JavaScript code, and event handlers (functions) that the browser needs to have for the Web page to be fully functional must be included in the code of the active Web page. Thus, the browser uses the Web-page context to respond to any interactions with the Web page. For example, if a Web surfer generates an event, the browser looks for its event-handler function within the code of the current Web page. If it does not find it, it throws a syntax error that the function is not defined.

This is a particularly important concept when we deal with on-the-fly Web pages. Let us consider the two Web pages of Example 21.5. `example215.html` is the parent Web page of the on-the-fly Web page defined inside the `newCooking()` function. Let us assume that the latter page requires a function called `newChef()`. Where should we include its JavaScript code? Should we include it inside the `<script>` tag of the parent Web page, `example215.html`? Or should we include it in `page`, the string that builds the on-the-fly Web page?

The answers to all these questions are easy if we think in terms of the Web-page context. The `newChef()` code should be included in the `page` string. After the on-the-fly Web page is displayed, its context becomes the current (active) one. Thus, including the code for `newChef()` in the parent Web-page context makes the code undefined to the browser, as that context is obsolete. The following example illustrates this concept further.

Example 21.6 Understand Web-page context.

Modify Example 21.5 to add `newChef()` to the on-the-fly Web page.

Solution 21.6 Using the AceHTML editor, generate the given code, and save it as `example216.html`. Render the Web page in a browser.

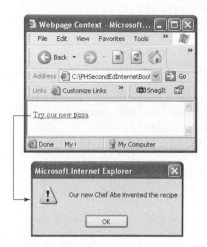

Code explained:

1. Lines 16–21 are added to the code of Example 21.5.

2. Line 33 is the same as line 27 of Example 21.5, but with `newChef()` added as another event handler. Thus, `newCooking()` and `newChef()` handle the hyperlink click.

Discussion:

Code lines 16–21 add a `<script>` section to the on-the-fly Web page. The `<script>` tag opens in code line 16 and closes in code line 21. Observer that, in code line 21, we must escape the / in order to avoid rendering problems. (See the Hands-on Exercise for this example.).

If we remove the \, the browser takes code line 21 as the closing `<script>` tag for the tag in code line 9. It therefore treats code lines 22–30 as part of XHTML and displays them in the Web page. We can replace the \ by using XHTML comment statement. Add `<!--` after code line 9, add `-->` after code line 28, and remove the \ from code line 21. This method should work just as well.

Hands-on exercise:

Remove the escaping character, \, from line 21. Save the file and render the page. What happens? Use the comment (`<!-- ... -->`) approach discussed previously to solve the problem. Now make `newChef()` a function belonging to the `example215.html` parent page by moving lines 17–19 to after line 28 and deleting lines 16 and 21. Render the new code. Explain the results.

```
1    <?xml version="1.0" encoding="iso-8859-1"?>
2    <!DOCTYPE html PUBLIC "-//W3C//DTD XHTML 1.1//EN"
3        "http://www.w3.org/TR/xhtml11/DTD/xhtml11.dtd">
4    <html xmlns="http://www.w3.org/1999/xhtml">
5    <!-- Generated by AceHTM http://freeware.acehtml.com -->
6    <head>
7    <meta http-equiv="Content-Type" content="text/html;
     charset=iso-8859-1" />
```

```
 8  <title>Web-Page Context</title>
 9  <script language="javascript">
10
11  //create an on-the-fly Web page
12  function newCooking() {
13  page   = "<html>";
14  page  += "<head>";
15  page  += "<title>On-the-fly Web page</title>";
16  page  += "<script language='javascript'>";
17  page  += "function newChef(name){";
18  page  += "alert('Our new Chef ' + name + ' invented the recipe')";
19  page  += "} //newChef()";
20  //must escape / by using \
21  page  += "<\/script>";
22  page  += "</head>";
23  page  += "<body>";
24  page  += "<h2 align='center'><div>We hope you like our
    pizza.</div><div>We spent a year developing the
    recipe.</div><h2>";
25  page  += "</body>";
26  page  += "</html>";
27  document.write (page);
28  } //newCooking()
29
30  </script>
31  </head>
32  <body>
33  <a href="#" onClick="newCooking(), newChef('Abe')">Try our new
    Pizza</a>
34  </body></html>
```

21.8 Nesting On-the-Fly Web Pages

Examples 21.5 and 21.6 show one-level nesting of on-the-fly Web pages. This means that each parent Web page (`example215.html` and `example216.html`) has one on-the-fly Web page only. We can extend this concept further by embedding an on-the-fly Web page inside another on-the-fly Web page, and so forth. Thus, we can nest these page to any depth we want.

However, we seldom go beyond two-level nesting. In two-level nesting, we have three Web pages in total: the parent Web page and two on-the-fly Web pages, one including the other. Figure 21.3 shows this case and the rendering sequence. The browser renders the parent Web page first, which includes the other two nested pages, as shown in step 1. When the Web surfer triggers the right event, the browser executes the related JavaScript function and renders the level-1 Web page, as shown in step 2. This page has in it the level-2 Web page. Again, when the Web surfer triggers the right event, the browser executes the related JavaScript function and renders the level-2 Web page, as shown in step 3. Assuming that each page has some JavaScript code, the code of steps 1, 2, and 3 should have three, two, and one `<script>` tags, respectively.

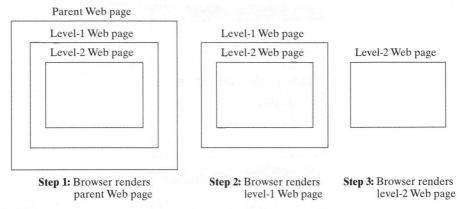

Step 1: Browser renders
parent Web page

Step 2: Browser renders
level-1 Web page

Step 3: Browser renders
level-2 Web page

Figure 21.3 Rendering order of nested on-the-fly Web pages.

Example 21.7 Understand how to nest on-the-fly Web pages.
Write a JavaScript application that uses two-level nesting of on-the-fly Web pages.

Solution 21.7 Using the AceHTML editor, generate the given code, and save it as `example217.html`. Render the Web page in a browser.

Code explained:

1. Lines 1–51 create the parent Web page.
2. Lines 15–38 create the first on-the-fly Web page (level-1 nesting).
3. Lines 21–28 create the second on-the-fly Web page (level-2 nesting)
4. The event handler in line 49 creates the first on-the-fly Web page.
5. The event handler in line 36 creates the second on-the-fly Web page.

Discussion:

We nest three Web pages in this example, the parent Web pages and two on-the-fly Web pages. The nesting of the three pages and their rendering order follow that depicted in Figure 21.3.

We use two string variables: `page` stores the code of the level-1 Web page, and `str` stores the code of the level-2 Web page. `page` is rendered when a Web surfer invokes the event handler of the hyperlink of screen capture ❶ (forthcoming) by clicking it. The click executes the `firstPage()` function. The rendering of `page` produces the Web page shown in screen capture ❷ (forthcoming). Line 36 has the event handler, `secondPage()`, that renders the level-2 page.

The Web page shown in screen capture ❷ has the hyperlink that executes the `second-Page()` function, which renders the `str` variable and creates the level-2 Web page. Screen capture ❸ (forthcoming) shows this Web page.

Observe that we toggle (alternate) the quotes from double to single as we nest them. Also, click `View => Source` (on the browser window) to view the source of each Web page in order to ensure that you have a proper understanding of the nesting concept.

Hands-on exercise:

Add a fourth Web page to this example, to create three-level nesting. This task would require the addition of the `<script>` tag after code line 23. Use double quotes for nesting, because the nesting occurs inside single quotes. Also, add more XHTML content to each of the four Web pages.

```
1   <?xml version="1.0" encoding="iso-8859-1"?>
2   <!DOCTYPE html PUBLIC "-//W3C//DTD XHTML 1.1//EN"
3       "http://www.w3.org/TR/xhtml11/DTD/xhtml11.dtd">
4   <html xmlns="http://www.w3.org/1999/xhtml">
5   <!-- Generated by AceHTM http://freeware.acehtml.com -->
6   <head>
7   <meta http-equiv="Content-Type" content="text/html;
    charset=iso-8859-1" />
```

```
8    <title>Nested Web pages</title>
9    <script language="javascript">
10
11   //begin hiding code, so we do not use "\" in line 32
12   <!--
13   function firstPage(){
14
15       page = "<html>";
16       page += "<head>";
17       page += "<title>The first on-the-fly Web page </title>";
18       page += "</head>";
19       page += "<script>";
20       page += "function secondPage(){";
21       page += "str  = '<html>';";
22       page += "str = '<head>';";
23       page += "str += '<title>The second on-the-fly Web page
             </title>';";
24       page += "str += '</head>';";
25       page += "str += '<body>';";
26       page += "str += '<h1> This is the second on-the-fly Web page
             </h1>'; ";
27       page += "str += '</body>';";
28       page += "str += '</html>';";
29       page += "document.write(str);";
30       page += "document.close();";
31       page += "} //secondPage()";
32       page += " </script>";
33       page += "<body>";
34       page += "<h1>This is the first on-the-fly Web page</h1>";
35       page += "</body>";
36       page += "<a href='#' onClick='secondPage()'>";
37       page += "Open the second on-the-fly Web page</a>";
38       page += "</html>";
39       document.write(page);
40       document.close();
41   } //firstPage()
42   //end code hiding
43   -->
44
45   </script>
46   </head>
47   <body>
48   <h1>This is the parent Web page</h1>
49   <a href="#" onClick="firstPage()">Open the first on-the-fly
     Web page </a>
50   </body>
51   </html>
```

21.9 Disabling XHTML Actions

Some XHTML elements have actions associated with them. Hyperlinks, image maps, and forms are examples. Clicking a hyperlink or a hot spot of an image map loads the Web page specified in the `href` attribute. Similarly, Clicking the `submit` button of a form executes the action specified in the form `action` attribute.

      Without JavaScript, all these actions are executed as soon a Web surfer generates a click. With JavaScript, however, we can make this execution conditional. For example, we can prevent it from executing it if one or more conditions are not met, and execute it if the conditions are met. We achieve this control in the event-handler function of the XHTML element. If the conditions are met, the function returns `true`, and the XHTML action is executed. Otherwise, the function returns `false`, which prevents the action from executing. In addition to simply using the return value from the function, we must capture that value in the tag of the XHTML element via use of the `return()` function.

Example 21.8 Disable XHTML actions.

Write a JavaScript program that creates conditional XHTML actions.

Solution 21.8 Using the AceHTML editor, generate the given code, and save it as `example218.html`. Render the Web page in a browser.

Code explained:

1. Lines 11–20 define a function that takes a number as input. It return `true` (line 14) if the number is positive or equal to zero. Otherwise, it returns `false` (line 18).

2. Line 26 uses the function as an event handler for a hyperlink with a positive condition.

3. Line 27 uses the function as an event handler for a hyperlink with a negative condition.

Discussion:

The JavaScript code of this examples makes the XHTML action, a link click, conditional. We simulate the case of course registration for a student. If the student owes money, the code prevents him or her from registering. Code line 26 simulates the case of a student who has a positive balance. The value of 200 is insignificant in itself. It is just a value. When you click this link, the first `alert` box shown in the set of screen captures (forthcoming) is displayed. After the user clicks OK, Northeastern's Web page is displayed. The display of this page is the XHTML action. If the student owes money, as shown in code line 27, Northeastern's Web page is never displayed. The key to this page's functionality is the `return ()` function in lines 26 and 27.

Hands-on exercise:

Remove the `return()` function from code lines 26 and 27. What happens in both cases?

```
1    <?xml version="1.0" encoding="iso-8859-1"?>
2    <!DOCTYPE html PUBLIC "-//W3C//DTD XHTML 1.1//EN"
3        "http://www.w3.org/TR/xhtml11/DTD/xhtml11.dtd">
4    <html xmlns="http://www.w3.org/1999/xhtml">
5    <!-- Generated by AceHTM http://freeware.acehtml.com -->
6    <head>
7    <meta http-equiv="Content-Type" content="text/html;
     charset=iso-8859-1" />
8    <title>Disable Event Handling</title>
9    <script language="javascript">
10
11   function checkIt(balance){
12       if (balance >= 0){
13       alert("Thank you!\nProceed to register.");
14       return true;
15       } //if
16       else {
17       alert("Sorry! You owe money.\nYou cannot register.");
18       return false;
```

```
19        } //else
20   } //checkIt()
21
22   </script>
23   </head>
24   <body>
25   <h1>Check if you can register for courses</h1>
26   <div><a href="http://www.neu.edu"
     onClick="return(checkIt(200))">Positive balance</a></div>
27   <div><a href="http://www.neu.edu"
     onClick="return(checkIt(-200))">Negative balance</a></div>
28   </body>
29   </html>
```

21.10 Tutorials

21.10.1 Handling all Hyperlink Events (Study Section 21.5)

This tutorial shows how to handle the `click`, `mouseOver`, and `mouseOut` events of a hyperlink. Using the AceHTML editor, generate the given code, and save it as `tutorial21101.html`. Render the Web page in a browser.

Code explained:

   1. Lines 10–24 define, the `whichEvent()` function.
   2. Line 25 creates a hyperlink with three events.

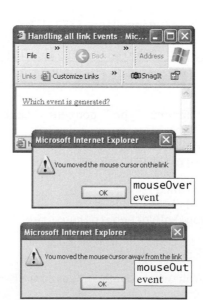

Discussion:

The `whichEvent(evtType)` function takes the type of a hyperlink event as its argument. The three values of `evtType` are 1, 2, and 3 for a `click`, `mouseOver`, and `mouseOut` event, respectively.

We call the function in code line 25 three times with three different values in order to process the link's three potential events. Clicking the link executes code lines 12–14. Moving the mouse cursor over the link executes code lines 16–18. Finally, moving the mouse cursor away from the link executes code lines 20–22.

Hands-on exercise:

There is a problem with this code: We are never able to click the link itself. Can you fix it while still being able to process the three events concurrently? If you find a solution, please send it to me at `zeid@coe.neu.edu`!

```xml
1   <?xml version="1.0" encoding="iso-8859-1"?>
2   <!DOCTYPE html PUBLIC "-//W3C//DTD XHTML 1.1//EN"
3       "http://www.w3.org/TR/xhtml11/DTD/xhtml11.dtd">
4   <html xmlns="http://www.w3.org/1999/xhtml">
5   <!-- Generated by AceHTM http://freeware.acehtml.com -->
6   <head>
7   <meta http-equiv="Content-Type" content="text/html;
    charset=iso-8859-1" />
8   <title>Handling all Link Events</title>
9   <script language="javascript">
10  function whichEvent(evtType){
11      switch (evtType) {
12      //click event
13      case 1:
14      alert("You clicked the link");
15      break;
16      //mouseOver event
17      case 2:
18      alert("You moved the mouse cursor on the link");
19      break;
20      //mouseOut event
21      case 3:
22      alert("You moved the mouse cursor away from the link");
23      } //switch
24  } //whichEvent()</script></head><body>
25  <a href="http://www.neu.edu" onClick="whichEvent(1)"
    onMouseOver="whichEvent(2)" onMouseOut="whichEvent(3)">Which
    event is generated?</a></body></html>
```

FAQs

Navigation Events (Section 21.5)

Q: My Web page has some hyperlinks it. When I use the `document.write()` function to handle events, nothing prints on the screen. What is the problem, and how can I fix it?

A: `document.write()` works well when the current (i.e., displayed in the browser window) Web page is blank, as was the case for the examples in Chapter 19. When the page has any content, such as links, `document.write()` does not work consistently. Sometimes it prints; many other times, it does not. Try to follow it by `document.close()` (to force a buffer flush). If this does not work, replace `document.write()` by `alert()`. `alert()` always works.

Q: How can I get around the `mouseOver` event if a script code uses it?

A: Look at the source code. For example, if the link is an image, the source code shows the image's full file name. Use it as a URL. Now you have the image alone, and you can do anything with it.

Blackbox

Section 21.1 (Introduction): JavaScript events make Web pages interactive.

Section 21.2 (Event Model) (Example 21.1): The JavaScript event model has event sources, the `event` object, and event handlers. The properties the event object are `type`, `target`, `width`, `height`, `layerX`, `layerY`, `pageX`, `pageY`, `screenX`, `screenY`, `data`, `modifiers`, and `which`. Valid event sources are a window (of a browser), a document (the Web page itself), a hyperlink (text and image), an image, an image map, a layer, a form (itself), and all form elements (text fields, checkboxes, radio buttons, buttons, select lists, passwords, hidden fields, files, the submit button, and the reset button).

Section 21.3 (Events): The JavaScript events are `abort`, `blur`, `change`, `click`, `dragDrop`, `error`, `focus`, `keyDown`, `keyPress`, `keyUp`, `load`, `mouseDown`, `mouseMove`, `mouseOut`, `mouseOver`, `mouseUp`, `move`, `reset`, `resize`, `select`, `submit`, and `unload`.

Section 21.4 (Event Handling): The general syntax for an event handler is

```
<tag_name onEventName="eventHandler1, eventHandler2, …">
```

For example, when a Web surfer click a hyperlink, the following tag handles it:

```
<a href="http://www.neu.edu" onClick="alert('Hello!')">
```

Section 21.5 (Navigation Events) (Examples 21.2–21.4): The `<a>` tag uses the `onClick`, `onMouseOver`, and `onMouseOut` events. The `<body>` tag uses the `onLoad` and `onUnload` events.

Section 21.6 (On-the-Fly Web Pages) (Example 21.5): An on-the-fly Web page is generated within the code of another Web page; it does not have an HTML file.

Section 21.7 (Web-Page Context) (Example 21.6): Web browsers can find code only within the source code of the currently displayed Web page.

Section 21.8 (Nesting On-the-Fly Web pages): (Example 21.7) An on-the-fly Web page may include the code of another on-the-fly Web page.

Section 21.9 (Disabling XHTML Actions) (Example 21.8): Event handlers can stop XHTML actions specified by the `href` attribute of any tag.

Section 21.10 (Tutorial): One tutorial shows how to handle the three events of the `<a>` tag.

Quick reference for the syntax presented in this chapter

Event source	Event-Handler name	When the event is generated	Example
`window`	`onBlur`	an area outside a window is clicked	`<... onBlur="abc()">`
	`onFocus`	an area inside a window is clicked	`<... onFocus="abc()">`
	`onLoad`	a Web page is loaded	`<... onLoad="abc()">`
	`onUnload`	a Web page is unloaded	`<... onUnload="abc()">`
`document`	`onLoad`	a Web page is loaded in a browser	`<... onLoad="abc()">`
	`onUnload`	a Web page is unloaded from a browser	`<... onUnload="abc()">`
`hyperlink`	`onClick`	a link is clicked	`<a ... onClick="abc()">`
	`onMouseOver`	the move cursor is moved over a link	`<a... onMouseOut="abc()">`
	`onMouseOut`	the move cursor is moved off of a link	`<a...onMouseOver="abc()">`
`image`	`onLoad`	an image is loaded	`<img...onLoad="abc()">`
	`onAbort`	the loading of image files is stopped	`<img...onAbort="abc()">`
	`onError`	there is an error in loading an image	`<img...onError="abc()">`
`image map`	`onClick`	a hot spot is clicked	`<area...onClick="abc()">`
	`onMouseOver`	the mouse cursor is moved over a hot spot	`<area... onMouseOver="abc()">`
	`onMouseOut`	the mouse cursor is moved off of a hot spot	`<area...onMouseOut="abc()">`

Event source	Event-Handler name	When the event is generated	Example
layer	onLoad	a layer is loaded into a Web page	`<div...onClick="abc()">`
	onMouseOver	the mouse is moved over a layer	`<div...onMouseOver="abc()">`
	onMouseOut	the mouse cursor is moved off of a layer	`<div...onMouseOut="abc()">`
form	onReset	a form's reset button is clicked	`<form ... onReset="abc()">`
	onSubmit	a form's submit button is clicked	`<form ... onSubmit="abc()">`
text field	onBlur	an area outside a text field is clicked	`<input ... onBlur="abc()">`
	onChange	a text field's text is changed	`<input...onChange="abc()">`
	onFocus	an area inside a text field is clicked	`<input ... onFocus="abc()">`
	onSelect	text in a text field is highlighted	`<input...onSelect="abc()">`
checkbox	onClick	a checkbox is clicked	`<input ... onClick="abc()">`
radio button	onClick	a radio button is clicked	`<input ... onClick="abc()">`
button	onClick	a button is clicked	`<input ... onClick="abc()">`
select list	onBlur	an area outside a select list is clicked	`<input ... onBlur="abc()">`
	onChange	select items are changed	`<input...onChange="abc()">`
	onFocus	an area inside a select list is clicked	`<input ... onFocus="abc()">`
password	onBlur	an area outside a password field is clicked	`<input ... onBlur="abc()">`
	onChange	password text is changed	`<input...onChange="abc()">`
	onFocus	an area inside a password field is clicked	`<input ... onFocus="abc()">`
	onSelect	text in a password field is clicked	`<input...onSelect="abc()">`
hidden field	none	a call to an event handler is forced	none

Event source	Event-Handler name	When the event is generated	Example
file	onBlur	an area away from a file is clicked	`<input ... onBlur="abc()">`
	onFocus	a file name is clicked	`<input ... onFocus="abc()">`
	onSelect	a file is selected	`<input...onSelect="abc()">`
submit button	onClick	the submit button is clicked	`<input ... onClick="abc()">`
reset button	onClick	the reset button is clicked	`<input ... onClick="abc()">`

Check Your Progress

At the end of this chapter, you should

✔ understand the need for JavaScript events (Section 21.1);
✔ understand the JavaScript event model (Section 21.2);
✔ know all the JavaScript events (Section 21.3);
✔ be able to identify the general syntax of an event handler (Section 21.4);
✔ have mastered the use of navigation events (Section 21.5);
✔ understand the concept of on-the-fly Web pages (Sections 21.6–21.8);
✔ have mastered how to disable XHTML actions (Section 21.9);
✔ have practiced the use of events and event handling (Section 21.10).

Problems

The exercises are designed for a lab setting, while the homework is to be done outside class time.

Exercises

21.1   Write a JavaScript application to handle the click event of the `<a>` tag.
21.2   Write a JavaScript application to handle the mouseOver event of the `<a>` tag.
21.3   Write a JavaScript application to handle the mouseOut event of the `<a>` tag.

Homework

21.4   Write a JavaScript application to handle the load event of the `<body>` tag.
21.5   Write a JavaScript application to handle the unload event of the `<body>` tag.
21.6   Write a JavaScript application that uses an on-the-fly Web page.
21.7   Write a JavaScript application that disables the href action of the `<a>` tag.

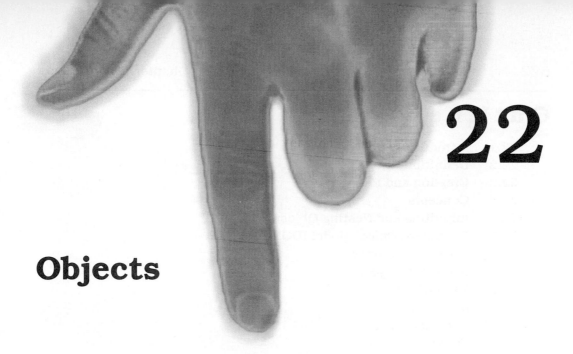

Objects

Goal

Understand JavaScript objects, how to create and use your own objects, how to use the JavaScript built-in objects, the impact of objects on JavaScript syntax, and the use of objects with XHTML tags.

Objectives

- The importance of objects in Web programming
- The definition of objects
- Concepts related to objects
- Implementation of objects
- Nesting of objects
- The Document Object Model (DOM)
- Associative arrays
- Built-in objects: document, Math, Date, and String

671

Outline

22.1 Introduction

Modern software development and computing are rooted in object-oriented programming (OOP). OOP resembles real life; it uses objects. Consider a car. The car has properties such as make, model, year, color, and so forth. It also is driven and needs maintenance. In OOP, the code for a "car object" can be related to this real-life definition.

Prior to the inception of OOP, procedural programming was the only programming method available. Procedural programming does not maintain the unity and integrity of objects. Today, both OOP and procedural languages exist. Example of OOP languages include Java, C++, Lisp, Perl, PHP, VBScript, and JavaScript. Examples of procedural languages include C, Fortran, Pascal, Basic, and Cobol.

Two important advantages of OOP over procedural programming are code reuse and modularity. Object-oriented (OO) code is relatively easier to read and understand than its procedural counterpart. Thus, it is easier to reuse and maintain. Consider an OO program for keeping track of bank account information. Any bank can use it in its own software because each bank needs the functionality it offers. Code reuse in OOP comes in the form of standard libraries and packages that programmers can import to and use in their own code.

The modules used in OOP are known today as software components (patterns). The idea here is to break big programs into stand-alone components that can be assembled together to build large software applications. This idea resembles the approach employed by the auto industry. A car is a collection of standard parts. Moreover, when a part breaks down, we simply replace it. Similarly, a software application is a collection of standard components. When a better version of a component becomes available, we use it to replace the old one. Software components include Java beans, EJBs (Enterprise Java Beans), servlets, JSPs (Java Server Pages), and ASPs (Active Server Pages).

JavaScript is based on the OO paradigm. However, it is a much simpler language than other OOP languages such as Java and C++. This characteristic fits well into its goal, as JavaScript is intended to be used with XHTML and Web pages, and neither requires heavy or complex computations or calculations. Actually, JavaScript is a powerful OOP language in the context of Web development.

22.2 Definition

The basic unit for thinking about, designing, building, and programming OO code is the object. Let us again consider a car in order to help us define an object. If we think of what characterizes a car, we come up with aspects such as make, model, year, color, drive, stop, maintain, and so forth. We can further divide these characteristics into two groups: attributes (properties) and behaviors. The attributes are make, model, year, and color. An **attribute** is just a value that we specify; it does not require any calculations; for example, the year is 2004, and the color is red. Object attributes become an object's *variables* in OOP.

The behaviors are drive, stop, and maintain. A **behavior** is the act of doing something; it takes input and produces output. For example, driving a car requires a sequence of steps, such as opening the car door, sitting down, turning the key in the ignition, and so on. Think of a behavior as an algorithm. Object behaviors become the object's *methods* in OOP. A **method** is a function associated with an object. We define a method the same way that we define a standard function. (See Chapter 20.)

To summarize, an **object** is defined as an entity (construct) that has attributes and behaviors. The attributes are its variables, and the behaviors are its methods. In JavaScript, the methods are functions.

In JavaScript, like other OOP languages, users can define their own objects, such as cars, houses, bank accounts, and so forth. JavaScript also provides its own built-in (predefined) objects, such as `Date` and `Math`, that programmers can readily use in their own code. Understanding objects is a prerequisite to creating one's own (custom) objects and using existing (predefined) ones.

We would like to point out that JavaScript functions have a dual meaning. When we use a function to define an object's behavior, we refer to it as a *method*. When we use a function as we did in Chapter 20, on the other hand, we refer to it as a *function*. In both cases, the `function` keyword is used.

Example 22.1 Define objects.

Write the definition of a house object and a bank account object.

Solution 22.1 Both of the objects have attributes and behaviors. Table 22.1 lists some of them. It also shows their mapping to JavaScript variables and methods.

Table 22.1   Object definition.

House object = {{owner, rooms, style, year built, garage}, {living space, maintain}}
Bank account object = {{number, owner, address, balance}, {deposit, withdrawal}}

Object		Definition		JavaScript mapping
House	Attributes	owner	Variables	`owner`
		rooms		`rooms`
		style		`style`
		year		`year`
		garage		`garage`
	Behaviors	living space	Methods	`livingSpace()`
		maintain		`maintain()`
Bank account	Attributes	account number	Variables	`accountNumber`
		account owner		`accountOwner`
		account address		`accountAddress`
		account balance		`accountBalance`
	Behaviors	deposit	Methods	`deposit()`
		withdrawal		`withdrawal()`

Observe that the JavaScript variables and methods have the same names as the corresponding attributes and behaviors of the object.

22.3 Creation and Use

We need to create and use objects in our programs in order to realize the full benefits of OOP. The definition of an object's variables and methods sets the stage for the implementation of the object. OOP languages use three concepts to implement objects: classes, instantiation, and the dot notation. Classes define objects, instantiation creates them, and the dot notation uses them. JavaScript uses these concepts, as Example 22.2 shows.

Example 22.2 Define, create, and use objects.

Write a JavaScript program that uses a house object.

Solution 22.2 Let us use the house object discussed in Example 22.1 and described in Table 22.1. Using the AceHTML editor, generate the given code, and save it as `example222.html`. Render the Web page in a browser.

Code explained:

1. Lines 10–15 define a generic `House` object.
2. Line 18 creates a specific `House` object.
3. Lines 21–24 use the `House` object created in line 18. They print the `House` object's variables.

Discussion:

This example shows the three steps (definition, creation, and use) that we need in OOP in order to utilize objects. The details behind the concepts used in this example are explained further in the upcoming subsections. We provide this example here to serve as background material for the reader, to make it easier to understand the abstract concepts we are about to cover.

Hands-on exercise:

Add two more properties to the `House` object: address and price. Define and use (display) them.

```
1   <?xml version="1.0" encoding="iso-8859-1"?>
2   <!DOCTYPE html PUBLIC "-//W3C//DTD XHTML 1.1//EN"
3       "http://www.w3.org/TR/xhtml11/DTD/xhtml11.dtd">
4   <html xmlns="http://www.w3.org/1999/xhtml">
5   <!-- Generated by AceHTM http://freeware.acehtml.com --><head>
6   <meta http-equiv="Content-Type" content="text/html;
    charset=iso-8859-1" />
7   <title>A House object</title>
8   <script language="javascript">
9   //define House object
10  function House (rms, stl, yr, garg) {
11      this.rooms = rms;         //attribute
12      this.style = stl;         //attribute
13      this.yearBuilt = yr;      //attribute
14      this.hasGarage = garg;    //attribute
15  }//House
16
17  //Create a house instance
18  myHouse = new House(5, "colonial", 1990, true);
```

```
19
20   //Use house instance
21   document.write("My house has " + myHouse.rooms + " rooms<br />");
22   document.write("My house style is " + myHouse.style + "<br />");
23   document.write("My house was built in " + myHouse.yearBuilt
     +"<br />");
24   document.write("My house has a garage: " + myHouse.hasGarage);
25
26   </script>
27   </head>
28   <body>
29   </body>
30   </html>
```

22.3.1   Constructor Function

OOP begins by creating a class for each object that a program uses. A **class** is a template that holds the object's definition. A class is considered a generic object. It is a one-size-fits-all object that defines a family of objects. Inside the class, we include all the variables and methods that define the object. Consider a class that defines a house. A house has an owner, a number of rooms, and a style, among other characteristics. *Any* house has these properties (attributes). As a result, the class is a generic object. A particular house, `myhouse`, still has these properties, but with *specific* values.

In class-based languages, such as Java and C++, we define an object by using the `class` keyword. Inside the class, we define one or more constructors. A **constructor** is a special method that creates and initializes instances. It assigns initial values for the instance variables (properties). An **instance** is a specific copy of a class.

JavaScript follows a similar model of defining and creating objects. However, being a prototype-based language, it does not separate a class definition from its constructor. Instead, JavaScript uses a function in place of the class and constructor; we refer to this function as the *constructor function*. Consider the `House` object defined in Example 22.2. Code lines 10–15 compose the constructor function that defines the `House` object. `House()` is a JavaScript function. We use an uppercase first letter in names of functions that define objects, to differentiate them from nonobject functions.

Code line 10 shows that `House()` has four parameters: `rms`, `stl`, `yr`, and `garg`. Code lines 11–14 define the `House` object. The four variables (`rooms`, `style`, `yearBuilt`, and `hasGarage`) define the `House` attributes. This `House` definition does not have behaviors yet. Code line 18 creates the `myHouse` instance with the shown values. These values are passed to `House()` as arguments and are assigned to the object variables in code lines 11–14 via the use of `this`.

In Example 22.3, we extend `House()` to include the two behaviors shown in Table 22.1. Each behavior requires us to define a method and include it in the `House` definition. We define a method in the same way that we define a standard function. Let us use `livingSpace()` and `maintain()`, as shown in Table 22.1. We use the following syntax to associate a method to an object:

```
this.methodName = functionName;
```

`methodName` is a name of our choice, and `functionName` is the name of the function. Both names may be the same. In fact, we recommend this style. Note that this name includes the function parentheses.

When we call the method on the object, we use `methodName` followed by the parentheses:

```
object.methodName(arguments);
```

Example 22.3 Define and use object methods.

Extend Example 22.1 to include object behaviors.

Solution 22.3 Let us use the two methods shown in Table 22.1. Using the AceHTML editor, generate the given code, and save it as `example223.html`. Render the Web page in a browser.

Code explained:

1. Lines 17 and 18 add two methods to the definition of the `House` object.
2. Lines 39 and 40 call the two methods on the `myHouse` object.

Discussion:
The implicit variable types we use are integers (code lines 13 and 15), string (code line 14), and Boolean (code line 16).

Code lines 22–24 and 27–29 define two functions. `livingSpace()` (code line 22) has three parameters. It calculates the living space as the product of the house's length, width, and the number of floors. Code line 23 returns the result. The other function, `maintain()` (in code line 27), does not have parameters. It returns a literal string.

Code lines 17 and 18 assign the two functions as two methods to the `House` object. When we call them in code lines 39 and 40, respectively, we must pass the correct number of arguments to each.

We have changed code lines 12–16 from Example 22.2 so that the variable names are the same on both sides of the equal signs (=). This format reduces the number of different names we use in a program. The scope (meaning) of each variable is different on each side. Consider code line 13: `rooms`, on the right side of the equal sign, is a function parameter, while `this.rooms`, on the left side, is an object attribute.

Code lines 39 and 40 capture the return values from the two methods (code lines 23 and 28, respectively) and use them in the `document.write()` methods.

Hands-on exercise:

Add one more behavior to the house: `paint()`. The method takes a color as an argument. Define and use `paint()`.

```
1   <?xml version="1.0" encoding="iso-8859-1"?>
2   <!DOCTYPE html PUBLIC "-//W3C//DTD XHTML 1.1//EN"
3       "http://www.w3.org/TR/xhtml11/DTD/xhtml11.dtd">
4   <html xmlns="http://www.w3.org/1999/xhtml">
5   <!-- Generated by AceHTM http://freeware.acehtml.com -->
6   <head>
7   <meta http-equiv="Content-Type" content="text/html;
    charset=iso-8859-1" />
8   <title>A House object</title>
9   <script language="javascript">
10
11  //define House object
12  function House (rooms, style, yearBuilt, hasGarage){
13      this.rooms = rooms;              //attribute
14      this.style = style;              //attribute
15      this.yearBuilt = yearBuilt;      //attribute
16      this.hasGarage = hasGarage;      //attribute
17      this.livingSpace = livingSpace;  //behavior
18      this.maintain = maintain;        //behavior
19  }//House
20
21  //define livingSpace()
22  function livingSpace (length, width, numFloors){
23      return (length*width*numFloors);
24  } //livingSpace()
25
26  //define maintain()
27  function maintain(){
28      return ("Keep the house in top shape");
29  }
30
31  //Create a house instance
32  myHouse = new House(5, "colonial", 1990, true);
33
34  //Use house instance
```

```
35    document.write("My house has " + myHouse.rooms +
      " rooms<br />");
36    document.write("My house style is " + myHouse.style +
      "<br />");
37    document.write("My house was built in " + myHouse.yearBuilt +
      "<br />");
38    document.write("My house has a garage: " + myHouse.hasGarage);
39    document.write("My house living space is: " +
      myHouse.livingSpace(30, 70, 2) + " square feet<br />");
40    document.write(myHouse.maintain());
41
42    </script>
43    </head><body></body>
44    </html>
```

22.3.2 Instantiation

As the class is a generic template, we use it to create specific objects; that is, we customize it. These specific objects are the instances. We instantiate the class to create an instance, using the new keyword (operator). Code line 32 in Example 22.3 demonstrates how to use this keyword. The instance name, myHouse. new, is followed by the constructor function, House(), and its arguments.

The keyword new performs three steps. First, it allocates memory space for the instance definition. This memory is known as heap. **Heap** is the memory where JavaScript, like Java and C++, keeps object definitions at run time. Because this memory allocation happens on the fly when the program executes, we refer to it as **dynamic memory allocation**. Second, new initializes (creates) the instance with the values passed as arguments to the constructor function and stores the instance in the heap. Third, new assigns the instance's variable name to the object's heap location. Figure 22.1 shows the heap of the myHouse instance of Example 22.3.

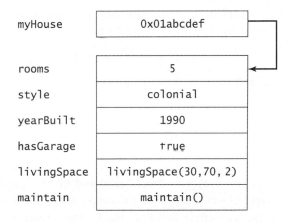

Figure 22.1   Heap memory for an instance.

22.3.3   The Dot Notation (.)

The dot notation (also known as the member operator) allows an instance to access its class members (variables and methods). To the left of the dot must come an instance (object) name, and to its right must come a variable or method name—for example, `myHouse.rooms` and `myHouse.livingSpace(30, 70, 2)`. Multiple dots can be used in the dot notation if subobjects exist; for example, `myHouse.myGarden.flowers` allows us to access the flowers in the garden of my house. In such cases, objects must exist in all the dots in the dot-notation chain, up to the left of the last dot; that is, the dot-notation chain must evaluate to an object. To the right of the last dot in the chain must come a variable or method of the object immediately to the left of the last dot. Consider the `window` object of JavaScript. This object has a **document** subobject. Thus, we can use `window.document.write()`.

22.3.4   The `this` Reference

The `this` reference (keyword or operator) is a powerful concept in OOP. It makes writing OO code efficient and elegant. There are a few uses of it:

- It is used to reference variables and methods within a constructor function. Code lines 13–18 of Example 22.3 show an example. In this context, we think of `this` as a future object (instance) for which we do not know yet know the name. For example, think of `this` as `myHouse` in code lines 13 and 35.
- It is used to reference the current object. The current object is the one used in the dot notation. See Example 22.4.

Example 22.4   Use the `this` reference.

Write a JavaScript application that uses `this`.

Solution 22.4   Using AceHTML editor, generate the given code, and save it as `example224.html`. Render the Web page in browser.

Code explained:

1. Lines 12–16 define a `Dog` object with two attributes and one behavior.
2. Lines 19–23 define the `Dog` behavior.
3. Lines 26–29 create four `Dog`s.
4. Lines 32–38 compare two `Dog`s at a time.

Discussion:

The `compareDogs()` function uses two objects: `dog` and `this`. The object is its parameter, and `this` is the current object. Code line 20 compares the attributes of both objects: `name` and `age`. If they are both equal in value, the function returns `true`; otherwise, it returns `false`.

Code lines 32, 35, and 38 compare two dogs each. Each time we call `compareDogs()`, we pass two objects to the method. The obvious one is the argument object. The less obvious one is the current object. Consider the method call in code line 32; the argument is `yourDog`, and the current object is `myDog`. `yourDog` replaces `dog` in code lines 19 and 20, and `myDog` replaces `this` in code line 20. While we did not pass `myDog` explicitly to `compareDogs()`, it is used inside it. The current object is the object used in the dot notation of the method call—`myDog.compareDogs(yourDog)`. If we were not aware of this concept, the code would be more cumbersome, as we would create the method with two parameters instead of one.

`myDog` and `yourDog` are not equal because both the `name` and `age` are different. `yourDog` and `johnDog` are equal. But `johnDog` and `lisaDog` are not equal, because although their names are the same, their ages are different.

Hands-on exercise:
Change the `compareDogs()` method to use two objects as parameters, `dog1` and `dog2`. Change code line 20 to use the two objects. Do you get the same results? Which approach is better?

```
1   <?xml version="1.0" encoding="iso-8859-1"?>
2   <!DOCTYPE html PUBLIC "-//W3C//DTD XHTML 1.1//EN"
3       "http://www.w3.org/TR/xhtml11/DTD/xhtml11.dtd">
4   <html xmlns="http://www.w3.org/1999/xhtml">
5   <!-- Generated by AceHTM http://freeware.acehtml.com -->
6   <head>
7   <meta http-equiv="Content-Type" content="text/html;
    charset=iso-8859-1" />
8   <title>The this Reference</title>
9   <script language="javascript">
10
11  //define Dog object
12  function Dog (name, age){
13      this.name = name;                //attribute
```

```
14        this.age = age;                        //attribute
15        this.compareDogs = compareDogs; //behavior
16   }//Dog
17
18   //define compareDogs()
19   function compareDogs(dog){
20        if (this.name == dog.name && this.age == dog.age)
21            return true;
22        else return false;
23   } //compareDogs()
24
25   //Create four dog instances
26   myDog    = new Dog("Splinter", 4);
27   yourDog = new Dog("Spotter", 3);
28   johnDog = new Dog("Spotter", 3);
29   lisaDog = new Dog("Spotter", 5);
30
31   //these two dogs are not equal
32   document.write("Comparing my dog and your dog produces: " +
     myDog.compareDogs(yourDog) + "<br />");
33   document.write("===================================<br />");
34   //these two dogs are equal
35   document.write("Comparing your dog and John's dog produces: " +
     yourDog.compareDogs(johnDog) + "<br />");
36   document.write("===================================<br />");
37   //these two dogs are not equal
38   document.write("Comparing John's dog and Lisa's dog produces: "
     + johnDog.compareDogs(lisaDog));
39   </script>
40   </head>
41   <body>
42   </body>
43   </html>
```

22.4 Concepts

Some of the OO concepts that we have used in Section 22.3 are abstraction, classes, constructors, encapsulation, instances, and inheritance. **Abstraction** can be defined as higher level thinking. Abstraction helps hide the details of implementation that may not be relevant to an application. Data and functional abstractions exist. Data abstraction hides the bits and bytes from a program. For example, when we use x = 5;, all we need to know is that x is an integer; we do not worry about how it is represented in the computer's memory. Similarly, document.write() hides the details of how the method works and is an example of functional abstraction.

We have already covered classes, constructors, and instances in Section 22.3. We cover inheritance in Section 22.5.

22.5 Inheriting and Nesting Objects

Inheritance promotes code modularity and reuse. **Inheritance** allows one object to use variables and methods of another object. The class (object) from which another object inherits is known as a **superclass**, and the class (object) that inherits is called a **subclass**. A subclass can define its own variables and methods, above and beyond what it inherits from its superclass(s). We can create an inheritance tree for a particular set of objects, as shown in Figure 22.2. The classes at the bottom of the tree are more specific that those at the top of the tree.

The inheritance tree shown in Figure 22.2 is used in class-based languages such as Java and C++. However, JavaScript implements inheritance differently. It associates a prototype object with any constructor function. We refer to this association as nesting of objects. Object nesting creates an object hierarchy that we represent in a tree structure. While this hierarchy seems to be one of inheritance, it is not. In terms of pure OO concepts, it is known as *association*. **Association** is defined as one object being used in (associated with) the definition of another object as an attribute. Association implements the **uses-a** relationship in OO design and analysis. For example, a person *uses a* computer, a pencil *uses a* sharpener, and a kitchen *uses a* stove.

We can nest objects in two different ways. First, we can pass an object as an argument to the constructor function of another object. In this way, nesting objects results in a chain dot notation, where each level of nesting translates to one dot in the chain. Consider nesting an engine object `myEngine` inside a car object `myCar`. If the engine has `cylinders` as a variable, we can access it through the car object by using `myCar.myEngine.cylinders`. Example 22.5 illustrates this way of nesting objects.

The other way of nesting objects is to prototype one object inside the constructor function of another object. In this way, the dot notation has only one dot. Prototyping one object inside the other somewhat resembles the true inheritance found in Java and C++. Example 22.6 illustrates this way of nesting objects.

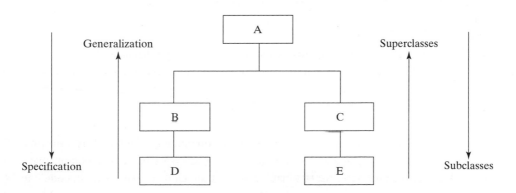

Figure 22.2   Inheritance tree.

When we design an object hierarchy for nesting purposes, we make the more general objects parts of the more specific objects, as shown in Example 22.5.

Example 22.5 Nest objects by passing them as arguments to another object definition.

Write a JavaScript application that nests an employee object in a manager object.

Solution 22.5 Using the AceHTML editor, generate the given code, and save it as `example225.html`. Render the Web page in a browser.

Code explained:

1. Lines 12–15 define an `Employee` object with two attributes.
2. Lines 18–21 define the `Manager` object with two attributes; one of them (`employee`) is an object.
3. Line 24 creates an employee object, `salesEmployee`, that we nest into the manager object `salesManager` in line 25.
4. Lines 26–28 print the `salesManager` object's variables.

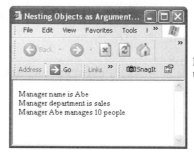

Nest objects
using arguments

Discussion:

We nest an employee in a manager, and not the other way around, because the former is more general than the latter. That is, each employee, including a manager, has a name and belongs to a department. However, only managers have the additional feature of having staff to manage. We create an `Employee` object with two attributes. We also create a `Manager` object with two attributes; one of them, `employee`, is an object.

Up to this point (code lines 1–22), nothing in the code indicates that `employee` (in code line 20) is an object. It is only in our mind that this is our plan. We execute this plan in code lines 24 and 25. We create an instance, `salesEmployee`, of the `Employee` object in code line 24. We pass this instance as an argument to the `Manager` constructor function in code line 25 in order to create the `salesManager` instance.

We access the three attributes of salesManager in code lines 26–28. Observe the effect of nesting in code lines 26 and 27, where we use two dots in the dot notation. Code line 28 uses only one dot, as staff is an attribute of the Manager object; it is not derived from the Employee object.

Hands-on exercise:

Write the dot notation to access attributes of the salesEmployee as a stand-alone object. Compare what you wrote with the corresponding terms in code lines 27 and 28. What are your conclusions about the relative simplicity of the dot notation vs. the notation used in code lines 27 and 28? Also, change the code to use three levels of nesting as follows: Person => Employee => Manager.

```
1   <?xml version="1.0" encoding="iso-8859-1"?>
2   <!DOCTYPE html PUBLIC "-//W3C//DTD XHTML 1.1//EN"
3       "http://www.w3.org/TR/xhtml11/DTD/xhtml11.dtd">
4   <html xmlns="http://www.w3.org/1999/xhtml">
5   <!-- Generated by AceHTM http://freeware.acehtml.com -->
6   <head>
7   <meta http-equiv="Content-Type" content="text/html;
    charset=iso-8859-1" />
8   <title>Nesting Objects as Arguments</title>
9   <script language="javascript">
10
11  //define Employee object
12  function Employee (name,department){
13      this.name = name;                    //attribute
14      this.department = department;        //attribute
15  }//Employee
16
17  //define Manager object
18  function Manager (staff, employee){
19      this.staff = staff;                  //attribute
20      this.employee = employee;            //nested object
21  }//Manager
22
23  //Create employee and manager instances
24  salesEmployee = new Employee ("Abe", "sales");
25  salesManager = new Manager(10, salesEmployee);
26  document.write ("Manager name is " + salesManager.employee.name
    + "<br />");
27  document.write ("Manager department is " +
    salesManager.employee.department + "<br />");
28  document.write ("Manager " + salesManager.employee.name +
    " manages " + salesManager.staff + " people");
29
30  </script>
```

```
31    </head>
32    <body>
33    </body>
34    </html>
```

Example 22.6 Nest objects by prototyping them inside another object definition.

Redo Example 22.5 to use prototyping to nest an employee object inside a manager object.

Solution 22.6 Using AceHTML editor, generate the code that follows, and save it as `example226.html`. Render the Web page in browser.

Code explained:

1. Line 31 prototypes the `Employee` object inside the `Manager` object.
2. Lines 37 and 38 assign attribute values to the `salesManager` instance.

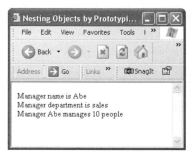

Nest objects
using prototypes

Discussion:

This example complements Example 22.5. It uses prototyping to nest an `Employee` object inside a `Manager` object. Example 22.5 does the nesting by passing `employee` as an argument to the `Manager` constructor function.

The code of this example is almost the same as the code of Example 22.5, with the following changes: Code line 29 has one parameter only, `staff`. Code line 31 uses the `prototype` and `new` keywords to nest `Employee` in `Manager`. Code lines 37 and 38 assign values to the instance `salesManager`. Lines 39–41 all use one-level dot notation to access the instance attributes.

Hands-on exercise:

Change the code to use three levels of nesting as follows: `Person => Employee => Manager`. Compare the resulting code with the code you wrote for the Hands-on Exercise part of Example 22.5. Which method of object nesting do you prefer, nesting objects via arguments (Example 22.5) or via prototyping (Example 22.6)? State your reasons.

```
1   <?xml version="1.0" encoding="iso-8859-1"?>
2   <!DOCTYPE html PUBLIC "-//W3C//DTD XHTML 1.1//EN"
3       "http://www.w3.org/TR/xhtml11/DTD/xhtml11.dtd">
4   <html xmlns="http://www.w3.org/1999/xhtml">
5   <!-- Generated by AceHTM http://freeware.acehtml.com -->
6   <head>
7   <meta http-equiv="Content-Type" content="text/html;
    charset=iso-8859-1" />
8   <meta name="description" content="" />
9   <meta name="keywords" content="" />
10  <meta name="author" content="zeid" />
11  <meta name="generator" content="AceHTML 5 Freeware" />
12  <!--
13  Compare the code of this example
14  with the code of Example 22.5
15  to understand to the differences between
16  nesting objects via arguments
17  and via prototyping
18  -->
19  <title>Nesting Objects by Prototyping</title>
20  <script language="javascript">
21
22  //define Employee object
23  function Employee (name,department){
24      this.name = name;                  //attribute
25      this.department = department;      //attribute
26  }//Employee
27
28  //define Manager object
29  function Manager (staff){
30      this.staff = staff;                //attribute
31      Manager.prototype = new Employee;  //nested object
32  }//Manager
33
34  //Create a manager instance
35  salesManager = new Manager(10);
36  //assign attribute (property) values to manager instance
37  salesManager.name="Abe";
38  salesManager.department = "sales";
39  document.write ("Manager name is " + salesManager.name
    + "<br />");
40  document.write ("Manager department is " + salesManager.department
    + "<br />");
41  document.write ("Manager " + salesManager.name + " manages " +
    salesManager.staff + " people");
42
```

```
43    </script>
44    </head>
45    <body>
46    </body>
47    </html>
```

22.6 Document Object Model (DOM)

JavaScript has many built-in objects that follows the DOM structure. When we load a Web page (document) into a browser window, the browser creates a number of JavaScript objects based on the XHTML code of the document. The DOM converts the XHTML elements of the Web page into built-in JavaScript objects. Each object has predefined variables and methods that become available for use by the JavaScript code of the Web page. These objects exist in a hierarchy that reflects the structure of the XMHTL Web page itself, as shown in Figure 22.3.

The association and the "uses-a" relationship is evident among the XHTML objects shown in Figure 22.3. For example, a `window` *uses a* a `location`, `document`, `history`, and `frame`. A `document` uses a `link`, `anchor`, `image`, and so forth. A `form` *uses a* `text`, `checkbox`, `radio`, and so forth. And a `navigator` uses a `mimeType` and `plugin`.

In the hierarchy shown in Figure 22.3, an object's "descendants" are attributes of the object. Consider a form `myForm` in a `document`. Both `document` and `myForm` are objects, and `myForm` is a property of `document`; we access it via the dot notation `document.myForm`. Each of these objects have properties (variables) and methods. See Example 22.6 for instruction on how to the access the attributes of an object.

Every Web page has the following objects:

1. `navigator`: has properties for the name and version of the browser being used, the MIME types it supports, and its plug-ins.
2. `window`,: the browser window. Also, each frame in a frame set has a `window` object.
3. `document`: refers to the Web page currently displayed in the browser window. `document` contains properties based on the content of the page, such as title, background color, links, and images.
4. `location`: contains the Web page's URL.
5. `history`: has the previously requested URLs that are stored in the browser's history list. This is the list we access via the browser's `Back` and `Forward` buttons.

The `document` of a Web page may contain some other of the objects listed in Figure 22.3, depending on the page's content.

The objects shown in Figure 22.3 follow the rule of nested objects when it comes to accessing their properties. We use the dot-notation chain to access them. For example, to access the `value` attribute of a text field `myField` in a form `myForm` in a `document`, we use

```
window.document.myForm.myField.value
```

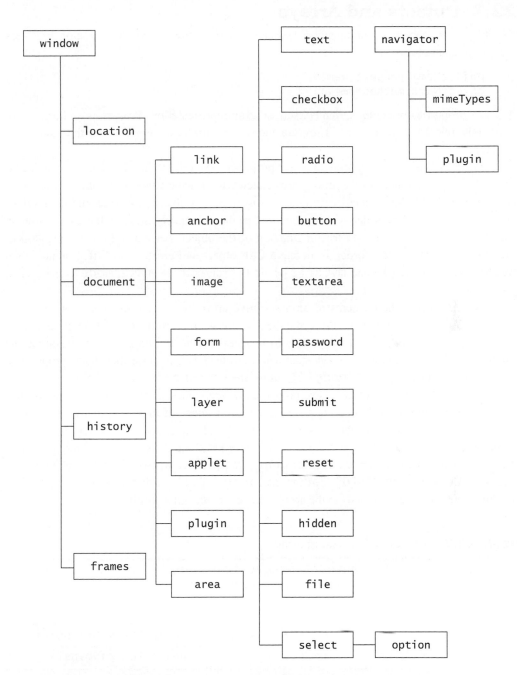

Figure 22.3   Hierarchy of JavaScript XHTML objects.

22.7 Objects and Arrays

An object has properties and behaviors associated with it. We use the dot notation to access them—for example,

```
objectName.propertyName;
objectName.methodName();
```

A list of properties of an object lends itself to array representation. Properties and arrays are intimately related in JavaScript. They are viewed as different interfaces to the same data structure.

JavaScript associates an array to object properties. We refer to this array as an **associative array** because each index of the array is associated with a string value; this value is a property name of the object. An associative array allows us to access object properties and their values via array elements. The order of the properties in the associative array is the same order in which they are used in the constructor function of the object. For example, if we use make, model, and year, in this order, to define a Car object and create a myCar instance, then myCar[0], myCar[1] and myCar[2] hold the values of the make, model, and year, respectively.

We can access the elements of an associative array by using a number or a string for the array element's index. If we use a number, we must do so in a for...in loop, as shown in Example 22.7. If we simply use myCar[1] to access the model property, JavaScript returns undefined. To access an array element via a string index, enclose the object property in quotes. For example, myCar["model"] returns the value of model.

Some of the browser objects have properties whose values are themselves arrays. We use these arrays to store information when we do not know ahead of time how many values there will be. Table 22.2 lists these objects. A particular XHTML tag creates the elements of an array in the order they are used. If we use, for example, the <img> tag three times in a Web page, then the document.images array has document.images.length = 3, and it has three elements: document.images[0], document.images[1], and document.images[2]. The first <img> tag corresponds to the array's first element, and so forth.

Table 22.2 Predefined JavaScript arrays.

Predefined arrays: links, anchors, images, forms, applets, embeds, elements, options, frames, history, mimetypes, and plugins

Object	Property	Arrays from	Associative-array access
navigator	mimeTypes	browser MIME types	navigator.mimeTypes[i]
	plugins	browser plug-ins	navigator.plugins[i]
window	history	browser session history list	window.history[i]
	frames	<frame> tags	window.frames[i]

Table 22.2   Predefined JavaScript arrays. (Continued)

Predefined arrays: `links`, `anchors`, `images`, `forms`, `applets`, `embeds`, `elements`, `options`, `frames`, `history`, `mimetypes`, and `plugins`

Object	Property	Arrays from	Associative-array access
document	links	<a> and <area> tags	document.links[i]
	anchors	<a> tags of Web-page anchors	document.anchors[i]
	images	<img> tags	document.images[i]
	forms	<form> tags	document.forms[i]
	applets	<applet> tags	document.applets[i]
	embeds	<embed> tags	document.embeds[i]
form	elements	<input> tags	document.forms[i].elements[j]
select	options	<option> tags	document.forms[i].elements[j].options[k]

Example 22.7 Use associative arrays.

Write a JavaScript application that uses an associative array.

Solution 22.7 Using the AceHTML editor, generate the given code, and save it as `example227.html`. Render the Web page in a browser.

Code explained:

1. Lines 1–21 are the same as in Example 22.5.
2. Lines 24–35 define a general function that can print the properties of any object.
3. Lines 38–43 are almost the same as in Example 22.5, with just a few modifications.
4. Line 48 calls the `print()` function from line 24.

Discussion:

We print the properties of the `salesManager` object, using the two ways (numbers and strings) of accessing the indexes of associative arrays. Code lines 41–43 use strings as indexes. Each string is a property name taken from code lines 13, 14, and 19. We use single quotes, as outer double quotes are already used.

Code line 48 prints the same properties by calling the `print()` function from code line 24. This function use the `for...in` loop (code lines 26–33). This loop has an inner `for...in` loop (code lines 28 and 29). We need it to cycle through the properties of nested object `salesEmployee`. Code line 27 uses the `instaceof` operator to check if a property is of type `Object`. If it is, we use a 2D array to access its properties, as shown in code line 29.

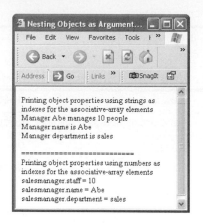

Let us apply code lines 26–34 to our examples. When $i = 0$, obj[0] is staff. When $i = 1$, obj[1] is employee, an object. (If we print this property, we get the bottom screen capture of the two shown above.) In this case, code line 27 returns true, and code lines 28 and 29 execute, to produce the results shown in the top screen capture of the two shown above.

Hands-on exercise:

Rewrite the print() function in code lines 24–35 to process properties of objects that are nested via prototyping. Do you still need the instanceof operator and the 2D array? Is the function much simpler now? Also, modify code lines 38–43 accordingly. (Refer to code of Example 22.6.)

```
1   <?xml version="1.0" encoding="iso-8859-1"?>
2   <!DOCTYPE html PUBLIC "-//W3C//DTD XHTML 1.1//EN"
3       "http://www.w3.org/TR/xhtml11/DTD/xhtml11.dtd">
4   <html xmlns="http://www.w3.org/1999/xhtml">
5   <!-- Generated by AceHTM http://freeware.acehtml.com -->
6   <head>
7   <meta http-equiv="Content-Type" content="text/html;
    charset=iso-8859-1" />
8   <title>Nesting Objects as Arguments</title>
```

```
 9    <script language="javascript">
10
11    //define Employee object
12    function Employee (name,department){
13        this.name = name;                    //attribute
14        this.department = department;         //attribute
15    }//Employee
16
17    //define Manager object
18    function Manager (staff, employee){
19        this.staff = staff;                  //attribute
20        this.employee = employee;            //nested object
21    }//Manager
22
23    //Use associative array to print any object properties
24    function print(obj, objName){
25        props = "";
26        for (i in obj){
27        if (obj[i] instanceof Object){
28            for (j in obj[i])
29            props += objName + "." + j + " = " + obj[i][j] +
    "<br />";
30        } //if
31        else
32        props += objName + "." + i + " = " + obj[i] + "<br />";
33        } //for
34        return props;
35    } //print()
36
37    //Create employee and manager instances
38    salesEmployee = new Employee ("Abe", "sales");
39    salesManager = new Manager(10, salesEmployee);
40    document.write("Printing object properties using strings as
    indexes for the associative-array elements<br />");
41    document.write ("Manager " + salesManager.employee['name'] +
    " manages " + salesManager['staff'] + " people<br />");
42    document.write ("Manager name is " +
    salesManager.employee['name'] + "<br />");
43    document.write ("Manager department is " +
    salesManager.employee['department'] + "<br />");
44    document.write("<br />============================<br />");
45
46    //print salesmanager another way
47    document.write("Printing object properties using numbers as
    indexes for the associative array elements<br />");
48    document.write(print(salesManager, "salesmanager"));
```

```
49
50    </script>
51    </head>
52    <body>
53    </body>
54    </html>
```

22.8 document Object

Beginning with this section, we cover four of the most popular JavaScript objects: document, Math, Date, and String. We list the variables and methods of each object, as well as the constants of the Math object. The reader is encouraged to write JavaScript programs to access them as the need arises. The variables and methods of the document object are as follows:

document variables: alinkcolor, anchors[], applets[], bgcolor, cookie, domain, embeds[], fgcolor, forms[], images[], lastModified, linkColor, links[], location, plugins, referrer, title, URL, and vlinkColor.

document methods: clear(), close(), open(), write(), and writeln().

Use document and any variable or method name in dot notation to access variables and methods—for example, document.alinkColor and document.write(). The writeln() method is like write(), but it forces a carriage return. It does not work in any browser because none of the browsers implemented it.

22.9 Math Object

The Math object (class) cannot be instantiated. Thus, all its constants, variables, and methods are *static*. A **static constant** is a constant that belongs to the class, and likewise for static variables and methods. This means that we can access it in dot notation via the class name; no instance name is needed. The constants, variables, and methods of the Math object are as follows:

Math constants:

Math.PI	(the constant π, truncated to 3.14159265)
Math.SQRT1_2	$(1/\sqrt{2})$
Math.SQRT2	$(\sqrt{2})$
Math.E	(the constant e = 2.171828182459045 truncated to)
Math.LN10	(natural logarithm for base 10)
Math.LN2	(natural logarithm for base 2)
Math.LOG10E	(the base-10 logarithm for base e)
Math.LOG2E	(the base-2 logarithm for base e)

Math variables: none.

> **Math** methods (all static): abs(), acos(), asin(), atan(), atan2(), ceil(),
> cos(), exp(), floor(), log(), max(), min(), pow(), random(), round(),
> sin(), sqrt(), and tan().

Example 22.8 Use the methods of the Math object.

Write a JavaScript application that uses the Math object.

Solution 22.8 Using the AceHTML editor, generate the given code, and save it as example228.html. Render the Web page in a browser.

Code explained:

Lines 12–30 use all the methods of the Math object.

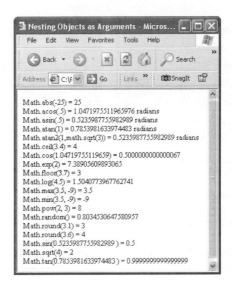

Discussion:

The methods of the Math object can be divided into a few groups. This example shows how to use each method. Math.abs(x) (code line 12) takes a number or variable x (positive or negative) and returns its absolute value. The trigonometric methods are

sin(x)	code line 28
cos(x)	code line 18
tan(x)	code line 30

and their inverse methods are

asin(x)(sin^{-1}(x))	code line 14
acos(x)(cos^{-1}(x))	code line 13

atan(x)(tan^{-1}(x))   code line 15
atan2(x)(tan^{-1}(x))   code line 16

sin(x), cos(x), and tan(x) take an angle x in radians. Use $(\theta \times 180)/\pi$ to convert an angle θ from degrees to radians. asin(x), acos(x), atan(x), and atan2(x) take a number x and find the corresponding angle in radians. Use $(\theta \times \pi)/180$ to convert an angle θ from radians to degrees. atan2(x, y) contains the angle's quadrant y(a value from 1–4), while atan(x) does not. This example uses the results from sin(x), cos(x), and tan(x) in the inverse methods asin(x), acos(x), atan(x), respectively. We get the expected results, within the numerical errors of the computations. For example, code line 30 should produce 1 (the value we used in code line 15) for a 45- degree angle.

Another group of methods is the limits and approximations. Math provides the following methods in this group:

ceil(x)	code line 17	returns the highest integer nearest to x
floor(x)	code line 20	returns the lowest integer nearest to x
round(x)	code lines 26 and 27	rounds x up or down to the nearest integer
max(x, y)	code line 22	returns the algebraic maximum of x and y
min(x)	code line 23	returns the algebraic minimum of x and y

The power and exponent groups have these methods, respectively:

exp(x)	code line 19	returns e^x; same as Math.pow(Math.E, x)
pow(x, y)	code line 24	returns x^y

The remaining methods are as follows:

log(x)	code line 21	returns the natural logarithm of x
random()	code line 25	returns number such that $0 <$ number < 1
random(x)		same as random(), but seeded with x
sqrt(x)	code line 29	returns the square root of x

Hands-on exercise:
Use the Math.random(x) method with the following different values of x: 0.7, 0.3, and 0.9. Does the seed value x influence the random-number generation by biasing it toward x?

```
1  <?xml version="1.0" encoding="iso-8859-1"?>
2  <!DOCTYPE html PUBLIC "-//W3C//DTD XHTML 1.1//EN"
3      "http://www.w3.org/TR/xhtml11/DTD/xhtml11.dtd">
4  <html xmlns="http://www.w3.org/1999/xhtml">
5  <!-- Generated by AceHTM http://freeware.acehtml.com -->
6  <head>
```

```
 7   <meta http-equiv="Content-Type" content="text/html;
     charset=iso-8859-1" />
 8   <title>Nesting Objects as Arguments</title>
 9   <script language="javascript">
10
11   //use methods of the Math object object
12   document.write("Math.abs(-25) = " + Math.abs(-25) + "<br />");
13   document.write("Math.acos(.5) = " + Math.acos(0.5) +
     " radians<br />");
14   document.write("Math.asin(.5) = " + Math.asin(0.5) +
     " radians<br />");
15   document.write("Math.atan(1) = "  + Math.atan(1) +
     " radians<br />");
16   document.write("Math.atan2(1,math.sqrt(3)) = " +
     Math.atan2(1,Math.sqrt(3)) +           " radians<br />");
17   document.write("Math.ceil(3.4) = " + Math.ceil(3.4) +
     "<br />");
18   document.write("Math.cos(1.04719755119659) = " +
     Math.cos(1.04719755119659) + "<br />");
19   document.write("Math.exp(2) = " + Math.exp(2) + "<br />");
20   document.write("Math.floor(3.7) = " + Math.floor(3.7) +
     "<br />");
21   document.write("Math.log(4.5) = " + Math.log(4.5) + "<br />");
22   document.write("Math.max(3.5, -9) = " + Math.max(3.5,-9) +
     "<br />");
23   document.write("Math.min(3.5, -9) = " + Math.min(3.5, -9) +
     "<br />");
24   document.write("Math.pow(2, 3) = " + Math.pow(2, 3) +
     "<br />");
25   document.write("Math.random() = " + Math.random() + "<br />");
26   document.write("Math.round(3.1) = " + Math.round(3.1) +
     "<br />");
27   document.write("Math.round(3.6) = " + Math.round(3.6) +
     "<br />");
28   document.write("Math.sin(0.5235987755982989 ) = " +
     Math.sin(0.5235987755982989 ) + "<br />");
29   document.write("Math.sqrt(4) = " + Math.sqrt(4) + "<br />");
30   document.write("Math.tan(0.7853981633974483 ) = " +
     Math.tan(0.7853981633974483 ) + "<br />");
31
32   </script>
33   </head>
34   <body>
35   </body>
36   </html>
```

22.10 Date Object

The Date object is essential to Web applications. For example, we can write a script that can display the current date in a Web page, thus making its content look current. There are canned scripts that Web developers can place in their Web pages in order to include dates. Also, some HTML editors, provide Date support. For example, Dreamweaver has an Insert => Date function that allows a developer to choose from among standard date formats.

The Date object has multiple constructors: Date(), Date(string), and Date(year, month, day, hours, minutes, seconds, or milliseconds). The Date() constructor returns the computer system's clock time, which can be processed and converted to the appropriate format.

The Date object uses set and get methods (also known as setters and getters, respectively). set methods assign values to the parameters of a Date instance, such as seconds, minutes, hours, day, week, month, and year. get methods perform the opposite task: They retrieve current values of a Date instance. The variables and methods of the Date object are as follows:

> **Date variables:** none.
> **Date methods:** getDate(), getDay(), getFullYear(), getHours(), get-Milliseconds(), getMinutes(), getMonth(), getSeconds(), get-Time(), getTimeZoneOffset(), getUTCDate(), getUTCDay(), getUTCFullYear(), getUTCHOurs(), getUTCMilliseconds(), getUTC-Minutes(), getUTCMonth(), getUTCSeconds(), getYear(), setDate(), setFullYear(), setHours(), setMilliseconds(), setMinutes(), set-Month(), setSeconds(), setTime(), setUTCDate(), setUTCFullYear(), setUTCHours(), setUTCMilliseconds(), setUTCMinutes(), setUTC-Month(), setUTCSeconds(), setYear(), toGMTString(), toLocal-String(), toString(), toUTCString(), and valueOf().

Example 22.9 Use the methods of the Date object.

Write a JavaScript application that uses the Date object.

Solution 22.9 Using the AceHTML editor, generate the given code, and save it as example229.html. Render the Web page in a browser.

Code explained:

1. Line15 creates an array of the days in a week.
2. Line 16 creates an array of the months in a year.
3. Lines 21–34 define the displayDate() function, which takes a date in a system clock format and returns a formatted date, as shown in the forthcoming screen capture.

4. Line 36 creates a `Date` instance, using the empty constructor.

5. Lines 43 and 48 use another constructor that takes numbers as input.

Discussion:

This example converts a `Date` instance `d` (code line 36) from a system clock format to a finished form, as shown in the foregoing screen capture. The `displayDate()` function does the conversion. It uses the `Date` object's `get` methods (code lines 23–25 and 31). The `getDate()` method returns the day of the month of a `Date` instance as a number between 1 and 31.

We create and use two arrays, one for the days of the week (code line 15) and one for the months of the year (code line 16). They are zero-based indexed arrays. We use them in code lines 23 and 24 to process and extract the day of the week and the month of the year, respectively, from the raw format used in `Date` instance `inDate`.

The `Date.getYear()` method returns different values, depending on the browser. In IE, for the year 2000 and beyond, it returns the actual year, as shown in the foregoing screen capture. See code lines 29 and 30 for more details. In the Netscape browser, it returns the actual year minus 1900. The method is implemented differently in each browser.

Hands-on exercise:

Convert the code given in this example to display the time in military format; that is, the hour should be 12 + the actual hour.

```
1  <?xml version="1.0" encoding="iso-8859-1"?>
2  <!DOCTYPE html PUBLIC "-//W3C//DTD XHTML 1.1//EN"
3      "http://www.w3.org/TR/xhtml11/DTD/xhtml11.dtd">
4  <html xmlns="http://www.w3.org/1999/xhtml">
5  <!-- Generated by AceHTM http://freeware.acehtml.com -->
6  <head>
7  <meta http-equiv="Content-Type" content="text/html;
   charset=iso-8859-1" />
```

```
 8    <title>Date Formatting in JavaScript</title>
 9    <script language="javascript">
10
11    //use methods of the Date object
12    <!-- Hide from ancient Browsers
13
14    // Global Day Names and Month Names for Date Formatting Routines
15    dayArray   = new Array("Sunday", "Monday", "Tuesday", "Wednesday",
      "Thursday", "Friday", "Saturday");
16    monthArray = new Array("January", "February", "March", "April",
      "May", "June", "July", "August", "September", "October",
      "November", "December");
17
18    // Function returns a string of the passed-in Date formatted as:
19    //        DayOfWeek MonthName Day, FourDigitYear
20    // e.g.   Thursday November 13, 2003
21    function displayDate(inDate)
22    {
23      str  = dayArray[inDate.getDay()];
24      str += " " + monthArray[inDate.getMonth()];
25      str += " " + inDate.getDate();
26
27      // Browsers return different values for Date.getYear()
28      // Netscape 4.x always shows 2-digit years
29      // IE and Netscape 3.x show 4 digits for 2000 and beyond and 2
      digits otherwise
30      // This formula is good through the year 2899, although other
      limits occur well before then!
31      theYear = inDate.getYear();
32      str += ", " + (theYear + (theYear < 1000 ? 1900 : 0));
33      return str;
34    }
35
36    d = new Date();
37    document.write("<BR>Date Value = " + d);
38    document.write("<BR>Date.getYear() = " + d.getYear());
39    document.write("<BR><B>Today = " + displayDate(d) +"</B>");
40    document.write("<BR>*********************************<BR>");
41
42    // Show the difference between a 19xx year and 20xx year
43    moonDate = new Date(1969, 6, 20);
44    document.write("<BR>Man walked on the moon on " +
      displayDate(moonDate));
45    document.write("<BR>The year was " + moonDate.getYear());
46    document.write("<BR>*********************************<BR>");
47
48    wtcDate = new Date(2001, 8, 11);
49    document.write("<BR>The world will remember " +
      displayDate(wtcDate));
```

```
50  document.write ("<BR>The year was " + wtcDate.getYear ());
51  document.close ();
52  //   End Browser Hiding -->
53
54  </script>
55  </head>
56  <body>
57  </body>
58  </html>
```

22.11 String Object

The String object is fundamental to Web applications. The String object has methods that allow us to control the appearance of strings (text) and manipulate them. The methods are intuitive and easy to use. We use the dot notation to implement the methods. Some of the methods achieve the same result as some XHTML tags. For example, the bold() and italics() methods are equivalent to the <b> and <i> tags, respectively.

The String methods treat strings as arrays of characters. For example, the string "I am here" is an array with 9 elements, where the index of the first character, I, is 0 and the index of the last character, e, is 8.

The String object has one property only, length. It returns the number of characters in a given string. For example, for the string "I am here", length returns 9. The variables and methods of the string object are as follows:

String variables: length.
String methods: anchor(), big(), blink(), bold(), charAt(), charCodeAt(), concat(), fixed(), fontcolor(), fontsize(), indexOf(), italics(), lastIndexOf(), link(), match(), replace(), search(), slice(), small(), split(), strike(), sub(), substring(), substr(), sup(), toLowerCase(), and toUpperCase().

Example 22.10 Use the methods of the String object.

Write a JavaScript application that uses the String object.

Solution 22.10 Using the AceHTML editor, generate the given code, and save it as example2210.html. Render the Web page in a browser.

Code explained:

1. Line 12 defines a literal string to which we apply the variables and methods of the String object.
2. Line 18 uses the length property of strings.
3. Lines 21–50 use all the methods of the String object.

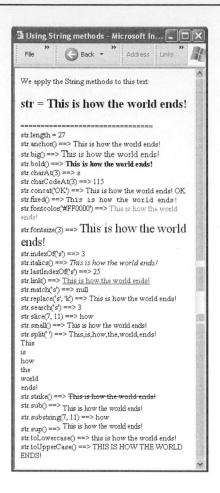

Discussion:

This example shows how to use each method of the `String` object. The following methods provide the same results as some XHTML tags:

`big()`	code line 22
`bold()`	code line 23
`fontcolor(x)`	code line 28
`fontsize(x)`	code line 29
`italics()`	code line 31
`small()`	code line 38
`strike()`	code line 44
`sub()`	code line 45
`sup()`	code line 48

The fontsize() method takes a number between 1 and 7, inclusive. The higher the number, the bigger is the font size of the text. The sub() method makes the text x into a subscript—for example, N_x. The sup() method does the opposite: It makes text into a superscript—for example, 2^x.

The remaining methods manipulate strings in order to perform tasks such as searching for characters, finding character indexes, extracting substrings, and splitting and slicing strings. These methods are listed as follows:

anchor(x)	code line 21	adds an <a> tag with the name x to the string
charAt(x)	code line 24	returns the character at location x
charCodeAt(x)	code line 25	returns the ASCII code of the character at location x
concat(x)	code line 26	concatenates x with a string
fixed()	code line 27	makes a fixed-width string with the <tt> tag
indexOf(x)	code line 30	returns the index of the character x
lastIndexOf(x)	code line 32	returns the index of the last occurrence of character x
link()	code line 33	converts a string to a hyperlink
match(x)	code line 34	returns null if none of the characters in a string matches x
replace(x, y)	code line 35	replaces character x by character y
search(x)	code line 36	returns the index of the first occurrence of character x
slice(x, y)	code line 37	returns characters between indexes x and y, inclusive
split(x)	code line 39	returns an array of words separated by delimiter x
substring(x, y)	code line 46	returns characters between indexes x and y, inclusive
toLowerCase()	code line 49	converts the string to lowercase
toUppercase()	code line 50	converts the string to uppercase

Observe that some of the foregoing methods are redundant; they achieve the same results. The reason that redundant methods exist is that some are more efficient to use than others, depending on the problem at hand. For example, the methods slice() and substring() produce the same results, as shown in the foregoing screen capture.

The split() method in code line 40 uses a whitespace character as a delimiter to split the string in to its component words. It returns an array that we capture in the words array. We print the elements of the array via the for loop in code lines 41–43. The split() method is most effective when working with structured strings. For example, we can use it to split a CGI name–value string into its pairs, using & as a delimiter. We then split each pair, using = as a delimiter, to retrieve the values (user input in a form).

Hands-on exercise:

Use different values for some of the String methods in this example. Observe how the resulting strings change.

```
1   <?xml version="1.0" encoding="iso-8859-1"?>
2   <!DOCTYPE html PUBLIC "-//W3C//DTD XHTML 1.1//EN"
3       "http://www.w3.org/TR/xhtml11/DTD/xhtml11.dtd">
4   <html xmlns="http://www.w3.org/1999/xhtml">
5   <!-- Generated by AceHTM http://freeware.acehtml.com -->
6   <head>
7   <meta http-equiv="Content-Type" content="text/html;
    charset=iso-8859-1" />
8   <title>Using String methods</title>
9   <script language="javascript">
10
11  //define a string
12  str = "This is how the world ends!";
13  document.write("We apply the String methods to this text:");
14  document.write("<h2>str = " + str + "</h2>");
15  document.write("===============================");
16
17  //use the only variable of the String object
18  document.write("<br />str.length = " + str.length);
19
20  //use the methods of the String object
21  document.write("<br />str.anchor('name') ==> " +
    str.anchor("name"));
22  document.write("<br />str.big() ==> " + str.big());
23  document.write("<br />str.bold() ==> " + str.bold());
24  document.write("<br />str.charAt(3) ==> " + str.charAt(3));
25  document.write("<br />str.charCodeAt(3) ==> " +
    str.charCodeAt(3));
26  document.write("<br />str.concat('OK') ==> " +
    str.concat(" OK"));
27  document.write("<br />str.fixed() ==> " + str.fixed());
28  document.write("<br />str.fontcolor('#FF0000') ==> " +
    str.fontcolor("#FF0000"));
29  document.write("<br />str.fontsize(3) ==> " + str.fontsize(5));
30  document.write("<br />str.indexOf('s') ==> " + str.indexOf('s'));
31  document.write("<br />str.italics() ==> " + str.italics());
```

```
32  document.write ("<br />str.lastIndexOf('s') ==> " +
    str.lastIndexOf ('s'));
33  document.write ("<br />str.link() ==> " + str.link());
34  document.write ("<br />str.match('k') ==> " + str.match ("k"));
35  document.write ("<br />str.replace('s', 'k') ==> " +
    str.replace ("s", "k"));
36  document.write ("<br />str.search('s') ==> " + str.search ("s"));
37  document.write ("<br />str.slice(7, 11) ==> " + str.slice (7,11));
38  document.write ("<br />str.small() ==> " + str.small ());
39  document.write ("<br />str.split(' ') ==> " + str.split (" "));
40  words = str.split (" ");
41  for (i=0; i<words.length; i++){
42  document.write ("<br />" + words [i]);
43  } //for
44  document.write ("<br />str.strike() ==> " + str.strike ());
45  document.write ("<br />str.sub() ==> " + str.sub ());
46  document.write ("<br />str.substring(7, 11) ==> " +
    str.substring (7, 11));
47  document.write ("<br />str.substr(7, 4) ==> " +
    str.substr (7, 4));
48  document.write ("<br />str.sup() ==> " + str.sup ());
49  document.write ("<br />str.toLowercase() ==> " +
    str.toLowerCase ());
50  document.write ("<br />str.toUpperCase() ==> " +
    str.toUpperCase ());
51
52  </script>
53  </head>
54  <body>
55  </body>
56  </html>
```

Example 22.11 Create a random-color generator.

Write a JavaScript application that generates hex code for colors randomly.

Solution 22.11 Using the AceHTML editor, generate the given code, and save it as example2211.html. Render the Web page in a browser.

Code explained:

1. Line 12 generates a random color.
2. Line 19 uses the fontcolor() method of the String object to assign the random color to the text of the str variable, defined in code line 18.

Discussion:

Code line 12 generates three random numbers, using the `Math.random()` method. It multiplies each number by a 100 to scale it up. Finally, it converts each number into an integer, using the `Math.floor()` method. It uses # for hex notation.

Hands-on exercise:

Replace the `Math.floor()` method by the `Math.ceil()` method. Does this change make a difference?

```
1   <?xml version="1.0" encoding="iso-8859-1"?>
2   <!DOCTYPE html PUBLIC "-//W3C//DTD XHTML 1.1//EN"
3       "http://www.w3.org/TR/xhtml11/DTD/xhtml11.dtd">
4   <html xmlns="http://www.w3.org/1999/xhtml">
5   <!-- Generated by AceHTM http://freeware.acehtml.com -->
6   <head>
7   <meta http-equiv="Content-Type" content="text/html;
    charset=iso-8859-1" />
8   <title>Random Color Generator</title>
9   <script language="javascript">
10
11  //generate a random hex color
12  color = "#" + Math.floor(Math.random()*100) +
    Math.floor(Math.random()*100) + Math.floor(Math.random()*100);
13
14  //display color hex code
15  alert (color);
16
17  //apply random color to text
18  str = "<h1>This is randomly colored text</font></h1>";
19  document.write(str.fontcolor(color));
20
```

```
21    </script>
22    </head>
23    <body></body></html>
```

22.12 Tutorials

22.12.1 Prime Numbers (Study Section 22.9)

Using the AceHTML editor, generate the given code, and save it as `tutorial22121.html`. Render the Web page in browser.

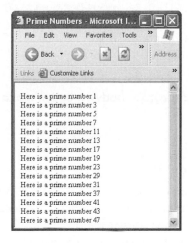

Code explained:

1. The `for` loop in lines 11–16 searches for prime numbers.

2. Line 19 calls `primeNumbers()`.

Discussion:

This example searches for prime numbers between 1 and 50, inclusive. A prime number is defined as a number that is divisible only by itself and 1. This definition leads us to believe that `if (n%1 == 0 && n%n == 0)` should work. It does not, however, as all numbers, prime or not, satisfy it. Code line 14 eliminates all possible numbers that are divisible by themselves and 1 and are not prime.

Hands-on exercise:

Can you find a better condition for the `if` statement in code line 14 than the current one? To find a new condition, remove some of the subconditions one at a time in order to understand their effects.

```
1    <?xml version="1.0" encoding="iso-8859-1"?>
2    <!DOCTYPE html PUBLIC "-//W3C//DTD XHTML 1.1//EN"
3        "http://www.w3.org/TR/xhtml11/DTD/xhtml11.dtd">
```

```
 4   <html xmlns="http://www.w3.org/1999/xhtml">
 5   <!-- Generated by AceHTM http://freeware.acehtml.com -->
 6   <head>
 7   <meta http-equiv="Content-Type" content="text/html;
     charset=iso-8859-1" />
 8   <title>Prime Numbers</title>
 9   <script language="javascript">
10
11   function primeNumbers (num) {
12       for(n =1; n <=num; n++){
13       //a prime number is only divisible by itself and 1
14       if((n%2!=0 && n%3!=0 && n%5!=0 && n%7!=0 && n%9!=0) || (n%2!=0
     && n%3!=0 &&n<=10) || (n ==3)){
15       document.write("Here is a prime number " +n+ "<br />");}
16       } //for
17   } //primeNumbers()
18   //call function
19   primeNumbers (50);</script><body></body></html>
```

FAQs

Creation and Use (Section 22.3)

Q: Can we define an object without using the `this` reference, as we do in Java and C++?

A: No. Even if you use a different name for a parameter of the constructor function than the name of the attribute variable, you get an `undefined` value for the variable. Use Example 22.2 as a test case, and remove the `this` keyword. What happens?

Blackbox

Section 22.1 (Introduction): JavaScript is an object-oriented (OO) scripting language. OO programming promotes reuse and modularity.

Section 22.2 (Definition) (Example 22.1): An object is defined as an entity (construct) that has attributes and behaviors. The attributes are its variables, and the behaviors are its methods. In JavaScript, methods are functions. In JavaScript, users can define their own objects, as well as utilize JavaScript's built-in (predefined) objects.

Section 22.3 (Creation and Use) (Examples 22.2–22.4): JavaScript uses three concepts to create and implement objects: classes, instantiation, and the dot notation. Classes define objects, instantiation creates them, and the dot notation uses them. JavaScript also uses the `this` reference.

Section 22.4 (Concepts): JavaScript uses the following OO concepts: abstraction, classes, constructors, encapsulation, instances, and inheritance.

Section 22.5 (Inheriting and Nesting Objects) (Examples 22.5–22.6): Inheritance allows one object (subclass) to inherit variables and methods from another object (superclass).

This hierarchy produces an inheritance tree. JavaScript implements inheritance via prototyping and via object nesting, where objects are used as parameters for functions.

Section 22.6 (Document Object Model (DOM)): The DOM converts qualified XHTML elements into JavaScript built-in objects. Every Web page has the following objects: `navigator`, `window`, `document`, `location`, and `history`. The `document` of a Web page may contain other objects.

Section 22.7 (Objects and Arrays) (Example 22.7): An associative array allows us to access object properties and their values via array elements. We can access the elements by using a number in a `for...in` loop, or a string as the array element's index (e.g., `myCar["make"]`). Some XHTML objects have array properties—for example, `document.images[]`.

Section 22.8 (`document` Object):

`document` variables: `alinkcolor`, `anchors[]`, `applets[]`, `bgcolor`, `cookie`, `domain`, `embeds[]`, `fgcolor`, `forms[]`, `images[]`, `lastModified`, `linkColor`, `links[]`, `location`, `plugins`, `referrer`, `title`, `URL`, and `vlinkColor`.

`document` methods: `clear()`, `close()`, `open()`, `write()`, and `writeln()`.

Section 22.9 (`Math` Object) (Example 22.8):

`Math` constants: `Math.PI`, `Math.SQRT1_2`, `Math.SQRT2`, `Math.E`, `Math.LN10`, `Math.LN2`, `Math.LOG10E`, and `Math.LOG2E`.

`Math` variables: none.

`Math` methods (all static): `abs()`, `acos()`, `asin()`, `atan()`, `atan2()`, `ceil()`, `cos()`, `exp()`, `floor()`, `log()`, `max()`, `min()`, `pow()`, `random()`, `round()`, `sin()`, `sqrt()`, and `tan()`.

Section 22.10 (`Date` Object) (Example 22.9):

`Date` variables: none.

`Date` methods: `getDate()`, `getDay()`, `getFullYear()`, `getHours()`, `getMilliseconds()`, `getMinutes()`, `getMonth()`, `getSeconds()`, `getTime()`, `getTimeZoneOffset()`, `getUTCDate()`, `getUTCDay()`, `getUTCFullYear()`, `getUTCHOurs()`, `getUTCMilliseconds()`, `getUTCMinutes()`, `getUTCMonth()`, `getUTCSeconds()`, `getYear()`, `setDate()`, `setFullYear()`, `setHours()`, `setMilliseconds()`, `setMinutes()`, `setMonth()`, `setSeconds()`, `setTime()`, `setUTCDate()`, `setUTCFullYear()`, `setUTCHours()`, `setUTCMilliseconds()`, `setUTCMinutes()`, `setUTCMonth()`, `setUTCSeconds()`, `setYear()`, `toGMTString()`, `toLocalString()`, `toString()`, `toUTCString()`, and `valueOf()`.

Section 22.11 (`String` Object) (Examples 22.10–22.11):

`String` variables: `length`.

`String` methods: `anchor()`, `big()`, `blink()`, `bold()`, `charAt()`, `charCodeAt()`, `concat()`, `fixed()`, `fontcolor()`, `fontsize()`, `indexOf()`, `italics()`, `lastIndexOf()`, `link()`, `match()`, `replace()`, `search()`, `slice()`, `small()`, `split()`, `strike()`, `sub()`, `substring()`, `substr()`, `sup()`, `toLow-erCase()`, and `toUpperCase()`.

Section 22.12 (Tutorials): One tutorial shows how to use the `Math` object.

Quick reference for the syntax presented in this chapter

Object Concept	How to implement	Name to use	Description	Example

Define object	Use constructor function	user choice	use the `this` reference	`function Obj(a, b){`
				`    this.prop1=a;`
				`    this.prop2=b;`
				`}`

Create instance	Use `new` keyword	user choice	instantiate object	`myInstance =` `new Obj(x, y);`
Use instance	Use dot notation	object variable or method name	access object variables and methods	`myInstance.prop1;` `myInstance.prop2;`

Object	Definition	Name	Description	Example
document	Variables	`alinkColor`	active-links color	`document.alinkColor`
		`anchors[]`	`<a>` tag	`document.anchors[i]`
		`applets[]`	`<applet>` tag	`document.applets[i]`
		`bgcolor`	background color	`document.bgcolor`
		`cookie`	Web page's cookies	`document.cookie`
		`domain`	Web page's domain	`document.domain`
		`embeds[]`	`<embed>` tag	`document.embeds[i]`
		`fgcolor`	foreground color	`document.fgcolor`
		`forms[]`	`<form>` tag	`document.forms[i]`
		`images[]`	`<img>` tag	`document.images[i]`
		`lastModi-fied`	Web page's last change	`document.lastModified`
		`linkColor`	link color	`document.linkColor`
		`links[]`	`<a>` tag	`document.links[i]`
		`location`	Web page's URL	`document.location`
		`plugins`	browser plug-ins	`document.plugins`
		`referrer`	invoking URL	`document.referrer`
		`title`	Web page's title	`document.title`

Object	Definition	Name	Description	Example
		URL	Web page's URL	`document.URL`
		`vlinkColor`	visited-link color	`document.vlinkColor`
	Methods	`clear()`	clear a document	`document.clear()`
		`close()`	close a document	`document.close()`
		`open()`	open a document	`document.open()`
		`write()`	write to a document	`document.write()`
		`writeln()`	write to a document on a new line	`document.writeln()`
`Math`	Constants	`PI`	$\pi = 3.14159265$	`Math.PI`
		`E`	$e = 2.171828182$	`Math.E`
	Variables	none		
	Methods	`abs(x)`	absolute value	`Math.abs(-4.5)`
		`acos(x)`	inverse of `cos(x)`	`Math,acos(.15)`
		`asin(x)`	inverse of `sin(x)`	`Math.asin(.3)`
		`atan(x)`	inverse of `tan(x)`	`Math.atan(.7)`
		`ceil(x)`	nearest highest integer	`Math.ceil(6.3)`
		`cos(x)`	cosine of `x`	`Math.cos(1.5)`
		`exp(x)`	e^x	`Math.exp(2)`
		`floor(x)`	nearest smallest integer	`Math.floor(5.8)`
		`log(x)`	natural logarithm	`Math.log(3)`
		`max(x,y)`	maximum of `x` and `y`	`Math.max(5.1, -2.0)`
		`min(x,y)`	minimum of `x` and `y`	`Math.min(98, 3.2)`
		`pow(x,y)`	x^y	`Math.pow(2, 3)`
		`random()`	random-number generator	`Math.random()`
		`round(x)`	round to nearest integer	`Math.round(9.3)`
		`sin(x)`	sine of `x`	`Math.sin(2.4)`
		`sqrt(x)`	square root of `x`	`Math.sqrt(49)`
		`tan(x)`	tangent of `x`	`Math.tan(.5)`

Object	Definition	Name	Description	Example
`Date`	Variables	none		
	Methods	`getDate()`, `getFullYear()`, `getHours()`, `getmilliseconds()`, `getMonth()`, `getSeconds`, `getYear()`, `setDate()`, `setFullYear()`, `setHour()`, `setmilliseconds()`, `setMinutes()`, `setMonth()`, `setSeconds()`, and `setTime()`		
`String`	Variables	`length`	number of characters	`myString.length`
	Methods	`anchor()`, `big()`, `blink()`, `bold()`, `charAt()`, `charCodeAt()`, `concat()`, `fixed()`, `fontcolor()`, `fontsize()`, `indexOf()`, `italics()`, `lastIndexOf()`, `link()`, `match()`, `replace()`, `search()`, `slice()`, `small()`, `split()`, `strike()`, `sub()`, `substring()`, `substr()`, `sup()`, `toLowerCase()`, and `toUpperCase()`.		

Check Your Progress

At the end of this chapter, you should

- ✔ understand object-oriented (OO) JavaScript (Section 22.1);
- ✔ understand object definitions (Section 22.2);
- ✔ understand object creation and use (Section 22.3);
- ✔ be able to identify the concepts of OOP (Section 22.4);
- ✔ have mastered use of object inheritance and nesting (Section 22.5);
- ✔ understand the document object model (DOM) (Section 22.6);
- ✔ have mastered use of associative arrays (Section 22.7);
- ✔ have mastered use of the JavaScript document, Math, Date, and String objects (Sections 22.8–22.12).

Problems

The exercises are designed for a lab setting, while the homework is to be done outside class time.

Exercises

22.1   Define a chair object.

22.2   Write a JavaScript application that implements the definition of the chair object from Problem 22.1.

22.3   Write a JavaScript application that nests an engine and a steering system in a car.

22.4   Use the associative-array concept to print the properties of the object of Problem 22.2.

22.5   Write a JavaScript program that creates a clock which functions in real time. The clock should display the hours, minutes, and seconds via the three hands of a traditional analog clock.

Homework

22.6 Define a car object.

22.7 Write a JavaScript application that implements the definition of the car object from Problem 22.6.

22.8 Write a JavaScript application that creates two levels of nesting. Nest a living room in a house, and a table in the living room. The attributes of the house object are owner, style, year in which it was built, and living room. The attributes of the living-room object are size, number of windows, and table. The attributes of the table object are maker and type of wood.

22.9 Use the associative-array concept to print the properties of the object of Problem 22.7.

22.10 Write a JavaScript program that uses as many of the methods of the `String` object as possible.

Windows and Frames

Goal

Understand the JavaScript window objects, how popup windows work, how to identify the browser that a client is using, how to use DHTML, and the relationship between frames and windows.

Objectives

- Windows and frames
- Browser-related objects
- `location` object
- `history` object
- `window` object
- Frames
- DHTML

715

Outline

23.1 Introduction

Quite often when we visit a website in a browser window, one or more windows popup with an advertisement. When we close them, others may popup—an effective way of getting our attention. If the same ad is instead included as a banner ad on the Web page, the surfer may not pay attention to it.

On other occasions, a Web page may tell its visitor the name and version of the client browser, being used. As a matter of fact, Web authors optimize their Web pages for particular browsers, typically IE or Netscape. This is usually done to address incompatibility between browsers. When a client requests a Web page, the correct version is sent because the HTTP header sends the browser type with the HTTP request to the server.

How are the aforementioned tasks done? As intriguing as they may look, JavaScript makes them easy to accomplish. It provides objects with properties and behaviors for these actions. The `window` and `navigator` objects provide all this functionality, as we explain in this chapter. The `window` object uses other subobjects, such as `location` and `history`. We also cover them here.

23.2 Browser-Related Objects

JavaScript's browser-related objects are `navigator`, `mimeTypes`, and `plugin`. We cover only the `navigator` object here. The `navigator` object contains information about the client-side browser in use. Table 23.1 summarizes the properties and methods of the `navigator` object.

Table 23.1   `navigator` object's properties and methods.

properties: `appCodeName`, `appName`, `appVersion`, `language`, `mimeType`, `platform`, `plugins`, and `userAgent`
methods: `javaEnabled()`, `preference()`, and `taintEnabled()`

Properties and methods	Name	Description
Properties	appCodeName	Returns the code name of the browser.
	appName	Returns the browser's name. The value of this property is usually `Microsoft Internet Explorer` or `Netscape`.
	appVersion	Returns the browser's software version.
	language	Returns the browser's language.
	mimeTypes	Returns an array of all the MIME types that the browser supports.
	platform	Returns the OS the browser is using.
	plugins	Returns an array of all the plug-ins currently installed on the client.
	userAgent	Returns the user-agent header.
Methods	javaEnabled()	Tests whether Java is enabled in the browser.
	preference()	Allows a script to `get` and `set` certain browser preferences. The syntax is `preference(prefName)` and `preference(prefName, setValue)`, respectively. `prefName` is the name of property we want to `get` or `set`. `setValue` is the value we want to assign to the preference.
	taintEnabled()	Determines whether data tainting is enabled. Tainting prevents scripts from passing secure data, such as the directory structure and session history list, to servers. It return `true` or `false`.

Example 23.1 Use the `navigator` object.

Write a JavaScript program that uses the `navigator` object.

Solution 23.1 Using the AceHTML editor, generate the given code, and save it as `example231.html`. Render the Web page in a browser.

Code explained:

1. Lines 12–19 print the browser's properties.
2. Lines 22–24 retrieve information about the browser.

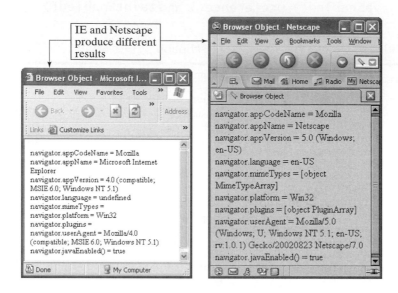

Discussion:

We retrieve all possible information about the client browser that is running the Web page. As shown in the screen captures, IE and Netscape produce slightly different results. IE does not recognize the `language`, `mimeTypes`, and `plugins` properties. It also ignores the `preference()` and `taintEnabled()` methods. Netscape ignore these two methods as well.

Hands-on exercise:

Disable Java and JavaScript in your browser and run the code of the example. Does it run?

```
1    <?xml version="1.0" encoding="iso-8859-1"?>
2    <!DOCTYPE html PUBLIC "-//W3C//DTD XHTML 1.1//EN"
3        "http://www.w3.org/TR/xhtml11/DTD/xhtml11.dtd">
4    <html xmlns="http://www.w3.org/1999/xhtml">
5    <!-- Generated by AceHTM http://freeware.acehtml.com -->
6    <head>
7    <meta http-equiv="Content-Type" content="text/html;
     charset=iso-8859-1" />
8    <title>Browser Object</title>
9    <script language="javascript">
10
11   //use properties of the navigator object
12   document.write("navigator.appCodeName = " +
     navigator.appCodeName + "<br />");
```

```
13    document.write("navigator.appName = " + navigator.appName +
      "<br />");
14    document.write("navigator.appVersion = " + navigator.appVersion +
      "<br />");
15    document.write("navigator.language = " + navigator.language +
      "<br />");
16    document.write("navigator.mimeTypes = " + navigator.mimeTypes +
      "<br />");
17    document.write("navigator.platform = " + navigator.platform +
      "<br />");
18    document.write("navigator.plugins = " + navigator.plugins +
      "<br />");
19    document.write("navigator.userAgent = " + navigator.userAgent +
      "<br />");
20
21    //use methods of the navigator object
22    document.write("navigator.javaEnabled() = " +
      navigator.javaEnabled() + "<br />");
23    document.write("navigator.preference('javascript.enabled') = "
      + navigator.preference('javascript.enabled') + "<br />");
24    document.write("navigator.taintEnabled() = " +
      navigator.taintEnabled() + "<br />");
25
26    </script>
27    </head>
28    <body></body></html>
```

23.3 location Object

The location object is a predefined JavaScript object that we can access through the location property of the window object. This object represents the URL associated with a window object (browser window).

The properties of the location object represent the different parts of a URL. The general form of a URL is

```
protocol://host:port/pathname#hash?search
```

The location object also has two more properties that are not obvious in the foregoing format of a URL. They are href and hostname.

The location object is a subobject of the window object; it must be accessed via the window.location dot notation. Table 23.2 summarizes the properties and methods of the location object.

Table 23.2   `location` object's properties and methods.

properties: `hash, host, hostname, href, pathname, port, protocol, search`
methods: `reload()`, and `replace()`

Properties and methods	Name	Description
Properties	`hash`	The anchor name in the URL.
	`host`	The host and domain name in the URL.
	`hostname`	The `host:port` part of the URL.
	`href`	The entire URL.
	`pathname`	The pathname part of the URL.
	`port`	The communication port that the server uses.
	`protocol`	The part of the URL before, and including, the colon.
	`search`	The part of the URL after, and including, the question mark (?). This part has the form of CGI name/value pairs.
Methods	`reload()`	Forces a reload of the window's current Web page (document).
	`replace()`	Loads the specified URL over the version in the history; the method call disables the **Back** button of the browser. After calling the `replace()` method, the user cannot navigate to previous URLs by using the browser's **Back** Button.

Example 23.2   Use the `location` object.

Write a JavaScript program that uses the `location` object.

Solution 23.2   Using the AceHTML editor, generate the given code, and save it as `example232.html`. Render the Web page in a browser.

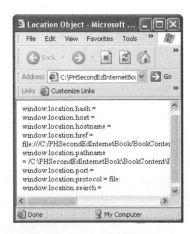

Code explained:

> **1.** Lines 12–19 print the `location` object's properties.
>
> **2.** Lines 22–23 uses the only two methods of the `location` object.

Discussion:

The foregoing screen capture shows the properties of the `location` object for the current URL, which is the file path of the code used in this example. There is no `hash` value, as we do not use an anchor in the file's URL. The `host` and `hostname` are not shown, because the URL is a local file. The `href` and `pathname` are identical, as expected. There is no `port` or `search` value, because we do not use them in the file's URL. The `protocol` of the URL is `file:`, as expected.

The two methods are shown in code lines 22 and 23. They are commented even though the syntax is correct and works fine. If it were not commented, code line 22 would hang up the browser because it attempts to reload the Web page indefinitely. If not commented, code line 23 would work, but we would never actually see the foregoing screen capture, as it would flash and get replaced very quickly by `http://www.neu.edu`. These two statements must be used with `if` statements or event handlers.

Hands-on exercise:

Find a way to get the `reload()` and `replace()` methods in code lines 22 and 23, respectively, to work properly. *Hint*: See Example 23.3.

```
1   <?xml version="1.0" encoding="iso-8859-1"?>
2   <!DOCTYPE html PUBLIC "-//W3C//DTD XHTML 1.1//EN"
3       "http://www.w3.org/TR/xhtml11/DTD/xhtml11.dtd">
4   <html xmlns="http://www.w3.org/1999/xhtml">
5   <!-- Generated by AceHTM http://freeware.acehtml.com -->
6   <head>
7   <meta http-equiv="Content-Type" content="text/html;
    charset=iso-8859-1" />
8   <title>Location Object</title>
9   <script language="javascript">
10
11  //use properties of the location object
12  document.write("window.location.hash = " + window.location.hash
    + "<br />");
13  document.write("window.location.host = " + window.location.host
    + "<br />");
14  document.write("window.location.hostname = " +
    window.location.hostname + "<br />");
15  document.write("window.location.href = "  + window.location.href
    + "<br />");
16  document.write("window.location.pathname = " +
    window.location.pathname + "<br />");
17  document.write("window.location.port = " + window.location.port
    + "<br />");
```

```
18   document.write ("window.location.protocol = " +
     window.location.protocol + "<br />");
19   document.write ("window.location.search = " +
     window.location.search + "<br />");
20
21   //use methods of the location object
22   //window.location.reload();
23   //window.location.replace('http://www.neu.edu');
24
25   </script>
26   </head>
27   <body>
28   </body>
29   </html>
```

23.4 history Object

The `history` object is a predefined JavaScript object that we can access through the `history` property of the `window` object. The `history` object contains the URLs that the client has visited (within a window) during a browser session. These URLs are stored in a history list or array `history[]`. Each array entry is a string composed of a visited URL. If we access the history array without specifying an array element, the browser returns all the URLs in the history list. Table 23.3 summarizes the properties and methods of the `history` object.

Table 23.3   `history` object's properties and methods.

properties: `length`, `current`, `next`, and `previous`		
methods: `back()`, `forward()`, and `go()`		

Properties and methods	Name	Description
Properties	`length`	Returns the length of the `history[]` array.
	`current`	Returns the current URL.
	`next`	Returns the next URL in the history list.
	`previous`	Returns the previous URL in the history list.
Methods	`back()`	Loads the previous URL in the history list.
	`forward()`	Loads the next URL in the history list.
	`go(x)`	Loads a URL from the history list. `x` could be zero, a positive number, or a negative number. `go(0)` means to reload.

Example 23.3 Use the history object.

Write a JavaScript program that uses the history object.

Solution 23.3 Using the AceHTML editor, generate the given code, and save it as example233.html. Render the Web page in a browser.

Code explained:

1. Lines 12–16 print the history object's properties.
2. Lines 19–22 use the methods of the history object.

Discussion:

The foregoing screen capture shows the properties of the history object for the current browser window. The only property that works is length. The others do not work for security reasons. If we were able to know what URLs a user has visited, we would be violating privacy rules of browsing. Thus, all the other properties have values of undefined.

The methods are shown in code lines 19–20 and 26–28. They all work fine. We use a positive number to move forward in the history list, and a negative number to move backward in the list. The methods in code lines 19 and 20 are commented in order to allow us to see the foregoing screen capture. Also, we must use the javascript: protocol in code lines 26 and 28; otherwise, the two methods will be interpreted as Web pages by the browser, and it will issue a message that the page cannot be displayed. Moreover, if the expression following javascript:URL evaluates to undefined, no new document is loaded. If the expression evaluates to a defined type, the value is converted to a string that specifies the URL. Thus, javascript:URL must evaluate to a valid URL.

We can use the javascript: protocol in many ways to add functionality to Web pages; it also becomes useful when we implement it with frames.

Verify the results of the two methods in code lines 26 and 28 manually by using the browser's Back button.

Hands-on exercise:

Move code lines 19 and 20 to the `<body>` section of the Web page. Reformat them according to XHTML rules. Make sure that you visit a number of Web pages before running the code, to build a history list in the browser window.

```
1   <?xml version="1.0" encoding="iso-8859-1"?>
2   <!DOCTYPE html PUBLIC "-//W3C//DTD XHTML 1.1//EN"
3       "http://www.w3.org/TR/xhtml11/DTD/xhtml11.dtd">
4   <html xmlns="http://www.w3.org/1999/xhtml">
5   <!-- Generated by AceHTM http://freeware.acehtml.com -->
6   <head>
7   <meta http-equiv="Content-Type" content="text/html;
    charset=iso-8859-1" />
8   <title>History Object</title>
9   <script language="javascript">
10
11  //use properties of the history object
12  document.write("window.history.length = " + window.history.length
    + "<br />");
13  document.write("window.history.current = " +
    window.history.current + "<br />");
14  document.write("window.history.next = " + window.history.next
    + "<br />");
15  document.write("window.history.previous = "  +
    window.history.previous + "<br />");
16  document.write("window.history[2] = "  + window.history[2]
    + "<br />");
17
18  //use methods of the history object
19  //window.history.forward();//same as clicking the browser's
    Forward button
20  //window.history.go(3);//same as clicking the Forward button 3
    times
21
22  </script>
23  </head>
24  <body>
25  <!-- same as clicking the browser's Back button -->
26  <div><a href="javascript:window.history.back()"> Reload previous
    Web page</a></div>
27  <!-- same as clicking the Back button 5 times -->
28  <a href="javascript:window.history.go(-5)"> Load fifth backward
    URL</a>
29  </body>
30  </html>
```

23.5 window Object

A window is created automatically when we launch a browser. The File menu of the browser window allows us to open another new window (File => New) or close the existing one (File => Close). We can also open and close windows via JavaScript code.

The window object is the root (top-level) object in the JavaScript DOM tree, as shown in Figure 22.3. A window object can also represent a frame in a frame set. We can refer to the current window of a browser in three ways: window, top, or self. The three names are synonyms. For example, we can close the current window by using window.close(), top.close(), or self.close(). Moreover, because the existence of the current window is assumed, we do not have to use dot notation; we can simply use the window's method name only—for example, close(). However, it is recommended to use dot notation, to make the code easier to read and follow.

A browser window lacks event handlers until XHTML that contains a <bod> or <frameset> tag is loaded into it.

Table 23.4 summarizes the properties and methods of the window object.

Table 23.4   window object's properties and methods.

properties: see table entries
methods: see table entries

Properties and methods	Name	Description
Properties	closed	Checks whether a window has been closed.
	defaultStatus	Displays the default message in the window's status bar.
	document	Contains the document displayed in the window.
	frames	An array of the window frames, if there are any.
	history	See Section 23.4.
	innerHeight	Vertical dimension, in pixels, of the window's content area.
	innerWidth	Horizontal dimension, in pixels, of the window's content area.
	length	Number of frames in a window.
	location	See Section 23.3.
	locationbar	Browser window's location (URL) bar.
	menubar	Browser window's menu bar.
	name	Name of the window.
	opener	The window that opens another (child) window.

Table 23.4   `window` object's properties and methods. (Continued)

properties: see table entries methods: see table entries		
Properties and methods	**Name**	**Description**
	`outerHeight`	Vertical dimension, in pixels, of the window's outside boundary.
	`outerWidth`	Horizontal dimension, in pixels, of the window's outside boundary.
	`pageXOffset`	Current *x* position, in pixels, of a window's viewed page.
	`pageYOffset`	Current *y* position, in pixels, of a window's viewed page.
	`parent`	Synonym for the window or frame.
	`personalbar`	Browser window's personal toolbar.
	`scrollbars`	Browser window's scrollbars.
	`self`	Synonym for the current window.
	`status`	Specifies a message to be displayed in the browser window's status bar.
	`statusbar`	Browser window's status bar.
	`toolbar`	Browser window's toolbar.
	`top`	Synonym for the current window.
	`window`	Synonym for the current window.
Methods	`alert()`	Displays an `alert` box.
	`back()`	Equivalent to clicking the browser's `Back` button.
	`blur(x)`	Removes focus from the specified object `x`.
	`capture Events()`	Sets the window or document to capture specified events.
	`clearInterval()`	Cancels a timeout that was set by the `setInterval()` method.
	`clearTimeout()`	Cancels a timeout that was set by the `setTimeout()` method.
	`close()`	Closes the specified window.
	`confirm()`	Displays a `confirm` dialog box.
	`disableExternal- Capture()`	Disables external event capturing set by the `enableExternalCapture()` method.

Table 23.4   window object's properties and methods. (Continued)

properties: see table entries
methods: see table entries

Properties and methods	Name	Description
	enableExternal-Capture()	Allows a window with frames to capture events in pages loaded from different locations (servers).
	find()	Finds the specified text string in the window's content.
	focus()	Gives focus to the specified object.
	forward()	See Section 23.4.
	handleEvent()	Invokes the handler for the specified event.
	home()	Points the browser to the home page specified in its preferences.
	moveBy()	Moves the window by the specified amount.
	moveTo()	Moves the top-left corner of the window to the specified screen location (coordinates).
	open()	Opens a new browser window.
	print()	Prints the content of a window or frame.
	prompt()	Displays a prompt dialog box.
	release Events()	Sets the window to release captured events and send them further along the event hierarchy.
	resizeBy()	Resizes a window by moving its bottom-right corner by the specified amount.
	resizeTo()	Resizes an entire window to the specified outer height and width.
	routeEvent()	Passes a captured event along the normal event hierarchy.
	scroll()	Scrolls a window to the specified location.
	scrollBy()	Scrolls a window by the specified location.
	scrollTo()	Scrolls a window to the specified location such that the specified point becomes the window's top-left corner.
	setInterval()	Evaluates an expression or calls a function every time a specified number of milliseconds elapses.
	setTimeout()	Evaluates an expression or calls a function once after a specified number of milliseconds elapses.
	stop()	Stops the current download.

We cover some of the window properties and methods listed in Table 23.4 in the upcoming examples. The `open()` method is of particular interest. It can be applied to a window or document. We use it to write on-the-fly Web pages into popup windows. In such cases, we recommend using this sequence to ensure that the JavaScript code works:

```
document.open();
document.write(page);
doocument.close();
```

When we use the `open()` method with windows, its general syntax is

```
window.open(URL, windowName, windowFeatures);
```

The three parameters are optional; we can use `window.open()` as well. `URL` specifies the Web page (document) that loads into the window. `windowName` is a string that forms a valid identifier. It could also be a JavaScript variable. `windowFeatures` is a string containing a comma-separated list, with no spaces at all in the string, that determines whether to create the standard window features. These features are `alwaysLowered` (hides the window behind others, whether it is active or not), `alwaysRaised`, `dependent`, `directories`, `height`, `hotkeys`, `innerHeight`, `innerWidth`, `location`, `menubar`, `outerHeight`, `resizable`, `screenX` (or `left`), `screenY` (or `top`), `scrollbars`, `status` (bar), `titlebar`, `toolbar`, `width`, and `z-lock` (the window does not rise above other windows when activated). Some of these features may not work in IE, Netscape, or both.

Example 23.4 Create an ad popup window.

Write a JavaScript program that uses the `open()` method of `window`.

Solution 23.4 This example opens a popup window upon the loading of a Web page in a browser window. It shows how these ad popups are created by websites. Using the AceHTML editor, generate the given code, and save it as `example234.html`. Render the Web page in a browser.

Code explained:

1. Lines 11–23 define the `popUp()` function that creates the popup window.
2. Line 12 creates the popup window. The long string containing the features must not have whitespace in it.
3. Line 13 defines a new document `ndoc`.
4. Lines 14–19 create an on-the-fly Web page.
5. Lines 20–22 display the Web page in the popup.
6. Line 27 calls the `popUp()` function, using an `onLoad` event.

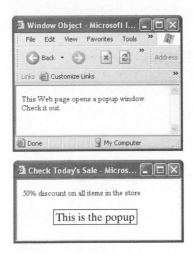

Discussion:

Code line 12 uses two variables to identify the popup window: awin and myPopUp. The first, awin, is a JavaScript variable that we use to refer to the popup window in code line 13. The second, myPopUp, is the name of the actual browser window that opens up. If we use this name again to create another window, the new window replaces the old one. If we use a different name, both the old and the new windows are displayed on the screen.

Code line 13 assigns the ndoc document to awin. We must make this assignment in order to distinguish between the parent and the child windows. We use ndoc in code line 21 to write the on-the-fly Web page onto it. We use the sequence in code lines 20–22 to ensure that the code works. We may use code line 21 only.

Hands-on exercise:

Replace code line 21 by document.write(page). What happens? Why? Also, modify the code given in this example to use two-level nested on-the-fly Web pages, so that when a Web surfer closes the first popup window, the second one pops up.

```
1   <?xml version="1.0" encoding="iso-8859-1"?>
2   <!DOCTYPE html PUBLIC "-//W3C//DTD XHTML 1.1//EN"
3       "http://www.w3.org/TR/xhtml11/DTD/xhtml11.dtd">
4   <html xmlns="http://www.w3.org/1999/xhtml">
5   <!-- Generated by AceHTM http://freeware.acehtml.com -->
6   <head>
7   <meta http-equiv="Content-Type" content="text/html;
    charset=iso-8859-1" />
8   <title>Open a Popup Window</title>
9   <script language="javascript">
10
11  function popUp(message) {
```

```
12        awin = window.open("", "myPopup",
    "toolbar=no,directories=no,status=no,scrollbars=no,resizable=yes,
    width=275,height=50");
13        ndoc = awin.document;
14        page  = "<html><head><title>Check Today's Sale</title>";
15        page += "</html>";
16        page += "<body>";
17        page += message;
18        page += "</body>";
19        page += "</html>";
20        ndoc.open();
21        ndoc.write(page);
22        ndoc.close();
23   } //popUp()
24
25   </script>
26   </head>
27   <body onLoad="popUp('50% discount on all items in the store')">
28   This Web page opens a popup window. Check it out.
29   </body>
30   </html>
```

Example 23.5 Control the location of a popup window.

Write a JavaScript program that controls the placement of a browser window.

Solution 23.5 Using the AceHTML editor, generate the given code, and save it as `example235.html`. Render the Web page in a browser.

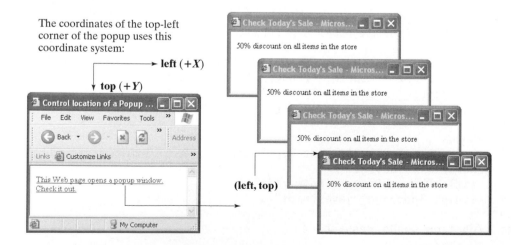

Code explained:

1. Line 11 initializes a counter i.
2. Line 13 increments the counter i by one for each function call.
3. Lines 18–23 create an on-the-fly Web page.
4. Line 16 is extended from line 12 in Example 23.4 by adding the (x, y) location of the popup window.
5. Lines 17–27 and 32 are the same as in Example 23.4.

Discussion:

This example extends Example 23.4 by controlling the location of the popup window's top-left corner. We use the left and top variables (from layers), as they both work in IE and Netscape. screenX and screenY work only in Netscape. The features string (code line 16) is now a concatenation of variables x and y and literal strings. The evaluated string must be continuous, with no whitespace, and all the features must be separated by commas.

Code lines 14 and 15 calculate a new popup location for each function call. When you click the hyperlink created by code line 32, popUp() is called. The value of i is preserved between (across) function calls. The numbers 50 and 75 used in code lines 14 and 15, respectively, could be any numbers.

Hands-on exercise:

Move code line 11 so that it comes after code line 12. Open three or four popups by clicking the hyperlink multiple times. What happens? Explain the result.

```
1   <?xml version="1.0" encoding="iso-8859-1"?>
2   <!DOCTYPE html PUBLIC "-//W3C//DTD XHTML 1.1//EN"
3       "http://www.w3.org/TR/xhtml11/DTD/xhtml11.dtd">
4   <html xmlns="http://www.w3.org/1999/xhtml">
5   <!-- Generated by AceHTM http://freeware.acehtml.com -->
6   <head>
7   <meta http-equiv="Content-Type" content="text/html;
    charset=iso-8859-1" />
8   <title>Control location of a Popup Window</title>
9   <script language="javascript">
10
11  i = 0;
12  function popUp(message){
13  i += 1;
14  x = 50*i;
15  y = 75*i;
16      awin = window.open("", i, "left=" + x + ",top=" + y +
    ",toolbar=no,directories=no,status=no,scrollbars=no,resizable=yes,
    width=275,height=50");
17      ndoc = awin.document;
18      page  = "<html><head><title>Check Today's Sale</title>";
19      page += "</html>";
```

```
20      page += "<body>";
21      page += message;
22      page += "</body>";
23      page += "</html>";
24      ndoc.open();
25      ndoc.write(page);
26      ndoc.close();
27  } //popUp()
28
29  </script>
30  </head>
31  <body>
32  <a href="#" onClick="popUp('50% discount on all items in the
    store')">This Web page opens a popup window. Check it out.</a>
33  </body>
34  </html>
```

23.6 Frame Objects

A frame set displays multiple frames on a single screen, each with its own URL. To convey the fundamentals of frame sets and frame objects, consider the following example:

```
1   <frameset rows="*, *">
2   <frameset cols="*, *">
3   <frame name="xxx" src="xxx.html">
4   <frame name="yyy" src="yyy.html">
5   </frameset>
6   <frame name="zzz" src="zzz.html">
7   </frameset>
```

The XHTML tree structure of the three frames xxx, yyy, and zzz (code lines 3, 4, and 6, respectively) has the following hierarchy according to XHTML: The outer frame set (code line 1) is the parent (parent or top). The inner frame set (code line 2) and frame zzz (code line 6) are its children. The two frames xxx (code line 3) and yyy (code line 4) are grandchildren of the outer frame set.

JavaScript does not use this tree structure to simplify dealing with nesting frames. When JavaScript creates the objects from frame sets, it "flattens" all frames. In other words, each frame, regardless of how deeply it is nested, is considered a child and is placed in the same frame array. JavaScript creates an array called frames that holds the frames of a frame set. All frames are placed into the array in the same sequence in which they appear in the XHTML code. All nesting is ignored. The sequence for the foregoing example is

frames[0].document.name is xxx
frames[1].document.name is yyy
frames[2].document.name is zzz

Think of each frame `frames[i]` as a subwindow in a `window` object. Just as we use `window.document` to access the properties of the `document` object, we use `document.name` to access the properties of the `frames[i]` object.

The flattening makes it easier to refer to a property in any frame. We do not need to know the relative relationship between frames, since they are each a child of the same parent (frame set).

JavaScript uses a `window` object to represent a frame. Every frame object is thus a `window` object and has all the properties and methods of a `window` object. The only difference between the two is that a frame is part (subwindow) of its top-level window (frame set). The keywords `window`, `self`, `top`, and `parent` can be used with frame objects; they refer to the frame-set window that contains the frames. For example, we can write `parent.frames[i].document.bgcolor="#FF0000"` to set the background color of `frames[i]` to red. We also can omit `parent`, as we do with `window`.

Example 23.6 Use frames.

Write a JavaScript program that uses frame objects.

Solution 23.6 Using the AceHTML editor, generate the given code, and save it as `example236.html`. Render the Web page in a browser.

Code explained:

1. Lines 12–14 define the `firstFrame()` function, which returns a Web page.
2. Lines 15–17 define the `initialize()` function, which displays the returned Web page in the top frame, as shown in the accompanying screen capture.
3. Lines 19–23 define the `randomNumbers()` function, which generates and prints five random numbers in the bottom frame, as shown in the accompanying screen capture.
4. Lines 26–29 define a frame set with two empty frames.
5. Line 26 uses two functions to handle the `onLoad` event.

Discussion:

Code line 16 uses the keyword `self` to refer to the frame-set window. This keyword is redundant; we could have removed it, as we did in code line 21. Code line 16 also uses the `javascript:` protocol. The keyword `parent` must be used, because it defines where the `firstFrame()` function is (in the frame-set document). Code lines 27 and 28 use a similar idea.

The `onLoad` event in code line 26 refers to the complete loading of the two frames of the frame set. After both frames and their content have been displayed, the JavaScript interpreter calls the two functions and executes them, thus replacing the content by the new content specified in the two functions and shown in the foregoing screen capture.

Hands-on exercise:

Remove the keyword `parent` from code line 16, and run the code. What happens? Explain the results. Also, replace code line 11 by some new XHTML content. Save and run the code. Do you ever see the new content? What is happening?

```
1   <?xml version="1.0" encoding="iso-8859-1"?>
2   <!DOCTYPE html PUBLIC "-//W3C//DTD XHTML 1.1//EN"
3       "http://www.w3.org/TR/xhtml11/DTD/xhtml11.dtd">
4   <html xmlns="http://www.w3.org/1999/xhtml">
5   <!-- Generated by AceHTM http://freeware.acehtml.com -->
6   <head>
7   <meta http-equiv="Content-Type" content="text/html;
    charset=iso-8859-1" />
8   <title>Using Frame Objects</title>
9   <script language="javascript">
10
11  empty= "";
12  function firstFrame(){
13      return ("<html><body bgColor='#FF0000' text='#FFFF00'>" +
    "<h1 align='center'>Hello World!</h1>" + "</body></html>");
14  }
15  function initialize(){
16      self.first.location = "javascript:parent.firstFrame()";
17  }
18
19  function randomNumbers(){
20      for (i=0;i<5;i++){
21          second.document.write("Here is a random number " +
    Math.round(Math.random()*100) + "<br />");
22      } //for
23  }
24  </script>
25  </head>
26  <frameset rows="100,*" onLoad="initialize(),randomNumbers()">
27  <frame name="first" src="javascript:parent.empty">
28  <frame name="second" src="javascript:parent.empty">
```

```
29   </frameset>
30   <noframes>
31   <h2 align="center">Your browser is not JavaScript enabled</h2>
32   </noframes>
33   </html>
```

23.7 Including JavaScript Files

Client-side JavaScript cannot read or write local data files. But it can load and use files stored in libraries (directories) on a Web server. Other programming languages operate in a similar manner. This is a useful way to store functions in their own files and then load the files at run time. Using JavaScript files

- simplifies the HTML files of Web pages,
- makes one function usable by more than Web page, and
- provides a central location where a function may be changed in order to affect every Web page that uses it.

External JavaScript files use the `.js` extension in their names—for example, `myLib.js`. One JavaScript file can contain one or more functions. We access these file via the `src` attribute of the `<script>` tag as follows:

```
<script src="myLib.js">...</script>
```

We can still use the `language` attribute, while allows us to embed JavaScript code in the XHTML code of a Web page, as we have done previously:

```
<script src="myLib.js">...</script>
<script language="javascript">...</script>
```

The pathnames of `.js` files follow the conventional pathname rules. If both the `.js` and the HTML files reside in the same folder, there is no need to use a pathname. We must use two separate `<script>` tags, as shown in the foregoing code.

Example 23.7 Use `.js` files.

Write a JavaScript program that creates and uses JavaScript libraries.

Solution 23.7 Using the AceHTML editor, generate the given code, and save it as `example237.html` and `mathLib.js`, respectively. Render the Web page in a browser.

Code explained:

1. Line 9 in the `example237.html` file includes the `mathLib.js` file in the Web page.
2. Lines 13–17 in the `example237.html` file call functions stored in the `mathLib.js` file.
3. Lines 2–16 in the `mathLib.js` file define four math functions.

Discussion:

We can use the four math functions stored in the `mathLib.js` file in any other Web pages. We can also change the file in order to affect all the Web pages that use it.

Hands-on exercise:

Create a file called `advancedMath.js`, and use it in the `example237.html` file. Include two more math functions in the `advancedMath.js` file, one that calculates x^y and another that generates a random number.

```
1   /* Generated by AceHTML Freeware http://freeware.acehtml.com */
2   function add(a, b) {
3       return (a + b);
4   }
5
6   function subtract(a, b) {
7       return (a - b);
8   }
9
10  function multiply(a, b) {
11      return (a * b);
12  }
13
14  function divide(a, b) {
15      return (a/b);
16  }
```

`mathLib.js`

```
1   <?xml version="1.0" encoding="iso-8859-1"?>
2   <!DOCTYPE html PUBLIC "-//W3C//DTD XHTML 1.1//EN"
3       "http://www.w3.org/TR/xhtml11/DTD/xhtml11.dtd">
4   <html xmlns="http://www.w3.org/1999/xhtml">
5   <!-- Generated by AceHTM http://freeware.acehtml.com -->
6   <head>
7   <meta http-equiv="Content-Type" content="text/html;
    charset=iso-8859-1" />
```

`example237.html`

```
 8   <title>Using JavaScript Libraries</title>
 9   <script  src="mathLib.js"></script>
10   <script language="javascript">
11
12   document.write ("Hello from the language attribute.<br />");
13   document.write ("These results use the src attribute:<br />");
14   document.write ("7 + 4 = " + add(7, 4) + "<br />");
15   document.write ("7 - 4 = " + subtract(7, 4) + "<br />");
16   document.write ("7 * 4 = " + multiply(7, 4) + "<br />");
17   document.write ("7/4 = " + divide(7, 4) + "<br />");
18   </script>
19   </head>
20   <body>
21   </body>
22   </html>
```

23.8 DHTML

Dynamic HTML (DHTML) is a loosely defined term. According to JavaScript, it refers to three concepts: CSS, content positioning (using layers), and downloadable fonts. These three concepts are the components of DHTML. Used together, the three components provide greater control over the appearance (CSS), layout (layers), and behavior (fonts) of Web pages. We already have covered CSS and layers.

Using downloadable fonts, Web developers can attach specific fonts to their Web pages. As a result, a page will always be displayed with its designed fonts; the browser does not have to substitute for missing fonts at display time of the page. This capability eliminates the need to use generic fonts to make the page look approximately similar on each platform, because downloadable fonts can be displayed on any platform. The browser locks the downloadable fonts in order to prevent Web surfers from copying and using them, thus protecting the rights of font designers.

Some people extend DHTML to include any dynamic action in a Web page that is generated by JavaScript—for example, event handlers and the action they take. Consider image rollovers: We swap one image for another via mouse events. Another example is the creation of popup windows. A third example is the creation of animated sequences. Web developers can also control the visiblity of Web-page elements via DHTML.

23.9 Tutorials

23.9.1 Animation Sequence (Study Section 23.5)

In this tutorial, we write a JavaScript program that creates an animation sequence of a popup window by changing the window's location on the screen. Using the AceHTML editor, generate the given code, and save it as `tutorial2391.html` and `lastPage.html`, respectively. Render the Web page in a browser.

Code explained:

`tutorial2391.html` code:

1. Line 11 specifies six frames for the animation sequence.
2. Line 12 specifies three images for use in the program.

3. Line 13 defines a variable that holds any new popup window (used in code line 59).

4. Line 14 defines an image counter (used in code line 33).

5. Lines 17–23 define and initialize the `myMessages` array. The array holds six messages for the six popup windows that the program opens, one per window.

6. Lines 26–29 define and initialize the `myImages` array.

7. Lines 32–36 define the `switchImage()` function, which assigns an image to the Web-page image in code line 35.

8. Lines 39–55 define the `startTheShow()` function. This is the main function of the program that starts the animation sequence. It calls the `wait()` and `closeup()` functions in code lines 42 and 43, respectively. It also loads up the last Web page in code lines 50–53, after the animation sequence is complete.

9. Lines 58–60 create a new popup window and call lines 64–73 to add a title and a message as content for the popup window.

10. Lines 76–83 define the `wait()` function, which uses the system clock to control the display of a new popup window every 3 seconds (3000 milliseconds).

11. Lines 86–91 close the current window.

12. Line 98 uses the `onMouseOver` event with the `<img>` tag.

13. Line 100 uses the `onClick` event with the `<a>` tag.

`lastPage.html` code:

1. Lines 11–13 define the `goBack()` function, which uses the `history` object in line 12.

2. Line 20 uses the `onClick` event with the `<a>` tag.

Discussion:

This example uses two Web pages and seven popups. The main Web page has the `Start The Show` link. When the Web surfer clicks it, the JavaScript interpreter calls the `startTheShow()` function, in the `tutorial2391.html` file. This function controls the entire program's execution. It creates six popups in code lines 40–44, each with a title and content. Code lines 58–61 create each popup, and code lines 64–73 add the title and content to it. Code line 42 calls `wait()`, which sets the time interval between the animation frames to 3 seconds. The `getTime()` method (code lines 77 and 80) of the `Date` object allows us to implement the idea of the time interval (lag) by using a `do ... while` loop (code lines 78–82). Code line 43 closes each popup after the 3-second interval by calling the `closePopUp()` method. Code lines 87–89 close the popup and set `currentWindow` to null in order to ensure that code line 87 is executed only if there is an open popup.

The `startTheShow()` function continues execution at code line 47. It creates the seventh (the last) popup and closes it after 3 seconds (code lines 48 and 49). It finally displays `lastPage.html` by executing code lines 50–53 and then stops. These lines extract the host name of the current Web page and add it to `lastPage.html`. Let us assume that the current URL is `http://www.aaa.bbb/example3291.html`. This URL is a location object. Code line 50 converts it to a string, via the `toString()` method, so we can manipulate it.

Code line 51 locates the index of "/" in the string, and code line 52 extracts the "`http://www.aaa.bbb/`" and adds "`lastPage.html`" to it, resulting in the "`http://www.aaa.bbb/lastPage.hml`" string, which is a valid URL. Code line 53 converts the string back to a URL, effectively displaying it in the browser window.

Once the `lastPage.html` Web page is displayed, its `Go back` hyperlink (code line 20 in the `lastPage.html` file) uses the `history` object (code line 12) to display the `example2391.html` Web page again if the Web surfer clicks the hyperlink. Code lines 17 and 18 simply add more content to the Web page, in addition to the hyperlink.

Hands-on exercise:

As the `tutorial2391.html` code shows, the current popup has a fixed size (code line 59), one background color (yellow, set in code line 71), and a predefined location (code line 41). Modify the code so that the popup has a random size, a random background color, and a random location. Check, in the code, to make sure that the popup is always visible on the computer screen; it should not be positioned outside the edges of the screen.

```
1   <?xml version="1.0" encoding="iso-8859-1"?>  | totorial2391.html |
2   <!DOCTYPE html PUBLIC "-//W3C//DTD XHTML 1.1//EN"
3       "http://www.w3.org/TR/xhtml11/DTD/xhtml11.dtd">
4   <html xmlns="http://www.w3.org/1999/xhtml">
5   <!-- Generated by AceHTM http://freeware.acehtml.com -->
6   <head>
7   <meta http-equiv="Content-Type" content="text/html;
    charset=iso-8859-1" />
8   <title>Creating Random Popups</title>
9   <script language="javascript">
10
11  numberOfWindows = 6;
12  numberOfImages = 3;
13  currentWindow = null;
14  currentImage = 0;
15
16  //List of popup messages
17  messages = new Array(numberOfWindows);
18  messages[0] = "Did you know that one out of two babies born in
    America uses a cradle?";
19  messages[1] = "In 1980, 10 percent of the baby girls born were
    named Layla.";
20  messages[2] = "Nobody in 1975 shot a sheriff.";
21  messages[3] = "10,000 babies born in 1997 had their father's
    eyes.";
22  messages[4] = "What guitar legend loves the blues?";
23  messages[5] = "If you guessed Eric Clapton, you are absolutely
    correct!";
24
25  //List of images to cycle through
```

```
26   myImages = new Array(numberOfImages);
27   myImages[0] = "eric.jpg";
28   myImages[1] = "jewel.jpg";
29   myImages[2] = "halloween.jpg";
30
31   //onMouseover, cycle through the image list
32   function switchImage(){
33       currentImage++;
34       if (currentImage >= numberOfImages) currentImage = 0;
35       document.images[0].src=myImages[currentImage];
36   }
37
38   //Start the animation
39   function startTheShow(){
40           for (i = 0; i < messages.length; i ++) {
41               createPopupWindow("Little Known Facts",
     messages[i], 30, 170 + i*70);
42               wait(3);
43               closePopup();
44           } //for
45
46       //Goto the last page
47       createPopupWindow("Location transition", "Taking you to the
     last page...", 700, 240);
48       wait(3);
49       closePopup();
50       newLoc = location.toString();
51       pos = newLoc.lastIndexOf('/');
52       newLoc = newLoc.substring(0,pos+1) + "lastPage.html"
53       location = newLoc;
54
55   }
56
57   //Create a popup window
58   function createPopupWindow(windowTitle, windowMessage, left,
     top){
59       currentWindow = window.open("", "",
     "scrollbars=yes,height=50,width=300,left=" +left +",top=" +top);
60       writeToPopupWindow(windowTitle, windowMessage);
61   }
62
63   //Fill in the document of the popup
64   function writeToPopupWindow(windowTitle, windowMessage){
65   newContent = "<html><head><title>" + windowTitle +
     "</title></head>";
66           newContent += '<body>'
67           newContent += windowMessage;
68           newContent += "</body></html>"
```

```
69
70                currentWindow.document.write (newContent);
71                currentWindow.document.bgColor = "#FFFF00";
72                currentWindow.document.close ();
73     }
74
75     //Wait for some seconds
76     function wait(waitSeconds){
77         startTime = new Date().getTime();
78         do
79             {
80                     currentTime = new Date().getTime();
81             }
82         while(currentTime - startTime <= (waitSeconds*1000))
83     }
84
85     //Close the current popup window
86     function closePopup (){
87         if (currentWindow != null){
88             currentWindow.close ();
89             currentWindow = null;
90         } //if
91     }
92
93     </script>
94     </head>
95     <body background="bground.gif">
96     <h4 align="center">Center for Popups.
97     Move the mouse cursor over this image to change it.
98     <div><img src="eric.jpg" width="73" height="112" onMouseOver=
       "switchImage()"></div>
99     <div>Please do not close the popup windows. They will
       automatically be displayed and closed every 3 seconds.</div>
100    <a href="#" onClick="startTheShow()">Start the show </a>
101    </h4>
102    </body>
103    </html>
```

```
1    <?xml version="1.0" encoding="iso-8859-1"?>
2    <!DOCTYPE html PUBLIC "-//W3C//DTD XHTML 1.1//EN"   lastPage.html
3        "http://www.w3.org/TR/xhtml11/DTD/xhtml11.dtd">
4    <html xmlns="http://www.w3.org/1999/xhtml">
5    <!-- Generated by AceHTM http://freeware.acehtml.com -->
6    <head>
7    <meta http-equiv="Content-Type" content="text/html;
     charset=iso-8859-1" />
8    <title>Last Page</title>
9    <script language="javascript">
```

```
10
11    function goBack(){
12        history.back();
13    }
14    </script>
15    </head>
16    <body background="bground.gif">
17    <h4 align="center">Thanks for taking me to the last page.
18    <div><img src="halloween.jpg" width="145" height="223"></div>
19    <div></div>
20    <a href="#" onClick="goBack()">Go back</a>
21    </h4>
22    </form>
23    </body>
24    </html>
```

FAQs

window Object (Section 23.5)

Q: I cannot get a popup window to open via the `window.open` method. What is wrong?
A: Check the features string of the method very carefully. Make sure that there is no whitespace in it and that all features are separated by commas.

Blackbox

Section 23.1 (Introduction): Popup windows are useful in some Web applications, as they grab the attention of Web surfers.

Section 23.2 (Browser-Related Objects) (Example 23.1): The `navigator` object contains information about the client-side browser in use. Its **properties** are `appCodeName`, `appName`, `appVersion`, `language`, `mimeType`, `platform`, `plugins`, and `user-Agent`. Its **methods** are `javaEnabled()`, `preference()`, and `taintEnabled()`.

Section 23.3 (`location` Object) (Example 23.2): The `location` object represents the URL of a browser a window. Its **properties** are `hash`, `host`, `hostname`, `href`, `path-name`, `port`, `protocol`, and `search`. Its **methods** are `reload()` and `replace()`.

Section 23.4 (`history` Object) (Example 23.3): The `history` object stores the history list of a browser window. Its **properties** are `length`, `current`, `next`, and `previous`. Its **methods** are `back()`, `forward()`, and `go()`.

Section 23.5 (`window` Object) (Examples 23.4–23.5): The `window` object represents a browser window. Its **properties** are `closed`, `defaultStatus`, `document`, `frames`, `history`, `innerHeight`, `innerWidth`, `length`, `location`, `location-bar`, `menubar`, `name`, `opener`, `outerHeight`, `outerWidth`, `pageXOffset`, pageYOffset, parent, personalbar, scrollbars, self, status, statusbar, toolbar, top, and window. Its **methods** are alert(), back(), blur(x), captureEvents(), clearInterval(), clearTimeout(), close(), confirm(), disableExternalCapture(), enableExternalCapture(), find(), focus(), forward(), handleEvent(), home(), moveBy(), moveTo(), open(), print(), propmt(), releaseEvents(), resizeBy(), resizeTo(), routeEvent(), scroll(), scrollBy(), scrollTo(), setInterval(), setTimeout(), and stop().

Section 23.6 (Frame Objects) (Example 23.6): JavaScript considers a frame as a window. Use parent or top to refer to a frame set.

Section 23.7 (Including JavaScript Files) (Example 23.7): Store JavaScript code in .js files. Use <script src="xxx.js"> to access them, where xxx is the file name.

Section 23.8 (DHTML): DHTML is loosely defined to include CSS, content positioning (layers), downloadable fonts, event handlers, and other dynamic actions.

Section 23.9 (Tutorials): One tutorial shows how to use the window object.

Quick reference for the syntax presented in this chapter

Object	Item	Name	Description	Example
navigator	Variables	appCodeName	browser code name	navigator.appCodeName
		appName	browser name	navigator.appName
		appVersion	browser version	navigator.appVersion
		language	browser language	navigator.language
		mimeTypes	supported MIME type	navigator.mimeType
		platform	browser OS	navigator.platform
		plugins	browser plug-ins	navigator.lpugins
		userAgent	user-agent header	navigator.userAgent
	Methods	javaEnabled()	checks if Java is enabled in the browser	navigator.clear()
		preference()	sets the browser preferences	navigator.preference()
		taintEnabled()	determines whether data tainting is enabled	navigator.taintEnabled()
location	Variables	hash, host, hostname, href, pathname, port, protocol, and search		
	Methods	reload() and replace()		

Object	Item	Name	Description	Example
`history`	Variables	`current`		
`history`	Variables	`length`	length of history list	`history.length`
		`current`	current URL in history list	`history.current`
		`next`	next URL in history list	`history.next`
		`previous`	previous URL in history list	`history.previous`
	Methods	`back()`, `forward()`, and `go()`		
`window`	Variables	`closed`, `defaultStatus`, `document`, `frames`, `history`, `innerHeight`, `innerwidth`, `length`, `location`, `locationbar`, `menubar`, `name`, `opener`, `outerHeight`, `outerWidth`, `pageXOffset`, `pageYOffset`, `parent`, `personalbar`, `scrollbars`, `self`, `status`, `statusbar`, `toolbar`, `top`, and `window`		
	Methods	`alert()`, `back()`, `blur(x)`, `captureEvents()`, `clearInterval()`, `clearTimeout()`, `close()`, `confirm()`, `disableExternalCapture()`, `enableExternalCapture()`, `find()`, `focus()`, `forward()`, `handleEvent()`, `home()`, `moveBy()`, `moveTo()`, `open()`, `print()`, `propmt()`, `releaseEvents()`, `resizeBy()`, `resizeTo()`, `routeEvent()`, `scroll()`, `scrollBy()`, `scrollTo()`, `setInterval()`, `setTimeout()`, and `stop()`		

Check Your Progress

At the end of this chapter, you should

- ✔ understand popup windows (Section 23.1);
- ✔ understand the browser-related objects (Section 23.2);
- ✔ understand the `location` object (Section 23.3);
- ✔ understand the `history` object (Section 23.4);
- ✔ have mastered use of the `window` and frame objects (Sections. 23.5–23.6);
- ✔ have mastered use of the `.js` files(Section 23.7);
- ✔ understand DHTML (Section 23.8);
- ✔ have practiced using the `window` object (Section 23,9).

Problems

The exercises are designed for a lab setting, while the homework is to be done outside class time.

Exercises

23.1 Write a JavaScript application that retrieves the browser language.

23.2 Write a JavaScript application that retrieves the URL of the current Web page in a browser window.

23.3 Write a JavaScript application that retrieves the inner width and height of the current browser window.

23.4 Write a JavaScript application that retrieves the outer width and height of the current browser window.

23.5 Write a JavaScript application that retrieves the status text of a browser window.

Homework

23.6 Write a JavaScript application that checks whether the client browser is IE or Netscape.

23.7 Write a JavaScript application that retrieves the protocol of the URL of the current Web page in a browser window.

23.8 Write a JavaScript application that scales the current browser window by half.

23.9 Write a JavaScript application that retrieves the default status message of a browser window.

23.10 Write a JavaScript application that retrieves the length of a browser window.

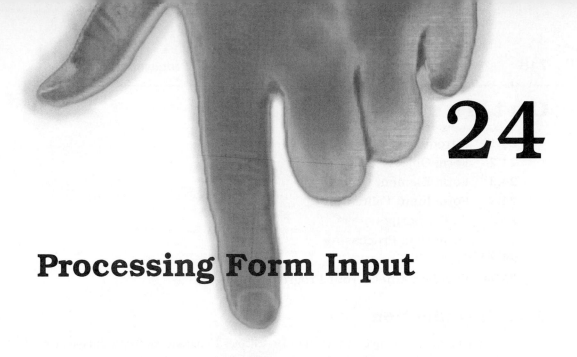

Processing Form Input

Goal

Understand JavaScript's `Form` object, the objects that correspond to form elements, client-side validation of form input, server-side storage of form data in a spreadsheet or a database, and the difference between header and footer scripts.

Objectives

- Back end of a Form
- Form object
- Objects of form elements
- Form input validation
- Accessing form elements in JavaScript: footer scripts
- Processing form data
- Processing needs: languages (Perl, PHP, and Java) and databases (Excel, and mySQL)
- Practice form validation and processing techniques

Outline

24.1 Introduction

We have covered forms in multiple chapters thus far. Chapter 15 introduced forms and their elements and discussed the front and back ends of forms. This chapter focused on the front end of a form and showed how to create all possible form elements. Chapter 18 focused on the back end of a form. It showed how the name/value pairs of a form input can be processed on the server side and how a CGI script sends a response to the client that has submitted the form.

While this coverage of forms may seem complete and comprehensive, it is not. We are still missing two important aspects of forms, if we want to be able to use them in practical and commercial applications. The first aspect is validating form input. How can we ensure that a Web surfer who fills in a form has done so correctly? Sure, a CGI script can decode a string of name/value pairs. But how good is the string if the input is wrong? We refer to a bad-input situation as GIGO (garbage in, garbage out). The second aspect is how to store the form's data in a spreadsheet or a database. We cover both aspects in detail here.

24.2 Form Object

Each form in a document creates a `Form` object. This object is a property of the **document** object, as shown in Figure 22.3. We can refer to form objects in a Web page by their names or by an associative array. JavaScript provides an array called `forms` for storing form objects, because a document can contain more than one form. The first form (the topmost in the Web page) is `forms[0]`, the second is `forms[1]`, and so forth. If a document has a form called `myForm`, we can refer to the form as `document.myForm` or `document.forms[0]`.

Table 24.1 summarizes the properties and methods of the form object. Notice that some of the method names are similar to event-handler names. For example, there is a `submit()` method and an `onSubmit` event-handler name. Here is how we use each:

```
<form name="myForm" onSubmit="validate()">
<form type="text" name="first" value="abe">
if (document.myForm.first.vlaue!="abe") document.myForm.submit();
```

Table 24.1   Form object's properties and methods.

properties: `action`, `elements`, `encoding`, `length`, `method`, `name`, and `target`
methods: `handleEvent()`, `reset()`, and `submit()`

Properties and methods	Name	Description
Properties	`action`	Reflects the `action` attribute—e.g., `myForm.action`
	`elements`	Array of form elements—e.g., `myForm.elements[i]`
	`encoding`	Reflects the `enctype` attribute—e.g., `myForm.encoding`
	`length`	The number of elements in a form—e.g., `myForm.length`
	`method`	Reflects the `method` attribute—e.g., `myForm.method`
	`name`	Reflects the `name` attribute—e.g., `myForm.name`
	`target`	Reflects the `target` attribute—e.g., `myForm.target`
Methods	`handleEvent()`	Invokes the handler for the specific event—e.g., `myForm.handleEvent()`
	`reset()`	Resets the form—e.g., `myForm.reset()`
	`submit()`	Submits the form—e.g., `myForm.submit()`

24.3 Form-Element Objects

Each element of a form creates a form-element object. These objects are shown in Figure 22.3. As with the form object, we can refer to each element by its name or by the `elements` associative array. The first form element (the topmost in the form, regardless of what it is) is `elements[0]`, the second is `elements[1]`, and so forth. For example, if a document has a form called `myForm` and the third element of the form is called `myElement`, we can refer to the element as `document.myForm.myElement` or `document.forms[0].elements[2]`.

Table 24.2 summarizes the properties and methods of the form-element objects. Notice that some of the method names are similar to event-handler names. For example, there is a `click()` method and an `onClick` event-handler name. Here is how we use each:

```
<input type="button" name="sport" value="golf" onClick="abc()">
if (xxx == yyy) document.myForm.sport.click();
```

24.4 Form Input Validation

JavaScript is a very valuable tool that enables us to validate form input at the client side, before sending it to the server. We can check for wrong input, missing input values, or both. We experience this validation all the time when we fill in forms online. If the input is wrong or incomplete, we are asked to correct or complete the form. Wrong input includes wrong data type (e.g., a number is required, but a string is entered) and wrong values (13 digits for a credit card number instead of 15 or 16). If the input is correct, a thank-you message is displayed and the form input is processed.

Table 24.2 Form-element object's properties and methods.

Form-element objects are text field, text area, password, checkbox, radio button, button, submit button, reset button, hidden, file, select list, and option.

Object	Item	Name	Description
text field text area password	Properties	defaultValue	Reflects the value attribute
		form	Specifies the form containing the element
		name	Reflects the name attribute
		type	Reflects the type attribute
		value	Reflects the current value
	Methods	blur()	Removes focus from the text field
		focus()	Adds focus to the text field
		handleEvent()	Invokes the handler for a specific event
		select()	Selects the input area of the text field
checkbox radio button	Properties	checked	Boolean reflecting the element's state
		defaultChecked	Boolean reflecting the checked attribute
		form	Specifies the form containing the element
		name	Reflects the name attribute
		type	Reflects the type attribute
		value	Reflects the current value
	Methods	blur()	Removes focus from the text field
		click()	Simulates a mouse-button click on the checkbox
		focus()	Adds focus to the text field
		handleEvent()	Invokes the handler for a specific event
button submit button reset button	Properties	form	Specifies the form containing the element
		name	Reflects the name attribute
		type	Reflects the type attribute
		value	Reflects the current value
	Methods	blur()	Removes focus from the text field
		click()	Simulates a mouse-button click on the checkbox
		focus()	Adds focus to the text field
		handleEvent()	Invokes the handler for a specific event

Table 24.2   Form-element object's properties and methods. (Continued)

Form-element objects are text field, text area, password, checkbox, radio button, button, submit button, reset button, hidden, file, select list, and option.

Object	Item	Name	Description
hidden	Properties	`form`	Specifies the form containing the element
		`name`	Reflects the `name` attribute
		`type`	Reflects the `type` attribute
		`value`	Reflects the current `value`
	Methods	`none`	
file	Properties	`form`	Specifies the form containing the element
		`name`	Reflects the `name` attribute
		`type`	Reflects the `type` attribute
		`value`	Reflects the current `value`
	Methods	`blur()`	Removes focus from the text field
		`focus()`	Adds focus to the text field
		`handleEvent()`	Invokes the handler for a specific event
		`select()`	Selects the input area of the file field
select list	Properties	`form`	Specifies the form containing the element
		`length`	Reflects the number of options in the list
		`name`	Reflects the `name` attribute
		`options`	Reflects the `option` tags
		`selectedIndex`	Reflects the index of the selected option, or the first selected option if multiple options are selected
		`type`	Specifies if the selection from the list is single or multiple
	Methods	`blur()`	Removes focus from the text field
		`focus()`	Adds focus to the text field
		`handleEvent()`	Invokes the handler for a specific event
option	Properties	`defaultSelected`	Specifies the initial selection state of the option
		`selected`	States the current selection state of the option
		`text`	Specifies the text of the option
		`value`	Reflects the `value` attribute
	Methods	`none`	

As Table 21.3 shows, there are two events associated with the `Form` object: `onReset` and `onSubmit`. Because the `<form>` tag creates the `Form` object, these two events are used with event handlers inside the `<form>` tag. The `onSubmit` event is key to validating form input, using JavaScript on the client side, as follows:

```
<form name="f" onSubmit="return(validate())" action="CGIScript">
```

The `validate()` function returns `true` if the form input is correct and complete; otherwise, it returns `false`. A `false` return disables the `action` attribute of the `<form>` tag and stops the name/value pairs from being sent to the server for processing. The `false` return also prevents the partially wrong input from being erased; that is, it prevents the form from being to its default state. This retention of the input values allows the user simply to correct the mistakes or input missing values and resubmit the form, a much easier task than filling out the entire form all over again.

We now focus our attention on the form validation process itself. The `<form>` tag creates the form itself. The `<input>`, `<select>`, and `<textarea>` tags create the form elements. Each of these tags has events associated with it, as listed in Table 21.3. The validation process begins by including an event handler with one of these tags. When the user generates the event associated with the event handler—for example, by clicking a button on the form, the event handler function—for example, `validate()`—is invoked and performs the checking.

We can validate form input at the form or element level. At the form level, we wait until the form user fills in the entire form and clicks the form's submit button. For this level, we use an `onSubmit` event handler that we add to the `<form>` tag. At the element level, we check the input for each and every element as the user inputs it. For this level, we use an element event that is specific to the element. We include the event-handler function in the element tag—for example, `<input type="button" onClick="vallidate()">` for a button.

Which level is better for validation? Practice has shown that validation at the form level is better. It becomes annoying and distracting to the user to be constantly prompted by messages warning of wrong input. Form-level validation mimics the experience of paper forms. We typically fill out a form on paper in its entirety and then look it over for errors.

We can design a form validation function in many ways. The central design structure is to pass user input to the function in a function call. Two design styles exist. First, the function could have arguments. In this style, we can pass an entire `Form` object, a form-element object, or just a value (property) of an element. The following three XHTML tags show the three cases, respectively:

```
<form name="myForm" onSubmit="return(validate(myForm))">
<input type="radio" name="sports" onClick="validate(sports)">
<input type="radio" name="sports" onClick="validate(sports.value)">
```

As shown in the third tag, we use the short dot notation to get to the form or the element object whose value we want to process. We can also use the long dot notation to traverse the

DOM tree hierarchy. With this method, the three foregoing tags become, respectively,

```
<form name="myForm" onSubmit="return(validate(document.myForm))">
<input type="radio" name="sports" onClick="validate(docu-
    ment.myForm.sports)">
<input type="radio" name="sports" onClick="validate(docu-
    ment.myForm.sports.value)">
```

We can also use the `this` reference. `this` takes the context of the XHTML tag with which it is used. If it is used in a `<form>` tag, it refers to the `Form` object. If it is used in the `<input>`, `<select>`, or `<textarea>` tag, it refers to the element object. The three foregoing tags can be rewritten using `this` as follows, respectively:

```
<form name="myForm" onSubmit="return(validate(this))">
<input type="radio" name="sports" onClick="validate(this)">
<input type="radio" name="sports" onClick="this.value)">
```

The second design style of the event-handler function uses no arguments—for example, `validate()`. In this case, the full long dot notation is used in the function body to access the form input and validate it.

There are no clear benefits to either style. The choice of style is a personal preference.

The remainder of this section presents an example for each form element, to show how to validate its input at the form level. Combining all the examples into one produces a function that can handle any form element, as shown in Section 24.7. The examples and tutorials we cover here are the same ones we used in Chapter 15, to provide continuity of coverage for better understanding.

Example 24.1 Validate the value of a text field.

Write a JavaScript program that validates the value of a text-field element of a form.

Solution 24.1 Retrieve your `example151.html` code. Using the AceHTML editor, edit it to generate the given code, and save it as `example241.html`. Render the Web page in a browser.

Code explained:

1. Lines 11–17 define the `isBlankField()` function, which returns `false` if the form's text-field element is left blank.
2. Lines 23–62 define the form's `validate()` function.
3. Lines 24 and 25 initialize `sErrText` (accumulates missing-data messages) and `bRetCode` (Boolean—returns either `true`, as in code lines 59 and 61, or `false`, as in code line 25).
4. Lines 28–42 check the input in all of the form's text fields by calling the `isBlankField()` function once for each text field.
5. Line 47 lists the missing data.

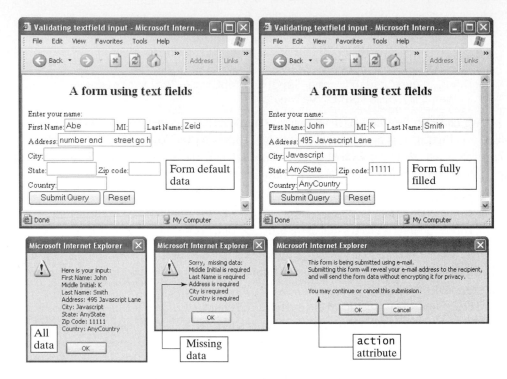

6. Lines 49–58 build the input string and print it, if no input is missing.

7. Line 68 uses the submit event to call `validate()`.

8. Lines 68–79 have been explained in Example 15.1.

Discussion:

The `validate()` function checks if the user has filled in the form elements. To do so, it calls the `isBlankField()` function, which checks the text fields. It retrieves the current value of a text field (code line13) and compares it with the empty string, `""`. We use this method throughout the examples and the tutorial in this chapter. We write a function for each form element, and we call it in `validate()`. We keep using `validate()` throughout the examples and the tutorial, but we replace its old code with the new code in each case, for ease of learning.

If any text fields are left blank, `validate()` informs the user; otherwise, it prints all of the user's input for a final check by the user. The return value (code line 61) is captured by the `return` statement in code line 68. If it is `true`, the form is submitted by executing the `action` attribute (as shown in the foregoing set of screen captures); otherwise, the submission is aborted. We can achieve the same results by using `onClick="return(validate())"` in the tag of the submit button.

The one thing that `validate()` does not do is check if the input is correct. For example, the user can input characters for a zip code instead of numbers. However, we can extend it to accomplish this task, as you will demonstrate in the Hand-on exercise.

Hands-on exercise:

Write another function, checkZipCode(), to ensure that we receive five digits for the zip code. Limit the function to checking for five digits; do not have it determine whether the digits are actually correct.

```
1   <?xml version="1.0" encoding="iso-8859-1"?>
2   <!DOCTYPE html PUBLIC "-//W3C//DTD XHTML 1.1//EN"
3       "http://www.w3.org/TR/xhtml11/DTD/xhtml11.dtd">
4   <html xmlns="http://www.w3.org/1999/xhtml">
5   <!-- Generated by AceHTM http://freeware.acehtml.com -->
6   <head>
7   <title>Validating textfield input</title>
8   <script language="javascript">
9
10  //check text-field input
11  function isBlankField(textObj)
12  {
13    if (textObj.value == "")
14      return true;
15    else
16      return false;
17  }
18
19  //**********************************
20  //Top-Level FORM Validation Function
21  //Calls the separate functions above.
22  //**********************************
23  function validate(formObj){
24    sErrText = ''; // Build error message - present all errors.
25    bRetCode = false; // set to true, if pass all validations
26
27    //Validate text fields
28    if (isBlankField(formObj.firstName))
29      sErrText += "\nFirst Name is required";
30      if (isBlankField(formObj.middleInitial))
31      sErrText += "\nMiddle Initial is required";
32    if (isBlankField(formObj.lastName))
33      sErrText += "\nLast Name is required";
34    if (isBlankField(formObj.address))
35      sErrText += "\nAddress is required";
36    if (isBlankField(formObj.city))
37      sErrText += "\nCity is required";
38    if (isBlankField(formObj.state))
39      sErrText += "\nState is required";
40    if (isBlankField(formObj.zipCode))
41      sErrText += "\nZip Code is required";
```

```
42      if (isBlankField(formObj.country))
43        sErrText += "\nCountry is required";
44
45   //If there are validation errors, sErrText holds them.
46      if (sErrText.length > 0)
47        alert("Sorry, missing data:" + sErrText);
48      else {
49          str = "\nHere is your input:";
50          str += "\nFirst Name: " + formObj.firstName.value;
51          str += "\nMiddle Initial: " + formObj.middleInitial.value;
52          str += "\nLast Name: " + formObj.lastName.value;
53          str += "\nAddress: " + formObj.address.value;
54          str += "\nCity: " + formObj.city.value;
55          str += "\nState: " + formObj.state.value;
56          str += "\nZip Code: " + formObj.zipCode.value;
57          str += "\nCountry: " + formObj.country.value;
58          alert(str);
59          bRetCode = true; //Set true enables submitting form!
60      }//else
61      return bRetCode;
62   }//validate()
63
64   </script>
65   </head>
66   <body>
67   <h2 align="center">A form using text fields</h2>
68   <form name="myForm" method="post"
     onSubmit="return(validate(myForm))"
     action="mailto:zeid@coe.neu.edu">
69   Enter your name:<br />
70   First Name:<input name="firstName" value="Abe" size="10" />
71   MI:<input type="text" name="middleInitial" size="1" />
72   Last Name:<input type="text" name="lastName" value="Zeid"
     size="10" maxlength="15" /><br />
73   Address:<input type="text" name="address" value="number and
     street go here" size="22" maxlength="30" /><br />
74   City:<input type="text" name="city" size="10"
     maxlength="15" /><br />
75   State:<input type="text" name="state" size="10"
     maxlength="15" />
76   Zip code:<input type="text" name="zipCode" size="5"
     maxlength="10" /><br />
77   Country:<input type="text" name="country" size="10"
     maxlength="15" /><br />
78   <input type="submit" name="submitButton" />
79   <input type="reset" name="resetButton" />
80   </form>
81   </body>
82   </html>
```

Example 24.2 Validate the value and state of a checkbox.

Write a JavaScript program that validates the value and state of a checkbox.

Solution 24.2 Retrieve your `example152.html` code. Using the AceHTML editor, edit it to generate the given code, and save it as `example242.html`. Render the Web page in a browser.

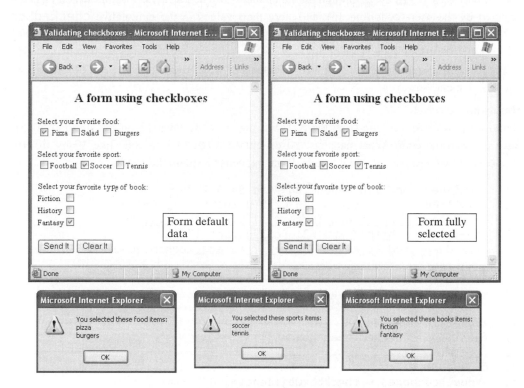

Code explained:

1. Lines 11–20 define the `isChecked()` function, which finds and prints the values of the checkboxes.
2. Line 13 defines `checkedStr` as an empty string.
3. Line 14 retrieves the length of the `checkboxObj` array.
4. Line 16 determines which checkbox the user has checked off (selected).
5. Line 17 stores the value of the selected (in line 16) checkbox in the `checkedStr` string.
6. Lines 29–31 validate the three groups of checkboxes that the Web page uses in lines 42–44, 46–48, and 50–52, respectively.

Discussion:

The validate() function determines which checkboxes are selected. It calls the isChecked() function three times. Each time, it passes the value of the name attribute of a checkbox group. When we use the same value of the name attribute for more than one form element, JavaScript creates an array whose name is the attribute's value and whose length is equal to the number of elements. Here, JavaScript creates food, sports, and books arrays, each with three elements. We use these arrays in the three function calls in code lines 29–31.

Code lines 15–18 cycle through all the elements of each array, determine which ones are selected by the user (code line 16), and store their values in the cumulative checkedStr (which we initialize in code line 13, so that we can use it as an accumulator in code line 17). Code line 19 prints the final value of this string. This line accesses the name of a group of checkboxes by using the name of the first array element, checkboxObj[0]; we could have used another element, however.

Hands-on exercise:

Remove the value attribute from the XHTML tags in code lines 42–44, 46–48, and 50–52. Save and run the code. What happens? Also, replace alert() in code line 19 by document.write(). Save and run the code. What happens? Explain the results.

```
1   <?xml version="1.0" encoding="iso-8859-1"?>
2   <!DOCTYPE html PUBLIC "-//W3C//DTD XHTML 1.1//EN"
3       "http://www.w3.org/TR/xhtml11/DTD/xhtml11.dtd">
4   <html xmlns="http://www.w3.org/1999/xhtml">
5   <!-- Generated by AceHTM http://freeware.acehtml.com -->
6   <head>
7   <title>Validating checkboxes</title>
8   <script language="javascript">
9
10  //check checkboxes
11  function isChecked(checkboxObj){
12
13  checkedStr="";
14    numCheckboxes = checkboxObj.length;
15    for (i=0; i<numCheckboxes; i++) {
16      if (checkboxObj[i].checked)
17          checkedStr += "\n" + checkboxObj[i].value;
18    } //for
19    alert ("You selected these " + checkboxObj[0].name + " items:
    " + checkedStr);
20  } //isChecked()
21
22  /****************************************
23  *Top-Level FORM Validation Function
24  *Calls the separate functions above.
25  ****************************************/
26  function validate(formObj){
```

```
27
28    //Validate checkboxes
29    isChecked(formObj.food);
30    isChecked(formObj.sports);
31    isChecked(formObj.books);
32
33  }//validate()
34
35  </script>
36  </head>
37  <body>
38  <h2 align="center">A form using checkboxes</h2>
39  <form name="myForm" method="post"
40  onSubmit="validate(myForm)" action="mailto:zeid@coe.neu.edu">
41  <div>Select your favorite food:</div>
42  <input type="checkbox" name="food" value="pizza" checked />
      Pizza
43  <input type="checkbox" name="food" value="salad" />Salad
44  <input type="checkbox" name="food" value="burgers" />
      Burgers<br /><p></p>
45  <div>Select your favorite sport:</div>
46  <input type="checkbox" name="sports" value="football" />Football
47  <input type="checkbox" name="sports" value="soccer" checked
      />Soccer
48  <input type="checkbox" name="sports" value="tennis"
      />Tennis<p></p>
49  <div>Select your favorite type of book:</div>
50  Fiction  <input type="checkbox" name="books"
      value="fiction" /><br />
51  History <input type="checkbox" name="books" value="history"
      /><br />
52  Fantasy<input type="checkbox" name="books" value="fantasy" checked
      /><br />
53  <p></p>
54  <input type="submit" name="submitButton" value="Send It" />
55  <input type="reset" name="resetButton" value="Clear It" />
56  </form>
57  </body>
58  </html>
```

☞──

Example 24.3 Validate the value and state of a radio button.

Write a JavaScript program that validates the value and state of a radio button.

Solution 24.3 Retrieve your example153.html code. Using the AceHTML editor, edit it to generate the given code, and save it as example243.html. Render the Web page in a browser.

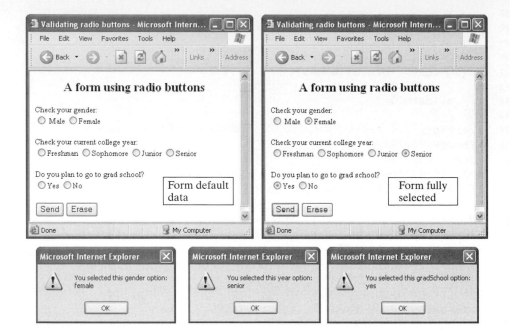

Code explained:

Refer to Example 24.2.

Discussion:

The JavaScript code for this example is identical to that of Example 24.2, with the exception of two changes: We replace `checkbox` by `radioButton` in code lines 11–19, and we use different group names in code lines 29–31. These names come from the XHTML `value` attributes used in code lines 41–42, 45–48, and 50–51.

Hands-on exercise:

Remove the `value` attribute from the XHTML tags in code lines 41–42, 45–48, and 50–51. Save and run the code. What happens? Also, replace `alert()` in code line 19 by `document.write()`. Save and run the code. What happens? Explain the results.

```
1   <?xml version="1.0" encoding="iso-8859-1"?>
2   <!DOCTYPE html PUBLIC "-//W3C//DTD XHTML 1.1//EN"
3       "http://www.w3.org/TR/xhtml11/DTD/xhtml11.dtd">
4   <html xmlns="http://www.w3.org/1999/xhtml">
5   <!-- Generated by AceHTM http://freeware.acehtml.com -->
6   <head>
7   <title>Validating radio buttons</title>
8   <script language="javascript">
9
10  //check radio buttons
```

```
11    function isChecked(radioButtonObj){
12
13    checkedStr="";
14      numradioButtons = radioButtonObj.length;
15      for (i=0; i< numradioButtons; i++) {
16        if (radioButtonObj[i].checked)
17          checkedStr += "\n" + radioButtonObj[i].value;
18      } //for
19      alert ("You selected this " + radioButtonObj[0].name + " option:
      " + checkedStr);
20    } //isChecked()
21
22    /***********************************
23    *Top-Level FORM Validation Function
24    *Calls the separate functions above.
25    **********************************/
26    function validate(formObj){
27
28      //Validate radio buttons
29      isChecked(formObj.gender);
30      isChecked(formObj.year);
31      isChecked(formObj.gradSchool);
32
33    }//validate()
34
35    </script>
36    </head>
37    <body>
38    <h2 align="center">A form using radio buttons</h2>
39    <form name="myForm" method="post"    onSubmit="validate(myForm)"
      action="mailto:zeid@coe.neu.edu">
40    <div>Check your gender:</div>
41    <input type="radio" name="gender" value="male" /> Male
42    <input type="radio" name="gender" value="female" />Female
43    <p></p>
44    <div>Check your current college year:</div>
45    <input type="radio" name="year" value="freshman" />Freshman
46    <input type="radio" name="year" value="sophomore" />Sophomore
47    <input type="radio" name="year" value="junior" />Junior
48    <input type="radio" name="year" value="senior" />Senior<p></p>
49    <div>Do you plan to go to grad school?</div>
50    <input type="radio" name="gradSchool" value="yes" />Yes
51    <input type="radio" name="gradSchool" value="no" />No<p></p>
52    <input type="submit"  name="submitButton" value="Send" />
53    <input type="reset"   name="resetButton" value="Erase" />
54    </form>
55    </body>
56    </html>
```

Example 24.4 Validate button selection.

Write a JavaScript program that identifies buttons selected by a user.

Solution 24.4 Retrieve your `example156.html` code. Using the AceHTML editor, edit it to generate the given code, and save it as `example244.html`. Render the Web page in a browser.

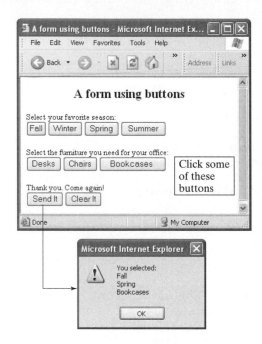

Code explained:

1. Line 11 defines and initializes `selectedStr`.
2. Line 13 accumulates the labels of clicked buttons in `selectedStr`.
3. Line 23 prints the labels of all selected buttons.
4. Line 24 resets the value of `selectedStr` back to empty.

Discussion:

The Web page of this example uses seven buttons, as shown in the foregoing screen capture. Their XHTML names are `button1–button7` (code lines 33–40). We could have used two names only to create two groups of buttons, as we did with checkboxes and radio buttons. But there is no value in using this method to validate buttons, as a button validation requires retrieving the label of the individual button after a user clicks it. The label is the `value` attribute assigned to the button in its XHTML tag, as shown in code lines 33–40.

Each button uses `isSelected()` as an `onClick` event handler. The form also uses `validate()` as an `onSubmit` event handler. Each time the user clicks a button, `isSelected()` is invoked and adds the button's label to `selectedStr`. When the user submits the form, `validate()` prints the labels of all clicked buttons and resets `selectedStr`.

Hands-on exercise:

Remove code line 24, and save and run the code. What happens? Why?

```
1    <?xml version="1.0" encoding="iso-8859-1"?>
2    <!DOCTYPE html PUBLIC "-//W3C//DTD XHTML 1.1//EN"
3        "http://www.w3.org/TR/xhtml11/DTD/xhtml11.dtd">
4    <html xmlns="http://www.w3.org/1999/xhtml">
5    <!-- Generated by AceHTM http://freeware.acehtml.com -->
6    <head>
7    <title>Validating form buttons</title>
8    <script language="javascript">
9
10   //check buttons
11   selectedStr = "";
12   function isSelected(label){
13     selectedStr += "\n" + label;
14   } //isSelected()
15
16   /*************************************
17   *Top-Level FORM Validation Function
18   *Calls the separate functions above.
19   *************************************/
20   function validate(formObj){
21
22     //Validate selected buttons
23     alert("You selected:" + selectedStr);
24     selectedStr=""; //reset value
25
26   }//validate()
27
28   </script>
29   </head>
30   <body><h2 align="center">A form using buttons</h2>
31   <form name="myForm" method="post"
     onSubmit="validate(myForm)" action="mailto:zeid@coe.neu.edu">
32   <div>Select your favorite season:</div>
33   <input type="button" name="button1" value="Fall"
     onClick="isSelected(value)" />
34   <input type="button" name="button2" value="Winter"
     onClick="isSelected(value)" />
35   <input type="button" name="button3" value="Spring"
     onClick="isSelected(value)" />
```

```
36  <input type="button" name="button4" value="Summer"
    onClick="isSelected(value)" /><p></p>
37  <div>Select the furniture you need for your office:</div>
38  <input type="button" name="button5" value="Desks"
    onClick="isSelected(value)" />
39  <input type="button" name="button6" value="Chairs"
    onClick="isSelected(value)" />
40  <input type="button" name="button7" value="Bookcases"
    onClick="isSelected(value)" />
41  <p></p>
42  <div>Thank you. Come again!</div>
43  <input type="submit" value="Send It" />
44  <input type="reset" value="Clear It" />
45  </form>
46  </body>
47  </html>
```

Example 24.5 Validate menu-item selection.

Write a JavaScript program that identifies menu items selected by a user.

Solution 24.5 Retrieve your `example157.html` code. Using the AceHTML editor, edit it to generate the given code, and save it as `example245.html`. Render the Web page in a browser.

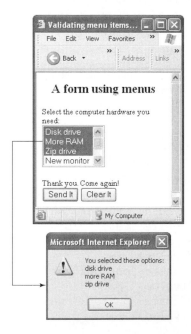

Code explained:

1. Line 13 defines and initializes `optionsStr`.
2. Line 17 accumulates the values of the selected menu items in `optionsStr`.
3. Line 19 prints the values of all selected menu items.

Discussion:

The Web page of this example uses a select list with six menu items, as shown in the foregoing screen capture. Their XHTML values are shown in code lines 40–45. A menu-item validation requires retrieving the value of the menu item after a user selects it. The value is the `value` attribute assigned to it in its XHTML tag, as shown in code lines 40–45.

JavaScript creates the `options` array, whose length is equal to the number of XHTML `<option>` tags used in the select list—six in this example. We pass this array as an argument to `isSelected()` in code line 30.

The form uses `validate()` as an `onSubmit` event handler. When the user submits the form, `validate()` calls `isSelected()`, which prints the values of all selected menu items.

Hands-on exercise:

Remove all the `value` attributes from code lines 40–45. What happens? Why?

```
1    <?xml version="1.0" encoding="iso-8859-1"?>
2    <!DOCTYPE html PUBLIC "-//W3C//DTD XHTML 1.1//EN"
3        "http://www.w3.org/TR/xhtml11/DTD/xhtml11.dtd">
4    <html xmlns="http://www.w3.org/1999/xhtml">
5    <!-- Generated by AceHTM http://freeware.acehtml.com -->
6    <head>
7    <title>Validating menu items</title>
8    <script language="javascript">
9
10   //check menu items
11   function isSelected(optionsObj){
12
13   optionsStr="";
14     numOptions = optionsObj.length;
15     for (i=0; i<numOptions; i++) {
16       if (optionsObj[i].selected)
17           optionsStr += "\n" + optionsObj[i].value;
18     } //for
19     alert ("You selected these options:" + optionsStr);
20
21   } //isSelected()
22
23   /***********************************
24   *Top-Level FORM Validation Function
```

```
25    *Calls the separate functions above.
26    ***************************************/
27    function validate(formObj){
28
29      //Validate menu items
30      isSelected(formObj.compHardware.options);
31
32    }//validate()
33
34    </script>
35    </head>
36    <body><h2 align="center">A form using menus</h2>
37    <form name="myForm" method="post" onSubmit="validate(myForm)"
      action="mailto:zeid@coe.neu.edu">
38    <div>Select the computer hardware you need:</div>
39    <select name="compHardware" multiple >
40    <option value="disk drive">Disk drive</option>
41    <option value="more RAM">More RAM</option>
42    <option value="zip drive" selected>Zip drive</option>
43    <option value="new monitor">New monitor</option>
44    <option value="faster printer">Faster printer</option>
45    <option value="new mouse">New mouse</option>
46    </select>
47    <p></p>
48    <div>Thank you. Come again!</div>
49    <input type="submit" value="Send It" />
50    <input type="reset" value="Clear It" />
51    </form>
52    </body>
53    </html>
```

Example 24.6 Validate the value of a text area.

Write a JavaScript program that validates the value of a `textarea` element of a form.

Solution 24.6 Retrieve your `example158.html` code. Using the AceHTML editor, edit it to generate the given code, that follows, and save it as `example246.html`. Render the Web page in a browser.

Code explained:

1. Line 12 ensures that there is text in the text area of the form. This text could be the seeding text or new text.
2. Line 13 prints the text area's text.

Discussion:

The Web page of this example uses a text area, as shown in the foregoing screen capture.

The text area is similar to a text field. Its text is stored in the `value` property of the `textarea` object.

The form uses `validate()` as an `onSubmit` event-handler. When the user submits the form, `validate()` calls `isBlankArea()`, which prints the current text of the text area.

Hands-on exercise:

Change the `soft` wrap in code line 33 to a `hard` wrap. Convert the inserted carriage return to `\n` in the `alert` box in order to prevent printing of the long lines of text shown in the foregoing `alert` box.

```
1   <?xml version="1.0" encoding="iso-8859-1"?>
2   <!DOCTYPE html PUBLIC "-//W3C//DTD XHTML 1.1//EN"
3       "http://www.w3.org/TR/xhtml11/DTD/xhtml11.dtd">
4   <html xmlns="http://www.w3.org/1999/xhtml">
5   <!-- Generated by AceHTM http://freeware.acehtml.com -->
6   <head>
7   <title>Validating text areas</title>
8   <script language="javascript">
9
10  //check text area
11  function isBlankArea(textareaObj){
12     if (textareaObj.value != "")
13       alert("You entered this text:\n" + textareaObj.value);
```

```
14   } //isBlankArea()
15
16   /***********************************
17   *Top-Level FORM Validation Function
18   *Calls the separate functions above.
19   ***********************************/
20   function validate(formObj){
21
22     //Validate text area
23     isBlankArea(formObj.myTextArea);
24
25   }//validate()
26
27   </script>
28   </head>
29   <body>
30   <h2 align="center">A form using text areas</h2>
31   <form name="myForm" method="post"
        onSubmit="validate(myForm)" action="mailto:zeid@coe.neu.edu">
32   <div>We love to hear from you:</div>
33   <textarea name="myTextArea" rows="7" cols="20" wrap="soft">
34   Please input up to 7 lines of text as your feedback and
        comments. Any additional lines beyond the first 10 are
        ignored by our database. Thank you for your cooperation!
35   </textarea>
36   <p></p>
37   <div>Thank you. Come again!</div>
38   <input type="submit" value="Send It" />
39   <input type="reset" value="Clear It" />
40   </form>
41   </body>
42   </html>
```

24.5 Footer Scripts

Footer scripts come after the **</body>** tag of a Web page, as opposed to header scripts, which come between the **<head>** tags and before the **<body>** tag, which is where we have been putting scripts all along so far. Footer scripts can access (see) all the XHTML objects created inside the **<body>** tag, while header scripts cannot. The only way for header scripts to access these objects is via event handlers such as **onClick**. The event-handlers can access these objects because the event handlers are not executed until all the XHTML tags are rendered, which means that all the XHTML objects are already created. If a header-script code tries to access XHTML objects before they are created, the JavaScript interpreter issues an **unde-fined** error. For example, if we make a footer script into a header script by moving it from after the **</body>** tag to before the **<body>** tag, errors occur, because the script cannot find the objects being referenced in it.

Footer scripts may not need event handlers. They can access XHTML objects in statements outside function definitions. Footer scripts have some useful applications. One of them is to place the cursor in a given form element, such as a text field, in order to guide users in filling out a form, or to focus their attention on errors made in filling out a form. The following example illustrates this idea.

Example 24.7 Use a footer script.

Write a JavaScript program that uses a footer script.

Solution 24.7 Using the AceHTML editor, generate the given code, and save it as `example247.html`. Render the Web page in a browser.

Code explained:

1. Lines 25–30 define a footer script.
2. Line 28 adds the focus to the `zip Code` text field, as shown in the foregoing screen capture.

Discussion:

The Web page of this example is the same as that of Example 24.1, without the event handlers. It uses a footer script that places the mouse cursor in the `zipCode` field. The script uses the `select()` method in code line 28. We can replace the `zipCode` name by any other text-field name in order to place the cursor there.

Table 24.2 shows all the methods that we can use with each form-element object. For this example, we could have used `focus()` instead of `select()`. Browsers exhibit inconsistent behavior, though. IE and Netscape 7.01 recognize and execute the `select()` method, while

Netscape 4.8 does not. On the other hand, Netscape 7.01 and 4.8 recognize the focus()
method, while IE does not.

Hands-on exercise:

Replace the select() method by focus(). Test the code in both the IE and Netscape
browsers. What happens? Also, change the code given in this example to place the mouse cursor
in the firstName field. Use both select() and focus(), and observe the difference.

```
1   <?xml version="1.0" encoding="iso-8859-1"?>
2   <!DOCTYPE html PUBLIC "-//W3C//DTD XHTML 1.1//EN"
3       "http://www.w3.org/TR/xhtml11/DTD/xhtml11.dtd">
4   <html xmlns="http://www.w3.org/1999/xhtml">
5   <!-- Generated by AceHTM http://freeware.acehtml.com -->
6   <head>
7   <title>Footer Script</title>
8   </head>
9   <body>
10  <h2 align="center">A form using text fields</h2>
11  <form name="myForm" method="post"
    action="mailto:zeid@coe.neu.edu">
12  Enter your name:<br />
13  First Name:<input name="firstName" value="Abe" size="10" />
14  MI:<input type="text" name="middleInitial" size="1" />
15  Last Name:<input type="text" name="lastName" value="Zeid"
    size="10" maxlength="15" /><br />
16  Address:<input type="text" name="address" value="number and
    street go here" size="22" maxlength="30" /><br />
17  City:<input type="text" name="city" size="10"
    maxlength="15" /><br />
18  State:<input type="text" name="state" size="10"
    maxlength="15" />
19  Zip code:<input type="text" name="zipCode" size="5"
    maxlength="10" /><br />
20  Country:<input type="text" name="country" size="10"
    maxlength="15" /><br />
21  <input type="submit" name="submitButton" />
22  <input type="reset" name="resetButton" />
23  </form>
24  </body>
25  <script language="javascript">
26
27  //this method call places the mouse cursor in zipCode field
28  document.myForm.zipCode.select();
29
30  </script>
31  </html>
```

24.6 Form Data Processing

Thus far, we are able to provide users with forms, validate user input via client-side JavaScript, and process the name/value pairs of form data on the server side (Chapter 18). We summarize form processing into four steps:

1. The user fills out a form (Chapter 15).

2. JavaScript verifies the user input on the client side before sending the form data to the server (Chapter 24 up to this point).

3. A CGI script processes the correct data on the server side by extracting the values (user input) from the name/value pairs (Chapter 18).

4. The values are stored in a spreadsheet or a database (this section).

We now focus our attention on form data processing. We need to be able to store the values that we extract from the name/value pairs (in step 3) in a spreadsheet or a database. This processing requires a knowledge of databases, SQL (Structured Query Language), and programming languages. Sample databases are Oracle, MySQL (Unix and Linux), and Microsoft Access and Excel (Windows). Programming languages include Perl and PHP (for Unix primarily), Servlets and JSPs (for Windows and Unix), and ASPs (for Windows).

To illustrate the ideas behind this important topic, we offer three concepts. Each concept uses a different programming language and database for data processing. The best way for readers to use these concepts is to select a programming language and a database of most interest to them and use the corresponding subsection. They should also consult with their system and database administrators about where the required libraries, databases, and cgi-bin directories are, as well as how to set database drivers, paths, and other system variables in order to run database applications.

24.6.1 Servlets and Spreadsheets

In this subsection, we use Microsoft Excel, which comes with MS Office. This approach saves us the burden of having to purchase, install, and learn how to use a database. However, we must create, configure, and load the database driver. A **database driver** is a computer program that acts as an interface between the database's native format and the application that uses it. The application sends requests (queries) to the driver in SQL format. The driver translates the queries to native format, passes them to the database, receives the results, translates them, and passes them to the application for display.

Microsoft ODBC (Open Database Connectivity) is a commonly used driver. It comes with Windows OS. Java also has its JDBC (Java Database Connectivity) driver, which builds on ODBC. It extends it by creating what is known as the JDBC–ODBC driver (bridge). Java Servlets may use the JDBC–ODBC driver to a connect to a Microsoft Excel spreadsheet.

A JDBC driver may require an ODBC driver (bridge), because they work together. Let us configure an ODBC driver for Excel on Windows XP. Double-click this sequence:

`My Computer => C:=>Documents and Settings=>All Users=>Start Menu=>Programs=>Administrative Tools`. The following screen capture shows the full path and the `ODBC` shortcut (for Windows 2000 97 and 95, the shortcut is under the `Control Panel`):

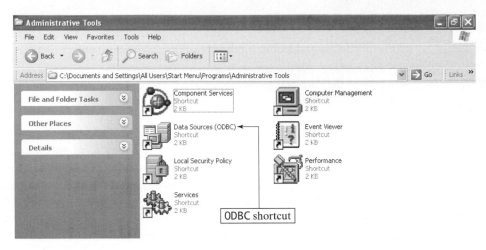

Double-click the `ODBC` shortcut to open the following window (`ODBC Data Source Administrator`), which displays the already existing data source names (`User DSN tab`) or drivers on the client (PC). Check for a Microsoft Excel database driver. There should already be one. If one does not exist, add it as follows: Click the **Add** button. This opens a new window (not shown here) that lists all the installed drivers on the client (PC). Select Microsoft Excel Driver (`*.xls`) and click the `Finish` button. The `ODBC Microsoft Excel Setup` window is opened. (See the first screen capture next page.) Type the name of choice, `Bank`, in the `Data Source Name` text field.

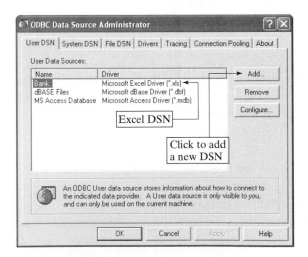

Click the `Select Workbook` button to specify an Excel sheet file. This is the file that has the database records. Click the `Options` button, and make sure to uncheck the `Read Only` checkbox (see the first screen capture in this page); otherwise, the servlet will not be able to write to the Excel file in order to update it. One tricky problem with databases is that neither the servlet nor the system generates any errors if database transactions fail during the servlet execution.

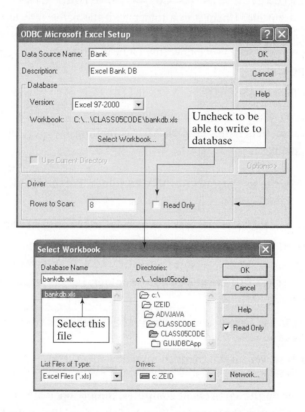

The result of the foregoing activities is an Excel spreadsheet with the name `Bank` that represents our database. This spreadsheet is also the data source name (DSN). The actual Excel file resides in the folder shown in the bottommost screen capture on this page. We open this file before and after we update it in order to ensure that the servlet has performed the planned updates.

With the configuration of the Excel database complete, we turn our attention to the Java servlet that uses it. While the servlet can query the database, the focus here is for the servlet to get the data from a form into the spreadsheet. When a Web surfer fills out the form's and submits it to the server, the form's `action` attribute executes the servlet. The servlet, in turn, retrieves the form's data and updates the database by writing the data into it as a new record.

The servlet we write inherits from the Java `HttpServlet` class that is part of the Java servlet API. This factor requires us to download and install both the Java 2 SDK (also known as the JDK) and the servlet API. We use the `j2sdk1.4.1` and the `Servlet 2.3` API. Visit `http://java.sun.com` and download and install both. While installing the j2SDK is straightforward, follow these steps for the servlet API: Click this sequence: `Downloads` (hyperlink on the top left side of the `http://java.sun.com` Web page) => `J2EE` => `Servlets Specification 2.4` => `Go` => `Download class files 2.3`. This sequence downloads a zip file. Unzip it to a folder with the name (create the folder) `javax`. Move the folder to `j2sdk1.4.1\jre\lib\ext`. Compiling a servlet's source code requires setting the path in the Windows OS window (the DOS window) by typing the following command at the system prompt:

```
set CLASSPATH=%CLASSPATH%;C:\j2sdk1.4.1\jre\lib\ext
```

The Tomcat server has containers (engines) that run both servlets and JSPs. We used JSPs in Chapter 18. We use servlets in this chapter. After compiling Java servlets, follow these steps to use Tomcat to run them:

1. **Move the HTML file to Tomcat's `servlets` folder.** Put the HTML file that uses the servlet, in its `action` attribute, in this folder:

   ```
   C:\tomcat-4.1.24\jakarta-tomcat-4.1.24\webapps\examples\servlets
   ```

2. **Compile the servlet's source code.** Compile the `.java` source file of the servlet on the client computer—for example, `>javac myServlet.java`.

3. **Move the servlet class to Tomcat's `classes` folder.** Put the resulting servlet class from step 2 in this folder:

   ```
   C:\tomcat-4.1.24\jakarta-tomcat-4.1.24\webapps\examples\WEB-
      INF\classes
   ```

4. **Run the Tomcat server on the client computer.** Follow steps 1–3 listed at the beginning of Section 18.7.2.

5. **Run the browser on the same client computer.** Simply open the browser window.

6. **Load the Web page into the browser.** Type the following URL in the browser's URL bar: `http://localhost:8080/examples/servlets/xxx.html`.

7. **Fill out and send the form.** Fill in all the form elements, and click the submit button. The `action` attribute of the `<form>` tag must reference the servlet class code as follows:

   ```
   <form action="../servlet/XxxYyy">
   ```

This path means that the servlet class code `XxxYyy` resides in the `servlet` directory that is one level above (`..`) where the form's HTML file resides (in the `servlets` folder). This path is somewhat confusing when compared with the path we use in step 3. The explanation is that Tomcat uses `servlet` as a logical (virtual) name that replaces the `WEB-IF/classes` part used in step 3. Steps 1 and 3 show that the Tomcat paths of the HTML file and its servlet are identical up to the examples directory, after which they divert. The HTML file folder (servlets) is used as a base for file-path specification because we run it first in the browser before clicking the form's submit button.

Now that we understand the client/server environment that uses an Excel ODBC driver, let us turn our attention to the servlet details. The servlet code defines, creates, opens, and uses a connection to the Excel database. It uses the JDBC API to achieve the communication with the database. The JDBC API comes bundled with Java 2 SDK 1.4.1. The servlet follows three steps to use the database: Establish a connection to the database, send SQL statements, and process the results set. These steps are general and are always used. The following example shows how to get all the concepts to work together.

Example 24.8 Use Java servlets and a Microsoft Excel spreadsheet.

Write a JavaScript program that stores form data into a database.

Solution 24.8 In this example, we develop, write, and test a database application for bank account information. We write a Java servlet that processes form input. The form receives account information from the user and employs the servlet in its action attribute in order to extract the form's data; then it updates the bank database by adding a new record to it. The user input consists of first name, last name, account number, and account balance. JavaScript verifies the user input, on the client side, before sending it to the server for processing. A Microsoft Excel database Bank is created and seeded with some initial records (rows) in it. Each record has four columns, one each for the account number, first name, last name, and account balance. New records are added to the Excel sheet automatically by the servlet. This bank application is a client/server application. We use the Tomcat server, discussed in Chapter 18. The servlet, the Web page, and the Excel sheet are hosted by Tomcat. The execution flow of the application begins when the Web page of the form is downloaded from the Tomcat server, which occurs when the user types the page's URL into the URL bar of a browser on the client side. A user then fills out the form and submits it to the server, thereby completing the transaction.

Three files are required here: bankdb.xls (database file), UpdateDB.java (servlet code), and example248.html (Web page containing the form). To create bankdb.xls, open Excel; type the records (rows) and the columns of the initial bank database, shown in the forthcoming screen capture; and save the file as bankdb.xls. The database has 13 records. The first record must be the field (column) names. We use these names in the Java code. A **database** is defined as a collection of tables; each table has records, (rows) and each record has fields (columns). Database manipulation begins with tables. The Excel sheet shown must be defined as a table with a name that we use in the Java code of the servlet. Select (highlight) all the data records in the initial database, including the field names, and then attach a name to these cells by clicking this sequence: Insert (menu on Excel's menu bar) => Name => Define => Type CustomerName as the table name => OK. Save bankdb.xls. See the following screen capture:

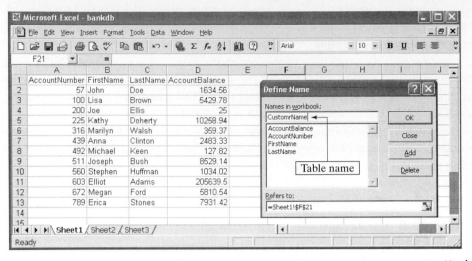

We use an IDE, such as NetBeans, to develop and debug the servlet code, `Updat-eDB.java`. Servlets require a server and interaction with a Web page in order to retrieve form input. We can simplify the development process by writing the code as a Java application with a `main()` method. Once the code is successful in handling the database transactions, we add and debug the servlet part of the code.

As usual, use the AceHTML editor to generate the given code, and save it as `example248.html`. and `UpdateDB.java`, respectively. Render the Web page in a browser.

Code explained:

`example248.html`:

1. Lines 11–46 are similar to the code of Example 24.1. They use JavaScript to validate form input.

2. Line 53 uses the `UpdateDB` servlet class in the `action` attribute.

3. Lines 53–61 create the Web page with the form.

4. Line 58 creates a validation button that has an `onClick` event handler.

5. Line 59 creates the form's submit button.

`UpdateDB.java`:

1. Lines 1–5 import some Java classes, including servlet classes.

2. Line 7 makes the `UpdateDB` class a servlet by inheriting from the Java `HttpServlet` class.

3. Lines 9–11 declare four variables that correspond to the four elements of the HTML form.

4. Lines 13–90 define the `doPost()` method, which reads form input (lines 17–20); send a congratulations on-the-fly Web page to the user (lines 22–29); and perform database transactions (lines 32–90).

5. Line 32 defines the JDBC–ODBC driver for the Excel `Bank` database.

6. Line 36 loads the JDBC–ODBC driver.

7. Line 40 creates a database connection.

8. Lines 41–47 print information about the connection. This information is helpful in debugging the code.

9. Lines 51–59 create an SQL statement and print the results set.

10. Lines 62–68 add a new record to the database, using the form data that the user inputs.

11. Lines 71–76 create an SQL statement and print the results set.

12. Lines 79–85 close all database-related objects, a good practice for security reasons.

13. Lines 92–117 define `displayResultSet()`, which cycles through the records of the SQL results and prints them to the screen.

Discussion:

Move the `example248.html` and `UpdateDB.class` files to the Tomcat `servlets` and `classes` directories, respectively. Begin running the example by starting the Tomcat server and typing the Web page's URL in a browser window. Fill in the form with some data. Click the `Confirm` button to validate the form's data. This validation is done on the client side via Java-Script. Once you are satisfied with the input, click the `Send It` button. This click executes the servlet.

The servlet has two objects. The `request` object communicates with XHTML via the `getParameter()` method. `request` allows the servlet to retrieve the form input, as shown in code lines 17–20 in the `UpdateDB.java` file. These lines of code must use the XHTML names of the form elements as specified by the `name` attribute in the `<input>` tags in code lines 54–57 in the `example248.html` file.

The other object that a servlet uses is `response`, which is used to specify HTML output from the servlet, as code line 21 of `UpdateDB.java` shows. The `out` object (code lines 16 and 22–29 of `UpdateDB.java`) prints results to the browser window.

New added record

Code lines 62–68 of `UpdateDB.java` insert the form data that the user inputs, as a new record in the Excel spreadsheet (see the foregoing screen capture), using a `preparedStatement` object—an SQL statement type. The question mark (`?`) in code line 62 signifies a variable. The first argument in the `set()` methods in code lines 64–67 indicates the order of the fields of the database record.

Each time the form's `Send It` button is clicked, a new record is added to the database. If too many records are added during the development process, select (highlight) them and click this sequence to delete them: Edit (menu on Excel's menu bar) => Delete => Select the Entire row radio button in the window that opens up => OK.

Code line 62 of UpdateDB.java uses the CustomerName table of the Excel spreadsheet. This table contains the records and fields of the database. Some databases are relational; a **relational database** consists of some tables that are related to each other, hence the term *relational.*

Hands-on exercise:

Add an Address field to the database, and add an address text field in the form. Modify the code accordingly.

```
1    <?xml version="1.0" encoding="iso-8859-1"?>     example248.html
2    <!DOCTYPE html PUBLIC "-//W3C//DTD XHTML 1.1//EN"
3        "http://www.w3.org/TR/xhtml11/DTD/xhtml11.dtd">
4    <html xmlns="http://www.w3.org/1999/xhtml">
5    <!-- Generated by AceHTM http://freeware.acehtml.com -->
6    <head>
7    <title>Online Banking</title>
8    <script language="javascript">
9
10   //check text-field input
11   function isBlankField(textObj)
12   {
13     if (textObj.value == "")
14       return true;
15     else
16       return false;
17   }
18
19   /**********************************
20   *Top-Level FORM Validation Function
21   *Calls the separate functions above.
22   **********************************/
23   function validate(formObj){
24     sErrText = ''; // Build error message - present all errors.
25
26     //Validate text fields
27     if (isBlankField(formObj.firstName))
28       sErrText += "\nFirst Name is required";
29     if (isBlankField(formObj.lastName))
30       sErrText += "\nLast Name is required";
31     if (isBlankField(formObj.acctNumber))
32       sErrText += "\nAccount number is required";
```

```
33      if (isBlankField(formObj.acctBalance))
34        sErrText += "\nAccount balance is required";
35
36  //If there are validation errors, sErrText holds them.
37      if (sErrText.length > 0)
38        alert("Sorry, missing data:" + sErrText);
39      else {
40          str  = "\nFirst Name: " + formObj.firstName.value;
41          str += "\nLast Name: " + formObj.lastName.value;
42          str += "\nAccount Number: " + formObj.acctNumber.value;
43          str += "\nAccount Balance: $" +formObj.acctBalance.value;
44          alert(str);
45      }//else
46  }//validate()
47
48  </script>
49  </head>
50  <body>
51  <h2 align="center">Welcome to ABC Online Bank</h2>
52  Open a new account:
53  <form name="myForm" method="post" action="../servlet/UpdateDB">
54  <div>First Name:<input name="firstName" value="Abe" size="10"
    /></div>
55  <div>Last Name:<input type="text" name="lastName" value="Zeid"
    size="10" maxlength="15" /></div>
56  <div>Account Number:<input type="text" name="acctNumber"
    size="10" /></div>
57  <div>Account Balance:<input type="text" name="acctBalance"
    size="10" /> </div>
58  <input type="button" name="confirm" value="Confirm"
    onClick="validate(myForm)"/>
59  <input type="submit" name="send" value="Send It" />
60  <input type="reset" name="erase" value="Erase It" />
61  </form>
62  </body>
63  </html>
```

```
1   import java.sql.*;
2   import java.io.*;                          UpdateDB.java
3   import javax.servlet.*;
4   import javax.servlet.http.*;
5   import java.util.*;
6
7   public class UpdateDB extends HttpServlet {
8
9       private int accountNumber;
```

```
10      private double accountBalance;
11      private String firstName, lastName;
12
13    public void doPost(HttpServletRequest request,
14                       HttpServletResponse response)
15       throws ServletException, IOException {
16      PrintWriter out = response.getWriter();
17      firstName = request.getParameter("firstName");
18      lastName = request.getParameter("lastName");
19      accountNumber =
    Integer.parseInt(request.getParameter("acctNumber"));
20      accountBalance =
    Double.parseDouble(request.getParameter("acctBalance"));
21      response.setContentType("text/html");
22      out.print("<h1>Congratulations!</h1>");
23      out.print("<h2>We added your following account information to
    our database:</h2>");
24      out.print("<ul>");
25      out.print("<li>First Name: " +  firstName);
26      out.print("<li>Last Name: " +  lastName);
27      out.print("<li>Account Number: " +  accountNumber);
28      out.print("<li>Account Balance: " + accountBalance);
29      out.print("<ul>");
30
31  //Database processing begins
32          String url = "jdbc:odbc:Bank";
33
34          try {
35          //Load the the jdbc-odbc bridge driver
36          Class.forName ("sun.jdbc.odbc.JdbcOdbcDriver");
37
38          //Establish a connection to the database driver.
39          //Connection connect = DriverManager.getConnection
    (url, logInName, password);
40          Connection connect = DriverManager.getConnection (url,
    "", "");
41          DatabaseMetaData connectData = connect.getMetaData();
42
43          //get and display information about the two connections
44          //via the DatabaseMetaDate object
45          System.out.println ("Connected to " +
    connectData.getURL());
46          System.out.println("Driver      " +
    connectData.getDriverName());
47          System.out.println("Version     " +
    connectData.getDriverVersion());
```

```
48
49          //Create a Statement object to submit SQL statements
50          //to the driver
51          Statement simpleStatement = connect.createStatement();
52
53          //Submit a query to database
54          //and store results in a ResultSet
55          String query = "SELECT * FROM CustomerName";
56          ResultSet myResultSet = simpleStatement.executeQuery
    (query);
57
58          //Display all rows and columns of the ResultSet
59          displayResultSet(myResultSet);
60
61          //Add a record to bank database
62          String upd = "INSERT INTO CustomerName VALUES (?, ?, ?,
    ?)";
63          PreparedStatement prepStmt =
    connect.prepareStatement(upd);
64          prepStmt.setInt(1,accountNumber);
65          prepStmt.setString(2, firstName);
66          prepStmt.setString(3, lastName);
67          prepStmt.setDouble(4, accountBalance);
68          prepStmt.executeUpdate ();
69
70          //print updated DB
71          query = "SELECT * FROM CustomerName";
72          //ResultSet rs = st.executeQuery( "Select * from
    [Sheet1$]" );
73          myResultSet = simpleStatement.executeQuery (query);
74
75          //Display all rows and columns of the ResultSet
76          displayResultSet(myResultSet);
77
78          //Close the result set
79          myResultSet.close();
80
81          //close the statement
82          simpleStatement.close();
83
84          //close the connection
85          connect.close();
86          }     //end try statement
87          catch (SQLException e) {}
88          catch (java.lang.Exception e) {}
89
90      }    //close doPost() method
```

```
91
92      public static void displayResultSet (ResultSet myResultSet)
    throws SQLException {
93
94      int count;
95
96      //get data to be used for column headings
97      ResultSetMetaData myData = myResultSet.getMetaData();
98
99      //get number of columns in the result set
100     int numberOfColumns = myData.getColumnCount();
101
102     //Display column headings
103     for (count=1; count <= numberOfColumns; count++) {
104         System.out.print(myData.getColumnLabel(count) + "|");
105     }   //end for loop
106     System.out.println();    //force a new line
107
108     //display data of the table row by row
109     boolean rowState = myResultSet.next();
110     while (rowState) {
111         for (count=1; count<=numberOfColumns; count++) {
112             System.out.print(myResultSet.getString(count) + "|");
113         }   //end for loop
114         System.out.println();   //force a new line
115     rowState = myResultSet.next();
116     }   //end while loop
117     }   //end displayResultSet() method
118
119 } //UpDateDB class
```

24.6.2   PHP and MySQL Database

PHP is a server-side embedded scripting language. It is similar to JSP. It works with XHTML to create dynamic Web pages (i.e. the Web-page contents vary according to the data involved and the actions of the user). By using PHP, we can create powerful applications that interact with a database and generate content dynamically.

PHP works with XHTML. As in XHTML, there is a tag that informs the server where the PHP code starts and where it ends. All the PHP code goes between these tags. The PHP tag is shown in the following template:

```
<html>
<? php
…. // php code goes here.
…..// php code goes here.
?>
</html>
```

All PHP variables have the dollar sign ($) as a prefix; thus, variables in PHP are written as $variablename.

Creating and querying a database from a Web page with PHP involve the following steps:

1. Set up a connection with the server.
2. Create a database, or select an appropriate database if one already exists.
3. If you create a database in step 2, create the tables for that database.
4. Query the database or update the database.
5. Retrieve the results set.

Steps 2 and 3 are usually performed once when creating a new application.

We use the MySQL database with PHP, as both are popular on Unix and Linux platforms. We now provide the general template that embeds PHP database-accessing code into XHTML code of a Web page. The template, which demonstrates the five foregoing steps is as follows:

```
1    <html>
2    <!-- Generated by AceHTML Freeware http://freeware.acehtml.com -->
3    <head>
4    <title>Database Aceess via PHP</title>
5    </head>
6    <body>
7    <h2>Database Aceess via PHP</h2>
8    <?php
9    //STEP 1:
10   $connection = mysql_connect("instruct.coe.neu.edu", "zeid",
     "xxxxx");
11   //STEP 2:
12   mysql select db("zeid");
13   //STEP 3: only if created database in STEP 2
14   $sqlstatement1 = "CREATE TABLE TesTable (... .parameters... .)";
15   mysql query($sqlstatement1);
16   $sqlstatement2 = "INSERT INTO TestTable VALUES (... .data1... .);
17       INSERT INTO TestTable VALUES (... .data2... .);";
18   mysql query ($sqlstatement2);
19   //STEP 4:
20   $query = "SELECT * FROM TestTable;";
21   $results = mysql_query($query);
22   //STEP 5:
23   $numResults = mysql num rows ($results);
24   for ($i = 0; $i < $numResults; $i++)
25   {
26       printf("<b>This is the results set </b>");
27       ......//process results
28       ......//process results
29   }
```

```
30    ?>
31
32    </body>
33    </html>
```

Example 24.9 Use PHP and the MySQL database.

Develop a Web page that accesses a MySQL database via PHP.

Solution 24.9 The Web page of this example runs on a server that has a PHP engine. It also uses the MySQL database. We use a server that has both the PHP engine and the MySQL database. Using the AceHTML editor, generate the given code, and save it as `example249.html`. Upload the file to the WWW server directory. Type the following URL into the URL bar of a browser: `http://www.coe.neu.edu/~zeid/example249.php`.

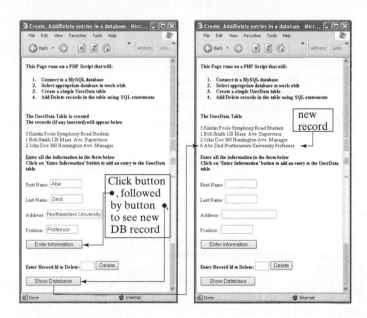

Code explained:

1. Line 1 specifies to the Web server where to find the PHP library.

2. The PHP tag opens in line 23 and closes in line 91.

3. Line 26 connects to the MySQL server.

4. Line 29 selects the MySQL database.

5. Lines 32–38 create the DB table, using the `CREATE TABLE` SQL statement.

6. Lines 43–48 insert a new record in the database table and inform the user.

7. Lines 53–60 delete records (rows) from the table if the user clicks the `Delete` button.

8. Lines 63–75 are executed if the user clicks the `Show Database` button.

9. Lines 78–90 display the original Web-page content.

10. Lines 93–110 create the Web page's form.

Discussion:

The Web page of this example uses dynamic content that is generated by PHP code. The Web page must run on a server in order to work properly. If it runs on a client, all the PHP code is displayed as part of the page's content, because the browser does not know how to render it; as a result, the browser treats it as part of the Web page's text.

   The database table comes seeded with some rows. The Web page adds new rows to it. The user fills in the form and clicks the Enter Information button to create a new record. The use must click the Show Database button in order to see the newly created record. The Delete button deletes the record whose number is entered.

Hands-on exercise:

Add a new database record with information about yourself. Also, delete one record.

```
 1   #!/usr/local/Free/bin/php #
 2   <html>
 3   <!This Code will create a PHP page that will:>
 4   <!  1. Connect to a MySQL database>
 5   <!  2. Select appropriate database to work with>
 6   <!  3. Create a simple UserData table>
 7   <!  4. Add/Delete records in the table using SQL statements>
 8
 9   <head>
10   <title>Create, Add/Delete entries in a database</title>
11   </head>
12   <body>
13   <b>This Page runs on a PHP Script that will:
14   <ol>
15       <li>Connect to a MySQL database</li>
16       <li>Select appropriate database to work with</li>
17       <li>Create a simple UserData table</li>
18       <li>Add/Delete records in the table using SQL statements</li>
19   </ol>
20   </b><br />
21
22   <!STARTING THE 'PHP' TAG>
23   <?php
24
25   //CONNECTING TO THE MySQL SERVER
26   $connection = mysql_connect("localhost", "zeid", "passwd");
27
28   //SELECTING THE DATABASE TO WORK WITH
29   mysql_select_db("zeid", $connection);
30
31   //CREATING THE UserData TABLE
```

```
32   $sqlstatement = "CREATE TABLE IF NOT EXISTS UserData
33           (id int(4) DEFAULT '0' NOT NULL AUTO_INCREMENT PRIMARY
     KEY,
34             fname varchar(20),
35             lname varchar(20),
36             address varchar(50),
37             position varchar(20))";
38   mysql_query($sqlstatement);
39
40   //THE STEPS COMPLETED SO FAR ARE APPLICABLE FOR EVERY APPLICATION
41   //THE REMAINDER OF THE PHP CODE DEALS WITH DYNAMIC CONTENT
42   //IF USER CLICKS 'ENTER INFORMATION' BUTTON, i.e., ADDS A NEW
     RECORD
43   if ($submit)
44   {
45   $newinsert="INSERT INTO UserData (fname, lname, address, position)
46           VALUES('$fname', '$lname', '$address', '$position')";
47   mysql_query($newinsert);
48   printf("THE RECORD HAS BEEN ADDED SUCCESSFULLY.<br>
49       To see the updated database click on 'Show Database' button at
     the bottom of the page.<br><br>");
50   }
51
52   //IF USER CLICKS 'DELETE' BUTTON, i.e., DELETES A RECORD
53   elseif ($delete)
54   {
55   $delete="DELETE FROM UserData
56       WHERE id=$del";
57   mysql_query($delete);
58   printf("THE RECORD HAS BEEN DELETED SUCCESSFULLY.<br>
59       To see the updated database click on 'Show Database'
     button at the bottom of the page.<br><br>");
60   }
61
62   //IF THE USER CLICKS 'SHOW DATABASE' BUTTON, i.e., TO SEE UPDATED
     DATABASE
63   elseif ($display)
64   {
65   printf("<b>The UserData Table</b><br><br>");
66   $displayquery="SELECT * FROM UserData";
67   $results=mysql_query($displayquery);
68   $numresults=mysql_num_rows($results);
69       for ($i=0; $i<$numresults; $i++)
70       {
71       $row=mysql_fetch_array($results);
72       printf("%s   %s   %s   %s %s<br>",
73       $row["id"],$row["fname"],$row["lname"],$row["address"],$row
     ["position"]);
```

```
74        }
75    }
76
77    //THIS PART OF THE CODE DISPLAYS THE DATABASE WHEN THE PAGE OPENS
78    else
79    {
80    printf("<b>The UserData Table is created<br>The records (if any
      inserted) will appear below</b><br><br>");
81    $displayquery="SELECT * FROM UserData";
82    $results=mysql_query($displayquery);
83    $numresults=mysql_num_rows($results);
84        for ($i=0; $i<$numresults; $i++)
85        {
86        $row=mysql_fetch_array($results);
87        printf("%s   %s   %s   %s   %s<br>",
88        $row['id'],$row["fname"],$row["lname"],$row["address"],$row
      ["position"]);
89        }
90    }
91    ?> <!CLOSING THE 'PHP' TAG>
92
93    <b><br />Enter all the information in the form below<br>
94    Click on 'Enter Information' button to add an entry to the
      UserData table<br /><br />
95    </b>
96
97    <!CREATE THE FORM>
98    <form method="post" action="<?php echo $PHP_SELF ?>" >
99    First Name: <input type="text" name="fname" size="10"
      maxlength="20" /><br /><br />
100   Last Name : <input type="text" name="lname" size="10"
      maxlength="20" /><br /><br />
101   Address   : <input type="text" name="address" size="20"
      maxlength="50" /><br><br>
102   Position  : <input type="text" name="position" size="10"
      maxlength="20" /><br /><br />
103   <input type="submit" name="submit" value="Enter Information"
      /><br /><br /><br />
104
105   <b>Enter Record Id to Delete:</b>
106   <input type="text" name="del" size="2" maxlength="4" /><t>
107   <input type="submit" name="delete" value="Delete" /><br /><br />
108
109   <input type="submit" name="display" value="Show Database" />
110   </form>
111
112   </body>
113   </html>
```

### 24.6.3	Perl and E-Mail Processing

Perl is yet another scripting language, like JSP and PHP. Perl is an acronym that stands for *Practical Extraction and Report Language*. Perl has eveloved over the years to become an OOP language. However, Perl is an interpreted language, so it runs slower than compiled languages. However, it is an easy language that Web developers can learn quickly and use to develop scripts to process form input and data. Perl is intended to be practical (easy to learn and use, efficient, and complete) rather than elegant (minimal). The strength of Perl lies in its powerful capabilities to process and manipulate text strings, and its straightforward I/O (input/output) utilities.

Perl was used to write CGI scripts before JSP and PHP became available. Perl embeds XHTML tags in its files. This approch is opposite to that of JSP and PHP, whose tags are embedded in HTML files. All Perl variables have the dollar sign ($) as a prefix; thus, variables in Perl are written as $variablename.

We can use Perl to process form data in three ways: Store data in a database (via SQL and the ODBC driver), write data to a file, or send data to someone via e-mail. The following example shows how to send data via e-mail. It also shows how to use files in Perl.

Example 24.10 Use Perl and e-mail processing.

Develop a Web page that e-mails an online order to a salesperson via Perl.

Solution 24.10 The Web page of this example runs on a server that has Perl installed on it. It creates and uses a text file. The Web page is a scaled-down version of a commercial Web page, to keep the example short. The Web page is an online store that sells cell-phone accessories.

Using the AceHTML editor, generate the given code, and save it as example2410.html, previewOrder.cgi, and processOrder.cgi, respectively. Upload the files to the www server directory. Type the following URL into a browser's URL bar: http://www.coe.neu.edu/~zeid/example2410.html.

Code explained:
example2410.html:

1. Line 11 defines an array whose elements are the unit prices of the website's products.
2. Lines 12 and 13 define two variables to hold total cast of orders and the product numbers.
3. Lines 15–63 define the checkAndCost() function, which ensures that the customer selects at least one product (lines 19–23), enters the required phone number (lines 26–29), the required credit-card type (lines 32–36), the required credit-card number (lines 38–42), and the required credit-card expiration date (lines 45–48).
4. Lines 51–62 calculate the total cost of an online order.
5. Lines 68–202 create the Web page's content.

Online Store - Microsoft Internet Explorer

File   Edit   View   Favorites   Tools   Help   Address   Links

Welcome To Our Online Store!

This Month's Special!	Descriptions	Unit Price and Quantity to Purchase
Nokia 6100 Series	Aftermarket Car charger and Leather Case	$30.94 Quantity to purchase: 1
Motorola StarTac Series	Aftermarket Car charger and Leather Case	$30.94 Quantity to purchase:

Nokia Accessories:	Descriptions	Unit Price and Quantity to Purchase
Nokia ACP-7U	Standard Travel Charger for the 5100/6100/7100/8200 Series Phones!	$19.95 Quantity to purchase: 5
Nokia LCH-9	Rapid Cigarette Lighter Charger for the 5100/6100/7100/8200 series phones. Lightweight and convenient, this charging option allows you to rapidly charge your phone while in your car.	$39.95 Quantity to purchase:
Nokia BCH-12U	Belt Clip BCH-12U Keeps your phone securely at hand while you are on the go. (Nokia 5100/6100/7100 Series Phones)	$19.95 Quantity to purchase: 3

Please fill in the following shipping information to complete your online purchase. Thank you.

First Name: John   Middle Initial: K   Last Name: Smith

Address 1: 25 New Street
Address 2: Apt.# 37

City: Boston   State: MA   Zip Code: 02115

Phone Number (10 digits only, including area code): 6173334444   **Required**

E-mail Address: amith@aaa.bbb.com

Quantities ordered

Items purchased

Would you like to receive our monthly *E-newsletter*? ● Yes ○ No

Credit Card Type: ○ Visa ● MasterCard ○ Discover **Required**

Credit Card Number (16 digits with no spaces please): 1111222233334444 **Required**

Credit Card Expiration date (4 digits, including zeros, with no spaces please): 1110 **Required**

Preview Order   Clear Form

Done   Internet

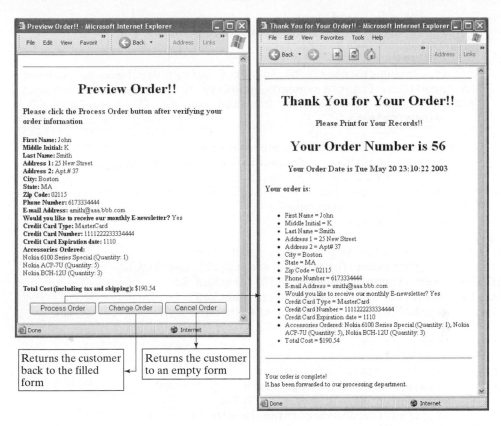

```
1   <?xml version="1.0" encoding="iso-8859-1"?>   example2410.html
2   <!DOCTYPE html PUBLIC "-//W3C//DTD XHTML 1.1//EN"
3       "http://www.w3.org/TR/xhtml11/DTD/xhtml11.dtd">
4   <html xmlns="http://www.w3.org/1999/xhtml">
5   <!-- Generated by AceHTM http://freeware.acehtml.com -->
6   <head>
7   <title>Online Store</title>
8   <script language="javascript">
9
10  //This array of prices matches the order of the products on the
    website
11  unitPrice = [30.94, 30.94, 19.95, 39.95, 19.95];
12  orderTotalCost=0;
13  productNumber =0;
14
15  function checkAndCost() {
16  orderTotalCost=0;
17  productNumber=0;
18  //check if any product is ordered in the Web page
```

```
19          for (i=0;i<=4;i++) {
20      if (document.forms[0].elements[i].value != "")
    productNumber += 1;
21          }//for
22      if (!productNumber > 0) {alert ("Sorry, you have not chosen
    any products. Enter a nonzero quantity for at least one product,
    and click the 'Preview Order' button again.  Thank you");
23          return false;}
24
25  //check for correct phone number entry
26      phoneNumberString = document.forms[0].elements[13].value;
27      if (phoneNumberString.length != 10) {
28      alert ("Please enter a 10-digit phone number with no spaces
    or parentheses.  Thank you");
29          return false;}
30
31  //check for choosing a credit card type
32      if (!document.forms[0].elements[17].checked &&
33  !document.forms[0].elements[18].checked &&
34  !document.forms[0].elements[19].checked) {
35      alert ("Please choose  a credit card type and click the
    'Preview Order' button again.  Thank you");
36          return false;}
37
38  //check for credit card number
39      creditCardNumberString =
    document.forms[0].elements[20].value;
40      if (creditCardNumberString.length != 16) {
41      alert ("Please enter a 16-digit credit card number with no
    spaces, and click the 'Preview Order' button again.  Thank you");
42          return false;}
43
44  //check for expiration date
45      creditCardExpirationDateString =
    document.forms[0].elements[21].value;
46      if (creditCardExpirationDateString.length != 4) {
47      alert ("Please enter a 4-digit credit card expiration date
    with no spaces, and click the 'Preview Order' button again..
    Thank you");
48          return false;}
49
50  //calculate total cost of order
51      for (i=0;i<=4;i++) {
52          //alert (unitPrice[i]);  //debugging
53          //alert (document.forms[0].elements[i].value); //debug
54          if (document.forms[0].elements[i].value != "") {
55          orderTotalCost +=
    parseInt(document.forms[0].elements[i].value) * unitPrice[i];
```

```
56              //alert ("Cost is " + orderTotalCost);   //debugging
57              }//if
58         }//for
59
60    //keep only two decimals
61    orderTotalCost=Math.round(orderTotalCost * 100)/100;
62    document.forms[0].Cost.value=orderTotalCost;
63    }//checkAndCost()
64
65    </script>
66    </head>
67    <body bgcolor="#FFFFFF">
68    <p align="center"><b>Welcome To Our Online Store!</b>
69
70    <form method="post" onSubmit ="return(checkAndCost())"
      action="previewOrder.cgi">
71    <table width="84%" border="1" bgcolor="#FF6600"
      bordercolor="#FF6600">
72         <tr bordercolor="#FF6600" bgcolor="#FFFFFF">
73           <td width="35%"><b>This Month's Special!</b></td>
74           <td width="42%"><b>Descriptions</b></td>
75           <td width="23%">
76             <p><b>Unit Price
77    and       
78                </b><b>Quantity to Purchase</b></p>
79           </td>
80         </tr>
81
82         <tr bordercolor="#FF6600" bgcolor="#FFFFFF">
83           <td width="35%"><b>Nokia 6100 Series</b></td>
84           <td width="42%"><b>Aftermarket Car charger and Leather
85    Case</b></td>
86           <td width="23%"><b>$30.94
87               &nb
      sp;   </b><b>   </b><b>
88             Quantity to purchase:
89             <input type="text" name="Nokia 6100 Series Special"
      size=1>
90           </b></td>
91
92         </tr>
93         <tr bordercolor="#FF6600" bgcolor="#FFFFFF">
94           <td width="35%"><b>Motorola StarTac Series</b></td>
95           <td width="42%"><b>Aftermarket Car charger and Leather
96    Case</b></td>
97           <td width="23%"><b>$30.94
98               &n
      bsp;   </b><b>   </b><b>
```

```
 99              Quantity to purchase:
100              <input type="text" name="Motorola StarTac Series
    Special" size=1>
101              </b></td>
102
103      </tr>
104      <tr bordercolor="#FF6600" bgcolor="#FF6600">
105        <td> </td>
106        <td> </td>
107        <td> </td>
108      </tr>
109
110      <tr bordercolor="#FF6600" bgcolor="#FFFFFF">
111          <td width="35%" bgcolor="#FFFFFF"><b>Nokia
    Accessories:</b></td>
112          <td width="42%"><b>Descriptions</b></td>
113          <td width="23%"><b>Unit Price
114    and       
115              </b><b>Quantity to Purchase</b></td>
116      </tr>
117
118      <tr bordercolor="#FF6600" bgcolor="#FFFFFF">
119          <td width="35%"><img src="Access/acp7u.gif" width="78"
120    height="64"><b>Nokia ACP-7U</b></td>
121          <td width="42%">Standard Travel Charger for the 5100/6100/
    7100/8200 Series Phones!</td>
122          <td width="23%" valign="top"><b>$19.95
123               &n
    bsp;   </b><b>   </b><b>
124              Quantity to purchase:
125              <input type="text" name="Nokia ACP-7U" size=1>
126              </b></td>
127      </tr>
128
129      <tr bordercolor="#FF6600" bgcolor="#FFFFFF">
130          <td width="35%"><b><img src="Access/lch9.gif" width="78"
    height="64">Nokia LCH-9</b></td>
131          <td width="42%">Rapid Cigarette Lighter Charger for the
132    5100/6100/7100/8200 series phones. Lightweight and convenient,
    this charging option allows you to rapidly charge your phone
    while in your car. </td>
133          <td width="23%" valign="top"><b>$39.95
134               &n
    bsp;   </b><b>   </b><b>
135              Quantity to purchase:
136              <input type="text" name="Nokia LCH-9" size=1>
137              </b></td>
138      </tr>
```

```
139
140          <tr bordercolor="#FF6600" bgcolor="#FFFFFF">
141            <td width="35%"><b><img src="Access/bch12u.gif"
     width="78" height="64">Nokia BCH-12U</b></td>
142            <td width="42%">Belt Clip BCH-12U Keeps your phone
     securely at
143     hand while you are on the go. (Nokia 5100/6100/7100 Series
     Phones)</td>
144            <td width="23%" valign="top"><b>$19.95
145               &nb
     sp;    </b><b>   </b><b>
146            Quantity to purchase:
147            <input type="text" name="Nokia BCH-12U" size=1>
148            </b></td>
149        </tr>
150
151        <tr bordercolor="#FF6600" bgcolor="#FFFFFF">
152          <td colspan="3">
153            <p>Please fill in the following shipping information
     to complete your online purchase. Thank you.</p>
154            <p>First Name:
155              <input type="text" name="First Name" size=20>
156                Middle Initial:
157              <input type="text" name="Middle Initial" size=1
     maxlength=1>
158                Last Name:
159              <input type="text" name="Last Name" size=20>
160            </p>
161            <p>Address 1:
162              <input type="text" name="Address 1" size=30><br>
163              Address 2:
164              <input type="text" name="Address 2" size=30>
165            </p>
166            <p> City:
167              <input type="text" name="City" size=20>
168              State:
169              <input type="text" name="State" size=2 maxlength=2>
170              Zip Code:
171              <input type="text" name="Zip Code" size=5 maxlength=5>
172            </p>
173            <p>Phone Number (10 digits only, including area code):
174              <input type="text" name="Phone Number" size=10
     maxlength=10>**Required**
175            </p>
176            <p>E-mail Address:
177              <input type="text" name="E-mail Address" size=30>
```

```
178                  <p>Would you
      like to receive our monthly <i><b>E-newsletter</b></i>?
179            <input type="radio" name="Would you like to
      receive our monthly E-newsletter?" value="Yes">Yes
180            <input type="radio" name="Would you like to
      receive our monthly E-newsletter?" value="No">No</p>
181         <p>Credit Card Type:
182            <input type="radio" name="Credit Card Type"
      value="Visa">Visa
183            <input type="radio" name="Credit Card Type"
      value="MasterCard">MasterCard
184            <input type="radio" name="Credit Card Type"
185      value="Discover">Discover **Required**</p>
186         <p>Credit Card Number (16 digits with no spaces please):
187            <input type="text" name="Credit Card Number"
      size=16 maxlength=16>**Required**
188         </p>
189         <p>Credit Card Expiration date (4 digits, including
      zeros, with no spaces please):
190            <input type="text" name="Credit Card Expiration
      date" size=4 maxlength=4>**Required**
191      <input type = "hidden" name = "Cost" value = 0>
192         </p>
193         <p align="center">
194            <input type="submit" name="submit" value="Preview
      Order">
195            <input type="reset" name="reset" value="Clear Form">
196         </p>
197      </td>
198    </tr>
199    </table>
200 </form>
201 </div>
202 </p>
203 </body>
204 </html>
```

previewOrder.cgi:

1. **1.** Line 1 specifies the path to the Perl library on the Web server.
2. **2.** It is a good habit to use line 2.
3. **3.** Line 3 allows the use (import) of CGI functions of Perl in our Perl script.
4. **4.** Lines 7–20 retrieve the form values (except the selected products) that a customer has input and assign them to Perl variables.
5. **5.** Line 21 retrieves the calculated cost from the example2410.html Web page and assigns it to the $costOfOrder Perl variable.

6. Lines 23–37 assign the Perl variables of lines 7–21 to another set of identical, "hidden" variables. Both sets have the same names, with `Hidden` added to the names of the second set. These `Hidden` variables are used to create a hidden Web page in lines 129–144.

7. Lines 39–88 check for the products selected by the customer and add them to the two aforementioned sets of variables.

8. Lines 90–98 format the ordered products for later printing. They store all product names and quantities ordered by concatenating them in the `accessoriesOrdered` and `accessoriesOrderedHidden` variables. The (`.`) is Perl's concatenation operator.

9. Lines 100–126 send an on-the-fly Web page summarizing the order to the customer for review.

10. Lines 128–148 create a hidden on-the-fly Web page that is used later by the `processOrder.cgi` script to process the order.

```
1   #!/usr/local/bin/perl  -w # change to path    previewOrder.cgi
    of perl on your machine
2   #use strict; # enforce declarations and quoting
3   use CGI qw(:standard);   # import shortcuts
4
5   my $query = CGI -> new; # These lines store the form fields
6
7   my $firstName = $query-> param('First Name'); # in some variables
8   my $middleInitial = $query-> param('Middle Initial');
9   my $lastName = $query-> param('Last Name');
10  my $address1 = $query-> param('Address 1');
11  my $address2 = $query-> param('Address 2');
12  my $city = $query-> param('City');
13  my $state = $query-> param('State');
14  my $zipCode = $query-> param('Zip Code');
15  my $emailAddress = $query-> param('E-mail Address');
16  my $enewsletter = $query-> param('Would you like to receive
    our monthly E-newsletter?');
17  my $phoneNumber = $query-> param('Phone Number');
18  my $creditCardType = $query-> param('Credit Card Type');
19  my $creditCardNumber = $query-> param('Credit Card Number');
20  my $creditCardExpirationDate = $query-> param('Credit Card
    Expiration date');
21  my $costOfOrder = "\$" . $query-> param('Cost');
22
23  my $firstNameHidden = "'" . $firstName . "'";
24  my $middleInitialHidden = "'" . $middleInitial . "'";
25  my $lastNameHidden =  "'" . $lastName . "'";
26  my $address1Hidden = "'" . $address1 . "'";
27  my $address2Hidden = "'" . $address2 . "'";
28  my $cityHidden = "'" . $city . "'";
29  my $stateHidden =  "'" . $state . "'";
30  my $zipCodeHidden = "'" . $zipCode . "'";
```

```perl
31    my $phoneNumberHidden = "'" . $phoneNumber . "'";
32    my $emailAddressHidden = "'" . $emailAddress . "'";
33    my $enewsletterHidden = "'" . $enewsletter . "'";
34    my $creditCardTypeHidden = "'" . $creditCardType . "'";
35    my $creditCardNumberHidden = "'" . $creditCardNumber . "'";
36    my $creditCardExpirationDateHidden = "'" .
      $creditCardExpirationDate . "'";
37    my $costOfOrderHidden = "'" . $costOfOrder . "'";
38
39    my $i = 0;
40    my @AccessoriesOrderedName = ();   #array of variable length
41    my @AccessoriesOrderedNameHidden = ();
42    my @AccessoriesOrderedQuantity = ();
43    my @AccessoriesOrderedQuantityHidden = ();
44
45    my $Nokia6100SeriesSpecial = $query-> param('Nokia 6100 Series
      Special');
46    if ($Nokia6100SeriesSpecial ne "") {
47        $AccessoriesOrderedName[$i] = 'Nokia 6100 Series Special';
48        $AccessoriesOrderedNameHidden[$i] = 'Nokia 6100 Series
      Special';
49        $AccessoriesOrderedQuantity[$i] = $Nokia6100SeriesSpecial;
50        $AccessoriesOrderedQuantityHidden[$i] =
      $Nokia6100SeriesSpecial;
51        $i =$i + 1;
52    }
53
54    my $MotorolaStarTacSeriesSpecial = $query-> param('Motorola
      StarTac Series Special');
55    if ($MotorolaStarTacSeriesSpecial ne "") {
56        $AccessoriesOrderedName[$i] = 'Motorola StarTac Series
      Special';
57        $AccessoriesOrderedNameHidden[$i] = 'Motorola StarTac Series
      Special';
58        $AccessoriesOrderedQuantity[$i] =
      $MotorolaStarTacSeriesSpecial;
59        $AccessoriesOrderedQuantityHidden[$i] =
      $MotorolaStarTacSeriesSpecial;
60        $i =$i+1;
61    }
62
63    my $NokiaACP7Ul = $query-> param('Nokia ACP-7U');
64    if ($NokiaACP7Ul != "") {
65        $AccessoriesOrderedName[$i] = 'Nokia ACP-7U';
66        $AccessoriesOrderedNameHidden[$i] = 'Nokia ACP-7U';
67        $AccessoriesOrderedQuantity[$i] = $NokiaACP7Ul;
68        $AccessoriesOrderedQuantityHidden[$i] = $NokiaACP7Ul;
69        $i =$i+1;
```

```perl
70   }
71
72   my $NokiaLCH9 = $query-> param('Nokia LCH-9');
73   if ($NokiaLCH9 != "") {
74       $AccessoriesOrderedName[$i] = 'Nokia LCH-9';
75       $AccessoriesOrderedNameHidden[$i] = 'Nokia LCH-9';
76       $AccessoriesOrderedQuantity[$i] = $NokiaLCH9;
77       $AccessoriesOrderedQuantityHidden[$i] = $NokiaLCH9;
78       $i =$i+1;
79   }
80
81   my $NokiaBCH12U = $query-> param('Nokia BCH-12U');
82   if ($NokiaBCH12U != "") {
83       $AccessoriesOrderedName[$i] = 'Nokia BCH-12U';
84       $AccessoriesOrderedNameHidden[$i] = 'Nokia BCH-12U';
85       $AccessoriesOrderedQuantity[$i] = $NokiaBCH12U;
86       $AccessoriesOrderedQuantityHidden[$i] = $NokiaBCH12U;
87       $i =$i+1;
88   }
89
90   my $arrayLength = @AccessoriesOrderedName;
91   my $accessoriesOrdered = "<br>\n";
92   my $accessoriesOrderedHidden = "";
93   for($j=0; $j<$arrayLength ; $j++){
94       $accessoriesOrdered =  $accessoriesOrdered .
     $AccessoriesOrderedName[$j] . " (Quantity: " .
     $AccessoriesOrderedQuantity[$j] . ")" . "<br>\n";
95           if ($j != ($arrayLength - 1)) {$accessoriesOrderedHidden
     =  $accessoriesOrderedHidden . $AccessoriesOrderedName[$j] . "
     (Quantity: " . $AccessoriesOrderedQuantity[$j] . ")" . ", ";}
96           else {$accessoriesOrderedHidden =
     $accessoriesOrderedHidden . $AccessoriesOrderedName[$j] . "
     (Quantity: " . $AccessoriesOrderedQuantity[$j] . ")";}
97   }
98   $accessoriesOrderedHidden = "'" . $accessoriesOrderedHidden . "'";
99
100  print header();                    # HTML page to respond to
     submission
101  print <<END_of_start;              # This is like a "here document"
     in a shell script
102    <html>
103    <head>
104    <title>Preview Order!!</title>
105    </head>
106    <body>
107    <hr noshade>
108    <h1 align="center">Preview Order!!</center></h1>
```

```
109   <h3>Please click the Process Order button after verifying your
      order information</h3>
110   <b>First Name:</b> $firstName<br>
111   <b>Middle Initial:</b> $middleInitial<br>
112   <b>Last Name:</b> $lastName<br>
113   <b>Address 1:</b> $address1<br>
114   <b>Address 2:</b> $address2<br>
115   <b>City:</b> $city<br>
116   <b>State:</b> $state<br>
117   <b>Zip Code:</b> $zipCode<br>
118   <b>Phone Number:</b> $phoneNumber<br>
119   <b>E-mail Address:</b> $emailAddress<br>
120   <b>Would you like to receive our monthly E-newsletter?</b>
      $enewsletter<br>
121   <b>Credit Card Type:</b> $creditCardType<br>
122   <b>Credit Card Number:</b> $creditCardNumber<br>
123   <b>Credit Card Expiration date:</b> $creditCardExpirationDate<br>
124   <b>Accessories Ordered:</b>$accessoriesOrdered<br>
125
126   <b>Total Cost (including tax and shipping):</b> $costOfOrder<br>
127
128   <center><form method='post' action='processOrder.cgi'>
129   <input type='hidden' name='First Name' value=$firstNameHidden>
130   <input type='hidden' name='Middle Initial'
      value=$middleInitialHidden>
131   <input type='hidden' name='Last Name' value=$lastNameHidden>
132   <input type='hidden' name='Address 1' value=$address1Hidden>
133   <input type='hidden' name='Address 2' value=$address2Hidden>
134   <input type='hidden' name='City' value=$cityHidden>
135   <input type='hidden' name='State' value=$stateHidden>
136   <input type='hidden' name='Zip Code' value=$zipCodeHidden>
137   <input type='hidden' name='Phone Number' value=$phoneNumberHidden>
138   <input type='hidden' name='E-mail Address'
      value=$emailAddressHidden>
139   <input type='hidden' name='Would you like to receive our monthly
      E-newsletter?' value=$enewsletterHidden>
140   <input type='hidden' name='Credit Card Type'
      value=$creditCardTypeHidden>
141   <input type='hidden' name='Credit Card Number'
      value=$creditCardNumberHidden>
142   <input type='hidden' name='Credit Card Expiration date'
      value=$creditCardExpirationDate>
143   <input type='hidden' name='Accessories Ordered'
      value=$accessoriesOrderedHidden>
144   <input type='hidden' name='Total Cost' value=$costOfOrder>
145   <input type='submit' value='Process Order'>
146   <input type='button' value='Change Order'
      onClick='javascript:history.back();'>
```

```
147   <input type='button' value='Cancel Order'
      onClick='javascript:location = "example2410.html"'>
148   </form>
149   END_of_start
150   print end_html;
```

`processOrder.cgi`:

1. Line 1 specifies the path to the Perl library on the Web server.
2. It is a good habit to use line 2.
3. Line 3 allows the use (import) of CGI functions of Perl in our Perl script.
4. Lines 5–11 open the `counter.dat` file (lines 5–7), read the `$visitor` counter from it (line 8), increment it by one (line 9), and close the file (lines 10 and 11).
5. Lines 13–18 open the `counter.dat` file (lines 13–15), write the `$visitor` counter to it (line 16), and close the file (lines 17 and 18).
6. Lines 22–37 read the values of the fields of the hidden Web page that we created in the `previewOrder.cgi` script.
7. Line 38 creates the order date.
8. Lines 39–63 e-mail the form's input and data for the customer's order.
9. Lines 65–99 print the sales receipt, as a Web page, to the browser.

```
1    #!/usr/local/bin/perl -w  # change to path      processOrder.cgi
     of perl on your machine
2    #use strict; # enforce declarations and quoting
3    use CGI qw(:standard);   # import shortcuts
4    #Generate order number
5    $orderNumber = "counter.dat";
6    open (FILE, $orderNumber) || die "Cannot read from counter
     file.\n";
7    flock (FILE, 2);
8    $visitors = <FILE>;
9    $visitors = $visitors + 1;
10   flock (FILE, 8);
11   close (FILE);
12
13   open (FILE, ">" . $orderNumber) || die "Cannot write to
     counter file.\n";
14   #open (FILE, ">$orderNumber") || die "Cannot write to
     counter file.\n";
15   flock (FILE, 2);
16   print FILE $visitors;
17   flock (FILE, 8);
18   close (FILE);
19   #end of order number generation
20   my $query = CGI -> new; # These lines store the form fields
21
```

```perl
22  my $firstName = $query-> param('First Name'); # in some variables
23  my $middleInitial = $query-> param('Middle Initial');
24  my $lastName = $query-> param('Last Name');
25  my $address1 = $query-> param('Address 1');
26  my $address2 = $query-> param('Address 2');
27  my $city = $query-> param('City');
28  my $state = $query-> param('State');
29  my $zipCode = $query-> param('Zip Code');
30  my $emailAddress = $query-> param('E-mail Address');
31  my $enewsletter = $query-> param('Would you like to receive
    our monthly E-newsletter?');
32  my $phoneNumber = $query-> param('Phone Number');
33  my $creditCardType = $query-> param('Credit Card Type');
34  my $creditCardNumber = $query-> param('Credit Card Number');
35  my $creditCardExpirationDate = $query-> param('Credit Card
    Expiration date');
36  my $accessoriesOrdered = $query-> param('Accessories Ordered');
37  my $costOfOrder = $query-> param('Total Cost');
38  my $orderDate = $query-> param('/usr/bin/date', scalar localtime);
39  # E-mail the form input
40  open (MAIL,"|/usr/lib/sendmail -t zeid\@coe.neu.edu")
41       or die "Can't open MAIL: $!";
42  print MAIL ("To: zeid\@coe.neu.edu
43  Subject: An Online Order
44  Order Number = $visitors
45  Order Date = $orderDate
46  First Name = $firstName
47  Middle Initial = $middleInitial
48  Last Name = $lastName
49  Address 1 = $address1
50  Address 2= $address2
51  City = $city
52  State = $state
53  Zip Code = $zipCode
54  Phone Number = $phoneNumber
55  E-mail Address = $emailAddress
56  Would you like to receive our monthly E-newsletter? $enewsletter
57  Credit Card Type = $creditCardType
58  Credit Card Number = $creditCardNumber
59  Credit Card Expiration date = $creditCardExpirationDate
60  Accessories Ordered = $accessoriesOrdered
61  Cost = $costOfOrder"
62  );
63  close MAIL or die "Can't close MAIL: $!";
64
65  print header(); # HTML page to respond to submission
66  print <<END_of_start; # This is like a "here document"
    in a shell script
```

```
67    <html>
68    <head>
69    <title>Thank You for Your Order!!</title>
70    </head>
71    <body>
72    <hr noshade>
73    <h1 align="center">Thank You for Your Order!!</h1>
74    <h3 align="center">Please Print for Your Record!!</h3>
75  <h1 align="center">Your Order Number is $visitors</h1>
76  <h3 align="center">Your Order Date is $orderDate</h3>
77  <h3>Your order is:</h3><BR>
78  <ul>
79  <li>First Name = $firstName
80  <li>Middle Initial = $middleInitial
81  <li>Last Name = $lastName
82  <li>Address 1 = $address1
83  <li>Address 2 = $address2
84  <li>City = $city
85  <li>State = $state
86  <li>Zip Code = $zipCode
87  <li>Phone Number = $phoneNumber
88  <li>E-mail Address = $emailAddress
89  <li>Would you like to receive our monthly E-newsletter?
      $enewsletter
90  <li>Credit Card Type = $creditCardType
91  <li>Credit Card Number = $creditCardNumber
92  <li>Credit Card Expiration date = $creditCardExpirationDate
93  <li>Accessories Ordered: $accessoriesOrdered
94  <li>Total Cost = $costOfOrder
95  </ul>
96    <hr noshade>
97    <p>Your order is complete!<br>
98     It has been forwarded to our processing department.</p>
99  END_of_start
100 print end_html;
```

Discussion:

This example illustrates how to process form data by sending it as an e-mail message. A customer browses the online store displayed on the Web page. The customer selects some products and fills out the form. The form encompasses the entire Web page, although it may not look like it. The quantities of product items shown on the Web page are text fields. The bottom part of the Web page is the last part of the form.

The Web page has many interesting design features. The minimal information that is needed to process the form is required—that is, at least one product quantity, a phone number, and credit card information (type, number, and expiration date). If the customer does not fill out the rest of the form, a sales representative can call and close the sale by requesting a name and an address to which to ship the order.

All the validation of these required fields is done on the client side via JavaScript. JavaScript also calculates the total cost of the order by using a `unitPrice` array (code line 11 in `example2410.html`). The order of the array elements matches the display order of the products on the Web page. Code lines 12–13 and 16–17 are identical, but they serve different purposes. (See the Hands-on exercise for this example.)

The `previewOrder.cgi` Perl script uses the form's hidden elements. We must do so in order to preserve the form's data across Web pages. This example creates three Web pages: the original one (`example2410.html`) and two on-the-fly Web pages. Perl generates the two on-the-fly Web pages; one is generated by `previewOrder.cgi`, and the other is generated by `processOrder.cgi`.

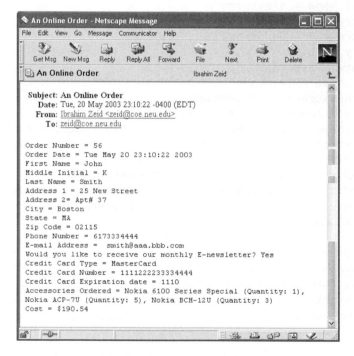

The `processOrder.cgi` Perl script uses the `$visitors` variable as a counter (code line 8 in the `processOrder.cgi` file) that is increments by one (code line 9 in the `processOrder.cgi` file) for each processed order. The counter acts as the order number that the customer can reference in any future inquiries. The counter is stored in the `counter.dat` file (code line 5 in the `processOrder.cgi` file). This file has only one number: the value of the counter. We use this approch to make the value of the `$visitors` variable (value is maintained) between script calls. The `processOrder.cgi` script also e-mails the form's data (code lines 40–63), as shown in the previous screen capture, and prints the receipt (code lines 73–98).

This Web page must be used with a secure Web connection in order to protect credit card information when receiving it from the customer and when sending the e-mail message.

Hands-on exercise:

Remove code lines 12 and 13 from the `example2410.html` file. Save and run the code. What happens? Explain the results. Also, add two more products to the Web page. Modify the code in the three files (`example2410.html`, `previeweOrder.cgi`, and `processOrder.cgi`) to process them.

24.7 Tutorials

24.7.1 Automatic Filling of Form Elements (Study Section 24.4)

This tutorial shows how we can use user input for some form elements in order to fill other elements automatically. Using the AceHTML editor, generate the given code, and save it as `tutorial2471.html`. Render the Web page in a browser.

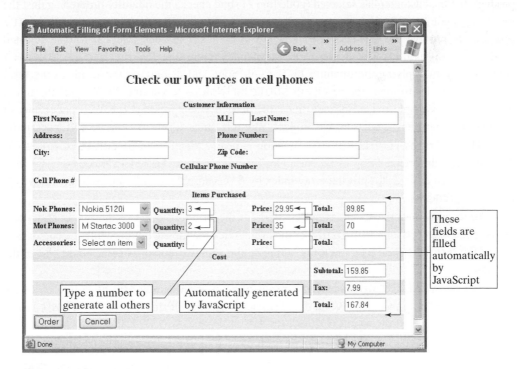

Code explained:

1. Lines 10–12 define three arrays whose elements correspond to each other.
2. Lines 14 and 15 define `subtotalNokia` and `subtotalMotorola`, which hold the customer's cost for Nokia and Motorola purchases, respectively, before taxes.

3. Lines 17–35 define the `automaticNokia()` function, which retrieves the customer's selection from Nokia products (lines 19–26), fills in the prices automatically (lines 27–32), calculates the tax (line 33), and calculates the cost after tax (line 35).

4. Lines 37–55 define the `automaticMotorola()` function, which retrieves the customer's selection from Motorola products (lines 19–26), fills in the prices automatically (lines 47–52), calculates the tax (line 53), and calculates the cost after tax (line 55).

5. Lines 14, 15, 18, and 38 are used to ensure that the script produces the right calculations of subtotals, tax, and totals all the time.

6. Lines 58–228 create a Web page that has a form which is formatted via tables.

Discussion:

The Web page of this tutorial is a scaled-down version of a commercial Web page. The page is created using an HTML editor. The page has one form. The customer can buy Nokia and Motorola cell phones and accessories. When the customer enters a quantity for a Nokia product, `automaticNokia()` is called as an event-handler (code line 134). The function finds the product that the customer has selected (code line 21) and checks the quantity ordered against the inventory (code line 22). If there is enough inventory to make the sale, `automaticNokia()` proceeds to retrieve the `unitSalePrice` (from the array in code line 12) for the selected product and display it in one of the form's text fields (code line 26). `automaticNokia()` continues by multiplying the quantity by the unit price and displaying the result in the form (code line 27). It also adds the results to `subtotalNokia` (code line 28). We set the initial value for this variable twice, in code lines 14 (needed when we start the Web page) and 18 (needed if the customer selects Nokia products multiple times during the same browser session).

The `automaticMotorola()` function is nearly identical to `automaticNokia()`, with the only difference lying in the variables' names. Also, `automaticMotorola()` uses `i-1+8` instead of `i-1`, to shift the array index by 8 (because the first 8 entries in the arrays are for Nokia products).

Both functions are used as event-handlers for the `onBlur` event of the two quantity text fields (code lines 134 and 159). To trigger the event, click the mouse button while the cursor is in one of the text fields, and then click the button again when the cursor is somewhere else in the window.

The form uses the `javascript:` protocol as its event-handler (in code line 60 of the `tutorial2471.html` file). When the customer clicks the `Order` button, an `alert` box is displayed.

The Web page is formatted using tables, as a result of our use of an HTML editor.

Hands-on exercise:

Remove code lines 18 and 38. Save and run the code. What happens? Now extend the code to verify the input to the form (in the `Customer Information` and `Cellular Phone Number` sections). Also, develop an automatic function similar to `automaticNokia()` to handle the last select list of the Web page.

```
1   <?xml version="1.0" encoding="iso-8859-1"?>
2   <!DOCTYPE html PUBLIC "-//W3C//DTD XHTML 1.1//EN"
3       "http://www.w3.org/TR/xhtml11/DTD/xhtml11.dtd">
4   <html xmlns="http://www.w3.org/1999/xhtml">
5   <!-- Generated by AceHTM http://freeware.acehtml.com -->
6   <head>
7   <title>Automatic Filling of Form Elements</title>
8   <script language="javascript">
9
10  products = ["Nokia 5120i", "Nokia 6120i", "Nokia 8260",
    "Nokia 5160i", "Nokia 6161", "Nokia 918", "Nokia 252",
    "Nokia 282", "Motorola Startac 7790i", "Motorola
    Startac 7797", "Motorola Startac 3000", "Motorola M3090",
    "Motorola Timeport", "Ericsson DF688"];
11  inventory = [10, 5, 3, 0, 20, 12, 7, 2, 1, 30, 22, 5, 7, 11];
12  unitSalePrice = [29.95, 50.00, 249.00, 60.00, 80.00, 0.0, 60.00,
    80.00, 100.00, 100.00, 35.00, 29.00, 100.00, 0.0];
13
14  subtotalNokia = 0.0;
15  subtotalMotorola = 0.0;
16
17  function automaticNokia() {
18  subtotalNokia = 0.0;
19      maxNokia = document.forms[0].nokia.options.length;
20      for (i=0;i<maxNokia;i++) {
21          if (document.forms[0].nokia.options[i].selected) {
22              if (document.forms[0].textfield723.value >
    inventory[i-1]){
23                  alert ("Low inventory; Only " +
    inventory[i-1] + " are available");
24                  break;
25              }//if
26              document.forms[0].textfield823.value
    =unitSalePrice[i-1];
27              document.forms[0].textfield923.value =
    unitSalePrice[i-1]*document.forms[0].textfield723.value;
28              subtotalNokia +=
    parseFloat(document.forms[0].textfield923.value);
29          }//if
30      }//for
31              subtotal = subtotalNokia + subtotalMotorola;
32              document.forms[0].textfield9222.value = subtotal;
33              document.forms[0].textfield92222.value = ((5*
    subtotal)/100).toFixed(2);
34              document.forms[0].textfield922222.value =
    (parseFloat (document.forms[0].textfield9222.value) +
    parseFloat
    (document.forms[0].textfield92222.value)).toFixed(2);
```

```
35   }//automaticNokia()
36
37   function automaticMotorola() {
38   subtotalMotorola = 0.0;
39      maxMotorola = document.forms[0].motorola.options.length;
40      for (i=0;i<maxMotorola;i++) {
41          if (document.forms[0].motorola.options[i].selected) {
42              if (document.forms[0].textfield72.value >
     inventory[i-1+8]){
43                  alert ("Low inventory; Only " +
     inventory[i-1+8] + " are available");
44                  break;
45              }//if
46              document.forms[0].textfield82.value
     =unitSalePrice[i-1+8];
47              document.forms[0].textfield92.value =
     unitSalePrice[i-1+8]*document.forms[0].textfield72.value;
48              subtotalMotorola +=
     parseFloat(document.forms[0].textfield92.value);
49          }//if
50      }//for
51              subtotal = subtotalNokia + subtotalMotorola;
52              document.forms[0].textfield9222.value = subtotal;
53              document.forms[0].textfield92222.value = ((5*
     subtotal)/100).toFixed(2);
54              document.forms[0].textfield922222.value =
     (parseFloat (document.forms[0].textfield9222.value) +
     parseFloat
     (document.forms[0].textfield92222.value)).toFixed(2);
55   }//automaticMotorola()
56
57   </script>
58   <body bgcolor="#FFFFFF">
59   <h2 align="center">Check our low prices on cell phones</h2>
60   <form method="post" action="javascript:alert('Observe the
     automatically filled form fields')">
61     <table width="8%" border="0">
62       <tr align="center">
63         <td colspan="20" align="left" bgcolor="#FFFF00">
64           <div align="center"><b>Customer Information</b></div>
65         </td>
66       </tr>
67       <tr>
68         <td colspan="2" align="left" bgcolor="#FFFFCC"><b>First
     Name:</b> </td>
69         <td colspan="11" bgcolor="#FFFFCC">
70           <input type="text" name="textfield524" size="21">
71         </td>
```

```
72      <td width="6%" bgcolor="#FFFFCC"><b>M.I.:</b></td>
73      <td width="2%" bgcolor="#FFFFCC">
74        <input type="text" name="textfield" size="1">
75      </td>
76      <td colspan="3" bgcolor="#FFFFCC"><b>Last Name:</b> </td>
77      <td colspan="2" bgcolor="#FFFFCC">
78        <input type="text" name="textfield53" size="20">
79      </td>
80    </tr>
81    <tr>
82      <td colspan="2" align="left"
   bgcolor="#CCFF99"><b>Address:</b> </td>
83      <td colspan="11" bgcolor="#CCFF99">
84        <input type="text" name="textfield523" size="21">
85      </td>
86      <td colspan="4" bgcolor="#CCFF99"><b>Phone Number:</b></td>
87      <td colspan="3" bgcolor="#CCFF99">
88        <input type="text" name="textfield5" size="20">
89      </td>
90    </tr>
91    <tr>
92      <td colspan="2" align="left" bgcolor="#FFFFCC"><b>City:
   </b></td>
93      <td colspan="11" bgcolor="#FFFFCC">
94        <input type="text" name="textfield522" size="21">
95      </td>
96      <td colspan="4" bgcolor="#FFFFCC"><b>Zip Code:</b></td>
97      <td colspan="3" bgcolor="#FFFFCC">
98        <input type="text" name="textfield52" size="20">
99      </td>
100   </tr>
101   <tr>
102     <td colspan="20" align="left" bgcolor="#FFFF00">
103       <div align="center"><b>Cellular Phone Number</b></div>
104     </td>
105   </tr>
106   <tr>
107     <td colspan="2" height="2" align="left"
   bgcolor="#FFFFCC"><b>Cell Phone
108         #</b></td>
109     <td colspan="18" height="2" bgcolor="#FFFFCC">
110       <input type="text" name="textfield32" size="25">
111     </td>
112   </tr>
113   <tr>
114     <td colspan="20" align="left" bgcolor="#FFFF00">
115       <div align="center"><b>Items Purchased</b></div>
116     </td>
```

```
117        </tr>
118        <tr>
119          <td colspan="2" align="left" bgcolor="#FFFFCC"><b>Nokia
     Phones:</b> </td>
120          <td colspan="3" bgcolor="#FFFFCC">
121            <select name="nokia">
122              <option selected>Select a Phone</option>
123              <option>Nokia 5120i</option>
124              <option>Nokia 6210</option>
125              <option>Nokia 8260</option>
126              <option>Nokia 5160</option>
127              <option>Nokia 6161</option>
128              <option>Nokia 918</option>
129              <option>Nokia 252</option>
130              <option>Nokia 282</option>
131            </select>
132          </td>
133          <td colspan="10" bgcolor="#FFFFCC"><b>Quantity:</b>
134            <input type="text" name="textfield723" size="4"
     onBlur="automaticNokia()">
135          </td>
136          <td colspan="2" bgcolor="#FFFFCC"><b>Price:</b> </td>
137          <td width="7%" bgcolor="#FFFFCC">
138            <input type="text" name="textfield823" size="7">
139          </td>
140          <td width="11%" bgcolor="#FFFFCC"><b>Total:</b></td>
141          <td width="28%" bgcolor="#FFFFCC">
142            <input type="text" name="textfield923" size="8">
143          </td>
144        </tr>
145        <tr>
146          <td colspan="2" align="left" bgcolor="#CCFF99"><b>Motorola
     Phones:</b></td>
147          <td colspan="3" bgcolor="#CCFF99">
148            <select name="motorola">
149              <option selected>Select a Phone</option>
150              <option>M Startac 7790i</option>
151              <option>M Startac 7797</option>
152              <option>M Startac 3000</option>
153              <option>M M3090</option>
154              <option>Mot Timeport</option>
155              <option>Eric DF688</option>
156            </select>
157          </td>
158          <td colspan="10" bgcolor="#CCFF99"><b>Quantity:</b>
159            <input type="text" name="textfield72" size="4"
     onBlur="automaticMotorola()">
160          </td>
```

```
161      <td colspan="2" bgcolor="#CCFF99"><b>Price:</b> </td>
162      <td width="7%" bgcolor="#CCFF99">
163        <input type="text" name="textfield82" size="7">
164      </td>
165      <td width="11%" bgcolor="#CCFF99"><b>Total:</b></td>
166      <td width="28%" bgcolor="#CCFF99">
167        <input type="text" name="textfield92" size="8">
168      </td>
169    </tr>
170    <tr>
171      <td colspan="2" align="left"
   bgcolor="#FFFFCC"><b>Accessories:</b></td>
172      <td colspan="3" bgcolor="#FFFFCC">
173        <select name="select3">
174          <option selected>Select an item</option>
175          <option>Nokia SKH</option>
176          <option>Det Faceplate </option>
177        </select>
178      </td>
179      <td colspan="10" bgcolor="#FFFFCC"><b>Quantity:</b>
180        <input type="text" name="textfield722" size="4">
181      </td>
182      <td colspan="2" bgcolor="#FFFFCC"><b>Price:</b> </td>
183      <td width="7%" bgcolor="#FFFFCC">
184        <input type="text" name="textfield822" size="7">
185      </td>
186      <td width="11%" bgcolor="#FFFFCC"><b>Total:</b></td>
187      <td width="28%" bgcolor="#FFFFCC">
188        <input type="text" name="textfield922" size="8">
189      </td>
190    </tr>
191    <tr>
192      <td colspan="20" align="left" bgcolor="#CCFF99">
193        <div align="center"><b>Cost</b></div>
194      </td>
195    </tr>
196    <tr bgcolor="#FFFFCC">
197      <td colspan="18" align="left" bgcolor="#FFFFCC"></td>
198      <td width="11%" bgcolor="#FFFFCC"><b>Subtotal:</b></td>
199      <td width="28%" bgcolor="#FFFFCC">
200        <input type="text" name="textfield9222" size="8">
201      </td>
202    </tr>
203    <tr bgcolor="#FFFFCC">
204      <td colspan="18" align="left" bgcolor="#CCFF99"></td>
205      <td width="11%" bgcolor="#CCFF99"><b>Tax:</b></td>
206      <td width="28%" bgcolor="#CCFF99">
207        <input type="text" name="textfield92222" size="8">
```

```
208        </td>
209        </tr>
210        <tr bgcolor="#FFFFCC">
211          <td colspan="18" align="left" bgcolor="#FFFFCC"><b>
    </b></td>
212          <td width="11%" bgcolor="#FFFFCC"><b>Total:</b></td>
213          <td width="28%" bgcolor="#FFFFCC">
214            <input type="text" name="textfield922222" size="8">
215          </td>
216        </tr>
217        <tr>
218          <td colspan="2" align="left" bgcolor="#CCFF99"><b>
219            <input type="submit" name="order" value="Order">
220          </b></td>
221          <td colspan="18" bgcolor="#CCFF99">
222            <input type="reset" name="reset" value="Cancel">
223          </td>
224        </tr>
225       </table>
226     </form>
227     </body>
228     </html>
```

FAQs

Form Input Validation (Section 24.4)

Q: A form must use names that look like arrays—for example, `<input name="mine[1]">`. However, when I use these names in a JavaScript program, it thinks they are array elements and gives me an error. How can I solve this problem?

A: The easy solution is to change the name. If you cannot, use the associative array to access the form elements—for example, `document.forms[0].elements[1]`. This way, you bypass all the names of the form elements.

Blackbox

Section 24.1 (Introduction): Form validation on the client side saves server time.

Section 24.2 (Form Object): The `Form` object contains information about a form. Its properties are `action`, `elements`, `encoding`, `length`, `method`, `name`, and `target`. Its methods are `handleEvent()`, `reset()`, and `submit()`.

Section 24.3 (Form-Element Objects): The form-element objects are text field, text area, password, checkbox, radio button, button, submit button, reset button, hidden, file, select lists, and option.

Section 24.4 (Form Input Validation) (Examples 24.1–24.6): Validate a form at the form level by using the onSumbit event.

Section 24.5 (Footer Scripts) (Example 24.7): A footer script comes after the </body> tag. Use it to access form elements without using event-handlers.

Section 24.6 (Form Data Processing) (Examples 24.8–24.10): Form data can be stored in spreadsheets and databases or sent via e-mail. Three specific methods of form data processing employ Java servlets and a Microsoft Excel sheets, PHP and a MySQL database, and Perl and e-mail processing.

Section 24.7 (Tutorials): One tutorial shows how to fill in form elements automatically.

Quick reference for the syntax presented in this chapter

Object	Item	Name	Description	Example
form	Variables	action	Reflects the action attribute	myForm.action
		elements	Array of the form elements	myForm.elements[i]
		encoding	Reflects the enctype attribute	myForm.encoding
		length	The number of elements in the form	myForm.length
		method	Reflects the method attribute	myForm.method
		name	Reflects the name attribute	myForm.name
		target	Reflects the target attribute	myForm.target
	Methods	handleEvent()	Invokes the handler for the specific event	myForm.handleEvent()
		reset()	Resets the form	myForm.reset()
		submit()	Submits the form	myForm.submit()
text field text area password	Variables	defaultValue	object's default value	myText.defaultValue
		forms	object's forms	myText.forms
		name	object's name	myText.name
		type	object's type	myText.type
		value	object's current value	myText.value
	Methods	blur(), focus(), handleEvent(), and select()		

Object	Item	Name	Description	Example
checkbox radio button	Variables	`checked`, `defaultChecked`, `form`, `name`, `type`, and `value`		
	Methods	`blur()`, `click()`, `focus()`, and `handleEvent()`		
button submit button reset button	Variables	`form`, `name`, `type`, and `value`		
	Methods	`blur()`, `click()`, `focus()`, and `handleEvent()`		
hidden	Variables	`form`, `name`, `type`, and `value`		
	Methods	`none`		
file	Variables	`form`, `name`, `type`, and `value`		
	Methods	`blur()`, `focus()`, `handleEvent()`, and `select()`		
select list	Variables	`list`, `form`, `length`, `name`, `options`, `selectedIndex`, and `type`		
	Methods	`blur()`, `focus()`, and `handleEvent()`		
option	Variables	`defaultSelected`, `selected`, `text`, and `value`		
	Methods	`none`		

Check Your Progress

At the end of this chapter, you should

- ✔   understand the need for form input validation (Section 24.1);
- ✔   understand the `Form` object and form-element objects (Sections 24.2 and 24.3);
- ✔   understand form input validation (Section 24.4);
- ✔   understand footer scripts (Section 24.5);
- ✔   understand form data processing via Servlets and spreadsheets (Section 24.6);
- ✔   understand form data processing via PHP and mySQL (Section 24.6);
- ✔   understand form data processing via Perl and e-mail PHP (Section 24.6);
- ✔   have practiced using methods of form input validation (Section 24.7).

Problems

The exercises are designed for a lab setting, while the homework is to be done outside class time.

Exercises

24.1   Write a JavaScript application that selects and prints the content of a text field and submits the form.

24.2   Write a JavaScript application that selects and prints radio button and submits the form.

24.3   Write a JavaScript application that selects and prints button and submits the form.

Homework

24.4   Write a JavaScript application that erases the content of a text field.

24.5   Write a JavaScript application that selects a checkbox and submits the form.

24.6   Modify Example 24.8 to create your own database, and apply new SQL queries to it.

24.7   Modify Example 24.9 to create your own database, and apply new SQL queries to it. Also, replace the form by one of your own creation.

24.8   Modify Example 24.10 to create your own form and process it.

24.9   Modify Tutorial 24.7.1 to place the cursor in the wrong text field after validation.

24.10 Modify Tutorial 24.7.1 to divide each array in code lines 10–12 of the `tutorial2471.html` file into two separate arrays: one for Nokia products and the other one for Motorola products. Change the code accordingly.

Bibliography

[1] ...

[2] ...

[3] ...

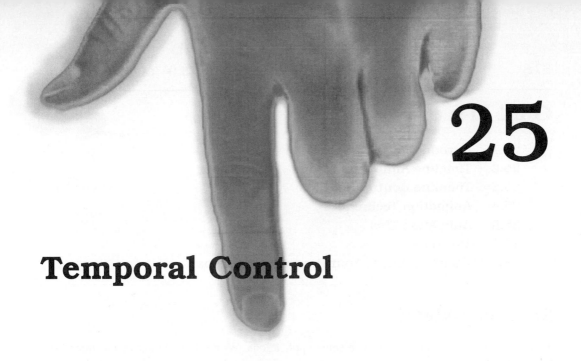

Temporal Control

Goal

Understand time control in JavaScript, how to time out user input, how to create timeline animation, how to use layers to create animation, and how to put animation to good use.

Objectives

- The need for timeline control
- JavaScript's timeline functions
- Timeline events
- Timeline event-handling objects
- Timeline animation techniques: source files and hidden layers
- Animation tips
- The use of HTML editors for animation

817

Outline

25.1 Introduction

Time can be an important element in some applications. Within the context of the Internet, a Web page may choose to display a sequence of elements over time to its surfers, creating what is known as a **timeline**. Elements of a timeline could be objects or events. Objects may be images that make up an animation. Events may be user inputs or program outputs. There is a time interval between the display of each timeline element in order to allow users to observe the sequence. We control this time interval, thus affecting the speed of display.

We identify two groups of timeline applications. The first group has to do with user interaction with a JavaScript program. We can get the user's attention by specifying a time interval—for example, 10 seconds—for the receipt of user input. When the time elapses, we prompt the user again. Many interesting applications belong to this group. Consider some game shows that have a time element, such as *Jeopardy* and *Wheel of Fortune* . A user must give an answer within a preset time interval. Internet versions of these games are thus an example of this group of timeline applications.

The second group of timeline applications has to do with a sequence of images that represents the progression of an event overtime. We refer to this group as timeline animation. **Animation** is the process by which the illusion of movement is achieved by creating and displaying a sequence of images that are different from each other or that show progressive motion. This group also has many interesting applications. For example, we can create an online storefront that cycles through and displays products for preview by Web surfers. Some engineering and science applications also belong to this group—for example, applications that simulate a projectile's motion under gravitational force, or the movement of a car under Newton's law.

As GIF animation seems easier to create, why do we need to use JavaScript animation? JavaScript animation is more universal and adaptable. We can manipulate an animation's behavior by editing the script of the animation, and we can alter the animation's content by replacing old image files by new ones. We can also use mathematical equations and formulas in JavaScript animation.

25.2 Timeline Animation

The definition of animation as the display of an ordered sequence of images is known as real-time playback animation. Each image represents an **animation frame** in the animation sequence. We create the frames (images) one by one, in the right order, and save them in files. A JavaScript program can display the frames later on in real time to create the animation.

The generation of the content and images of animation frames can be done in many ways. One way is to save some images in files. For example, we can scan and save images of people, cars, social events, meetings, products, or other objects. We then write a JavaScript program that displays the images in the correct order to create the effect of a timeline.

Another way is to use some scientific principles to generate frame content. For example, we can use the equations of motion to derive the path of motion of an object such as a baseball that has been hit by a batter. We generate points in the time domain and place the ball there. Each point and its ball compose the content of a frame. When we play all the frames back, we see the baseball flying from the batter's location.

The generation of animation frames can be time consuming. We can use the concept of keyframes and inbetweening to speed up the process. A **keyframe** is an important frame in the animation sequence. **Inbetweening** (also known as tweening) is an interpolation process that generates in-between frames to fill in the gaps between keyframes. Consider the animation of raising a flag on a pole. We can create two keyframes: one showing the position of the flag at the start, and the other showing the position of the flag at the end. We can then use an animation program that can generate the in-between frames by interpolating the two keyframes linearly. Macromedia Dreamweaver implements this idea.

How do we control the duration of animation during playback? We typically specify the number of frames and the **frame rate**—the number of frames per seconds (fps). In JavaScript, we can specify the number of frames and the interval (delay) between frames. If we have 10 frames and we use a 0.1-second interval, the frame rate becomes 10 fps. Browsers use a default setting of 15 fps. This is a good average rate to use for a browser. Browsers always play back every frame of the animation, even if they cannot attain the specified frame rate on the client computer.

25.3 Timeline Control

The two key issues in timeline control are frame generation and the frame rate. Frame generation entails creating and saving files containing images. JavaScript provide four functions to control the frame rate. The four functions belong to the `window` object. They are `setInterval()`, `clearInterval()`, `setTimeout()`, and `clearTimeout()`. Table 25.1 describes each method.

Table 25.1   JavaScript's timeline methods.

methods: `setInterval()`, `clearInterval()`, `setTimeout()`, and `clearTimeout()`	
Method	Description
`setInterval()`	❶Evaluates an expression or calls a function *every time* a specified number of milliseconds elapses, until canceled by a call to `clearInterval()`. ❷Syntax: `setInterval (expression|function, delay)`. The | means "OR". The `delay` is the time interval between each invocation of the `expression` or `function`, specified in milliseconds. ❸Returns a value, call it `intervalID`, that can be passed to the `clearInterval()` method.
`clearInterval()`	❶Cancels a timeout that was set by the `setInterval()` method. ❷Syntax: `clearInterval (intervalID)`. `intervalID` is the value returned by the corresponding `setInterval() method`.
`setTimeout()`	❶Evaluates an expression or calls a function *once* after a specified number of milliseconds elapses. ❷Syntax: `setTimeout (expression|function, delay)`. The | means "OR". The `delay` is the time interval between each invocation of the `expression` or `function`, specified in milliseconds. ❸Returns a value, call it `timeoutID`, that can be passed to the `clearTimeout()` method.
`clearTimeout()`	❶Cancels a timeout that was set by the `setTimeout()` method. ❷Syntax: `clearTimeout (timeoutlID)`. `timeoutID` is the value returned by the corresponding `setTimeout() method`.

Example 25.1 Use the `setInterval()` and `clearInterval()` methods.

Write a JavaScript program that creates a timeline, using time intervals.

Solution 25.1 Using the AceHTML editor, generate the given code, and save it as `example251.html`. Render the Web page in a browser.

Code explained:

1. Lines 11–13 define the `setTimer()` function, which uses the `setInterval()` method.
2. Lines 15–19 define the `clearTimer()` function, which uses the `clearInterval()` method.
3. Lines 23–25 create a form with a button.

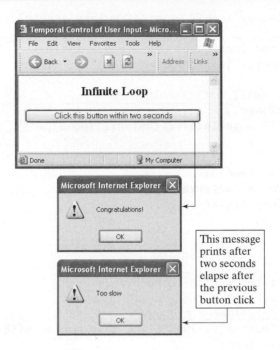

Discussion:

This example requests that a Web surfer clicks the button shown in the foregoing topmost screen capture within two seconds (2000 milliseconds). When the Web surfer clicks the button, `clearTimer()` calls `clearInterval()` (in code line 16). `clearInterval()` prints a message (code line 17) and calls `setTime()` (code line 18). `setTime()` calls `setInterval()` (code line 12), which runs indefinitely and prints a message (code line 12) every two seconds. Click the `OK` button anytime to close the message. The only way to stop the infinite loop set by `setInterval()` is to call `clearInterval()` (via code line 24) and pass the `intervalID` variable to it. It is this variable that identifies to `clearInterval()` which `setInterval()` method to stop if the JavaScript program uses more than one. (See Example 25.2.)

Hands-on exercise:

Replace `setInterval()` and `clearInterval()` by `setTimeout()` and `clearTimeout()`, respectively. Also, replace `intervalID` by `timeoutID`. Save and run the code. What is the difference? *Hint*: `setTimeout()` runs only once.

```
1   <?xml version="1.0" encoding="iso-8859-1"?>
2   <!DOCTYPE html PUBLIC "-//W3C//DTD XHTML 1.1//EN"
3       "http://www.w3.org/TR/xhtml11/DTD/xhtml11.dtd">
4   <html xmlns="http://www.w3.org/1999/xhtml">
```

```
5    <!-- Generated by AceHTM http://freeware.acehtml.com -->
6    <head>
7    <title>Temporal Control of User Input</title>
8    <script language="javascript">
9
10   intervalID = null;
11   function setTimer(){
12       intervalID = setInterval("alert('Too slow')", 2000);
13   }
14
15   function clearTimer(){
16       clearInterval(intervalID);
17       alert("Congratulations!");
18       setTimer();
19   }
20
21   </script>
22   <h2 align="center">Infinite Loop</h2>
23   <form name="myForm" method="post"
     action="mailto:zeid@coe.neu.edu">
24   <input type="button" value="Click this button within two seconds"
     onClick="clearTimer()"/>
25   </form>
26   </body>
27   </html>
```

Example 25.2 Use multiple setInterval() methods.

Write a JavaScript program that uses multiple setInterval() methods.

Solution 25.2 Using the AceHTML editor, generate the given code, and save it as example252.html. Render the Web page in a browser.

Code explained:

1. Lines 12 and 13 both call the setInterval() method; the particular method call used depends on which button was clicked by the user.
2. Lines 25 and 26 create two buttons.

Discussion:

This example extends Example 25.1. It creates two buttons: one with a 3-second time delay and the other with a 1-second time delay. We pass the button label (in code lines 25 and 26) to clearTimer(), which then calls setInterval() with the proper time delay.

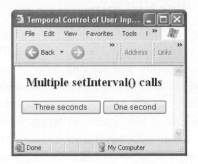

Hands-on exercise:

Replace setInterval() and clearInterval() by setTimeout() and clearTime-out(), respectively. Also, replace intervalID by timeoutID. Save and run the code. What is the difference? *Hint*: setTimeout() runs only once.

```
1   <?xml version="1.0" encoding="iso-8859-1"?>
2   <!DOCTYPE html PUBLIC "-//W3C//DTD XHTML 1.1//EN"
3       "http://www.w3.org/TR/xhtml11/DTD/xhtml11.dtd">
4   <html xmlns="http://www.w3.org/1999/xhtml">
5   <!-- Generated by AceHTM http://freeware.acehtml.com -->
6   <head>
7   <title>Temporal Control of User Input</title>
8   <script language="javascript">
9
10  intervalID = null;
11  function setTimer(label){
12      if(label == "Three seconds") {intervalID =
    setInterval("alert('Too slow')", 3000);}
13      else {intervalID = setInterval("alert('Too slow')", 1000);}
14  }
15
16  function clearTimer(label){
17      clearInterval(intervalID);
18      alert("Congratulations!");
19      setTimer(label);
20  }
21
22  </script>
23  <h2 align="center">Multiple setInterval() calls</h2>
24  <form name="myForm" method="post"
    action="mailto:zeid@coe.neu.edu">
25  <Input type="button" value="Three seconds"
    onClick="clearTimer(value)"/>
26  <input type="button" value="One second"
    onClick="clearTimer(value)"/>
27  </form></body></html>
```

25.4 Animation Techniques

DHTML is used to create timeline animation. Two animation techniques exist. One technique changes the properties of layers in a series of frames over time. The animation effect is created by changing the position, size, visibility, and stacking order of layers over time. We include all the layers in the Web page and make all of them, but one, invisible. We start the timeline effect by displaying the invisible layers, one at a time, in an ordered fashion.

The other technique uses image files instead of layers. It loads one file per frame during the animation sequence. This technique is slower than the layers technique.

The two animation techniques can be viewed in the larger context of timelines in general. In addition to animation, timelines are useful for other actions that occur after a Web page has been loaded. For example, timelines can change the source file of an image, and they can execute behaviors at a particular time. They can also display sequences of visual instructions, PowerPoint slides, charts, and other documents that illustrate progression over time. For example, we can display a timeline that show the growth or contraction of a budget, fundraising results, or student enrollment.

Example 25.3 Use layers for animation.

Write a JavaScript program that uses layers for animation.

Solution 25.3 Using the AceHTML editor, generate the given code, and save it as `example253.html`. Render the Web page in a browser.

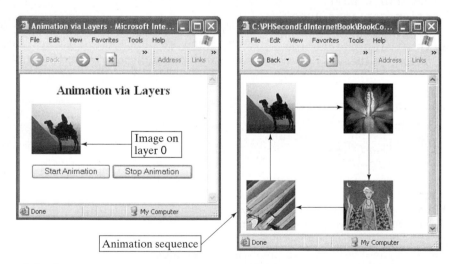

Code explained:

1. Lines 10 and 11 initialize `frame` (used as a counter) and `timeoutID` (used by the `setTimeout()` and `clearTimeout()` methods).

2. Lines 12–20 define the `prepareAnimation()` method, which creates an array of image objects, using the JavaScript `Image` class.

3. Lines 22–29 define a recursive function `animate()` `animate()` calls itself in line 28.

4. Lines 34–36 and 43–49 define four layers, 0–3, each of which holds one image. Layer 0 is visible, while layers 1–3 are invisible.

5. Lines 38–41 define a form that has two buttons to control the animation. One button starts animation, while the other stops it.

Discussion:

We animate, via layers, a sequence of four images in the order shown in the forgoing screen capture. The idea behind animation via layers is to have one visible layer at a time. We start by setting layer 0 as visible and layers 1–3 as invisible. When a Web surfer clicks the Start Animation button, we call two functions to handle the event: `prepareAnimation()` specifies that we have four frames for the animation, and `animate()` does the animation. Code line 13 is required in order to make n global, as we need it in code line 26. Code lines 14–18 create the `myImageArray`, whose elements are `Image` objects; each element holds an image file. All the image files reside in the `images` subfolder, and each file has the `.jpg` file extension, as shown in code line 18. The `example253.html` file and the `images` folder must be in the same directory (folder).

Code lines 23–25 set layer 1–3 to be invisible, to ensure that the animation works correctly. Code line 26 resets the `frame` counter to 0 each time it reaches the value 3, its maximum allowable limit. Code line 27 sets the layer whose Id is `frame` to visible. Code line 28 sets the animation speed (how fast to display the frames) to 500 milliseconds.

The animation buttons (code lines 39 and 40) check the current value of `timeoutID`. Only if it is `null` does animation should begin; this value disables the Start Animation button during animation, should the user happen to click it. Similarly, the Stop Animation button is effective only if animation is running. Code line 40 must set `timeOutID` to `null` in order for both buttons to work correctly.

Hands-on exercise:

Remove code lines 23–25. Save and run the code. What happens? Explain the results. *Hint*: Although all the layers are visible, only the last one (layer 3) is always displayed, because it is the last layer to be rendered (code lines 48–49). Animation is still running, although it does not seem so visually. Also, remove code lines 10, 11, and 13. Save and Run the code. What happens?

```
1   <?xml version="1.0" encoding="iso-8859-1"?>
2   <!DOCTYPE html PUBLIC "-//W3C//DTD XHTML 1.1//EN"
3       "http://www.w3.org/TR/xhtml11/DTD/xhtml11.dtd">
4   <html xmlns="http://www.w3.org/1999/xhtml">
5   <!-- Generated by AceHTM http://freeware.acehtml.com -->
6   <head>
7   <title>Animation via Layers</title>
8   <script language="javascript">
```

```
9
10    frame=0;
11    timeoutID = null;
12    function prepareAnimation (n) {   //build array of Image objects
13        totalFrames = n; //to make n available globally
14        myImageArray=new Array(n);
15        imagenames=new Array("camel",  "flower", "night","surf");
16        for (i=0;i<n;i++){
17            myImageArray[i]=new Image();
18            myImageArray[i].src="images/" + imagenames[i] + ".jpg";
19        }//for loop
20    }
21
22    function animate() {
23        for (i=1;i<totalFrames;i++){
24        document.getElementById(frame).style.visibility = "hidden";
25        }
26        frame =(frame+1)%totalFrames;
27        document.getElementById(frame).style.visibility = "visible";
28        timeoutID = setTimeout("animate()", 500);
29    }
30
31    </script>
32    <body>
33    <h2 align="center">Animation via Layers</h2>
34    <div id="0" class="page" style="position:absolute; left:20px;
      top:50px;  width:50; height:50; visibility: visible;">
35    <img src="images/camel.jpg">
36    </div>
37    <div id="form" class="page" style="position:absolute; left:20px;
      top:150px; visibility:visible;">
38    <form>
39    <input type="button" value="Start Animation"
      onClick="if(timeoutID==null){prepareAnimation(4);animate()}"/>
40    <input type="button" value="Stop Animation"
      onClick="if(timeoutID)clearTimeout(timeoutID);timeoutID=null" />
41    </form>
42    </div>
43    <div id="1" class="page" style="position:absolute; left:20px;
      top:50px;  width:50; height:50; visibility: hidden;">
44    <img src="images/flower.jpg">
45    </div>
46    <div id="2" class="page" style="position:absolute; left:20px;
      top:50px;  width:50; height:50; visibility: hidden;">
47    <img src="images/night.jpg"></div>
48    <div id="3" class="page" style="position:absolute; left:20px;
      top:50px;  width:50; height:50; visibility: hidden;">
49    <img src="images/surf.jpg"></div></body></html>
```

Example 25.4 Use image files for animation.

Write a JavaScript program that uses source files for animation.

Solution 25.4 Using the AceHTML editor, generate the given code, and save it as `example254.html`. Render the Web page in a browser.

Code explained:

1. Line 23 assigns an image object to the Web-page image.
2. Line 30 must be used to create a placeholder to display the images of the animation sequences in the Web page.

Discussion:

This example achieves the same animation of Example 25.3 by displaying the four images in the same location (`document.images[0]`, in code line 23) in the Web page.

Hands-on exercise:

Is there any way you can display the animation as four images shown one next to the other horizontally? If not, use layers to achieve this objective.

```
1   <?xml version="1.0" encoding="iso-8859-1"?>
2   <!DOCTYPE html PUBLIC "-//W3C//DTD XHTML 1.1//EN"
3       "http://www.w3.org/TR/xhtml11/DTD/xhtml11.dtd">
4   <html xmlns="http://www.w3.org/1999/xhtml">
5   <!-- Generated by AceHTM http://freeware.acehtml.com -->
6   <head>
7   <title>Animation via Image Files</title>
8   <script language="javascript">
```

```
9
10   frame=0;
11   timeoutID = null;
12   function prepareAnimation(n) {  //build array of Image objects
13       totalFrames = n; //to make n available globally
14       myImageArray=new Array(n);
15       imagenames=new Array("camel",  "flower", "night","surf");
16       for (i=0;i<n;i++){
17           myImageArray[i]=new Image();
18           myImageArray[i].src="images/" + imagenames[i] + ".jpg";
19       }//for loop
20   }
21
22   function animate() {
23       document.images[0].src = myImageArray[frame].src
24       frame =(frame+1)%totalFrames;
25       timeoutID = setTimeout("animate()", 500);
26   }
27
28   </script>
29   <h2 align="center">Animation via Image Files</h2>
30   <img src = "images/camel.jpg">
31   <form>
32   <input type="button" value="Start Animation"
     onClick="if(timeoutID==null){prepareAnimation(4);animate()}"/>
33   <input type="button" value="Stop Animation"
     onClick="if(timeoutID)clearTimeout(timeoutID);timeoutID=null" />
34   </form>
35   </body>
36   </html>
```

25.5 Animation Tips

One key issue in creating animations is dealing with the large number of image files and their large sizes. The general advice is to keep the number and sizes as small as possible. Here are some specific tips:

1. **Use (show and hide) layers instead of changing the source files of the images.** Switching the source file of an image can slow down the animation, because the new image file must be downloaded.
2. **Use more frames if the animation looks choppy.** More frames create smoother animation. Create a small number of keyframes, and use software to create many in-between frames.
3. **Avoid animating large image files.** Improve the animation speed by animating only small parts of a large image. For example, show a car moving by animating the wheels only.
4. **Create simple animations.** Avoid creating complex animations that browsers cannot handle.

25.6 Tutorials

25.6.1   Creation of Random Popup Windows
(Study Sections 25.3 and 25.4)

Example 23.5 showed how to control the location of a popup window. We extend this idea in this tutorial by creating a popup window that has a random location, random size (width and height), and random background color.

Using the AceHTML editor, generate the given code, and save it as `tutorial2561.html`. Render the Web page in a browser.

Code explained:

1. Lines 9 and 10 initialize the `win` and `intervalID` variables, respectively.

2. Lines 11–32 define the `bounce()` function, which creates a new popup window.

3. Lines 34–38 define the `startwin()` method, which uses the `setInterval()` method in line 36.

4. Lines 40–46 define the `stopwin()` function, which uses the `clearInterval()` method in line 45.

5. Lines 51 and 52 create two buttons that control the window generation.

Discussion:

The foregoing screen captures show the Web page (with the two buttons) and two sample random popup windows. When a Web surfer clicks the `Start Windows` button, the `startwin()` method is invoked (code line 51). This method checks (in code line 35) whether any popup windows are currently open. If not, it starts generating them (in code line 36) by calling the `bounce()` method with a time delay of 1.5 seconds (1500 milliseconds).

The `bounce()` method generates a random `width` (in code line 13) and random `height` (in code line 14). We use `screen.availWidth` and `screen.availHeight` to ensure that the size of any popup window size is a fraction of the screen size. The screen size could be that of a 15-, 17-, 19-, or 21- inch monitor.

Code lines 21 and 22 set the location of the popup window randomly and ensure that the location and size of the window are within the screen's limits.

Code lines 23–26 create a random color by generating three RGB hex signals (code lines 23–25) and combining them (in code line 26) to create the random background color. The `toString(16)` method converts the random decimal value generated to a hex (base 16) value. Code lines 27–30 create a popup window with a `(0, 0)` location. Code line 31 moves it to the `(x, y)` location.

Hands-on exercise:

Change the code given in this tutorial to use the `setTimeout()` and `clearTimeout()` methods instead of the `setInterval()` and `clearInterval()` methods, respectively.

```
1    <?xml version="1.0" encoding="iso-8859-1"?>
2    <!DOCTYPE html PUBLIC "-//W3C//DTD XHTML 1.1//EN"
3       "http://www.w3.org/TR/xhtml11/DTD/xhtml11.dtd">
4    <html xmlns="http://www.w3.org/1999/xhtml">
5    <!-- Generated by AceHTM http://freeware.acehtml.com -->
6    <head>
7    <title>Random Windows</title>
8    <script language="javascript">
9    win = null;
10   intervalID = null;
11   function bounce() {
12
13       width = Math.floor((Math.random()) * screen.availWidth);
14       height = Math.floor((Math.random()) * screen.availHeight);
15        if(win != null){
16          if(!win.closed)
17            win.close();
18        }
19       win = window.open("", "",
```

```
20                "width=" + width + ",height=" + height);
21       x = Math.floor((Math.random()) * (screen.availWidth -
   width) );
22       y = Math.floor((Math.random()) * (screen.availHeight -
   height) );
23       red = Math.floor((Math.random() * 256)).toString(16);
24       green = Math.floor((Math.random() * 256)).toString(16);
25       blue = Math.floor((Math.random() * 256)).toString(16);
26       col = "#" + red + green + blue;
27       ndoc = win.document;
28       ndoc.write("<body bgcolor='" + col + "'>");
29       ndoc.write("<h1> Random window </h1></body>");
30       ndoc.close();
31       win.moveTo(x,y);
32    }
33
34    function startwin(){
35       if(win == null || win.closed){
36          intervalID = setInterval("bounce()", 1500);
37       }
38    }
39
40    function stopwin(){
41       if(win != null){
42         if(!win.closed)
43            win.close();
44       }
45     clearInterval(intervalID);
46    }
47    </script>
48    <body>
49    <h2 align="center">Random Windows</h2>
50    <form>
51    <input type="button" value="Start Windows" onclick="startwin();">
52    <input type="button" value="Stop Windows" onclick="stopwin();">
53    </form></body></html>
```

FAQs

Animation Techniques (Section 25.4)

Q: I cannot get code for an animation to work correctly. What could be the problem?

A: Make sure that the animation function that you call in the `setInterval()` or `setTimeout()` method is enclosed between quotes.

Blackbox

Section 25.1 (Introduction): Timeline control and animation are useful JavaScript applications.

Section 25.2 (Timeline Animation): Timeline animation uses frames, keyframes, and a frame rate. Timeline animation is a playback animation.

Section 25.3 (Timeline Control) (Examples 25.1 and 25.2): JavaScript provides four functions to control timelines: `setInterval()`, `clearInterval()`, `setTimeout()`, and `clearTimeout()`. They all belong to the `window` object.

Section 25.4 (Animation Techniques) (Examples 25.3 and 25.4): Create animation via two techniques: layers and image files. Change the position, size, visibility, and stacking order of layers over time. Use image files by loading one file per frame during the animation sequence.

Section 25.5 (Animation Tips): Use these tips to increase the quality of your animations: Use (show and hide) layers instead of changing the source files of the images; use more frames if the animation looks choppy; avoid animating large image files; create simple animations.

Section 25.6 (Tutorials): One tutorial shows how to animate a series of popup windows.

Quick reference for the syntax presented in this chapter

Method	Description	Example
`setInterval()`	❶Calls a function *periodically*. ❷Syntax: `setInterval (expression|function, delay)`.	`intervalID = setInterval("bounce()", 300);`
`clearInterval()`	❶Cancels a timeout that was set by the `setInterval()` method.	`clearInterval (intervalID);`
`setTimeout()`	❶Calls a function *once* after a given time increment. ❷Syntax: `setTimeout (expression|function, delay)`.	`timeoutID = setTimeout("bounce()", 300);`
`clearTimeout()`	❶Cancels a timeout that was set by the `setTimeout()` method.	`clearTimeout (timeoutID);`

Check Your Progress

At the end of this chapter, you should

✔   understand timelines (Section 25.1);

✔   understand timeline animation (Section 25.2);

✔   understand timeline control (Section 25.3);

✔ have mastered some animation techniques (Section 25.4);
✔ know some animation tips (Section 25.5);
✔ have practiced implementing animation (Section 25.6).

Problems

The exercises are designed for a lab setting, while the homework is to be done outside class time.

Exercises

25.1 Write a JavaScript application that prints a statement every 5 seconds.

25.2 Write a JavaScript application that plays a sound clip every 5 seconds.

25.3 Write a JavaScript application that animates assembly instructions for a particular item.

25.4 Write a JavaScript application that animates driving instructions.

25.5 Write a JavaScript application that animates filling a cup with liquid.

Homework

25.6 Write a JavaScript application that plays a video clip every 5 seconds.

25.7 Write a JavaScript application that animates a bouncing ball.

25.8 Write a JavaScript application that animates a flying bird.

25.9 Write a JavaScript application that animates a moving boat.

25.10 Write a JavaScript application that animates a person running.

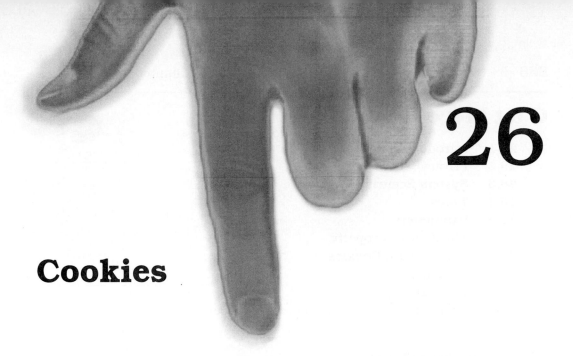

Cookies

Goal

Understand cookies, why servers need to use them, how to use them to identify repeat visitors to a website, how to create website hit counters, and how to deal with cookies.

Objectives

- Cookie files on a client computer
- The relationship between cookies and privacy
- The relationship between cookies and system security
- Types of cookies: client or server, and temporary or persistent
- Parameters of cookies
- The `cookie` property
- Dealing with cookies: read, write (create), overwrite, and delete
- Visibility of cookies

835

Outline

26.1 Introduction

The use of cookies on the Web sometimes generates mystery. How does a Web server "remember" its repeat visitors from previous sessions? How does a Web server "remember" someone's password after the person has entered his or her username? The answer to these puzzling questions is cookies.

A **cookie** is a small amount of information stored on the client or server computer that can be retrieved by a JavaScript program, using the document.cookie property. Cookies might contain information such as login or registration data, online shopping cart information, user preferences, and so forth. When a server receives a request from a browser that includes a cookie, the server is able to use the information stored in the cookie. For example, the server might customize what is sent back to the user or keep a log of particular user's requests.

Cookies are usually set to expire after a predetermined amount of time and are typically saved in memory until the browser software is closed down, at which time they may be saved to disk if their expiration date has not been reached.

Cookies are developed to make up for the stateless nature of the HTTP protocol. HTTP is designed to be stateless in order to make the Web more efficient. Each time a browser requests a URL of a Web page from a Web server, the server treats each request as a completely new interaction, with no knowledge of whether the same browser (client) has been a previous visitor. However, the stateless nature of HTTP makes it difficult to create, for example, online shopping carts that "remember" the user's actions and choices over an extended period of time.

When a browser connects to a server for the first time, the server sends a cookie to the browser. Thereafter, the browser returns a copy of the cookie to the server each time it connects. This exchange creates the illusion of an interaction that spans multiple sessions and multiple Web pages.

Cookies are not intended for use as a general-purpose communication tool to transfer data between a client and a server. Other technologies, such as servlets and JSPs, are better suited for that purpose. Cookies are intended for infrequent storage of small amounts of data. Browsers set limits on how many cookies they accept from one server (usually 20) and the size of a cookie (usually 4 KB).

26.2 Privacy

Cookies cannot be used to steal information that a Web surfer has not provided, information that is not available through JavaScript objects such as `navigator` and `location`, or information that is not part of the client/server connection process, such as an IP address. Cookies can store only information that a surfer has provided when filling out a form or responding to a survey. If the surfer, for example, indicates a preference for a particular color in a survey, the server may change a Web page's background color to the preferred one before sending it to the surfer.

Web surfers must remember that the vast majority of cookies are benign good-faith efforts to improve the Web-browsing experience, not to intrude on one's privacy. Very few websites and Internet companies collect information about users and implement to create profiles (including information on users' tastes and interests) that are used for targeted and customized advertising banners. This type of audience profiling is controlled by the U.S. law, as we have discussed in chapter 6. Moreover, users can refuse to accept cookies from suspicious websites by configuring their browsers appropriately.

26.3 System Security

In addition to privacy issues, cookies carry security implications. Many websites uses cookies for authentication and state preservation. For example, cookies can be used as a sort of admissions ticket. A website that requires a username and a password may store this information in a cookie on the user's computer. When the user attempts to log in by typing in his or her username, the password is entered automatically via the cookie. This approach has the advantages of speeding up the login process and not requiring the user to remember the password. For the server, this approach avoids the overhead of looking up the username and password in a centralized database each and every time a user accesses a Web page.

However, this approach, unless carefully implemented, may compromise system security. Hackers and eavesdroppers armed with a packet sniffer (a program that tries to read TCP packet content) could simply intercept cookies during their journeys from browsers to servers, thus gaining free access to websites.

Cookie interception can be minimized, if not eliminated, by using secure (SSL) Internet connections and by employing techniques to encrypt the entire data set of a cookie. Cookies themselves can provide some security measures as well. For example, a cookie should have an expiration date so as to minimize and contain the damage if it is stolen, as it can then be used for only a finite period of time, after which it becomes invalid. Also, including the client's IP address in cookies renders a stolen cookie unusable through another IP address.

26.4 Types

Cookies can be classified into client-side and server-side categories, according to their storage location. A **client-side cookie** is stored on the client computer. A **server-side cookie** is created on the client computer, but returned to the server for storage. To the user, the type is not important. To the server, server-side cookies have an advantage, as the server can then ensure that they are not deleted. In formed users can delete all the cookies stored on their computers, because they know where they are stored. (See Section 26.5.)

Cookies can also be classified as transient (session) or persistent. A **transient cookie** is a cookie that is active only during a particular browser session; it dies (is deleted) once the user leaves the Web page or kills the browser window. A **persistent cookie** lasts for a predefined amount of time that goes beyond the session that creates it. Persistent cookies are stored in the browser's memory cache (RAM) during the session and in the browser's disk cache (the computer's hard disk) once the session ends. When the user revisits the server that created the cookie, the browser returns the cookie to the server for use.

26.5 Parameters

Thus far, cookies are still a bit of a mystery to us. A knowledge of where they are stored on the client computer and an understanding of their parameters will unravel their secrets and show how they work. As powerful as cookies may seem, the concept behind their design is simple. Think of a cookie as an object with some parameters (attributes). In this chapter, we focus on client-side persistent cookies.

Where are cookies stored on the hard disk of a computer? The answer depends on the browser. The IE browser stores cookies in the `cookies` directory (folder). Each cookie is stored in its own file. There is also an `index.dat` nontext file that contains all the cookies. The full path to this directory depends on the Windows version being used. For Windows XP, it is

`C:\Documents and Settings\zeid\Cookies`. The name of the subfolder `zeid` is provided by the user upon configuration of Windows XP.

The Netscape browser stores all cookies in the `cookies.txt` file. It resides in this directory:

`C:\Program Files\Netscape\Users\default`

Cookies are stored in text files, so we can read them. IE's individual cookie files and Netscape's `cookies.txt` file are all text files. Figure 26.1 and 26.2 show both the IE and Netscape cookie files.

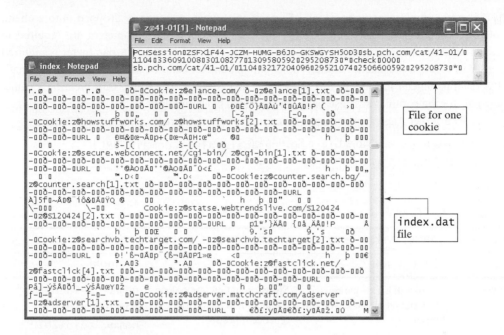

Figure 26.1 IE cookie file.

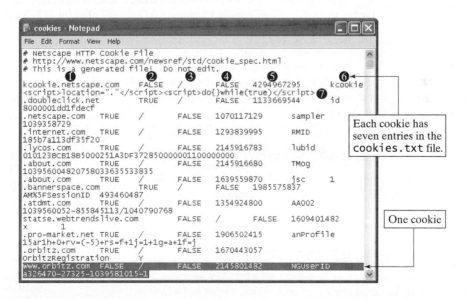

Figure 26.2 Netscape `cookies.txt` file.

A cookie has six parameters, all of which exist when a cookie is dropped onto a client. Table 26.1 describes the parameters. Only the `name` and `value` parameters are required in order to create a cookie; the others are optional. However, the `expires` parameter is required in order to create a persistent cookie. The cookie parameters can be set manually or automatically. Each parameter has a keyword as its name and is assigned a value, thus creating a name/value pair for the parameter. These pairs are separated by semicolons (;).

A Web server uses the parameters listed in Table 26.1 to create a cookie as follows:

```
set cookie: name=value; expires=dateValue; domain=URL;
    path=pathName; secure=false
```

Table 26.1 Cookie parameters.

Parameters: `name`, `value`, `expires`, `path`, `domain`, and `secure`

Parameter	Description	Value	Example
`name`	Cookie ID. This parameter is assigned by the JavaScript program.	String excluding semicolons, commas, and whitespace (encode if needed).	`name="zeidCookie"` `name="zeidID"` `name="zeid%20ID"`
`value`	Cookie value. This parameter could be null (i.e., assigned no value).	String.	`value="red and sports"` `value=`
`expires`	Expiration date. Should be a value in the future.	A date in the form weekday, dd-mm-yy hh:mm:ss GMT	`expires=Tuesday,` `09-12-04 23:12:45` `GMT`
`path`	The URL path within which the cookie is valid. Web pages that are located outside of the path cannot read or use the cookie.	A valid URL. If no value is used, the browser uses the path of the document (Web page) creating the cookie.	`path=sales/` `households`
`domain`	The cookie's domain. Cookies can be assigned to an entire domain name or to individual machines. For security reasons, the server creating the cookie must belong to the domain it assigns to the cookie.	A domain name. This value must contain at least two dots for top-level domains and three dots for extended domains. If no value is specified, the browser uses the host name of the server creating the cookie.	`domain=.aaa.bbb` `domain=www.ccc.ddd` `domain=.eee.fff.ggg` (*not* `eee.fff.ggg`)
`secure`	Specifies whether the Internet connection using the cookie should be secure (via SSL and HTTPS).	`true` (secure connection) or `false`. For most connections, it is set to `false`.	`secure=false`

Here is an example:

```
set cookie: name=abe_zeid; expires=Tuesday, 09-12-04 23:12:45 GMT;
    path=/
```

After the server creates the cookie, it sends the cookie's information to the client in the HTTP header when responding to the client's HTTP request during a session. For example, the user fills in a form and clicks the submit button. This set of actions constitutes an HTTP request. The server extracts what it needs about the user from the form's data, creates the cookie, and sends it in the HTTP header to the browser along with a response to the user. The user sees the response, but never sees the cookie. The browser stores the cookie as shown in Figure 26.1 and 26.2 for future use. Any future HTTP requests made by the client, such as requesting the Web page from the server again, will include transmittal of the cookie from the client back to the server, which takes the following form:

```
cookie: name=abe_zeid
```

The server now knows that it is `abe_zeid` who is requesting the Web page; it can then send a personalized greeting message such as, `Welcome back abe_zeid`. This example of communication between the client and the server should remove the mystery surrounding cookies.

The cookie parameters are stored by the IE and Netscape browsers in the formats shown in Figure 26.1 and 26.2, respectively. In addition to the six parameters shown in Table 26.1, Netscape stores flag with a `true` or `false` value indicating whether all machines within a given domain can access the cookie. The browser sets this value automatically. A mapping of the cookie parameters to the second cookie in Figure 26.2,

```
.doubleclick.net TRUE / FALSE 113669544 id 8000001dd1fdecf
```

is as follows: `domain` = `.doubleclick.net`, `flag` = `TRUE`, `path` = `/`, `secure` = `FALSE`, `expires` = `113669544` (milliseconds), `name` = `id`, and `value` = `8000001dd1fdecf`.

26.6 The cookie Property

HTTP requests made by a client (browser) to a server include the transmittal of cookies from the client back to the server in the following format:

```
cookie: name=abe_zeid
```

We raise two questions here. The first is, How does the browser determine the valid cookies that it should send to the server for a particular URL? The browser searches the list stored in its cookies file (`cookies.txt` for Netscape) for valid cookies. The browser performs two screening tests. First, it compares the `domain` parameter of each cookie in its list with the domain name of the host from which the URL is retrieved. If there is a match, the browser performs a `path` matching to determine whether the cookie should be sent to the server, where the browser compares the `path` parameter of the cookie with the pathname of the URL. Only if they match does the browser send the cookie to the server. Refer to Section 26.8 for more discussion on this topic.

The second question is, How does the browser send valid cookies to the server in the HTTP request? The browser includes the name/value pairs of all valid cookies in the `cookie` string (we use the terms property and string interchangeably) in the following format:

```
cookie: name1=value1; name2=value2; ...; namen=valuen
```

Observe that the name/value pairs are separated by semicolons. Each semicolon is followed by a single whitespace character. It is important to know this format, as a JavaScript script can be written to extract the values of cookies for processing.

What the browser does is include name/value pairs of the valid cookies in the `cookie` property of the `document` object. This way, the manipulation of valid cookies is done on the client side. A JavaScript program can then access the `document.cookie` property in order to extract the values of the cookies via the methods of the `String` object.

Example 26.1 Print the information in the `document.cookie` property.

Write a JavaScript program that prints the name/value pairs of a document's cookies.

Solution 26.1 Using the AceHTML editor, generate the given code, and save it as `example261.html`. Render the Web page in a browser.

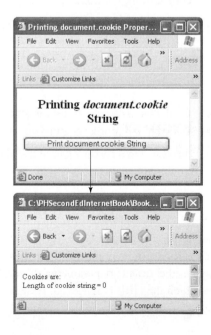

Code explained:

1. Lines 10–13 define the `printCookies()` function, which accesses the `document.cookie` property in line 11.
2. Lines 18–20 create a form with one button.

Discussion:

When the user clicks the form button shown in the first screen capture on the previous page, the `onClick` event handler (code line 19) is called. `printCookies()` prints the `cookie` string (code line 11) and its `length` (code line 12).

As expected, the Web-page document `example261.html` did not create any cookies. When the browser applied its `domain` and `path` matching rules to find valid cookies, none matched. Thus, the `document.cookie` string is null and therefore has a zero length.

Hands-on exercise:

Move the `example261.html` file into different directories in order to change the `path` property, and run it for each change. Does movimg it make a difference?

```
1   <?xml version="1.0" encoding="iso-8859-1"?>
2   <!DOCTYPE html PUBLIC "-//W3C//DTD XHTML 1.1//EN"
3       "http://www.w3.org/TR/xhtml11/DTD/xhtml11.dtd">
4   <html xmlns="http://www.w3.org/1999/xhtml">
5   <!-- Generated by AceHTM http://freeware.acehtml.com -->
6   <head>
7   <title>Printing document.cookie Property</title>
8   <script language="javascript">
9
10  function printCookies(){
11      document.write("Cookies are: " + document.cookie + "<br />");
12      document.write("Length of cookie string = " +
    document.cookie.length);
13  }
14
15  </script>
16  <body>
17  <h2 align="center">Printing <i>document.cookie</i> String</h2>
18  <form>
19  <input type="button" value="Print document.cookie String"
    onClick="printCookies()">
20  </form></body></html>
```

26.7 Dealing with Cookies

Cookies can be thought of as small files. Thus, we can perform any of the following four activities on any cookie:

1. **Create (bake, write, or drop) the cookie.** We can create only persistent cookies; we must specify a name, value, and expiration date. The browser creates the other parameters. We write the cookie to the `document.cookie` property, and the browser saves it in its cookie file (e.g., `cookies.txt` for Netscape). We should not edit the `cookies.txt` file manually and insert cookies there. Even if we do, the browser ignores our changes. We must use `document.cookie` to create cookies legitimately. We must also write cookies one at a time. If we try to write more than one cookie at one time, the browser writes only the first one and ignores the others.

2. **Read (eat) the cookie.** We read the name/value pairs from the `document.cookie` string that the browser hands to us, decode them, and extract the values of the cookies. We can use `split()`, `substring()`, and other methods of the `String` object to manipulate the `cookie` string. Although we can write only one cookie at a time, we can read multiple cookies at one time.

3. **Overwrite (change) the cookie.** Saving a cookie with the same `name` and `path` parameters as an existing cookie overwrites the existing cookie. Thus to replace a cookie's old value, overwrites it with a new value. Overwriting a cookie can be useful in some applications. If the value of a cookie is the last date that a user has visited a website, we should update the value every visit.

4. **Delete (throw away) the cookie.** To delete a cookie, we make it expire in the past. To do so, we overwrite the cookie, replacing its `expires` parameter with a value in the past. Because the `name` and `path` must match exactly, the cookie's originating script will then delete it.

Example 26.2 Create a cookie.

Write a JavaScript program that creates persistent cookies.

Solution 26.2 Using the AceHTML editor, generate the given code, and save it as `example262.html`. Render the Web page in a browser.

Code explained:

1. Lines 10–14 define the `createCookie()` function, which takes three arguments and creates a cookie.
2. Lines 16–19 define the `printCookies()` function, which is the same as in Example 26.1.
3. Lines 24–26 create a form with one button.

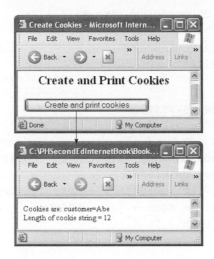

Discussion:

When the user clicks the form button shown in the foregoing screen capture, the `onClick` event handler (code line 25) is called. We call two functions to handle the click event. `createCookie()` creates a cookie that expires a day later. `printCookies()` prints the `cookie` string (code line 17) and its `length` (code line 18). In this example, the string is `customer=Abe`, whose length is 12 characters.

We create the `expires` value of the cookie by first retrieving the current date (in code line 11). We then add one to the current day, retrieved via `getDate()`, as shown in code line 12. Code line 13 creates the cookie, following the appropriate rules. The forthcoming screen capture shows the cookie file that IE creates. This file is in `C:\Documents and Settings\zeid\Cookies`.

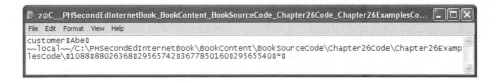

Hands-on exercise:

Create two more cookies, and print the `document.cookie` string and its length. Make one cookie expire 15 hours from the current date, and the other expire one month from the current date. The name/value pairs for the two cookies are, respectively, `visitor=James` and `personID=123455678`.

```
1    <?xml version="1.0" encoding="iso-8859-1"?>
2    <!DOCTYPE html PUBLIC "-//W3C//DTD XHTML 1.1//EN"
3        "http://www.w3.org/TR/xhtml11/DTD/xhtml11.dtd">
4    <html xmlns="http://www.w3.org/1999/xhtml">
5    <!-- Generated by AceHTM http://freeware.acehtml.com -->
6    <head>
7    <title>Create Cookies</title>
8    <script language="javascript">
9
10   function createCookie(name, value, expiredays) {
11       todayDate = new Date();
12       todayDate.setDate(todayDate.getDate() + expiredays);
13       document.cookie = name + "=" + value + "; expires=" +
     todayDate.toGMTString() + ";"
14   }
15
16   function printCookies(){
17       document.write("Cookies are: " + document.cookie + "<br />");
18       document.write("Length of cookie string = " +
     document.cookie.length);
19   }
20
21   </script>
22   <body>
23   <h2 align="center">Create and Print Cookies</h2>
24   <form>
25   <input type="button" value="Create and print cookies"
     onClick="createCookie('customer', 'Abe', 1), printCookies()">
26   </form>
27   </body>
28   </html>
```

☞ ───

Example 26.3 Read a cookie.

Write a JavaScript program that reads persistent cookies.

Solution 26.3 Using the AceHTML editor, generate the given code, and save it as example263.html. Render the Web page in a browser.

Code explained:

1. Lines 10–40 define the readCookies() function, which reads all the cookies that are included in the document.cookie string.

2. Line 42 calls readCookies() explicitly.

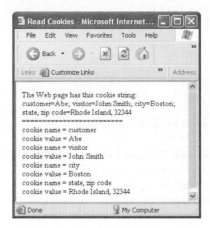

Discussion:

We use the `example262.html` code to create four cookies. When we render the Web page of this example, `example263.html`, it reads the four cookies and prints them as shown in the foregoing screen capture.

Code lines 12 and 13 ensure that the `cookie` string is not null; if it is, the program prints the message in code line 39. Code line 18 uses the `split()` method of the `String` object to break up the cookie string into its name/value pairs. It uses the fact that these pairs are separated by semicolons. `split()` returns an array of these pairs, which we save in the `args` array.

We continue parsing the cookies' name/value pairs in code lines 19–35. We use the array length (in code line 19) to split each pair at the = sign (in code line 22); we know that the name is to the left of = and that the value is to its right. As a result, the two elements of the `name-Value` array now hold the names and values, respectively (in code lines 22–24). Code lines 26–28 remove the leading space, required by the format of the `cookie` string, from the cookie name. Code lines 30 and 31 unescape the name and value, respectively in case they have hex values (%xx). Code lines 33 and 34 print the cookies.

Hands-on exercise:

Change the code given in this example to read the value of only one cookie, whose name is passed to `readCookie()`. Change the function to take one argument as input. Also, change the code to prompt the user with the names of the available cookies and ask the user to select one or more to read.

```
1   <?xml version="1.0" encoding="iso-8859-1"?>
2   <!DOCTYPE html PUBLIC "-//W3C//DTD XHTML 1.1//EN"
3       "http://www.w3.org/TR/xhtml11/DTD/xhtml11.dtd">
4   <html xmlns="http://www.w3.org/1999/xhtml">
5   <!-- Generated by AceHTM http://freeware.acehtml.com -->
6   <head>
```

```
7    <title>Read Cookies</title>
8    <script language="javascript">
9
10   function readCookies()
11   {
12      allCookies = document.cookie.length;
13      if (allCookies > 0)
14      {
15       document.write("The Web page has this cookie string:<br />"
     + document.cookie + "<br />");
16           document.write("=========================" + "<br />");
17      //split the cookie string into name/value pairs
18      args = document.cookie.split(';');
19      for (i=0;i<args.length;i++)
20      {
21        //split each name/value pair into its name and value
22        nameValue = args[i].split("=");
23        name =  nameValue[0];
24        value = nameValue[1];
25      //Remove leading whitespace from cookie name
26        if (name.length != 0)
27          if (name.charAt(0) == " ")
28            name = name.substr(1,name.length-1);
29          //unescape the values
30          name = unescape(name);
31          value = unescape(value);
32          //print the names and values
33          document.write("cookie name = " + name + "<br />");
34          document.write("cookie value = " + value + "<br />");
35      }//for
36      }//if
37
38      //a case of null cookie string
39      else alert ("Sorry! This page cannot access any cookies");
40   }
41   //call function explicitly
42   readCookies();
43
44   </script>
45   <body>
46   </body>
47   </html>
```

Example 26.4 Overwrite a cookie.

Write a JavaScript program that overwrites a cookie.

Solution 26.4 Using the AceHTML editor, generate the given code, and save it as `example264.html`. Render the Web page in a browser.

Code explained:

1. Lines 11–15 define the `overwriteCookie()` function, which changes the value of an existing cookie.
2. Line 16 calls `overwriteCookie()` explicitly.

Discussion:

Overwriting and creating cookies are the same. The only difference is that overwriting uses the name of an existing cookie. The code of `createCookie()` in Example 26.2 and of `overwriteCookie()` in this example are thus the same. In this example, we change the value of the first cookie in Example 26.3 from `Abe` to `Mary Brown`.

Hands-on exercise:

Change the code given in this example to prompt the user with the names of the available cookies and ask the user to select one or more to overwrite.

```
1   <?xml version="1.0" encoding="iso-8859-1"?>
2   <!DOCTYPE html PUBLIC "-//W3C//DTD XHTML 1.1//EN"
3       "http://www.w3.org/TR/xhtml11/DTD/xhtml11.dtd">
4   <html xmlns="http://www.w3.org/1999/xhtml">
5   <!-- Generated by AceHTM http://freeware.acehtml.com -->
6   <head>
7   <title>Overwriting a Cookie</title>
8   <script language="javascript">
9
10    //overwriting a cookie is exactly the same as  re-creating it
      with different values
11   function overwriteCookie(name, value, expiredays) {
12       todayDate = new Date();
13       todayDate.setDate(todayDate.getDate() + expiredays);
```

```
14        document.cookie = name + "=" + value + "; expires="
   +todayDate.toGMTString() + ";"
15  }
16  overwriteCookie("customer", "Mary Brown", 1);
17
18  </script>
19  <body></body></html>
```

Example 26.5 Delete a cookie.

Write a JavaScript program that deletes cookies.

Solution 26.5 Using the AceHTML editor, generate the given code, and save it as `example265.html`. Render the Web page in a browser.

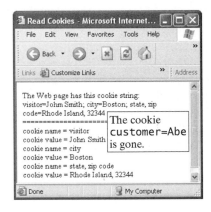

Code explained:

1. Lines 11–15 define the `deleteCookie()` function, which deletes an existing cookie.

2. Line 16 calls `deleteCookie()` explicitly.

Discussion:

We delete the first cookie (`customer=Abe`) that we created using the `example262.html` code. When we render the Web page of this example, `example265.html`, it deletes the cookie and does nothing else; there is no display. But when we read the cookies via the `example263.html` code, we confirm the deletion, as shown in the foregoing screen capture.

`deleteCookie()` takes the cookie's name as input (`customer` in code line 16). It changes the cookie's expiration date to yesterday, by subtracting 1 from today's date (in code line 13). It writes the cookie to the `cookie` string with the newly expired date. It also assigns an empty value to the cookie; we must do so in order to create the cookie successfully.

Hands-on exercise:

Remove the "=' ' "+ from code line 14, save and run the code. What happens? Why?

```
1    <?xml version="1.0" encoding="iso-8859-1"?>
2    <!DOCTYPE html PUBLIC "-//W3C//DTD XHTML 1.1//EN"
3        "http://www.w3.org/TR/xhtml11/DTD/xhtml11.dtd">
4    <html xmlns="http://www.w3.org/1999/xhtml">
5    <!-- Generated by AceHTM http://freeware.acehtml.com -->
6    <head>
7    <title>Deleting (Expiring or Removing) a Cookie</title>
8    <script language="javascript">
9
10   //to delete an existing cookie is to make it expire on a past
     date.
11   function deleteCookie(name) {
12       todayDate = new Date();
13       todayDate.setDate(todayDate.getDate() - 1);
14       document.cookie = name +  "=''" +"; expires=" +
     todayDate.toGMTString() + ";";
15   }
16   deleteCookie("customer");
17   </script><body></body></html>
```

26.8 Visibility

As discussed in Section 26.6, the browser determines, through the `document.cookie` property, the valid cookies to which a Web page can have access. The browser matches the `domain` and `path` parameters in order to make this determination. We refer to this matching as cookie visibility. Understanding cookie visibility enables us to design websites effectively. Let us assume that all Web pages have the same `domain` so that we can investigate the effect of the `path` parameter.

A cookie created by a Web page in a directory path is visible by all Web pages at the same level as or below the Web page. Consider the website structure shown in Figure 26.3. If the `dir1/index.html` document creates a cookie (`sales`), then `doc2.html` and `dir2/index.html` should see this cookie through the `document.cookie` string. `doc2.html` should see it because it is in the same directory, `dir1`, as `dir1/index.html`. `dir2/index.html` should see it because it is in a subdirectory, `dir2`, of `dir1`. However, `doc1.html` does not see this cookie, because it is not in the path.

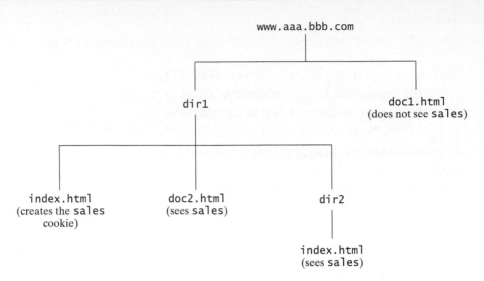

Figure 26.3 Cookie visibility.

Example 26.6 Investigate cookie visibility.

Write a JavaScript program that investigates cookie visibility.

Solution 26.6 Using the AceHTML editor, generate the given code, and save it as `example266.html`. Render the Web page in a browser.

Code explained:

Lines 10 and 11 print the cookie string and its length, respectively.

Discussion:

We use a brute-force approach in this example to show how the cookie visibility rules, as illustrated by Figure 26.3, work. Move the `example266.html` file around from one directory to another, and observe the results. The accompanying screen captures show two sets of results. The Web page sees different cookies, depending on where it is in the file directory structure.

Hands-on exercise:

Move the file around, and render the Web page after each move. What results do you get?

```
1   <?xml version="1.0" encoding="iso-8859-1"?>
2   <!DOCTYPE html PUBLIC "-//W3C//DTD XHTML 1.1//EN"
3       "http://www.w3.org/TR/xhtml11/DTD/xhtml11.dtd">
4   <html xmlns="http://www.w3.org/1999/xhtml">
5   <!-- Generated by AceHTM http://freeware.acehtml.com -->
6   <head>
7   <title>Visible Cookies</title>
8   <script language="javascript">
9
10  document.write("Cookies are " + document.cookie + "<br />");
11  document.write ("cookie string length is " +
    document.cookie.length);
12
13  </script>
14  <body>
15  </body>
16  </html>
```

26.9 Tutorials

26.9.1   Web-Page Hit Counter (Study Sections 26.5 and 26.6)

In this tutorial, we create a hit counter that keeps track of the number of visitors to a Web page. Each time the Web page is requested, the counter is incremented by 1.

Using the AceHTML editor, generate the given code, and save it as `tutorial2691.html`. Render the Web page in a browser.

Code explained:

1. Lines 11–15 define the standard `createCookie()` function. (See Example 26.2.)
2. Lines 17–48 define the `readCookie()` function, which is a modified version of that in Example 26.3.
3. Line 42 converts the type of `value` from string to integer via JavaScript's `parseInt()` built-in function.
4. Lines 51–62 define the `showHits()` function, which increments the `visits` counter (line 58) and calls the `createCookie()` function (line 60).
5. Line 65 calls `showHits()` explicitly.

Discussion:

We put the cookies concept to good use in this example. We create a Web-page hit counter that shows how many visitors have visited our Web page. While HTML editors, such as Dreamweaver, have built-in (canned) hit-counter functions that Web developers can use, this tutorial offers insight into how they work.

The siteVisits cookie keeps track of the number of visitors to the Web page. Code line 58 increments value by 1 for each new visit. Code line 35 checks for the siteVisits cookie by name. If it finds it, it breaks out of the for loop (in code line 36). After ensuring that the cookie exists (in code line 40), the program returns the current value of the cookie.

Hands-on exercise:

Change the code to sort the Web page's visitors by gender (male or female), and print the number of visitors in each group. you need to add an element that queries the user about his or her gender.

```
1    <?xml version="1.0" encoding="iso-8859-1"?>
2    <!DOCTYPE html PUBLIC "-//W3C//DTD XHTML 1.1//EN"
3       "http://www.w3.org/TR/xhtml11/DTD/xhtml11.dtd">
4    <html xmlns="http://www.w3.org/1999/xhtml">
5    <!-- Generated by AceHTM http://freeware.acehtml.com -->
6    <head>
7    <title>Webpage Hit Counter</title>
8    <script language="javascript">
9
```

```
10   // Standard cookie create and read functions
11   function createCookie(name, value, expiredays){
12       todayDate = new Date();
13       todayDate.setDate(todayDate.getDate() + expiredays);
14       document.cookie = name + "=" + value + "; expires=" +
     todayDate.toGMTString() + ";"
15   }
16
17   function readCookie(cookieName){
18      allCookies = document.cookie.length;
19      if (allCookies > 0){
20      //split the cookie string into name/value pairs
21      args = document.cookie.split(';');
22
23        for (i=0;i<args.length;i++){
24          //split each name/value pair into its name and value
25          nameValue = args[i].split("=");
26          name =  nameValue[0];
27          value = nameValue[1];
28        //Remove leading whitespace from cookie name
29          if (name.length != 0)
30            if (name.charAt(0) == " ")
31              name = name.substr(1,name.length-1);
32            //unescape the values
33            name = unescape(name);
34            value = unescape(value);
35            if (name == cookieName)
36            break;
37        }//for
38
39        //first visit, cookie does not exist
40        if (value == "NaN") value = 0;
41        //after first visit, there is a value
42        else value = parseInt(value);
43        return value;
44      }//if, line 19
45
46        //a case of null cookie string
47        else return value =0;
48   }
49
50   //hit-counter function
51   function showHits() {
52     // First we'll check if the user has visited this
53     // page before by examining the siteVisits cookie:
54     value = readCookie("siteVisits");
55     if (value == 0)
56        visits = 1;   //this is the first visit
57     else
```

```
58        visits =  value + 1;
59        // Create or update existing cookie:
60        createCookie("siteVisits", visits, 1);
61        document.write("This site has been visited  <b>" + visits +
   "</b> times<hr>");
62     }
63
64     document.write ("cookies are " + document.cookie + "<BR>");
65     showHits();
66     </script>
67     </head>
68     <body>
69     </body>
70     </html>
```

26.9.2   Remember Web-Page Visitors
(Study Sections 26.5 and 26.6)

This tutorial uses cookies to store data that a Web surfer inputs in a form on a Web page. When the surfer visits the Web page again, a personalized welcome message is displayed along with the form as it was filledout. This tutorial simulates how we can collect data about website visitors and send them targeted information. Remember a surfer's profile uses only information that the surfer provides.

The Web page uses a frame set consisting of two frames: `header` and `body`. The borders between the two frames are not visible, as we suspend them by using `frameborder=0`. The page also uses a style sheet to format the its elements.

Using the AceHTML editor, generate the given code, and save it as `tutorial2692.html`. Render the Web page in a browser.

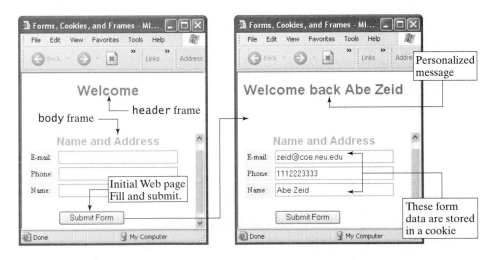

Code explained:

`tutorial2692.html`:

1. Line 11 shows that the form has three fields, as shown in the foregoing screen captures.
2. Lines 13–32 define the `validateStringLength()` function, which ensures that the user input in a text field is within the minimum and maximum values.
3. Lines 34–52 define the `validateStringRestrictedChars()` function, which ensures that the user does not use an asterisk (*) or an equal sign (=) as characters. These are reserved characters.
4. Lines 54–66 define the `validateEmail()` function, which checks for the correct formatting of an input e-mail address.
5. Lines 68–100 define the `validateForm()` function, which validates form input.
6. Lines 102–107 define the `writeCookie()` function as we have done before.
7. Lines 109–150 define the `readCookie()` function, which reads the form data from a cookie.
8. Lines 152–176 define the `headerFrame()` function, which creates the content of the header frame of the frame set.
9. Lines 187–238 define the `bodyFrame()` function, which creates the content of the body frame of the frame set. It gets the content from the `cookieArray` that is filled by the `readCookie()` function.
10. Lines 240–247 define the `initialize()` function, which fills both frames of the frame set with their initial content. This function is an event handler and is used in line 251.
11. Lines 251–254 define the frame set and is with two frames.
12. Lines 255–260 are for browsers that do not support frames.

`class.css`:

1. Lines 1–14 define the text styles.
2. Lines 18–24 define the spaces styles.
3. Lines 28–34 define the bold and italic styles.
4. Lines 40–49 define the background-color styles.
5. Lines 52–57 define the header styles.
6. Lines 60–65 define the subheader styles.
7. Lines 68–91 define other styles.

Discussion:

This tutorial uses frames, cookies, and style sheets to store user input to a form for use later. When the user revisits the Web page, a personalized greeting message is displayed in the Web page. While the tutorial may seem complex, it builds on the basic concepts that have been covered throughout this book. This tutorial provides an idea of what one can do by combining the Internet, XHTML, and JavaScript.

Hands-on exercise:

Extend the form to include four checkboxes for user interests: sports, crafts, reading, and music. Modify all the functions and the cookie to process the checkboxes.

```
1    <?xml version="1.0" encoding="iso-8859-1"?>        tutorial2692.html
2    <!DOCTYPE html PUBLIC "-//W3C//DTD XHTML 1.1//EN"
3        "http://www.w3.org/TR/xhtml11/DTD/xhtml11.dtd">
4    <html xmlns="http://www.w3.org/1999/xhtml">
5    <!-- Generated by AceHTM http://freeware.acehtml.com -->
6    <head>
7    <link rel=stylesheet type="text/css" href="class.css" title="Style
     Sheet">
8    <title>Forms, Cookies, and Frames</title>
9    <script language="javascript">
10
11   totalInputFields = 3;
12
13   function validateStringLength
     (inputLabel,inputText,minLength,maxLength){
14       inputLabel = inputLabel;
15       inputText = inputText;
16       inputTextLength = inputText.length;
17       minLength = minLength;
18       maxLength = maxLength;
19       if (inputTextLength > maxLength) {  //open if - input string
     too BIG
20           differenceChars = (inputTextLength - maxLength);
21           alert("The field " + inputLabel + " is too big. Please
     enter a string between " + minLength + " and " +  maxLength + "
     characters. \nYou entered: " + inputText + " (remove " +
     differenceChars + " characters).");
22           return(false);
23       }  // close if - input string too BIG
24       else if (inputTextLength < minLength) {  // open if - input
     string too SMALL
25           differenceChars = (minLength - inputTextLength);
26           alert("The field " + inputLabel + " is too small.
     Please enter a string between " + minLength + " and " +
     maxLength + " characters. \nYou entered: " + inputText +
     " (add " + differenceChars + " characters).");
27           return(false);
28       }  // close if - input string too SMALL
29       else {
30           return(true);
31       }
32   }
33
```

```
34   function validateStringRestrictedChars (inputLabel,inputText){
35        inputLabel = inputLabel;
36        inputText = inputText;
37        inputTextLength = inputText.length;
38        asteriskIndex = inputText.indexOf("*");
39        equalIndex = inputText.indexOf("=");
40
41        if (asteriskIndex !== -1) {
42             alert("The field " + inputLabel + " contains an
     asterisk (*). This is a reserved character. Please reenter the "
     + inputLabel + "field. \nYou entered: " + inputText + ".");
43             return(false);
44        }
45        if (equalIndex !== -1) {
46             alert("The field " + inputLabel + " contains an equal
     sign (=). This is a reserved character. Please reenter the  "
     + inputLabel +" field. \nYou entered: " + inputText + ".");
47             return(false);
48        }
49        else {
50             return(true);
51        }
52   }
53
54   function validateEmail (inputLabel,inputText) {
55        inputLabel = inputLabel;
56        inputText = inputText;
57        inputTextLength = inputText.length;
58        atSignIndex = inputText.indexOf("@");
59        if (atSignIndex == -1) {
60             alert("The field " + inputLabel + " must contain an at
     sign (@). This is a reserved character. Please reenter the  "
     + inputLabel + "field. \nYou entered: " + inputText + ".");
61             return(false);
62        }
63        else {
64             return(true);
65        }
66   }
67
68   function validateForm (personForm) {
69   // validate e-mail field
70   returnCode = validateStringLength("E-mail",
     personForm.email.value, 1, 50);
71        if (returnCode == false) {
72             return(false);
73        }
```

```
74   returnCode = validateStringRestrictedChars("E-mail",
     personForm.email.value);
75       if (returnCode == false) {
76           return(false);
77       }
78   returnCode = validateEmail("E-mail", personForm.email.value);
79       if (returnCode == false) {
80           return(false);
81       }
82   // validate phone field
83   returnCode = validateStringLength("Phone", personForm.phone.value,
     10, 13);
84       if (returnCode == false) {
85           return(false);
86       }
87   returnCode = validateStringRestrictedChars("Phone",
     personForm.phone.value);
88       if (returnCode == false) {
89           return(false);
90       }
91   // validate name field
92   returnCode = validateStringLength("Name",
     personForm.fullName.value, 1, 50);
93       if (returnCode == false) {
94           return(false);
95       }
96   returnCode = validateStringRestrictedChars("Name",
     personForm.fullName.value);
97       if (returnCode == false) {
98           return(false);
99       }
100  }
101
102  function writeCookie(expiredays){
103    todayDate = new Date();
104    todayDate.setDate(todayDate.getDate() + expiredays);
105      validateForm(top.body.document.personForm);
106      document.cookie = "formData"  + "=" + "email" + "=" +
     top.body.document.personForm.email.value + "*" + "phone" + "="
     + top.body.document.personForm.phone.value +"*" +"fullName" + "="
     + top.body.document.personForm.fullName.value + "*" +
     "*" + "; expires=" + todayDate.toGMTString() + ";"
107  }
108
109  function readCookie(){
110      // create array for field data
111      fieldDataArray = new Array(totalInputFields);
112      // read in the raw cookie data
```

```
113     rawCookieText = document.cookie;
114     rawCookieTextLength = document.cookie.length;
115     // find the start of the FormData
116     indexFormDataLabel = rawCookieText.indexOf("formData=");
117     if (indexFormDataLabel !== -1) { //process formData cookie
118       indexFormData = indexFormDataLabel + 9;
119     // create a string that starts with the formData (but
  may include other cookie data at the end)
120       subCookieText =
  rawCookieText.substr(indexFormData,(rawCookieTextLength -
  indexFormData));
121       subCookieTextLength = subCookieText.length
122       // create a string called formDataText that contains
  the formData only (no other cookie data at the end)
123       indexTrailingSemiColon = subCookieText.indexOf(";");
124         if (indexTrailingSemiColon == -1) {
125           formDataText = subCookieText;  // no other
  cookie data at the end
126         }
127         else {
128           formDataText =
  subCookieText.substr(0,indexTrailingSemiColon);  // remove other
  cookie data from end
129         }
130         formDataTextLength = formDataText.length
131     // loop through formDataText, pulling out pair of form
  fields and data
132       currentPosition = 0;
133       workingData = formDataText;
134       workingDataLength = workingData.length;
135       for (i=0;i<totalInputFields;i++) {
136         // e-mail processing
137         asteriskPosition = workingData.indexOf("*");
138         equalPosition = workingData.indexOf("=");
139         fieldCharPosition = (equalPosition + 1);
140         fieldData =
  workingData.substr(fieldCharPosition,(asteriskPosition -
  fieldCharPosition) );
141         fieldDataArray[i] = fieldData;
142         workingData = workingData.substr((asteriskPosition
  + 1),(workingDataLength - asteriskPosition) );
143         workingDataLength = workingData.length;
144       } // close for loop
145       return (fieldDataArray);
146     } // close if - process formData cookie
147     else {  // open else - there is no form data cookie
148       return (fieldDataArray);
149     }  // close else - there is no form data cookie
```

```
150   }  // close function
151
152   function headerFrame(){ //build header HTML
153       cookieArray = readCookie();
154       headContent  = "<html>";
155       headContent += "<head>";
156       headContent += "<title>Navigation Bar</title>";
157       headContent += "<link rel=stylesheet type='text/css'";
158       headContent += "href='class.css'";
159       headContent += "title='Style Sheet'>";
160       headContent += "</head>";
161       headContent += "<body>";
162           if (cookieArray[2] == null) {//there is no cookie
163               headContent += "<p class=header>Welcome</p>";
164           }
165           else {  //there is a cookie
166               if (cookieArray[2].length == 0) {// there is a cookie,
      but no data
167                   headContent += "<p class=header>Welcome</p>";
168               }
169               else {  //there is a cookie with data
170                   headContent += "<p class=header>Welcome back "
      + cookieArray[2] + "</p>";
171               }
172           }
173       headContent += "</body>";
174       headContent += "</html>";
175       return (headContent);
176   }//headerFrame function
177
178   function bodyFrame(){//build body HTML
179       cookieArray = readCookie();
180       bodyContent  = "<html>";
181       bodyContent += "<head>";
182       bodyContent += "<title>Body</title>";
183       bodyContent += "<link rel=stylesheet type='text/css'";
184       bodyContent += "href='class.css'";
185       bodyContent += "title='Style Sheet'>";
186       bodyContent += "</head>";
187       bodyContent += "<body>";
188       bodyContent += "<form name = 'personForm'>";
189       bodyContent += "<table border=0 width='100%'>";
190       bodyContent += "<tr>";
191       bodyContent += "<td colspan=2><p class=subheader>Name and
      Address</p></td>";
192       bodyContent += "</tr>";
193       bodyContent += "<tr>";
```

```
194       bodyContent += "<td
     class=background> E-mail: </td>";
195           if (cookieArray[0] == null) {
196               bodyContent += "<td><input type='text' name='email'
     size='30' maxlength=50></td>";
197           }
198           else {
199               bodyContent += "<td><input type='text' name='email'
     size='30' maxlength=50 value='" + cookieArray[0] + "'></td>";
200           }
201       bodyContent += "</tr>";
202       bodyContent += "<tr>";
203       bodyContent += "<td
     class=background> Phone: </td>";
204           if (cookieArray[1] == null) {
205               bodyContent += "<td><input type='text' name='phone'
     size='30' maxlength=50></td>";
206           }
207           else {
208               bodyContent += "<td><input type='text' name='phone'
     size='30' maxlength=50 value='" + cookieArray[1] + "'></td>";
209           }
210       bodyContent += "</tr>";
211       bodyContent += "<tr>";
212       bodyContent += "<td
     class=background> Name: </td>";
213           if (cookieArray[2] == null) {
214               bodyContent += "<td><input type='text'
     name='fullName' size='30' maxlength=50></td>";
215           }
216           else {
217               bodyContent += "<td><input type='text'
     name='fullName' size='30' maxlength=50 value='" +
     cookieArray[2] + "'></td>";
218           }
219       bodyContent += "</tr>";
220       bodyContent += "<tr>";
221       bodyContent += "<td colspan=2> </td>";
222       bodyContent += "</tr>";
223       bodyContent += "<tr>";
224       bodyContent += "<td> </td>";
225       bodyContent += "<td>";
226       bodyContent += "<input type='button' value='Submit Form'
     name='writeCookieButton'
     onClick='javascript:parent.writeCookie(7)'>";
227       bodyContent += "</td>";
228       bodyContent += "</tr>";
229       bodyContent += "</td>";
```

```
230     bodyContent += "</tr>";
231     bodyContent += "</td>";
232     bodyContent += "</tr>";
233     bodyContent += "</table>";
234     bodyContent += "</form>";
235     bodyContent += "</body>";
236     bodyContent += "</html>";
237     return (bodyContent);
238 }
239
240 function initialize() {//load header and body frames
241     top.header.location = "javascript: parent.headerFrame()";
242     top.body.location = "javascript: parent.bodyFrame()";
243 }
244
245 function blank() {//build empty HTML page
246     return "<html></html>";
247 }  // close blank function
248
249 </script>
250 </head>
251 <frameset rows="100,*" onLoad = "initialize()">
252 <frame name="header" src="javascript:parent.blank()"
        frameborder="0">
253 <frame name="body" src="javascript:parent.blank()"
        frameborder="0">
254 </frameset>
255 <noframes>
256 <body>
257 <p>Your browser does not support frames.</p>
258 </br />
259 </body>
260 </noframes>
261 </html>
```

```
                                                              class.css
1 .test   {        text-align: justify;
2               text-decoration: line-through;
3               text-indent: 50px;
4               text-transform: capitalize;
5
6               border-color: green;
7               border-width: 12px;
8               border-style: outset;
9
10              margin-left: 100px;
11
12              padding: 10px;
13              padding-top: 25px;
```

```
14              }
15
16    <!-- Space tags -->
17
18              <!-- used with the paragraph tag - to build in 6 points
      of space  -->
19    .6space      {     font-size: 6pt;
20              }
21
22              <!-- used with the paragraph tag - to build in 350
      points of space  -->
23    .bigspace    {     font-size: 350pt;
24              }
25
26    <!-- Generic tags -->
27
28              <!-- used with the span tag - to make text bold  -->
29    .bold        {     font-weight: 700;
30              }
31
32              <!-- used with the span tag - to make text italic  -->
33    .italic      {     font-style: italic;
34              }
35
36
37    <!-- Home/welcome tags -->
38
39              <!-- used with the body tag - used to apply a
      background color  -->
40    .background {      background: #ffff66;
41              }
42
43              <!-- used with the body tag - used to apply a
      background color  -->
44    .backgroundBlue {    background: blue;
45              }
46
47              <!-- used with the body tag - used to apply a
      background color  -->
48    .backgroundGreen    {     background: green;
49              }
50
51              <!-- used with the list tag - used to display list of
      products  -->
52    .header      {     font-family: Arial, Helvetica, sans-serif;
53              text-align: center;
54              font-size: 18pt;
55              font-weight: 900;
```

```
56              color: red;
57         }
58
59     <!-- used with the list tag - used to display list of
   products  -->
60  .subheader    {    font-family: Arial, Helvetica, sans-serif;
61              text-align: center;
62              font-size: 14pt;
63              font-weight: 800;
64              color: orange;
65         }
66
67         <!-- used with the list tag - used to display list of
   products  -->
68  .none       {   font-family: Arial, Helvetica, sans-serif;
69              list-style-type: none;
70         }
71
72         <!-- used with the paragraph tag - default tag  -->
73  .normal     {   font-family: Arial, Helvetica, sans-serif;
74         }
75
76         <!-- used with the paragraph tag - used to center text
   -->
77  .center     {   font-family: Arial, Helvetica, sans-serif;
78              text-align: center;
79         }
80
81  <!-- Specific Tags -->
82
83         <!-- Tags for logo slide tags -->
84  .demotext   {   font-family: Arial, Helvetica, sans-serif;
85              font-size: 36pt;
86              color: blue;
87              position: absolute;
88              top: 0px;
89              left: 0px;
90              visibility: visible;
91         }
```

FAQs

Introduction (Section 26.1)

Q: Where does the "name "cookie" come from?

A: A cookie is a computer science term that is used to describe a piece of data held by an intermediary. The term fits the usage of cookies precisely. Cookie also sounds like the Greek word for transcending, or going above and beyond. This Greek meaning indicates that cookies use in computer science facilitates the communication between two parties.

Parameters (Section 26.5)

Q: Do browsers set limits on the number of cookies they accept from a server?

A: Yes. Netscape, for example, can receive and store 300 cookies in total, 4 KB per cookie (for its name/value pairs) and 20 cookies per server or domain. When the 300-cookies limit or the 20-cookies-per-server limit is exceeded, Netscape deletes the oldest cookies. When the 4-KB-per-cookie limit is exceeded by a particular cookie, the cookie is trimmed to fit; however, its name is untouched as long the name it fits within the 4-KB limit.

Blackbox

Section 26.1 (Introduction): Cookies convert the stateless HTTP protocol into a stateful protocol.

Section 26.2 (Privacy): Cookies store only the information that a user provides.

Section 26.3 (System Security): Use cookies over a secure (SSL) Internet connection to minimize hacking of the data they carry.

Section 26.4 (Types): Cookies may be client-side cookies or server-side cookies, and they may be transient or persistent.

Section 26.5 (Parameters): Cookies are stored in files in directories on the client computer. For Windows XP, the directory is

```
C:\Documents and Settings\zeid\Cookies.
```

The name of the subfolder `zeid` is provided by the user upon configuration of Windows XP.

The Netscape browser stores all cookies in the `cookies.txt` file, in this directory:

```
C:\Program Files\Netscape\Users\default
```

The cookie parameters are `name`, `value`, `expires`, `path`, `domain`, and `secure`.

Section 26.6 (The `cookie` Property) (Example 26.1): The browser includes the name/value pairs of all valid cookies in the `cookie` property, in the following format:

```
name1=value1; name2=value2; ...; namen=valuen
```

Section 26.7 (Dealing with Cookies) (Example 26.2–26.5): We can create (write), read, overwrite, and delete cookies.

Section 26.8 (Visibility) (Example 26.6): A cookie created by a Web page in a particular directory path is visible by all Web pages at the same level as or below the Web page.

Section 26.9 (Tutorials): Two tutorials show how to use cookies in applications.

Quick reference for the syntax presented in this chapter

Cookie parameters: `name`, `value`, `expires`, `path`, `domain`, and `secure`

Parameter	Description	Value	Example

`name`	Cookie ID. This parameter is assigned by the Java-Script program.	String excluding semi-colons, commas, and whitespace (encode if needed).	`name="zeidCookie"`
			 `name="zeidID"`
			 `name="zeid%20ID"`

`value`	Cookie value. This parameter could be null (i.e., assigned no value).	String.	`value="red and sports"` `value=`
`expires`	Expiration date. Should be a value in the future.	A date in the form weekday, dd-mm-yy hh:mm:ss GMT.	`expires=Tuesday, 09-12-04 23:12:45 GMT`
`path`	The URL path within which the cookie is valid. Web pages that are located outside of the path cannot read or use the cookie.	A valid URL. If no value is used, the browser uses the path of the document (Web page) creating the cookie.	`path=sales/ households`

`domain`	The cookie's domain. Cookies can be assigned to an entire domain name or to individual machines. For security reasons, the server creating the cookie must belong to the domain it assigns to the cookie.	A domain name. This value must contain at least two dots for top-level domains and three dots for extended domains. If no value is specified, the browser uses the host name of the server creating the cookie.	`domain=.aaa.bbb`
			 `domain=www.ccc.ddd`
			 `domain=.eee.fff.gg g` (not `eee.fff.ggg`)

`secure`	Specifies whether the Internet connection using the cookie should be secure (via SSL and HTTPS).	`true` (secure connection) or `false`. For most connections, it is set to `false`.	`secure=false`

Check Your Progress

At the end of this chapter, you should

- ✔ understand cookies (Section 26.1);
- ✔ understand the effect of cookies on privacy and system security (Sections 26.2 and 26.3);
- ✔ know the types of cookies (Section 26.4);
- ✔ have mastered the use of cookie parameters (Section 26.5);
- ✔ have mastered use of the `cookie` property (Section 26.6);

✔ have mastered ways to deal with cookies (Section 26.7;)
✔ understand cookie visibility (Section 26.8);
✔ have practiced using cookies (Section 26.9).

Problems

The exercises are designed for a lab setting, while the homework is to be done outside class time.

Exercises

26.1 Write a JavaScript application that prints the `cookie` string.

26.2 Write a JavaScript application that creates a cookie for your daily schedule.

26.3 Write a JavaScript application that creates a cookie for a list of phone numbers.

26.4 Write a JavaScript application that creates a cookie for names of friends.

26.5 Write a JavaScript application that creates a cookie for science facts.

Homework

26.6 Write a JavaScript application that creates a cookie for a daily quote.

26.7 Write a JavaScript application that creates a cookie for weekly reminders.

26.8 Write a JavaScript application that creates a cookie for sorting numbers.

26.9 Write a JavaScript application that creates a cookie for adding numbers input in a form.

26.10 Write a JavaScript application that creates a cookie for calculating sales tax.

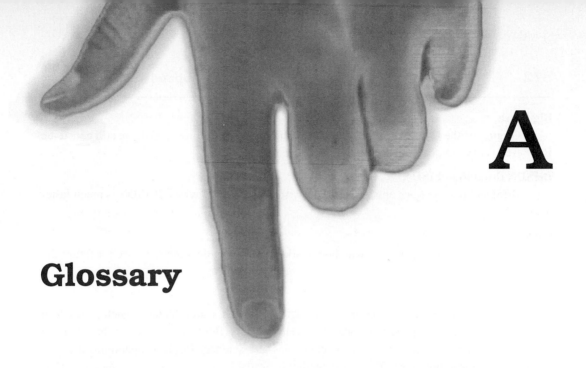

Glossary

A

This appendix serves as a quick reference to many of the terms and abbreviations that are widely used with respect to the Internet, the World Wide Web, and XHTML. It is also a compilation of the important terms and abbreviations that are used throughout the book. The terms and abbreviations are listed alphabetically.

address book
    E-mail tools provide their users with address books in order to allow them to store all their e-mail addresses in one location and use them to send e-mail to individuals or mailing lists.

ADSL (asynchronous digital subscriber line)
    This is a technology that allows Internet users to connect to the Internet at high speed over an ordinary phone line.

alink (active link)
    During the time between when the user presses the mouse button and holds it down while the cursor is on a link and when the user releases the mouse button, the link is said to be active and is called an active link.

Apache server
    The Apache server is one of the most widely used Web servers on the Internet. Apache is a Unix-based server; however, Windows-based and Mac-based versions are available as well.

Big Seven

Originally, the Usenet groups were divided into seven subgroups, which are still called the Big Seven. They are `comp`, `sci`, `rec`, `news`, `talk`, `soc`, and `misc`.

B-ISDN (broadband ISDN)

B-ISDN lines use fiber optics instead of twisted-pair copper wires. B-ISDN is much faster than ISDN.

bookmarks

Browsers provide their users with bookmarks in order to allow them to save for future use URLs they have visited.

Boolean search

Some search engines provide their users with advanced search features, such as Boolean search. These features help users to focus their search results. Boolean searches are based on the classical Boolean operations found in mathematics and science. Boolean operations are performed via Boolean operators. The most commonly available Boolean operators are union (OR operator), intersection (AND operator), and subtraction (NOT operator).

cache

Browsers, like other applications, use the concept of cache to improve access to documents. A cache is a storage location. A browser uses two types of caching schemes: memory and disk. The memory cache is a portion of the computer's RAM that the browser uses to store the most recently downloaded Web pages during the current Internet session. The disk cache is a portion of the computer's hard disk that the browser uses to store previously downloaded Web pages.

CATV (cable access TV)

Cable TV companies provide Internet access. They act as service providers. Internet access through cable TV companies is called CATV.

CDPD (cellular digital packet data)

This is the protocol, similar to TCP/IP, that is used to transmit data over wireless (cellular) Internet connections used by cellular phones.

CGI (Common Gateway Interface) script

A CGI script is a computer program that a Web author writes in order to process the input to a form in a Web page. A CGI script runs on a Web server.

`cgi-bin` directory

Webmasters designate a special directory, usually with the name `cgi-bin`, that stores all CGI scripts. They set up all types of security restrictions on this directory. This directory is under their direct control.

checkbox

This is a form element. Checkboxes are mutually inclusive; thus, a use can select multiple check boxes simultaneously. Checkboxes are displayed as squares. Selecting and deselecting them is accomplished with a mouse-button click. Checkboxes that are already selected (checked) are shown with checkmarks inside them.

codec

Video compression schemes use codec (*co*mpression/*dec*ompression) algorithms. These algorithms compress the video to store and transmit it, and decompress it to play it.

color palette and lookup table

The available colors are usually known as the color palette, and the mappings from pixel values to colors are stored in the monitor's color lookup table. The browser-safe color palette uses 216 colors.

Common Gateway Interface (CGI)

The Common Gateway Interface is a standard method of communication between clients and Web servers which ensures that each understands the other in a clear, unambiguous manner. As a result, when the client sends information, the server knows what to do with it. Likewise, when the server sends back a response, the client handles it correctly.

dial-up connection

A dial-up connection typically uses a PC, a modem, and a phone line to connect to the Internet via a phone call.

digital certificate

Digital certificates are used for digital signatures. A digital certificate is an electronic ID similar to, say, a credit card or driver's license. It is issued by a certification authority. The certificate includes the user's name, the certificate's expiration date, the public key, and the digital signature of the issuer of the certificate. These certificates are kept in registries, so that their owners can look up their public keys, just as one might look up a deed for a house.

digital sound

Sound generated by computers is known as digital sound.

digital-to-analog (D/A) converter

This device converts continuous natural (analog) sound into digital sound.

digital video

Video as generated by computers is known as digital video.

dithering

Dithering can be thought of as a method of interpolation to resolve missing colors. The method is used by browsers during the rendering of Web pages.

DNS (Domain Name System)

This is application software that provides name-to-address translation. For example, the name ftp.netscape.com corresponds to the IP address 198.95.249.66. It is easier and more logical to use names as Internet addresses. The IP addresses are used to send packets through the

Internet. DNS servers maintain lists of domain name and IP address correspondences. A DNS server maps a domain name to its IP address.

DSL (digital subscriber line)
A DSL connection is one of the methods of connecting to the Internet. It allows Internet users to connect into the Internet at high speed over an ordinary phone line.

E-mail (electronic mail) address
Each node, computer, or user on the Internet has a unique e-mail address. E-mail addresses are used to send and receive e-mail messages and files.

encryption and decryption
Encryption and decryption use complex computer and mathematical algorithms to respectively scramble and unscramble data and content for secure transmission across the Internet.

Ethernet
Ethernet is a network that was developed by Xerox during the 1970s and is still popular today. It provides open-architecture networking.

Extranet
An Extranet is a network outside an organization. It facilitates intercompany relationships. Extranets typically link companies and businesses with their customers, suppliers, and partners over the Internet. An Extranet may be viewed as an intermediate network between the Internet and an Intranet.

form
An XHTML form consists of a collection of elements organized in a certain layout.

frame rate
Frame rate (also known as refresh rate) is defined as the number of frames displayed per second. For TV, the frame rate is 30 frames per second.

frame size
Frame size is defined as the pixel size of a video image. For TV, the frame size is the size of the TV screen itself, unless the screen is split between multiple channels.

FTP (File Transfer Protocol)
FTP is the Internet tool you use when you know that the information you seek is stored in a large file in a given location. FTP lets you download a copy of the file from a remote host to your local computer. FTP can transfer ASCII and binary files. It is a client/server application.

helper applications
These are external applications that a browser launches which can open or save files that the browser cannot handle on its own.

hidden field

This is a form element. Hidden fields are elements that are never displayed on the screen. They are used by Web authors for tracking purposes.

HTML editor

This is an editor that generates XHTML code and tags automatically. HTML editors provide Web authors with an automation tool for writing XHTML code. By using HTML editors, Web authors can focus on page design and layout while the editor generates the code automatically.

HTML hybrid editor

The hybrid editors are a mix of WYSIWYG and tag editors. HotMetal Pro is an example. These editors allow authors to use XHTML tags if they need to.

HTML tag editor

This is a type of HTML editor. HotDog Pro is an example. These editors provide Web authors with menus of XHTML tags and their attributes, to help the authors develop their Web pages.

HTML WYSIWYG (what you see is what you get) editor

These editors show the Web page as the Web author creates it. The XHTML tags are hidden during the editing session. Netscape Composer and Microsoft FrontPage are examples.

HTTP (HyperText Transport Protocol)

The protocol that is used to transfer Web pages from websites or servers to client browsers so that Web surfers can view them.

hyperlinks

Hyperlinks create hypertext. They produce two effects when Web authors include them in Web pages. First, they link other Web pages and files to the current Web page. Second, the reader of an HTML document can click any link in the page, at any time, at random. Despite its simplicity, the link has been one of the driving forces behind the success of the Web.

image formats

Among the many image formats, three are supported by browsers by default. They are Graphics Interchange Format (GIF), Joint Photographic Experts Group (JPEG or JPG), and Portable Network Graphics (PNG).

image hyperlink

Images can be used as hyperlinks. Instead of text, an image is used as the link. As with text hyperlinks, the mouse cursor changes to a hand when a Web surfer moves the cursor over an image hyperlink.

image (clickable) map

An image map is defined as a single image that links to multiple URLs or HTML documents. The image is divided into regions, sometimes known as "hot spots" or "hotlinked" regions.

IMAP (Internet Message Access Protocol)

Incoming e-mail servers use the IMAP protocol to receive e-mail messages.

Internet

The Internet is a giant network. It is also known as the information superhighway. It consists of computers located all over the world that communicate with each other.

interdocument links

Hyperlinks that connect Web pages to a particular external Web page are known as interdocument links.

Intradocument links (anchors)

Hyperlinks that connect different sections within the same Web page are known as intradocument links, or anchors.

Intranet

An Intranet is a computer network that is contained within an organization; that is, it is an internal or private network.

IP address

This is an identification number that is assigned to a computer that is connected to a network. Without IP addresses, the Internet would not work. IP addresses allow successful communication between the different networks, servers, and computers that make up the Internet. An IP address is a 32-bit number. An example of an IP address is `129.10.1.13`.

ISDN (integrated service digital network) Line

This is a fast Internet connection. An ISDN connection operates at speed of 128–144 Kbps.

ISO Latin-1 (8859-1) character set

This character set contains the Latin characters. It represents each character by a unique code, allowing Web authors to include Latin characters in their Web pages.

ISP (Internet service provider)

ISPs offer direct Internet connections as well as dial-up access for individual and home users. They do not offer content; they offer only access. Examples of ISPs are AT&T WorldNet, IBM Internet Connection, MCI Internet, and Prodigy Internet.

Kbps (Kilobits per second)

The Kbps is a measuring unit that shows how fast data are transmitted throughout the Internet.

LAN (local area network)

This is a network that connects computers. The computers must be within a certain physical distance for the network to work. Ethernet LANs are quite popular.

list

This is an XHTML element that can be used in a Web page to organize its contents in a list or bullet form. Three types of lists exist: bullet (unordered), numbered (ordered), and definition lists. Lists can be nested to support different hierarchical levels.

listserv

Listserv discussion groups combine elements of e-mail and Usenet news.

Mbps (Megabits per second)

The Mbps is a measuring unit that shows how fast data are transmitted throughout the Internet.

menu

This is a form element. Menus allow users to choose one or more items at the same time. Other names that are frequently used for an XHTML menu are option list or menu, select list or menu, and drop-down list or menu.

metadata

Metadata are data about an HTML document itself rather than the document's content. Browsers do not render metadata. Such data are used by search engines for indexing and ranking page hits in a given search.

metasearch engine

This is a search engine that searches several other search engines at once for every search request—that is, it performs a multiengine search. Metasearch engines speed up the searching of the Web.

MIME (multipurpose Internet mail extension)

A variety of audio, video, and animation formats, collectively known as MIME data types, is now found on a large number of websites. There are seven main MIME types. They are text, application, image, audio, video, multipart, and message. All browsers support them and their formats.

Mosaic

The first graphically oriented browser, Mosaic was developed at the National Center for Supercomputing Applications (NCSA) at the University of Illinois at Urbana–Champaign (UIUC).

MP3 sound format

The MP3 format allows near-CD-quality digital music and songs to be played over the Internet and on PCs.

name/value pairs

When a Web surfer fills in a form on a Web page, the browser encodes the data into name/value pairs before sending them to the server for processing via a CGI script. The name is the name of the form element, and the value is what the Web surfer inputs into this form element.

newsgroups (discussion groups)

On a practical level, discussion groups and newsgroups refer to the same thing. Discussion groups are groups of people who are interested in certain topics and usually share opinions and ideas about these topics. Newsgroups are the collections of the messages that the discussion groups post to a news server about a given topic or subject. Newsgroups are also known as Netnews.

newsreader

A newsreader is software (e.g., a browser) that helps users navigate newsgroups and their messages.

NNTP (Net News Transport Protocol)

Usenet software employs the NNTP protocol to organize messages and distribute copies of and replies to these messages to users.

playback video

Playback video is video that is created, stored in files, and included in Web pages as video clips.

plug-ins

A plug-in is a program that, after installation, runs within the browser window, extending its capabilities. Even though it is a separate program, a plug-in appears to be part of the browser. Plug-ins are better to use than helper applications.

POP (Point Of Presence, or Post Office Protocol)

This is an access point to the Internet with an IP address. Service providers have many POPs in various geographical locations, to allow customers to connect to the Internet vial local phone calls.

POP3

POP3 is a popular e-mail-server type.

PPP (Point-to-Point Protocol)

This protocol allows two hosts, say your PC and an Internet server, to connect over a direct link such as a telephone connection. The connection is known as a PPP connection.

public and private keys

These two keys are used as part of encryption–decryption technology. The public and private keys are used to encrypt and decrypt data, respectively. The two keys are a set of two numbers that are generated randomly. The private key is used to decrypt data that have been encrypted by the public key. The keys come in pairs that are not interchangeable.

radio button

This is a form element. Radio buttons are mutually exclusive, allowing a user to make only one choice at a time. Radio buttons are displayed as circles. Selecting and deselecting them is done with a mouse-button click. A radio button that is already selected is shown with a filled circle inside it.

reset button

This is a form element. Each form must have this button. Clicking the reset button erases all the form's input and replaces it with the form's default values.

RGB (red, green, and blue) color model

This model is used to create colors in Web pages. It generates colors additively by mixing the three primary colors: red, green, and blue.

router

This is a device that controls traffic on a network. It finds the fastest route along which to deliver Internet content and information.

search engine

This is an application software that helps Web surfers search and navigate the Internet and the Web.

SGML (Standard Generalized Markup Language)

This is the superset language that defines XHTML tags. XHTML is a subset of SGML.

signature file

A signature file is a file that you develop yourself, often in a word processor such as Microsoft Word. The file usually contains your affiliation, including name, company name and address, phone and fax numbers, e-mail address, and company logo. The e-mail tool appends your signature file automatically to every e-mail message you send out. Thus, you save time by not typing that same information over and over. In other words, your signature file acts as a rubber stamp for you.

single-tier client/server model

The single-tier client/server model uses one computer as both the client and the server.

SMTP (Simple Mail Transfer Protocol)

Outgoing e-mail servers use the SMTP protocol to communicate with client computers. The SMTP protocol allows the sender to identify him- or herself, specify a recipient, and transfer an e-mail message.

sound formats

The available sound formats are AU (Sun), WAV (Microsoft), MIDI, and AIFF. The file extensions (types) for these formats are `.au`, `.wav`, `.mid`, and `.aif`, respectively.

SSL (Secure Sockets Layer)

Both Web servers and browsers use SSL technology, which was developed by Netscape, to manage the security of data transmission between them.

static sound

Static sound is sound stored in files and included in Web pages as sound clips.

streaming sound

Streaming sound is the sound coming from broadcast stations operating on the Internet. This sound is similar to that of conventional radio stations.

streaming video

Streaming video is real-time video. Streaming video allows Web surfers to view video as it is downloaded. Web surfers can use streaming video to watch live events from all over the world. Video cards that come with PCs can play streaming video if the software that can handle streaming video is installed.

submit button

This is a form element. Each form must have this button. Clicking the submit button activates the browser to send the form's input as name/value pairs to a CGI script installed on the Web server containing the form for processing.

T1 and T3 lines

These lines provide dedicated access to the Internet. A T1 line provides a bandwidth of 1.5 million bits per second (Mbps). A T3 line provides a bandwidth of 45 Mbps.

table

A table is defined as a region that has rows and columns of small rectangles, called cells, that are arranged relative to each other in a certain way that makes up the table layout.

table border

The table border is the outside boundary of a table. We can think of it as the table's container.

table caption

The table caption is the title of a table. It provides a short description of the table's purpose. It can be placed at the top of a table or at the bottom.

table cell

This is the basic unit of a table. Each table cell holds its own content (data). In Web pages, cell data could consist a any XHTML element, such as text, hyperlinks, images, and so forth.

table cell padding

Cell padding is equivalent to specifying the top, bottom, left, and right margins for the cell. It describes the amount of horizontal and vertical spacing between cell content (data) and the cell's borders.

table cell spacing

Cell spacing describes the amount of the horizontal and vertical whitespace between cells.

table directionality

Table directionality describes how the cells of table rows are laid out. For example, they can be laid out from left to right or from right to left. The former is the default.

table header

The table header is the first row in a table. Each cell in this row is a header for the column underneath it. It holds the title of the column.

table nesting

This term refers to the embedding of an entire table inside another table. Web authors may nest tables in order to achieve certain design goals and layouts of their Web pages.

table rows and columns

Table rows are the horizontal layouts of the cells. Similarly, table columns are the vertical layouts of the cells.

table summary

The table summary provides a long description of the table that may be used by people utilizing speech- or Braille-based browsers.

table width and height

The width and height of a table are a representation of the number of its rows and columns, respectively.

TCP/IP (Transmission Control Protocol/Internet Protocol)

This is the communication method that the Internet uses to transmit content and information from one location to another. TCP/IP can be viewed as Internet rules similar to the rules of the postal service.

TCP and IP packets

The TCP/IP protocol breaks the data to be transmitted, for example an e-mail message, into chunks (called TCP packets) of a maximum size of 1500 bytes each. These packets are enclosed in IP packets. The IP packets travel through the telephone lines and the fiber-optic cables of the Internet to their final destinations.

Telnet

Telnet is an important tool for accessing the resources of the Internet. Rather than providing a method to obtain files, it provides a way to obtain computing services from the hosts that can be reached on the Internet. Telnet allows you to log into a remote computer (host) and use it. You must be a valid user and have an account on that computer. When you telnet to a host from a remote location, it asks you for your username and password.

text area

This is a form element. Text areas allow users to input multiple lines of text. Each text area has a width (number of columns) and a height (number of rows). Both parameters are specified as numbers of characters.

text field

This is a form element. Text fields are typically used when only one line of text is needed as input. A text field is displayed as a rectangle and has a size and a maximum length.

tiling

   An image can be used as the background for a Web page. In some cases, the browser repeats the image horizontally and vertically across the page to create a pattern. This pattern is known as a tile or tiling effect.

three-tier client/server model

   The three-tier client/server model uses one client computer and two server computers. One server acts as an intermediate between the client and the other server. It is used for security reasons.

two-tier client/server model

   The two-tier client/server model uses two computers, one for the client and one for the server.

URL (Uniform Resource Locator)

   The name that corresponds to an IP address in the DNS is known as a URL or an Internet name. A URL identifies a node on the Internet uniquely. The Internet DNS follows a standard format to assign a URL (IP address) to any of its nodes.

Usenet

   The network of computers (news servers) that exchange Netnews is known as Usenet. News servers are maintained by companies, groups, and individuals and can host thousands of newsgroups.

vCard

   This is an electronic business card that users can create and use in their e-mail messages. E-mail tools such as Netscape e-mail and Microsoft Outlook Express use vCards. The e-mail tool attaches the vCard at the end of each e-mail message a user sends.

video formats

   There are many video formats available for producing playback video. The available common formats are AVI (Audio Video Interleave), QuickTime, MPEG (Moving Picture Experts Group), and MJPEG (Motion JPEG). The file extensions (types) for these formats are `.avi`, `.mov`, `.mpg`, and `.mjpg`, respectively.

vlink (visited link)

   After the user clicks a link and releases the mouse button, the link becomes a visited link.

WAN (Wide Area Network)

   A WAN is a network that connects computers. The computers must be within a certain physical distance for the network to work. WANs cover a much larger geographical area than LANs do.

Web browser

   A Web browser is an application that has a GUI (Graphical User Interface) that allows its users to read their e-mail, participate in discussion groups, display Web pages, search the Internet, run Java applets, and so forth.

Web page

This is the outcome of displaying, in a browser, a document that is written in XHTML. A Web page can contain hyperlinks that lead to other Web pages. The formatting of a Web page is achieved by XHTML tags.

Web portals

"Web portal" (also portal site, or just portal) is a metaphor used to describe websites that work as gateways, launching pads, or starting points to the Internet. They act as tables of contents (information meccas) for the Web. Web portals aggregate a lot of content in one place for users' convenience. They also offer a variety of online services, such as travel information, chat rooms, news, forums, e-mail, weather forecasts, stock quotes, sports information, shopping, search engines, and so forth.

Web server

A Web server is a software program. A Web server runs on a fast networked computer with a large hard disk and a large amount of memory (RAM). The server software performs many tasks, such as hosting Web pages and CGI scripts.

Winsock (Windows socket) protocol

Winsock is the Windows Sockets API (Application Programming Interface). It enables Windows to work with the Internet, thereby allowing Windows-based PCs to be connected to the Internet. The protocol became available in 1993.

World Wide Web (WWW)

The World Wide Web (WWW or W3) is the section of the Internet that features such multimedia capabilities as video, audio, images, graphics, and text. In 1989, the World Wide Web was conceived by Tim Berners-Lee of the European Laboratory for Particle Physics, or CERN (an acronym for the group's original, French name), in Geneva, Switzerland. The Web began to take off after graphical Web viewers, called browsers, were developed in 1993.

World Wide Web Consortium (W3C)

This is the group that manages the XHTML standards. To find out what is current for XHTML, visit its website at `http://www.w3.org`.

XHTML (Extensible HyperText Markup Language)

This is a simple and easy-to-use scripting language for writing code to format and create Web pages. The code is stored in HTML documents. The two main characteristics of XHTML are its markup and hyperlinks.

XHTML document structure

A well-structured HTML document should have three parts: header, body, and footer. The header identifies the document as an HTML document, establishes its title, and includes its `<meta>` tag. The body contains the content of the Web page. The footer has the website address information that Web surfers can use to get in touch with the site's webmaster.

XHTML frame

XHTML frames enable Web authors to display multiple HTML documents (multiple Web pages) in multiple views rendered by the browser in its one window. Each frame displays a Web page.

XHTML frame set

A collection of XHTML frames is referred to as a frame set.

XHTML frame size

A frame size is specified by the number of columns (`cols`) and the number of rows (`rows`) in XHTML. The units of `rows` and `cols` could be pixels or a percentage of the browser window.

XHTML nested frames

There are two types of frame sets: simple and complex. Simple frame sets divide a browser window into rows or columns only. Complex frame sets create nested frames by dividing the window both horizontally and vertically.

XHTML tags

XHTML tags are special keywords enclosed in brackets (< and >). Web authors use them to format Web pages. Browsers execute them and thereby display the Web pages.

XHTML target frames

Target frames are defined as frames that receive content from other frames.

Index

USER'S TUTORIAL AND REFERENCE MANUAL

CREDITS

Family Members

Thanks to our family members: Robert and Rebecca Baron; Branka Billante;
Gary Corda; Walter and Joan Detjens; Carlota Corona, Ruben Miyar, and Cao Nguyen;
Gau Bu Bu; Marylou and the Geoffrion family; Karen and Kayla Gill; Phillip Howard;
Abby Hyde; Mason Lang; Joheem Loh; Victoria and Cristian Lopez; David Madwin;
Hjäner Mortensen; Daniel Kopelovich; Julie Thiel; Sam Turner; Abe VanGoor;
Jamiee Wade; WellerWorks; and Annie and William Huang — for all their support and
understanding during the months and many late hours it took to complete this project.

Program Design, Coding, and Management

Ben Au-Yeung; Doreen DeSalvo; Timothy Detjens; Roger Dunn; Randall Eike;
Jeff "Gee-Zooks" Gill; Peter Hollingsworth; Jeff Levinsky; Ed Mortensen; Drew Satica;
Kevin Tsay; Keith Yamamoto; Derek Wade; Manhong Zhou

Quality Assurance

J.P. Aragon; Christian Billante; Gigi Geoffrion; Esther Kopelovich;
Rick Lopez; Steve Madwin; Gwen Zierdt

Documentation

Bruce Storie; with assistance from Peter Hollingsworth

Packaging

Michelle Baron; Courtney Corda; Laura Howard; Christina Lang; Liz Lieber;
Andria Strelow; Woods & Woods Design